W9-AHF-630

Red Square, Moscow

NORTHEAST
HIGH SCHOOL
MEDIA CENTER

Peter the Great, St. Petersburg

The World Today Series®
Stryker-Post Publications, Harpers Ferry, WV • USA

RUSSIA AND THE COMMONWEALTH OF INDEPENDENT STATES

M. Wesley Shoemaker

38th edition
Next Edition: August 2008

2007

M. Wesley Shoemaker . . .

Professor emeritus, Lynchburg College, Lynchburg, Virginia. B.A *Magna Cum Laude*, Waynesburg College (History); M.A. and Ph.D., Syracuse University (Russian History). Before he entered the teaching profession, he served for a number of years as a Foreign Service Officer with the Department of State. He had assignments in the European Bureau of the Department and abroad at the American Embassy in Kingston, Jamaica, the American Embassy in Bonn, Germany, and the American Consulate General in Stuttgart, Germany. He travels extensively in Eastern Europe.

Photographs used to illustrate *The World Today Series* come from many sources, a great number from friends who travel worldwide. If you have taken any which you believe would enhance the visual impact and attractiveness of our books, do let us hear from you.

First appearing as a book entitled *The Soviet Union and Eastern Europe 1970*, revised annually, published in 1970 and succeeding years by

Stryker–Post Publications
P.O. Drawer 1200
Harpers Ferry, WV 25425
Telephones: 1–800–995–1400 (U.S.A. and Canada)
     Other: 1–304–535–2593
     Fax: 1–304–535–6513
     www.strykerpost.com
     VISA–MASTERCARD–AMERICAN EXPRESS

Copyright © 2007 by Stryker–Post Publications

All rights reserved. This publication, or parts hereof, may not be reproduced without permission in writing from the publisher.

International Standard Book Number: 1–887985–87–5

International Standard Serial Number: 1062–3574

Library of Congress Catalog Number 67–11537

Cover design by nvision graphic design

Historical Research: Robert V. Gross

Cartography by William L. Nelson

Typography by Barton Matheson Willse & Worthington

Printed in the United States of America
by United Book Press, Inc.
Baltimore, MD 21207

The World Today Series has thousands of subscribers across the U.S. and Canada. A sample list of users who annually rely on this most up-to-date material includes:

Public library systems
Universities and colleges
High schools
Federal and state agencies
All branches of the armed forces & war colleges
National Geographic Society
National Democratic Institute
Agricultural Education Foundation
Exxon Corporation
Chevron Corporation
CNN

Contents

Moldovan students in National Gallery of Art, Chișinău

Russia and the Commonwealth of Independent States 2007

The twelve republics which constitute the membership of the Commonwealth of Independent States have much in common, in spite of their many different languages, religions and cultures. All were part of the Russian Empire for at least a century; all were part of the Soviet Union from its inception. Perhaps most important, their economic and political cultures were essentially formed during the communist era as a part of the industrialization that guided the Soviet State in the 74 years of its existence. Russians were, of course, the dominant political, social and cultural force in both the Russian Empire and the Soviet Union, but the break-up of the Soviet Union at the end of 1991 freed each of the other fourteen republics of the old USSR to go its own way. Estonia, Latvia, and Lithuania have since opted for membership in NATO and the European Union.

Developments in the other republics have not been as clear. Although the remaining eleven republics sought their freedom from the Kremlin, they recognized that they had to find a way to coexist with Russia. All knew that, because of its size, its potential wealth, and a long tradition as a Great Power, Russia would remain an important player in the area; moreover, the long years of communist rule meant that the economies of the eleven remaining republics were heavily intertwined with the Russian economy.

Until recently, Russia actively used the mechanism of the Commonwealth of Independent State to facilitate its relations with the other 11 republic members. But Russia's recent great economic success seems to have convinced many Russian officials that granting other members of the CIS special economic benefits no longer served Russian interests. Russia continues to use some of the sub-organizations associated with the CIS, but, increasingly, Russia deals with other members of the CIS on a bilateral basis. The Russian decision, announced in 2006, to begin charging CIS member states world market prices for oil and natural gas reflects this new Russian viewpoint.

Russian actions in support of separatist movements in Georgia and Moldova—and the 2006 decision to ban products such as wine, fruits and vegetables from these republics—have also exacerbated relations with these republics. Of Russia's neighbors to the west and in the Caucasus, Russia currently has good relations only with Armenia. Russia's decision to begin charging Belarus world market prices for oil and natural gas has soured a formerly good relationship.

President Vladimir Putin's political and economic programs since his election have contributed to this decline in relationships, but developments in other republics have played a role as well. The Russia of 2000 was politically and economically weak. Putin saw this situation as being one of near anarchy. From the beginning, he was determined to take control of the main political forces and put an end to the various forces tearing Russia apart.

Putin's political accomplishments during his first term are best exemplified by the result of the December 2003 Duma elections. *United Russia*, the pro-government bloc, took 300 of the 450 seats, giving it a two-thirds majority in the new Duma. To accomplish this result, Putin brought NTV, the only independent television network, under government control. This gave the government monopoly control over the media during the 2003 legislative elections, a control it used to discredit opposition to the government.

Putin took a number of other political actions which contributed to increasing authoritarianism in Russia. He abolished elections for regional executive officers and made them presidential appointees. He persuaded the Duma to change the electoral law to abolish single member constituencies and have all deputies elected on the basis of proportional representation and party slates. The Duma also gave President Putin greater authority to appoint judges, thus increasing his authority over the judiciary.

Even as Russia retreats from political pluralism, however, the trend in some of the other CIS republics has been toward greater democracy. Georgia's "Rose Revolution" began the process in the fall of 2003. Ukraine followed suit in the fall of 2004 and Kyrgyzstan became the third republic to have a popular revolution in the spring of 2005.

One could argue that, except for Georgia's "Rose Revolution," none of these popular revolutions turned out very well. That is, perhaps true, but there is no indication that any of these peoples would like to return to a more authoritarian system. What we see, instead, is that the individual CIS republics have divided on the issue; Turkmenistan, Belarus, and Uzbekistan—and to a lesser extent Tajikistan, Azerbaijan, and Kazakhstan—may be said to be in the Russian camp. The other republics are going their own way.

Opposition political parties exist in Moldova, Armenia, Kazakhstan, Kyrgyzstan, Azerbaijan and Tajikistan. Pluralism is strongest in Moldova and Armenia. In most of the other republics, opposition political parties are relatively weak. Although they are permitted to field candidates, they have little possibility of coming to power legally. Kyrgyzstan may be a partial exception to that; in March 2007, President Bakiev appointed a prominent opposition political figure as his new prime minister.

The 2007 Armenian elections were judged by international observers to have been relatively clean and fair. Greater political pluralism is also possible in Kazakhstan, Azerbaijan and Moldova.

In Belarus, Turkmenistan and Uzbekistan, on the other hand, almost no political pluralism had been permitted to develop. In the case of Belarus an early political pluralism was suppressed. In these three republics, peaceful revolutions are probably impossible. The situation in Turkmenistan has changed somewhat since the death of President Niyazov in December 2006. The new president, Gurbanguly Berdymukhammedov, has reversed a number of Niyazov's policies since taking office; he is no democrat, but his policies thus far appear to be an improvement over those of his predecessor.

President Lukashenka fears just such a development in Belarus, and he has recently moved to further restrict any form of independent political activity. Belarus's 2005 presidential elections were, if anything, an even greater travesty than previous elections. Although a small political opposition continues to challenge government policies, it is so repressed that it represents no real threat to Lukashenka's authority.

Uzbekistan's government is also authoritarian, but what one can say of President Karimov is that he rules the country in much the same way he did when he was head of the *Communist Party of Uzbekistan*. There is, to be sure, a façade of democracy. Although there are five political parties, no true opposition parties are permitted to exist.

When a local revolt broke out in 2005 in the city of Andijon, Karimov did not hesitate to use significant force to reestablish control, even though it led to the death of as many as 500 citizens. Karimov is currently being criticized for his government's actions, but his policy is unlikely to change in the future. He sees any popular movement as a threat and a challenge to the government's authority, and he therefore fears it. Little is likely to change here either.

M.W.S.
Arlington, VA
May 2007

The Russian Federation

Area: 6,592,692 sq. mi. (17,075,200 sq. km.).
Population: 142.8 million (July 2006 estimate).
Capital City: Moscow (metropolitan population: 9 million).
Other Major Cities: St. Petersburg (5.1 million), Nizhny Novgorod—formerly Gorky (1.5 million), Ekaterinburg—formerly Sverdlovsk (1.4 million), Samara—formerly Kuibyshev (1.3 million), Omsk (1.2 million), Kazan, Perm (1.1 million each).
Climate: Russia lies within the temperate, sub–arctic, and arctic zones. Most of European Russia is within the temperate zone, while most of Siberia lies in the arctic zone.
Neighboring Countries: (counter–clockwise from the northwest) Norway, Finland, Estonia, Latvia, Belarus, Ukraine, Georgia, Azerbaijan, Kazakstan, Mongolia, China, North Korea, Japan. Kaliningrad (separated from the rest of the nation) is lodged between Lithuania (north and east) and Poland (south).
Official Language: Russian.

Ethnic Composition: Russians (82.7%), Tatars (3.7%), Ukrainians (2.9%), Chuvash (1.2%), Bashkirs (0.9%), Belarusians (0.8%), Mordovins (0.8%), Chechens (0.7%), Other (6.3%)
Principal Religions: Russian Orthodox and Protestant Christianity, Islam, Judaism.
Chief Commercial Products: Russia is a major industrial power, albeit highly polluted, largely self–sufficient insofar as the domestic economy is concerned. Exports consist of petroleum and natural gas, many commercial and precious metals, including manganese, nickel, chromium, copper and lead, gold, silver and platinum, diamonds, furs, and, almost alone among processed goods, military equipment. Imports include grains, tropical produce, manufactured goods, including consumer goods and machinery. Russia has more than 90 percent of the former USSR's oil reserves.
Currency: *ruble*.

Per Capita Annual Income (Purchasing Power Parity): $10,700.
Former Political Status: Core of the Russian Empire for centuries to November 7, 1917. Russian Soviet Federative Socialist Republic, member of the Union of Soviet Socialist Republics from 1922 to 1991.
Federal Structure: Under the new constitution, Russia is defined as a Federative Republic consisting of republics, provinces, autonomous provinces, districts, autonomous districts and territories. Republics enjoy greater rights of self–government than other subdivisions and some of the republics have negotiated separate agreements with the national government.
National Day: June 12 (Russia Day).
Chief of State: Vladimir Putin, President (Reelected in March 2004).
Head of Government: Mikhail Fradkov, Prime Minister (March 2004).
National Flag: Three equal horizontal stripes of white, pale blue, and red (the same as used by the Russian Imperial Empire).

The Land and the People

The Russian Federation, which became a separate, independent nation in December 1991 after the collapse of the Union of Soviet Socialist Republics, consists of the Russian–speaking core of that former union. Still the largest country in the world, it stretches 5,500 miles (9,200 km.) from the Kaliningrad enclave in the west to the Kamchatka Peninsula in the east, encompassing the lands of historic Russia west of the Ural Mountains and all of Siberia. Expressed in another way, the Russian Federation reaches 172 degrees around the globe (from longitude 19°39'E to 169°W).

Ten time zones separate the Kaliningrad Region in the west from the Chukotka Peninsula in the east. Thus, even though fourteen republics broke away and established themselves as independent nations in 1991, the Russian Federation continues as one of the great nations of the world.

The heart of this enormous land is a seemingly endless plain that stretches from the Polish border in the west to beyond the Yenisei River in the east and into Central Asia in the south. This Eurasian plain, actually three interconnected plains partially separated by the low–lying Ural Mountains, is known as the Russian Plain west of the Ural Mountains. East of the Urals, it becomes the Western Siberian Lowlands. That part of the plain that extends across Kazakhstan and into Central Asia is known as the Turan Lowland.

The Russian Plain is part of the even larger East European Plain. It begins at the Baltic Sea in the north and extends to the Black Sea and the Caucasus Mountains in the south. Not totally flat, it is broken up by a series of higher elevations, the most significant of which is the Valdai Hills (also known as the Central Russian Upland), located in the northwest.

The somewhat higher elevations of the Valdai Hills give rise to several large rivers which, flowing outward to the seas, connect most parts of the Russian Plain. Although the Valdai Hills cover an area of only about 100 square miles, they are the birthplace of four rivers, including the two largest rivers of the Russian Plain, the Dnieper and the Volga. The other two rivers are the Western Dvina (known in Latvia as the Daugava) and the Lovat.

Today, the Valdai Hills form part of the border between the Russian Federation and the Republic of Belarus (formerly Byelorussia). However, this area, including the Pripet Swamps to the southwest, is usually accepted as the birthplace of all the Eastern Slavs, which include Russians. The Dnieper River flows west, then south, crossing the border into Belarus. It then continues southward, passing through the Republic of Ukraine before entering the Black Sea.

The Volga flows eastward, then southward, finally emptying into the Caspian Sea. The Western Dvina flows northward into Latvia, where it undergoes a name change and becomes the Daugava. It

Russia

flows through Latvia into the Gulf of Riga, an arm of the Baltic Sea. The Lovat flows north into Lake Ilmen. When its waters leave the lake, they become the Volkhov, on which the historic city of Novgorod is located. The Volkhov, in turn, flows into Lake Ladoga. As they go from the lake, they become the Neva River. The Neva, on which St. Petersburg is located, flows into the Gulf of Finland, another arm of the Baltic Sea.

The origins of the Russian state are associated with a north–south water trade route that arose in the ninth century using the western part of this river system. The major river involved was the Dnieper, along whose middle reaches the city of Kiev is located. Kiev, capital of the Republic of Ukraine, was also the capital of Kievan Rus, the first Russian state. The other river system was the Lovat–Volkhov–Neva, and here the other important Russian city was Novgorod, located on the Volkhov at the northern edge of Lake Ilmen. These two cities guarded the trade route, and their unification under a single ruler marked the beginning of the then small Russian state.

There is one other river of the Russian Plain that needs to be mentioned, though its significance is more recent. The Don River lies between the Dnieper and Volga Rivers in the south. It flows into the Sea of Azov, an arm of the Black Sea. Because it is connected to the Volga by the Volga–Don canal, it provides a link between the Caspian and Black Seas.

The Western Siberian Lowlands, though nearly as large as the Russian Plain, have little of its importance, largely because of the climate. All of Russia lies quite far to the north, but most of European Russia benefits from weather patterns that give it a milder climate than its northern location would indicate. The warm waters of the Gulf Stream, pushing up through the English Channel and into the Baltic Sea, greatly modify the climate of northern Russia. Other weather patterns associated with the Mediterranean Sea have a similar effect on the southern part of Russia.

The influence of these weather patterns is not found east of the Ural Mountains. Moreover, they are replaced by countervailing weather patterns whose effect is to make the climate even more severe than

would be expected at similar latitudes. In addition, much of Siberia lies further north than the European part of the Russian Federation.

Nearly half of Siberia is situated north of the 60° parallel, the same parallel as St. Petersburg, and perhaps one–fifth of it lies north of the Arctic Circle. Another influence is that the land tends to slope downward from south to north, meaning that Arctic fronts can sweep unhindered southward across the landscape. This means also that Siberia's rivers flow from south to north—and their mouths in the north freeze earlier in the fall and thaw later in the spring than their more southerly upstream sections. The northern two–thirds of the Western Siberian Lowlands are, accordingly, a land of mixed evergreen forest and swamp.

This is the western third of a broad band of forest stretching from the Ural Mountains to the Pacific Ocean known as the Taiga. Agriculture is possible only in the south, in a fairly wide band just east of the Ural Mountains, but sharply narrowing as one travels eastward, ending west of Irkutsk. It is easy to locate this fer-

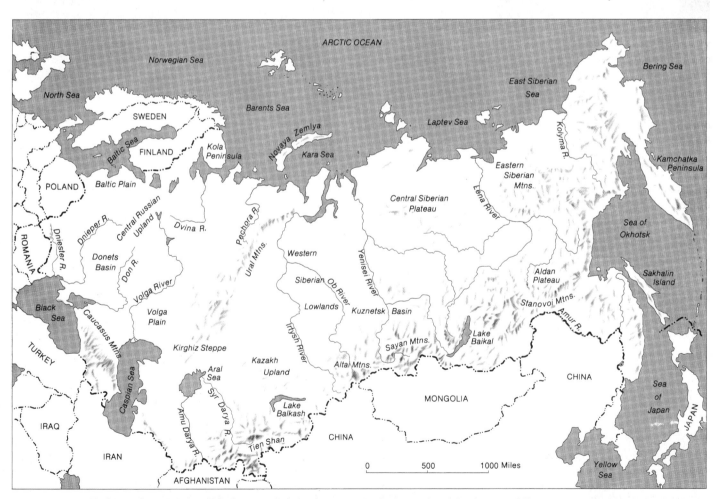

To keep the map simplified, names of the former, now independent, Soviet republics, are not shown.

2

The first helicopter tour by an American journalist of the main harbor of Vladivostok (eastern coast of Siberia facing on the Sea of Japan) produced this aerial view. In the foreground is a naval shipyard now serving the Russian Pacific fleet, with the aircraft carrier Minsk (center) undergoing maintenance.

Photo by Bryan Hodgson © 1990 National Geographic Society

tile band on a map for here are found all of the major cities of western Siberia, connected by the Trans–Siberian Railway, which passes through the region.

The Western Siberian Lowlands are dominated by two great river systems, the Ob–Irtysh and the Yenisei. The Ob–Irtysh drains the western and central part of the plain; the Yenisei drains the eastern part plus the western edges of the Central Siberian Plateau. Because they both flow northward, their economic usefulness is very limited.

To the east of the Western Siberian Lowlands, the land rises and becomes known as the Central Siberian Plateau. Here the land is still mostly flat or slightly rolling, but the climate is much harsher, partly because of the higher elevation. In the north, the area is all treeless tundra, while the rest of the land is covered by evergreen forests, a continuation of the Taiga. The entire plateau is classified as an area of permafrost—the land is permanently frozen to a depth of 50–60 feet and in the short Siberian summers only the top 3–4 feet thaw. Subsistence agriculture is carried on in openings in the forests in the south, but this is generally not an area suitable for agriculture.

The Lena River, mightiest of Siberia's rivers, divides the Central Siberian Plateau from the Eastern Siberian Mountains. The southern, upstream portion of the Lena River Valley has been developed somewhat more because of extensive mineral deposits that have been found in the area. Yakutsk, capital of the Republic of Yakutsk–Sakha, which is located on the banks of the Lena River, boasts a population of over 200,000 inhabitants.

The Eastern Siberian Mountains are a series of ranges that run for 1,500 miles from west to east, up to the Bering Strait and the Pacific Ocean. Like the Central Siberian Plateau, it is an area of permafrost, with tundra in the north and taiga in the south. The tallest of these mountains is only about 10,000 feet in height, but the area is largely uninhabited except for wandering tribes of reindeer herders because of the extreme climate. Temperatures average above freezing for only about two months out of the year, partly because of the northern location, but also because of the effect of cold Arctic Ocean currents just offshore.

South of the Eastern Siberian Mountains, the Amur River forms the boundary between the Russian Federation and the People's Republic of China for a distance of about 700 miles before it turns northeastward and eventually empties into the Sea of Okhotsk. The Amur is the only major Siberian river to flow from west to east and the Amur River Valley is the only area of extensive cultivation in the eastern part of Siberia. The amounts produced are insufficient to supply the population, however, so this, like the rest of Siberia, is a net food–importing area.

The last major feature of the Siberian landscape is a series of very high mountain chains that stretch all along the southern border. Starting from the west, they are the Altai, Sayan and Yablonoi, plus the Stanovoi Mountains. The Stanovoi Mountains, which begin north of the Amur River, are separated from the Eastern Siberian Highlands by the Aldan Plateau. Together, the four high, rugged, mountain chains hem in the land and isolate Russian Siberia from its southern neighbors.

Natural Regions

The Russian Federation includes within its limits climatic belts varying from the temperate to the arctic, stretching from west to east in wide bands across the country. Two of these, the Tundra and the Taiga,

Russia

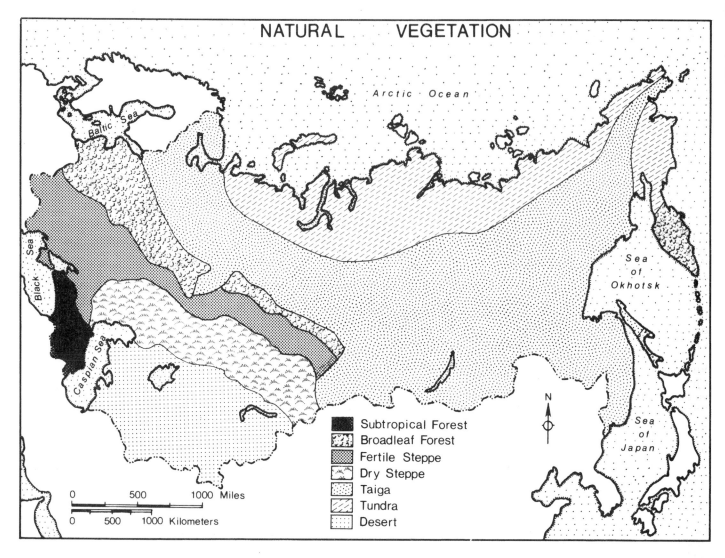

NATURAL VEGETATION

Arctic Ocean

Baltic Sea

Black Sea

Caspian Sea

Sea of Okhotsk

Sea of Japan

Legend:
- Subtropical Forest
- Broadleaf Forest
- Fertile Steppe
- Dry Steppe
- Taiga
- Tundra
- Desert

0 500 1000 Miles

0 500 1000 Kilometers

N

are found primarily in Siberia. The Tundra stretches across the northern part of the land that borders on the Arctic Ocean from the Ural Mountains in the west to the tip of the Chukotka Peninsula in the east. It is almost entirely uninhabited and nothing but moss and swamp shrubs will grow there. Migratory herds of reindeer graze briefly in the southernmost part of the Tundra during the brief summer.

Immediately south of the Tundra is the Taiga, a zone of evergreen forest that begins at about Archangel in the west and gradually widens toward the east until it takes in an area as far south as Lake Baikal. The belt then bends somewhat northward before continuing on to the Sea of Othotsk.

To the south of the Taiga is a zone of mixed forest which stretches from west to east across the entire country. West of the Urals, this takes in about two–thirds of the Russian Plain, reaching as far south as Kiev, capital of the Republic of Ukraine. On its southern edge, it gradually thins out, becoming mixed wooded steppe and

grassy meadow. The northern slope of the Caucasus Mountains also belongs in this climatic zone.

The last vegetation zone is the Steppe, or prairie area. The Steppe begins as a 150–mile band north of the Black Sea and stretches eastward into Central Asia. It was originally a natural grassland, but today this area is mostly cultivated land. The chief city of the Russian Steppe is Stavropol, the main city of the region where Mikhail Gorbachëv grew up.

Ethnic Diversity:
The Symbolism of Chechnya

According to the Russian Federal Statistics Service, the population was 142.8 million as of December 1, 2005. This figure is down by 675,000 from a year earlier. The population drop during the corresponding period of 2004 was 683,400.

There is little doubt that the population of native-born Russians has been dropping for several years and that the population is down by approximately 4.2 million since the 1989 census. The reasons for

the decline are also well-known; the birth rate has been declining for several years while the death rate has been increasing.

But that is not the entire story; another part of the story is that immigrants are not counted in the population statistics. According to Russia's Federal Migration Service, more than 20 million migrants enter Russia each year, most of them citizens of CIS member states. Except for Georgians, none of citizens of the other CIS states require visas to enter Russia; their numbers are therefore largely unknown. The Federal Migration Service estimates, however, that there are between 10 and 14 million illegal migrant workers in Russia. The Russian Government has taken the position that at least some of these migrants should be legalized, since they take jobs that would otherwise remain unfilled. Native-born Russian citizens are often hostile toward foreign workers, however—particularly those from the Caucasus and Central Asia—so the government has limited itself to calling on citizens to be more accepting of migrants.

4

Russia

The Russian Federation, with 82.7 percent of the population ethnic Russians, is relatively homogeneous. Nevertheless, it is home to numerous non–Russian ethnic groups and this is reflected in its federal structure—which divides the country into 21 republics, 49 regions, six territories, ten autonomous areas, two cities of federal importance—Moscow and St. Petersburg, plus the Jewish autonomous region. After the collapse of communism in 1991, a number of the republics declared their "sovereignty" vis–à–vis the Russian Federation and several modified their names. For example, the Tatar Autonomous Republic became the Republic of Tatarstan, while the Yakutsk Autonomous Republic, changed its name to the Republic of Sakha (Yakutia). In the area of the northern Caucasus, one group, the Chechens seceded from the Chechen–Ingush Autonomous Republic to establish their own Republic of Chechnya. Under the leadership of Dzhokhar Dudayev, a former Soviet Air Force general, Chechnya then declared its independence.

President Yeltsin attempted to reassert Russian authority over the Republic of Chechnya in November 1991, but discovered he had neither the force nor the political support to carry it out. He backed down when the Russian Supreme Soviet refused to endorse his policy. Over the next three years, a series of attempts were made to get Chechnya to drop its independence bid, but without success. Chechnya also refused to sign the general Federation treaty which Yeltsin negotiated with the various republics in 1992. And General Dudayev refused to accede to the new constitution of the Russian Federation, approved in December 1993, even though, under its terms, Chechnya would have had extensive autonomy, including its own constitution.

It has been suggested that one reason why the Chechens continued to hold out for independence is that most of the republic's 1.3 million inhabitants are Muslims who want to separate from Russia for religious reasons. It is true that General Dudayev did, at times, make references to the creation of an Islamic nation. Yet that is not the only reason, for other Muslim–majority areas have accepted the new constitution. In any case, President Yeltsin's patience was exhausted by December 1994 and he then authorized the use of military force against the Republic of Chechnya.

Although greatly outnumbered, the Chechnyan defenders resisted strenuously and even managed to create a temporary stalemate. It took the Russian army approximately three months to capture Grozny, the capital and, even so, additional units had to be brought in to accomplish this. By April 1995, most of Chechnya had been brought under Russian control and a new Chechen government, headed by Salambek Khadjiev, a longtime opponent of General Dudayev, had been installed.

General Dudayev and his embattled forces retreated into the mountains in the south. They had not been finally defeated, however, so guerrilla fighting continued, with occasional Chechnyan forays even into nearby parts of Russia.

Though Russian forces managed to kill General Dudayev in early 1996, anti–war sentiment continued to grow in Russia, eventually forcing President Yeltsin to begin seeking a way out of the impasse. After his reelection, therefore, Yeltsin named

European Russia's Heartland
showing principal cities

Russia

General Lebed as his new security adviser and gave him responsibility for Chechnya.

Using his new authority, Lebed negotiated a settlement with the new Chechnyan leadership, agreeing to a withdrawal of all Russian forces from the republic in return for a Chechnyan pledge not to press for formal independence for five years. Although Lebed later lost his job, the agreement held until 1999, partly because no one on the Russian side wanted to restart the war. As for the Chechnyans, they selected Aslan Maskhadov, the man who negotiated the agreement with Lebed, as their new president in January 1997, and he subsequently did his best to adhere to the agreement.

Unfortunately, Maskhadov often found his relatively moderate policies challenged by insubordinate military commanders, in particular the legendary guerrilla leader Shamil Basayev, who dreamed of ridding the entire north Caucasus area of Russian influence and bringing it together in a new Islamic state. In August 1999, then, Basayev joined his forces with those of a radical commander of Jordanian origin by the name of Khattab and

launched an invasion into neighboring Dagestan as a first step in accomplishing this ultimate goal. Russian military forces in Dagestan managed to drive the invading forces back into Chechnya after about six weeks of fighting, but a series of bomb explosions in Moscow and Rostov that killed about 300 individuals, which were blamed on Chechnyan terrorists, convinced Moscow to carry the war to Chechnya itself. Moscow began bombing what it termed "strongholds of Islamic militants" in late September, at the same time breaking all links to Maskhadov's government in Grozhny. Moscow launched its ground campaign against Chechnya on September 30.

As the war proceeded, hundreds of thousands of Chechnyan refugees fled across the border into neighboring provinces as Russian forces leveled Grozny and other urban areas. It took the Russian forces about four months to overrun most of Chechnya, though several thousand of the remaining Chechnyan forces withdrew into the Caucasus mountains region of southern Chechnya and remained undefeated. Russian military campaigns car-

ried out since that time, plus periodic offers of amnesty, have led to a reduction in the numbers of Chechnyan forces still holding out in the south, but guerilla attacks continue to occur in various parts of the republic.

Still, President Yeltsin's decision to once again authorize the use of force against Chechnya should be viewed as something of an aberration. Yeltsin was, in fact, a consistent advocate of local sovereignty for the republics and other autonomous political subdivisions and it is this position that is essentially enshrined in the December 1993 constitution. Yeltsin's decision to take action in Chechnya resulted from his concern that Russia's authority in some of the other autonomous republics might be threatened if Chechnya were not punished for its challenge to Russian authority. There is at least some basis for this fear. There are still separatist tendencies in several of the republics, in particular Tatarstan and Bashkortostan, both of whom have large Muslim populations and occupy a strategic location along the Volga River. Any movement toward independence in these republics would have to be viewed extremely seriously, for they are situated astride all the major railroad lines and oil pipelines connecting Siberia to European Russia. Thus the war in Chechnya was essentially a war on behalf of Russia's territorial integrity.

Vladimir Putin's election as president in March 2000 changed that equation in some respects. First of all, Yeltsin's selection of Putin as his successor was partly based on the actions he took with regard to Chechnya while he was serving as prime minister. Secondly, Putin made it clear after he became president that he intended to reassert the power of the center and bring all of the straying regions back into line. His Chechnyan policy has reflected this position. Militarily, the war against the rebels has continued; at the same time, Chechnya has been reconstituted as a republic within the Russian Federation and given a new constitution.

History

The origins of both the Russian state and nation are found in the area north of the Black Sea and in the steppe lands to the north and east of that strategic body of water. Although there is evidence of human settlement in the area dating back to the neolithic period of the Stone Age, significant history begins with the Slavs. These people were and are identified by a common or similar language rather than by any other common features. The Russians are part of an Eastern Slav group, the other members of which speak Ukrainian and Byelorussian (Belarusian).

The Poles, Czechs and Slovaks belong to a second major group, the West Slavs. There is also a South Slav branch represented by the Bulgarians, Macedonians, Serbs, Montenegrins, Croats and Slovenes.

Little is known about the original home of the early Slavs and many theories have been developed and discarded by scholars. As early as the beginning of the Christian era, however, Slavic people were found throughout most of the Russian Plain west of the Dnieper River and in Eastern Europe as far west as the Vistula River in what is now central Poland. References to the Slavs are also found in the writings of the Greek and Roman historians of the early Christian era, but very little is known about them in this time period. Essentially, they were cut off from classical civilization by the fact that they occupied only the center of the Russian Plain, the more southern part bordering the Black Sea not being suitable for medieval agriculture. The Slavs were traditionally agricultural people and left the grassy steppe of southern Russia to others.

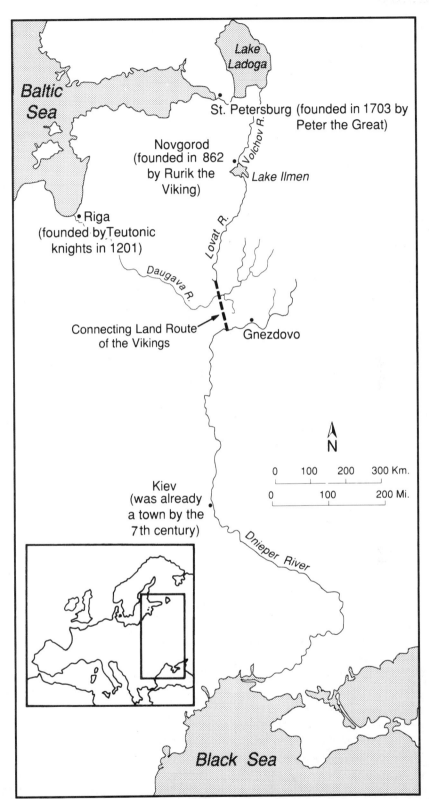

ROAD FROM THE VARANGIANS TO THE GREEKS

The early political organization of the Slavs was basically tribal, with groups of self–governing villages cooperating in such areas as defense. By the seventh century, towns had begun to develop and trade between the tribes became more important. Kiev, later the capital, was founded at about this time and probably owed its existence to the trade that had started along the Dnieper River. Located

Russia

N.C.B.

**Christian Orthodox (Byzantine) cross
and pagan symbols**

1. Goddess
2. God of the Under–World
3. Hammer of a God
4. Sky God
5. Male God

high on the bluffs that overlook the western shore of the river, Kiev was ideally located to dominate all such trade.

Novgorod, located at the northern edge of Lake Ilmen, was established somewhat later. Begun as a trading post for amber and other products of the Baltic Sea area, it soon developed as a manufacturing center for jewelry, metals and wood products. Its chief significance, however, was as the northern terminus of the trade route known as the "Road from the Varangians to the Greeks." It was the existence of the trade route that led to the creation of the first organized Russian state.

"Varangian" was the old Slavonic word for a Norseman or Viking. Ancestors of today's Scandinavians, the Vikings were great seamen and from about the seventh century onward, they had been pushing out of Scandinavia, carrying out raids and explorations in all directions. Eventually they established settlements in eastern England, northern France and along the southern coastline of the Baltic Sea. This brought them into contact with Novgorod. According to tradition, Rurik, leader of one of these Viking bands, established himself at Novgorod in 862.

The story of the coming of the Vikings is told in *The Primary Chronicle*, a twelfth century compilation of history from unknown earlier sources. According to the *Chronicle*, Rurik and his band of Varangians were invited to set themselves up as the local rulers—"Our land is great and abundant, but there is no order in it; come rule and reign over us." It is more likely that the Novgorodian merchants hired Varangians as mercenaries and then Rurik decided to take complete control himself. Twenty years later, Oleg the Norwegian, Rurik's successor, "set himself up as prince in Kiev." Since he retained control in Novgorod, he then controlled the two chief cities of the "Road from the Varangians to the Greeks."

Kievan Russia

This was the beginning of "Kievan Rus," the first organized Russian state. Oleg lived until 913 and he spent the rest of his life extending his control over neighboring Slavic tribes and building up the trade route upon which the prosperity of the new state was based. His most spectacular gesture, according to Russian sources, was an attack on Constantinople which he launched in 907. Byzantine sources make no reference to such an attack but they do record that in 907 the

Byzantine Emperor signed a treaty with Oleg which granted access to Byzantine markets on very favorable terms. Oleg was succeeded by Igor in 913; the latter was either the son or grandson of Rurik and from that time onward the descendants of Rurik sat on the throne of Kievan Rus. The Rurikovichi ("sons of Rurik") dynasty later made the transfer when the capital was moved to Vladimir and, later to Moscow, so that it remained the ruling dynasty of Russia until 1598, when Fedor, son of Ivan Grozny ("the Terrible"), died without an heir.

The first ruling family of Russia was thus Varangian in origin, but it must be emphasized that they became rulers of a land that had already developed an extensive "Slavic" culture. The Varangians were fine warriors and good leaders, but the Viking culture did not replace the native Slav culture. In fact, the opposite happened—the Varangian rulers were soon enveloped by Slavic culture.

This can be seen in the names of subsequent rulers. Igor was killed in 945 while on an expedition to collect tribute from a neighboring Slavic tribe. He was succeeded by his wife, Olga, because his son was still only a child. But that son, who succeeded to the throne in 962, was named Sviatoslav—the third generation of Varangian rulers already had Slavic names and, one can reasonably assume, were speaking the local Slavic language.

The subject of early Slavic culture is complex. It was indeed fairly well developed by this time, but it was centered round a belief in pagan Slavic deities. The trade connection between Kievan Rus and Constantinople meant that the Russians were exposed to Byzantine culture and religion.

Constantinople was the leading city of Europe, the capital of the Byzantine Empire and the home of the Patriarch of Constantinople, leader of Greek Orthodox Christianity. It was a center of wealth, power and culture. Further, the Orthodox Church was actively committed to a policy of conversion of the Slavs. Its missions had been active among the Bulgarians for some time and two Orthodox monks, Cyril and Methodius, had translated the *Bible* into Old Slavonic. In the process, they created the Cyrillic alphabet, which kept letters from the Greek alphabet for those sounds common to both languages but created new letters for *sounds* unique to Slavonic. The first written Slavic language was thus created.

Oleg permitted an Orthodox mission to open in Kiev, but the first breakthrough did not occur until 955 when Olga underwent Christian baptism by missionaries from Constantinople. Her son, Sviatoslav, never converted, however, so Christianity remained a minority belief. The largest conversion to Orthodox Christianity occurred during the reign of Sviatoslav's son, Vladimir (978–1015). It was somewhat ironic that Vladimir was responsible for the conversion to Christianity, since he assumed the throne as a champion of the old Slavic gods. Paganism was a dying force, however. Poland, Hungary and Bulgaria had already become Christian and the kings of Denmark and Norway were converted shortly after Vladimir's accession to the throne.

Thus, when the Byzantine Emperor found himself faced with revolts in various parts of the empire and called upon Vladimir for assistance, offering his own sister to Vladimir as a bride, the offer was irresistible—Vladimir sent help and looked forward to the added power his anticipated bride would bring. But he found that the marriage could only take place if he converted to Christianity. Without hesitation, with the intent of allying himself with the most powerful state of that age, he underwent baptism in 988. After the marriage arrangements had been completed, he ordered the mass baptism of the entire population of Kiev and began the construction of St. Sophia Cathedral, the first of the great Orthodox cathedrals built during the time of Kievan Rus. The Byzantine style of architecture was thus introduced into Russia, a style that would remain dominant until Peter the Great introduced the neo–classical style at the beginning of the eighteenth century.

Kievan Rus also officially adopted the Cyrillic alphabet at this time, and Vladimir ordered that schools be set up for the education of the sons of the upper classes. Kievan Rus had, in fact, completely opened itself to Byzantine influence and, gradually, much of its culture was transformed.

Vladimir and his successor, Yaroslav (1019–1054), were responsible for much of this transformation; for this reason, the combined reigns of these Grand Princes is known as the height of Kievan Rus. Influenced by the Byzantine example, the relationship of the Grand Prince to the people changed and, because of this change, Kievan Rus could be, for the first time, defined as a nation. Earlier princes had merely levied tribute on the various tribes, each spring traveling about the country collecting goods, which were then traded in Constantinople. Vladimir replaced the tribute system with taxation. Yaroslav was responsible for having the Bishop of Kiev named a *Metropolitan*, meaning that he became the head of an autonomous Russian Church. The Patriarch of Constantinople still retained the authority to *name* the Metropolitan, but this made Kiev the religious as well as political capital of the state. Yaroslav's other important achievement is

that he was responsible for the first Russian law code, the *Russkaya Pravda*.

After the death of Yaroslav, there was a period of decline, partly because of the "Rota" system, a method of inheritance in which all brothers inherited before any of the sons. The Rota system contributed to the division of the kingdom into separate principalities by encouraging competition for the throne among brothers and cousins. Occasionally, uncles and nephews struggled with each other to determine which would occupy the dominant throne of Kiev.

New Asian invaders, the *Polovtsy*, also appeared on the scene at about this time, contributing further to the decline of Kiev. Then, in 1169, Kiev was attacked by a contender for the throne who, having achieved his purpose, moved the capital to his own city of Vladimir. Kiev thus lost its position as capital of the Russian states at this time.

It was then almost completely destroyed in 1240 by a massive invasion of Mongols (Tatars) led by Batu, grandson of the renowned Ghengis Khan, founder of the Mongol Empire. Batu Khan would later establish his own capital at Sarai, near the mouth of the Volga River, and this became the origin of the "Golden Horde."

What came to be called the "Mongol Yoke" had to be endured by the Russians until it was finally overthrown in 1480 by Ivan III, Prince of Moscow. An earlier attempt in 1380 ended in failure, despite the dashing military exploits of the Russian forces led by Dmitri Donskoi, also a Prince of Moscow.

The Effects of Mongol Occupation

Historians disagree about the exact significance of the period of Mongol (Tatar) occupation. Generally speaking, the three-fold division is between those who point to the catastrophic effects of Tatar rule, those who feel it was beneficial, and those who feel that the importance of the occupation has been exaggerated.

It is hard to deny, however, that the strong, centralized and autocratic state that arose at Moscow between the thirteenth and fifteenth centuries differed greatly from the loosely organized confederation that had been Kievan Rus. In addition, it is possible to point to specific developments, such as the legal concept of land–holding, military techniques and organization, and forms of tax collection, as things taken over by the Moscovites from the Mongols. Certain Russian words also represent borrowings, although the words appear, in each case to be Chinese in origin. These include *chai* (tea) and *chin* (rank).

Some historians have also stressed the disruption of contact between the Russian people and important centers of culture

19th century drawing of a Mongol general

such as Byzantium and the developing European states to the west that resulted from the Mongol conquest. It is certainly true that Russia missed most of the European Renaissance and the Reformation, but it is possible to exaggerate the extent of isolation as a result of the Mongol conquest. Moscow always maintained contact with the Byzantine Empire though its connection with the Patriarch of Constantinople. And in the fifteenth century, Ivan III obtained his wife, Sophia Paleologue, niece of the last Byzantine Emperor, through negotiations with the Pope; he also imported Italian builders to construct the "Faceted Palace" for him in the middle of the Kremlin.

Regardless of what judgment is placed on the effect of Tatar rule, there is agreement on one result—the growth and rise to power of a new center of leadership in the Russian lands: the Grand Duchy of Moscow. The emergence of this area as a leader compensated for the destruction of Kiev and the breaking away of other states which remained detached from Russia for centuries.

To understand the contribution of the Tatars to the growth of Moscow, it is necessary to know of the way they exercised their power over the conquered Russian lands. With few exceptions, the Tatars usually left the native princes on their thrones and converted them into collectors of tribute and taxes. They also permitted them to continue to act as the law

Russia

An Italian map (1560) of the Principality of Moscow

the Great." The most significant trading place in western Russia, Novgorod also possessed a unique form of government. Although a prince was the head of state, he was required to keep his throne outside the city walls; the internal affairs of the city were managed by the *Veche*, a broadly representative town council which could be summoned into session when any citizen rang the town bell. This early experiment in democracy came to an end when Novgorod was absorbed by autocratic Moscow.

Ivan further achieved prestige in 1472 when he married Sophia Paleologue, niece of the last Byzantine emperor, killed when the Turks conquered Constantinople in 1453. Ivan occasionally styled himself *Tsar*, a Slavic contraction of the word *Caesar*, and he also added the titles *Autokratar* (Greek for "independent ruler") and *Gosudar* ("sovereign").

About this time, the monk Philotheus of Pskov also developed the theory of the "Third Rome," which identified Moscow as the true capital of Christendom, in a line of succession through Rome and the recently fallen Constantinople. In later centuries, this doctrine became a justification for imperial expansion, although it had only a religious significance when first expounded.

Ivan the Terrible

The "ingathering of lands" was continued by Ivan the Great's successors. His grandson, Ivan IV (1533–1584) came to be known as "The Terrible." Actually the English word "terrible" is not an entirely accurate translation of the Russian word *grozny*, which is better described by the term "awe–inspiring." But there is much to justify Ivan's nickname regardless of the translation—he was a ruler impressive enough to inspire awe and he was undoubtedly cruel and unpredictable enough to be called "the terrible."

Well–educated by comparison with other princes of his time, this shrewd man with a deep interest in theology was given to uncontrolled outbreaks of violence and cruelty. His pattern alternated between exaggerated acts of pious behavior and periods of unrestrained viciousness.

Ivan was a child of three in 1533 when his father died and he became the titular ruler of Russia. When his mother, Elena Glinskaya, died mysteriously five years later, Ivan found himself at the mercy of two competing *boyar* families: the Belskys and the Shuiskys. In their struggle for power, the two families paid public homage to Ivan, but ignored him in private. They exploited the state and pillaged the treasury. Ivan put an end to the situation in 1543 when the 13-year-old boy turned to his guards and ordered them to

enforcement officials of their territories. Working as a tax collector for the Tatars was one of the many factors that helped to transform the insignificant village of Moscow, first mentioned in the year 1147, into the center of a future empire. It is also important to point out that, first as pagans and later as Muslims, the Tatars exempted the Orthodox Church from the payment of all taxes and, in this way, contributed to the growth of its authority and power.

The Rise of Moscow

Moscow profited from its location close to frequently traveled river routes. Called Moskva in Russian, the city is located on a river of the same name that flows to the Oka River, the most important western tributary of the mighty Volga. The rise of the small principality of Moscow was made possible by the Rota—the traditional inheritance system—which encouraged battles to determine the successor to the throne and thus weakened Moscow's rivals for leadership. Moscow made its own contributions through a clever policy of expansion through purchase, conquest, service agreements with lesser princes and, finally, clever dealings with the Tatar leaders that appeared to be part of a pattern of obedient behavior. Moscow also had to provide occasional military help to the Tatars in their battles to suppress rebellious princes and populations.

Moscow benefited also from the loyalty of the large landowners, called *boyars* in

Russian, and from the support of the Church. The boyars, whose lands suffered from the constant feuds among the lesser princes, wanted a strong prince who could enforce his authority and thus bring greater law and order to Russia. The Orthodox Church, which had transferred the seat of the Metropolitan, as the head of the Russian Church was known, from Kiev to Vladimir in 1300. However, the Metropolitan Theognostus formally established Moscow as the seat of the Metropolitan during the reign of the Grand Prince Ivan Kalita (i.e., Ivan "Moneybags"), thereby making it the spiritual capital of "all Russia." The Grand Prince of Moscow thus added to his status as a national leader and gradually came to be looked upon as the protector of the Russian lands against the Mongols.

As the power of the *Golden Horde* began to wane, the leading position of Moscow became less and less contested. The amount of territorial gain was tremendous—from the time of Ivan Kalita to the second half of the fifteenth century, the area of Moscow control expanded from about 600 to 15,000 square miles. In still further expansion, the ruler Ivan III ("The Great") added another 40,000 square miles by a combination of purchases, inheritance and conquest.

Ivan the Great

Ivan the Great's most important military effort resulted in the capture of the powerful city of Novgorod, referred to in its own official title as "Lord Novgorod

Ivan IV—the boy and the man

Nell Cooke Byers

cate as Tsar unless he was given a free hand to deal with his enemies, both real and imagined, as he wished. His terms were spelled out in two letters he had delivered to the Metropolitan of Moscow. What Ivan proposed was to set up half of the realm as a personal domain, free from normal governmental administration and supervision by the "Chosen Council." In effect, half of Russia was to become Ivan's private property, and he would be free to take the lands of all the *boyars* located within the *Oprichnina*—"area set apart."

To enforce his will, he set up an *oprichnik* army of 6,000 men. Black–robed and riding black horses, each *oprichnik* had a dog's head fixed to his saddle and carried a broom, all to symbolize the Tsar's determination to hound traitors and to sweep corruption from the land.

As Ivan obviously intended, the *oprichniki* struck terror throughout the land and the operation was successful from his viewpoint. The ability of the *boyars* to oppose the Tsar was destroyed completely. The purges lasted seven years and, its purpose accomplished, Ivan dissolved the *Oprichnina* in 1572, after executing some of the chief executioners.

The Time of Troubles

Two years before his death in 1584, Ivan quarreled with his eldest son and namesake and, in a fit of passion, struck and killed him. He was succeeded, therefore, by his second son, Fedor, who was mentally retarded. Under Fedor, actual power was exercised by a regency council headed by Boris Godunov. Fedor had no children, so the Rurikovichi dynasty came to an end when he died in 1598.

This left the throne vacant and meant that the Russian people had to choose a new tsar. There were a number of candidates but three men eventually emerged as serious contenders—Boris Godunov, Fedor Romanov and Basil Shuisky. Each had some connection to the previous ruling family. Boris Godunov was married to the sister of Fedor; Fedor Romanov was the son of Nikita Romanov, brother of Anastasia, Ivan IV's first wife; and Basil Shuisky was descended from the elder branch of the Rurikovichi line.

To give legitimacy to the choice, the Patriarch proposed calling a *Zemskii Sobor* and allowing this popular assembly to select the new tsar. It chose Boris Godunov, who took the throne as Boris I (1598–1605).

Boris's reign started out well but, when a combination of early frosts and droughts produced widespread crop failures, the superstitious Russian people began to believe that they had made a mistake in choosing Boris, and opposition mounted to his rule. He managed to hold on to power during his lifetime but things be-

take Prince Andrew Shuisky away and kill him. At 13, Ivan was not yet ready to take the rule himself, but no one dared to oppose his will from that day onward.

Ivan was crowned "Tsar of All the Russias" in 1547, the first ruler to assume the title at the time of his coronation. In this same year, he married Anastasia Romanova, daughter of a minor *boyar* family. Ivan proved to be an energetic ruler whose reign was characterized by both reforms and military conquests. The reforms were, first of all, intended to reduce the traditional powers of the *boyars*, but they also included a new code of laws, the *Sudebnik*, issued in 1550, and an attempt to reform the Church through the calling of a church council in 1551.

Ivan was also responsible for creation of Russia's first parliament, the *Zemskii Sobor* ("Assembly of the Land"), which he convened in 1550 and again in 1566.

Ivan defeated and annexed the Khanate of Kazan in 1552, thus giving him control over the middle Volga. Four years later, he attacked and defeated the Khanate of Astrakhan, adding those domains to his realm. This gave him control of the entire course of the Volga River and access to the Caspian Sea. To celebrate his victory over the Tatars, Ivan ordered the construction

of St. Basil's Cathedral in what is now Red Square in Moscow.

Problems began in 1558 when he decided to launch an invasion of Livonia—modern Estonia and Latvia—in an attempt to gain access to the Baltic Sea. When Livonia disintegrated, Poland–Lithuania and Sweden moved in to pick up the pieces and Ivan found himself at war with both of these nations plus Denmark. The war dragged on until 1582 and left Russia badly depleted.

The war also was at least partly responsible for Ivan's creation of the *Oprichnina*, a separate administration which was intended to finally destroy the traditionally separate power of the *boyars*. During the Livonian war, some of the *boyars* engaged in open treason and joined the side of Poland–Lithuania. One of the most distinguished of the *boyars* was Prince Andrei Kurbsky, one of Ivan's army commanders. He defected to the enemy side in 1564 after having been defeated by Lithuanian forces. The event is remembered through a fascinating exchange of correspondence between the Tsar and the prince; the Tsar called the prince a traitor, while Kurbsky maintained that he "chose freedom."

Ivan became determined to deal with all "traitors" and he threatened to abdi-

11

Russia

From Act I of Musorgski's opera Boris Godunov.

Courtesy of OPERA NEWS

gan to fall apart when he died suddenly in April 1605. Within a month, his son, who had succeeded him, was overthrown by the first would–be Dmitri, an impostor who claimed to be the youngest son of Ivan IV.

This marked the beginning of a period of great turmoil in Russian history known as the "Time of Troubles." Dmitri (1605–1606) survived for approximately a year before he was murdered by Basil Shuisky, who then ascended the throne as Basil I (1606–1610).

Basil, who represented the interests of the old *Boyar* class, was unable to consolidate his control and was overthrown in 1610. Russia was once again without a tsar. In addition, a Polish army occupied Moscow while a Swedish army occupied parts of northern Russia. A number of Russian nobles proposed to offer the throne to Wladyslaw, the 15–year old son of Sigismund, the Polish king. Sigismund rejected the offer and claimed the throne for himself.

This posed a basic threat to the power of the Russian Orthodox Church. Sigismund was a Roman Catholic and proba-

bly would have tried to force a union of the Church with the Roman Church. The Patriarch of Moscow, Hermogen, called urgently for the Russian people to drive out the Poles. A national revival to save "Mother Russia" began, led by Kuzma Minin, a wealthy commoner from Nizhni Novgorod. Minin assembled an army representing all classes of Russian society from *boyar* to serf and the Polish army was driven out of Moscow. A *Zemskii Sober* was then summoned and proceeded to choose Michael Romanov as the new tsar.

The First Romanovs

Michael Romanov (1613–1645) was a boy of sixteen when he was elevated to the throne of Russia. The *Zemskii Sober* wanted Michael's father, Fedor Romanov, as tsar, but that proved impossible for two reasons. The first was that Boris Godunov, after his own election as tsar, had forced Fedor to become a monk. He did this in order to remove a potential rival to the throne since Fedor, as a monk, would be ineligible for the throne. The second reason was that Fedor, now the Metropolitan Filaret, was in prison in Poland.

He had gone to Poland in 1610 as a member of the Russian delegation sent to negotiate with the Polish king with regard to his son Wladyslaw's accession to the Russian throne. When Sigismund decided to claim the throne for himself, he threw the entire Russian delegation into prison. When Filaret was finally permitted to return to Moscow in 1619, he was named Patriarch of the Russian Church and made co–ruler with Michael. He effectively ruled Russia until his death in 1633. Thus Michael remained in the shadow of his father most of his life.

Michael was succeeded by his son, Alexis (1645–1676), who also was sixteen when his father died. Like his father, he was a gentle person, easily dominated by those about him. Dominated in his youth by his tutor Morozov, he later fell under the influence of the Patriarch Nikon and, still later, by his last favorite, Artamon Matveev. Most of the accomplishments of his reign are more the product of these men than of Alexis.

Fedor III was the third Romanov Tsar (1676–1682), son of Alexis, who came to the throne as a boy of fourteen. An in-

Michael

Alexis

Fedor

valid, Fedor left most of the decision–making of the state to his advisors; he died after six years on the throne.

The first Romanovs were thus not very impressive, either as individuals or as rulers. Cautious and conservative, always looking to the past rather than the present or future, manipulated by those around them, their greatest contribution was that they survived. Yet this was a significant period since a number of things occurred during the reigns of these three tsars that would have an important bearing on subsequent Russian history.

The first thing is that the Russian state had to recover from the effect of the Time of Troubles and the Livonian War. The situation in 1613 was less than positive. The economy was in a shambles with large parts of the countryside going untilled and whole villages abandoned. Rebellious peasants and gangs of soldiers from the various disbanded armies roamed the countryside, robbing civilians and looting property. Novgorod was under Swedish occupation and Russia was still at war with Poland. Prince Wladyslaw of Poland continued to press his claim to the Russian throne.

Sweden agreed to return Novgorod in 1617 but, in that same year, Prince Wladyslaw invaded Russia at the head of a Polish army and laid siege to Moscow. The invasion actually helped Michael to establish his authority since he became identified with defense of the Russian homeland against the foreign invader. Wladyslaw's forces were driven out and a truce was signed between the two sides in 1618.

To further bolster his authority, Michael kept the *Zemskii Sobor* in more or less continuous session in Moscow and all important decrees were issued under the joint authority of the Tsar and that body. This might have led to the creation of a permanent representative institution in Russia, but as he became more firmly established, Michael made less use of the *Zemskii Sobor*. A policy emerged whereby sessions were called only to discuss unusually important issues, such as whether Russia should go to war against Poland in the 1630s. A new *Zemskii Sobor* was also called to confirm Alexis' succession to the throne in 1645.

Alexis called two further sessions—in 1649 to issue a new law code and in 1651–1653 to address the question of war with Poland. It did not meet thereafter. The *Zemskii Sobor* was thus used to create and reinforce the authority of the Tsar at a time when that authority was not firmly established. When this purpose was fulfilled, it was no longer called into session and so it just disappeared.

Another major development had to do with the revolt of the Ukraine against Polish rule and its acquisition by Russia. The area of the Ukraine had originally become part of the Principality of Lithuania in the 14th century. Subsequently, a dynastic marriage brought Poland and Lithuania together under a single monarch; they merged into a single state in 1569.

Poland was Roman Catholic and the Ukrainians were Russian Orthodox. Efforts to catholicize the Ukrainians were intermittent until 1589, when the Metropolitan of Moscow was raised to the rank of

Patriarch and given authority over all Russian Orthodox believers. Poland refused to recognize the authority of the Patriarch within any of its territories and attempted to force all its Orthodox subjects to join a new "Uniate" church that recognized the authority of Rome.

In addition, economic pressure was applied as the estates of upper class Orthodox were seized and redistributed to Polish nobles while attempts were made to turn the mass of Ukrainian peasants into serfs.

Bogdan Khmelnitsky, who had himself lost lands to a Polish nobleman, was elected *Hetman* (chief) of the Zaporozhian Cossacks, a group of adventurous independent soldiers and mercenaries. He became the leader for Ukrainian autonomy. Khmelnitsky was successful initially, but a defeat at the hands of Polish forces convinced him that the Ukrainians could not hope to maintain their independence for long. Believing that a victory by Poland would mean the end of the Orthodox Church and the enslavement of the people, Khmelnitsky offered to bring the Ukraine under Russian rule.

Tsar Alexis and his advisers discussed the matter for two years before accepting the offer because they recognized that, if they did so, it would mean war with Poland. The *Zemskii Sobor* finally decided in 1653 to incorporate the Ukraine into Russia and declare war on Poland. The war lasted until 1667, ending with the Truce of Androsovo, under the terms of which Russia obtained all of the Ukraine east of the Dnieper and was permitted to occupy the city of Kiev for two years. Rus-

Russia

Nikon, Patriarch of Moscow

sia never gave back Kiev, however, and the terms of the truce were made permanent by the treaty of peace of 1686.

Another important territorial addition that occurred in the 17th century was the extension of Russian control over Siberia. The penetration of Western Siberia first occurred in the sixteenth century during the reign of Ivan IV, when the famous merchant family of the Stroganovs became interested in Siberian furs. It was this family that hired Yermak, an *ataman* of the Volga Cossacks, to explore east of the Ural Mountains. He led an expedition to the Irtysh River, defeated the Siberian ruler and claimed Siberia west of the Ob and Irtysh rivers for Russia.

Territorial acquisition was resumed in the seventeenth century. The Stroganovs continued to be involved, but now they were joined by other enterprising types; these merchant traders and explorers advanced from the Ob to the Yenisei, then from the Yenisei to the Lena. As they ad-

vanced, they left fortified trading posts behind them. By the middle of the century, they had reached the Amur River and had come into contact with the Chinese. The Chinese attempted to starve out the Russians by withdrawing the entire population from the Amur River valley. The matter was resolved in 1689 by the Treaty of Nerchinsk whereby Russia gave up all claims to the area of the Amur River Valley, but was conceded the rest of Siberia north of the Amur. Thus, by the end of the seventeenth century, Russian territory in the east extended to the sea.

The last development associated with the first Romanovs had to do with a church reform carried out by the Patriarch Nikon. Russian church books contained many errors that had crept in over the centuries as a result of mistakes of copyists. Nikon was determined to correct them according to the Greek originals. The changes were not very significant—correcting the spelling of the name Jesus,

making the sign of the cross with three fingers instead of two, three Hallelujahs instead of two at a certain time during the worship service—but the old ways had been entrenched by tradition. Nikon found himself opposed by a significant element among the clergy who resisted the changes. Avvakum, the chief spokesman for the "Old Believers," called Nikon "a mocker of God and a heretic." Nikon retaliated by banishing the supporters of the old order.

A church council eventually approved Nikon's changes and Avvakum was sentenced to be burned at the stake. That, however, only resulted in a division in the church as the Old Believers continued to oppose the reforms. Since Tsar Alexis supported the measures, he became the "Anti–Christ" as far as the Old Believers were concerned, a term they applied to subsequent tsars as well. The government outlawed them as heretics but there were too many of them for this to be effective. Overall, the effect of the schism was to weaken the power of the church and to make it more dependent on the government for support. That soon became an important consideration, for it is unlikely that Peter the Great could have carried out many of his reforms against the united opposition of the church.

Peter the Great

Peter the Great (1682–1725) is usually conceded to have been the greatest of Russia's rulers and to have had a greater impact on the Russian land and people than any of his predecessors or successors. Yet, his was a disputed succession to the throne and for seven years after he became co–tsar in 1682, there was a serious question whether he would be permitted to rule in his own right.

The problem was that his father, Alexis, had married twice and Peter was born of the second marriage. Alexis' first wife, Maria Miloslavska, had given him two sons, Fedor and Ivan, as well as several daughters, including the ambitious and strong–willed Sophia. When Fedor came to the throne in 1676, he chose his advisors from among the Miloslavsky family and shunted the relatives of his stepmother, Natalia Narishkina, aside. When Fedor died in 1682, the next in line for the throne was Ivan, Fedor's younger brother. Ivan, however, was mentally retarded, subject to fits and nearly blind.

The Narishkin clan proposed that the ten–year–old Peter become the next tsar. Sophia, recognizing that this would mean her total exclusion from power, appealed to the *streltsy*, the hereditary tsarist guard created by Ivan the Terrible, to intervene on behalf of the weak Ivan, suggesting that his life was in danger. She promised

became more and more proficient. Eventually the two regiments were given the names of Preobrazhensky and Semenovsky and became the nucleus of a new army that Peter later created.

When Peter was fourteen, he found an old English sailboat that was in storage. He had it brought out and launched on a nearby lake. Soon he found a Dutch shipmaster to instruct him, and he began building other boats, working along-side Dutch carpenters from the foreign quarter. Peter also liked to sit in the foreign quarter drinking with his friends, so it is not surprising that his first mistress was the daughter of the Dutch innkeeper Mons.

Peter's mother disapproved of Peter's choice of pastimes and decided that he needed a wife to settle him down. He was therefore married at the age of sixteen to Eudoxia Lopukhina, a rather pious and uninteresting young woman. Peter was distracted long enough for her to become pregnant, but within a few weeks he returned to his military games and his boats. Some years later, Peter banished Eudoxia to a convent. His son, Alexis, was partly raised in that convent, and he grew up hating his father and all he stood for.

In 1689, when Peter was seventeen, Sophia decided that she should become ruler of Russia in her own right and began making plans to dethrone both Ivan and Peter. Peter, learning of the plot, fled to the Trinity Monastery and called his "toy regiments" to his side. Sophia's support began melting away and she was forced to surrender power. Peter banished her to a nunnery.

Never particularly interested in the more ordinary aspects of governing, he turned the day–to–day control of Russia

Peter I

pay increases to the *streltsy* to encourage their support. They invaded the Kremlin, killed a number of Peter's relatives and demanded a reordering of the succession to the throne. As a result, Peter and Ivan were named "co–tsars" and Sophia became regent and the real ruler of Russia. Peter and his mother were permitted to take up residence in a palace in the village of Preobrazhenskoe outside Moscow, and it was here that he spent the next seven years.

Moscow's "foreign quarter" was located in a suburb near Preobrazhenskoe, and Peter, bored with life in the village, soon made the acquaintanceship of a number of foreigners who had come to Russia to take service with the Russian government. These included a Swiss, Franz Lefort, a Scot, Patrick Gordon, and a Dutchman, Franz Timmerman.

Another of Peter's diversions was to organize the young nobles assigned to him as playmates into opposing "toy regiments" and to have mock battles. He also discovered that a note dispatched to the Royal armory would bring him any piece of military equipment he asked for. So, he combined his two diversions, using

Lefort, Gordon and Timmerman, who were all military men, as advisors. Gradually Peter learned military engineering, artillery and even geometry as part of these war games, and the "toy regiments"

The Winter Palace of the Tsars in St. Petersburg

15

Russia

to his wife's relatives and returned to his military training. He participated in his first military campaign in 1695–1696 which resulted in the capture of a Turkish fortress at Azov, at the mouth of the Don River. It was to seek allies for a general war against Turkey that Peter next organized a "Grand Embassy" to travel to Western Europe.

Peter accompanied the embassy in the guise of an apprentice shipbuilder, Peter Mikhailov. He went to Brandenburg–Prussia, Holland, England and Vienna, capital of the Holy Roman Empire. He spent six months in Holland working as an ordinary shipbuilder.

Although he learned a great deal, he found no potential ally for a war against Turkey. Charles XI of Sweden had recently died, however, and several countries—Poland, Brandenburg–Prussia and Denmark—were eager to go to war to despoil Sweden of territories won during the seventeenth century in the Baltic Sea area. This offered Peter an even better chance to gain a seaport, so he agreed to go to

war against Sweden as soon as he could bring the war against Turkey to an end.

Peter was in Vienna when he learned of another revolt by the *streltsy*. Although the revolt had been quashed by the time he got back to Moscow, Peter took terrible revenge upon the mutineers. The leaders were beheaded and hundreds of others were tortured or killed and their bodies left to lie out on display as an object lesson for others. Sixteen *streltsy* regiments were ultimately disbanded; Peter had managed to destroy the political power of the *streltsy*, but he had also left himself without an army.

Peter is remembered as the "Great Westernizer" and it is true that he introduced many things into Russia from the west, particularly dealing with culture and manners. Peter was not an uncritical admirer of the west, however, and his primary motivation for introducing western styles was to make Russians more acceptable to Europeans. Thus beards, which were out of style in the west, were forbidden at court and Peter personally took a pair of shears

and cut the hair of his chief courtiers. Nobles who chose to keep a beard were required to pay a tax of 100 rubles and to wear a badge indicating that they had paid it. Peasants were permitted to keep their beards, but had to pay a fine of 1 kopeck each time they entered Moscow. Western-style clothing became mandatory for members of the upper classes. Women, previously kept in isolation, were now invited to public entertainments and dinners, and court balls were organized where men and women danced in the western manner.

Peter kept changing Russian ways of doing things all the rest of his life, but most of the other changes which he introduced might more properly be characterized as modernizations. He simplified the Russian alphabet, eliminating what he considered useless letters, and ordered that the new characters be used in all lay books. Church books continued to use the old style, which came to be known as Old Slavonic.

He also set up the first newspaper in Russia in 1703, established all sorts of

ROMANOV DYNASTY

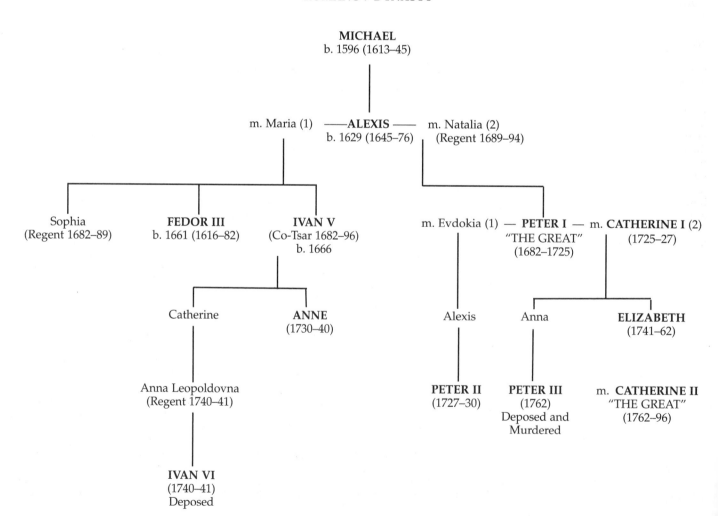

MICHAEL
b. 1596 (1613–45)

m. Maria (1) ——ALEXIS—— m. Natalia (2)
b. 1629 (1645–76)
(Regent 1689–94)

Sophia
(Regent 1682–89)

FEDOR III
b. 1661 (1616–82)

IVAN V
(Co-Tsar 1682–96)
b. 1666

m. Evdokia (1) — PETER I — m. CATHERINE I (2)
"THE GREAT"
(1682–1725)
(1725–27)

Catherine

ANNE
(1730–40)

Alexis

Anna

ELIZABETH
(1741–62)

Anna Leopoldovna
(Regent 1740–41)

PETER II
(1727–30)

PETER III
(1762)
Deposed and
Murdered

m. CATHERINE II
"THE GREAT"
(1762–96)

IVAN VI
(1740–41)
Deposed

technical institutes, laid the foundations for the Universities of Moscow and St. Petersburg, created the Russian Academy of Sciences, sponsored expeditions to explore the Kamchatka Peninsula, the Kuril Islands and the Bering Strait, carried out extensive administrative reforms, reorganized the government of the Orthodox Church, established an iron industry, a munitions industry, textile factories, and in general encouraged the development of trade.

Peter also built a modern army and navy and he fought a long, 21–year war with Sweden for control of the southern shores of the Baltic Sea. The war was ultimately successful, and Russia became established as one of the "great powers" of Europe as a result, but it was extremely costly. Taxes had to be increased on the peasantry and other commoner classes, while a lifetime service obligation beginning at age 15 was instituted for the nobility. Peasants were also drafted into the military for the first time. Although military service became a lifetime obligation for them, it did have the advantage that they ceased to be serfs upon taking the military oath.

After Peter's death, the term of military service for both nobility and commoners was reduced to 25 years. His proudest achievement was the city he built at the mouth of the Neva River on land newly liberated from the Swedes. St. Petersburg, whose foundations were laid in 1703, was to be his capital, his chief seaport on the Baltic and his "window to the west." It was here—and at Tsarskoe Selo ("the Tsar's village"), twelve miles away—that he began the magnificent palaces which were to signify Russia's new great power status. His new capital was partly responsible for his death, however, for St. Petersburg was built on a swamp and was subject to periodic flooding. Peter died in early 1725 as the result of a chill he caught while helping to rescue victims of such a flood.

An Era of Palace Revolutions

One of Peter's greater disappointments was his son, Alexis, who in the normal course of events would have succeeded him. Alexis opposed everything that Peter stood for, however, and he made no secret of the fact that he planned to undo all of Peter's reforms if he came to power. He embarrassed his father further in 1716 by fleeing abroad and requesting sanctuary from the Holy Roman Emperor. Two years later, he returned home at his father's urging, where Peter forced him to renounce his claim to the throne, then had him put on trial for treason. He was found guilty and sentenced to death, but it was later announced that he had died while under interrogation.

Peter issued a decree abolishing succession of the oldest son or child of the tsar, which stated that the tsar would name his successor. He never got around to designating his own, however, and his sudden death left the succession unsettled. It was resolved by Prince Alexander Menshikov, one of Peter's close associates, who called upon the Guards regiments to support Catherine, Peter's second wife, as his successor. The Guards regiments, descendants of Peter's original "toy regiments," thus set a tradition of intervention which would continue throughout the eighteenth century. It was not until 1796, under Emperor Paul, that Peter's succession decree was finally repealed and primogeniture was reinstituted as the method of succession.

The weird succession to the throne of Russia following the death of Peter the Great at the age of 53 is best understood with the help of a diagram. The rulers between Peter the Great and Catherine the Great were as follows:

CATHERINE I, a peasant woman, Peter's second wife (two years)

PETER II, son of the dead Prince Alexis (three years)

ANNE, Duchess of Courland, half–niece of Peter I (ten years)

IVAN VI, half great–great nephew of Peter I (one year)

ELIZABETH, younger daughter of Peter I by his second wife (twenty–one years)

PETER III, son of Elizabeth's older sister Anna and the Duke of Holstein, grandson of Peter I (less than one year; deposed)

This peculiar succession reflects the sequence of intrigues, plots and *coups* by a series of advisers, court favorites, and lovers. The amazing thing is that Russia's international position did not decline during this period because other powers failed to take advantage of the internal upheaval.

Of these rulers, only one, Elizabeth, made any important contribution to Russian development. She consciously took up Peter's reforms where they had been left hanging in 1725 and carried them forward. It was Elizabeth who completed the Winter Palace in St. Petersburg, who hired the famous Italian architect, Rastrelli, to rebuild the Peterhof at Tsarskoe Selo and who established Moscow University. She also emulated Peter's foreign policy by signing alliances with Paris and Vienna and by intervening in the Seven Years War against Frederick the Great of Prussia. She partially neutralized that accomplishment, however, when she named Peter III as her successor to the throne.

When he succeeded her at the beginning of 1762, he immediately set out to undo nearly everything she had accomplished. Although a grandson of Peter the

Great, Peter III was completely German by upbringing and was Lutheran in religion. He was not at all happy about becoming Tsar of Russia, a position for which he was totally unfit, both physically and mentally.

His marriage to the daughter of a minor German princely family, Sophie of Anhalt–Zerbst, had been arranged by his aunt, the Empress Elizabeth. It had been Peter the Great who had begun the practice of "arranged marriages" for political purposes (a pattern followed by German and other western European dynastic alliances), and she continued the policy. But the 1745 marriage remained "in name only" for nine years because the young Grand Duke had a physical disability which made it impossible for him to consummate the relationship.

Peter eventually had an operation to cure his disability, but Catherine, as the young Grand Duchess, was known after her conversion to Russian Orthodoxy, had already been urged by Empress Elizabeth to take a lover in order to assure an heir to the throne. In her memoirs, Catherine identified the young lover, Sergei Saltykov, as the father of her son, Paul. Whether true or not, Peter III evidently believed it because, when he became Tsar in 1762, he decided to disinherit Paul and send Catherine to a convent. This led to his overthrow and to his death in a *coup d'etat* which installed Catherine as Empress of Russia.

Catherine the Great

Catherine had no personal claim to the Russian throne, but she did win the support of the Guards regiments—partly because her latest lover, Gregory Orlov, was an officer of the Guards. For thirty–four years, the growing Russian Empire was governed by a woman of great talent and even greater determination to excel in everything and to control all things. She was hard–working and devoted to matters of state. She saw herself as both a figure of the Enlightenment and as Peter the Great's successor. She had a lively correspondence with Voltaire and Frederick the Great of Prussia and at one point she invited Diderot, the French Encyclopedist, to St. Petersburg and set aside an hour each evening for conversation with him.

When she first came to the throne, she had great hopes for further reforms and she did a great deal to encourage culture and learning. At one point, she spent two years drafting instructions for a Legislative Conference which she called to draw up a new code of law. The instructions, heavily based on the writings of Montesquieu and other Enlightenment thinkers, were considered so radical that they were banned in France. The instructions were apparently

Russia

Catherine the Great

also too radical for members of the Legislative Conference; they were unable to draft a new code based on them.

When Catherine first came to the throne, she expressed her dislike for serfdom. But she ultimately found that she could do nothing about it, for serfdom formed the economic basis of the nobility, the class that staffed the army and civil administration.

In her role as an enlightened despot, therefore, Catherine didn't accomplish very much. On the other hand, she proved to be a good publicist whose writings and correspondence created a good impression of Russia in the West.

Something more should perhaps be said about her lovers. It is a matter of record that she had, over a period of many years, at least 21 lovers. In this regard, Catherine was not greatly different from other 18th century monarchs. The Empress Elizabeth, at whose court she grew up, had a succession of lovers who were given the official title of "Gentleman of the Bedchamber." Louis XIV of France was famous for his succession of official mistresses, known as "Ladies of the Bedchamber." The practice

was so well accepted that one Prussian monarch had an officially appointed Lady of the Bedchamber even though he personally preferred men.

Catherine had more lovers than most, but only four had any significance insofar as Russian history is concerned. Two of these, the presumed father of Paul and the officer who helped her come to power, have already been mentioned. A third was Stanislaw Poniatowski, a handsome Polish nobleman whom she later made King of Poland. The fourth was Gregory Potemkin (Poh–*tyom*–kin), who was responsible for a number of Russia's military victories during her reign, including the conquest and annexation of the Crimea. Potemkin became her lover and chief adviser—and there may even have been a private marriage ceremony. But when the two functions conflicted, he chose to remain her chief adviser—and over the next several years personally selected the young Guardsmen who became Catherine's "Gentleman of the Bedchamber."

Catherine deserves to be called "the Great" primarily because of her successful wars and because of Russia's extensive

territorial expansion during her reign. Perhaps the most important of her territorial expansions is associated with her participation with Prussia and Austria in the partitions of Poland that resulted in an end of the Polish–Lithuanian state.

The liquidation of Poland brought into the Russian empire all the lands which had been claimed as "Russian" during earlier history. This was not the only success of Catherine—under her leadership the first major victory was scored against the Ottoman Turkish empire to the south, hastening the decline of a once–powerful foe. Russia obtained access to a considerable portion of the Black Sea in 1774 and secured the right of passage through the Turkish Straits into the Mediterranean. It was also recognized as the official protector of Orthodox Christians living under Turkish rule. Further expansion led to the acquisition in 1792 of a little–known fortress called Ochakov and the right to control the Crimean Peninsula. These events caused the first alarm in England over the possibility of Russian expansion into areas of interest to the British.

During the struggle between England and the American colonies, Russia played an important role in the League of Armed Neutrality. This was a group of nations that insisted on the right of passage of neutral ships across the Atlantic Ocean and other bodies of water in spite of British objections. Catherine followed with interest the developments in Western Europe and broke off relations with France after revolutionaries executed King Louis XVI. She apparently intended that Russia would be part of an armed intervention in France. She also entertained a greater scheme for the creation of a Christian empire out of Greece and other Turkish possessions, but nothing came of this.

The French Revolution and Russia

For a century prior to the French Revolution, Russia had been governed by a series of rulers committed to the concept of a "revolution from above." In the process, the nobility and urban classes had been transformed, but the peasantry—90 percent of the people—remained the same. It was this obstacle that Catherine was unable to overcome and when the French Revolution popularized the ideas of "liberty, equality and fraternity" and announced the end of serfdom and legal distinctions based on class, this made the ideas of the French Revolution subversive within the Russian part of Europe.

An even greater difficulty was that Russian rulers from Catherine onward, educated in the Enlightenment traditions, agreed with many of the ideals of the French Revolution, but could not see how to achieve them in Russia without completely disrupting the very fabric of Russian society. All agreed, for example, that serfdom was a clearly seen evil and ought to be abolished, but none before Alexander II could bring himself to do so. As a result, the distance between convictions and actions widened, and the actions of Russian rulers became more and more conservative as the nineteenth century progressed. Half–hearted and partial reforms were still proposed and sometimes implemented, but they were never sufficient to transform the basic organization of the Russian society; the ideals of the French Revolution continued to be regarded as suspect and unworthy in Russia.

Further change was afoot in Western Europe—the Industrial Revolution—transforming social and economic relationships. As England, France and Germany industrialized, Russia, with a social and economic system incompatible with capitalism, fell further behind. In spite of all of its efforts, therefore, Russia's system of government and its role as a great power were both in decline throughout most of the nineteenth century. Even as its rulers attempted to catch up, Russia remained "on hold."

Romanov Monarchs After Catherine

We continue to refer to monarchs after Catherine the Great as Romanovs even though she was a German, and if her memoirs are correct, they are all descendants of Catherine and Sergei Saltykov. Before the Romanov dynasty ended its historical role, a sprawling and multi–national Russia was ruled by six tsars—Catherine's son, Paul, his two sons, Alexander I and Nicholas I, Nicholas I's son, grandson and great–grandson—Alexander II, Alexander III and Nicholas II.

Paul, who succeeded his mother in 1796, had been alienated from her because he believed that she had usurped his rightful throne. He therefore spent the first part of his reign attempting to undo his mother's accomplishments. Possessing a military mentality and a foul temper, his was an unstable reign that ended after five years in a *coup d'etat* made on behalf of his son, who gave his advance approval. Paul was murdered during the *coup*, a fact that was said to prey on Alexander's conscience and may explain some of his otherwise unexplainable actions. As one historian has pointed out, this was the last "indoor" assassination—the Tsar was killed in his bedroom by an "inside" group of conspirators and officers of the Guards regiments. In the next century, "assassinations were to take place in the open street." With this last palace revolution, Russia drifted into the nineteenth century, loaded down with traditions of

the past, with autocratic rule, a privileged upper class and with serfdom weighing as heavily as ever on the shoulders of the Russian people.

The first Alexander has presented a puzzle to both historians and psychologists. At first, he was inclined toward liberal ideas and was determined to continue efforts to westernize Russia. He ended up in a fanatically conservative and mystical stupor, dying in southern Russia apparently during an attempt to run away from it all. Typical for Russia, there was a legend that he didn't really die, but chose the life of a saintly hermit to ask forgiveness for his sins. His knowledge of the plot to kill his father may have been the sin that really bothered him.

At the beginning of his rule, Alexander asked the outstanding statesman, Michael Speransky, to plan basic reforms, including a constitution, a modern code of laws and an educational system. He even gave half–hearted consideration to abolishing serfdom, but the only result of this was a law of 1803 that permitted the voluntary emancipation of serfs by landlords. Needless to say, few were inclined to make use of this opportunity.

On Alexander's orders, Speransky drew up a constitution which would have created a national legislature and guaranteed various civil rights. Most of the nobility opposed the plan, however, and Alexander, needing the nobility's support in his confrontation with France, was forced to dismiss Speransky.

Alexander did carry out an administrative reorganization, turning the Colleges he had inherited from Peter the Great into Ministries and organizing them into something analogous to a cabinet, called the Committee of Ministers. In addition, he created an appointed legislature called the Council of State, to draw up legislation for the Tsar's approval and increased the authority of the Senate. None of these changes or new institutions actually restricted the Tsar's authority, but they did regularize procedures and increase the size of the circle of advisers.

The War of 1812

The most famous achievement of Russia in this period was the spectacular defeat of Napoleon I of France when he tried to invade the endless land mass of Russia.

Russia had joined in the so–called Third Coalition to fight against Napoleon in 1805. It and its allies, Prussia and Austria, were beaten and had to submit to rather harsh conditions of the Treaty of Tilsit. A period of relative peace and cooperation with Napoleon, then the master of the European continent, followed.

Russia profited from it by securing areas remote from Napoleon's control at the

expense of Persia and Turkey. Georgia was annexed in the south; to the southwest, Bessarabia was added, giving rise to a greater Russian influence on the neighboring Balkan area of Eastern Europe. At the same time, Russia also seized Finland from Sweden, converting it into a Grand Duchy with the Tsar as ruler. It was also during this period that forts were established in "Russian America"—first in Alaska and then close to what is now San Francisco.

Mutual jealousy between France and Russia emerged in 1811–1812. Napoleon, swayed by his past successes, decided to invade Russia and did so on June 21, 1812, with an army of almost one–half million; the French constituted only about half of this force. A great number of Poles joined the effort, expecting Napoleon to liberate and restore to them all or most of the territory of the defunct Polish–Lithuanian commonwealth.

As in the past, the peasant masses, in spite of their grievances, rallied to the support of "Mother Russia." Another significant factor in turning Napoleon's invasion into a major defeat was the well–known Russian winter, which in 1812–1813 was unusually severe. This completely disrupted the extremely long supply lines of the French.

Hoping for a speedy surrender of the Tsar's forces, Napoleon rejected the advice to retreat to winter quarters and before long his glorious army was in tatters and without food. "Scorched earth" tactics and roaming bands of guerrillas were used against the invader by the Russian general, Mikhail Kutuzov. The departure of Napoleon's forces was not just a retreat—it was a rout.

Russia played a major role at the Congress of Vienna which was convened to settle the affairs of Europe. The supposed allies of Russia had some success in trying to contain the "undue" expansion of Russian political power in Europe. Great Britain and Austria in particular opposed the demands of Alexander I for reestablishment of a large Kingdom of Poland with himself as king under a constitutional government with an independent Polish army.

Although such a kingdom was created, it was much smaller than desired by the Russians, and substantial portions of what used to be Poland were kept until after World War I by Austria and Prussia.

While haggling over the boundaries of Europe in Vienna, the Russian Tsar tried to promote a scheme for a "Holy Alliance" of monarchs. This was to bind the rulers of Europe in a spirit of Christian brotherhood. It was a rather unclear plan that had no important practical results in the field of international relations.

Russia

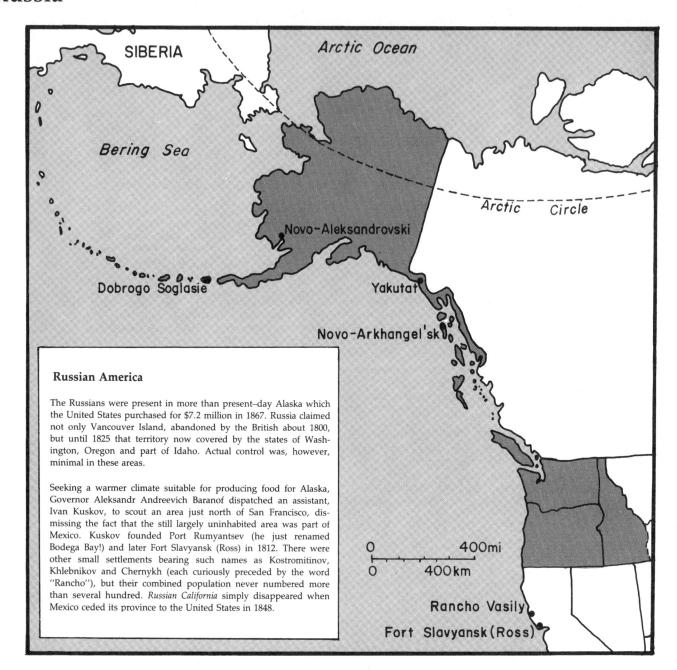

SIBERIA

Arctic Ocean

Bering Sea

Arctic Circle

Novo-Aleksandrovski

Dobrogo Soglasie

Yakutat

Novo-Arkhangel'sk

Russian America

The Russians were present in more than present–day Alaska which the United States purchased for $7.2 million in 1867. Russia claimed not only Vancouver Island, abandoned by the British about 1800, but until 1825 that territory now covered by the states of Washington, Oregon and part of Idaho. Actual control was, however, minimal in these areas.

Seeking a warmer climate suitable for producing food for Alaska, Governor Aleksandr Andreevich Baranof dispatched an assistant, Ivan Kuskov, to scout an area just north of San Francisco, dismissing the fact that the still largely uninhabited area was part of Mexico. Kuskov founded Port Rumyantsev (he just renamed Bodega Bay!) and later Fort Slavyansk (Ross) in 1812. There were other small settlements bearing such names as Kostromitinov, Khlebnikov and Chernykh (each curiously preceded by the word "Rancho"), but their combined population never numbered more than several hundred. *Russian California* simply disappeared when Mexico ceded its province to the United States in 1848.

0   400mi
0   400km

Rancho Vasily

Fort Slavyansk (Ross)

Of greater significance was the Quadruple Alliance, signed by Russia, Great Britain, Austria and Prussia, which made provision for periodic conferences to review matters of common interest and to assure continued peace. The consensus about what it meant to maintain the peace settlement did not last very long, however. The British wished to limit international cooperation to international attempts to overthrow the *status quo*, while Russia, Prussia and Austria argued for international cooperation to put down revolutionary movements within individual states. Great Britain broke with the other three nations on this issue in 1820, but Russia, Prussia and Austria continued to cooperate.

Alexander I put domestic policies on hold during the War of 1812. After Napoleon's defeat, he turned his attention back to domestic affairs, but a large foreign debt and a budget deficit precluded major new programs such as had marked the earlier part of his reign. His antipathy toward serfdom continued, however, and in 1816 he abolished serfdom in Estonia. Another decree the next year ended serfdom in Courland, while a third decree abolished it in Livonia in 1819.

But Alexander I began to lose interest in secular change after he fell under the influence of a Russian monk known for his piety during the Napoleonic Wars. Another influence on him was Prince Metternich, chief minister of the Austrian Em-

pire, who persuaded Alexander that revolutionary forces threatened the political stability of Europe. Alexander began to collect more conservative advisers about him and, increasingly, to act on their advice. The most influential of these was General Alexis Arakcheev, who drew up and implemented plans for "military colonies" in the western part of Russia. Recruits assigned to the military colonies helped to support themselves by growing most of their food. Hated by both soldiers and officers, the military colonies were abolished by Nicholas I after Alexander's death.

Alexander also appointed religious conservatives to major posts such as the Ministry of Education with predictable results.

A new regime of censorship was imposed and religious instruction was given a more prominent place in the curriculum.

The Decembrists

The end of Alexander's reign in 1825 is associated with the first Russian revolution—that of the Decembrists. Although this was exclusively a revolt by army officers and lasted only one day, it is labeled a revolution because the leaders had specific plans about changing the nature of the Russian state and society and did not merely wish to change rulers. The Decembrists were all nobles who had served in Western Europe and who wished to rid Russia of its backwardness. Their specific goals included the abolition of serfdom and the creation of a constitutional government. They were particularly aggrieved that Alexander I had granted a constitution to Poland and had permitted Finland to retain a constitution it had when it was annexed in 1809, but refused to grant one in Russia.

Organized into secret societies, they carried on discussions for a number of years, but were unable to agree on any specific action to take. They were galvanized into action by Alexander I's death, when no new Tsar was immediately sworn in as his successor. The confusion about the succession arose because Constantine, the nominal heir, had married a Polish countess and relinquished his claim to the throne—but this was not known. It was compounded by the fact that Constantine was in Warsaw, where he was regent, and all communications were by mail.

By the time the matter was sorted out and Nicholas was ready to officially take over as Tsar, the Decembrists had decided "to refuse to take the oath of allegiance to Nicholas and . . ." But it seems that they had gotten no further than that for, on the appointed day, 3,000 troops, assembled on the Senate Square, refused to take the oath to Nicholas, but then did nothing further. Nicholas surrounded the square with 10,000 loyal troops and demanded their surrender. When they refused, he ordered the artillery to fire on the insurgents, who then broke and ran. The revolt was over.

The Decembrist revolt was therefore only a minor affair. Five of the top leaders were executed, while approximately a hundred others were imprisoned and later exiled to Siberia. But what made it important was the myth that grew up about the Decembrists; Alexander Herzen, Russian revolutionary publicist, later took up the cause of the Decembrists and made them heroes to subsequent generations. Another importance of the Decembrist revolt was the breach it opened between the government and Russian liberals, who never forgave Nicholas for his harsh treat-

ment of the Decembrists and remained alienated throughout his reign. Conversely, Nicholas was never able to overcome his suspicion that all liberals were potentially disloyal.

Nicholas was 29 years old when he became Tsar and ruled Russia for 30 years until his death in 1855. He was not particularly well educated and he had no practical experience in administration before he succeeded to the throne. His background was entirely in the military, where he held the rank of brigade general. He liked the military and during his lifetime he surrounded himself with soldiers, preferring them as advisers and chief administrators.

Nicholas I

He distrusted public opinion and did not believe that solutions could arise from among the people. He therefore prohibited public discussion of current problems, and books, journals and newspapers were censored. Since he also distrusted the bureaucracy but needed sources of information, he created "His Majesty's Third Section" as his eyes and ears; this organization was no more than a secret police organization.

However, he kept a report of the testimony of the Decembrists on his desk and conscientiously attempted to meet some of the criticism contained in their statements. One of his early successes was the new code of laws which was issued in 1833—the first new code since 1649. He was also deeply concerned about serfdom and appointed a series of committees to work on the problem, but he could not bring himself to the point of abolishing the system. He did, however, improve the lot of the State Peasants by commuting all labor service into taxes and by setting up local government for them. Just over 50 percent of

all peasants were State Peasants—people who lived on state land rather than on the land of individual nobles.

Nicholas I's reign has also been referred to as "the reign of outer repression and inner liberation," since it was during his reign that Russian literature and culture first attained international stature and recognition. Great Russian writers of this period included the poet Alexander Pushkin, the novelist Mikhail Lermontov, author of *A Hero of Our Time*, and Nicholas Gogol, famous for novels, plays and short stories. Nicholas I, who attended the premiere of Gogol's play *The Inspector General*, a biting satire on Russian officialdom, afterwards commented "Everybody got what was coming to him and I got more than anyone."

Other Russian creative artists who began their work during the reign of Nicholas I included Ivan Turgenev, who wrote *A Sportsman's Sketches* during this time, and Mikhail Glinka, founder of Russian classical music and famous for his operas. The Bolshoi Theater, constructed in 1824, also provided a showcase for Russian ballet, comparable to that of France from where it came.

There were economic changes of some note as well, though the prohibitive tariff system adopted at the close of the Napoleonic Wars tended to isolate Russia from the momentous changes in Western Europe as a result of the spread of the Industrial Revolution. The continued existence of serfdom was another factor hindering change.

In spite of that, there was a dramatic growth in textile manufacturing in the province of Moscow and in and around the city of Lodz, in Russian Poland, during the reign of Nicholas I. Most of the early factories were relatively primitive, for powered machinery was beginning to be introduced only toward the end of his reign. This new industry was significant, however, because it was the first to make widespread use of free wage labor in Russia.

What made it even more interesting is that most of the workers were serfs who also compensated a master for labor services not performed in return for permission to take an outside job. The success of the new factories using wage labor foreshadowed the end of serfdom in Russia, for they established that free labor was more efficient than serf labor.

Nicholas I was also responsible for construction of the first railways in Russia, against the advice of his ministers. The first line, between St. Petersburg and Tsarskoe Selo, the royal palace complex located 12 miles away on the Baltic, was constructed as an experiment. The second line connected St. Petersburg with Moscow. Nicholas I authorized a third line

Russia

St. Isaac's Orthodox Cathedral in St. Petersburg was commissioned by Tsar Nicholas I. It was designed by French architect Auguste Montferrand and under construction from 1818–1858. The workers who applied the magnificent gold–mercury amalgam knew when they breathed the toxic fumes that they would die, often within 2 years.
Photo by Miller B. Spangler

linking St. Petersburg and Warsaw, but the Crimean War intervened and the project was put on hold.

In foreign affairs, Nicholas carried out a mainly peaceful policy, though he did fight a war against Turkey in 1828–29 which gave Russia the mouth of the Danube River and the eastern coast of the Black Sea. His troops were used again in 1830–31 to put down a Polish insurrection. Nicholas then punished the Poles by abolishing their constitution and declaring Poland an integral part of the Russian Empire. Troops were also dispatched to Hungary in 1849 to end a revolt there and force the Hungarians back within the Austrian Empire.

Two years before his death, Nicholas involved the Russians in his first major war, the Crimean War. The basis of the original quarrel with Turkey—Russia's claim to be the protector of all Orthodox Christians under Turkish rule—would not have justified a war involving three great powers, but England and France intervened because England believed that Russia was attempting to partition Turkey. The war began with naval attacks against coastal Russian towns on the Baltic Sea, the White Sea, and the Pacific Ocean, but the main attack came in 1854 when 60,000 allied troops began a siege of the Russian naval base at Sevastopol on the Crimean Peninsula.

Although faced with superior forces, the siege of the Russians lasted almost a year. One episode of the senseless loss of many lives is known to most pupils from Alfred Tennyson's "Charge of the Light Brigade." Tsar Nicholas died in the midst of the war, which was brought to an end by the Treaty of Paris in 1856. Russia had to surrender some territory, including Bessarabia, and give up the right to have naval forces or fortifications on the Black Sea.

The Tsar Emancipator

Alexander II (1855–1881), who succeeded to the throne upon the death of his father, Nicholas I, went down in history as the "Tsar Emancipator," the greatest westernizer since Peter the Great. Yet, he was not particularly well-liked during his reign, and he died the victim of a terrorist's bomb. The problem was that, though he saw the need for reforms, he wished to implement them in the form of another "revolution from above," in the manner of previous tsars. Perhaps that was inevitable, but the result was that, first, his reforms were modified in their application by a conservative bureaucracy and, second, his unwillingness to involve the newly educated elites created by his reforms meant that he lost a chance to develop a popular constituency to support his measures.

Alexander II came to the throne much better prepared than his father, for Nicholas had appointed him to the State Council (the appointed legislative assembly created by Alexander I) and the Committee of Ministers (the Tsar's cabinet, also created by his predecessor). He held a series of military commands and had also sat on a committee on serfdom appointed by Nicholas. At the conclusion of one session, Alexander petitioned his father to abolish serfdom. Nicholas said he recognized that serfdom was a present, existing evil, but to touch it might perhaps create greater evils.

Russia's defeat in the Crimean War convinced Alexander that Russia could no longer afford to do nothing; its continued existence as a great power was now at stake. The industrialization that had spread across Europe in the first half of

Alexander II

the nineteenth century had left Russia largely untouched. Serfdom, with its mass of peasant workers tied to the soil, was incompatible with industrialization. Russia stood still while Europe progressed.

Moreover, serfdom, which had been abolished everywhere else in Europe, had come to be viewed as a moral evil whose continued presence in Russia excluded it from the company of civilized Europe. This moral revulsion toward serfdom had been an important factor in the harsh terms applied to Russia in the Treaty of Paris. Alexander II thus had two important reasons to move for the abolition of serfdom.

Alexander appointed his first committee to consider ways to abolish serfdom in 1857. Four years later, in 1861, he gave his approval to the emancipation manifesto which immediately freed all serfs from personal bondage. Since Russia had an overwhelmingly agricultural economy, it was decided to free the serfs with a type

of land tenure. Since the land legally was the property of the nobles, however, the law stipulated that the ex–serfs would get the amount of land they had worked for themselves before emancipation, but they would have to pay for it. Since the ex–serfs had no money, the government arranged to pay the nobles for the land and to have the ex–serfs pay off their debt to the government over a period of 49 years.

Direct and personal ownership of the land was not given to the peasants; the so–called peasant commune was to be collectively responsible for the payments of its members and had the right to allot the land to peasant families. This was to be done according to the size of the family, and the allotments were open to revision every few years. Because of the financial responsibility, the commune hindered the attempts of the peasants to move away, causing overpopulation and land hunger in some areas.

Emancipation ended the control of the nobility over the serfs and necessitated the creation of local government and judicial institutions for the newly–freed peasants. Both of these reforms were carried out in 1864. The *Zemstvo* reform created elective councils at the district and provincial level and gave them responsibility for the local economy, health protection and education. Although voters were organized into three classes—nobles, townsmen and peasants—and voted separately, the *Zemstvo* assemblies were genuinely democratic institutions in which all classes participated and they became an important voice for rural interests.

The judicial reform was even more radical, because it abolished traditional Russian judicial practices and created an entirely new system that introduced trial by jury, public trials, defense attorneys and an independent judiciary, none of which had hitherto existed in Russia.

Cities were granted local government in 1870 along the lines of the *Zemstvo* reform. Elected city councils were created and an executive board was headed by a mayor. Although weighted voting systems meant that a relatively few large taxpayers could control the city council, the effect of the overall reform was positive.

An army reform, introduced in 1874, initiated the principle that every man, regardless of class, was liable for military service. The ordinary term of service was reduced to six years, schools for officers were modernized and specific provisions were made to ensure that all enlisted men were taught how to read and write. Since illiteracy was quite high in Russia, the army thus became a significant adjunct to the nation's educational system.

Alexander also reorganized the secondary school system, granted autonomy

Russia

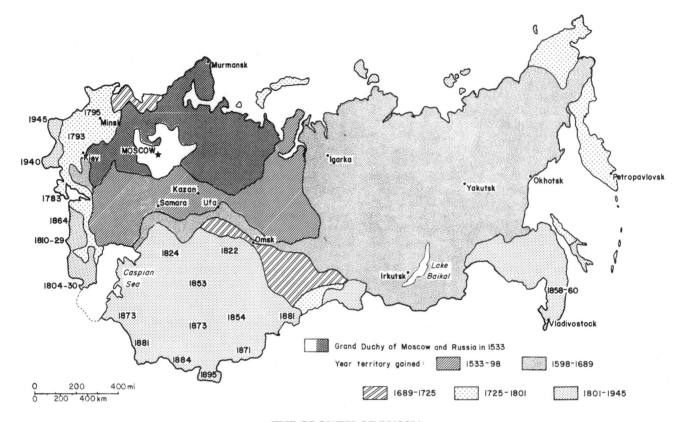

THE GROWTH OF RUSSIA

Grand Duchy of Moscow and Russia in 1533
Year territory gained: 1533–98 | 1598–1689
1689–1725 | 1725–1801 | 1801–1945

to the universities and waived university fees for those too poor to pay. The *Zemstvos* had been given responsibility for primary education, but Alexander did approve a law calling for the establishment of a system of primary education throughout Russia. Many *Zemstvos* were slow to follow through on the Tsar's orders, but primary schools slowly came into existence; by 1914, *Zemstvos* were spending approximately one–third of their budget on primary education.

Alexander's economic reforms were—aside from serf emancipation—his most important measures, but they were more long–term and so took longer to show an effect. In addition, Alexander's commitment to industrialization was closely connected to his desire that Russia remain a great power. One of the major reasons for Russia's defeat in the Crimean War was the inability of the Russian government quickly to move men and supplies to the Crimean area. Because of the nature of the climate and the soil, getting about on land was nearly impossible for several months every year—roads turned into quagmires in the spring and fall. Russia's rivers were important transport links, but they were frozen during six winter months.

Alexander, whose mother and wife were both German and who visited Germany regularly, had been impressed by the extensive railway building in Ger-

many in the 1840s and 1850s and the thrust this had given to German industrialization. The Tsar conceived of a similar program for Russia. But since there was little capital in Russia for investment and even fewer entrepreneurs—and the Russian government had no funds adequate for such railway construction—Alexander and his advisers set out to encourage the creation of private railway companies in Russia financed by foreign private capital investment.

Railway companies were permitted to bring in duty–free all equipment and material needed to construct a railroad; in addition, dividends and interest on stocks and bonds issued by the railway companies were guaranteed by the Russian government. Investors were, in effect, guaranteed against all losses.

The plan worked. By the time of Alexander II's death in 1881, approximately 7,500 kilometers of railroad had been constructed, metal–working and machine–building companies had sprung into existence and the beginnings of a modern iron and steel industry had been laid. It was still only a beginning, but railroad construction continued in the 1880s and 1890s and, after a financial and political crisis that lasted for several years, again began between 1907 and 1914. By 1914, European Russia was covered by an extensive network of railways and the Trans–

Siberian Railway had been built across Siberia down to Vladivostok.

Alexander II was obsessed with Russia's defeat in the Crimean War and was determined to undo at least the more onerous clauses of the 1856 treaty. This became the main thrust of his foreign policy; his efforts to win over the French resulted in a friendship treaty between the two nations in 1857, but the Polish uprising six years later disrupted this relationship, since the French were sympathetic to the Poles. Alexander next turned to Prussia as a potential ally and this led to Russian support for German unification and a growing economic relationship between the two.

When the Franco–Prussian War broke out in 1870, the Russian government took advantage of the situation by denouncing the Black Sea clauses of the earlier treaty. England protested, but agreed to drop the offending clauses when it became clear that the new German government supported Russia.

Russia and the Austro–Hungarian Empire tended to be rivals in the Balkan area and their relations had been strained since the Crimean War. However, Russia, Germany, and Austria signed an agreement in 1873—The Three Emperor's League—which brought them together in a quasi-alliance. It was Bismarck, the German Chancellor, who sponsored the agreement;

24

he hoped to end the Russo–Austrian rivalry in the Balkans. Russia and Austria could, however, only agree to maintain the *status quo*, so when an uprising began in Bosnia in 1875 and quickly spread to Serbia and Bulgaria, relations between the two countries soured.

Russia and Austria signed the Reichstadt Agreement in 1876 whereby Austria agreed to remain neutral in case of war, while Russia agreed to a suitable territorial compensation for Austria and promised that it would not sponsor the creation of a single large Slavic nation. War broke out between Russia and Turkey in 1877; Russian armies were victorious. In the ensuing treaty, Russia got back southern Bessarabia plus three small towns east of the Black Sea; Turkey agreed to recognize the independence of Serbia, Romania and Montenegro. The remaining Slavic territories in the eastern Balkans would be organized into a single, autonomous state with an elected Christian Prince. No mention was made of any territorial compensation for Austria.

A bitter Austria threatened to go to war and England also objected to the terms of the treaty, sending its fleet into the eastern Mediterranean. War appeared imminent and Bismarck quickly agreed to host a conference of the powers in Berlin.

At the Congress of Berlin, the powers modified the terms of the treaty as follows: Bulgaria was reduced to one–third of its former size; another third was set up as the autonomous region of Eastern Rumelia and the final third, Macedonia, was returned to Turkey. Austria received the right to administer Bosnia and Herzegovina and was allowed to station troops in the Sanjak of Novibazar. England got Cyprus. Even as modified, the Treaty of Berlin was a triumph for Russia for, with the return of Bessarabia, the last of the offending clauses of the 1856 treaty had been overturned. But instead, the Congress of Berlin was considered to be a humiliation for Russia and Alexander's foreign policy was judged to be a failure. The Three Emperors' League was dead; relations between Russia and Germany cooled; and Russia drew more and more into self–isolation for the next three years.

Although often at odds with the European powers, Russia was quite friendly with the United States of America. For example, the North was pleased to have

squadrons of the Russian fleet pay visits to New York and San Francisco during the Civil War, though the Americans might have been less pleased had they known that the purpose of the naval visits was to avoid being trapped inside Russian bases in the event of a European war—they were not interested in helping the North. Even so, the North was determined to see the naval visits as evidence of the mutual friendship that existed between our two countries, and they also compared serf emancipation with America's abolition of slavery.

In this atmosphere, the United States Government responded favorably when the Russian Government suggested that it was willing to sell Alaska to America. After some negotiations, then, the United States purchased Alaska from Russia in 1867 for the sum of $7.2 million. Although this turned out to be one of America's greatest bargains, many Americans denounced it at the time as "Seward's Folly," a reference to the U.S. Secretary of State who arranged the purchase.

In spite of Alexander II's preoccupation with relations with the West, the Russian nation continued to expand in Asia during his reign. In East Asia, China was involved in a struggle with the western powers encroaching on its coastal areas. Taking advantage of this, Russia coerced China into ceding it the regions around the Amur and Usuri Rivers. The city of Vladivostok, meaning "Ruler of the East," was founded in 1860 as a symbol of Russian power on the Pacific shores.

Central Asia was another area of expansion for Russia in the nineteenth century. This was Russia's southern frontier and, as settlers pushed southward, they came increasingly into contact with central Asian peoples who resented their presence and showed this by carrying out periodic raids against Russian settlements. This would be followed in turn by punitive forays by the Russian army against central Asian settlements. As the raids continued, the army would begin building a new line of forts along the frontier and a new piece of territory would be added to the Russian empire.

By 1846, when a large part of Kazakhstan was incorporated into Russia, central Asia had been reduced to three independent Islamic khanates, Bokhara, Khiva and Kokand. Great centers of trade and export in the middle ages which had made them legends of wealth and power, all three khanates had subsequently declined in importance. By the middle of the nineteenth century, their main cities had been reduced to regional trading centers and the khanates were pale shadows of their former selves. Moreover, the writ of their rulers extended mainly to the larger

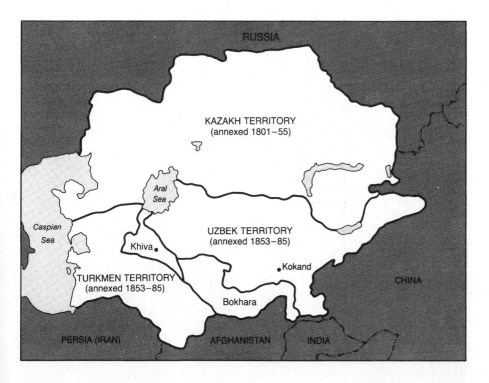

Russia

NIHILISM

The following is an excerpt from Ivan Turgenev's *Fathers and Sons*. In this scene, Arkady, son of a large land-owner, has just returned home from St. Petersburg, having graduated from the university. He is accompanied by a classmate, Bazarov, who has just gotten his medical degree. Arkady's father, Nikolai Petrovich and his uncle, Pavel Petrovich, both old liberals, ask about Bazarov:

"What is Bazarov?" Arkady smiled. "Would you like me, uncle, to explain?"

"If you will be so good, nephew."

"He's a nihilist."

"How?" inquired Nikolas Petrovich, while Pavel Petrovich lifted a knife in the air with a small piece on its tip, and remained motionless.

"He's a nihilist," repeated Arkady.

"A nihilist," said Nikolai Petrovich, "That's from the Latin, *nihil, nothing*, as far as I can judge; the word must mean a man who . . . who accepts nothing?"

"Say, who respects nothing," put in Pavel Petrovich, and he set to work on the butter again.

"Who regards everything from the critical point of view," observed Arkady.

"Isn't that just the same thing?" inquired Pavel Petrovich.

"No, it's not the same thing. A nihilist is a man who does not bow down before any authority, who does not take any principles on faith, whatever reverence that principle may be enshrined in."

settlements and they made no significant attempt to control the undisciplined tribesmen of the countryside or to stop them from carrying out raids on Russian settlements across the border.

In the 1860s, the Russian armies began a final conquest of the area. Kokand, with its ancient cities of Tashkent and Samarkand, took three years to subdue. Its final conquest came in 1868. Bokhara fell the same year and Khiva was conquered in 1873.

Revolutionary Stirrings

While Russia was having general success in the area of international relations, the situation at home was deteriorating. Alexander II's promise of reforms brought a wave of enthusiasm among the people at the beginning, and even support from old revolutionaries such as Alexander Herzen in his exile in London. But disillusionment set in as implementation of the reforms began, for it became clear that,

first, from the point of view of liberals, there were flaws in the legislation itself and, second, that a conservative bureaucracy would do its best to limit even further the benefits to come from the new legislation. Moreover, the very fact of reform from above brought a questioning of the *status quo* among educated Russians because it legitimated the question—"what further should be changed?" One writer who wrote on this theme was Nicholas Chernaevsky, whose novel, *What Is To Be Done?*, became almost a sacred text for the questioning youth of the 1860s.

This questioning occurred mainly among the greatly increased numbers of young men streaming into the universities—as yet young women had to go abroad if they wanted a university education. Exposed for the first time to the latest scientific and philosophical theories from Western Europe—revolution, positivism, French Utopian Socialism—many of these young people began questioning everything about Russian culture and the Russian way of life. Although women were denied access to the universities, some of them soon became important leaders in this new movement.

We speak of this movement as *nihilism* and it was perhaps best summed up by the great Russian novelist Turgenev in his novel *Fathers and Sons*. Turgenev saw the development as a kind of generation gap, a clash between the ideas of the "fathers and sons."

The *nihilists* of the 1860s were in general not revolutionaries, but there were some exceptions. In 1866, one such "student" decided to shoot the tsar and he actually went to the garden of the palace, walked up to Alexander II, pulled out his revolver and shot at him. What saved Alexander II's life at that moment is that a worker in the gardens, seeing what was happening, grabbed his arm.

By the 1870s, the vague and somewhat negative revolutionary stirring of the previous decades merged into the so–called *Narodnik* (populist) movement. The *Narodniki* were heavily influenced by the writing of the French Utopian Socialists. Appalled by what they thought of as the evils of industrialism, they advocated a kind of agrarian socialism based on the traditional Russian peasant commune. The leadership expected to stir the Russian masses by going among the simple people, teaching them, but also learning from their supposedly pure and simple outlook which they allegedly had because they had not been "contaminated" by urban life. It became fashionable to "go to the people" to bring education and sanitary habits to the primitive, rural folk. Often the peasants repaid this by denouncing the uninvited tutors to the police.

Some of the populist leaders concluded that someone else would have to work for the peasants, because the masses were not mature and thinking enough to stage a general uprising against the Russian system. A decision was made to engage in acts of terrorism, the most spectacular of which was the attempt to kill the military governor of St. Petersburg. By the end of the 1870s, the revolutionary organization *Zemlya i Volya* (Land and Freedom) split into two major groups, one of which favored gradual change. The other, *Narodnaya Volya* (Will of the People), chose more terror in the somewhat questionable belief that removal of a few high personalities would change things in Russia. The Tsar was selected as the chief target for assassination. After several unsuccessful attempts, Alexander II was killed by terrorists in 1881. This apparently came on the very day when he was about to sign a new decree granting more political freedom to the people.

An Age of Reaction

The death of Alexander II brought to an end the age of reforms that originally began with Peter the Great. "Western" and "liberal" took on sinister meanings in the eyes of the government and upper classes. Alexander III (1881–1894), who was in narrow political terms a reactionary, believed it was impossible to come to terms with the liberals and that his father's assassination had partly resulted from his attempts to do so. He made it clear that liberals could expect nothing from him when, in his accession address, he declared his "complete faith in the strength and truth of autocracy" and that "for the good of the people" he would "maintain and defend the autocratic power from attack."

Alexander III

He was 36 when he came to the throne. A great bear of a man, he referred to himself as the "peasant Tsar," and he was very proud of the fact that he could straighten horseshoes with his bare hands. He was honest and hard–working, but intellectually somewhat dull. He recognized his limitations, however, and left many decisions to his ministers, supporting them and keeping them in office even when he didn't understand what they were trying to do.

His most important political advisers were Constantine Pobedonostsev, Michael Katkov and Dmitri Tolstoy. Curiously enough, all had been supporters of Alexander II's reforms. Pobedonostsev had helped to draft the judicial reforms, for example, and Tolstoy had been minister of education in the previous regime. Katkov had been a well–known westernizer and liberal.

By 1881, however, they had rejected their earlier admiration for foreign ideas and now sought Russia's salvation in its own past. Alexander III, strongly nationalistic with Pan–Slav leanings, accepted their advice about the need to Russify the minorities and to bring the entire population into the Russian Orthodox Church.

In Poland and in the Baltic provinces, Russian was made the language of instruction in the schools. Catholics, Protestants and Old Believers found themselves affected by government policies aimed at the conversion of these groups to Russian Orthodoxy.

More affected were the Jews, for even more restrictive policies were applied to them. Laws forbidding their settlement in central Russia were tightened, and they were confined to an area called the "Pale of Settlement." Limitations were placed on the entry of Jews to universities; they were excluded from most government service; and forbidden to acquire land in rural areas. In addition, agencies of the government were frequently engaged in stirring up *pogroms* (violent outbreaks) of the people against their Jewish countrymen. Repeated outbreaks caused a massive migration of Jews from the lands of the Russian empire. Many came to America.

The nature of Alexander III's reign was thus quite different from that of his father. Yet, though he disagreed with his father politically, he was loath to undo the work which his predecessor had begun. The substance of reform survived, although the new Tsar did approve some amendments aimed at reducing popular participation. Provincial governors were, for example, given greater control over the *Zemstvo* assemblies and the franchise was changed to increase the representation of the nobility. The government also increased its administrative powers over the judiciary.

Alexander III shared his father's commitment to industrialization, so there was no essential change in economic policy. Government policy continued to encourage the construction of railroads, though more state–owned railroads were built in this period. Tariffs were also raised several times in order to encourage "infant industries." The policy worked in the sense that there was a good deal of foreign investment in Russia in the 1880s, but it also led to a tariff war with Germany from 1887 to 1893.

The policy of Alexander III toward the peasantry was probably his most important personal contribution toward the economic policy of his reign. Genuinely interested in the welfare of the peasantry, the Tsar set out to do what he could to improve their lot—at least insofar as that could be done within the framework of Russia at that time. The redemption debt was reduced in 1881 and again in 1884. Two taxes that weighed heavily on the lower class, the salt tax and the poll tax, were repealed. They were replaced by two taxes which applied mainly to the upper and middle classes: an inheritance tax and a tax on bonds.

The increase in population after emancipation had also reduced the average size of peasant allotments. To remedy this, the government set up a Peasant Land Bank to lend money. The bank also made loans to those who were willing to move to Siberia. In spite of these measures, the true state of Russia became evident in 1891 when crop failures led to famine in the countryside.

Although Russia remained at peace during the 13 years that Alexander III was on the throne, Russia's foreign relations were often abrasive, for, as one historian says of him, Alexander III attempted to obtain peacefully objectives that are usually obtained only as the result of a successful war. Russia's quarrels were primarily with Austria–Hungary and Germany and led to Alexander's decision to sign an alliance with France in 1892.

Alexander III's quarrels with Germany were of a two–fold nature, but they were exacerbated by his pan–Slav leanings. In the 1870s, Alexander III, then the heir to the throne, had supported pan–Slav aspirations in the Balkans and was deeply angered when Austria refused to accept the Treaty of San Stefano, negotiated at the close of Russia's victorious war against the Ottoman Empire in 1878. He favored a connection with Germany, however, and, in 1881, accepted his foreign minister's advice that a renewal of the Three Emperors' League was the only way this could be arranged.

Things went smoothly until 1885, when the Bulgarians, at that time protégés of the Russians, decided to carry through a union with East Rumelia without consulting with the Russian Government. Alexander III "punished" the Bulgarians by withdrawing all Russian military advisers. When Austria took advantage of the situation to increase its own influence in Bulgaria, Alexander III felt betrayed and denounced the Three Emperors' League. His real quarrel, therefore, was with Austria. Alexander III still wanted a connection with Germany, however, and suggested a bilateral alliance with Germany in 1887, "not against Austria, but without Austria." This became the Re–insurance Treaty, which existed for three years, until 1890.

Alexander III also had a grievance with Germany having to do with economic relations between the two countries. In the 1880s, Germany was Russia's chief trading partner and the source of most foreign capital investment in the Russian economy. Russia had an adverse trade balance with Germany, which it attempted to solve by raising tariffs on the main goods coming in from Germany. This led a good number of German firms to open affiliates in Russian Poland as a way to retain the Russian market. However, this large German commercial presence in Russian Poland became another problem, because Russian nationalists felt it threatened Russian political control in this borderland area. In 1887, the Russian Government issued a decree prohibiting foreigners from owning land in border areas such as Russian Poland, and Germany retaliated by an attack on Russian securities, known as the *Lombard Verbot*. Thus began an economic war that lasted until 1894 and brought the two nations as close to war as they were to come in the nineteenth century.

It was these poor economic–political relations with Germany which led Alexander III to sign an alliance with France in 1892. That alliance, still in force in 1914, would bring Russia and France into World War I as allies against Germany and Austria.

The Last Tsar

Alexander III has sometimes been referred to as the last Russian autocrat; whatever else can be said of him, it is generally agreed that he personified the policy of his reign. Nicholas II (1894–1914), by contrast, was a weak–willed individual who, all his life, was dominated by those about him. Moreover, he hated confrontations and got around them by seeming to agree with whomever he was talking. This made it extremely difficult for government ministers, for they never knew whether his approval of one of their suggestions was apparent or real. This also inclined him against strong–willed ministers, for that increased the possibility of disagreement. This trait became

Russia

Nicholas II and Alexandra

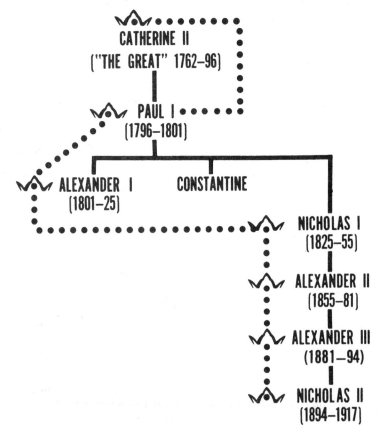

even more noticeable as he grew older, probably the result of the influence of his wife, Alexandra.

Alexandra, who also attempted to dominate him, called him weak–willed to his face and demanded that he stand up to his ministers. Other examples of her advice follow. Her baleful influence came primarily toward the end of his reign, however, as she undoubtedly saw the future crumbling.

Nicholas II was 26 years old when he succeeded to the throne. Professing his admiration for his father, he retained his father's ministers and promised to continue his policies. Meeting with representatives of the *Zemstvo* of Tver, for example, Nicholas told them that:

> It has come to my knowledge that there have been heard in some Zemstvos the voices of those who have indulged in senseless dreams that the Zemstvos might participate in the direction of the internal affairs of the state. Let all know that I shall devote my energy to the service of the people, but that I shall maintain the principle of autocracy as firmly as did my father.

In spite of his promise, Nicholas did modify his father's policies in one area. He did not share his father's dislike for German culture and this showed up domestically in his reversal of his father's Russification policy as it applied to the Baltic Germans. It showed up internationally in the much better relations that developed with both Austria and Germany after 1894.

Russia was already in the midst of an economic boom when Nicholas came to the throne. The minister of finance was Sergei Witte (*Vi–teh*), a strong proponent of industrialization. Witte put the country on the gold standard, encouraged the inflow of foreign investment and pushed the construction of railroads. The boom lasted until 1899; by that time, the production of large–scale industry as a whole had doubled.

One ominous sign on the horizon was the lack of domestic entrepreneurs, however. Of 14 new steel mills built during the 1890s, only one was Russian. The other 13 were foreign–owned and had foreign management. Other branches of industry dominated by foreign capital included the electric and electro–technical industry, the gas industry, chemicals and dyes. Many metal–working and machine–building companies were also foreign–owned and run. Using the terminology of Karl Marx, whose economic theories were to have such a dynamic impact on Russia, it was *creating capitalism but very few capitalists.*

The Revolution of 1905

A worldwide financial crisis in 1899 halted the flow of new foreign capital into

Russia, leading to a wave of bankruptcies and mounting unemployment. Just as business was starting to recover, the economy was set back by crop failures in the countryside in 1901–2. A period of unrest followed, with strikes in the cities and peasant demonstrations in the villages. Illegal political parties began to appear and agitation for basic reforms increased.

Then came the Russo–Japanese War of 1904. It was badly fought, and the defeat of Russian forces at Port Arthur swelled the numbers of those who had come to believe that the government was unfit to rule.

In this tense atmosphere, the government made yet another blunder and set off the Revolution of 1905. Father Gabon, a Russian Orthodox priest who had started an organization for workers with the permission of the secret police, was asked by them to lead them in a march to the Winter Palace to present a petition for redress of grievances to the Tsar. The peaceful crowd of workers, accompanied by their wives and children, were fired upon by the police as they approached the Winter Palace.

Approximately a hundred people were killed and another hundred wounded. Although it had been one of the Russian Grand Dukes who had given orders to fire on the crowd—Nicholas II was not in residence at the Winter Palace at the time—Nicholas was blamed for what happened. Thus this event, which has gone down in history as "Bloody Sunday," had a significance beyond the immediate deaths and injuries. On that day, a myth died. The peasants had always thought of the Tsar as the "Little Father" who cared for his people. With the events of Bloody Sunday, that myth could no longer be sustained.

It triggered a wave of resentment and protests that continued throughout the spring and summer of 1905 and led, then, to a general strike that began in early fall. The general strike established that Nicholas II's government had lost the confidence of all Russian society, with the possible exception of the nobility and some of the military.

On the advice of Sergei Witte, Nicholas issued a manifesto promising constitutional government, civil liberties to all citizens and a national legislature or (*Duma*). This was termed the "October Manifesto;" Nicholas also named Witte as his new chief minister.

Elections to the first *Duma* took place in March 1906. A plurality of the seats was won by members of the *Constitutional Democratic (Cadet) Party*, a liberal group supported by Russia's professional classes, because the more radical political parties boycotted the elections.

Learning that Witte had been sounding out *Cadet* representatives about joining his cabinet, Nicholas dismissed him as chief minister just before the legislature convened, replacing him with a colorless bureaucrat by the name of Goremykin. Perhaps Witte would not have been able to work with the *Cadets* either, but Goremykin never even tried.

As a result, there was a bitter clash between the representatives and the government and Nicholas reacted by dissolving the first *Duma*. The second *Duma* was even more radical and it also was dissolved.

In calling for elections to a third *Duma*, Nicholas changed voting regulations to reduce the representation of those elements of the population that had been voting for more radical candidates. He also appointed Peter Stolypin as his new Chief Minister.

The change in voting made the new *Duma* less representative, but it also produced a body willing to work with the Tsar and his ministers. Stolypin turned out to be a strong individual who managed to save the Tsar from himself for the next several years.

Stolypin's name is particularly associated with a land reform which broke up the peasant communes and redistributed the land to the peasants as their private property. He hoped that, by giving the peasants something to lose, he would wean them away from their support of the radicals. But the reforms came too late and took too much time; by 1914, only about 25 percent of the peasants had managed to exchange their scattered strips for a single, contiguous plot of land. Stolypin was assassinated by revolutionaries in 1911. With his strong presence gone, Nicholas II again began to exercise a greater say in the government.

World War I

The good relations that Nicholas had cultivated with Germany and Austria came to an end in 1908 when a new quarrel erupted between Russia and Austria over events in the Balkans. Austria's annexation of Bosnia began the dispute, but it soon spread and involved Germany—because of its support of Austria. Russia then became a patron of Serbia, which had been anti–Austrian since the Karageorgovic dynasty seized the Serbian throne in 1903. The assassination by a Serbian nationalist of Archduke Francis Ferdinand, heir to the Austrian throne, led Austria to declare war on Serbia.

The general system of alliances transformed this Balkan war into World War I and it was not long before the continent of Europe was aflame. Russian war plans were predicated on a war with Austria, and the Russian army had no plans drawn up at the beginning of the war for an attack on Germany. However, as the war be-

---

SAMPLES OF THE FATEFUL ADVICE GIVEN TO THE TSAR BY EMPRESS ALEXANDRA

". . . You know you are too kind and gentle . . .

Sometimes a good loud voice and a severe look can do wonders. Do, my love, be more decided and sure of yourself . . . Humility is God's greatest gift, but a sovereign needs to show his will more often."

". . . Be more autocratic, my very own sweetheart . . . Be the Master and Lord, you are the autocrat."

". . . We are not a constitutional country and dare not be; our people are not educated for it . . . Never forget that you are and must remain an autocratic Emperor. We are not ready for constitutional government."

". . . For Baby's sake, we must be firm, otherwise his inheritance will be awful, since with his character he won't bow down to others but be his own master, as one must be in Russia while the people are still so uneducated." . . . Listen to our friend (Rasputin) . . . I fully trust in our friend's wisdom, endowed by God to counsel what is right for you and our country."

(Quoted from *Letters of the Tsarina to the Tsar, 1914–1916*. London: Duckworth, 1923).

---

gan, the German military, working on the basis of the Von Schlieffen Plan, pushed rapidly through Belgium and into France, and soon threatened Paris. The French Government then made a desperate plea to Nicholas II to launch an invasion into eastern Germany in order to take the pressure off France.

Nicholas II ordered three Russian armies to invade East Prussia in August 1914. The Russian armies, operating without a specific plan of invasion and both ill–prepared and poorly equipped, suffered a humiliating defeat. The action did accomplish France's purpose, however, for the German Emperor responded to the invasion by pulling off forces from the right wing of the German armies invading France and ordered them to East Prussia. Shortly thereafter, the German forces were halted in the west and Paris was saved.

The Russian military was not that well prepared at the beginning of the war, but it did have fairly consistent success on the Austrian front in 1914 and 1915. It was, in fact, only when it came up against German forces that the Russian army proved to be not up to the task. However, a greater problem than the purely military one was the inability of the Russian gov-

Russia

Nicholas II: A Prisoner at Tsarskoe Selo, 1917

ernment to work with the public organizations that were willing to assist in the war effort. Distrustful of the motives of these organizations, the government rejected their help and insisted on doing everything itself. The government thereby alienated a large part of the educated classes who were involved in these organizations, and such individuals tended thereafter to see every mistake and blunder of the government as a sign of its incompetence.

Tsar Nicholas made things worse for himself by assuming direct command of the armed forces in September 1915, leaving the Empress Alexandra in charge back

Grigori Efimovich Rasputin

in the capital. Although raised at the court of Queen Victoria, the German–born Alexandra had extremely conservative political ideas but, more importantly, she was obsessed by a tragic family problem—the fact that her only son, Alexis, the heir to the throne, suffered from hemophilia, an incurable bleeding disease. Alexandra probably also suffered from a feeling of guilt, for hemophilia can only be inherited through the mother.

This led to another unhealthy influence in the palace, for Alexandra, seeking help for her son, put her complete faith in an itinerant Siberian monk called Rasputin—because she believed that Rasputin was a "Holy Man" sent by God, who could stop her son's bleeding when an attack started. Rasputin, often characterized as an illiterate, immoral and filthy peasant, did apparently have some success in this regard, though no one knows how.

Many members of the educated classes of Russia objected to Alexandra's associating with such a man, but the real problem was that she soon began seeking Rasputin's advice on extremely important matters of state, and even dismissed officials who had anything negative to say about Rasputin. Such actions eventually convinced most educated Russians that the government was corrupt and incapable of governing competently. This also led several members of the Russian aristocracy, including two related to the royal family, to plan Rasputin's murder in December 1916; they were successful in their plan, but by that time it was too late.

The effects of the war at first caused unrest mainly among the city dwellers who suffered from fuel shortages and high food prices caused by disrupted supplies. Soon the countryside also became restive. Major military defeats in 1915 and 1916 also contributed to a feeling that the government was incompetent. In addition, the demands of the military often overtaxed the hauling capabilities of the railroads, resulting in shortages of food in the cities.

By the beginning of 1917, the number of strikes and demonstrations was on the increase. Then food riots broke out in the capital city after bakeries began running short on flour, and bread became scarce in the stores. Troops summoned to restore law and order tended to side with the angry people. Nicholas was then advised by the *Duma* leaders that the only way to save the monarchy was for him to abdicate in favor of his son, Alexis.

Nicholas first considered doing so, but he then decided that it would be too great a burden on Alexis. He therefore changed the order of succession and named his brother, the Grand Duke Mikhail, as his successor. However, Mikhail refused the offer, and overnight the Russian monarchy came to an end. The royal family was later put under arrest, then executed by the Bolsheviks in July 1918 in a cellar in Ekaterinburg.

An Experiment With Democracy

During the war years, the *Duma* had continued to meet periodically and to debate current issues. In September 1915, for example, the *Duma* had called for a government having the confidence of a majority in the legislature. Nicholas, of course, ignored this advice and, instead, appointed himself commander–in–chief and went off to the front.

A second series of debates in October 1916 was even more negative in its evaluation of the government but they, too, represented points of view that the Tsar was not interested in hearing, so he ignored them as well.

By February 1917, however, the leaders of the *Duma* had come to the conclusion that they could no longer ignore their own responsibilities so, when Nicholas again issued a decree dissolving the *Duma*, they ignored the order and remained in Petrograd. When the tsarist regime "evaporated," the *Duma* first organized a Temporary Committee with representation from all political groups except the extreme right and the extreme left. The Bolsheviks who had been elected to the *Duma* during the last elections in 1912 were, in any case, either in jail or in Siberian exile. The Temporary Committee then established a Provisional Government under the chairmanship of Prince George Lvov, a liberal aristocrat.

It was intended that the Provisional Government would run the affairs of Russia until a Constituent Assembly charged with writing a constitution could be elected by the people. The Provisional Government lasted for a total of seven months and after July was headed by Alexander Kerensky, a moderate socialist, who held power until overthrown by the *Bolsheviks* on October 25 (or November 7 by the new calendar), 1917.

In order to understand how the Provisional Government came to be deposed, it is important to know that, on the very day that the *Duma* organized its Temporary Committee, the Provisional Executive Committee of the Soviet of Worker's Deputies also came into existence. This was actually a revival of the institution that briefly functioned as a command post during the Revolution of 1905.

The Soviet was soon enlarged by adding representatives of the soldiers in revolt. It was led by moderate socialists at this time, though *Bolsheviks* such as Stalin and Molotov soon joined the deliberations. The moderate socialists, using Karl Marx as their guide, believed that Russia, a backward country in terms of industrial development, would have to go through a *bourgeois-democratic* stage before it could proceed to socialism. This *bourgeois–democratic* stage would bring Russia to the level of a mature, capitalist nation, at which time it would be ripe for a socialist revolution. The workers, or *proletariat*, would grow in numbers in the democratic capitalist period and would become aware of their power and historical role; another revolution would then usher in socialism.

Accordingly, the leftist parties, including the *Bolsheviks* prior to Lenin's return to Russia, gave their conditional support to the Provisional Government, although

---

FROM LENIN'S "APRIL THESES"

(A few days after his return to Russia, Lenin published on April 7, 1917, a set of brief "theses" stating his view of the situation in the war-torn country. He outlined a program for the "second stage" of the revolution. Below are some excerpts.)

1. In our attitude toward the war, which unquestionably remains on Russia's part a predatory imperialist war under the new government of Lvov Company because of the capitalist nature of that government, not the slightest concession to "revolutionary defencism" is permissible.

The class–conscious proletariat can give its consent to a revolutionary war which would really justify "revolutionary defencism" only if (a) the power passes to the proletariat, (b) all foreign annexations be renounced in fact and not just in word, and (c) that a complete break be made in fact with all capitalist interests. . .

5. There should not be a parliamentary republic—to return to a parliamentary republic from the Soviets of Workers' Deputies would be a step backwards—there must be a republic of Soviets of Workers', Agricultural Laborers' and Peasants' Deputies throughout the country, from top to bottom.

There also must be abolition of the police, the army and the bureaucracy. . .

9. (c) (We must) change the Party's name. Instead of "Social Democracy," the world leaders of which have betrayed Socialism and deserted to the bourgeoisie . . . we must call ourselves a Communist Party.

10. There must be a new International. We must take the initiative in creating a new revolutionary International. . .

(except for Alexander Kerensky) refusing to serve in it. A peculiar pattern of power therefore emerged; although the Soviet enjoyed substantial support from the workers and soldiers, it reserved for itself the position of being a critic and "watchdog" of the revolution and refused to govern directly. Meanwhile the Provisional Government, the official governing body, had no mass following and was forced to rely on the Soviet for support. This was particularly true in matters involving the army. Although the Provisional Government was in nominal control of the armed forces, the Soviet actually had representatives from all of the military units and its "Order Number 1," which granted full civil rights to enlisted personnel, also instructed them to form company committees to assume control of arms and keep them out of the reach of officers, in order to prevent a counter–revolution.

Lenin's Return

Events took a decisive new turn when Vladimir Lenin, the leader of the *Bolshevik* faction of the *Social Democratic Party*, returned to Russia on April 3, 1917. A natural politician, Lenin believed strongly in the ideas of Marx, but he was, at the same time, flexible enough to deal with situations not covered by Marx. In line with ideas expressed in 1916 in *Imperialism, the Highest Stage of Capitalism*, Lenin believed that Russia was ready for the socialist revolution. He therefore proposed in his "April Theses" that the Provisional Government be pushed aside in favor of the new revolutionary government of the Soviets. He also called for an end to the war, arguing that the proletariat could "give its consent to a revolutionary war" only if "all power passes to the proletariat."

Lenin was aware that, at that moment, the *Bolsheviks* were a minority in the Soviet, but he fully expected to win over the masses to his ideas. In fact, many of his own *Bolsheviks* did not support his position when he first announced it, but they soon fell in line. His opposition to the war soon won him additional support because the Provisional Government continued to insist that Russia had an obligation to continue to fight Germany, an idea that was becoming increasingly unpopular. Another factor was the failure of moderate elements to deal with pressing internal problems such as distribution of land to peasants and creating an orderly supply of food. Propelled by Lenin's determined will and by simplified slogans such as "Peace, Bread, and Land," the *Bolsheviks* began their quest for power.

In July 1917, there was a *Bolshevik*–inspired uprising in Petrograd (the Russian version of St. Petersburg adopted in 1914) which was suppressed, and Lenin

Demonstration against the Provisional Government, July 1917

Russia

Lenin

was forced to flee across the border to Finland. In spite of this temporary setback, the influence of the *Bolsheviks* grew steadily, particularly among the soldiers and sailors.

The opposition of the *Bolsheviks* toward continuing the war with Germany was especially helpful in winning additional support. The Provisional Government, besides failing to solve internal problems, made no real effort to get out of the unpopular war because it felt bound by an agreement with Russia's allies not to make a separate peace. Its decision to mount one more military offensive in July 1917 not only lost it additional support but it also contributed to the near collapse of army organization and morale. This played right into the hands of the *Bolsheviks*.

Lenin's slogan, "all power to the soviets," was picked up by radicals not under his control and it became the basis for an uprising known as the "July Days." Lenin supported the uprising, even though he considered it to be premature. When it collapsed after three days, therefore, Lenin had to go into hiding across the border in Finland.

After the "July Days," the Provisional Government tried to turn the anger of the people against Lenin and his followers by accusing them of being German agents. It further charged that Lenin had spent the war years away from Russia, mainly in neutral Switzerland; that he was an "internationalist" who had opposed the war from its very beginning in 1914; that he had returned to Russia with the assistance of the German army's High Command, who arranged for his travel through Germany in a sealed railway car; and that he had been the recipient of sums of money

from Germany since his arrival in Russia. Lenin never denied the first three charges and there is some evidence that the fourth accusation was true as well. But Lenin was never a German agent. The German army High Command helped Lenin to get back to Russia because he was a known opponent of the war and they hoped his presence in Russia would weaken the Russian resolve to continue the war. Any financial assistance they may have given Lenin was for the same reason. And Lenin was willing to take assistance from any source, provided it promoted his own particular goals.

Although Lenin was forced to remain in hiding because of these charges against him, the *Bolsheviks* continued to grow in popularity, primarily because of incompetence and failures on the part of the Provisional Government and the other political parties. One such case was the "Kornilov Affair."

General Lavr Kornilov had been appointed commander–in–chief of the armed forces shortly before with the support of Alexander Kerensky, who had been head of the Provisional Government since July 20, 1917. In late August, an unscrupulous financier by the name of Zavoyko convinced Kornilov, who was honest and patriotic but politically naive, that Kerensky was willing to relinquish power to him as a way to combat the growing influence of the *Bolsheviks*. Meanwhile, Kerensky, learning that Kornilov had made plans to lead his troops to Petrograd, accused him of planning a coup and fired him.

When Kornilov refused to give up his post and issued a statement directed against the Provisional Government, Kerensky called upon the workers of the threatened capital, including groups that were known to be under *Bolshevik* influence, to come to his assistance. The "Kornilov Affair" ended with the arrest of the general. That seemed to strengthen Kerensky's position for a while but, in reality, the prestige of the Provisional Government had all but vanished.

Lenin's attitude at the time of the "Kornilov Affair" is reflected in his response to Kerensky's plea for support against Kornilov—"We will support him the way a noose supports a hanged man." Lenin apparently liked analogies about ropes and nooses for, on another occasion, he characterized capitalists as being willing to "sell you the rope with which to hang them."

The Kornilov affair rehabilitated the Bolsheviks and prepared the way for their eventual seizure of power. In September, the Petrograd Soviet returned a *Bolshevik*

majority; a week later, the Moscow Soviet did likewise. The new chairman of the Petrograd Soviet was Lev D. Bronstein, better known by his revolutionary name, Trotsky. Although a longtime revolutionary and radical ideologist, he had only joined the Bolshevik faction in the summer of 1917. With Lenin still in hiding, however, it was Trotsky who took charge and actually carried out the *coup d'etat* against the Provisional Government which was to go down in history as the "Great October Socialist Revolution."

However, even Trotsky later conceded that Lenin was the one indispensable individual in the Russian Revolution. It was Lenin who was convinced that the time was ripe to move against the Provisional Government and who persuaded the Central Committee of the Bolsheviks to begin preparations for the seizure of power.

Trotsky accepted that decision and set about to implement it. He persuaded the Executive Committee of the Petrograd Soviet that a Military Revolutionary Committee needed to be created for the defense of the revolution. This Military Revolutionary Committee then sent "political commissars" to each of the military units stationed in Petrograd. Their instructions were to persuade the soldiers and sailors to accept no orders from their officers unless they were countersigned by the political commissar of the Petrograd Soviet. In this manner, Trotsky managed to neutralize the entire Petrograd Garrison.

After many hesitations, the attempt to seize power was timed to coincide with the sessions of the All–Russian Congress of Soviets called for October 25, 1917 (November 7 by the new calendar). However, events came to a head a day earlier—the government had been tipped off about the impending *coup* and began to move some loyal troops into position. It also ordered the soldiers to occupy the premises where the Bolshevik newspaper *Pravda* (Truth) was printed.

By this time, the Bolsheviks were in control of the major military units of the Petrograd Garrison, and easily secured a number of important points. The seat of government in the Winter Palace was defended briefly by a detachment of military cadets and a women's battalion but, when the guns of the cruiser Aurora were trained on the palace, resistance ceased. Most members of the Provisional Government were put under arrest. Kerensky escaped in disguise in a car flying the American flag. He died in New York in 1970; his writings blame everyone but himself for the events of 1917.

The Bolsheviks march into Moscow

THE COMMUNIST ERA (November 1917–August 1991)

What is Communism?

Communism, the official dogma of the Communist Party of the Soviet Union, was a modified version of a theory developed in the 19th century by Karl Marx and Friedrich Engels. Since the modifications are primarily those introduced by Vladimir I. Lenin, this dogma is also referred to as Marxism–Leninism. Let us begin with the theory of communism as developed by Marx and Engels.

First of all, Marxian communism includes, and to a great extent derives from, a theory of history called "historical materialism." According to this theory, the "mode of production in material life determines the general characteristics of the social, political, and spiritual processes of life." Marx illustrated the operation of this theory in the *Communist Manifesto* when he wrote that "the history of all hitherto existing society is the history of class struggles."

Marx, who was a heavy borrower of the ideas of others, took the basic mechanism for "historical materialism" from the dialectic of the philosopher Hegel. Hegel, concerned with historical change, developed a mechanism that focused on the evolution of ideas. His conclusion was that ideas evolved through a "dialectical" process based on the concepts of a thesis, antithesis, and synthesis. The original idea (thesis) is challenged by a second idea (antithesis). The challenge is resolved by a merging of what is true from both ideas to form a new idea (synthesis). The term "dialectic" refers to this process of conflict and reconciliation.

Marx borrowed Hegel's dialectical process but rejected his premise that ideas shape the nature of the real world. He concluded that Hegel had it backwards; that it is the real world (materialism) that

determines what we think. Or as Marx phrased it in the *Communist Manifesto*,

Does it require deep intuition to comprehend that man's ideas, views, and conceptions, in one word, man's consciousness, changes with every change in the conditions of his material existence, in his social relations and in his social life? What else does the history of ideas prove, than that intellectual production changes its character in proportion as material production is changed? The ruling ideas of each age have ever been the ideas of its ruling class.

If the controlling mechanism is materialism, however, Hegel's original question, "what causes historical change?," still required an answer. Marx's answer was that historical change was the result of *changes in the mode of production—and*

Russia

that changes in the mode of production were themselves the result of "internal contradictions."

This explains why Marx saw all history as "class struggles." Each mode of production produces its own ruling class; as the internal contradictions bring about a change in the mode of production, a new class, representing the new mode of production, struggles to come to power.

Applying his ideas to the 19th century, Marx labeled the epoch as "capitalistic" and the ruling class as the "bourgeoisie." This class had been progressive within its own time for it had rid the world of feudalism and serfdom. Moreover, because of its identification with the economic idea of "free competition," it "historically, has played a most revolutionary part" and, in fact, "cannot exist without constantly revolutionizing the instruments of production." As a result,

the bourgeoisie, during its rule of scarce one hundred years, has created more massive and more colossal productive forces than have all preceding generations together. Subjection of nature's forces to man, machinery, application of chemistry to industry and agriculture, steam–navigation, railways, electric telegraphs, clearing of whole continents for cultivation, canalization of rivers, whole populations conjured out of the ground—what earlier century has even a presentiment that such productive forces slumbered in the lap of social labor?

And yet, said Marx, competition, the very mechanism that released those productive forces, produces internal contradictions within capitalism that doom it inevitably to eventual extinction. These internal contradictions, which Marx identified as "laws," are (1) the Law of Capitalist Accumulation; (2) the Law of the Concentration of Capital; and (3) the Law of Increasing Misery.

These "laws" are based on Marx's presupposition that *labor alone creates value and, accordingly, all profits are derived from unpaid labor time.* Their essence is that competition forces capitalists to invest more capital in labor saving machinery, which results in a higher ratio of capital to labor and, Marx asserts, a consequent drop in profit; this leads to bankruptcies as less efficient capitalists are driven out of business. The effect of the operation of laws one and two is increased unemployment and a general lowering of employee wages as each capitalist attempts to increase his profits by increasing the amount of unpaid labor time.

As a result of the operation of these three "laws," capitalistic society eventually reaches the stage of monopoly capitalism, whereby nearly all wealth is in the hands of a few capitalists and the overwhelming mass of the people have been driven down into the ranks of the proletariat. As Marx puts it,

And here it becomes evident, that the bourgeoisie is unfit any longer to be the ruling class in society, and to impose its conditions of existence upon society as an overriding law. It is unfit to rule because it is incompetent to assure an existence to its slave within his slavery, because it cannot help letting him sink into such a state, that it has to feed him, instead of being fed by him. Society can no longer live under this bourgeoisie, in other words, its existence is no longer compatible with society.

At this point, "the more or less veiled civil war . . . breaks out into open revolution," overthrowing the bourgeoisie and raising the proletariat to the position of the ruling class." Once in power, the proletariat will nationalize all the means of production and institute state planning to replace the now discarded mechanism of free competition. The state—"nothing more than a machine for the oppression of one class by another"—will wither away and mankind will have entered the highest and last stage of development, communism.

Marxism thus claims to be a scientific doctrine that, having mastered the general laws that govern human society, can apply them to understand the future. The logical test of Marxism is, therefore, whether the predictions that constitute Marx's "laws" subsequently came true.

In fact, none of Marx's predictions came true. The total number of capitalists continued to grow throughout the remainder of the 19th century as inventions such as the electric dynamo, the internal combustion engine, the light bulb, and the telephone brought whole new industries into being. As for Marx's proletariat, living standards improved as wages began an upward spiral that actually accelerated toward the end of the century. By 1900, it was generally conceded that Marx's Law of Increasing Misery was not operating, and among his followers efforts were being made to update and correct him.

Vladimir I. Lenin was not, properly speaking, one of these revisionists. He thought of himself as primarily a revolutionary, not a theoretician, but it was precisely for this reason that he wanted to know why the revolution had not yet occurred and what could be done to bring it about. He set forth his conclusions in *What Is To Be Done?*, a book he wrote in 1902. In essence, he argued that the revolution hadn't occurred because the proletariat wasn't capable of carrying out a socialist revolution—that, left to itself, it

was only "able to develop trade union consciousness." The revolution would be made by "a revolutionary youth, armed with Social–Democratic theory." What was needed, therefore, was an organization of full–time professional revolutionaries who, acting as "the vanguard of all the revolutionary forces," would bring about the revolution in the name of the proletariat.

Lenin thus presented an "organizational" solution to the question "what could be done to bring the revolution about?" This "organizational" solution had additional implications, however, for it effectively excluded the proletariat from control of the revolutionary party. Only individuals trained in Marxist ideology would have the necessary "socialist consciousness" to be able to provide proper guidance to the proletariat.

Lenin's position on the nature of the party became the chief issue at the Second Congress of the *Russian Social Democratic Labor Party* when it met in 1903. Lenin's supporters became known as *Bolsheviks,* while his opponents became known as *Mensheviks.* There was, in effect, a split in the party.

The Bolsheviks became a small band of professional revolutionaries, whose chief common characteristic was their personal loyalty to Lenin. Lenin's control was further reinforced in July 1917 when a Bolshevik party congress adopted the principle of *democratic centralism* as the basis of party organization. *Democratic centralism,* which remained the basis of Soviet Communist Party organization until Gorbachëv abandoned the concept in the late 1980s, meant in practice that subordinate party units were mere agents of the party leadership, bound to follow all instructions from above.

Lenin made a somewhat broader contribution to Marxist theory in 1916 when he wrote *Imperialism, The Highest Stage of Capitalism.* Most of the book is rather unoriginal, but it does contain an argument which tends to modify Marx's theory that the socialist revolution occurs in a country only after capitalism has been fully developed. According to Marx,

a social system never perishes before all the productive forces have developed for which it is wide enough; and new, higher productive relationships never come into being before the material conditions for their existence have been brought to maturity within the womb of the old society itself.

According to Lenin, however, imperialism created a new situation which called for a modification of Marx's statement insofar as colonial or semi–colonial people were concerned. Under imperialism, monopoly capitalists exploit backward, colonial peoples, first, as markets and, secondly, as a cheap source of raw materials. This exploitation permits the capitalists to pay their own workers higher wages than they would otherwise be able to pay, and accounts for the improvement in the lot of the workers, contrary to Marx's theory. At the same time, it has given a new form to the proletariat—which now included the "toiling masses of the backward countries."

Accordingly, every country that was subject to capitalistic exploitation was a suitable target for revolution, *regardless of the extent of its industrial development*. Russia was thus a proper target for revolution. The Russian Revolution of February 1917 further reinforced Lenin's conviction that Russia was ready for a socialist revolution. He returned to Russia in April 1917 and immediately began to implement his vision. The rest is history.

Creation of the New Soviet Regime

Although the *coup d'etat* that brought the *Bolsheviks* to power was made in the name of the Second Congress of Soviets, it was actually carried out by the Military Revolutionary Committee of the Petrograd Soviet, and the *Bolsheviks* announced the overthrow of the Provisional Government before the Congress of Soviets convened on the evening of October 25/ November 7. The Congress was dominated by the *Bolsheviks* and their allies, the Left *Socialist Revolutionaries*, however, so they accepted their new role and passed are solution written by Lenin proclaiming the transfer of all power to the Soviets. Executive power was vested in a Soviet of People's Commissars (*SOVNARKOM*).

Lenin became chairman, and he filled the other positions on the *SOVNARKOM*

Karl Marx

(equivalent to a cabinet) with *Bolsheviks*. Thus the *Bolsheviks* managed to clothe themselves in the legitimacy of the Soviet movement and to use it to gain political power in Russia. The Congress of Soviets, having installed the *Bolsheviks* in power, had completed its usefulness. A Central Executive Committee was therefore elected, composed of 2/3 *Bolsheviks* and 1/3 Left *Socialist Revolutionaries*, and given full authority to pass legislation in the name of the Congress, which now adjourned. Just in case that wasn't sufficient, the *SOVNARKOM* was authorized to issue decrees which would have the force of law.

Soviets had sprung up spontaneously over all Russia after the February Revolution, but they only existed at the local level and were not universal. In December 1917, a decree of the *SOVNARKOM* called for the creation of Soviets at the local, district, regional, and provincial level, these Soviets to replace the Zemstvos as organs of government. Soviet officials were in theory to be elected, but only workers and peasants had the right to vote.

Since the Soviets only recognized socialist political parties, all others had become illegal as of the creation of the new Soviet government. *Mensheviks* and *Socialist Revolutionaries* lost their representation when the Congress of Soviets adjourned and they soon found themselves subject to some repression as well. *Menshevik* newspapers were closed first, but this ban was soon extended to all opposition newspapers. By the spring of 1918, all opposition political parties had been outlawed and the *Communist Party* (the new name the *Bolsheviks* had adopted in March 1918) had become the sole legal party in Soviet Russia.

War Communism

The period of Soviet history down to March 1921 is usually referred to as the period of War Communism. Once it got itself organized, the new regime set out to communize the country—or at least those parts that recognized its authority, since at this time the various minority nationalities had broken away and were in the process of establishing separate governments.

First priority was given to the nationalization of the means of production. A decree on land, issued immediately after the takeover, abolished private property in land but permitted the peasants to continue to use the land, provided they did not make use of hired labor. Banks, railroads, shipping and foreign trade were nationalized almost immediately, and the Supreme Economic Council was set up to begin state planning. Another decree established worker control over production

and distribution of industrial output. Lenin would probably have preferred to move more slowly with nationalization of the rest of the economy, but he found his pace forced by so–called "nationalizations from below" as individual workers expelled owners and seized control of factories on their own. By the spring of 1918, most industry had been nationalized. Meanwhile, the economy continued to deteriorate.

During the summer of 1918, the Soviet Government implemented new policies aimed at further increasing Soviet control over the countryside. In June, the government created "Committees of Poor Peasants," and gave them the task of carrying "the class war to the village." The government also used these committees to help implement a policy of grain requisitioning, which essentially meant that the government took what grain it could find and seized it in order to be able to feed the cities. To be sure, the peasants received promises that they would receive manufactured goods from the cities in compensation, but there never was any surplus to distribute. The peasant response was to plant less the next year, setting the stage for a future famine.

In the cities, in the meanwhile, the government completed the nationalization of all major industries and placed them under the direction of the Supreme Economic Council. In November, the government extended its control over all internal trade. At about this same time period, partly in response to the beginning of the civil war and partly due to a continuing drop in production, new decrees were issued forbidding workers from leaving their jobs or striking. Even so, as the civil war progressed, more and more workers fled the cities and went back to their villages in search of food.

The Treaty of Brest–Litovsk

Of all the things *Bolshevik* propaganda had promised the people, peace had perhaps been the most significant. But the *Bolsheviks* also needed peace in order to have time to consolidate their government. They attempted a "decree on peace" on the very first day after seizing power, but that had no more than a propaganda effect. For real peace, they had to find a way to negotiate with those making war on Russia—the German Imperial General Staff. Preliminary negotiations resulted in the signing of a temporary truce in December. But when peace negotiations began in January, the German terms were so harsh that Trotsky, in charge of the negotiations as people's commissar for foreign affairs, rejected them out of hand. Lenin argued that there was no alternative to acceptance of the German terms, but it was

Russia

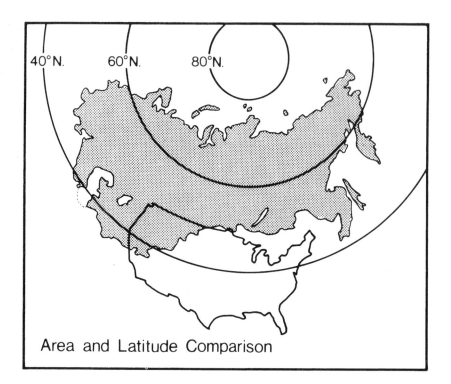

40°N. 60°N. 80°N.

Area and Latitude Comparison

not until the Germans began a new advance that he could get his associates to agree. The Treaty of Brest–Litovsk, signed on March 3, 1918, ended the state of war between Russia and the Central Powers, Germany and Austria.

By the terms of the treaty, the Soviet government obligated to give up any claim to Georgia (in the Caucasus area of southern Russia), the Ukraine (to the south–west, between Russia and Poland) and Finland (to the north). In addition, Poland plus Lithuania, Latvia and Estonia, three small states located along the Baltic which were attempting to establish themselves as independent states, were recognized by the treaty as falling within Germany's sphere of influence. The Aaland Islands, in the Baltic Sea off the coast of Finland, were to be evacuated as well. Finally, the Turks, then allied with Germany, were given land in or near the cities of Kars, Ardahan and Batum.

Profiting from Russia's weakness, the Romanians occupied the province of Bessarabia which had been a part of south–western Russia. Altogether, the terms of the treaty meant a loss of 1.3 million square miles of Russian territory. This represented about 32 percent of the agricultural land, about one–third of the factories and approximately 75 percent of the coal and iron mines of Russia.

Harsh as the terms of the Treaty of Brest–Litovsk were, they gave the hard–pressed *Bolsheviks* an opportunity to consolidate their power in areas outside the two main cities of the country. Trotsky, who became people's commissar for war

after Brest–Litovsk, undertook the gigantic task of building an army to defend the revolution beginning in April 1918. But this was to be no revolutionary army. Known as the *Workers and Peasants Red Army*, it was based on conscription, authority, and discipline. Trotsky even recruited old tsarist officers to command the units he was creating, though they were now referred to as "military specialists" and their second in command was a political commissar whose job was to countersign all military orders to assure that they were not counter–revolutionary.

Intervention and Civil War

Russia's departure from the war with Germany was followed by a civil war within Russia, waged by elements opposed to the new regime. There had been, in fact, some fighting in the south during the early part of 1918, but most people date the real beginning of the civil war to the fighting which broke out between the Czechoslovak Legion and the Bolsheviks in May.

The Czechs were at that time in Cheliabinsk, in the Urals, making their way to Vladivostok by way of the Trans–Siberian Railroad, from whence they intended to make their way to France in order to rejoin the war on the western front. The Soviet Government had actually agreed to this arrangement in March, but a clash between Czech and Hungarian soldiers caused Trotsky to order the Czechoslovak soldiers to be disarmed. They refused to allow themselves to be disarmed, however, and began taking control of towns

along the Trans–Siberian Railroad as clashes between Czechs and *Bolsheviks* spread. The French Government intervened at this time to urge the Czechs to remain where they were, for the French were now planning an allied intervention. Allied forces were, in fact, already in the port cities of Murmansk, Archangel and Vladivostok with the permission of the Soviet Government. Their stated purpose for being there was to reclaim war supplies sent to the Russian Government before it had left the war. Even as the allies began to intervene, however, they were never in agreement about what they might accomplish by intervening. None of the allies liked the *Bolsheviks*, to be sure, but probably only the French were totally committed to their overthrow. The result was a half–hearted intervention, in Winston Churchill's words, "a wretched half–measure." The allies cooperated to some extent with anti–*Bolshevik* groups, but this assistance was never decisive.

The intervention was, in fact, a series of badly coordinated military efforts which, in European Russia, became tied in with the attempts of opposition groups to hold parts of the vast Russian territory and to form counter–governments in a series of uncoordinated attempts to overthrow the *Bolshevik* regime. Various groups were sponsored and supported by foreign powers. A period of short–lived resistance by former tsarist generals in the winter of 1918 was followed by a major effort of General Anton Denikin to deny the Soviet government access to the food and oil producing regions of the south. Elsewhere, an uprising against the *Bolsheviks* was staged by the right wing of the *Social Revolutionaries*, who were in favor of rejoining the war on the side of the Allies. After the Czech revolt, an anti–*Bolshevik* government was established in the Siberian city of Omsk by socialist elements. This was quickly taken over by Admiral Alexander Kolchak, who proclaimed himself "Supreme Ruler" of Russia. In still another area, General Peter Wrangel fought the *Bolsheviks* in the Caucasus, largely with French support. The British provided some support to both General Denikin and Admiral Kolchak.

The civil war dragged on until 1920, marked by heroism and cruelty on both sides. By that time, the allied intervention had come to an end and most of the anti–*Bolshevik* armies had been defeated. During the year also, Russia signed peace treaties with Estonia, Latvia, Lithuania and Finland, recognizing their independence and establishing agreed boundaries.

Poland was another problem, however, for the Pilsudski government claimed Poland's "historic" boundaries and insisted that the Soviet government surrender all land west of the 1772 border—in other words, prior to the first partition of Poland. This included areas with significant Byelorussian and Ukrainian populations and the Soviets therefore refused.

Pilsudski launched an invasion of the Ukraine in the spring of 1920, capturing Kiev. His victory was short–lived, however. A Soviet counterattack drove the Polish army back out of the Ukraine and shortly thereafter a Soviet army was threatening Warsaw. But then the tide of battle turned once again, forcing the Soviet troops to retreat. The Soviets and Poles now agreed to a compromise territorial settlement, with the Poles getting much of what they wanted, and the Peace of Riga was signed in October 1920. The settlement left about 4.5 million Byelorussians and Ukrainians inside Poland, however, a factor that continued to influence Soviet–Polish relations until 1939.

In the autumn of 1920, the Soviets supported the establishment of socialist governments allied with Soviet Russia in Georgia, Azerbaijan and Armenia. Shortly thereafter, Central Asia came back under Russian rule as well. This effectively brought peace to Russia, for only the area east of Lake Baikal—organized as the Far Eastern Republic—remained outside of Soviet control. And, in late 1922, the Far Eastern Republic also rejoined Russia.

New Economic Policy

With the end of the civil war and the war with Poland, a new situation existed. The economy had deteriorated over the preceding three years to such an extent as to make a mockery of *Bolshevik* claims to have improved the lot of the worker. Industrial output had fallen to 20 percent of its 1914 level and half of all industrial jobs had evaporated. Cities were being deserted as people fled to the countryside to find food. The population of Petrograd had declined from a pre–war total of 2.3 million to 900,000. Agricultural output had also declined significantly, partly because of the ravages of the civil war, but also in response to the government's food requisition policy.

Neither the workers nor the peasants had supported the anti–*Bolsheviks*, but many were also unhappy with *Bolshevik* policies. They now felt free to put pressure on the government to change its policies. The result was peasant unrest, strikes by workers and, finally, a revolt of sailors at Kronstadt in early 1921. Lenin now recognized that some compromises were necessary and he announced a *New Economic Policy* (NEP) in March 1921.

The *NEP*, as it came to be called, reestablished a market economy in Russia. Food requisitions were to cease, to be replaced by a tax on agriculture to be paid with produce. After the individual peasant had paid the tax, he could dispose of the remainder of his crops as he saw fit. That meant that internal trade had to be reestablished within the private sector for, otherwise, the peasant would not have been able to dispose of his crops. An important feature of this era was the *NEP–Man*, the private trader who bought the peasant's produce and furnished him with the products he wanted to buy. In the cities, private ownership of shops and factories employing fewer than 20 workers was also permitted. Money, which had largely lost its value, came back into use and a new currency was issued with gold backing.

The "commanding heights"—all large factories, mines, steel mills, transportation, banking and foreign trade—remained in government hands, however. For that reason, eighty–five per cent of all industrial workers continued to work in nationalized industry. But even government plants that were part of the "commanding heights" were formed into separate combines or trusts and ordered to operate on the basis of market principles. In addition, the government invited foreign capitalists to invest in Russia and it also recruited foreign technicians by offering contracts to come to Russia to teach their skills to Soviet workers. The Ford Motor Company opened a tractor factory in Russia at this time but, in general, the attempt to secure foreign capital investment was unsuccessful.

The *NEP* brought new life to Soviet Russia. By 1927, agricultural production had surpassed the levels of 1913 and consumer goods were again in ample supply. Only the large nationalized plants had not regained their pre–war levels—but even they had made great progress.

The *NEP* was never intended to exist for any given length of time, however, and Soviet state planning for industrialization continued throughout the period of the NEP. GOSPLAN, or the State Planning Commission, which subsequently became responsible for the *Five Year Plans*, was actually set up on February 22, 1921, that is, immediately prior to the adoption of the NEP. Thus, one might say that Lenin ordered the beginning of planning to make it possible to eliminate the *NEP* at the very same time he was approving the new program.

Constitutional Arrangements

It was also during the period of the *NEP* that the Union of Soviet Socialist Republics (USSR) came into being—though nearly all the territories included in the new USSR had been under communist control since 1920. The first piece in the new constitutional structure was the *Russian Soviet Federated Socialist Republic* (RSFSR), created in July 1918 when the communists adopted the first Soviet constitution. As they extended their control to Byelorussia, the Ukraine and the Caucasus, these areas were given similar constitutions and the designation of Soviet Socialist Republic. Although they had signed treaties with the RSFSR, they remained technically independent republics. That situation created all kinds of legal and bureaucratic problems, so these four republics were brought together as the USSR in December 1922. The RSFSR institutions were then enlarged and somewhat modified to become "union" institutions. A new constitution for the USSR—essentially a copy of the 1918 RSFSR constitution—was drawn up and adopted in 1924. These constitutional arrangements were extended to Central Asia in 1924 with the admission of the Turkmen and Uzbek Republics to the USSR. By 1936, five more republics had been created, raising the number of union republics to eleven. Then the Soviet Union added the three Baltic Republics plus Moldavia in 1940, spoils of its Non–Aggression Pact with Nazi Germany, bringing the number of republics to fifteen.

CONSTITUENT REPUBLICS OF THE USSR

1. Russian S.F.S.R.1922
2. Ukrainian S.S.R.1922
3. Byelorussian S.S.R.1922
   Transcaucasian S.S.R.1922
   (Dissolved in 1936 into three
   constituent Republics, 4–6):
4. Armenian S.S.R.1936
5. Azerbaijan S.S.R.1936
6. Georgian S.S.R.1936
7. Uzbek S.S.R.1924
8. Turkmen S.S.R.1924
9. Tadzhik S.S.R.1929
10. Kazakh S.S.R.1936
11. Kirghiz S.S.R.1936
12. Moldavian S.S.R.1940
13. Lithuanian S.S.R.1940
14. Latvian S.S.R.1940
15. Estonian S.S.R.1940

The Struggle For The Succession

Lenin suffered a cerebral hemorrhage in May 1922 which left him incapacitated for several months. By September, he had recovered enough to be able to work again at his desk, but he then suffered a new apoplexy in December, followed by a third reoccurrence in March 1923 that left him speechless. He died on January 21, 1924. After his death, Lenin's body was embalmed and placed in a mausoleum in Red Square. Petrograd was renamed Leningrad in his honor at this same time.

Russia

Once Lenin's illness removed him from the active leadership of the party, a struggle broke out among Lenin's chief lieutenants to determine who would lead the party. In his "testament," Lenin himself identified four possible successors—Trotsky, Kamenev, Zinoviev and Stalin. To the rank–and–file, Trotsky appeared to be the most logical choice, for he was the only one of Lenin's associates whose contributions to the revolution rivaled those of Lenin. In fact, according to a document reported on by a Soviet historian, Lenin offered Trotsky the number two position in the government in 1922, but he turned it down. His reason, according to what he told the Central Committee in 1923, was that "we should not give our enemies the opportunity to say that our country was being ruled by a Jew."

As Lenin's deputy, Trotsky would have been in a good position to outmaneuver Stalin when Lenin's stroke set off a struggle for the succession. Instead, it was Stalin, Kamenev and Zinoviev who formed a *troika* (a three–member team) with the express purpose of excluding Trotsky from the leadership.

Trotsky had his own levers of power—he was People's Commissar for War and a member of the Politburo—and he decided to carry the battle to the Party Congress. A great orator, he expected to win over the delegates to his side. Two things made that impossible. First, Lenin had gotten the Party Congress to outlaw factions in 1921. This meant that Trotsky could not do any pre–Congress organizing. Second, Stalin had been made General Secretary in 1922, and this gave him control over selection of the delegates to the Party Congress. Trotsky found the battle had been lost before it had begun.

Stalin later fell out with Kamenev and Zinoviev and this led them in turn to form a "United Opposition" with Trotsky against Stalin. But Stalin's control over the administrative levers of the party allowed him to defeat all three. Trotsky was expelled from the Politburo and then from the party; in 1928 he was exiled to Siberia, then a year later deported to Turkey. Stalin rapidly filled the Politburo with his supporters and was well on his way to establishing his "dictatorship over the party."

The struggles between Stalin and Trotsky involved apparent differences over policy and these were also aired during the period. Trotsky was an advocate of world revolution and he also wanted to end the NEP and embark on a rapid, large–scale industrialization of Russia. Stalin developed a theory of "socialism in one country" and defended the NEP. These turned out to be differences without a difference, however, for Stalin

Leon Trotsky

adopted Trotsky's policy on industrialization immediately after eliminating Trotsky as a source of competition.

Foreign Policy During the NEP

When the communists first came to power in November 1917, their first consideration was to end the war with Germany. They considered it an "imperialistic" war that they had opposed from the beginning, but Lenin also recognized the need for peace in order to allow communism to be firmly established in Russia. Because of Russia's withdrawal from the war after the *Bolsheviks* came to power, France and England excluded Russia from the peacemaking at Versailles. Russia reciprocated by condemning the Treaty of Versailles and the League of Nations. Russia was thus hostile to the postwar settlement and the allies responded by attempting to isolate the new government of Russia, and all that it stood for, diplomatically.

This didn't bother the Russian communists too much, for it essentially coincided with their own perception that the capitalistic countries would inevitably be hostile to the new Soviet government. In addition, Lenin was convinced that the world communist revolution predicted by Marx would break out at any moment and he was primarily concerned with what Russian communists could do to bring it about.

This led to the creation of the Communist International (*COMINTERN*) in March 1919 as a sort of coordinating body for the

coming world revolution. Efforts such as these only reinforced the British and French in their opinion that Soviet Russia was a radical nation that had to be quarantined internationally.

With the adoption of the NEP in 1921, however, Russian policy began to change. The revolutionary tide in Europe had begun to ebb and Lenin opted for a policy which he called "peaceful coexistence." His emphasis was now on rebuilding the Russian economy and for that he wanted outside assistance. He therefore called for the establishment of trade and diplomatic relations with all countries willing to live in peace and offered to reopen the country to foreign capital investment.

The free market aspects of the NEP also helped to convince many people that Russia was moving away from communism—and that, too, had a good effect abroad. Trade talks took place with England and Germany in 1921, but neither nation wanted to be the first to open diplomatic relations with Russia.

The breakthrough came in 1922 when the allies called for an international conference to discuss reparations. The Soviets had to be invited because, according to the Treaty of Versailles, they were also entitled to reparations from Germany. The Genoa Conference failed to resolve the reparations issue (in fact, France refused to allow the subject to be raised), and this convinced the German delegates that they had nothing to lose by signing an agreement with Russia—particularly since the

38

Soviets were willing to give up any claim to reparations from Germany. Over the weekend, the Russian and German delegates got together in the nearby town of Rapallo and signed an agreement reestablishing diplomatic relations between the two countries.

The Rapallo Agreement became the basis for a Russo–German relationship that was to continue throughout the 1920s and to serve the interests of both countries. What they had in common is that both were outcast nations who opposed the post–World War I settlement. Germany used the Russian connection to obtain concessions from England and France; for Russia, it served the purpose of ending its diplomatic exile. A major British trade delegation led by ex–Prime Minister Baldwin visited Russia in 1923, and this was followed by the resumption of diplomatic relations between the two countries in 1924. Italy, Austria, Greece, Norway and Sweden followed almost immediately thereafter and before the year was out they had been joined by China, Denmark, Mexico and France. Of the major countries, only the United States continued to withhold diplomatic recognition. Although there were fairly extensive trade relations between the two countries, formal recognition did not come until 1933.

Building Socialism—The Five–Year Plans

Although Marx had written that "new, higher productive relationships never come into being before the material conditions for their existence have been brought to maturity within the womb of the old society itself," Lenin's revolution had brought the communists to power in an, at best, imperfectly industrialized country, one that obviously lacked the material conditions for communism. There could be no real guidance in Marx on how to remedy the lack, for Marx had never anticipated that this situation would arise. Lenin, guided by a reference in the *Communist Manifesto* to increasing "the total of productive forces as rapidly as possible" and, elsewhere, by references to *state planning* as the mechanism that would replace free competition as the driving force within a society under communism, did create the *Supreme Economic Council* in 1917 and the *State Planning Commission (GOSPLAN)* in 1921; he also linked the creation of large–scale industry with the electrification of the country. But he favored government efforts in this direction within the context of the *NEP*.

The policy of "socialist" industrialization was first proclaimed at the 14th Party Congress in late 1925, the first victory for Stalin's "socialism in one country." The measure did not come into effect immedi-

Stalin: Ruler of Soviet Union

ately, however, for there were serious disagreements at the time as to how industrialization was to be carried out. Two years later, the Party Congress ordered *GOSPLAN* to prepare a Five–Year Plan for expansion of the national economy. This first Five–Year Plan went into operation in 1928.

The purpose of the plan was to carry out a large–scale, state–directed rapid industrialization. The priority was on heavy industry. Specifically, the government embarked on the construction of steel mills, opening of coal mines, building of dams for the production of hydro–electricity, and building of factories for the manufacture of a host of products, including tractors, agricultural machinery, automobiles, and chemicals. The goals for increased production were impressive: steel produc-

tion was to go from 4.2 million tons to 10 million tons; coal from 35 million to 150 million tons; electric power from 5 million to 22 million kilowatt–hours. Some of these higher levels were to come from increased production at already existing plants, but it mostly involved new productive capacity.

In all, the plan called for the creation of 1,500 new enterprises and a capital construction budget of 64.5 billion rubles. Such funds were not available to the state under the conditions of the NEP market economy. Stalin's solution was to phase out the NEP and to replace it with a "command model" which gave the state direct control over all economic activity. For the urban sector, this meant a return to the situation as it had existed under War Communism; for the villages, it meant an end

Russia

to individual agriculture and the forcible creation of collective farms.

The Collectivization of Agriculture

Although collectivized agriculture eventually came to be an integral part of the economic system of nearly every communist country, Marx had, in fact, little to say about the organization of agriculture under communism. Some of the more pertinent references are found in the Communist Manifesto, where he referred to

the bringing into cultivation of wastelands, and the improvement of the soil generally in accordance with a common plan. . . . Establishment of industrial armies, especially for agriculture. . . Combination of agriculture with manufacturing industries; gradual abolition of the distinction between town and country, by a more equitable distribution of the population over the country.

After the revolution, the communists took over the estates formerly owned by the Imperial family and organized them into state farms (*sovkhozy*). These units, owned and operated by the state, were run like "factories in the field," with the peasants receiving daily wages. The object was to turn the peasants into proletariat in line with Lenin's theory, expressed in *The Agrarian Program of Russian Social Democracy*, that hired agricultural workers belonged to the "working class." The communists also had in mind to create examples of good farming methods which the peasants could follow.

The *sovkhozy* represented—and until Gorbachëv's agricultural reforms continued to represent—the communist ideal for organization of the countryside, but the obligation to pay year–around wages means that they are expensive to run. The communists therefore developed a second type of farm organization which they called the *kolkhoz*. This was, in theory, a cooperative organization formed on a voluntary basis by a group of peasants. Land, livestock and farm machinery were pooled and then became the property of the *kolkhoz*.

The unit was farmed collectively by the group of peasants, and all income after expenses and taxes was shared on the basis of the total number of workdays performed by each member of the collective. The farmers were permitted an individual "private plot" of not more than an acre for use as a garden. They also could keep a cow, pigs and chickens. In the 1920s, the government offered special subsidies and favorable tax treatment to those who would join a *kolkhoz*, but they were not popular with the peasants and, by 1928, only about one peasant in 60 had joined.

The first Five Year Plan called for 17.5 percent of the cultivated land to be organized into *kolkhozy*, which would have entailed persuading between 4 and 5 million peasants to join collective farms. There was strong resistance to the collectivization, however, and even the offer of seed, credit and the use of state–owned machinery brought a meager response, primarily among poorer peasants having little to lose. The communists, recalling how the peasants had frustrated them during the period of War Communism, decided to force the issue. Peasants opposing collectivization were labeled kulaks and were declared to be class enemies. Communist squads from the cities were sent into the countryside to seize the grain of the *kulaks*. Committees of poor peasants were also set up to cooperate with the government and report on their wealthier neighbors. In effect, the communists deliberately promoted class warfare in the countryside. At first, Stalin made it look as if the new measures of the government and party were only directed against the *kulaks*, who were said to constitute less than 1 million out of a total of over 25 million peasant families. It was not long, however, before the bulk of the peasant population was involved. The progress of collectivization is shown by the following figures:

Year	Per Cent Collectivized
1928	1.7
Oct. 1929	4.1
Jan. 1930	21.0
Mar. 1930	58.0

A temporary halt was called in early 1930. Collectivization was slowed down and many kolkhozy were dissolved and the land was returned to individuals. This occurred after Stalin criticized those carrying out the forced collectivization in a famous article entitled "dizziness with success." But the program was soon resumed and those collectivized grew to 61.5 percent by the end of 1932. By the end of 1938, the 25 million peasant households were almost completely gathered into some 240,000 collective farms.

Because of extensive resistance, the former voluntary nature of the *kolkhoz* ceased and the farm manager, formerly elected by the membership, was selected by and subordinate to the higher *Communist Party* authorities. In addition, Machine–Tractor–Stations (MTS's), directly controlled by the state, were set up in the countryside. The MTS's got all the new farm machinery that was being manufactured and, using their own crews, performed all of the mechanical labor on the collectives. They usually contained the local *Communist*

Party cell as well, so they also exercised a control function in rural areas.

At the end of the harvest, each collective farm first delivered a set amount of its total production to the state at a controlled price, then paid off the MTS. Any remaining production was divided among the peasants. In many years, the amount remaining to be divided was relatively small and the peasants had to rely on produce raised on the garden plots to feed themselves.

There were several important reasons for the collectivization of agriculture, but the most important reason was that it allowed the *Communist Party* to gain control of the countryside in a predominantly rural nation and to force the peasantry to serve the interests of the communist state. In one of his moments of candor, Stalin explained that, since Russia had no colonies to exploit, it could only find the funds for industrialization by taking them from its own people. And this is what was done.

[For a discussion of the man-made famine (*Holodomor*) in Ukraine in 1932–33, see the historical section of the chapter on Ukraine entitled *Collectivization and the Great Famine*, beginning on page 151.]

During the period of the first Five–Year Plan, the living standard for the average Soviet citizen diminished by an estimated 35 percent, meaning that the living standard of the workers, the darlings of the *Communist Party*, suffered a drop during these years; but it was the peasantry whose privations during this period primarily paid for the first Five-Year Plan. As the government and the *Communist Party* saw it, however, by pouring 35 percent of the gross national product into new productive facilities, the government managed to more or less meet the goals of the plan.

Second and third Five–Year Plans followed and continued the process of industrialization. Nearly all of the investment continued to be in heavy industry, however, so the Soviet people saw very little change in their standard of living. But the heavy pace wore out the country, and criticism of Stalin's harsh policies increased even among his supporters. His reaction was to launch a purge—massacre—that eventually enveloped all parts of Russian society.

Terror and Purges

Stalin resorted to terror not only to deal with temporary emergencies; terror became a permanent and prominent feature of his style of governing. Lenin and other Bolshevik leaders had used terror on a smaller scale, and they had employed a special organization to combat "counter-revolution"—the Cheka. It came into existence soon after the Bolsheviks seized power. The name of the organization was changed several times; known by its Russian initials, it has been the GPU, OGPU, NKVD, MVD, MGB and KGB. Whatever its name, however, its function was always the same—a highly secret police looking everywhere for saboteurs, spies and counter–revolutionaries. Abroad, it came to be used as a highly active espionage organization, more often than not in the guise of members of the Russian diplomatic corps.

Stalin changed the nature of the secret police, however, when, in the 1930s, he made them a major instrument of his ruthless purges. Stalin's first targets were the non–communist technicians and specialists, both Russian and foreign, who had been enlisted to help in the first Five–Year Plan. This had the effect of providing an excuse for failure to achieve some of the goals of the plan. Accused of espionage and sabotage, they were convicted with the help of manufactured evidence and forced confessions.

The next group subjected to terror and liquidation were those peasants who were accused of sabotaging the collectivization drive. This action was officially known as the "liquidation of the *kulaks* as a class," but it actually affected millions who could by no stretch of the imagination be called "rich" peasants. Besides the million or so peasants who suffered death, there were others who filled forced–labor camps and were used in digging canals, mining gold and other enterprises under unbelievably inhuman conditions.

What is known as the *Great Purge* lasted from 1934 to 1938 and differed from earlier periods of Stalinist terror. This time it was directed against the leading echelons of the *Communist Party*. The concept of a "purge" goes back to the era of Lenin, when it meant removal from the party only. It was Stalin who changed the meaning of the "purge," transforming it into an action that might include criminal prosecution, exile or death. The *Great Purge* began in December 1934 with the assassination of Sergei M. Kirov, a member of the Politburo and Zinoviev's successor as first secretary of the Leningrad party organization. Although supporters of Zinoviev were blamed for the assassination, it is now known that Stalin engineered the murder because Kirov was questioning the wisdom of continuing the break–neck tempo of change in Russia. He was also seen as a possible successor to Stalin as party leader.

Purge at the Top

Stalin used Kirov's death as an excuse to unleash a purge of suspect party members and, particularly, party leaders. Most significantly, the Society of Old *Bolsheviks*, whose members had worked closely with Lenin, was dissolved in mid–1935. A "verification" of party membership cards was ordered, and some 10 percent were expelled; by 1936, at least one–quarter of the membership had been dropped from the party. Next came, in 1936, the first of three public trials, when sixteen Old *Bolsheviks*, including Zinoviev and Kamenev, were charged with treason, convicted and executed. Michael P. Tomsky, leader of the trade unions, committed suicide. In early 1937, at the second trial, seventeen prominent communists, diplomats, economists and writers, including Karl Radek, who had closely collaborated with Lenin, were tried as alleged German and Japanese spies. At the trials, an attempt was made to "expose" Trotsky and to condemn his activities abroad as being directed against the USSR. Thirteen of the accused were shot, while the other four were sentenced to long prison terms; none of them was ever heard from again.

Then, in June 1937, there was a brief press announcement which told of the secret trial and execution of Army Marshal Michael Tukhachevsky and seven other leading generals of the Red Army. This was followed by a mass purge of officers which eventually included two of the five Soviet marshals, 13 out of 15 army generals, 62 out of 85 corps commanders, 110 out of 195 divisional commanders and 220 out of 406 brigade commanders. It has been estimated that 65 percent of all military officers holding the rank of colonel or above were liquidated.

The last of the public trials came in 1938 when several former Politburo members, including Nikolai Bukharin, Alexei Rykov and N.M. Krestinsky, plus distinguished provincial party leaders were found guilty of treason and shot. The public "show trials" were the most spectacular aspect of the Great Purge because they included public "confessions," but they were only a minor aspect of the overall purge. Eventually, large numbers of trade–unionists, managers, intellectuals, and party and Comintern functionaries were arrested and liquidated. Finally, at one point, orders went out to the secret police to arrest an arbitrary percentage of the entire population. These individuals were given summary trials, then shipped off to prison camps in Siberia where they provided the regime with a large quantity of unpaid labor. Finally, two different secret police heads, Yagoda and Yezhov, eventually became victims of the purges themselves. Yagoda was shot as a spy upon Yezhov's orders, while Yezhov simply disappeared in 1938 after Lavrenti Beria had replaced him as head of the secret police.

One observer has aptly called this period "a reign of terror without parallel in Soviet history" in which "no sphere of Soviet life, however lofty, was left untouched." The destructive fury of the *Great Purge* can only be explained on the assumption that Stalin was determined to eliminate once and for all any possible challenge to his personal power within the party leadership.

Many westerners, while accepting the fact of the purges, have been loath to believe that Stalin was directly responsible for them. They have argued that the purges must have been the product of overzealous subordinates who carried out the executions on their own. But a book published in the Soviet Union in 1989, *Stalin: Triumph and Tragedy*, answers those doubts. According to a review in the *Economist*, the author, Dmitri Volkogonov, "examined Stalin's personal papers and found his marginal comments or initials on thousands of execution lists and reports of mass repressions. His scribbled remarks invariably call for harsher measures."

Cauldron of intrigue: Hotel Lux in Moscow, where foreign Communists were housed during purges

Russia

Death of a Commissar (1928)

K. S. Petrov–Vodkin

Stalin's Cultural Counter–Revolution of the 1930s

Marx had very little to say about the implications of his philosophical system insofar as the performing and creative arts were concerned, though it follows that, since the creative arts would be considered part of the superstructure of society, they must, according to Marx's general theory, reflect the social and economic environment in which they appear. Marx did indicate that the proletariat would take over that which was good in the previous bourgeois society, but he also stipulated that much would be discarded—and he made a specific attack on the bourgeois family. In most respects, however, Marx had conventional tastes in art and literature.

Lenin was also rather ordinary in his tastes, but he never attempted to enforce his personal viewpoint on the new communist state and his first people's commissar for education specifically proclaimed the right of individual creation. Lenin never permitted the printing of anything anti–revolutionary or anti–communist but, with that limitation, there was considerable artistic freedom in Russia under Lenin. Among the excellent works produced in the 1920s were Alexander Blok's *The Twelve*, Mikhail Bulgatov's *The Master and Margarita*, Mikhail Sholokov's *Quiet Flows the Don*, poems by Boris Pasternak and Vladimir Mayakovsky and, finally, the music of Dimitri Shostakovich.

In the schools, all sorts of experimental ideas were tried out—such as abolishing discipline—and courses in mathematics and chemistry, geography and physics were phased out in favor of vocational education. Traditional family values also came under attack as divorce became a mere registration process and the emancipation of women from home life was stressed. Religious training, traditionally also a function of the family, came under attack.

All of this came to an end in 1929 when Stalin, launching his Five–Year Plan, decided that the creative arts had to be mobilized in support of the industrialization program of the *Communist Party*. Publishers were instructed on the types of books they were to publish. Specific "proletarian" goals were announced for art, music and literature. Experiments in style were condemned and creative workers were informed that what they produced had to be intelligible to the masses. Themes suggested to the creative artists included industrial construction, the fight against external aggression and internal subversion and the glory of life on collective farms.

Schools were reorganized and traditional courses reinstated. Examinations were reintroduced, and teachers were again given control in the classroom. Family life was again emphasized and the parents were instructed that they were responsible for training and disciplining their children.

Socialist Realism

During this period also, the state developed a specific theory for the arts called *socialist realism*—defined as a portrayal of reality in its revolutionary development in order to remake and re–educate the workers in the spirit of socialism. What this meant in practice was that artists were to depict Soviet reality *as it would be, or should be*, rather than as it was. As one his-

Militarized Communist Youth (1933)   A. N. Samokhvalov

torian has expressed it, it was communism with a smiling face. No morbid or pessimistic themes were allowed; music was to be melodic and life was to be portrayed as good and getting better.

The effect of these restrictions was predictable. Soviet paintings tended to be either poster art in the revolutionary style or Soviet versions of *Saturday Evening Post* covers. Favorite painting subjects included portraits of Lenin and Stalin, scenes from the Russian revolution and civil war, and landscapes that included factories or glamorized collective farms. Modern dance and jazz were outlawed and Soviet ballet returned to the classical style. Composers such as Shostakovich and Prokofiev began to base their compositions on folk music. Abstract and semi-abstract art were out, and this led to a purge of paintings in Russian museums. Artists whose works were now labeled decadent included Vincent Van Gogh, Paul Gauguin, Georges Seurat, Henri Matisse, Pablo Picasso, Marc Chagall and Vasili Kandinsky. Their paintings were taken down from display and locked away in storerooms.

Soviet Foreign Policy In The 1930s

The Soviet Union had established friendly relations with Germany as a result of the Rapallo Pact in 1922 and those relations continued after Stalin came to power. Trade between the two countries actually increased after 1928 as the Soviet Union began its first Five–Year Plan. Political relations also remained good and the two nations signed an agreement in 1931 prolonging the Berlin Treaty on neutrality which the two nations had signed in 1926.

The Soviet Union was willing to continue good relations even after Adolf Hitler came to power in 1933; it was Hitler's decision, not Stalin's, that changed the course of German–Soviet relations—and eventually led to a change in overall Soviet foreign policy.

The change in course by Hitler, plus his extreme anti–communist speeches, convinced the Soviet Union that it would have to seek new friends. Russia had always been an opponent of the League of Nations, but when Nazi Germany left the League, the Soviet Union decided to join. Stalin appointed Maxim Litvinov, a Jew, as the new Soviet foreign minister—a move that must have been intended to irritate Hitler. Litvinov became a familiar figure at Geneva and the Soviet Union be-

came a leading advocate of "collective security" between 1934 and 1939.

Although it appeared that the Soviet Union was interested in active opposition to Nazism and Fascism, Stalin's actual policies at the time can best be described as isolationism with a substantial amount of appeasement. This reflected his caution and his obsessive fear of having to fight alone against a united capitalist world. The Soviet Union also chose a policy of appeasement towards Japan when it began to assert its strength on the Asian mainland beginning in 1931. Although Stalin encouraged the Chinese nationalists and communists alike to resist the Japanese, he obviously considered events in East Asia to be less significant than what was happening in Europe and he was also unwilling to expose the USSR to direct Japanese attack. To lessen the threat of conflict, therefore, he arranged to sell the Russian share in the Chinese Eastern Railway to the Japanese–controlled puppet state of Manchukuo.

The main driving force behind Soviet foreign policy in the 1930s was the USSR's domestic industrialization program. Before 1934, therefore, foreign policy initiatives tended to be aimed at protecting the country from attack from abroad, and this took the form of negotiating non–aggression pacts with its neighbors. Thus, in 1932, it signed non–aggression pacts with Finland, Estonia, Latvia, Poland and France. Its second main concern was to obtain access to modern technology and, complementary to that, to find markets for its grain, so as to be able to pay for foreign technology needed for industrialization.

After 1934, Litvinov's policy of cooperating with the Western democracies to oppose the growing menace of Nazi Germany led to mutual security pacts with France

Kolhkoz Festival (1937)   S. V. Gerasimov

Russia

and Czechoslovakia, both signed in 1935. Soviet policy in the Spanish Civil War (1936–1939) took a slightly different direction. Here, the Soviet Union became actively involved as a supporter of the loyalist side against the insurgents led by General Francisco Franco. Although Great Britain and France opposed the Franco insurgency, they adopted a policy of strict neutrality. By comparison, the Soviet Union appeared to be supporting intervention in support of the loyalists, a position many people in the West attributed to the fact that the Spanish communists constituted a major part of the loyalist forces. The fact that the COMINTERN helped organize "international brigades" to fight on the side of the Spanish Republic merely reinforced this interpretation, causing great disquiet in Great Britain and France.

In 1938, when Hitler demanded that areas of Czechoslovakia where German-speakers were in the majority be turned over to Germany, it appeared that the Soviet Union might be called upon to honor its mutual security pact and come to the aid of Czechoslovakia. However, France and Great Britain, after giving Czechoslovakia some initial support, eventually acquiesced in Hitler's demand and signed the Munich Agreement ceding the area of the Sudetenland to Germany.

It could not have pleased Stalin that the Soviet Union was not even invited to the Munich Conference, in spite of its mutual security pact with Czechoslovakia. But the British and French act of appeasement represented by the Munich Pact also went a long way toward convincing Stalin that a foreign policy based on cooperation with the West against Hitler was worthless. On the other side, there was an extremely negative reaction in the West to the gruesome purges Stalin was then conducting in the Soviet Union. Stalin probably realized that this Western revulsion would make any close cooperation between the Soviet Union and the Western democracies extremely difficult.

The appeasement policies of the Western Powers may have also led Stalin to suspect that they were hoping to encourage Hitler to attack the Soviet Union and thereby remove the threat from themselves. Some groups in the West did indeed nourish such hopes, although it never became the official policy of any of the Western governments.

Hitler's seizure of the rest of Czechoslovakia in March 1939 reinforced Stalin's perception that neither Great Britain nor France could be depended upon, since neither took any action, even though both had guaranteed Czechoslovakia's remaining territories. It is true that Prime Minister Chamberlain condemned the German

Stalinist die-hards demonstrating for their hero in late 1990s

actions in Czechoslovakia in his Birmingham speech of March 17 and promised that his country would resist any further act of aggression by Germany, in particular against Poland—but Great Britain had made promises before and then ignored them. In March 1939, Stalin spelled out the position of the Soviet Union in a famous speech to the 18th Party Congress in which he declared that the Soviet Union was not willing to "pull the chestnuts out of the fire" for the benefit of others.

Chamberlain's promise that Great Britain would resist any German aggression against Poland meant that Hitler had to expect war with Great Britain, and possibly France, if he pursued his objectives on Poland. On the other hand, the position of the Soviet Union now became all important. Hitler would need to come to an understanding with the Soviet Union before he could invade Poland, unless he was willing to chance the possibility of having to fight a war on two fronts.

As the crisis deepened, the Soviet Union became involved in two sets of negotiations in Moscow—official alliance discussions with the French and British on one hand and unofficial discussions under the guise of trade negotiations with Nazi Germany on the other. Stalin had to ask himself whether an alliance with Great Britain and France would deter Hitler—or whether it would only mean that the Soviet Union would be drawn into the war from the very beginning of an armed conflict.

The Nazi–Soviet Non–Aggression Pact

The German side had an offer that looked much more appealing—the division of Poland between Germany and Russia. From Stalin's point of view, this offered the opportunity to keep the Soviet Union out of the war and yet to receive the eastern third of Poland as a reward from Hitler for remaining neutral. In addition, Hitler was willing to recognize the Baltic area and Bessarabia as falling within the Soviet Union's "sphere of influence."

The agreement between the Soviet Union and Germany was announced on August 23, 1939. Though it came as a shock and surprise to the world, it was the most logical choice among the alternatives facing Stalin at the time. Soviet–Polish relations had never been particularly good, and the Soviet Union had no substantial reason to come to Poland's assistance. Moreover, what Stalin feared most of all was to be dragged into a war against Germany by Great Britain and France, and then be forced to bear the brunt of that war while those countries sat on the sidelines.

Hitler's invasion of Poland came on September 1, 1939, its purpose, in the language of the war order, "to destroy Polish military strength and create, in the East, a situation which satisfies the requirements of defense." The end was not long in coming. The Polish forces collapsed under the onslaught of the first German *Blitzkrieg*.

The fighting was mostly over by September 17, when Soviet troops entered from the east to claim the Soviet share of

Russia

Map legend:
- Hitler's Germany
- Under German rule
- Axis military occupation
- Axis satellites

of the Nazi–Soviet Non–Aggression Pact. In May 1940, the three Baltic republics were forced to join the Soviet Union. Next, Romania was asked to cede the province of Bessarabia, taken from Russia during World War I, and parts of Bukovina, about which there had been no clear arrangement with the Germans in 1939. The Soviet Government also protested when Hitler sent German troops into Finland and signed an alliance with Romania which involved dispatching German troops to that country as well.

Soviet Entry Into World War II

In late 1940 and early 1941, relations between the Soviet Union and Germany acquired an air of unreality. Stalin alternately appeased and challenged Hitler, while the *Führer*, who had already ordered planning to begin for an invasion of the Soviet Union, tried to persuade Stalin to look to Iran and British India for future spoils. The Soviet Foreign Minister, V.M. Molotov, was presented with such a proposal during a visit to Berlin in late 1940, but the Soviets took the position that it was too early to discuss cutting up the British Empire.

By the autumn of 1940, Hitler was in a quandary. His plan for the invasion of England, Operation Sea Lion, had to be aborted when his air force was unable to gain control of the air over England. Now America was throwing its support behind England, and that support was sure to grow. There was no immediate threat in the west, but also no chance to bring the British to the negotiating table. Was this the time to turn on the Soviet Union and, in another lightning onslaught, destroy his long–term foe in the east? On December 18, he answered that question by signing Operation Barbarossa "to crush Soviet Russia in a quick campaign even before the end of the war against England."

It mattered very little what the Soviet Union did at that point. However, one question arises with regard to what Stalin did prior to the German attack. He had received reports of an impending German invasion from more than one source, but he ordered no preparations for the invasion, supposedly because he believed that they were bits of "disinformation" spread by the Western intelligence services to force a break between the Soviet Union and Nazi Germany. Although nothing has emerged from the Soviet files since the collapse of communism to disprove this theory, an equally plausible explanation for his inaction is that he was aware of the damage to the reputation of the Soviet Union as a result of the deal with Hitler in 1939 and understood that the Soviet Union could be accepted as an ally of the

the spoils. The last member of the Polish Government had already left the country to seek refuge abroad. The Soviet Union then claimed that its troops were entering a no–man's land; Stalin even had the nerve to suggest to Hitler that he be permitted to state that Soviet troops were entering the former Polish territory in order to save the largely Ukrainian and Byelorussian population of the area *from the Germans!*

The Soviet side also suggested a change in the terms of the secret agreement. They wanted less Polish territory than what had been given them in the original deal, and asked instead to have Lithuania included in the Soviet "sphere" along with Latvia and Estonia. Hitler agreed and the swap was made. In October 1939, the Soviet Union forced the three Baltic republics to sign offensive and defensive alliances which provided for the stationing of Soviet troops on their territory.

Finland also came under similar pressure, but the Finns resisted the Soviet demands. As a result, Stalin ordered the invasion of Finland in November 1939. Although the Finns managed to stop the first Soviet offensive—and in doing so to inflict

embarrassing losses on the Soviet forces—the small country was forced to sue for peace after three months and to cede some Finnish territory to the Soviet Union.

The Soviet Union's use of military force against its small neighbor added to the bad reputation which the Soviet Union had in the West, already resentful of the Soviet deal with Hitler. Unrealistic ideas of coming to the assistance of Finland almost resulted in British and French declarations of war *against the Soviet Union*, then looked upon as an ally of Adolf Hitler. Fortunately for the future of Europe, the British decided against any such action when it became clear that they would be unable to provide any meaningful assistance to the Finns.

German troops conquered Denmark and Norway in April 1940, then began their sweep across France, Belgium and the Netherlands in May. Their swift military success disturbed Stalin, who apparently expected a much longer involvement of German troops on the Western front. This is evident in the fact that he moved quickly to consolidate his hold on the territories he had obtained as a result

45

Russia

West only if it were clear that it was the target of unprovoked aggression by Hitler. Therefore, the Soviet Union was forced to let the Germans fire the first shot.

Nevertheless, Stalin's failure to improve the combat readiness of the Soviet armed forces during this period exposed millions of soldiers to slaughter and capture in the very first weeks of the war, launched by Hitler on June 22, 1941. Even Soviet sources now admit that Stalin "failed to take full advantage" of the time gained by the Soviet Union as a result of the 1939 agreement.

Ally of the West

Hitler's unprovoked attack changed the Soviet Union's international position literally overnight. British Prime Minister Winston Churchill, though a life–long enemy of communism, welcomed the Soviet Union as an ally of Great Britain. Churchill summed up his reasons for doing so in one of those pithy statements for which he became famous. "If I heard that Hitler invaded Hell," Churchill was quoted as saying, "the least I could do would be to say a few nice words about the Devil." The United States, not yet engaged in the war, also extended lend–lease to the Soviet Union in September 1941. There were, however, serious doubts in the West about Russia's ability to resist Hitler's offensive for very long, and the speedy advance of German troops in July and August seemed to justify gloomy predictions. Although it was felt that the Soviet Union should be supported in its struggle against Germany because it was tying down masses of German troops, it did not appear that the Soviet Union was an important factor to reckon with at the time.

In this period, the Soviet Government yielded to British pressure to reestablish relations with the Polish government–in–exile in London. However, even at this darkest time of military fortune, Stalin made it clear that the Soviet Union intended to retain all the territorial gains made as a result of the Non–Aggression pact with Hitler.

The Nazi offensive consisted of three attacking forces whose destinations were Leningrad, Moscow and the Ukraine. It achieved tremendous success in the beginning as Soviet units at the border disintegrated and Germany's mechanized armies swept eastward across the Russian plain, surrounding and conquering whole Soviet armies. Stubborn Soviet defenses halted the German armies for a time at Pskov and Smolensk, but reinforced German armies eventually overcame the Soviet defenders and continued their advance to the east. In the north, the Ger-

mans forces reached Leningrad in August, and then laid down a siege around the city. But the Germans were unable to close the ring entirely, so the city continued to be reprovisioned across the ice on Lake Ladoga. The ring of the blockade was broken in January 1943 and the siege was lifted by a German retreat a year later. About 650,000 people died in Leningrad during the blockade.

On the Soviet Central Front, the German forces got within 35 miles of Moscow before being ground to a halt by the Russian winter. In the south, Kiev was captured on September 19th. Between then and December, German armies overran the rest of the Ukraine, reaching as far east as the Donets River. However, Hitler, enraged that neither Leningrad nor Moscow had been captured, dismissed his chief generals in December and assumed personal command himself.

This was a gift for the Russians—Hitler, although occasionally capable of brilliant insights, was not a military strategist. In 1942, for example, he held his forces on the north and center on the defensive while he attempted to make a breakthrough in the south. His original goal was the oil fields of the Caucasus, an entirely logical one under the circumstances. But in June he ordered part of his southern armies to turn directly east and open a drive toward Stalingrad. Apparently he intended to humiliate Stalin by destroying the city named after him. But Stalingrad (since renamed Volgograd) was a city of no particular strategic significance, while Hitler's diversion of part of his southern armies meant that the remaining forces were not strong enough to seize the Caucasus oil fields.

Stalingrad was reached in September 1942, after slow progress in the face of heavy Russian resistance. In late 1942, most of the city had been captured after bloody street–to–street fighting. Now, Stalin launched an artillery offensive that came up to the city from the East. The Soviet forces began an enveloping movement from both south and north of the city and the German Sixth Army was soon encircled. The German forces could have broken out of the trap at this time, but Hitler ordered the 285,000 men trapped by the Soviets not to retreat. After attempts to relieve the army failed, the 90,000 survivors of the battle of Stalingrad surrendered on January 30, 1943. Later, Stalin would have them marched in triumph through the streets of Moscow.

After Stalingrad

The reversal of Soviet military fortunes represented by the victory at Stalingrad

created an entirely new political situation. Although the Soviet Union remained heavily dependent on the lend–lease supplies that were flowing into Russia in very large amounts from the United States at the cost of many lives lost to German submarines, the Soviets developed the feeling that they had managed to live through the darkest moments of the war largely by their own efforts. It also did not help that the Allies now informed the Soviet Union that the "second front" in the West would have to be put off until 1944.

It was also at this time that another situation arose which acted as a wedge between the Soviet Union and its Western allies. In the spring of 1943, Germany announced the discovery of a mass grave in the Katyn Forest containing the bodies of thousands of Polish army officers who had fallen into the hands of the Soviet forces in September 1939. They had been shot in the back of the head, a standard method of execution practiced by the Soviet secret police. Alarmed by the discovery, the Polish Government–in–exile in London asked for an investigation by the International Red Cross.

Stalin accused the Polish government–in–exile of aiding German propaganda and used this as an excuse to break off diplomatic relations. Soon a new organization was formed from among Polish refugees in the Soviet Union. This organization, the Union of Polish Patriots, became the nucleus of the Soviet–sponsored Lublin Government, which was installed in power by the Soviet army after the liberation of Poland.

Wartime Conferences and the Occupation of Eastern Europe

The Soviet military occupation of Eastern Europe and the Soviet decision to set up communist governments in the area are usually considered to be important factors in the origins of the Cold War that developed between the Soviet Union and its Western allies after World War II. The matter is somewhat more complex, however.

First of all, there were always differences between the Soviet Union and its allies over Soviet territories obtained as a result of the Nazi–Soviet Non–Aggression Pact of 1939. In particular, neither the United States nor Great Britain ever recognized the incorporation of Latvia, Estonia, Lithuania and Bessarabia into the Soviet Union.

When the United States and Great Britain drew up the Atlantic Charter in 1941, setting forth their wartime goals, they stipulated there were to be no territorial changes without the freely registered approval of the people involved. They also promised to respect the right of

"The Big Three:" Stalin, Roosevelt and Churchill at Tehran

all peoples to determine the form of government under which they would live. When, six weeks later, the Soviet Union gave its approval to the Atlantic Charter, American policy–makers accepted that as a basis for cooperation. And in September 1941, although the United States was not yet at war, it extended a billion dollar "lend–lease" grant to the Soviet Union for the purchase of supplies in the United States. By the end of the war, the United States had shipped approximately $11 billion worth of equipment and supplies to the Soviet Union.

Presumably the Soviet Union signed the Atlantic Charter because it wanted the "lend–lease" agreement with the United States. Again, it would have been for the same reason that it agreed to the incorporation of the Atlantic Charter into the Declaration of the United Nations which the USA, Great Britain, the USSR and 23 other nations signed on January 1, 1942. That it never intended to apply the terms of the Atlantic Charter to territories annexed in 1939–1940 can be seen by the fact that it

continued to pressure the USA and Great Britain to recognize the incorporation of these territories into the USSR after signing the Atlantic Charter.

Another factor was Franklin D. Roosevelt's opposition to concepts such as "balance of power politics" and "spheres of influence." The United States was committed to allowing the peoples of Eastern Europe to set up their own freely elected governments and FDR attempted to bind his allies to a similar position. What he forgot, however, is that Nazi Germany's defeat would bring about a power vacuum in Eastern Europe and, *one way or the other*, that power vacuum would be filled. But perhaps the most important factor influencing American foreign policy at this juncture was FDR's belief that Stalin didn't want anything for himself in Eastern Europe. As he commented to Ambassador Bullitt just prior to the Tehran Conference,

I have just a hunch that Stalin doesn't want anything but security for his country, and I think that if I give him everything I possibly

can and ask nothing in return, noblesse oblige, he won't try to annex anything and will work for a world of democracy and peace.

Roosevelt's "hunch" seemed to be confirmed when he, Churchill, and Stalin met in Tehran in November 1943, for it was here that the "Big Three," in a general declaration which they drew up, promised an enduring peace in which "all the peoples of the world may live free lives untouched by tyranny and according to their varying desires and their consciences."

In delineating spheres of military operations, however, Romania, Bulgaria, Hungary, Yugoslavia, Czechoslovakia, Poland and Finland were designated areas of Soviet operations. If Roosevelt was right about Stalin, it wouldn't matter; but if he was not, he was putting his stamp of approval on whatever policy Stalin chose to carry out in Eastern Europe. Churchill, recognizing the potential danger in such an arrangement, pushed for an allied invasion up through the Balkans, but he was overruled.

Russia

Soviet troops began entering Eastern Europe in August 1944; by the time of the Yalta Conference in early 1945, Soviet armies occupied Romania, Bulgaria, Poland and parts of Hungary and Czechoslovakia. The Yalta Conference was primarily concerned with the problem of Germany, and it was at this time that allied zones of occupation were established. The Soviet Zone would eventually become the German Democratic Republic.

Poland was also considered. Its eastern and western borders were established; the Communist Provisional Government was to be enlarged by the inclusion of democratic leaders from abroad, and the broadened Provisional Government was to hold "free and unfettered elections as soon as possible on the basis of universal suffrage and secret ballot." The rest of Eastern Europe was covered by a general declaration that other people of the region would be encouraged to

form interim governmental authorities broadly representative of all democratic elements in the population and pledged to the earliest possible establishment through elections of governments responsive to the will of the people.

It has often been charged that the United States essentially yielded to Soviet demands concerning territorial matters and the composition of the government of postwar Poland because it was eager for Soviet military assistance in the Far East. It is true that Stalin agreed at Yalta to enter the war against Japan within 90 days of victory in Europe. It is also true that an American military study had estimated that, without Soviet assistance, the war against Japan would last until 1947 and might mean another million American lives. The study obviously did not take into consideration the development of the atomic bomb, and it is possible that Roosevelt didn't either. On the other hand, the essential fact is that the American armies were only approaching the Rhine River at the time when Soviet troops were in western Poland and approaching the German border at a point much closer to the main prize, Berlin. Political and strategic decisions made much earlier meant that the United States could only hope that the Soviet Union shared American perceptions about the future of Eastern Europe.

The Cold War

The Cold War essentially began when the Soviet Union, in occupation of Eastern Europe, began to implement its intentional misunderstanding of the various wartime agreements. The problem arose over the differing Soviet and western Al-

lied understandings of such terms as "democratic," "free elections" and "governments friendly to the Soviet Union." The United States, recognizing the Soviet Union's concern for its security, agreed that the Russians could demand governments "friendly to the Soviet Union" in Eastern Europe. The problem was that Stalin believed that any non-communist government would be *hostile* to the Soviet Union. The same thing applied to such terms as "democratic" and "free elections." According to communist dogma, both terms applied only to states in which communism prevailed.

Stalin was probably not certain that his Western Allies would permit him to communize Eastern Europe. He also recognized that it was necessary to mobilize as much popular support as possible for the new regimes he was installing. That is why "Popular Front" governments were installed nearly everywhere in Eastern Europe in the beginning and why they were normally headed by a non-communist. This transition phase lasted approximately three years. In the meantime, Soviet–Allied relations worsened as it became clear just what Stalin was doing.

It is difficult to pinpoint an exact date for the beginning of the Cold War, but revisionist historians who suggest that President Truman's suspension of "lend–lease" assistance to the Soviet Union in May 1945 was motivated by anti–Soviet feelings place it too early. Actually, Truman was merely following the mandate of Congress which, in passing the original legislation, specified that it would continue only for the duration of the war. Moreover, a quarrel over the political make–up of the new Polish Government was resolved just prior to the Potsdam Conference (July 1945) when the USA and Great Britain extended diplomatic recognition in return for Stalin's promise to add non–communist elements to it.

At Potsdam (a suburb of Berlin), the USA and Great Britain threatened to withhold recognition from the communist–dominated governments of Romania and Bulgaria unless they were enlarged to include a broader political spectrum. But on the major topic, Germany, the Big Three were in general agreement on policies of disarmament and de–Nazification. The USA and Great Britain also agreed that the Soviets were entitled to reparations from Germany, although they insisted that the Soviets extract them primarily from their own zone of occupation. That may have been hard on the East Germans, but did not affect the Soviets unduly.

Averill Harriman, who was U.S. Ambassador to Russia at the time, dates the beginning of the Cold War to a conver-

sation he had with Stalin in the fall of 1945. Stalin had apparently just come from a meeting of the Politburo, and he told Harriman that "we have decided to go it alone." Stalin expanded on this theme in a speech which he gave in early 1946, just prior to new elections to the Supreme Soviet. It was a long speech, but its essence was that the alliance between the Soviet Union and the western democracies had been for limited purposes— to defeat fascism—and now that the purpose had been accomplished there was no longer any basis for co-operation. From now on, the emphasis would be on strengthening the "Soviet social order," which had established its superiority over any non–Soviet form of social organization.

If we place Stalin's comments into the context of the widespread destruction that occurred in the Soviet Union during World War II, they take on a more specific meaning. Large parts of the country had been occupied by foreign troops, and the effects of the actual fighting plus the Soviets' *scorched earth* policy during the retreat of 1941 and the willful destruction of the Germans as they retreated in 1943–44, left very little intact in the western part of the Soviet Union. In addition, an estimated 20 million Soviet citizens had died during the war—seven million of them in action. Even though the blame for much of this destruction is historically that of Stalin, it was realized that the rebuilding of Russia would require tremendous sacrifices on the part of the Soviet people. Some who lacked a sufficient "proletarian consciousness" might be *seduced* by capitalist promises of a better life. This explains why, as Alexander Solzhenitsyn has documented, hundreds of thousands of Soviet soldiers and prisoners of war were shipped off to labor camps in the GULAG Archipelago rather than being treated as heroes. They had become ideologically contaminated because they had seen and might bear witness to what Soviet propaganda endlessly continued to deny—*that even in devastated Germany the people were better off than those living in the land of the victorious proletariat.*

It also helps to explain Stalin's policy toward Eastern Europe. If these economies could be tied to the Soviet economy, exploitation would make the rebuilding much easier. To accomplish this, trade agreements and mutual friendship and alliance treaties were forged with the Eastern European countries as soon as new governments were formed, with the purpose of reorienting their trade toward the Soviet Union. By 1947, a third of the Soviet Union's imports were coming from Eastern Europe, and the figure continued to grow thereafter. Slowly, Eastern Europe was being cut off and isolated from Western Europe. When Winston Churchill made his famous speech stating that a curtain of iron had been erected between East and West by Stalin in 1946, he was partly referring to this occurrence.

Though disturbed by developments in Eastern Europe, the United States continued to maintain an ambivalent attitude toward the Soviet Union. Something of a break in that pattern came in March 1947 when President Truman, in a speech to Congress, enunciated a policy toward Greece and Turkey that subsequently became known as the "Truman Doctrine." The Greek government was fighting a communist insurgency supported by Bulgaria and Yugoslavia, while Turkey was under pressure from the Soviet Union to cede certain frontier districts. In Truman's words, it was to be "the policy of the United States to support free people who are resisting attempted subjugation by armed minorities or by outside pressure." Neither communism nor the Soviet Union was mentioned, but the meaning was clear.

Three months later, Secretary of State George Marshall, speaking at the Harvard commencement, offered a broader response, insisting that

> . . . our policy is directed not against any country or doctrine but against hunger, poverty, desperation and chaos . . . governments, political parties or groups which seek to perpetuate human misery in order to profit . . . politically will encounter the opposition of the United States . . .

He thus spelled out a policy which later became known as the "Marshall Plan." The purpose of this was to assist Europe in the restoration of its destroyed economies, and it was to be open to all European nations. For a short while, it appeared that the Soviet Union was interested in the American offer, and Foreign Minister Molotov even attended a preliminary meeting in Paris to discuss details. Czechoslovakia and Poland also expressed their interest. Then Molotov abruptly denounced the Marshall Plan as an attack on the sovereignty of Europe and announced that the Soviets would not participate after all. Czechoslovakia and Poland withdrew their applications as well. As American economic assistance began to pour into Western Europe, the gulf between East and West widened even further.

The Soviet Union, recognizing that a resurgent Western Europe might prove such an attraction that it would weaken the Soviet hold over Eastern Europe, decided to tighten its controls by organizing the Council for Mutual Economic Assistance (CMEA) in 1949. While Stalin was alive, the CMEA was used primarily as a tool to exploit the Eastern European economies. After 1953, however, it became more of a coordinating body to facilitate economic planning and effort.

A second reaction to the Marshall Plan was the creation of a successor organization to the COMINTERN, which had been dissolved in 1943. The Communist Information Bureau (COMINFORM) came into being in the fall of 1947 with its headquarters in Belgrade, Yugoslavia. This turned out to be a poor choice—a scant year later, Yugoslavia was expelled from the COMINFORM upon Stalin's orders because of Marshal Tito's objection to Moscow's meddling in Yugoslavia's domestic economic affairs.

Stalin would have driven Tito from power had he been able to. But Stalin had no Soviet troops stationed in Yugoslavia and the *Yugoslavian Communist Party* remained loyal to Tito. And, compounding his treason, Tito turned to the United States for support.

Concerned that there might be other Titos, Stalin ordered a purge of other communist parties of Eastern Europe. Individuals suspected of "national deviationism"—putting the interests of one's own country above the interests of the Soviet Union—were removed from office and sometimes put on trial and executed. As the number of executions grew, the American distaste for what was going on inevitably also grew, and so American–Soviet relations deteriorated even further.

The year 1948 also brought a direct Western–Soviet confrontation over Berlin, when Stalin cut off all land access routes between West Germany and Berlin. The Western response was an "airlift" that kept West Berlin supplied with food and fuel for nearly a year until Stalin lifted the blockade.

The Berlin Blockade was a double failure, for it, plus the communist *coup d'etat* in Czechoslovakia, convinced the West that a more long–term response was needed. The North Atlantic Treaty Organization (NATO) came into being in April 1949 with General Dwight D. Eisenhower as Supreme Commander of the Allied Forces in Europe. Agreement was also reached on merging the three western zones of occupation of Germany, a decision that led to the founding of the Federal Republic of Germany in May 1949. Conceding defeat, the Soviet Union ended the Berlin Blockade in May 1949. Five months later, it organized a separate government for its own zone of occupation, which became the German Democratic Republic.

As the European situation turned into a stalemate, Soviet interest began to turn to the East Asia. Here, the victory of Mao Zedong's communists and the establishment of the People's Republic of China seemed to open new vistas for communist expansion. In mid–1949, *Pravda*, the Soviet Communist Party newspaper, carried a long article by Liu Shaoqi, one of the main leaders of the Chinese revolution, reporting on Asian communist parties. The article explicitly endorsed armed struggle as the primary tactic to be pursued by them. Since the article was followed by several similar articles, it soon became evident that the party line on armed struggle had changed. Thus, when the communist government of North Korea launched an invasion of the south in June 1950, the United States assumed that it was operating under Soviet direction. The United States, therefore, brought the matter before the Security Council of the United Nations, which declared the North Korean invasion to be an act of aggression and called upon all members of the United Nations to join in a united "police action" to defend South Korea. This action was possible because the Soviet delegate had been boycotting meetings of the Security Council since January 1950 in protest of the failure to seat communist China.

The Korean "police action" turned into a full–scale war that lasted until after Stalin's death in March 1953. It soon became obvious that neither side would be permitted to resolve the issue by force, but too much prestige had been invested on both sides to allow for a compromise. News of the gray–haired old dictator's death was therefore greeted with relief, for it was hoped that a compromise might now be reached. The armistice came approximately four months later—on July 27, 1953.

Domestic Developments During and After World War II

When Nazi Germany launched its invasion of the Soviet Union in June 1941, Stalin, recognizing that the vast bulk of the Soviet citizenry had no particular reason to love communism, decided almost immediately to phrase his public messages in the language of Russian patriotism. Communist ideology almost disappeared from public utterances and World War II became the "Great Patriotic War." When, somewhat later, the Russian Orthodox Church offered its assistance and support, Stalin even went so far as to arrange for the election of a new Patriarch. The Russian Orthodox Church continued to benefit from its enhanced role after World War II as well.

Russia

But if Stalin was willing to make nationalist gestures where large numbers of citizens were involved, he still retained his suspicious nature and he did not hesitate to make use of the secret police to uproot whole groups of the population when he became suspicious of their loyalty to the Soviet regime. Thus, the Crimean Tatars and the Volga Germans were forcibly removed from their homes in southern Russia and resettled in Siberia or Central Asia. As the war progressed, other ethnic groups who were suspected of being willing to collaborate with the Germans, or who deserted from the Red Army in too large numbers, were also affected.

After the war, the main task of the NKVD, as it was then called, was to screen and "reintegrate" Soviet citizens who had spent some time in Germany as prisoners of war or as forced labor. Many people also were deported from the areas acquired by the Soviet Union during and after the war.

The Fourth Five Year Plan, 1946–51

The stated economic goals of the fourth Five Year Plan, initiated in 1946, were to restore war–ravaged areas of the country and to rebuild heavy industry and agriculture to their pre–war levels. These goals would have been challenging enough but, in February 1946, Stalin committed the nation to tripling industrial production in order to make the USSR "ready for every eventuality."

Although the Soviet Union announced in April 1951 that these goals had been met, Western scholars subsequently concluded that, while the assigned targets for raw industrial priority goods had been met, the production of low priority consumer goods fell far short of assigned goals. Agriculture, in particular, was an area in which production bore little relationship to stated goals. Most of the major grain–producing areas of the Soviet Union had, of course, been overrun by the Germans in World War II, and one effect of that was that the collective farms had been dissolved and most farm machinery was destroyed. Yet the fourth Five Year Plan allocated a pitiful 12.3 billion rubles to agriculture for 1946, while allocating 68.8 billion rubles to industry and a further 10 billion rubles to transport.

A famine beginning in late 1946 convinced the Party that something more would have to be done for agriculture, so a separate Three Year Plan for agriculture was instituted in 1947. The goals—50 percent increase in the production of meat, milk, lard, eggs and wool; a 20 percent increase in the number of cattle, hogs, sheep and goats—were impressive but, ultimately, they were not achieved. And the reason is simple—heavy industry had first claim on resources and there weren't enough capital resources left over to finance stated agricultural needs.

When the Three Year Plan for agriculture failed to increase agricultural production significantly, Nikita Khrushchëv, who at that time was Party secretary in charge of agriculture, put forth a plan for amalgamating several small collective farms into single, larger collective farms. Khrushchëv argued that amalgamation could cut costs and increase efficiency, making it possible to reallocate funds for the purpose of increasing production. The plan reduced the number of collective farms from 254,000 in April 1950 to 97,000 in October 1952. Khrushchëv's original plan had also called for razing the old peasant village houses and moving all of the collective farm workers in new, *agrogoroda* (literally, farm cities) consisting of high rise apartments. Although peasants were promised that the *Agrogoroda* would come with theaters, parks, and other amenities, peasant opposition to the loss of their traditional village homes (and the garden plots attached to them) was strong enough that this aspect of the reform was never implemented. Still, this "reform" had an important effect on country life, even if there is no evidence that it increased efficiency in any way.

Cultural Purges and Anti–Zionism

One remaining aspect of this last period of the Stalin era should be mentioned here. That is the program of cultural and ideological "rehabilitation" that Stalin instituted beginning shortly after the end of World War II, remnants of which continued until his death in 1953. Some reference has already be made to the treatment of soldiers and prisoners of war who were shipped off to prison camps when they arrived back in the Soviet Union. That was because they had seen conditions in central Europe at first hand and could have told their fellow citizens how much worse it was in the Soviet Union.

But the loosening of restrictions during World War II meant that even citizens who had never left home had been exposed to "foreign influences" and become tainted. To counteract that, the Party launched a virulent anti–Western campaign in the summer of 1946. The man in charge of this Soviet "cultural revolution" was Andrei Zhdanov who, in explaining the campaign, said

Does it suit us, the representatives of the advanced Soviet culture, to bow before bourgeois culture or play the role of its disciples? Our job is to scourge boldly and to attack bourgeois culture, which is in a state of miasma and corruption.

Among the Soviet creative artists whose works came under attack during this time were the poet Anna Akhmatova, the composers Sergei Prokofiev and Dmitri Shostakovich, the film director Sergei Eisenstein, the philosopher G. F. Alexandrov, and the economist Eugene Varga.

Zhdanov died in 1948 and Soviet cultural policy then changed or, perhaps it might better be said, found another target. The targets were still intellectuals but, now, the target was Jewish intellectuals, who were accused of being unpatriotic, "rootless cosmopolitans." The real issue here appears to be that Israel emerged as an independent state in 1948 and some in the *Communist Party* worried that Jews, who often held important positions in the society, might be more loyal to Israel than they were to the Soviet Union. Many Jewish intellectuals were arrested and, in 1952, several Jewish writers were executed without a trial.

Was Stalin personally involved in these events? The greatest evidence pointing in that direction is connected with a so–called "doctors' plot" that developed during the last months of Stalin's life. The top echelons of the *Communist Party* had their own doctor–specialists whose job was to look out after their health. Many of these individuals happened also to be Jews. Stalin evidently came to believe that these Jewish doctors had drawn up a plan aimed at killing or undermining the health of leading Soviet officials. The investigation into the "doctors' plot" quickly came to an end after Stalin's death and Nikita Khrushchëv stated in a "secret" speech in 1956 that the "doctors' plot" was fabricated from beginning to end.

The Post-Stalin Era

The Struggle for Succession

The announcement of Stalin's death came on March 5, 1953. It was a strange announcement, for it spoke of the need to prevent "any kind of disorder and panic." The disarray in the leadership which this indicates derived from the fact that Stalin had never permitted his lieutenants any independent authority and squelched any discussion of who his successor would be; now, for the first time, they were on their own. In his memoirs, Nikita Khrushchëv reminisced about this period:

Right up until his death Stalin used to tell us, "you'll see, when I'm gone the imperialistic powers will wring your necks like chickens." We never tried to reassure him that we would be able to manage. We knew it wouldn't do any good.

The disorder did not last very long, but it did result in some policy reversals in the first few days. Georgi Malenkov, who was silently looked upon as Stalin's logical successor, was permitted to succeed to both of Stalin's positions—General Secretary of the Central Committee of the Communist Party and Chairman of the Council of Ministers—but after one day he gave up the position of General Secretary for unexplained reasons. Nikita Khrushchëv unofficially got the top party position. It was obvious that the *Presidium* (the new name for the Politburo, adopted at the 19th Party Congress in 1952), was attempting to prevent the rise of a new "sole leader," and had decided to split the top party and state offices. Malenkov chose to remain as Chairman of the Council of Ministers—apparently because he believed that the more immediate power position lay with that title. For a while, it appeared that he had made the correct choice for, in the party, collective leadership of the entire Presidium was stressed while Malenkov was treated in the Soviet press as spokesman for the regime.

A Soviet history written in the 1980s characterizes this period as one of "restoration of Leninist norms and the collective principle in the work of the Party and state." There was actually a great deal of agreement in the Presidium about the need for modifications in the system. Some of these changes were inevitable. Stalin had concentrated all decision-making in his own hands—now, some decentralization was in order. The Central Committee, which had fallen into disuse, was revived and regular meetings scheduled. The various ministries were given a greater say in decision-making and there was a great deal of talk about streamlining and rationalizing the ministerial and planning bureaucracies.

In foreign affairs, the turn away from confrontation that led to an armistice in Korea also had an effect on Eastern Europe. In East Germany, the political leadership, concerned about the lack of domestic support, announced a "new course" aimed at reducing popular dissatisfaction. But before the "new course" could be put into action, worker demonstrations and strikes broke out in East Berlin and in other cities. When Soviet tanks were brought in to quell the demonstrations, the workers rebelled and had to be put down with force. June 17th, the date of the workers' rebellion in East Berlin, was subsequently established as a legal holiday in the Federal Republic of Germany.

In July 1953, the Central Committee met in a plenary session to hear that Lavrenti Beria, head of the secret police and a top member of the party leadership since 1939, had been arrested. The charge was that he had been attempting a bid for total power based on his control of the secret police. To forestall such an attempt in the future, the secret police were brought firmly under party control by taking them out of the ministry of the interior and creating a separate committee for state security (KGB) directly accountable to the Presidium. The powers of the KGB were also somewhat restricted by the issuance of new regulations specifying when arrests could be made. Beria, who was executed in December, was to be the last leading communist to be physically eliminated after losing in a struggle for power. From 1953 until the collapse of communism in 1991, the maximum penalty was expulsion from the party.

The Beginning of the Khrushchëv Era

In September, the first indication that Khrushchëv might be a claimant for power came when it was announced that the title of the chief party post had been changed from *General* Secretary to *First* Secretary and that Khrushchëv had been confirmed in this office. He now became a vigorous advocate of strengthening the party after years of Stalin's neglect.

The first sign that there were policy differences between Malenkov and Khrushchëv also appeared in September—though in the carefully phrased way in which Party speeches were made this was easy to see only in retrospect. In August, Malenkov had addressed the Supreme Soviet, setting forth the future direction of the regime. Bidding to reverse Stalin's traditional emphasis on heavy industry, Malenkov's program called for additional investment in the areas of consumer goods and agriculture. His theme was that people had a "right to demand consumer goods of high quality."

Khrushchëv, addressing a plenum of the Central Committee of the party after

Nikita Khrushchëv

Russia

having been installed as First Secretary, argued that something had to be done for agriculture, but rejected a change in investment priorities to finance it.

The battle continued in 1954 and, in fact, became clearer. Khrushchëv wanted to retain the priority of heavy industry and wanted to pour additional funds into modernizing defense—while greatly increasing agricultural production. He proposed to accomplish this through what later became known as the "virgin lands" program. This involved opening up huge quantities of steppe land in Kazakhstan for cultivation that had traditionally been considered too dry for normal agriculture. Khrushchëv's program was approved by a Central Committee plenum in March 1954; it was started in that year, but primarily was carried forward in 1955.

In the meantime, Khrushchëv had continued his attacks against Malenkov and managed to get him removed as Chairman of the Council of Ministers in early 1955. His replacement was Marshal Nikolai Bulganin. Khrushchëv had won a victory, but it was only partial. Bulganin belonged to the same faction on the Presidium as Malenkov.

Although it is largely coincidental, the period of joint leadership by Bulganin and Khrushchëv is associated with a number of breakthroughs in the foreign policy area. Calling for a resurrection of the old Leninist doctrine of "peaceful coexistence," the team of "B and K," as they became known to the West, engaged in a number of spectacular trips abroad, the most notable of which was a trip to Belgrade, Yugoslavia, to heal the breach with Marshal Tito. In a gesture to the West, the Soviet Union also agreed to end the joint military occupation of Austria, which regained its independence in 1955. This was the first withdrawal of Soviet troops without leaving a communist regime behind since World War II.

The good feeling engendered by the Soviet action in Austria was an important factor in producing the first meeting of major heads of government since the Potsdam Conference in 1945. This was the Geneva Summit of 1955. No specific agreements were reached but there was an exchange of views on German rearmament and reunification, European security, disarmament and the improvement of East–West contacts. The major Soviet proposal dealt with the opposing military alliances. It offered to disband the newly created (in May 1955) Warsaw Pact in return for the disbanding of NATO and the withdrawal of all "foreign troops" from the European continent. The proposal was so obviously one–sided that the West was unwilling to even consider it seriously. The summit was valuable from the Soviet point of view, however, for

it signified that the West was willing to accept the Soviet Union as an equal in diplomatic discussions.

The 20th Party Congress, which met in February 1956, represented a new high for Khrushchëv, for it confirmed that he had taken control of the party apparatus. It also represented a new foreign policy departure, for it was here that Khrushchëv first articulated the view that war between capitalism and communism was no longer "fatalistically inevitable"—the view held by Stalin. Khrushchëv justified his position on the basis of the emergence of socialism into a world system which made possible a world–wide peaceful transition to communism.

It appears, however, that the real basis for the change was Khrushchëv's recognition that the existence of nuclear weapons had changed the basic nature of war and rendered it no longer "thinkable."

De–Stalinization

Khrushchëv's most important speech at this Congress did not take place in the public session, however. In a separate "secret" session of the Congress, Khrushchëv launched a major attack on the record of Stalin and what he called the "cult of personality." The speech set forth in great detail the many crimes of Stalin. Its content soon became known in the Soviet Union, however, and the actual text, first available in the West, has since been made public.

Khrushchëv gave the speech to smash the "Stalin myth" and so to free himself to carry out wider changes in the system than conservatives favored. Khrushchëv and his supporters apparently believed that it was possible to condemn Stalin's "errors" and at the same time maintain and even strengthen their own position. This was an effort to make communist rule more respectable by moving back toward older, "Leninist" norms. It signaled no basic change in the nature of communist rule, but it did suggest an end to harsh, terrorist tactics.

The impact of Khrushchëv's speech went far beyond what he had obviously intended. Stalin had defined the nature of communism for so long that the move to repudiate him unleashed forces which threatened the very foundations of Soviet power. Only weeks after the Congress, riots in Tbilisi, the capital of Soviet Georgia, resulted in the deaths of over a hundred persons.

The most serious and direct consequences of de–Stalinization occurred in Eastern Europe, however. In the Polish cities of Poznan and Warsaw, armed clashes occurred between the workers and police. In Hungary, university students demanded, and obtained, an end to compulsory Russian language instruction.

The situation continued to build in both countries. In October, a Polish Party plenum elected Wladislaw Gomulka as First Secretary and called for internal reforms. In Hungary, the clash between university students and the Hungarian secret police led to large–scale fighting and, when it was ordered to intervene, to the disintegration of the Hungarian army.

The Soviet Ambassador to Hungary, Yuri Andropov, met with the new Hungarian Government and arranged for the withdrawal of Soviet troops from Budapest on October 28. One week later, on November 4, they returned and put down the uprising. The Soviet intervention in Hungary brought revulsion abroad and a wave of resignations among prominent foreign communists. Jean–Paul Sartre of France and Howard Fast of the United States were among those who turned in their party cards at this time.

Khrushchëv now began to downplay de–Stalinization, but he had lost the confidence of a number of the leading members of his own party. In June 1957, the Presidium voted seven to four to dismiss him as First Party Secretary. Khrushchëv refused to accept the decision of the Presidium, however, and demanded that the full Central Committee be convened to vote on the matter. Khrushchëv won in the larger forum and managed to obtain the removal of his opponents from the Presidium. Malenkov was sent to manage a remote installation in Central Asia while Molotov was named Soviet Ambassador to Mongolia. Nine months later, in March 1958, Khrushchëv assumed the additional office of Chairman of the Council of Ministers (head of government).

One of those who benefited from Khrushchëv's victory was Leonid Brezhnev, who became a full member of the Presidium in June 1957. Three years later, in May 1960, Brezhnev became Chairman of the Presidium of the Supreme Soviet (titular head of state). That same month, Alexei Kosygin and Nikolai Podgorny were promoted to full membership in the Presidium.

The 22nd Party Congress met in Moscow in October 1961. Its major theme was de–Stalinization. Following the Congress, Stalin's body was removed from alongside Lenin in the mausoleum on Red Square and buried outside the Kremlin wall. The city of Stalingrad had its name changed and became Volgograd, and other cities named after Stalin had their names changed as well. Yevgeni Yevtushenko, already well–known because of his poem about Babi Yar (where the Nazis carried out a massacre of Soviet Jews during World War II), now produced his poem entitled "The Heirs of Stalin" in which he spoke of those who *from rostrums, even heap abuse on Stalin but, at night, hanker after the good old days*

and warned that

As long as the heirs of Stalin walk this earth Stalin, I fancy, still lurks in the mausoleum.

This was followed in November 1962 by the publication of *One Day in the Life of Ivan Denisovich*, Alexander Solzhenitsyn's bold novel about life in Stalin's concentration camps.

Writings with a specific political content were not published in the Soviet Union except with approval from high up, and it was said that Khrushchëv authorized publication of Solzhenitsyn's book. But this was the surface reality. None of the "heirs of Stalin" denounced as criminals at the 22nd Party Congress suffered anything more than verbal abuse. They kept their jobs and bided their time. And in October 1964 they took their revenge by casting their votes for Khrushchëv's ouster from power.

De–Stalinization was only one of several factors involved in Khrushchëv's dismissal from power, however. Foreign policy was an issue and in particular, the Cuban missile crisis. It was an American who characterized Khrushchëv's foreign policy as one of "overextension followed by capitulation" but this appears to have been the opinion of some of those on the Presidium itself. One of the few specific charges brought against Khrushchëv in October 1964 was that he had caused a Soviet defeat at the time of the Cuban missile crisis. The theme of overextension was specifically taken up by Brezhnev the following month when he asserted that, in the future, Soviet foreign policy would take into consideration the "military power of the countries of the socialist camp."

The other chief issue was domestic. Khrushchëv had staked a great deal on economic development and he had promised the Soviet people that the USSR would catch up with the United States economically by 1980. He had carried through a partial economic decentralization in 1957 when he created 105 new regional *sovnarkhozy* (economic councils). In November 1962, he announced a division of the party into separate industrial and agricultural sections, the object to turn the party into an economic administrative apparatus. This move threatened the power position of the regional first party secretaries and created a great deal of dissatisfaction throughout the party.

In the end, it was probably the failure of Khrushchëv's agricultural policies that did him in. After the initial success of his "virgin lands" program, agricultural production stagnated and the country began to suffer chronic food shortages. The 1962 division of the party was an attempt to deal with the problem administratively, but it was a failure. In August 1964, Khrushchëv announced yet another reorganization of agriculture which he intended to submit to a November party plenum. But by this time the other members of the Presidium had enough. On October 15, 1964, Moscow's TASS (the official news "wire") announced that Khrushchëv had been relieved of his duties as First Party Secretary and Chairman of the Council of Ministers, and that Leonid Brezhnev had been elected First Party Secretary in his place. Alexei Kosygin became Chairman of the Council of Ministers. Anastas Mikoyan, who had succeeded Brezhnev as Chairman of the Presidium of the Supreme Soviet (titular head of state) in July 1964, retained that position until his retirement in December 1965; he was succeeded by Nikolai Podgorny, who continued to serve in that position until his death.

Soviet Foreign Policy under Khrushchëv

Of key importance to the leadership of the Soviet Union was the problem of relations with the United States, the country which, after World War II, was the leader of the Western alliance. Stalin, knowing that he could not both keep control over Eastern Europe and continue good relations with the United States, chose confrontation. His successors, perhaps frightened at the turn that confrontation had taken and more aware of the threat that nuclear weapons represented, attempted to reach an accommodation with the West while retaining Stalin's empire. This led to some easing of tensions and to increased diplomatic contacts. A Geneva Summit Conference in 1955 after Stalin's death represented the culmination of this trend. No significant agreements were reached, but the "spirit of Geneva" continued to influence relations between the two powers for about five years.

The refusal of the United States to accept Soviet domination of Eastern Europe always remained a factor in U.S.–Soviet relations, however, and when, as in 1956, the Soviet Union resorted to the use of force to retain its control, bilateral relations suffered. Not all of the Soviet Union's problems with regard to maintaining control were amenable to the use of force, however. One such case was Berlin, established under separate four–power occupation in 1945. In the 1950s, West Berlin (representing a union of the three western zones of occupation) was a free enterprise, democratic island in the middle of a communized East Germany and it had become a place of refuge for East Germans fleeing communism. Determined to put an end to the constant drain of manpower, Khrushchëv demanded in November 1958 that the occupation of West Berlin be terminated and that it be turned into a "free city" within the territory of the communist German Democratic Republic. Khrushchëv's position, put in the form of an ultimatum, created the Berlin Crisis of 1958.

It is difficult to determine whether Khrushchëv expected his viewpoint to prevail, but it did result in a four–power foreign ministers' conference in Geneva in May 1959 and an invitation to Khrushchëv to visit the United States in September. Khrushchëv stayed for 18 days, which included three days spent at Camp David in private conversation with President Eisenhower.

Though the talks produced only an agreement for additional summit level negotiations, the Soviets subsequently referred to them as having created the "spirit of Camp David." When Khrushchëv returned to Moscow, he publicly characterized Eisenhower as a man who

First Secretary Khrushchëv and President Kennedy, Vienna, 1961

Russia

"sincerely wants to liquidate the cold war and improve relations between our two great countries." That also led Khrushchëv to suggest, in early 1960, that the Soviet armed forces would be reduced by about one–third.

This was the high–water mark in U.S.–Soviet relations under Khrushchëv. In May 1960, the Soviets shot down an American U–2 photo–reconnaissance plane that had penetrated Soviet air space. Khrushchëv demanded an apology from Eisenhower and, when it was not forthcoming, he torpedoed a summit meeting scheduled to take place in Paris in mid–May. This also was one of the factors that explains Khrushchëv's extraordinary performance at the United Nations General Assembly in September when he took off his shoe and banged it on his desk to show his disapproval of one of the speeches.

A meeting between Khrushchëv and President Kennedy in May 1961 proved to be unproductive and, in fact, Khrushchëv resurrected the Berlin Crisis by demanding a settlement by the end of the year. Further, he coupled this with a statement that the Soviet defense budget would be *increased* by one–third. Then, on August 13, 1961, the Soviet Union instituted a unilateral solution to the Berlin Crisis by beginning to build a wall between West and East Berlin. Since the wall was being built on the territory of East Berlin, there was little that the United States and its allies could do other than to issue a diplomatic protest—but it obviously had a negative effect on U.S.–Soviet relations. Barriers were later placed to totally divide East Germany from West Berlin. This was the first time in history that a fortified wall had been erected to keep people *in* instead of *out*.

The next test of wills came in October 1962—the Cuban missile crisis. In his memoirs, Khrushchëv relates that:

It was during my visit to Bulgaria (May 14–20, 1962) that I had the idea of installing missiles with nuclear warheads in Cuba without letting the United States find out they were there until it was too late to do anything about them.

But the United States found out what the Soviet Union was up to as the missiles were being installed and demanded their removal. Khrushchëv had to acquiesce, but he attempted to save face by claiming that he had preserved world peace and obtained (an oral) guarantee for Cuba's Fidel Castro against any future attempts to overthrow him by troops launched from the U.S. In fact, he did have some gains to show. In the final settlement, the United States confined its objective to the withdrawal of Soviet missiles, thereby conced-

ing Castro's right to remain a Soviet ally and to retain a communist form of government if he wished. This was a tacit repeal of the Monroe Doctrine. In addition, the U.S. soon afterwards began removing its intermediate range ballistic missiles from Turkey, which Khrushchëv could claim as an additional victory on his part.

Moreover, in retrospect, the United States was as appalled as the Soviet Union at how close the two nations had come to all–out war and the result was further steps toward *detente*. This led to the installation of a Washington–Moscow "hot line" and the signing of a limited test ban treaty in 1963.

Domestically, however, Khrushchëv drew different conclusions from the Cuban missile crisis and in March 1963 he pushed through a revision of the last two years of the Seventh Five Year Plan to allow for a large–scale deployment of Soviet ICBMs. As he records in his memoirs,

the experience of the Caribbean crisis also convinced us that we were right to concentrate on the manufacture of nuclear missiles.

The Brezhnev Era

During the years that followed Khrushchëv's ouster, the Soviet Union was governed by a relatively stable coalition of leaders that included Brezhnev, Kosy-

gin and Podgorny, but also included Michael Suslov, the party's chief ideologist, as well. Brezhnev gradually consolidated his position as first among equals, however, and, starting in the late 1960s, he became the dominant figure in foreign policy. Brezhnev's style of leadership was undramatic, however, and both his successes and his failures tended to be associated more with the system than with the man.

The immediate period following Khrushchëv's departure was characterized by a reversal of many of his policies. Most importantly, the November 1962 division of the party into separate industrial and agricultural units was reversed and a unitary party structure was recreated. The regional economic councils created in 1957 were also gradually phased out and replaced by centralized ministries.

In 1965, at a Central Committee plenum, Brezhnev announced a change in agricultural policy which, he said, would place the emphasis on farm autonomy. The real thrust of the new program was *not* farm autonomy, however, but increased incentives—diffused in such a way that they probably had little economic effect. Ever since their creation in the 1930s, collective farms had been required to deliver a set quota of grain to the government at artificially low prices. Brezhnev now lowered that quota by 11 million tons and increased the price that

Leonid Brezhnev

View of Moscow and the Moscow River

the government would pay for above–quota deliveries. The price of various types of agricultural equipment was also lowered at this time. These changes increased retained earnings for the collective farm administrations, but they did not filter down in a meaningful way to the individual peasant. Two other reforms did, however; peasants for the first time became eligible for old age pensions and were guaranteed a minimum monthly income. In addition, there was an attempt to encourage the production of more fruit, vegetables and meat for sale in the free peasant markets of the big cities by easing restrictions and reducing taxes on small private plots. All of these changes under Brezhnev had the effect of blurring the distinction between state and collective farms.

Major changes in the industrial sector were also experimented with at this time. These experiments, collectively known as the *Liberman Plan*, were actually suggested in 1962 when a Kharkov (Ukraine) University professor by the name of Yevsei Liberman wrote an article for *Pravda* setting forth general principles for economic reform. Under the Soviet economic system, manufacturing enterprises operated on the basis of detailed instructions drawn up by planning experts in centralized ministries. Liberman proposed that much of this planning be dismantled and that individual plant managers be given authority to run their enterprises themselves, subject only to overall production figures and fulfillment of delivery dates. Profitability, rather than the meeting of production norms, would be the new test of the effi-

ciency of an enterprise, and supply and demand would replace the exchange of goods on the basis of pre–planned indexes. Wages and salaries would also be tied to the profitability of individual enterprises.

The Liberman article in *Pravda* had been personally approved and endorsed by Khrushchëv, and in August 1964 the first test of the *Liberman* ideas began with an experimental tryout of the system in two textile plants. After Khrushchëv's fall, Alexei Kosygin made the Liberman Plan his own and ordered that a reform program be drawn up for the entire economy. The new program was put into effect beginning in September 1965. There was considerable opposition from among those who believed that it would tend to decrease the role of the party in the economy, however, and Brezhnev apparently aligned himself eventually with this group. As a result, the Central Committee plenum that instituted the reform also re-instituted central industrial and technical ministries, at least partially negating the reform from the very beginning. *Liberman-ism* was subsequently adopted by many Eastern European regimes, most notably Hungary, but in the Soviet Union it was phased out beginning in 1970.

Another program reversal that followed the ouster of Khrushchëv was the gradual end of de–Stalinization, accompanied by a generally harder line on the cultural front. A *Pravda* article in 1965 by Professor Sergei Trapeznikov, chief of the Central Committee's department of science and education, characterized the Stalin era as "one of the most brilliant in the history of the Party and the Soviet State" and sug-

gested it as a pattern for the theoretical and practical activity of the Party.

A month earlier, in September 1965, A.M. Rumiantsev, editor of *Pravda*, had been dismissed after he came to the defense of Andrei Voznesensky, a Soviet writer who had been accused of *nihilism*. In that same month, Andrei Sinyavsky and Yuri Daniel were arrested and tried for publishing abroad works critical of the Soviet Union. They were sentenced to 7 and 5 years at hard labor.

The 23rd Party Congress of 1966 appeared to confirm the trend toward re–Stalinization. The Presidium again became known as the Politburo while the First Party Secretary resumed the title of General Secretary. Both names dated from the Stalinist era and had been dropped by Khrushchëv.

The Dissident Movement

Re–Stalinization was accompanied by the rise of a dissident movement that grew in numbers and in significance in the late 1960s. In 1966, an underground journal, *Phoenix 61*, began to appear. Four writers associated with the journal were arrested at the beginning of 1967 and later sentenced. This, in turn, led to several public and private petitions of protest, signed by increased numbers of distinguished Soviet intellectuals. The situation was further worsened when Stalin's daughter, Svetlana Allilueva, defected in April 1967 and in a subsequent book, *Twenty Letters to a Friend*, expressed her solidarity with the Soviet intellectuals in their struggle for intellectual freedom. Also, about this time, two of Alexander Solzhenitsyn's novels,

Russia

Russian student with her classmates at the College of Europe

First Circle and *Cancer Ward*, were published abroad—without Solzhenitsyn's permission, to be sure, but the mere fact of publication abroad was considered to be an act of dissidence.

As the dissident movement continued to grow, it gained a widening circle of recruits. In July 1968, Andrei Sakharov, a distinguished physicist and father of the Soviet Union's hydrogen bomb, allowed a manuscript of his entitled *Thoughts on Progress, Peaceful Coexistence and Intellectual Freedom*, to be published abroad. Sakharov had joined the ranks of active dissidents two years earlier when he wrote a letter to Brezhnev protesting the arrest of four persons whose crime was that they had protested against the trial of Sinyavsky and Daniel. Since Sakharov was a prominent member of the Soviet Academy of Sciences and a recipient of both the Stalin Prize and the Lenin Prize, nothing had happened then or subsequently when he signed a letter to the Party warning against a resurgence of Stalinism. In August 1968, however, Sakharov was removed from all secret work and transferred to another academic institute in Moscow; he and his wife were later sent to the official detention city of Gorky, where they remained until their release by Gorbachëv in 1986.

The Soviet invasion of Czechoslovakia in 1968 brought both renewed protests and a harsher crackdown on dissidents. One of the seven individuals who staged a brief demonstration in Red Square against the invasion was Pavel Litvinov, grandson of Maxim Litvinov, Stalin's Foreign Minister in the 1930s. Litvinov was

sentenced to five years internal exile in a Siberian village. After his return to Moscow in 1973, Litvinov and his wife applied for exit visas as Jews and emigrated shortly afterwards.

One of the more interesting developments of the Brezhnev era was the adoption of a policy of allowing Jewish emigration. There were a little over two million Jews in the Soviet Union and the large majority of them considered themselves to be assimilated and at home. In 1970, for example, only 17.7 percent of all Jews listed either Hebrew or Yiddish as their mother tongue. There had always been some anti–Semitism in Russia, but the Soviet Union, to its credit, had seldom encouraged the attitude. In 1967, however, following Israel's defeat of the Soviet Union's Arab clients, Egypt and Syria, the Soviet Union unleashed a violent anti–Zionist campaign. For some of the Russian public, the distinction between anti–Zionism and anti–Semitism was too fine a difference to draw. As a result, an increasing number of Jews began applying for visas to emigrate to Israel; eventually over 100,000 Jews applied to emigrate. In 1968, the ministry of interior notified a few Jewish families that, if they still wanted to leave, they could. The flow of Jewish emigrants grew steadily thereafter, and by 1973 an average of 30,000 Jews were leaving every year.

The question of Jewish emigration became a foreign policy matter in 1974 when the U.S. Congress, following the leadership of Senator Henry Jackson of Washington State, approved an amendment to the 1972 trade agreement on "most-favored–nation" status for the Soviet Union which made approval contingent on increased Jewish emigration from the Soviet Union. The Soviets, calling the Jackson Amendment an interference in their domestic affairs, rejected the trade agreement in 1975.

Jewish emigration continued at a decreased level for awhile after 1975, but then began growing again. By 1979, an average of 4,000 Jews were departing monthly. Then came a policy reversal. From a peak of 51,320 in 1979, the number of emigrants declined to 2,688 in 1982, the last year of Brezhnev's regime.

Non–Jewish dissidents did not, in general, have the right to apply for emigration but the Brezhnev regime rediscovered, in the period of the 1970s, that emigration or expulsion sometimes provided a suitable alternative to imprisonment for individuals too prominent to treat as ordinary criminals. Alexander Solzhenitsyn, expelled in February 1974, was the most famous of these, but the list of those given permission to go abroad temporarily who thereafter had their Soviet citizenship withdrawn was much longer. Thus by the end of the Brezhnev regime in 1982, most individuals who had joined the ranks of the dissidents in the 1960s or early 1970s were either living abroad, in prison, a psychiatric hospital, or in internal exile.

A few new dissidents did appear in the late 1970s, particularly in association with attempts to demand implementation of the human rights provision of the Helsinki Accord, signed in 1975. They were small in number, however, and quickly rounded up. There was also some dissident activity in connection with the 1980 Summer Olympics and again at the time of the 1980–81 Madrid follow–up conference to the Helsinki Conference on Security and Cooperation in Europe.

Yet the movement, although troublesome because of its international ramifications, was never more than an annoyance to the regime. The actual number of dissidents was always quite small. Thus, a Western study which attempted to identify all those who were in any way involved in the dissident movement was able to come up with names of only 3,400 persons for the period 1956 to 1975. The disturbing element from the point of view of the regime was that the dissidents originated in a social base that consisted essentially of the scientific–cultural *intelligentsia*. Their significance was that they said aloud what other people could only think.

A Regime In Crisis

A more serious problem in the long run was that the Soviet economy, which began

Russia

a slowdown by 1970, continued in that pattern to the end of the Brezhnev era. Moreover, wage increases granted to the workers after 1965 exacerbated the situation for there was no accompanying increase in consumer goods.

The Five Year Plan for 1971–1975 attempted to deal with this situation by calling for vast investment in agriculture and increased investments in consumer industry. For the first time in Soviet history, consumer goods were to be favored over heavy industry. But by the end of 1972, the planners had to admit that their priorities did not permit the planned investments in consumer goods and the plan was revised to renew the emphasis on heavy industry. The Tenth Five Year Plan (1976–1980) continued the revised priorities of the preceding plan. These targets were also not met.

The 11th Five Year Plan (1981–1985) called for a slightly larger growth in consumer industry than heavy industry. Some of its goals, particularly those with regard to agriculture were unrealistic, however, and were never met. The essential problem—and it is one that the Soviets never solved—is that Soviet productivity slowed to a negligible rate in the 1960s and all the tinkering with the economy after that time did nothing to reverse that trend. Any effective economic reform would have had to decrease the role of the cadre of the Communist Party in the economy. Under Brezhnev, this was always unacceptable.

The Brezhnev era has one last characteristic worth mentioning. The Soviet Union had a huge bureaucracy which ran all things under the guidance of the Party. Khrushchëv had feared that the bureaucracy was becoming ingrown and in 1961 he had sponsored a new Party statute which attempted to deal with the problem. Under the terms of the statute, there was to be a normal turnover of personnel on each of the Party committees, with a certain percentage of the membership to be replaced at each election. There was considerable opposition to this policy among Party bureaucrats and, at the 23rd Party Congress in 1966, the policy was reversed. Although a general clause was added stressing the intention of the Party to promote "energetic and competent young cadres," this was generally ignored in the period of the 1970s.

The result was an unparalleled continuity in office at all levels of government, and an aging Party and government elite. One can see how this operated with regard to membership on the Central Committee. In 1966, 76 percent of those elected at the 24th Party Congress were already full members. The percentage of full members reelected subsequently remained at this level. In fact at the 26th Party Congress in 1981, the figure was actually 75 percent; it would have been much higher, but the Central Committee was also growing during these years, having increased by 44 persons since the previous Congress.

Soviet Foreign Policy under Brezhnev

When Brezhnev replaced Khrushchëv as Party chief in October 1964, a subtle change occurred. Without repudiating *detente*, Brezhnev began to speak about the necessity of maintaining Soviet defense potential at the highest possible levels. In July 1965, he spoke of a five–year defense plan to "increase the defensive might of the USSR." The subsequent 1966–1970 Soviet defense budget nearly doubled defense spending; it continued to grow in the period of the 1970s, though a CIA report issued in the middle 1980s indicated that the annual growth rate may have dropped somewhat for the period 1979–1982.

Brezhnev's push for increased defense expenditures was, from the Soviet point of view, entirely compatible with a policy of *detente* and, in some respects, a precondition for it. Cooperation between the two super powers was made somewhat more difficult because of the United States' increasing involvement in Vietnam but, in spite of this, a treaty to ban nuclear weapons in outer space was negotiated in 1967. This was followed in 1968 by a treaty on the non–proliferation of nuclear weapons.

Negotiations to limit the size of both countries' strategic nuclear forces were to begin in 1968, but were canceled by President Johnson after a Soviet invasion of Czechoslovakia. The Strategic Arms Limitation Talks (SALT) concept was revived by President Nixon, however, and this led to a visit by President Nixon to Moscow in May 1972 and the signing of the SALT–1 accords. SALT–1 primarily limited the deployment of antiballistic missiles (ABMs) but it also contained a five–year interim agreement freezing the number of land and sea–based offensive missiles. In late 1974, President Ford met with Brezhnev in Vladivostok and there the two leaders agreed on general guidelines for a SALT–2 pact which would deal with strategic nuclear missiles. SALT–2 was finally initialed in 1979, but President Carter later withdrew the treaty from consideration by the United States Senate after a Soviet invasion of Afghanistan.

Military Intervention in Afghanistan

A group openly claiming to be Marxist–Leninist came to power in Afghanistan in a bloody *coup* in late 1978. The U.S. government recognized the new regime, but became more and more disquieted by subsequent events. A large number of "advisers" were imported from the Soviet Union and the regime began an attempt to bring about a social revolution within the country. This produced strong resistance among the Afghan population, however, and it wasn't long before armed uprisings throughout the country threatened the very existence of the regime. In late 1979 therefore, the Soviet Union intervened with 80,000 Soviet troops to prop up the

Presidents Carter and Brezhnev exchange signed copies of the SALT II Treaty agreement, Vienna, June 1979

Russia

Mujahidin **resistance fighters look down on a village after a Soviet aerial attack. At left are terraced crop fields.**
AP/World Wide Photos

faltering Afghan communist regime. But Afghanistan is mostly rugged mountain country with a population of about 20 million people; the Soviet troops were only sufficient to keep the communist regime from being overthrown, but not enough to put down the rebellion.

Soviet intervention in Afghanistan had an adverse effect on the Soviet Union's relations with most of the rest of the world, however. A number of countries, including the United States, boycotted the 1980 Moscow Olympics.

President Carter also announced a partial embargo on the sale of grain to the Soviet Union and began negotiating an agreement with Pakistan to provide military support to the *mujahidin*, the Afghan resistance. In addition, the Carter Administration reversed its earlier position on the adequacy of American military power and began a new buildup of U.S. forces. Further, it sponsored resolutions in the United Nations condemning the Soviet military presence in Afghanistan.

The Reagan Administration continued and intensified most of these policies. Agreement with Pakistan was reached and significant aid began flowing to the *mujahidin*. Military budgets were greatly enlarged and the administration openly boasted about beginning a new arms race which they expected to win. The B–1 bomber aircraft, canceled by the Carter Administration, was reinstated and a number of new weapons systems, including the multiple–warhead MX and the Trident submarine, were proposed.

This was the stick. At the same time, the Reagan Administration stipulated its willingness to negotiate arms reductions and symbolized this by changing the name of the arms negotiations process from SALT—Strategic Arms Limitation Talks—to START—Strategic Arms Reduction Talks.

The START negotiations began in June 1982. The American position, set forth by President Reagan, called for a reduction of missile launchers to 850 each (down from 2,000 for the USA and 2,700 for the USSR) and a reduction of nuclear warheads by about a third. No more than half of the missile launchers could be land–based. Agreement on these points would lead to a second round of talks aimed at reducing other elements of the two nations' "balance of terror."

Brezhnev rejected Reagan's proposal in May 1982, apparently disturbed by its proposed limits on land–based ICBMs. His own proposal called for a two–thirds reduction in nuclear warheads, a ban on the development of new types of strategic weapons, and a freeze on strategic weapons at current levels, to begin concurrently with the negotiations. The United States rejected the freeze on the basis that it would codify existing Soviet advantages, but welcomed Brezhnev's willingness to negotiate.

The United States and USSR were at least talking with each other in the area of strategic weapons. One other area of American concern, that of theater nuclear weapons in Europe, remained totally stalemated. The problem dated from 1977, when the Soviet Union began installing SS–20 missiles in Eastern Europe. A mobile missile with three warheads, the SS–20 caused great concern among Western European leaders and they be-gan pushing for NATO to match these missiles.

In 1979, therefore, NATO voted for the emplacement of American Pershing II and Cruise missiles in Europe, if talks with the Soviet Union did not produce another solution. The Soviets refused to discuss the removal of their missiles, however, so President Reagan offered his Zero Option—if the Soviet Union would pull its SS–20s out of Eastern Europe, then the USA would refrain from installing Pershing IIs and Cruise missiles in Western Europe—in a public speech in September 1981. The Soviet Union had not yet responded as of November 1982, when Brezhnev died.

Government Transition

November 1982–March 1985

Prior to Brezhnev's death in November 1982, there was a widespread feeling that the last years of his regime had been ones of stagnation and even decline. Many felt that what was needed was a strong, vigorous, but tested leader who could get the country going again.

Konstantin Chernenko was Brezhnev's *protégé* and therefore represented continuity; Yuri Andropov, who had been head of the KGB for 15 years, was a man from outside Brezhnev's inner circle, and therefore represented change. The choice fell to Andropov. It turned out, however, that Andropov was a frail reed on which to lean. He was personally honest and hardworking, and he had attached to himself a number of younger individuals committed to change. But he was also suffering from a heart condition and diabetes, and was temporarily incapacitated only five months after becoming General Secretary. Moreover, although a majority of the

Pravda **announces Brezhnev's death**

Politburo had chosen him over Chernenko, it soon became clear that there was no firm majority for reform. As a result, there were only three major policies associated with Andropov's name. The first of these was his campaign against corruption and slack labor discipline. There was undoubtedly corruption and slack discipline, but if western observers were correct that these things were only symptoms and that the major problems were systemic—arising from or pertaining to the system *itself*—then Andropov's campaign was relatively meaningless.

Andropov was also interested in renewing the leadership of the Party by retiring older individuals and promoting younger men in their places. He succeeded to a certain extent at secondary levels, but the average age of the Politburo remained well past the usual age of retirement.

He also introduced two economic "reforms," a system of brigades for farm workers that permitted some wage differentiation based on actual production, and an experiment, limited to five ministries, in which work teams were set up in factories and encouraged to compete with each other. The factory reform was begun as of January 1, 1984. Both reforms constituted "tinkering with the system" and therefore made no significant contribution to higher productivity. They did represent Andropov's commitment to economic reform, however, and provided a beginning upon which Gorbachëv could later build.

Foreign relations under Andropov deserve comment. He essentially represented a hard–line faction in this area, but he was extremely vigorous in his negotiating stance. Thus it was Andropov who issued the first formal reply to President Reagan's "Zero Option" speech of September 1981. In November 1982, shortly after becoming General Secretary, Andropov gave a speech in which he proposed to reduce the number of SS–20s in Eastern Europe to the same number of missiles held by Great Britain and France if, in return, NATO would cancel deployment of Pershing IIs and Cruise missiles in Western Europe. The offer was unacceptable because the British and French missiles, being part of their "national" arsenals, were not under NATO control. It did open the way for formal negotiations to begin, however.

The United States continued to push its Zero Option until March 1983. Then President Reagan gave another speech in which he introduced his "Interim Proposal." He proposed that the United States and the USSR agree to an equal number of theater nuclear warheads on each side, with the expectation that talks on an eventual Zero Option would continue. The Soviets rejected this proposal.

Negotiations nevertheless continued and there was at least the possibility that an agreement would have been reached, except for the unfortunate circumstances of the Soviet shooting down of a commercial airliner, South Korean Flight 007, in September 1983. The mutual recriminations that followed that event doomed the Theater Nuclear Weapons discussions.

Izvestia announces Andropov's death

In order to preserve their real or imaginary advantage, the Soviets embarked on a vigorous campaign to drive a wedge between the USA and its Western European NATO allies through mountains of propaganda describing the horrors of nuclear war. This did, in fact, succeed in attracting the sympathies of a substantial number of people in Western Europe and led to numerous anti–nuclear demonstrations. However, in November 1983, with no agreement in sight, the United States began delivering the first of the Pershing II and Cruise missiles to Western Europe. The Theater Nuclear Force discussions were then abruptly recessed by the Soviets in December 1983. They announced that they would not return to the negotiating table unless the United States agreed to withdraw all nuclear missiles emplaced in Western Europe.

Andropov fell ill at just about this point. He was last seen in public shortly before the downing of the airliner, and it is not known what role, if any, he had in foreign affairs during those last five months when he remained sequestered from the world.

This is the record which the members of the Politburo had to evaluate when they met to choose Andropov's successor in February 1984. The promise he represented had been largely unfulfilled, but even the pallid reforms instituted had been negatively received by a large part of the bureaucracy. In particular, Andropov's attempts to weed out incompetents and to promote younger persons to positions of higher responsibility threatened the security of the tenure of the "old guard" Party cadre, and they mobilized their forces accordingly. Chernenko, passed over once precisely because he represented the poli-

General Secretary Konstantin Chernenko of the U.S.S.R.

Russia

tics of the waning years of the Brezhnev era, became their candidate.

The other two candidates were Mikhail Gorbachëv and Grigori Romanov. Gorbachëv and Romanov represented the younger generation of the Politburo and tended to be classified as economic specialists because both probably favored greater experimentation in the area of the economy. The Politburo chose Chernenko—although it appeared that Gorbachëv moved into a clear number two position and was the heir apparent.

And how did Chernenko change things after becoming General Secretary? Serge Schmemann, Moscow correspondent for the *New York Times*, wrote, quoting from an interview he had with a knowledgeable figure in Moscow:

We have come to peace with Mr. Chernenko. He has contributed nothing new, the pace has slowed, the results are humble, but at least he has not turned back the clock.

Chernenko was a transitional figure, chosen to hold the fort a little longer before transferring power to a new generation. As such, his initiatives, or lack of them, reflected the will of a majority of the Politburo. When he first took over, there apparently were high–level disagreements on a number of policy issues, most importantly, on foreign policy. The result was several months of hibernation, exemplified by a Soviet boycott of the 1984 Summer Olympics in Los Angeles and a cancellation of a visit to China by Ivan V. Arkhipov, Vice Chairman of the USSR Council of Ministers.

But Chernenko, who suffered from emphysema and a weak heart, disappeared from view for two months in mid–1984 and reportedly was brought back to Moscow in a wheelchair. It was shortly afterwards that Foreign Minister Gromyko agreed to a meeting with President Reagan. The seriousness of Chernenko's illness had apparently broken the stalemate in the Kremlin and a new majority favoring negotiations with the USA had emerged. At the beginning of November, it was announced that new high–level economic talks would be held in Moscow in January 1985. Two weeks later, Gromyko and Secretary of State George Shultz agreed to meet in Geneva in early January to discuss resumption of arms talks. It was also at about this time that Moscow announced that Arkhipov's delayed visit to China would take place in December.

The Moscow talks were inconclusive, but there was agreement to resume arms talks in Geneva beginning March 12, 1985. Arkhipov's visit to China also resulted in some improvement in Soviet–Chinese relations.

These events occurred in Chernenko's absence, for he had disappeared from sight on December 27 and was never again seen in public. In February, it was officially confirmed that he was ill. A short television clip showed him voting in the Republic elections on February 24th, but it appeared to have been "doctored," since its background matched another clip reported to be at another time and place. Fifteen days later, his death was announced. According to the official medical report, his death resulted from a combination of factors which included emphysema, a heart condition and chronic hepatitis which had developed into cirrhosis. Evidently his death was quite expected, for the Central Committee had already met and decided on his successor.

The Gorbachëv Era

A new General Secretary

The story of Gorbachëv's formal installation as General Secretary is well–known—how Gromyko made the nominating speech at the meeting of the Central Committee and how he concluded his remarks with the observation that "Comrades, he has a nice smile, but he has iron teeth." No other candidates were presented to the Central Committee and acceptance was therefore assured.

In March 1987, however, a somewhat different report surfaced about a secret Politburo meeting which took place prior to the Central Committee meeting that installed Gorbachëv as General Secretary. This report, which appeared in a Finnish newspaper, *Svomen Kuvalehti*, was based on an interview with Mikhail Shatrov, a Soviet playwright and Gorbachëv adviser. According to Shatrov, nine persons were present at the Politburo meeting. With Gromyko as chairman and abstaining, the vote was tied four to four between Gorbachëv and Viktor Grishin, Moscow party leader. Gromyko then intervened to cast the deciding vote.

Not every good story is true, of course, and according to Dmitri Volkogonov—who reviewed the files of that particular politburo meeting during preparation of his book *Autopsy for an Empire*—this is another example of a good story not supported by the written record, or at least not all of it. According to Volkogonov, Gromyko did nominate Gorbachëv for the position of party General Secretary, Gromyko was later named Chairman of the Presidium of the Supreme Soviet (head of state), and Grishin and three other members of the Politburo did shortly afterwards lose their seats on the Politburo. But Gromyko supported Gorbachëv because he believed that only a young man

could "pump new energy into the Party;" Gromyko was named Chairman of the Presidium of the Supreme Soviet because Gorbachëv wanted to replace him as Minister of Foreign Affairs; and Grishin and three other members lost their Politburo seats as part of a remaking of the Politburo in Gorbachëv's image.

Born on March 2, 1931, Gorbachëv was at the time the youngest man on the Politburo. He was also the best educated, having graduated from Moscow University in 1955 with a degree in law. He later would add a second degree when he earned the qualification of "agronomist–economist" from the Stavropol Agricultural Institute in 1967.

It was at Moscow University that Gorbachëv first began to take an active interest in politics. He became the head of the Moscow University branch of the *Komsomols* (Young Communists) and it was at this time that he joined the Communist Party. After graduation, Gorbachëv joined the Stavropol Agricultural Institute. East of the Black Sea, this is an important agricultural district in southern Russia. It was also Gorbachëv's home region, so he probably had political contacts there. He began work as a researcher, agronomist and economist, but he soon moved over into full–time party work. By his thirty–fifth birthday, he was Stavropol party chief; four years later, he had become the party chief of the entire region.

Gorbachëv was brought to Moscow in 1978 to become a member of the Central Committee Secretariat with responsibility for agriculture. A year later, he was made a candidate member of the Politburo; in 1980 he became a full member.

When Andropov became General Secretary in 1982, he apparently began grooming Gorbachëv as a possible successor. The first evidence of this came in May 1983 when Gorbachëv made a visit to Canada. This was his first official trip outside the Communist Bloc and he acquitted himself very well. A trip to England in December 1984 was equally successful. Domestically, Gorbachëv had been in charge of the Secretariat since at least October 1984. By March 1985, it was clear that Gorbachëv was well–qualified to handle the General Secretary position.

In making his acceptance speech at the CPSU Central Committee meeting on March 11, 1985, Gorbachëv broke no new ground but he did make a number of points which gave some indication of his thinking. First of all, he referred to "enhancing the independence of enterprises, raising their interest in the end product of their work." This implied a commitment to greater economic reform. Second, he made the assertion "we want a real and major reduction of the arms stockpiles."

Although again somewhat vague, it appeared to be a commitment to pursue arms reductions talks with the United States with a definite goal in mind rather than simply exploring areas of disagreement.

Manipulation of the Politburo

The first order of business of the new leader was to consolidate his power base. He began the process a little over a month later, on April 23, at a special session of the Central Committee. Three men, all obviously Gorbachёv allies, were promoted to full membership on the Politburo and one other individual was made a candidate member. The elevation of Viktor Chebrikov, the KGB chairman—who was already a candidate member—came as no surprise. But the promotions of Yegor Ligachёv and Nikolai Ryzhkov were different, because both were elevated to full membership without having to go through the intermediate step of candidate member. Moreover, both worked in the Secretariat under Gorbachёv and were closely tied to him personally. The other promotion, that of Minister of War Sokolov to non–voting candidate membership, was probably an effort to appease the "old guard" and military at the same time. Sokolov, already 74, was viewed at the time as an interim appointee.

The April 1985 changes gave Gorbachёv a firm majority and he used it to begin remaking the Politburo and the government. At the regular plenary session of the Central Committee on July 1, 1985, Georgi Romanov—another of Gorbachёv's rivals for the position of General Secretary—was retired from the Politburo "on health grounds." His Politburo seat went to Eduard Shevardnadze, First Secretary for the Georgian Republic. Gorbachёv's promotion and Romanov's retirement had also created two vacancies in the Secretariat and these were filled by Boris Yeltsin and Lev Zaikov.

Some additional reasons for the changes became evident the next day when the Supreme Soviet met. One of its tasks was the selection of a new Chairman of the Presidium (often referred to in the West as the Soviet President), vacant since the death of Chernenko. It had been thought that Gorbachёv would assume this position but, in a switch, he announced that, having been requested to devote all of his time to Party affairs, he was nominating Andrei Gromyko to the position. He then added that Eduard Shevardnadze would replace Gromyko as minister of foreign affairs. Gromyko thus got the honor of becoming head of state, while Gorbachёv got a new minister of foreign affairs, untainted by any connection with previous Soviet foreign policies.

When he took over his new job, Shevardnadze was totally without experience in foreign affairs. He did have a reputation for being honest and hard–working, however, and had, it was said, waged an energetic and effective campaign against corruption and laziness in his native Georgia. Shevardnadze's appointment suggested that Gorbachёv intended to have the principal voice in foreign affairs. That indeed proved to be the case, although Shevardnadze earned high marks during his tenure as foreign minister.

Gorbachёv continued his rebuilding in the fall of 1985. In September, Nikolai Tikhonov stepped down as Chairman of the Council of Ministers and was replaced by Nikolai Ryzhkov. A Gorbachёv ally now occupied the office responsible for implementing economic reforms approved by the Politburo.

Additional changes occurred in October when Tikhonov retired from the Politburo and Nikolai Talyzin became a candidate member. Talyzin, a telecommunications specialist, became head of GOSPLAN at the same time. Now an individual closely associated with Gorbachёv was also in

Gorbachёv speaks at the Kremlin's Palace of Congresses

Russia

charge of economic planning. The move was particularly significant, since Gorbachëv had already rejected the draft Five Year Plan drawn up by Nikolai Baibakov, the man whom Talyzin replaced at GOSPLAN. But Talyzin proved to be the wrong choice. At the mid–1987 meeting of the Central Committee, he was singled out for criticism by Gorbachëv for failure to embark upon economic change with sufficient rapidity. Somewhat later, he was replaced at GOSPLAN and named permanent representative to the Council for Mutual Economic Assistance.

Economic leadership changes were particularly important to Gorbachëv. As he made clear at the 27th Party Congress in February 1986, the Soviet leader intended an economic transformation of his country and was well aware of the human factor in any such transformation. This almost certainly is why he forced the resignation of the relatively young Georgi Romanov, an economic specialist, but also a conservative on programs of economic reform. Tikhonov, 81, and Baibakov, 75, on the other hand, were probably replaced primarily because of advanced age.

Having promoted four of his allies to the Politburo within six months of becoming General Secretary and accepted the resignation of two others, it is clear that Gorbachëv had carried out a rapid transformation of this ruling body. As it turned out, however, the transformation was not complete. In January 1986, Viktor Grishin resigned his Politburo seat and simultane-ously turned over his position as Moscow City First Secretary to Boris Yeltsin. One month later, a number of other personnel changes were announced. Lev Zaikov became a full member of the Politburo while Boris Yeltsin and Nikolai Slyunkov became candidate members. Two candidate members, Boris Ponomarev, 81, and Vasily Kuznetsov, 85, were edged into retirement.

There were also two interesting additions to the Secretariat at this time. The first of these was Anatoli Dobrynin, who had served as Soviet Ambassador to the United States since 1962. Gorbachëv, probably hoping to make use of his extensive personal knowledge of the United States, appointed a new ambassador to replace him in Washington and added him to the Secretariat. The second addition was Alexandra Biryukova, who thus became the highest ranking woman in the Soviet Communist Party. Biryukova, whose background was that of a national trade union leader, had been a member of the Central Committee since the early 1970s, but this marked her transition to full–time party work.

Gorbachëv's extensive changes since becoming General Secretary placed a new generation of leadership in power in the Soviet Union. At the 27th Party Congress in February 1986, this new leadership committed the Soviet Union to a Five Year and a Fifteen Year Plan whose goal was to tri-ple the rate of productivity growth by the year 2000 and at the same time double living standards. The goals for the five years 1986–91 were less ambitious—basically an increased growth of approximately one percent over what had taken place during the previous five years. As the end of that plan came, however, it became clear that it had not been achieved.

Gorbachëv's greatest problem was that, while the top leadership favored reform, the working level bureaucrats who had to implement any reform remained unconvinced, particularly when it involved the potential loss of their jobs. It was this opposition in both the party and administrative bureaucracy that explained why Gorbachëv began waging a major public relations campaign following the 27th Party Congress designed to generate support for reform, going over the "heads" of the bureaucracy with a direct appeal to the people.

Glasnost, Perestroika and Democracy

In the process, Gorbachëv introduced three slogans, *glasnost*, *perestroika*, and *demokratiya*, which came to symbolize for the West what he wanted to accomplish in the Soviet Union. However, none of these words has the same meaning in Russian that they have in the West. For example, we have translated *glasnost* as "openness." The actual root of the word is "voice," thus a more appropriate translation might be "speaking out." That was what Gorbachëv was stating when he used the term—that people who supported what he was trying to do should speak out to make their support known. His campaign resulted in a greater openness within So-

The legendary summer palace—*Tsarskoe Selo* ("The Tsar's Village"), 15 miles south of St. Petersburg

viet society, but that was a by–product of what he sought to accomplish.

Gorbachëv's second key word, *perestroika*, is usually translated as "restructuring." Again, the translation here is adequate, but also does not really reflect what was understood by the term within the Soviet Union. When Gorbachëv first used the term, he meant it in the purely economic sense of reorganizing economic activity to make it more productive. At that point, the principles associated with it were "socialist" and "self–financing." But later people began applying it to all aspects of the society, speaking of the restructuring of science, the media or even politics. Thus it became a synonym for general societal change.

Demokratiya or democracy, Gorbachëv's third slogan, is perhaps the most difficult word to explain in the Soviet context. At least in the beginning, it did not mean democracy in the sense of political democracy and it was not meant to challenge the monopoly of the *Communist Party of the Soviet Union* as the directing agent of Soviet society. Yet Gorbachëv did mean greater popular participation in decision making at the local and possibly even up to the Republic level. Partly, this was once again an attempt to mobilize popular support behind his reform program, but it was also an attempt to give the people a feeling that they had a real stake in their country's future. Because more than one candidate was to be nominated for each position, it also gave the people somewhat more control at the local level and moved toward something like genuine democracy.

Additional Politburo and Leadership Changes

This campaign was accompanied by changes in the Politburo related to Gorbachëv's campaign for reform. The first such change came in December 1986, when Dinmukhamed Kunaev was dismissed as First Secretary for Kazakhstan. Accused of corruption, he lost his Politburo seat in January 1987. Kunaev may have been corrupt for it was the policy of the Brezhnev regime to co–opt non–Slavic leaders by not paying too much attention to what they did within their own jurisdictions so long as they remained loyal supporters of Moscow's policies nationally. On the other hand, he was dismissed primarily because he was an old–line conservative unable to adjust to Gorbachëv's new technocratic vision.

But Gorbachëv's decision to put his own man in charge backfired in this case. When word reached Alma–Ata, the Kazakh capital, that Kunaev had been dismissed and that he was being replaced by Gennady Kolbin, an ethnic Russian, violent rioting broke out and several persons were killed. Kolbin's appointment violated a long– standing tradition that the first secretary of a republic always represented the dominant ethnic group (i.e., in this case, the Kazakhs). Kolbin was later reassigned and a Kazakh was appointed First Secretary in his place.

The next changes came at a plenary session of the Central Committee on June 26, 1987. Three men, Aleksandr N. Yakovlev, Nikolai Slyunkov and Victor Nikonov, were added to the Politburo, while Dmitri Yazov, the new defense minister, became a candidate member. Yakovlev, who had served for a number of years as ambassador to Canada, quickly established himself as a strong voice for reform. Nikonov, a member of the Secretariat, had picked up the agriculture portfolio from Gorbachëv when he became General Secretary. Slyunkov, who had been First Secretary of the Republic of Byelorussia, was considered to be a protege of Ryzhkov's.

These additions to the Politburo must have strengthened Gorbachëv politically, even though two stalwarts of the Brezhnev era, Geidar Aliyev and Vladimir Shcherbitsky, retained their positions.

Geidar Aliyev announced his resignation three months later, in October, ostensively because of ill health. Although there were some rumors earlier that Aliyev had suffered a heart attack, it is still not clear whether Aliyev left voluntarily or was pushed out. What was significant, however, is that Aliyev was the last Central Asian on the Politburo and his departure left Foreign Minister Shevardnadze as the sole non–Slav on the ruling body.

If Aliyev's departure may have been voluntary, the dismissal, in the same month, of Boris Yeltsin as First Secretary for Moscow clearly was not. His dismissal, after a speech criticizing the pace of reform, came as something of a shock because he had been closely associated with Gorbachëv up to that time. His "crime" was apparently that he favored a more confrontational approach with the bureaucracy than Gorbachëv and wanted to force the pace of reform even against growing opposition. He was subsequently accused of holding the "political illusion" that reform "could be achieved through vigorous and honest guidance from above alone, that is, by using 'purified' but still high– handed methods."

It appears that Yeltsin fell victim to an emerging split in the top leadership ranks over the issue of how quickly economic reform should be implemented. Everyone in the top leadership accepted the necessity of economic reform but several wanted the reform to be as narrow and technical as possible. At this time, Ligachëv, Chebrikov and Yazov were the most outspoken exponents of this point of view. All three pub-

Boris Yeltsin

licly criticized aspects of the reform. Gorbachëv obviously felt that he needed their general support, however, and when Yeltsin took a confrontational stance and attacked Ligachëv and others, Gorbachëv abandoned him and he lost his leadership position in the party.

Even though Yeltsin was subsequently made first deputy chairman of the state construction committee, meaning that he was not totally disgraced, his dismissal had a chilling effect on the more outspoken reformers. In February 1988, Yeltsin lost his seat as an alternate member of the Politburo, though he retained his membership on the Central Committee.

However, the same Central Committee meeting that dropped Yeltsin also added two persons as alternate members of the Politburo. They were Yuri Maslyukov, 50, a defense expert, and Georgi Razumovsky, 52, an agricultural expert. Maslyukov subsequently replaced Nikolai Talyzin as head of GOSPLAN. Razumovsky, who was supposed to have close ties to Gorbachëv, became a member of the Secretariat with responsibility for personnel.

And a New Definition of Democracy

The next event of significance in 1988 was the 19th All–Union CPSU Conference, which met in Moscow on June 28–July 1. Gorbachëv, who presided over the conference, encouraged an atmosphere of open expression and, occasionally, debate among the delegates. The delegates eventually voted to accept six resolutions, the most important of which called for "democratization of Soviet society and the reform of the political system."

Russia

The *das* have it: Gromyko is voted out as Chairman of the Presidium of the Supreme Soviet. He sits dejected while Ryzhkov and Gorbachëv vote "yes".

The resolution provided only a bare outline of a new political system, but it did put the party on record as favoring a restructuring of the political system. Not everyone was happy with the resolutions, however. In August, two Politburo members, Yegor Ligachëv and Viktor Chebrikov, gave speeches critical of the direction Gorbachëv was taking the party.

Gorbachëv responded by calling a meeting of the Central Committee which met at the end of September. The meeting led to a major reshuffle within the top leadership, several retirements, and some promotions. Among those retired were Andrei Gromyko, who also stepped down as Chairman of the Presidium of the Supreme Soviet (informally, President), and Mikhail Solomentsev. Vladimir Dolgikh, and Pyotr Demichev, who had been alternate members of the Politburo, were retired at the same time. The meeting also nominated Gorbachëv as Gromyko's successor as Chairman of the Presidium of the Supreme Soviet, and this was subsequently confirmed by the Supreme Soviet.

Yegor Ligachëv retained his seat on the Politburo, but he lost his position as chief ideologist and his informal position as Second Secretary, by virtue of which he had

chaired meetings of the Secretariat. He gained the title of chairman of the agricultural commission. Chebrikov was removed as head of the KGB and made chairman of the legal affairs commission. Both moves were considered to be demotions.

Vadim Medvedev, considered to be an ally of Gorbachëv, was added to the Politburo and made chief ideologist. His official title was chairman of the ideologi-cal commission. In addition, Alexandra Biryukova, Aleksandr Vlasov, and Anatoly Lukyanov were made alternate members of the Politburo. Biryukova thus became the first woman on the Politburo since the Khrushchëv era.

In yet another change, Anatoli Dobrynin was relieved of his duties as secretary of the Central Committee and sent into honorable retirement. Increasingly, Gorbachëv's chief adviser on relations with the United States would be Aleksandr Yakovlev.

Although these personnel shifts helped Gorbachëv to further consolidate his power, structural changes adopted at the same time may have had an even more important long–term significance. Essentially, the Central Committee voted to abolish the old Secretariat in the form in which it

had previously existed—that is, as a body charged with implementing Politburo decisions. Instead, secretaries of the Central Committee were appointed as chairmen of six newly created commissions. In addition to those mentioned above, commissions were created for party building and cadre policy (Razumovsky), socio-economic policy (Slyunkov), and international policy (Yakovlev).

The secretaries thus became responsible for longer–term policy planning, while shorter–term decisions became the prerogative of persons occupying state positions. The obvious purpose of the change was to remove the party from the day–to–day supervision of affairs and to have it concentrate on matters of broad policy. Similar instructions—that is, to stop interfering in the day–to–day affairs of the Soviets and the economy—were sent out to party secretaries at subordinate levels at this same time. The continuing evidence indicated that it had little effect on how party secretaries operated, however.

A Legislature?

The party had, in fact, long decided everything. If it were to be restricted to long–term planning, then a power vacuum would be created unless the governmental institutions were strengthened. This was the thrust of the reorganization plan which Gorbachëv submitted to the Supreme Soviet in late November. An elaboration of the outline approved by the party conference in June, it created a 2,250–member Congress of People's Deputies, to be elected on the basis of a competitive ballot. The new Congress, when it met, would elect a Chairman of the USSR Supreme Soviet (informally, President), plus a two chamber standing legislature, the USSR Supreme Soviet.

In effect, Gorbachëv had redesigned the political system to allow for at least a partial transfer of power from the *Communist Party* to popularly elected legislative bodies. In addition, by creating strong executive ties to the new legislative bodies, he had partially freed himself from having to consult constantly with other members of the Politburo.

Elections to the Congress of People's Deputies took place on March 26, 1989, with the most interesting part being the campaign that preceded the actual election. Every candidate had to present an election platform, so the voters were able to choose between candidates based on issues. Most seats were contested. Of 1500 seats, only 384 had a single candidate; the rest had two or more. Seven hundred and fifty other seats were filled by various officially recognized organizations, including 100 filled by the *Communist Party*. But, although only this small number were elected directly by the *Communist Party*, it is significant that 82 percent of all the candidates were members of the *Communist Party* and the party endorsed candidates in most of the districts.

Approximately 80 percent of those endorsed by the party won. The party was, therefore, in no way repudiated. However, a number of individuals who, a few years ago, were considered to be dissidents were among the winners. These included Andrei Sakharov and historian and writer Roy Medvedev. A third individual who won running against a candidate endorsed by the party was none other than Boris Yeltsin, who got almost 90 percent of the vote in a Moscow at-large seat. There were also some prominent losers. The highest ranking of those was Yuri Solovyev, First Secretary for the Leningrad area, who failed to muster 50 percent of the vote, even though he was running unopposed. As a result, he eventually lost both his position as First Secretary and his seat on the Politburo.

The new Congress was scheduled to convene at the end of May but, before that occurred, Gorbachëv called a meeting of the Central Committee at the end of April and asked for the retirement of 110 people, or approximately one–third of the membership of that body. In turn, 24 persons were added to the Central Committee. In one sense, this was not a purge, however, as most of those who were retired from the Committee had already retired from the jobs that had earned them entry to the Central Committee in the first place. As one official associated with Gorbachëv expressed it, since there was to be a genuine working legislative body for the first time, Gorbachëv needed a Central Committee which was also made up of currently active individuals.

The Congress, when it did meet, proved to be lively but, ultimately, Gorbachëv dominated the session. The Congress first grilled Gorbachëv, then proceeded to elect him Chairman of the USSR Supreme Soviet (informally, President). The new USSR Supreme Soviet, the smaller, standing legislature, was then elected, and remained in session over the summer.

Although Gorbachëv set the agenda and tended to dominate discussions, it established itself as a genuine independent voice and a valuable forum. The second session showed itself to be even more independent and less subject to Gorbachëv's control.

Gorbachëv's greatest problem was to find groups who were not only loyal but were also committed to his programs. Again and again he made it clear that commitment to his goals came even before loyalty. This was shown once again in 1989, when he directed another major reshuffle. Three members of the Politburo, Viktor Nikonov, Viktor Chebrikov and Vladimir Scherbitsky, were "relieved of their duties" as Politburo members. They were joined in retirement by two alternate members, Yuriy Solovyev and Nikolay Talyzin.

Shcherbitsky was the last remaining member of the old Brezhnev Politburo (except for Gorbachëv) and his dismissal had been long predicted. Chebrikov, Nikonov, Solovyev and Talyzin, on the other hand, were early allies of Gorbachëv who had shown a general lack of commitment to reform.

The additions were equally telling. Vladimir Kryuchkov, head of the KGB, and Yuriy Maslyukov, head of GOSPLAN, had both been early Gorbachëv supporters. Their promotion to full membership appeared to give Gorbachëv two strong allies on the Politburo. The two new alternate members, Yevgeny Primakov and Boris Pugo, were also viewed as Gorbachëv loyalists though they later would turn on him. Primakov, chairman of the Council of the Union of the USSR Supreme Soviet, was also an academician of the USSR Academy of Sciences with a doctorate in economics. Pugo, chairman of the Party Control Commission, and a former head of the Latvian Communist Party, was also a deputy of Latvia's Supreme Soviet.

Nationality Problems

The major agenda topic at the Central Committee Plenum at which these political changes were made was nationality policy. The *Communist Party* had always boasted that it had solved the nationality problems in the USSR but, in fact, the problems were merely suppressed.

Gorbachëv's policies, which among other things encouraged people to get involved and to demand reform, and which also tolerated the creation of unofficial groups and promised economic autonomy to the individual republics, had led to the creation of national fronts in nearly every republic and other groups organized along ethnic or nationality lines whose function was to air grievances and demand redress. In the Caucasus region, this had eventually led to a state of virtual war between Armenia and Azerbaijan over the mixed area called Nagorno–Karabakh and autonomy movements in the Baltic republics, in Moldavia, and within Western Ukraine (where the Ukrainian Catholic Church is predominant).

At the Central Committee Plenum, Gorbachëv, arguing that "the need for profound changes is long overdue in ethnic relations," promised a new federation under which "the right of each ethnic group to enjoy all the fruits of sovereignty and to decide all issues of its development—economic, political, and cultural," would be guaranteed.

Although Gorbachëv's position was endorsed by the Central Committee plenum, the subsequent collapse of communist governments throughout Eastern Europe in the last three months of 1989—even though in one sense orchestrated by Gorbachëv—changed the equation and brought calls for greater change.

A Distressed Economy

In addition, the domestic economic situation had been deteriorating for some time and this added to the pressures as shortages of consumer goods continued to grow worse, producing greater public dissatisfaction. Reform–spirited communists, now organized into the *Democratic Platform*, threatened to split the party unless they got their way. Conservatives, on the other hand, reacted by urging a slowing down in the pace of reform.

In December, Nikolai Ryzhkov, Chairman of the USSR Council of Ministers, brought in a new draft five–year plan that represented a clear retreat from economic change. It looked like the planners would remain in charge for another five years.

Russia

As had become his practice, it was at this moment that Gorbachëv opted for more political reform. First of all, he accepted the idea of a multi-party system and formally proposed that the constitution be changed to delete the *Communist Party's* leading position. This was accomplished in January–March 1990.

Next he proposed that, under the new circumstances, what the Soviet Union needed was an executive president, able to take action in an emergency without consultations with other bodies such as the Presidium of the Supreme Soviet.

This led, in March, to creation of the office of President of the USSR, to which Gorbachëv was subsequently elected. It also led to creation of a presidential council, which appears to have been an attempt to create a Soviet version of a national security council or, possibly, a "super cabinet." Its membership, originally 16, included the foreign, interior, and defense ministers, the head of the KGB, other government and party officials, and two prominent writers, Valentin Rasputin and Chingiz Aitmatov. In addition, the Chairman of the Council of Ministers sat as an ex-officio member. It didn't work out and was later disbanded.

The first challenge which the new president had to handle came from Lithuania. Following multiparty elections which were won by *Sajudis*, the Lithuanian national front, the Lithuanian legislature installed Vytautas Landsbergis as president and passed a declaration of independence. Similar declarations were adopted by Latvia and Estonia, although in a somewhat different form. Gorbachëv condemned all three as illegal and initiated a partial economic blockade of Lithuania. He then offered that, if the three republics suspended their declarations, talks leading to independence within two years could begin.

Gorbachëv also said that he would not use force against the would-be breakaway republics. Since he was scheduled to meet with President Bush on May 30, that obviously acted as a restraint on his actions. Although President Bush raised the subject, he apparently did not press it with vigor. The United States found itself in an awkward position at this time. The three republics had been incorporated into the Soviet Union as a result of the Nazi–Soviet Non-Aggression Pact signed in August 1939. In the Pact, Hitler had recognized these nations as being in the Soviet sphere of influence in return for a Soviet

promise of neutrality when Hitler invaded Poland.

The United States had never recognized the incorporation of the three republics into the USSR and its legal position was that they were still sovereign nations. In fact, embassies of the three republics were still to be found in Washington, D.C. At the same time, the United States favored closer relations with the Soviet Union.

However, the Soviet position articulated by Gorbachëv was even more awkward. Although the Soviet Government had repudiated the Nazi–Soviet Non-Aggression Pact and considered it invalid, it continued to maintain that the three republics were factually a part of the USSR and therefore had to apply for and receive permission to leave.

Rumblings of Change

Gorbachëv also had other concerns. In the spring of 1990, elections in the Russian, Byelorussian, and Ukrainian republics produced a strong showing for the radical reformers, who won majorities in the largest cities, including Moscow and Leningrad. In Moscow, Gavriil Popov, a member of the Congress of People's Deputies and one of the leaders of the radical

Just weeks before his dream collapses, a giant portrait of Lenin, father of modern communism, rises in front of KGB headquarters in Moscow.

Photo by Steve Raymer © National Geographic Society

inter–regional group in the USSR Supreme Soviet, was elected mayor on the promise to move Moscow quickly toward a market economy.

Perhaps more important, Boris Yeltsin, was elected Chairman of the RSFSR Supreme Soviet (popularly, Russian President) on the third ballot in May. Gorbachëv thus lost control of the all–important Russian Republic.

Essentially, all of this happened because the party had split into three factions, conservatives, Gorbachëv supporters and democrats. The democrats wanted to move more quickly on reforms than Gor-

Gavriil Popov
Former Mayor of Moscow

bachëv did, and threatened to leave the party and form a new political party if Gorbachëv didn't go along. Gorbachëv, citing the need for party unity, urged them to stay. The conservatives, on the other hand, urged the democrats to leave.

This was the background to Gorbachëv's other concern, the party congress which was scheduled to take place in late June/early July 1990. Gorbachëv decided to use the party congress to remake the party, getting rid of the Politburo and replacing it with a larger, less powerful Presidium, the majority of whose members would be *ex officio*—the party chairman and his deputies plus the 15 republic party secretaries. Gorbachëv intended the new Presidium to concentrate on coordinating the activities of the party. Broad policy functions would then become the prerogative of the Soviet Government.

The draft made no mention of the office of General Secretary but it did specify that there would continue to be a secretariat. The leader of the party would be the

"chairman," and he was to be elected by the party congress, as was the case under Lenin.

The draft was modified at the party congress but Gorbachëv got most of what he wanted. The office of General Secretary was retained, but he was elected by the party congress. The Politburo was retained, but its membership and function were modified as Gorbachëv desired.

The delegates also adopted a document called "Toward Humane, Democratic Socialism." Although the word socialism is in its title, the document actually moved the party a long way toward a rejection of what traditionally has been understood as Marxism–Leninism. Instead, the document spoke of the ideology of the party being based on "the legacy of Marx, Engels and Lenin, freed from dogmatic interpretation."

This document broke with traditional ideology in two basic ways. Socialism, it declared, should be based on individual, not collective, interests; and "private ownership must have a place in the system of forms of ownership" of equal validity with collective ownership. What this meant is that the *Communist Party* was now claiming to represent the interests of Soviet citizens as individuals, not as members of a class or socio–economic grouping. Thus Marx's entire class–based analysis was discarded. And granting private property equal status with collective property flaunted Marx's premise that ownership of the means of production provided the basis for exploitation of man by man. In ideological terms, this programmatic statement moved the *Communist Party* a long distance from Marxist–Leninist orthodoxy. It could still claim to be a socialist party, of course.

Two other issues preoccupied Gorbachëv in 1990–91, the economy and the negotiation of a new union treaty. The two issues were intricately linked to each other, since one of the demands of the republics was control over economic activity and natural resources. An economic plan that would devolve authority to the republics would go a long way toward meeting this demand.

That is why the Shatalin Plan, which proposed transforming the Soviet Union to a market economy in 500 days, had the support of fourteen of the fifteen republics. Proposed in August 1990 as an alternative to the government's plan to retain the old system of state orders for another 18 months, it even got Gorbachëv's backing for a short while.

But Gorbachëv backed down when Ryzhkov, chairman of the Council of Ministers, threatened to resign rather than take responsibility for implementing a plan he disagreed with. Gorbachëv then told Ryzhkov to take the two approaches

and combine them. The result, which was mainly the Ryzhkov plan, was approved by the Supreme Soviet in November. But Gorbachëv's economic advisers were disappointed by the compromise and most left to work for Boris Yeltsin and the Russian Government.

Gorbachëv did get one good bit of news in October when he learned that he had been awarded the Nobel Peace Prize. Even that could not distract from worry about the economy, however. As Georgi Arbatov, the traditionalist director of the USA and Canada Institute, commented at the time, "I am sure that he deserves the Peace Prize. I wouldn't think he has deserved the Nobel Prize for economics."

In late 1990, under prodding from the Supreme Soviet, Gorbachëv changed the organizational structure once more. The presidential council and council of ministers were abolished and their place was taken by a strengthened council of the federation (created in March 1990) and a streamlined cabinet of ministers. There continued to be a chairman who headed up the cabinet, but he was made directly subordinate to Gorbachëv. These provisions were more or less implemented while some other provisions, such as Gorbachëv's suggestion that the Congress of People's Deputies be replaced by a directly elected Supreme Soviet, were not.

Gorbachëv lost his most valuable ally in December 1990 when Foreign Minister Eduard Shevardnadze resigned after charging that the Soviet Union was headed toward a dictatorship. He was replaced by Alexandr Bessmertnykh, whose previous position had been Soviet ambassador to Washington. After his resignation, Shevardnadze became head of a new independent foreign policy research institute, the Soviet foreign policy association.

Gorbachëv lost a second adviser in December when Nikolai Ryzhkov suffered a heart attack and resigned as chairman of the newly created cabinet of ministers. He was replaced by Valentin Pavlov, who had been Ryzhkov's finance minister. A conservative, Pavlov's first major action was to attempt to reduce the money overhang by a partial repudiation of the currency. All 50 and 100 ruble notes were withdrawn from circulation, with individuals given three days to redeem a limited amount related to monthly salary. Pavlov's overall economic program was a continuation of the Ryzhkov program. Gorbachëv also dismayed many people when he appointed Gennadi Yanayev, a *Communist Party* bureaucrat, as his vice president.

The Baltic Republics became the center of attention once again in January 1991, when ministry of the interior troops stormed the Lithuanian press center and a building occupied by the Lithuanian

Russia

The Supreme Soviet of the USSR discussing problems of stabilizing the national economy and transition to a market system, October 1990.

Union of Soviet Socialist Republics as a renewed federation of equal sovereign republics, in which human rights and the freedoms of all nationalities will be fully guaranteed?"

Six republics refused to participate in the referendum, and four other republics modified the question in some way. Gorbachëv nevertheless claimed a victory on the basis of the 76 percent who voted "yes" among those who participated.

The next month, Gorbachëv and the heads of the nine republics who had participated in the referendum announced their agreement on an outline for a new union treaty that would create a Union of Sovereign Soviet Republics. The draft called for a great deal of decentralization, particularly in the economic area, plus a remaking of the national government, including new elections for a national legislature and president. In early May, Gorbachëv agreed to turn coal mines over to the Russian Government as part of a deal to end a miners' strike.

Later in the month, Gorbachëv also endorsed a new plan for economic reform drawn up by Grigory Yavlinsky, who had also contributed to the Shatalin Plan. This new plan called for significant international economic assistance to act as a "shock absorber of social costs and shocks" as the Soviet Union moved to a market economy.

Events tumbled on at a faster and faster rate. In May–June there was a resolution of differences over the CFE Treaty and a new immigration law was passed by the Supreme Soviet. It was announced that President Bush would travel to Moscow for a summit meeting sometime during the summer. And, in a new test of public opinion, Boris Yeltsin won 60 percent of the popular vote in his run for the newly created office of president of the Russian Federation. The official communist candidate came in a dismal third. Gorbachëv, reversing his previous position, warmly embraced Yeltsin's victory.

Communist conservatives, evidently alarmed by this development, began to plot a "constitutional *coup*" against Gorbachëv in late June. It took the form of a request by Premier Pavlov that the Supreme Soviet transfer from Gorbachëv to him the power to rule by decree. The President, Pavlov explained, was "overworked." Pavlov's request was supported by Defense Minister Yazov, KGB Chairman Vladimir Kryuchkov and Minister of Interior Boris Pugo.

The attempt failed. Forewarned of Pavlov's attempt to strip away some of his powers, Gorbachëv counterattacked and defeated the move. In the process, however, Gorbachëv did two things that he would later rue. He permitted all four of

civilian militia on January 13, killing 14 persons. Gorbachëv's role in all this was ambivalent. He did not repudiate the attack, but claimed to have found out about it only after it happened. The following weekend, five more persons were killed when ministry of interior troops seized the Latvian ministry of interior building.

The European Parliament then moved to block $1 billion in food aid to the Soviet Union, and a number of European nations began threatening other sanctions. In Washington, the Bush administration began discussing postponement of an up-

coming summit meeting, which was in fact postponed, though publicly it was because of the Iraq conflict. Responding to this international pressure, Gorbachëv backed down in early February and agreed to appoint a commission to consult with the Baltic Republics about their demands for independence.

Gorbachëv's great concern was the national referendum on the question of the future of the USSR which was scheduled for March 17, 1991. The question asked of the Soviet people was whether they considered it "necessary to preserve the

his disloyal subordinates to retain their positions of power, while he attacked their political arguments. He told these four representatives of the military–industrial complex that the Soviet Union was over–militarized and that "we have to remove this burden and turn the economy over to the people. Otherwise my mission will be useless and I will have to resign."

Gorbachëv had a busy summer. In July, he traveled to London to meet with the "Group of Seven" (United States, Great Britain, Canada, Germany, France, Italy and Japan). His purpose in requesting the meeting was to try to get a promise of economic assistance. He basically used the Yavlinsky Plan as the basis of his discussions. He got no promises of cash, though the Group did offer the Soviet Union some technical assistance and a "special associate status" with the IMF and World Bank.

President Bush came to Moscow at the end of July. The summit meeting included

two days of discussions and a ceremonial signing of the completed START agreement. Gorbachëv then left for a vacation in the Crimea with his family.

He planned to return to Moscow on August 19 since, the following day, he and the leaders of nine of the republics were to sign a new union treaty that conceded significant powers to the individual republics. Instead, Gorbachëv was placed under house arrest on the evening of August 18. The next day, the world learned that a *coup d'etat* had been launched by conservative communists in the top echelons of government—their goal to preserve the Soviet Union and the communist system. Among the top leaders were Pavlov, Yazov, Kryuchkov, and Pugo, the four participants in the attempted "constitutional *coup*" against Gorbachëv in late June. They were joined this time by Vice President Gennadi Yanayev. These five, plus three other conservatives, took con-

trol as the "State Committee for the State of Emergency."

The *coup* lasted approximately 60 hours and eventually failed, thanks primarily to Boris Yeltsin and supporters of reform and democracy throughout the country. But the complicity of the *Communist Party* in the *coup* was so great that there were few objections when Boris Yeltsin, on the morning after the *coup* was defeated, banned *Communist Party* activities in the Russian Republic. Two days later, Gorbachëv resigned as General Secretary and called upon the Central Committee to dissolve itself. He then issued a decree suspending the activities of the party and seizing all party property. After 74 years, the communist era had come to an end.

Foreign Policy Under Gorbachëv

Soviet foreign policy began changing in 1985, not only with regard to the United States, but with regard to the Third World

Soviet President Mikhail Gorbachëv joins the Group of Seven leaders in London. First row (l. to r.) President Bush, Gorbachëv, British Prime Minister Major, French President Mitterrand, German Chancellor Kohl. Second row: EC President Jacques Delors, Italian Prime Minister Andreotti, Canadian Prime Minister Mulroney, Japanese Prime Minister Kaifu, Dutch Prime Minister Lubbers.

Reuters/Bettmann

Russia

President–Elect George H.W. Bush, President Ronald Reagan and General Secretary Mikhail Gorbachëv check out their "where to stand" marks for a photo–taking session at Governor's Island, NY., December 7, 1988. AP/Wide World Photo

and Eastern Europe as well. Soviet support for a settlement in southern Africa led to an agreement to pull Cuban troops out of Angola. It was Soviet pressure on Vietnam that caused that country to pull its troops out of Cambodia. The Soviet Union also eventually halted the shipment of military equipment to Nicaragua and then tacitly supported the free elections that resulted in a non–Communist government coming to power there in April 1990.

When Iraq invaded Kuwait, Gorbachëv gave his support to the various UN Security Council resolutions demanding that Iraq pull out of Kuwait and then those authorizing the use of force against Iraq, even though Iraq had been a long–time ally of the Soviet Union. Gorbachëv also presided over the demise of the Council for Mutual Economic Assistance and the

Warsaw Pact, thus formally dissolving the ties that bound the various countries of Eastern Europe to the Soviet Union. And, of course, he presided over a series of military negotiations that helped to bring an end to the Cold War.

Changing Relations with
Eastern Europe under Gorbachëv

The pattern of foreign relations established by Stalin with Eastern Europe after World War II was one of almost total subordination on the part of the communist leaderships of those countries, exemplified after 1948 by Stalin's campaign to remove from office those communist leaders who showed any independence whatsoever. During this period, Soviet ambassadors acted as virtual proconsuls, whose orders had the force of law.

Poland's Wladyslaw Gomulka, one of those who resisted and, as a result, was purged, described this phenomenon:

> In this bloc of socialist states, it was Stalin who stood at the apex of this hierarchic ladder of cults. All those who stood on lower rungs of the ladder bowed their heads before him. . . The first secretaries of the central committees of the parties of the various countries who sat on the second rung of the ladder of the cult of personality, in turn donned the robes of infallibility and wisdom.

Soviet–East European relations were thus, for Stalin, an extension of domestic Soviet politics.

All of that began to change after Stalin's death. The new Soviet leadership, which had been subject to the same treatment during Stalin's lifetime, committed itself to a "new course" in intra–bloc relations. Modifying the previous relationship, they allowed Eastern European leaders greater independence and encouraged them to develop policies designed to win them greater popularity among their people. This was, they concluded, the best way to ensure the long–term success of communism in Eastern Europe.

There were limitations to this independence, of course. All were required to join the Warsaw Pact when it was established in 1955 and even Khrushchëv, chief spokesman for this viewpoint, didn't hesitate to intervene militarily in Hungary in 1956, when the communist leadership there began to lose control. Khrushchëv's decision to allow Gomulka to take power in Poland in 1956 was another part of this loosening of control.

Khrushchëv sought to further integrate the Soviet and East European economies, but he permitted Romania to opt out when that country opposed the international division of labor proposed by the Soviet Union. Khrushchëv also did nothing when, in April 1964, Romania claimed the right to develop its own policies. Romania would later go on to develop its own, independent foreign policy, though it always remained an orthodox communist society domestically.

Brezhnev intervened in Czechoslovakia in 1968 when that country's communist party moved to give up its monopoly of political power. He also put strong pressure on the Polish communist leadership to reverse its decision legalizing the independent trade union *Solidarity* in 1981. But he quietly permitted Hungary to implement ever more far–reaching economic reforms without interference. Gorbachëv's attitude toward Eastern Europe when he became General Secretary in 1985 appeared to be relatively orthodox, though from the beginning he tended to treat individual communist leaders as though he considered them partners in a common enterprise. His first plans for economic reform relied heavily on Eastern Europe as a source of new technology and he confidently expected them to join him in implementing similar reforms in their own countries. The Soviet Union already got many of the more sophisticated products that it imported, such as computers, computer software and machine tools, from Eastern Europe, and he expected that they would want to upgrade their technology and become a source of ever more sophisticated technology.

He was disappointed by the first response to his reform ideas. Only Hungary, already well along in its own reform program, was enthusiastic. For a while, he attempted to lead by example and by persuasion, speaking of his economic reform and pointing out its advantages on visits to Eastern Europe, but making no effort to coerce communist leaders into adopting the same approach. On the other hand, the Soviet Union did chide Eastern European leaders for the poor quality of their exports and it put behind the scenes pressure on them to upgrade the quality and technological level of their products, though with little success. Czechoslovakia and the German Democratic Republic, the Eastern European countries with the most developed economies, were both led by conservative leaders who believed that a program of economic reform would undermine their own legitimacy.

Gorbachëv slowly came to realize that the Eastern European countries weren't going to provide the significant assistance in the area of technology that he had been counting on to help him with his own *perestroika*. Their unreformed economies simply weren't up to it. Finland, the only non–communist neighbor, proved to be much more valuable as a source of technology than any of the communist countries of Eastern Europe.

Meanwhile, the Soviet Union was providing Eastern Europe with energy supplies and raw materials below world prices, while receiving shoddy consumer goods and old technology in return. The question Gorbachëv had to ask himself was whether the conservative and unreformed communist leaderships were more of a burden than an asset. Was Finland a better model? A number of articles appeared in the Soviet press at about this time discussing the merits of a "Finlandization" of Eastern Europe.

The 1989 Revolutions

Thus we come to the events and decisions of 1989, when communism collapsed nearly everywhere in Eastern Europe. In country after country, ruling communist parties were first forced to compromise with their opponents and then, in most cases, to relinquish part or all of their power to them. Communism, a doctrine imposed from the outside by Soviet armies after the defeat of Nazi Germany, never was popular among the people of Eastern Europe. Yet the communist elites remained in power, partly because they controlled a monopoly of power and partly because they could always count on the support and backing of the Soviet Union, spelled out after 1968 in the "Brezhnev Doctrine."

So no one predicted the events of 1989, precisely because no one expected that the Soviet Union would permit such changes to occur in Eastern Europe. And that points out the most important difference about 1989—that the Soviet Union did not merely acquiesce in these changes; it was, in fact, an active agent in bringing them about. In hindsight, it was predictable. The Soviets had become economically exhausted and their only choice to continue control in Eastern Europe was military, which would have enraged world opinion.

Gorbachëv had several times said things that sounded like a repudiation of the Brezhnev Doctrine after becoming General Secretary, but no one was certain whether he meant it. It was his intervention in Poland in the latter part of 1988

October 1989: On a stone lion in front of parliament a Hungarian youth hoists the flag of his country—with the hammer and sickle surgically removed. AP/Wide World Photos

71

Russia

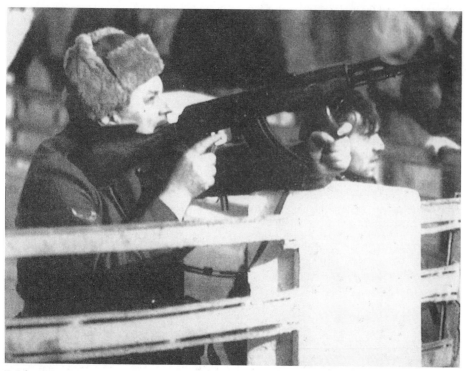

Bucharest, Romania, Christmas Eve 1989. A Romanian soldier points his rifle at enemy positions during street fighting.

AP/Wide World Photos

that gave the first indication that he meant what he had said.

After outlawing *Solidarity* in December 1981, General Jaruzelski and the ruling *Polish United Workers' Party* introduced a program of economic reform to remake the Polish economy and to deal with the conditions that had brought *Solidarity* into existence in the first place. That attempt at economic reform from above was unsuccessful and the government, under challenge from the official trade unions, collapsed in September 1988.

It was at this moment that the first indication of a reversal of Soviet policy occurred, in the form of a series of articles in the Soviet press portraying Lech Walesa and *Solidarity* in a favorable manner. This led to formal talks between the Polish Government and *Solidarity* and the now famous April 1989 agreement re-legalizing *Solidarity* and setting new elections for June 4.

Those elections provided for only 35 percent of the seats in the *Sejm* (lower house of parliament) to be freely contested, but did include elections to a new Senate, all of whose seats were competitive. *Solidarity* took 99 out of 100 seats in the Senate, plus all of the open seats in the *Sejm*. In addition, most of the top communist leadership, running unopposed for *Sejm* seats, were rejected because they failed to get 50 percent of the valid votes. These seats, reserved for communists, were filled in a second round of voting

only because *Solidarity* instructed its supporters to endorse the new candidates.

The failure of the communists at the polls meant that they were in practice unable to form a government. Their allies, the *United Peasants' Party* and the *Democratic Party*, refused to support the communist candidate for Chairman of the Council of Ministers and opened discussions with *Solidarity*. This led Lech Walesa to propose a *Solidarity*–led coalition government which would include communists. Now came a second decisive Soviet intervention. After Mieczyslaw Rakowski, the new head of the *Polish United Workers' Party*, announced his opposition to such a coalition, he got a 40 minute telephone call from Gorbachëv, the essence of which was that Gorbachëv expected the Polish party to accept a *Solidarity*–led coalition government.

The psychological effect on the rest of Eastern Europe of the installation of a non–communist government in Poland was enormous; and even more important, it was known that Gorbachëv not only gave his support to the change but actually intervened to help bring it about. This was seen as making change possible all over Eastern Europe. Surprisingly, Gorbachëv continued to support change in Eastern Europe, even as those changes led to the collapse of communist governments throughout the region.

After Poland, the next development occurred in Hungary, where a reform com-

munist leadership had been installed in May 1988. Over the next year, opposition political parties were legalized and free elections were scheduled. New laws were also passed guaranteeing Hungarians the right to travel abroad and to emigrate. And in March 1989, Hungary signed a United Nations protocol on refugees in which it obligated itself not to force refugees to go back home. In signing the protocol, the Hungarian Government obviously had in mind Hungarian–speaking Romanians who were infiltrating across the border from Romania. By August 1989, however, tens of thousands of East German citizens had gathered in Hungary, drawn there by Hungary's decision to begin dismantling the barbed wire on its border with Austria. Refusing to return to East Germany, they wanted to go west.

The problem was a treaty that Hungary had signed with the German Democratic Republic in 1968 under which the Hungarian Government promised to obtain clearance from the GDR before permitting GDR citizens to travel from it to a third country, a permission that was not forthcoming. The Hungarian Government now decided to let the East Germans go, but there was some concern about the Soviet reaction. When informal sounding established *that the Soviet Government would not object*, Hungary opened the border for the East Germans on September 10.

The third break occurred in the German Democratic Republic, largely as a result of the decision of the Hungarian Government to allow East Germans to depart for the west. After the Hungarian action, other East Germans, unable to obtain visas to Hungary, began traveling in large numbers to Czechoslovakia, where no visa was required. Gathering in Prague, they began to inundate the grounds of the West German Embassy. Here they were given West German passports, but they still needed permission to depart Czechoslovakia for the west. The Czechoslovakian Government, not wanting to be caught in the middle, requested clearance from the GDR Government. The GDR eventually gave in and began arranging for trains to carry its citizens directly to West Germany.

The flight of hundreds of thousands of East Germans began to have repercussions at home, however. Protest demonstrations which were already occurring in a number of East German cities grew in size and number. The most organized of the demonstrations occurred in Leipzig. At first, the regime tried to handle the situation through the use of force. In addition to its usual riot police, it called out special "battle groups" of its party militia and fighting teams of the state security police, equipped with water cannons and armored cars. And on October 3, the East German Government closed its borders with Czechoslovakia.

The matter came to a head on October 9 in Leipzig, when the local party leadership rejected orders from East Berlin to put down demonstrations scheduled for that day and instead called for a dialogue, promising to "use our full power and authority to ensure that this dialogue will occur, not only in the Leipzig area but with our national government."

At the Politburo meeting called to discuss the Leipzig decision, Egon Krenz, the number two man in the party, supported the Leipzig leaders over Erich Honecker's objections. This led to a Central Committee meeting eight days later and to Honecker's ouster as General Secretary on October 18.

Egon Krenz took over as General Secretary and promised reforms. He reopened the borders with Czechoslovakia and promised East Germans 30 days a year travel abroad. The flight through Czechoslovakia immediately resumed. Krenz next gambled that he could stabilize the situation by granting all citizens the right of unrestricted travel to the west, symbolized by the opening of the Berlin Wall on November 9, 1989. He accompanied this with promises of freer elections, economic liberalization, and power–sharing with other parties. Within a week, an estimated one–third of all East Germans had visited either West Berlin or West Germany.

After the initial euphoria, however, the pressure for change continued. On November 17, Hans Modrow, Dresden party chief, who had a reputation as a reformer, became the new head of government. Modrow proposed round–table discussions with the opposition and these began on December 7.

In the meanwhile, Egon Krenz and the other members of the Politburo submitted their resignations and a caretaker committee was appointed to run the party. At a special party congress that began five days later, Gregor Gysi, an attorney who had made his reputation as a defender of critics of the state and people caught fleeing the country, was appointed the new party leader. The delegates also voted to change the name of the party and to set the goal of the party as "democratic socialism."

At the congress, Hans Modrow spoke in favor of a confederation between the two Germanys. Helmut Kohl, the West German Chancellor, had proposed a ten– point plan for unification in November, but this was the first time that any East German leader had endorsed the concept. Unification received another boost when Chancellor Kohl paid an official visit to East Germany on December 19. Kohl spoke in Dresden to cheering crowds and then he and Modrow joined the mayors of West and East Berlin in a ceremony opening a pedestrian crossing at the Brandenburg Gate.

Reunification was the big issue in the elections on March 18 and they were won by the conservative *Alliance for Germany*, led by the GDR *Christian Democratic Union*. On April 12, Lothar de Maizere, leader of the *Christian Democratic Union*, became the first non–communist head of government, leading a "Grand Coalition" of the main non–communist parties, including the *Social Democrats*.

The new government immediately began preparing for German reunification. For a while, Gorbachëv maintained that the Soviet Union would not agree to German unification, unless Germany either suspended its membership in NATO or maintained its membership in the Warsaw Pact as well. After negotiations with the Federal Republic, however, he accepted continued German membership in NATO. An economic, social and currency union went into effect on July 1 and final unification took place on October 3, 1990.

November 11, 1989: With the Reichstag in the background, young Germans sit on the Berlin Wall in its final hours.

73

Russia

Czechoslovakians had not reacted to the large numbers of East Germans fleeing west by way of their country, but subsequent events in East Germany did lead to the beginning of massive demonstrations in Prague. On November 17, three thousand young people gathered near Wenceslas Square in Central Prague and began demanding free elections. The Government reacted by ordering the police to put down the demonstration by force. It was a fatal mistake. The Czechoslovak people, aroused by the government's brutality, went into the streets in great numbers, singing, chanting, and demanding the ouster of Milos Jakes, the party General Secretary who had approved the police action. It was at this moment that Mikhail Gorbachëv intervened by sending a message that the Soviet Government would not tolerate violence.

As the demonstrations continued and grew in size, a Central Committee meeting was called for November 24 and Milos Jakes and his entire Presidium resigned. The party had begun to crumble. Prime Minister Ladislav Adamec opened negotiations with the opposition, now organized as the *Civic Forum*. But Adamec, who wanted to retain a communist-dominated government, was forced to resign on December 6. His replacement, Marian Calfa, organized a new government in which the communists were in a minority.

The Czechoslovak parliament was subsequently purged and on December 28 Alexander Dubãek, leader of the 1968 Prague Spring, was elected chairman. The next day, Vaclav Havel, the Czech playwright whose opposition to the previous regime had landed him repeatedly in prison, was elected president. Czechoslovakia thus had its first non-communist president since 1948. *Civic Forum* won the multiparty elections that took place on June 6, 1990 while the communists were reduced to a tiny remnant.

Change also came to Bulgaria, though in the beginning at least it was engineered to a greater extent from above. On November 9, Todor Zhivkov was forced out as communist party leader and replaced by Petar Mladenov. Zhivkov had been in power for 36 years. Mladenov, who had served as Bulgarian foreign minister for the previous 19 years, immediately instituted a policy of liberalization that soon led to legalization of opposition groups and the beginning of demonstrations in the streets. Broad-based talks began in January between the party and the opposition and a few days later the parliament voted to end the party's monopoly of power. At a hastily called party congress, the party voted to change its name and to become the *Bulgarian Socialist Party*.

Mladenov also stepped down as party leader in April, after he had been elected to a new executive Presidency.

Multi-party elections that took place in June were won by the ex-communists, but they had lost in the cities and the opposition, emboldened by this, continued their attacks on the government. In July, Mladenov was replaced by Zhelyu Zhelev, a leader of the opposition. After continued demonstrations, Dimitar Popov, a non-communist, was appointed prime minister. There was never any direct Gorbachëv intervention in the political events occurring in Bulgaria in 1989–90. However, Gorbachëv's responses with regard to events in other parts of Eastern Europe were well known in Bulgaria and undoubtedly were a factor influencing events in Bulgaria as well.

Romania experienced perhaps the greatest change of any country in Eastern Europe in 1989 when Nicolae Ceaucescu, who had ruled the country since 1965, was overthrown in a violent uprising that ended in Ceaucescu's death by firing-squad on December 25. Ceaucescu, who was proud of his independence from Moscow, had rejected Gorbachëv's policy of reform and made every effort to isolate his countrymen from events going on elsewhere in Eastern Europe. In November 1989, he had reaffirmed his policies at a party congress and had been reelected head of the party for a further five-year term. It was probably this reaffirmation of policies that was responsible for his downfall, for they had been responsible for a significant decline in the standard of living of Romanians over the previous nine years.

The revolt, which actually began as an ethnic dispute in the city of Timisoara, in the western part of Romania, spread to Bucharest, the capital, when Ceausescu called a mass meeting for December 21 to denounce the events in Timisoara. Instead, the people began shouting "freedom" and "democracy" and Ceausescu stalked off. That afternoon, the streets were full of people demonstrating against Ceausescu. That evening, Ceausescu ordered the secret police to begin firing on the people. A similar order to the army brought a refusal from General Milea, the Defense Minister. General Milea was executed the next morning, but the army now joined the revolution. Ceausescu and his wife fled the capital, but they were captured, brought back to Bucharest, and summarily tried and executed.

The *Securitate*, Ceausescu's secret police, fought on for a few days more but the army gradually managed to restore order. In the meantime, a group calling itself the *National Salvation Front* emerged as the new political leadership in the country. The Front, at first made up almost exclu-

sively of former establishment figures who had fallen out with Ceausescu, was enlarged within a few days to take in various non-communist elements. It then began referring to itself as the *Council of National Salvation*. In the third week of January, the *Council* announced that multi-party elections would take place in May and that it intended to run its own candidates. This brought a condemnation from the leaders of the three largest opposition parties. After a series of negotiations, the *Council* agreed to make room for representatives of other parties. On February 1, the *Council* brought the representatives of 29 other political parties into the government coalition.

By this time, it had grown to approximately 180 members. It also underwent a name change and became the *Provisional Council for National Unity*. A new ten member executive committee, headed by Acting President Ion Iliescu, also came into existence now. Meanwhile, the original *National Salvation Front* reorganized itself as a political party and announced that it, not the *Council*, would field candidates in the upcoming May 20 elections. As its candidate for president, it nominated Ion Iliescu. Most of the leadership of the *Front* had been members of the old *Romanian Communist Party* and the local branches of the *National Salvation Front*, set up at the time of the revolution, were largely made up of ex-officials. Thus, while the old communist party structure had collapsed, a large percentage of its membership transferred their loyalties to the *National Salvation Front*.

Eventually, some 80 political parties came into existence, though only three of them had any significant political support in the country. Two of these, both parties that were outlawed when the communists took over, were the *Liberals* and the *Peasant Party*. The third, the *Hungarian Democratic Union*, represented the interests of ethnic Hungarians. Although the opposition attacked the *National Salvation Front* because of its high component of ex-communists, there was, in fact, little to differentiate between them as far as programs were concerned. All were committed to the creation of a multi-party democracy and a market economy.

In the May elections, Ion Iliescu was elected president with approximately 83 percent of the vote while the *National Salvation Front* took 66 percent of the seats in the National Assembly. Election observers announced that there had been some irregularities in the voting but that, overall, the election was free.

An Overview

The events of 1989 and 1990 transformed east-central Europe and laid the basis for a new relationship with the Soviet Union. In the beginning, all of the new governments promised to remain in the Warsaw Pact and the Council for Mutual Economic Assistance (CMEA), but the basis for those organizations no longer existed. The CMEA was changing in any case, having agreed to carry on all trade in dollars as of January 1, 1991. This turned out to be so destabilizing that the CMEA effectively ceased to exist after the changeover and was formally dissolved on July 1, 1991. The military aspects of the Warsaw Pact were phased out in April after Hungary had announced that it intended to resign its membership; on July 1, 1991, the Warsaw Pact was also dissolved.

The Soviet Union pulled the last of its troops out of Hungary and Czechoslovakia in June 1991. It also signed an agreement with Germany to withdraw all Soviet troops by 1994 and gave a similar promise to Poland.

The various East European countries had begun to reorient their exports toward hard currency areas and away from the Soviet Union, a process that speeded up after the Soviet Union canceled standing orders with eastern European companies because of an inability to pay for the products in the now required hard currency. In a curious twist, the Economic Community actually helped to recreate some of those ties in 1991 as part of an agreement giving Hungary, Czechoslovakia and Poland associate membership status in the EC (now EU). France, concerned about agricultural imports from east-central Europe, persuaded the EC to buy a part of the production from these countries for delivery to the Soviet Union.

U.S.–Soviet Relations Under Gorbachëv

In 1985, the overriding factor in U.S.–Soviet relations was the military rivalry between the two superpowers and how it was managed. Arms negotiations had occurred at intervals since the 1960s. There had been the occasional, successful negotiations, but the period 1979–85 was basically one of stalemate. The two sides had continued to talk, but no agreements were reached. Meanwhile, the size of the arsenals continued to grow on both sides. Gorbachëv's first policy speech after becoming General Secretary outlined a traditional Soviet position, but even that speech contained the phrase, "we want a real and major reduction of the arms stockpiles." The sticking point was President Reagan's Strategic Defense Initiative (SDI), launched in March 1983.

The SDI was a proposal to use emergent technology to develop a shield to stop incoming missiles, using a combination of laser beams, computers, satellites and radar. SDI promised to reduce the threat

Foreign ministers meet in Bonn, West Germany, May 1990. Third from left is Foreign Minister Eduard Shevardnadze

of Soviet missiles to the United States. The failure of international negotiations gave it much of its political support, for it promised to achieve unilaterally what could otherwise be achieved only by successful negotiations.

The threat of having its missile force neutralized alarmed the Soviet leadership, and led to a Soviet proposal for talks on space weapons in mid–1984. The first discussions actually took place on March 12, 1985, one day after Gorbachëv succeeded Chernenko as General Secretary. The beginning Soviet position was that the USA cease *research* on development of a SDI system.

Officially, the Soviet opposition to American development of an SDI system was based on the premise that a successful one would give the United States a first strike capability *since it would not have to worry about retaliatory Soviet missiles.* The actual reasons for this opposition were far more complex, but were associated with Soviet weakness in the area of technological innovation and a Soviet recognition that the western world was experiencing a technological revolution in the areas of computers and automation that was leaving the Soviet further and further behind.

This new computer technology had significant military applications and constituted, in fact, the heart of any successful SDI system. The Soviets thus feared SDI for the emerging technology it could produce. There was also the possibility of SDI "spin-offs" which could revolutionize conventional warfare, thus reducing Moscow's huge advantage in this area. It is no coinci-

dence that Gorbachëv's opposition to SDI internationally was coupled with a domestic program aimed at giving the Soviet Union mastery of advanced technology.

Although arms negotiations talks continued in Geneva, no progress was possible because of the deadlock over SDI. To break this, Reagan and Gorbachëv decided to hold a summit conference in Geneva in November 1985. The talks were relatively cordial, and the two spoke privately for about five hours. There was no breakthrough on SDI, but Gorbachëv did accept an invitation extended by Reagan to visit the United States in 1986.

Negotiations at Geneva continued in 1986. They were serious, and differences were narrowed, but a final agreement still remained beyond their grasp—because of SDI differences. When Gorbachëv, as a consequence, postponed his visit to the United States, it was decided to hold a "pre–summit" in Reykjavik, Iceland. The two leaders met on October 11–12, 1986 for what turned out to be a wide–ranging discussion of the entire field of arms control.

No accord was reached, but the astonishing thing is how close they came, considering the topics discussed during that historic weekend. Insofar as intermediate range ballistic missiles stationed in Europe, Gorbachëv agreed to the U.S.–proposed "zero option." On strategic offensive weapons, the two sides agreed to 50 percent cuts in five years and elimination of *all* such weapons in ten years.

Negotiations with regard to SDI proved to be most intractable, but even here progress in resolving differences was made.

Russia

Thus, the Soviet position was that each side agree to adhere to the ABM Treaty for ten years; that during this time all SDI testing be confined to the laboratory, and that the two sides negotiate about SDI stationing at the end of ten years. Prior to the summit, the United States had been offering not to withdraw from the ABM Treaty for a term of 7–1/2 years. At Reykjavik the U.S. agreed to adhere to the ABM Treaty for ten years if, during that same time period, strategic nuclear ballistic missiles were reduced to zero.

The two sticking points were the question of confining SDI testing to the laboratory and the question of whether the United States could begin deploying SDI at the end of ten years without further negotiations with the Soviet Union. When agreement could not be reached on these two points, the negotiations fell through, because the Soviet position was that the arms-talks proposals were a single package, and agreement on any part of the package depended on acceptance by both sides of the *entire* package.

The first reaction to the Reykjavik summit was one of disappointment, but as both sides began looking back at what *had been accomplished*, the many areas of agreement became clear. In January 1987 the Soviet Union indicated its desire to continue discussions by naming a new chief Soviet negotiator at Vienna, Yuli Vorontsov, who held the rank of first deputy foreign minister.

Because of the lack of breakthrough, Gorbachëv launched a new initiative on February 28. Reversing his position at Reykjavik, he called for urgent negotiation of a separate agreement on intermediate–range nuclear missiles. He accompanied this with the promise that once agreement on intermediate–range missiles was reached, the Soviet Union would withdraw its shorter–range missiles from East Germany and Czechoslovakia. In April, he further modified his proposal by indicating that the Soviet Union would eliminate all shorter–range missiles from Europe as part of an agreement on intermediate–range missiles. He was also quoted by TASS at this time as saying that he was ready to meet Reagan in order to "conclude" a treaty on intermediate–range missiles and to reach agreement on "key provisions" regarding strategic offensive arms, space defense, arms and nuclear tests.

Negotiations between the two countries continued over the summer of 1987 but became stalled when the Soviet side insisted that West Germany's 72 Pershing 1A missiles (with U.S.–controlled warheads) had to be included in the deal. This obstacle was removed in August when West German Chancellor Kohl agreed conditionally to dismantle the Pershing 1A missiles. It took a visit to Washington by Foreign Minister Shevardnadze in September and a visit of Secretary of State Shultz to Moscow in October, but the result was a draft agreement banning intermediate-range (and Soviet shorter–range) missiles, known as the INF agreement. It was this INF agreement that General Secretary Gorbachëv signed when he made his first visit to the United States on December 8–11, 1987.

The successful conclusion of the INF treaty did not, as it turned out, provide enough momentum for agreement on strategic arms in time for President Reagan's visit to the USSR on May 29–June 2, 1988. As a result, the Moscow summit was largely ceremonial, though not less important for that reason.

Negotiations on strategic arms continued, but no agreement was reached, partly because of the change of American administrations and partly because of the complexity of the subject. There were other major developments in this area, however. The most important of these came in December 1988, when Gorbachëv, during an address to the United Nations General Assembly, announced that the USSR would make unilateral cuts of 500,000 troops and 10,000 tanks, with 50,000 troops and 5,000 tanks to be pulled out of Eastern Europe. He also promised that, in addition to the tanks, other equipment used in an attack, including river–bridging equipment would also be withdrawn.

The new Conventional Forces in Europe (CFE) talks—the enlarged version of the old MBFR talks—also began in Vienna in March 1989. The talks went very well from the beginning for it was the Soviet Union which proposed eliminating "imbalances and asymmetries" over a period of two years. Since they had an overwhelming advantage in ground equipment, their proposal meant that the Soviet

Presidents Gorbachëv and Bush at dinner aboard the Soviet Ship *Gorky*, off Malta, December 1989

76

Union would have to eliminate about 10 tanks for each tank eliminated by NATO.

The Soviet plan also suggested "equal collective ceilings which would be 10 to 15 percent lower than the lowest level possessed by either of the politico–military alliances." The ceiling proposed by NATO had been only slightly higher than this.

Finally, the Soviets also acknowledged the need for "the most stringent and rigorous verification, including inspections without right of refusal," thus meeting yet another of NATO's concerns.

A further significant breakthrough came in May 1989 when Gorbachëv announced that the Warsaw Pact was prepared to withdraw from Eastern Europe 40,000 of 58,470 tanks, 42,000 out of 70,330 armored vehicles and 47,000 out of 71,500 artillery pieces, and finally that it was willing to "make similar reductions in manpower and other types of weaponry." This was precisely the area of NATO's greatest concern and, therefore, Gorbachëv's offer was accepted with enthusiasm.

Two weeks later, President Bush, at a NATO summit in Brussels, proposed an equal ceiling of 275,000 troops which the two super–powers would be permitted to station in Europe outside their own territory and suggested that the CFE talks be expanded to include helicopters and land–based combat planes. He further called for demobilization of all troops to be withdrawn and for destruction of all equipment thus removed. Bush also suggested that it would "be possible to reach agreement in six months or even a year."

Since the Soviets had earlier suggested troop reductions and had wanted to include combat aircraft in the discussions all along, they welcomed President Bush's proposals. The CFE talks subsequently became stalled, however, partly because of the political changes that occurred in Eastern Europe in 1989. With non–communist leaderships in power throughout the region and with the German Democratic Republic moving toward unification with the Federal Republic of Germany, the old political basis of the Warsaw Pact no longer existed. In addition, the Soviet Union had agreed to withdraw its troops from Hungary and Czechoslovakia by the end of 1991 and those in Germany and Poland by 1994.

The CFE Treaty was initialed in November 1990 at a meeting of the CSCE. Shortly afterwards, the Soviet armed forces leadership reclassified three divisions as naval forces and claimed that these divisions were not covered by the CFE, since naval forces had not been included in the discussions. The United States and other western nations objected and the treaty was put on hold. The disagreement was resolved in May 1991 when Gorbachëv sent General Moiseyev, the chief of the Soviet Staff, to Washington, D.C. to work out a compromise. The compromise stipulated that the three divisions could be excluded from overall figures, provided commensurate reductions were made in forces not originally covered by the agreement.

Two months later, the USA and the Soviet Union announced that they had reached agreement on a START Agreement and that it would be signed at the end of July when President Bush traveled to Moscow for a Summit Conference with President Gorbachëv. The agreement, signed on July 31, 1991, required the two signatories to reduce the number of nuclear warheads to 6,000 each, though an involved method of counting raised this figure by about one–third. Nevertheless, it was the first treaty to achieve actual reductions in the number of nuclear weapons on each side. This was, it turned out, Gorbachëv's swansong. Less than three weeks later, conservative communists tried to oust him in an attempted *coup*. Although the *coup* was defeated, it discredited the *Communist Party* and led to the collapse of the Soviet Union.

An Independent Russia is Reborn

Gorbachëv still thought to save the union, even if under another name and with reduced powers, but it was not to be. By the end of August, nine of the fifteen republics were committed to independence. With the three Baltic Republics already receiving international recognition, Gorbachëv called a special session of the Congress of People's Deputies for September 2. After three days of debate, the Congress accepted Gorbachëv's proposal for the creation of a new interim government whose chief purpose would be to negotiate a new union treaty.

Gorbachëv remained president of this new interim government, but final executive authority was lodged in a state council made up of Gorbachëv and the leaders of the participating republics. A separate inter-republic economic committee, appointed by the state council, assumed the economic functions of the former Council of Ministers. Finally, a two chamber legislature was established, the membership of the second chamber to be appointed by and represent the governments of the individual republics. In this chamber, voting would be by delegation, with each republic having one vote.

From the beginning, only ten of the republics participated in the interim government. The first act of the state council was to recognize the independence of the Baltic Republics. Moldova refused to participate at all and Georgia sent only observers. In addition, over the next several days, all of the remaining republics other than the Russian Federation, Kazakhstan and Turkmenistan declared their independence. Later, even Kazakhstan and Turkmenistan would join the list.

Gorbachëv knew that his new interim government existed on sufferance and that Boris Yeltsin's support was the first requisite. Gorbachëv therefore dismissed all of his former advisers and accepted Yeltsin's advice on the make–up of his new government. He thus surrounded himself with liberals. He even appointed Ivan Silayev, prime minister of the Russian Federation, as chairman of the inter-republic economic committee, a post that effectively made him the caretaker prime minister of the union government.

Determined to save some form of union, he asked the reform economist Grigori Yavlinsky to draw up a plan for economic union and he and the state council began working on a plan for a new political union. Yavlinsky's draft for a new economic union was submitted to the state council in late September and won general approval. It was then submitted to the individual republics in October.

Most of the republics accepted the language of the economic union treaty, but the big exception was the Republic of Ukraine. Opposition was centered in the Ukrainian parliament, which drew up two pages of objections. The parliament demanded the right to set up an independent Ukrainian national bank, to issue a separate Ukrainian currency and, in general, to control its own fiscal policy. Later that same month, the Ukrainian parliament withdrew the mandate from its delegates to the USSR Council of the Republic and instructed them to participate as observers.

It came as no surprise, then, when the Republic of Ukraine decided to boycott the November 14 session of the state council, called to consider Gorbachëv's draft for a new union treaty. In the event, only seven republics gave their preliminary approval to a new treaty creating a "Union of Sovereign States." Two weeks later, the state council met again, supposedly to initial the draft agreement. Instead, they voted to submit it to the individual republic legislatures for approval, a process that put the proposed treaty into severe jeopardy.

Up to this point, Boris Yeltsin had consistently maintained that he favored a continuation of the union. But he had also said that he could not envisage a union without the Ukraine. Yet Leonid Kravchuk, the Ukrainian leader, said on No-

Russia

President Reagan and General Secretary Gorbachëv, Reykjavik, Iceland, October 11, 1986

vember 12 that he would "never sign" a treaty which contained "even the slightest hint of certain governing central bodies" and he had refused to participate in discussions in the state council on the new union treaty.

Yeltsin's own actions during this time indicate that he was also having second thoughts about the advisability of maintaining a strong center. At the end of October, he took over as his own prime minister and then announced that Russia would unilaterally begin a sweeping program of economic reform that included freeing prices, privatizing industry and land, and creating a strong Russian currency. He requested the Russian parliament to grant him the power to suspend Soviet laws that "hamper economic reforms." He also announced that, effective November 15, the Russian Government would no longer finance union ministries which it did not utilize.

Yeltsin's program got the Russian parliament's endorsement on November 1. Two weeks later, he assumed control of Soviet diamonds and gold production and took charge of issuing oil export licenses.

He followed this up with another decree taking over the remaining structures of the Soviet finance ministry, including its controls over foreign currency. This was accompanied by an announcement that Russia would no longer be responsible for any new debts incurred by the union government.

In effect, Yeltsin had begun a unilateral dismantling of the central government. This was carried a step further at the end of the month when Yeltsin stepped in and offered to finance the Soviet payroll after the central government had run out of funds. An integral part of the agreement was that Yeltsin henceforth controlled the union budget. He used his new power to order most central ministries to be closed.

Very little of the central government remained on December 1 when the Ukrainian people went to the polls to elect a new president and to vote on a referendum on independence. Leonid Kravchuk won the presidential race with 61.5 percent of the vote. Nearly 90 percent of all Ukrainians voted yes on independence.

"The independence of the Ukraine is a new political reality," commented Boris

Yeltsin upon receiving the results of the Ukrainian vote. Yeltsin recognized that the draft union treaty drawn up by Gorbachëv was dead, but he still felt that some kind of coordinating mechanism was necessary to handle the many problems of the now–separating republics. He therefore contacted President Kravchuk and Stanislav Shushkevich, president of Belarus, and suggested that the three presidents meet the following weekend to discuss the future. Shushkevich agreed to host the meeting and offered the use of a hunting lodge located not far from the Belarusian city of Brest. "We came to the conclusion," Shushkevich commented after the meeting, "that we had to sort out the concept of the kind of union we are capable of building."

The three leaders talked for two days, December 7–8. At the end of the second day, they returned to Minsk, where they signed an agreement creating a "Commonwealth of Independent States." Its most significant clause stated that "the USSR has ceased to exist as a subject of international law and as a geopolitical reality." This was, in effect, the Russian Federation's declaration of independence. Eight other republics—the sole holdout was Georgia—joined the CIS at a conference in Alma–Ata on December 21.

Gorbachëv resigned as president of the USSR on December 25, turning the Kremlin and authority over the Soviet Union's nuclear arsenal to Boris Yeltsin. The Russian Federation succeeded to the Soviet Union's membership in the United Nations and its seat on the Security Council.

Economic Reform

Boris Yeltsin launched his economic reform on January 2, 1992. Over the next several months, his government was mainly occupied with the implementation of that program, assuming the Soviet Union's international obligations, including its various diplomatic missions abroad, and carrying on negotiations with the other members of the CIS over economic relations and the future of the Soviet military forces. The republics had agreed to maintain strategic and nuclear forces under a single command, but three republics, Ukraine, Moldova and Azerbaijan, opted from the beginning to establish their own national armies. Plans for a unified command under the CIS for the remaining forces were gradually discarded as the remaining republics moved toward creating their own national armies.

The original CIS agreement called for the republics to maintain a single economic space, but that proved impossible in practice. One problem was that the other republics wanted to buy more from Russia than it needed to buy from them.

As a result, Russia had built up a positive balance of 1.2 trillion rubles with the other republics by the end of 1992. The Russian Government abandoned its commitment to maintaining a single ruble zone for the CIS about the middle of 1992. In view of the growing trade imbalance coupled with Moscow's perception that the governments of the other republics were not doing enough to control spending, the Russian Government began limiting the amount of rubles they were willing to make available to the other republics and it began encouraging the other republics to develop their own currencies. Most eventually moved to do so, though in a number of cases "coupons" rather than a new currency were authorized.

A number of the other republics complained about the speed of Russia's economic reform, particularly the wide–ranging freeing of prices, but most grudgingly went along with it. At home, however, Yeltsin soon found that a majority of the members of the Supreme Soviet were also appalled at the speed of the reform. Even though they had, in December 1991, granted Yeltsin the right to rule by decree for the period of one year, by June 1992 they were strongly attacking his program and doing what they could to frustrate it or slow it down. Between June and December, they undermined his economic reform mainly through an enormous increase in credit, accomplished through taking control of the Russian State Bank. And in those same months, Speaker Khasbulatov emerged as the chief spokesman for the anti–reform majority in the Supreme Soviet.

This raises an important question, for Khasbulatov had been elected chairman in 1991 with the support of reformers associated with Yeltsin; further, he had stood at Yeltsin's side in August 1991 in opposition to the attempted coup. Why did he now abandon his former allies and throw in his lot with many of the same individuals he had opposed in August 1991? It appears clear that he did it, not primarily for ideological reasons, but because his own position was threatened. Khasbulatov was elected in 1990 to represent the autonomous republic of Chechnya. Since that time, Chechnya had declared its independence and was attempting to secede from Russia. An extremely ambitious individual, Khasbulatov's one chance for continued power on the national level was if secessionist movements were put down resolutely.

Thus he made common cause with a coalition of ex–communists and Russian nationalists dreaming about a restoration of the old Soviet Empire. Because he is an able man and a facile speaker, his joining the parliamentary opposition to President Yeltsin gave that grouping more success than it would have been able to achieve on its own.

That became clear in December 1992, when the Congress of People's Deputies met to decide what policy to take toward President Yeltsin and his reforms. At issue was whether to extend President Yeltsin's power to name his own government ministers and to issue decrees with the force of law. Under the leadership of Speaker Khasbulatov, the Congress failed by a narrow four votes to pass a constitutional amendment that would have stripped President Yeltsin of most of his powers. The Congress then voted a resolution condemning Acting Prime Minister Yegor Gaidar's reform program and calling his methods of work unsatisfactory. They subsequently rejected Yegor Gaidar as prime minister.

President Yeltsin stalked out of the Congress, then threatened to organize a referendum on his policy of economic reform. Apparently frightened by the possibilities inherent in such a referendum, the Congress leadership proposed additional talks with Yeltsin. Valeri Zorkin, chairman of Russia's constitutional court, also offered his services as an honest broker during any talks. The result was a compromise whereby Yeltsin would retain his decree–issuing powers for another four months while a nation–wide referendum on a new constitution would be scheduled for April. In return, President Yeltsin agreed to nominate as prime minister a person acceptable to the Congress. The Congress's choice fell on Viktor Chernomyrdin, a centrist who had been vice prime minister for oil and gas production since July. Chernomyrdin was undoubtedly a disappointment to the Congressional majority, however, for he continued the basic thrust of Gaidar's economic program.

Frustrated in its attempts to put an end to economic reform, the Supreme Soviet continued its attacks on Yeltsin and his government. In addition, a majority of the Supreme Soviet began having second thoughts about a referendum which might lead to a new constitution and new elections which might see them removed from office. Things came to a head in February 1993 when Speaker Khasbulatov denounced the idea of a referendum. A few days later, Valeri Zorkin added his voice in opposition to a referendum. In addition, the leaders of Russia's regional governments, meeting with Yeltsin on February 9, told him that a referendum might lead to an explosion in the country. Faced with this wide–spread opposition, Yeltsin backed down and agreed to postpone the referendum indefinitely, provided a power– sharing arrangement could be reached with Khasbulatov and the Supreme Soviet. Yeltsin and Khasbulatov finally reached an agreement of sorts, subject to approval by the Congress of People's Deputies, which was reconvened on March 10.

But the full Congress was not in a mood to compromise. Rejecting Khasbulatov's efforts, the Congress voted to severely limit Yeltsin's right to rule by decree and canceled the referendum scheduled for April. Yeltsin temporized for seven days,

Inside St. Petersburg's nuclear power plant   Courtesy: NOVOSTI

Russia

then went on national television on March 20 to announce that he would organize his own referendum to take place on April 25. The Russian people would be asked to cast a vote of confidence on his presidency and to approve a new constitution that would serve as a basis for new elections. In the meantime, Yeltsin added, he planned to ignore the Supreme Soviet and rule by decree.

Vice President Rutskoi and Valeri Zorkin, chairman of Russia's constitutional court, immediately denounced Yeltsin's plan as unconstitutional. On the other hand, at an emergency meeting of the Supreme Soviet the next day, the prime minister and the defense, security and interior ministers all threw their support behind Yeltsin. The Supreme Soviet then requested the constitutional court to rule on Yeltsin's plan. The court declared Yeltsin's decree to be unlawful on the basis of his television speech, since it had not yet received a copy of the decree itself. On that basis, Khasbulatov called for Yeltsin's impeachment and the Supreme Soviet voted to convene the Congress of People's Deputies on March 26.

A motion to impeach was supported by a majority of the Congress members voting, but fell 72 votes short of the two-thirds vote necessary to convict. Having failed to impeach Yeltsin, the Congress acceded to the idea of a referendum, but demanded that four questions be submitted to the people instead of Yeltsin's two: "Do you have confidence in the president? Do you approve of the socioeconomic policy carried out by president and government in 1992? Do you think early presidential elections are necessary? And do you think early parliamentary elections are necessary?"

The Congress further stipulated that Yeltsin would have to win the votes of a majority of all registered voters on the first two questions in order to claim a popular mandate. Such a stipulation would have been almost impossible to obtain. In 1991, Yeltsin won 57 percent of all votes cast but that constituted only 42 percent of registered voters. The constitutional court subsequently ruled that Yeltsin could claim a victory on the first two questions if he won a majority of votes cast, but that the last two questions were constitutional and required the support of a majority of all registered voters to be binding.

In the event, Yeltsin won a 57.4 percent approval on the first question and 53.7 percent on the second. On the third question, 49.1 percent favored immediate presidential elections; however, 70.6 percent voted in favor of immediate parliamentary elections. Nevertheless, this constituted only 44.8 percent of the registered electorate, so it was not legally binding.

But Yeltsin had won only a battle, not the war. Speaker Khasbulatov dismissed the voting results as meaningless and divisive and announced that neither he nor the Congress of People's Deputies were prepared to accept the results as decisive. Vice President Rutskoi, for his part, argued that:

there can be no talk of overall popular support. Those who said 'no' or remained silent are also Russian citizens, and we have to ask ourselves why they did so.

Rutskoi later added:

There is no popular support. That is why all these reform policies should be changed.

Yeltsin's reaction to his victory was predictably different. Saying that the referendum had created "a fundamentally new political situation" which required a new constitution, he summoned the political leaders from Russia's regions and republics to Moscow in April. Here he presented them with copies of a new draft constitution. Yeltsin proposed that each region and republic examine the draft and submit comments to him within a month. He asked them also to appoint two delegates to a constituent assembly which would convene to complete work on the document.

This procedure, not specified anywhere in the old Soviet constitution—which gave the power to amend to the Congress of People's Deputies—was Yeltsin's attempt to circumvent the opposition of the Congress of People's Deputies. The 585 member constituent assembly met for about a month. After closely examining and modifying the constitution, they approved it by a better than two-thirds majority and sent it on to President Yeltsin. He then submitted it to the 88 republics and regions for their approval.

As this was going on, the Supreme Soviet took up the government's draft budget and proceeded to gut it. Declaring that the budget was "anti-social," they increased spending to 40 trillion rubles ($40 billion), which according to the chairman of the Supreme Soviet's own budget committee would have meant a budget deficit of 25 percent of GDP. That would have destroyed the government's reform program entirely and unleashed hyperinflation. Not content with that, the Supreme Soviet tried to sabotage the privatization program of the government by voting to cancel a presidential decree requiring state-owned firms to swap at least 20 percent of their shares for privatization vouchers. Instead, it announced that from October these vouchers could be replaced by "privatization accounts" at the government-

owned savings bank. Cutting short his holiday, President Yeltsin returned to Moscow and issued a new decree guaranteeing that privatization would continue. There was little he could legally do about the budget, however. He could veto it, but his veto could be overruled by a two-thirds vote in the Supreme Soviet.

President Yeltsin did, in fact, veto the budget twice over the next month and a half, but the Supreme Soviet was preparing to pass it for a third time on September 22. It was this which finally caused President Yeltsin, on the evening of September 21, to go on television to announce that the Russian parliament had been disbanded and that elections to a new parliament would take place on December 11-12. Within an hour, the rump Supreme Soviet, under Ruslan Khasbulatov's leadership, voted to strip Yeltsin of his powers, then installed Alexander Rutskoi, the vice–president, as a rival president.

In the succeeding confrontation, Prime Minister Chernomyrdin and his cabinet, plus the police and the army, remained loyal to Yeltsin. The stand–off continued for nearly two weeks. The parliamentary forces, refusing to disband, barricaded themselves in the parliament building and began to collect arms. Yeltsin surrounded the building with a cordon of police, then ordered that electricity, heat and water be cut off from the building.

Things turned violent on the night of October 3, when a mob broke through the police cordon and entered the parliament building. Urged on by Vice–President Rutskoi, the mob attempted to seize Ostankino, the main television building. A number of television channels were knocked off the air, but the mob never managed to gain control of the entire building.

President Yeltsin then called on the army to restore order and after some hesitation they agreed to do so. The first tanks arrived at the parliament building at 5:20 the next morning. Systematically firing into the building, then beginning a room by room movement through the building, the army rounded up the last of the defenders that afternoon. Kasbulatov and Rutskoi were arrested and imprisoned. That cleared the way for the December parliamentary elections. President Yeltsin set them for December 12 and enlarged the scope of the vote by specifying that the Russian people would also vote in a referendum on a new constitution and elect new regional and local councils.

The results of the elections were a disappointment for the reformers, however. Although the people approved the new constitution, that was the last good news. It was the elections to the State Duma, the lower house of the Federal Assembly, that were the most disappointing. There were 450 seats to be filled, half by proportional representation and half by first–past–the–post voting. The largest vote getter for the proportional seats was the badly mis-named *Liberal Democratic Party* of Vladimir Zhirinovsky, the ultranationalist leader, which got 22 percent of the vote. The reform party of Yegor Gaidar, *Russia's Choice*, came in second with 20 percent.

Because Zhirinovsky's party did poorly in the first–past–the–post voting, how-ever, *Russia's Choice* was the largest party in the State Duma with 76 seats. The *New Regional Policy* faction, formed after the election by individuals who had run with-out a party label, was second with 65 seats. The third largest faction was Zhiri-novsky's *Liberal Democratic Party* with 63 seats. Other parties included the *Agrarian Party* (53 seats), the *Communist Party* (45 seats), the *Party of Russian Unity and Ac-cord* (30 seats), *Yabloko* (25 seats), *Women of Russia* (23 seats), and the *Democratic Party of Russia* (15 seats). The remaining 35 seats were held by independents not affiliated with any party.

That makes the result sound better than it actually was, however. Except for *Yabloko*, the party of reform economist Gregory Yavlinsky, nearly every one of the remaining parties was cool to reform; to-gether they controlled a majority of the seats in the State Duma. Reflecting this fact, the man they selected as their Speaker was Ivan Rybkin, a member of the *Agrarian Party*.

The situation in the Federation Council, the upper house of the Federal Assembly, was more positive. Here a majority of the members supported reform. Vladimir Shumeiko, the Speaker, was a former dep-uty chairman of the Russian Council of Ministers.

One of the powers given to the State Duma in the new constitution is the right to grant amnesty. One of the first things the State Duma did after it met was to de-clare an amnesty to all those involved in the August 1991 and October 1993 at-tempted *coups*. This was widely seen as a rebuke to President Yeltsin, though it did have the advantage of cutting short what was turning into a long political trial.

Despite a stormy beginning, relations between the government and the legisla-ture subsequently settled down into a form of cohabitation that occasionally be-came even cooperation. The best sign of this was the peace accord which President Yeltsin managed to get most of the factions in the State Duma to sign in the spring of 1994 giving the government two years of calm to focus on economic recovery.

That truce largely came to an end in De-cember 1994 after President Yeltsin autho-rized the military to send troops into

President Boris Yeltsin shares microphones with Chairman Ruslan Khasbulatov
Courtesy: NOVOSTI

Chechnya to put down a separatist move-ment there. Curiously, however, it was his former supporters among the reformers who led the attack against the interven-tion. In January, the State Duma passed a resolution supporting a political solution in Chechnya and calling on the govern-ment to "take all necessary measures" to bring an end to the fighting. The resolu-tion was in the form of a recommendation to the president, however, and lacked the force of law. Only 172 out of 450 members voted for a separate resolution which would have barred the army from fight-ing in domestic conflicts. Yet even those who objected to the use of force in Chech-nya made it clear that they considered Chechnya to be an integral part of Russia.

Much the same was true of interna-tional opinion. Although the U.S. Govern-ment accused Russia of violating interna-tional agreements by failing to notify other countries about large–scale troop movements into Chechnya, it was also clear that it considered Chechnya to be strictly an internal affair. Senator Jesse Helms was more critical, commenting that he would oppose aid to President Yeltsin's government "if he can't control his people in terms of killing women and children and other innocent people."

The drop in domestic and international popularity was not surprising. Most peo-ple were appalled by the news stories coming out of Chechnya and reacted ac-cordingly. The decline would undoubt-edly have been temporary had the Rus-

sian military been able to restore order in Chechnya and bring all fighting to an end. Unfortunately, this was not the case. In fact, General Dudayev managed to main-tain a guerilla force in the mountainous areas of southern Chechnya and had twice showed—through terrorist raids on Rus-sian hospitals in Budyonnovsk in June 1995 and in Kizlyar in January 1996—that he could make the Russian occupation of Chechnya costly.

Yet the results of the legislative elections which took place in December 1995, though clearly not favorable to either President Yeltsin or his government, indi-cate that political opinion has changed very little since the previous elections in December 1993. The first thing about these most recent elections was the extreme po-litical fragmentation as each ambitious politician, it seemed, founded his own po-litical party as a vehicle for his preten-sions. Ultimately, forty–three parties, blocs and movements contested them. This proved to be self–defeating for a party needing a minimum showing of 5 percent of the national vote to enter the Duma on a party list. Since it was the re-formers who had splintered the most—of-ten concentrating their venom on other re-formers during the campaign—their final representation showed the greatest drop. The more disciplined *Communist Party of Russia* was the runaway winner with 22.3 percent of the vote—up ten percentage points from 1993. Vladimir Zhirinovsky's ultranationalist *Liberal Democratic Party*

Russia

came in second with 11 percent—though that was only half what the party had gotten in 1993. The only other parties to surmount the 5 percent barrier were two reform parties, *Our Home is Russia*, the party of Prime Minister Viktor Chernomyrdin, which came in third with 10 percent, and *Yabloko*, the party of Grigory Yavlinsky with 7 percent. Since only these four parties entered parliament on a party list, almost 50 percent of the votes were wasted because they had been cast for parties that failed to enter parliament on party lists.

Since only half of the seats were filled by party vote, the remainder being single–seat constituencies, there were several additional parties represented in the Duma. These included the *Agrarians* (21 seats), *Power to the People* (10 seats), *Russia's Democratic Choice* (10 seats), *Congress of Russian Communists* (5 seats) and *Women of Russia* (3 seats). A number of additional parties won one or two seats, and 76 individuals won as independents. Finally, the *Communist Party of Russia* won 58 single–constituency seats, *Our Home is Russia* won ten seats, *Yabloko* won 14 seats, and the *Liberal Democrats* won one single–constituency seat.

When parliament convened in January, it proved to be dominated by the *Communists*. Although they held only 149 out of the 450 seats themselves, they had a voting strength of 212 seats because of the support of a large number of individuals who ran and won as independents, meaning that they were just 14 seats short of a majority. After a stiff fight, they managed to elect one of their own, Gennadi Seleznyov, a former editor of *Pravda*, as the new speaker of the Duma. They also obtained the chairmanships of more than a third of the committees, including almost half of the major committees.

Although the position of the *Communists* was that economic reform has been a failure and should be ended, they were able, in fact, to find a lot of common ground with the government following the elections. One reason for this is that President Yeltsin also drew his own conclusions from the election results and essentially put economic reform on hold. Even more important, he got rid of the remaining reformers in his administration, replacing them with individuals more acceptable to the new majority in the Duma. Those departing included Anatoly Chubais, who as first deputy prime minister in charge of economic policy had been in charge of privatization, Sergei Shakrai, also a deputy prime minister, and Andrei Kozyrev, foreign minister.

But these dismissals were probably more symbolic than anything else, since all were ultimately implementers of Yeltsin policies rather than independent figures in their own right. More importantly, everyone understood that Yeltsin's term of office would expire in less than six months and that it would be the winner of the June 1996 elections who would determine the future course of government policy.

The major candidates in the presidential race were Yeltsin, Gennady Zyuganov, the *Communist* leader, Grigory Yavlinsky, founder of *Yabloko*, Vladimir Zhirinovsky, leader of the *Liberal Democrats*, and General Alexander Lebed, a Russian nationalist considered to be somewhat more moderate than Zhirinovsky.

From the beginning, Zyuganov was the favorite in the polls, first of all because the *Communists* had the best party organization and, secondly, because of the *Communist Party's* victory in the December 1995 Duma elections. Yeltsin, technically not a member of any party, had the additional disability of being the incumbent responsible both for the economic situation and the continuing Chechen conflict. Even he admitted that he could not be elected if the Chechen conflict were not settled by June. Another factor arguing for a Zyuganov win was that the *Communists* had no competitors on the left, while Zhirinovsky and Lebed were competing for the nationalist vote and Yeltsin and Yavlinsky were dividing the reform vote. Zyuganov was not expected to win a majority of the vote in the first round of voting, however; the important question, therefore, was who would come in second and so get to run against Zyuganov in the second round.

From the beginning, Yeltsin's strategy was to win enough votes to come in second. Sensing that most Russian voters wanted stability most of all, he told the electorate that the reforms had accomplished their purpose and now it was time for consolidation, not change. To make this point even clearer, he dismissed all of the reformers in the government and promised new, costly social programs that would benefit pensioners and others hurt by the collapse of the old command system. Reformers were extremely critical of him in the beginning, but he picked up the endorsement of a number of prominent reformers after they had pondered the various alternatives. He also picked up a surprise endorsement from the *Women of Russia* party and had the support of *Our Home is Russia*, the party founded by Prime Minister Chernomyrdin.

Yeltsin's chances improved in March when the *Communists* pushed through a resolution in the Duma declaring the 1991 dissolution of the Soviet Union to be illegal. They almost certainly hurt their case also when they promised that a *Communist* victory would lead to extensive renationalizations and a rebuilding of state control over the economy.

The Russian weekly, *Arguments and Facts*, predicts the outcome of the April 1993 referendum. Pictured are President Yeltsin and Ruslan Khasbulatov, Chairman of the Russian Federation's Supreme Soviet.

The Russian public were well aware that any attempt to reestablish the Soviet Union was likely to result in many more Chechnyas. Except for Belarus, a *Communist* victory would have been viewed with dismay throughout the region and any attempt to recreate the Soviet Union would have been opposed. Even the various Central Asian republics, though they had rebuilt some of the military and economic connections with Russia that existed prior to 1991, made it clear that they wished to retain their political independence and would react negatively to any attempt to bring them under Moscow's control. All of the Caucasus republics felt the same way.

Yeltsin evidently read the Russian populace correctly. When the election finally took place, Yeltsin came in first with 35 percent of the vote to Zyuganov's 32 percent. The third place winner was General Alexander Lebed, with 15 percent of the vote. Zhirinovsky and Yavlinsky trailed much further behind.

Courted by both sides, Lebed decided to throw his support to Yeltsin. Since the choice was now either Yeltsin or the *Communists*, the rest of the reformers came aboard as well. Yeltsin won in the second round with approximately 54 percent of the vote to Zyuganov's 40 percent. The remaining ballots were cast "against" both candidates.

Yeltsin went into seclusion after the election, however, and it was announced that he needed a heart bypass operation. The only positive development during those months is that Yeltsin named General Lebed as his security adviser and Lebed used this authority to negotiate an end to the war in Chechnya. Yeltsin had a successful heart bypass operation on November 5, receiving five arterial grafts. Almost immediately after returning to work in January 1997, however, he developed pneumonia. Though this was apparently not directly connected to his heart bypass operation, it incapacitated him for a further six weeks.

Little got done in the government during the several months that he was ill. Prime Minister Chernomyrdin, supposedly in charge, ran the day–to–day affairs of government but he was no leader. Meanwhile the Duma, dominated by *Communists* and nationalists, attempted to take control of the country's agenda, and there were repeated calls for Yeltsin's resignation.

The calls ceased soon after Yeltsin's return in March, however, for he soon made it clear who was in charge. Moreover, Yeltsin had clearly decided that further reform was needed to deal with such continuing economic problems as the widespread failure of employees to be paid on

Russia's parliament building—The White House   Courtesy: NOVOSTI

time. He therefore brought Anatoly Chubais back into the government as first deputy prime minister, even though he was aware that Chubais had few friends in the Duma. Also significant but symbolic as well, he appointed Boris Nemtsov as the other first deputy prime minister. Nemtsov, governor of Nizhny Novgorod province for the previous five years, had been among the first regional leaders to privatize small business enterprises and to promote land reform. As a result, Nizhny Novgorod, a closed city under the Soviets, had come to boast a fashionable pedestrian shopping mall, a glittery trade fair, a Coca Cola bottling plant, a branch office of the accounting firm Price Waterhouse, and regular service by Lufthansa Airlines. Yeltsin was obviously hoping that Nemtsov could do something similar for the country. In any case, Yeltsin's selection of Nemtsov was undoubtedly a good political move, for the youthful Nemtsov was quite popular with the Russian people and provided a good "public face" for reform.

Over the summer, Chubais and Nemtsov pushed policies designed to lower the rate of inflation, pay off pension arrears, and carry out the sale of Svyazinvest, Russia's large telecommunications company. Their policies had some positive effect, but it became increasingly clear as time went by that some larger measures would be necessary to get the Russian economy growing again.

Yeltsin sought to spell out just what was still needed in an address to the Federation Council, the Russian parliament's upper house, in September 1997. The message was an interesting one, for Yeltsin essentially pledged to put an end to the era of free–wheeling crony capitalism that had come in with the fall of communism in 1991. What was needed, Yeltsin said, was a "new economic order" in which government, not big business, made the

rules. The speech, in other words, was an explicit attack on the new industrial barons and bankers who had bankrolled his reelection campaign. However, these same men were now attempting to extend their economic power even further and refusing to pay taxes to the state. This was, undoubtedly, their chief "crime," for the government had recently been able to collect only about ten percent of GDP in taxes, which provided an insufficient amount of money to pay back wages and pensions and meet the government's pressing current needs. That same week, Boris Nemtsov reinforced Yeltsin's message when he warned the bosses of Avtovaz, a car–maker, that they had until October 1 to pay their back taxes or see the company forced into bankruptcy.

Two things now occurred that largely derailed reform, however. First, the economic crisis in Asia led to a world–wide decrease in investor confidence that resulted in some significant disinvestment in Russia in the fall of 1997. Second, Anatoly Chubais found himself caught up in a scandal when he and a team of colleagues agreed to accept a "publisher's advance" worth $450,000 for a book on privatization from a publishing firm linked to a bank that had made significant profits from participating in a number of privatizations overseen by Mr. Chubais. To his enemies, the "publisher's advance" looked like a bribe or a payoff. Chubais offered his resignation as first deputy prime minister and minister of finance on November 15, but Yeltsin refused it, though he subsequently downgraded Chubais's position in the administration by stripping him of the minister of finance title.

Although President Yeltsin's administration had a few accomplishments over the next three months that he could point to—most salary and pension arrears were paid off by the end of the year and the

Russia

Anatoly Chubais   NOVOSTI

1998 budget was finally approved by the Duma in February 1998—this was essentially a period of drift. That came to an end toward the end of March when Yeltsin dismissed Prime Minister Chernomyrdin and his cabinet and appointed Sergei Kirienko, a 35–year old junior minister, in his place. This also set up a confrontation with the opposition–controlled Duma, which had to confirm Kirienko before he could actually assume the job.

The only explanation that Yeltsin gave for his firing of Chernomyrdin—that he wanted the prime minister to "concentrate on political preparations for the forthcoming election," which would "decide the future of Russia"—didn't satisfy most people, so there were numerous speculations as to the "real" reasons. These ranged from speculations about Yeltsin's failing health to his anger at Chernomyrdin for moving too quickly to establish himself as a candidate for election to the presidency in 2000. None seemed adequate, particularly since they all had in common that they ignored the increasing drift of the previous three months. It appears more likely that Yeltsin, recognizing that this drift was discrediting reform in the minds of Russian voters, decided that some decisive action would have to be taken to get Russia back on track. His gamble was an extremely large one, but he did win the first part of his bet. The Duma, after rejecting Kirienko twice, finally confirmed him as prime minister by a vote of 251 to 25 on April 24. Kirienko needed 226 votes to win.

It is interesting to see which political parties voted for and against him. Gennady Zyuganov, the *Communist Party* leader, urged his followers to vote against Kiriyenko—and they did so during the first two rounds of voting. In the third round of voting, however, a significant number voted to confirm Kirienko. It helped that Duma Speaker Gennady Seleznev, a member of the *Communist Party*, threw his support to Kirienko in the third round, arguing that "Russia will not forgive us if we sacrifice the State Duma over a nomination for the prime minister." Seleznev was referring to the fact that, had Kirienko been defeated in the third round of voting, President Yeltsin would have been required by the constitution to dissolve the Duma and call for new elections.

Most members of *Our Home is Russia*, the party led by Chernomyrdin, voted for Kirienko, even though a successful Kirienko might have threatened Chernomyrdin's own run for the presidency in 2000. Kirienko had the support of Vladimir Zhirinovsky and his *Liberal Democrats*,

Victor Chernomyrdin   NOVOSTI

though Zhirinovsky also publicly negotiated for seats in the cabinet in return for his support. No public promises were made to him, though that is not to say that he expected to have no influence in the new government.

Curiously, perhaps the most consistent opponent was Grigory Yavlinsky, along with his *Yabloko* party. Yavlinsky, a self-billed reformer, had consistently opposed the government from 1993. However, the real reason for opposition to Kirienko was that Yavlinsky planned to run for the presidency in 2000 and a successful reform government would diminish his chances of winning. Yavlinsky and *Yabloko* refrained from taking part during the third round of voting to make clear their united opposition to Kirienko.

Kirienko promised to put together a cabinet of technicians who would push through necessary reforms and get the Russian economy growing again, but the specific programs he laid out mainly dealt

with additional subsidies for the energy sector. It must be assumed that Kirienko's program was really President Yeltsin's program and that he intended to change directions in order to win greater support for his government.

If that is indeed the case, then, this time, President Yeltsin gambled and lost, for the Kirienko government was almost immediately overwhelmed by the economic crisis sweeping out of Asia. On August 17, the Kirienko government panicked and announced a series of economic measures that included a devaluation of the currency and a partial repudiation of Russia's debt. In response, President Yeltsin dismissed Kirienko as prime minister.

President Yeltsin then nominated Victor Chernomyrdin as prime minister, but this time he did not get his way. A weakened Yeltsin had to agree to appoint a prime minister acceptable to the majority in the Duma. That turned out to be Yevgeny Primakov, an old bureaucrat who had been foreign minister in the two preceding cabinets.

Primakov served as prime minister from September 1998 to May 1999. During that time, the government printed new money to pay back wages of workers, thereby further depressing the value of the ruble. At the same time, the government negotiated with the IMF for several billions dollars worth of loans. The IMF finally agreed, though primarily to prevent a total economic collapse in Russia. The Duma approved a reasonably austere 1999 budget at the end of the year, but it continued to press the government to increase spending. Surprisingly, some privatization continued under the Primakov government, though primarily because the

Gennady Zyuganov   NOVOSTI

government was in desperate need of additional funds.

Primakov did calm the political atmosphere to some extent, since he was personally acceptable to the majority in the Duma. Yet the Duma continued to work on plans to begin impeachment proceedings against President Yeltsin, a step they finally took in May. It also did not help that Yeltsin was hospitalized several times in late 1998 and early 1999 because of a bleeding ulcer and appeared to be acting erratically in those periods when he did reemerge for a few days.

Things came to a head when the Duma leadership announced impeachment proceedings against President Yeltsin, to begin on May 13. Most of the five charges filed were purely political in nature, such as being responsible for the dissolution of the Soviet Union and for taking unconstitutional actions against the Duma in October 1993. The Duma leadership had been threatening to impeach Yeltsin for months and Prime Minister Primakov had been attempting to negotiate an arrangement whereby the Duma leadership would drop impeachment proceedings in return for a guarantee from Yeltsin that he would allow Primakov's government to remain in power until new parliamentary elections in December. When it had become clear that Primakov had failed, Yeltsin dismissed Primakov as prime minister one day before the impeachment proceedings were to begin.

President Yeltsin then nominated Sergei V. Stepashin as his candidate for the office of prime minister. Stepashin, whose background was in law enforcement, was an unlikely candidate for the office of prime minister, and most observers assumed that he would never be confirmed by the Duma. But Primakov's removal presented the Duma with a very unpleasant situation; should it vote to remove Yeltsin in impeachment proceedings before it confirmed a new prime minister, there would be no *constitutionally authorized* person available to assume power from Yeltsin upon his removal. Thus it appeared that the confrontation between the president and the Duma had landed Russia in another crisis.

What happened next was something of an anti-climax, however, for the Duma leadership first opted to proceed with impeachment, then failed to win the required two–thirds majority on behalf of its motion to impeach. Having been frustrated in its attempt to remove Yeltsin, the Duma then voted to confirm Stepashin as prime minister by a lop-sided 298 to 55 on May 19.

Yet, only two months after he had been confirmed by the Duma, Yeltsin dismissed Stepashin as prime minister. Yeltsin never

Sergei Kirienko   NOVOSTI

Yevgeny Primakov   NOVOSTI

said why he decided to replace Stepashin, but it is suggestive—particularly considering what happened afterwards—that Stepashin was fired only hours after he had flown back to Moscow from the Russian province of Dagestan, where Russian forces were fighting to repulse an armed invasion from neighboring Chechnya led by Shamil Basaev, one of Chechnya's more militant Muslim generals. The threat that Basaev represented was the possibility of a general Muslim rebellion against the Russian presence throughout the north Caucasus area.

What appears likely is that Stepashin's advice on Dagestan convinced Yeltsin that he wasn't up to the job of becoming president. This second point is supported by the fact that, when Yeltsin announced that he was nominating Vladimir V. Putin (pronounced POO-teen) as Stepashin's successor, he praised him as

the person capable of consolidating society, the person who basing himself on the broadest political forces, is capable of ensuring a continuation of reforms in Russia.

Putin, a former K.G.B. agent who became associated with St. Petersburg Mayor Anatoly Sobchak, one of the early leaders of Russia's democratic movement, moved to Moscow in 1996 where he served as Yeltsin's deputy chief of staff, then head of the internal intelligence agency, before being named secretary to the Security Council in 1998.

Although little known before being named prime minister, Putin very quickly showed himself to be a force to be reckoned with. From the beginning, he took a hard line toward Chechnya, but he did not push for decisive military action until after a series of bomb attacks in Russian cities were blamed on militants from

Chechnya, and even then he did not press for action until the Russian army indicated it was ready to move. Partly because of the bombings in Russian cities, the renewed campaign against Chechnya proved to be immensely popular, so Putin's popularity increased as the Russian military began to extend its control over the republic.

Although he had never stood for public office, Putin also showed himself to have a flair for politics as well. With new parliamentary elections set to take place on December 19, Russia's politicians prepared by building political alliances such as that represented by *Fatherland–All Russia*, which brought together Yuri Luzhkov, Mayor of Moscow; Alexander Yakovlev, governor of St. Petersburg region; Mintimir Shamiev, boss of Tatarstan; and Yevgeny Primakov, prime minister in 1998–99. A second, competing, political grouping, *Unity*, came into existence in September 1999 with the explicit purpose of increasing the political clout of regional leaders, and from the beginning its membership included many of the members of the Federation Council. Then, in November, Prime Minister Putin explicitly endorsed *Unity*, which then ran on a platform of supporting the government. A third new party, the *Union of Rightist Forces*, brought together most of Russia's reformers, including Sergei Kirienko, Boris Nemtsov, and Egor Gaidar. The *Communist Party of Russia* also set up an electoral alliance, *For Victory*, with the *Patriots* plus a faction of the *Agrarians*. Shortly before the elections, the *Fatherland–All Russia* bloc announced that it had agreed to "coordinate positions" in the new Duma with the *Communist Party of Russia*.

Six political parties surmounted the five percent barrier to win proportional representation seats in the December 19 elec-

Russia

tions. The *Communist Party of Russia* came in first with 123 seats (67 proportional seats plus 56 single mandate seats). *Unity* came in second with 72 seats (64 proportional seats plus 8 single mandate seats). *Fatherland–All Russia* came in third with 67 seats (37 proportional seats plus 30 single mandate seats). *The Union of Rightist Forces* came in fourth with 29 seats (24 proportional seats plus 5 single mandate seats). *Zhirinovskii's Bloc* won 18 seats (17 proportional seats plus one single mandate seat). Finally, *Yabloko* won 16 proportional seats. Eight other political parties entered the new Duma on the basis of winning one or more single mandate seats. Nine single mandate seats were won by *Our Home Is Russia*, led by Viktor Chernomyrdin, the former prime minister. The other seven political parties won an additional 10 single mandate seats.

The largest significance of the December 1999 parliamentary elections was that they produced a Duma that was more centrist and reformist. As a result, although the *Communist Party of Russia* was still the largest party in the Duma, the defeat of its former allies meant that it had become an isolated minority no longer able to dominate the agenda of the Duma. This fact was obscured but not negated when Putin, in January 2000, brokered a deal for a division of the leadership positions in the Duma between *Unity* and the *Communist Party of Russia* that resulted in a communist, Gennady Seleznev, being elected speaker. As it turned out, this agreement dealt only with process and not program.

Putin subsequently negotiated agreements with the smaller reform parties in which the government committed itself to support tax reform, passage of a land code, a labor law, and legislation limiting the right of legislators to immunity from criminal prosecution. Most of this program had already been achieved by the spring of 2001.

The Putin Presidency

Yeltsin's decision to resign as president as of December 31, 1999 made Vladimir Putin acting president and guaranteed that new presidential elections would have to take place within three months. They actually took place on March 26. Although eleven candidates competed in the election, Putin won in the first round of voting, garnering an impressive 52.5 percent of the vote—a 22 percent spread between himself and Gennady Zyuganov, the number two candidate, who polled just under 30 percent.

Putin was formally inaugurated as president in May and named Mikhail Kasyanov, his former deputy prime minister, as the new prime minister. Putin had not put forth any comprehensive program prior to his election, but he remedied that situation shortly after his inauguration— first of all, through the persons he selected as members of the cabinet. Although Putin retained several ministers from his

President Vladimir V. Putin

earlier cabinet, he placed liberals in charge of all the traditional top economic posts— finance, tax, and labor—and then created a fourth economic ministry—economic development.

In the following year, this group of ministers shepherded a new tax code through the Duma that created a 13 percent flat tax on all incomes. The flat tax was well received and greatly increased government revenues from income taxes. A new land code setting up procedures for the sale of non–agricultural land was passed by the Duma in March 2001.

In November 2001, the Duma passed a reform of the judicial code which, in addition to extending professional require-

Outside of the MIR

NOVOSTI

Prime Minister Mikhail Fradkov Itar-Tass

ments for judges and establishing norms for disciplinary and criminal responsibility, mandated the nationwide establishment of jury trials by January 2003 for cases involving crimes such as murder and rape. Based on the experience of regions such as Inanovo, Moscow and Saratov oblasts, where jury trials have been in use since 1993, the Duma passed follow-up legislation in July 2002 which made 3,500 changes in the criminal code aimed at making jury trials work better. Three of the most important reforms incorporated in the new legislation include the fundamental concept of presumption of innocence, the right to habeas corpus (i.e., anyone accused of a crime must be charged in court within 48 hours), and a new role for the judge as a neutral arbitrator (not as a prosecutor's helper, his role under the old Soviet code). These reforms were gradually implemented over the remainder of 2002 and jury trials resumed formally in 61 Russian regions as of January 2003.

Through his appointments and subsequent actions, Putin established that he is, in some respects, an economic liberal. But it has also become clear that, politically, he is a conservative. Although he has always insisted that he is a democrat, the policies he has pursued as president make clear that there a strong streak of authoritarianism in his make-up. That became even more evident after his reelection in 2004.

The first of those policies, announced within days of assuming the presidency, was the division of Russia into seven federal administrative districts and the appointment of seven presidential representatives to head these new administrative districts. Putin intended that these seven men would eclipse regional governors and help to reassert the control of the center over the regions. Although this reform has not been particularly effective in bringing the regions under centralized control, it has acted as a complement to other policies that Putin has implemented.

Putin's second announced policy was to remake the Federation Council (the upper house of parliament) by replacing regional governors with representatives elected from each region. Under the law passed in June 2000, each region sends two representatives, the first to be nominated by the governor with the consent of the regional legislature and the second to be elected from among candidates nominated by the legislature's speaker or by no less than one-third of the chamber's deputies. The reform, which was phased in over the next 18 months, worked in some ways to strengthen the voice of the regions at the center, since the new Federation representatives remain permanently in Moscow, unlike the governors they replaced.

Putin created a State Council at the same time he instituted the Federation Council reform. The State Council is a smaller body whose membership, appointed by the president, includes a number of regional governors. That fact led some commentators to suggest that the State Council might eventually replace the Federation Council as spokesman for the regions. In fact, Putin appears to use the State Council solely as an advisory body. Moreover, the constantly changing make-up of the council resulting from the fact that appointees serve for a six-month period would suggest that it constitutes no threat to the position of the Federation Council.

Putin's third policy program, which was actually launched soon after he became acting president, was more diffused, but its essence was to bring all of the regions into compliance with the Russian constitution and Russian Federation laws. The government used such terms as "harmonization of federal and regional legislation" and "conformity of all laws with each other," but the essence was that the center would no longer permit regions to have constitutions or pass laws that conflicted with the Russian constitution or Russian law. As a part of that, Putin had also, by April 2002, cancelled 28 of the 42 power-sharing treaties that President Yeltsin had negotiated with regions such as St. Petersburg and Nizhnii Novgorod and autonomous republics such as Komi, Bashkortostan, Sakha (Yakutia), and Tatarstan. In general, Putin's position has been to negotiate new power-sharing treaties with autonomous republics while cancelling those with regions. In addition, he has forced several autonomous republics to redraw their constitutions to bring them into agreement with the federal constitution. These policies have undoubtedly increased central control over the regions and autonomous republics and this has led some commentators to express the worry that Putin's policies toward the re-

gions might lead to so large an increase in the center's powers that Russia would cease being a federation in fact, even if not in name. That was still only a threat during Putin's first term in office, but actions that he has taken since his reelection in 2004 suggest that that is, indeed, a real possibility.

Chechnya

President Putin's policy toward Chechnya—in some ways his most controversial domestic policy—is related to his commitment to bring all of the regions into compliance with the Russian constitution and Russian Federation laws. Putin was President Yeltsin's deputy chief of staff in 1996 when General Lebed, as Yeltsin's security adviser, negotiated an end to the war in Chechnya—the terms of which specified the withdrawal of all Russian forces from Chechnya in return for a Chechnyan pledge not to press for formal independence for five years.

Unfortunately, Aslan Maskhadov, elected president in 1997, found his policies, which were based on secular separatism, challenged by insubordinate military commanders who dreamed of ridding the entire north Caucasus area of Russian influence and uniting it in a new Islamic state. The chief spokesman for this point of view, Shamil Basayev, was originally a Chechen patriot who came under the influence of a radical commander of Jordanian origin by the name of Khattab in the middle 1990s. Khattab, who came to Chechnya in 1995, had fought with bin Laden as a teenager and the message he brought to Chechnya was of an international movement to free Muslims everywhere from foreign rule. In the case of Chechnya, this meant merging the two majority Islamic states of Chechnya and Dagestan into a single Islamic state. Under Khattab's tutelage, Basayev visited al Qaeda training camps in Afghanistan on three separate occasions, then he and Khattab established their own training camp in Chechnya.

Islamic radicals had also been active in Dagestan since the early 1990s. One of them was a Jordanian cleric by the name of Khabib Abdurrakhman, who established a headquarters in the town of Karamakhi and here, heavily financed from outside, managed to build up an armed cadre of religious fundamentalists committed to jihad and the town into an armed enclave stockpiled with weapons. Khattab visited Karamakhi, even going so far as to take a local 17-year old girl as his wife. Together, Abdurrakhman and Khattab plotted a takeover of Dagestan.

Basayev launched his invasion into Dagestgan in August 1999, but the operation failed miserably within a few weeks as Russian troops drove the rebels under

Russia

Basayev and Khattab back into Chechnya. Russian forces took control of Karamakhi in September and began purging the hamlet of radical Islamic forces. Most Dagestani, it turned out, rejected radical Islam, preferring to remain part of Russia.

But this marked the beginning of the second Chechnyan war. When Maskhadov did not immediately repudiate Basayev and Khattab, Moscow broke off all relations with his government; by October, 80,000 Russian troops had begun their ground campaign in Chechnya. Chechnyan forces were soon forced to abandon Grozny, the capital, and retreat southward into the Caucasus Mountains, though they remained undefeated. Khattab was killed by Russian forces in 2002.

The continuing conflict has had significant diplomatic repercussions for Russia, first of all as it has affected Russia's relations with Georgia and Azerbaijan and, secondly, with the countries of the European Union and, to a lesser extent, the United States. Russia has been critical of Azerbaijan for permitting a representative of the Chechen rebel authority to maintain an office in Baku until October 2002. It has been even more critical of Georgia, which it has accused of allowing Chechen rebels to find sanctuary in the Pankisi Gorge, and it has even threatened to carry "preventive strikes" against Chechen bases in Georgia. Further, the European Union sponsored a resolution in the UN Human Rights Committee condemning Russia for human rights violations in Chechnya. The United States, which had frequently been critical of Russian military operations in Chechnya, announced in February 2003 that it was adding three Chechen rebel groups to its blacklist of terrorist organizations. That was undoubtedly viewed as good news by the Russian Government, for this can be seen as an endorsement of the Russian position that the Russian army is fighting an "anti–terrorist" campaign in Chechnya. Even so, the overall U.S. Government position remains that "the broader conflict in Chechnya cannot be resolved militarily" and human rights reports issued by the U.S. State Department have criticized reports of mistreatment of citizens in Chechnya.

An incident in the latter part of 2002 has also made it clear that the Chechen rebels have now turned to terror tactics as an integral part of their war against Russia. It all began on October 23 in Moscow when a group of approximately 40 Chechen militants led by Movsar Barayev, a 25–year old fledgling guerrilla leader, seized a packed Moscow theater, taking more than 800 persons hostage. Refusing to negotiate with the Russian authorities, Barayev demanded that all Russian military forces be withdrawn from Chechnya within one

week. Armed with explosives strapped to their bodies and having placed additional explosives throughout the theater, the Chechen militants threatened to begin killing their hostages unless the Russian Government complied with their ultimatum. The Russian authorities waited three days, then used sleeping gas to resolve the hostage standoff. During the rescue action, all of the militants were killed while at least 129 hostages died as a result of a gas overdose.

The situation was made worse by the fact that Chechen President Maskhadov refused to condemn the hostage–taking while it was going on. It was further compounded when Shamil Basayev, whom Maskhadov had named to head his government's Military Committee in June 2002, claimed responsibility for the hostage taking. This is, of course, the same Shamil Basayev who started the second Chechen war when he launched his invasion of Dagestan in August 1999. President Putin responded by launching a massive retaliatory military operation in Chechnya, accompanying it with a promise to expand Russia's war on terrorism, targeting "all places where terrorists and their ideological supporters and financial backers are based."

He also decided to put an end to any possibility of eventual Chechen independence by organizing a referendum in Chechnya on a new draft constitution establishing Chechnya as an autonomous republic within the Russian Federation. That referendum, which took place on March 23, 2003, received the overwhelming approval of the people voting in Chechnya and new elections, held in October 2003, resulted in the election of Akhmed-hadji Kadyrov as president.

These actions have not brought an end to the continuing conflict in Chechnya, nor have they prevented radical elements of the Chechnyan resistance from launching terror attacks in Moscow, in Chechnya, and in the neighboring republics of Daghestan, Ingushia and North Ossetia.

Kadyrov himself was killed on May 9, 2004 when a bomb planted under the stands blew up as he was attending celebrations in Grozny stadium to mark the anniversary of the end of World War II. But Kadyrov's assassination did not change the Russian Government's policy in Chechnya; in fact, his son, Ramzan Kadyrov, was appointed prime minister of Chechnya soon after his father's death. Ramzan Kadyrov was appointed acting president in February 2007, then subsequently won election as president in his own right.

Aslan Maskhadov, the separatist leader, was killed by the Russian military in March 2005. Maskhadov's successor was

Abdul-Khalim Sadulayev, a lesser known Islamic fundamentalist, who was himself killed in June 2006. The current leader of the Chechnyan resistance is Doku Umarov, a veteran field commander who had served as vice president under Sadulayev. Umarov chose Shamil Basayev as his vice president in June 2006; two weeks later, Basayev was killed while leading a terrorist attack in southern Russia, the probable target a Russian military base in North Ossetia.

The separatist cause in Chechnya has been weakened by the loss of much of its top leadership, but it appears determined to fight on—and to extend the war to other parts of the north Caucasus area. Meanwhile, an amnesty plan, announced after Shamil Basayev's death, was, according to the government, accepted by 647 former militants. Most of those who sought amnesty were low-level militants, however; no one knows how many militants continue to support the resistance.

Since President Putin's policies at the national level are aimed at strengthening the power of the central government in all of its dealings with the various political subdivisions, events in Chechnya have been used as an argument to reinforce control at the center by stripping all of Russia's subdivisions of some of their autonomy, lest they turn into other Chechnyas. Thus events in Chechnya have directly contributed to a growth in authoritarian throughout Russia.

Media

Another policy area of the Russian Government that has caused some concern is the attitude toward the media, and in particular Russia's independent television network NTV. Russia has three television networks—two state–run networks, ORT and RTR—and NTV, a privately owned network started in the mid–1990s by Vladimir Gusinsky. NTV, noted for its lively and critical news and current affairs programs, was a strong supporter of President Yeltsin and his policies until 1999, but it became a critic of the Russian Government after Russian troops were sent back into Chechnya in that year. Not coincidentally, Vladimir Gusinsky came under increasing attack from the government shortly thereafter. Gusinsky was jailed briefly in the summer of 2000, then fled to Spain, fighting extradition when the Russian Government attempted to force his return. The Spanish Government eventually refused to return Gusinsky, but, at home, the Russian Government moved against Gusinsky's media empire, arresting a number of the NTV's employees, including its finance chief, Anton Titov.

But the main attack was indirect. This attack was made possible by the fact that

Russian campaign poster for Vladimir Zhirinovsky's Liberal Democratic Party of Russia

Gusinsky had started NTV with financial support from Gazprom, Russia's national gas company, and Gazprom got 46 percent of the shares in the company as a result. Gusinsky subsequently found himself in financial difficulties and borrowed an additional $300 million from Gazprom, pledging 19 percent of NTV's shares as collateral for the loan. When he was unable to repay the loan, Gazprom demanded the additional shares and sued the company in court when Gusinsky refused to turn them over. Gazprom won in court in April 2001; it then took control of the company and replaced its previous management.

All of this might have been viewed as a straight–forward business arrangement, were it not for the fact that Gazprom is partially owned—and effectively controlled—by the state. Did all of this happen because the government was determined to gain control of the sole independent television network in Russia? Would the government henceforth control this network as it already did the other two networks? Many of NTV's employees thought so and quit to work elsewhere after the new management took over. In addition, when Ted Turner offered to buy the 19 percent interest in NTV from Gazprom in return for a promise from the Russian Government that NTV could continue to operate as an independent network, President Putin said that the government was not involved in the matter and so could make no such promises.

Although Gazprom's takeover of NTV certainly represents a loss for Gusinsky, it is less clear that it was the result of a decision by President Putin to bring all of the media under government control. In fact, Michael Wines, writing in *The New York Times* in April 2001, concluded that it did not. Wines wrote that, while Russians did not enjoy freedom as Westerners know it, a great media variety continued to exist in Russia.

There has been a continued deterioration in press freedom in Russia since 2001, however. In November 2004, Reporters Without Borders issued a new press freedom index which ranked Russia 140th out of 167 countries. Commenting on the current situation, Mikhail Berger, Editor in Chief of *Yezhenedelnyi*, wrote in January 2005 that "it is amazing how the print media are willing to cater to the ruling elite's needs rather than to society's information needs." Dealing with the same topic, Igor Yakovenko, Secretary-General of the Russian Union of Journalists, wrote about "the problem of the government monopoly of the media market [which] has not been resolved and has even grown worse." Vladimir Ryzhkov, an independent Duma Deputy, commented somewhat more cynically in April 2005 that "there are just two strategic resources for keeping power in this country—oil and television."

Two years later, that evaluation is still applicable. Freedom of the press as it is understood in the United States does not exist in Russia. On the other hand, the situation in Russia is not as bad as it is sometimes portrayed abroad. Television and much of the national press is controlled either by the government or by wealthy individuals allied with the government, but many independent newspapers and regional radio stations still exist. It is also still possible to find most of the major western newspapers and newspapers for sale in Russia, at least in the major cities. An independent press can continue to exist so long as it is careful to maintain a stance of genuine neutrality between the government and its political opponents; the danger comes when a radio station or a newspaper is perceived as being an instrument of the political opposition. That's certainly not the American definition of press freedom, but it is still a vast improvement over the controlled press of the Soviet era.

Recent Political Developments

In April 2002, there was a realignment of leadership positions in the Duma which ousted the *Communists* from most of their committee chairmanships and threatened the position of the Duma speaker, Gennadii Seleznev, a member of the Communist faction. The genesis of this development goes back to October 2001, when two of the parties of the pro–government party coalition, *Unity* and *Fatherland–All Russia* voted to merge to create a new centralist political party, *Unified Russia*. This merger was completed in February 2002.

Russia

Meanwhile, public opinion polls taken in October 2001 indicated that the *Communist Party of the Russian Federation (KPRF)* was losing support and would win fewer seats than *Unity* in any new legislative elections. This led Zyuganov, the *Communist* leader, to call an emergency congress of the *KPRF* to meet in January 2002 to deal with the situation. In spite of a warm letter from President Putin to the congress in which he referred to the *KPRF* as "a creative and constructive political association that united a considerable part of society," Zyuganov used the forum to launch a sharp criticism of President Putin's policies, while the congress adopted a resolution placing the *KPRF* in "irreconcilable opposition" to the government and its policies.

Since Putin's party, *United Russia*, together with the other parties of the pro–government coalition—the *People's Deputy* faction, the *Union of Rightist Forces*, and the *Russian Regions* group—controlled a majority of the seats in the Duma, it was only a question of what action they would take to counteract the *Communist* challenge. The move came in March 2002, when the government coalition threatened to replace Seleznev as Duma speaker. That threat was subsequently withdrawn, but Seleznev did lose the right to cast a deciding vote in the Duma Council, the organization which sets the agenda for the lower house. In addition, the coalition began to push for a reassignment of Duma committee chairmanships. That vote took place on April 3.

This realignment put a formal end to the working arrangement brokered between the pro–government *United Russia* and the Communist leadership in the Duma as the Duma had organized itself after the December 1999 legislative elections. Under the new arrangement, seven of the nine committee chairmanships held by the *Communists* were transferred to pro–government political parties of the center and right. The pro–government coalition also voted to restrict Speaker Seleznev's authority.

The *Communist Party* then ordered the two chairmen who had been scheduled to retain their chairmanships to resign these positions and the *Agro–Industrial Group*, traditional allies of the *Communists*, voted to relinquish control of their two committees as well. In response to these actions, the Duma Mandate Commission voted to abolish three of the affected committees, assigning their functions to other committees. The fourth of the committees, the Committee on Culture and Tourism, was retained, with the position of chair going to a *United Russia* member. Before this decision could be implemented, however, Nikolai Gubenko, the *Communist* chair of the Committee on Culture and Tourism, withdrew his resignation and reclaimed his chairmanship. In addition, Svetlana Goryacheva withdrew her resignation as chair of the Committee on Women's Issues, Families and Youth, so she retained her position as chair of that committee as well.

Threatened by a general breakdown in party discipline, the presidium of the central committee of the *Communist Party* voted to expel from the party those *Communist* deputies who refused to relinquish their leadership seats—and made it clear that this applied to State Duma Chairman Gennady Seleznev as well. When Seleznev refused to step down, he was expelled from the *Communist Party* in June. Seleznev's expulsion was not that significant in itself, but it was an indication of a further breakdown in party discipline.

The 2003 Duma elections were scheduled to take place on December 7. With President Putin's popularity running at about 75 percent, it was a foregone conclusion that the pro-presidential *United Russia* would do well at the polls. But Putin was apparently determined to reduce the clout of the *Communist Party* and so his political operatives encouraged the creation of a new political alliance on the left led by Dmitrii Rogozin, a nationalist who was chairman of the Foreign Affairs Committee of the Duma, and Sergei Glazev, a member of the *Communist* faction in the Duma. This new party, which took the name *Motherland*, billed itself as a leftwing but patriotic party, thus presenting itself as an alternative to all those

Original Königsberg University (now in Kaliningrad), where Imanuel Kant taught.

who had traditionally supported the *Communists*, but who were turned off by the position of total opposition adopted by the *Communist Party*. It also didn't hurt that the mostly government-controlled media gave the new party wide favorable coverage while largely ignoring the campaign of the *Communist Party*.

The December 7 vote brought a fundamental political shift with pro-government parties sweeping the field. *United Russia*, the pro-government bloc, took 37.1 percent of the vote, while the *Communists* came next with 12.7 percent. The other parties that surmounted the five percent hurdle to obtain proportional seats were Zhirinovsky's *Liberal Democratic Party* with 11.6 percent and *Motherland* with 9.1 percent. Support for the two so-called liberal or reform parties, *Yabloko* and the *Union of Right Forces*, fell to under five percent so they lost their party representation in the Duma. In the final enumeration, *United Russia* took 300 of the 450 seats, which gave the government a two-thirds majority in the new Duma.

The results of the parliamentary elections were actually a prelude to presidential elections scheduled to take place on March 14, 2004. With his public approval ratings a consistent 70–75 percent, Vladimir Putin was always considered likely to win reelection, but the astonishing showing of the pro-government bloc in the December parliamentary elections convinced all of the potential major candidates to drop out of the race.

Faced only with minor opposition, Putin never formally campaigned for reelection, though he did manage to create some excitement in February when he fired his prime minister, Mikhail Kasyanov, and named Mikhail Fradkov, a political unknown, as his replacement. Fradkov, a career bureaucrat, is a former head of the tax police and was serving as Russia's representative to the European Union when he was appointed prime minister. Putin said that he was changing prime ministers before the presidential vote because he wanted the Russian people to know precisely what they would be getting in his second term. However, the real message that Putin was sending had to do with the campaign that the government had launched the previous fall against the Russian oligarchs and, in particular, Mikhail Khodorkovsky, then head and chief shareholder of the energy company Yukos. When Kasyanov publicly objected to the government's decision to impound 44 percent of the shares of Yukos as a way to guarantee that it could collect on any future judgment against Yukos, most people were convinced that it was only a matter of time before Putin replaced him as prime minister. Of course, Putin was also mak-

ing it clear that it was he who would be totally in charge in the new administration.

The March 14 election came out as expected, with Putin garnering 71.2 percent of the vote. *Communist Party* candidate and Duma Deputy Nikolai Kharitonov came in second with 13.7 percent of the vote. The other two candidates, Sergei Glasev and Irina Khakamada came in third and fourth with 4.1 percent and 3.9 percent of the vote.

A Shift Toward Authoritarianism

President Putin promised at the time of his reelection to translate his landslide victory into a new season of reform, but the new policies introduced since that time have all tended toward authoritarianism rather than reform. In September 2004, Putin proposed to eliminate the direct election of governors and other regional executive-branch heads—including the heads of the so-called ethnic republics. In place of the election process, the president of the Russian Federation would submit the name of a candidate to the appropriate regional legislature, which would have to "give its consent" to the nominee before he was appointed to office. One can imagine how often a regional legislature would reject a candidate proposed to them by the president of the Federal Republic. However, should that occur, and the candidate be rejected a second time if resubmitted, the president would have the authority to appoint an acting regional head. If the candidate were rejected a third time, the president could dissolve the legislature and call for new elections. This particular "reform" was passed by the Duma in December 2004.

President Putin next submitted a bill to the Duma to change how deputies are elected. Under the new legislation, single-mandate districts will be abolished, and all deputies will be elected from party lists according to a proportional-representation system. In addition, the new legislation bans the formation of electoral blocs to contest federal, regional, or local elections. The new legislation, which the Duma passed in April 2005, will eliminate independent candidates and place selection of all deputies in the hands of the political parties. Some democratic countries do have proportional-representation systems, but in the Russian system, where the largest political party is an instrument of the government with no party platform other than loyalty to the government, the possibilities for political manipulation of the electorate are enormous.

Another law, passed in December 2004, appears to have as its purpose to limit the number of new political parties coming into existence. Under this legislation, a party must have 50,000 members nation-

First Deputy Prime Minister Dmitry Medvedev: possible candidate for president in 2008

wide, while half of the regional branches must have no fewer than 500 members each. A new party which fails to reach a sufficient membership will have to become a public association unless it achieves a minimum membership within the following year.

In yet another "reform," Putin proposed—and the Duma passed—a law creating a Public Chamber of 126 members whose function is apparently to co-opt non-governmental organizations. The chamber will meet in Moscow at least twice a year to discuss state initiatives to promote civic society. President Putin has appointed 42 of the members, public organizations have selected a further 42, and the remaining 42 members are representatives of the regions. The bill approved by the Duma in March 2005, gives the Public Chamber a weekly 60-minute program on state television, its own print organ, and a website. Aleksei Makarkin, deputy director of the Center for Political Technologies, told the *Nezavisimaya gazeta* that the chamber would provide an opportunity for nongovernmental organizations to prove their loyalty to the Kremlin. Selection to the chamber "will mean that the state regards these organizations as respectable and reputable and recommends that its representatives in the regions do the same." The new Public Chamber has probably had a marginal effect on public opinion, but it does not appear to have the clout that some critics of the president had feared.

Putin's latest reform relates to nongovernmental organizations (NGOs) operating in Russia. The new law, which went into effect on April 17, 2006, has set new rules for the more than 400,000 NGOs operating in Russia. Essentially, the new

Russia

First Deputy Prime Minister Sergei Ivanov: possible candidate for president in 2008

law requires foreign and domestic NGOs to re-register with a state body that will examine their work before deciding whether they will be permitted to continue operations. An important reason for the legislation is the fear that foreign money could promote the sort of popular revolt that led to the color revolutions in Georgia, Ukraine and Kyrgyzstan. The legislation permits the Federal Registration Service to prevent the funding of certain activities to safeguard the "constitutional' order. In addition, the legislation states that NGOs can be closed if they threaten "Russia's sovereignty, independence, territorial integrity, national unity and originality, cultural heritage and national interests." Although a number of prominent NGOs initially had some difficulty in getting re-registered, most have since been successfully registered.

Two advisers to Putin during his first term in office who have subsequently broken with him are former Prime Minister Mikhail Kasyanov and Andrei Illarionov, who resigned as Putin's top economic adviser in December 2005. Kasyanov, who has often spoken critically about Putin's "restoration of Soviet order" since stepping down as prime minister, announced the formation of a new political movement, called the *People's Democratic Union*, in 2006. At the time, many people thought that Kasyanov was positioning himself for a political run for the presidency in 2008. That may still occur, but Kasyanov will be only a minor candidate if he does run.

Illarionov, on the other hand, does not appear to have political ambitions and for that reason his criticisms of government policy have had more resonance. Six days before he resigned, he told a press conference that Russia "is no longer a democratic country. It is no longer a free country." Since his resignation, he has criticized Putin for turning Russia into a corporate state. "Russia," he wrote in January 2006, "has become richer over the past six years but has seen its economic, political, and so-

cial freedoms diminish." But as Masha Lipman, editor of the Carnegie Moscow Center's *Pro et Contra journal*, wrote in September 2005:

> While public opinion polls show unrelenting discontent with government policies, Putin's own approval rating, which had dropped somewhat, popped back up to 70 percent in August.

It is true that criticism such as those of Illarionov have had no effect on Putin's popularity, which according to the latest polls hovers between 70 and 80 percent. This was also reflected in regional elections that took place in March 2007. Putin's *United Party* won about 60 percent of the seats in 14 regional assemblies. The *Communist Party* came second with 12.5 percent. *Just Russia*, the second pro-government party formed late in 2006 through the merger of the *Party of Life, Motherland,* and the *Party of Pensioners*, came in third with 12 percent. The other party to make a significant showing was Vladimir Zhirinovsky's *Liberal Democrats*, which took about 5 percent.

New Duma elections, which are scheduled for December 2007, will take place under a pure proportional representation system. All candidates will run on a party list, and the individual party will have to win a minimum of 7 percent of the national vote in order for any of its candidates to win a seat in the Duma. Moreover, parties are barred from forming coalitions to get over the 7 percent minimum vote requirement. The outcome is expected to be similar to that of the 2007 regional elections.

President Putin's second term will be coming to an end in March 2008, and the government has already begun preparing for that eventuality as well. It is expected that Putin will, at some point, designate an intended successor. The current front-runners are Dmitry Medvedev and Sergei Ivanov. Both are first deputy prime ministers in the current government. Medvedev, who holds the social portfolio in the cabinet, is also the chairman of Gazprom, the massive, state-controlled gas giant. Ivanov has a military background; he was defense minister until last year, when he was made a first deputy prime minister. The political opposition is talking about a united opposition presidential candidate. Names that have been mentioned include Mikhail Kasyanov, *Yabloko* leader Grigory Yavlinsky, State Duma Deputy Vladimir Ryzhkov and *United Civic Front* leader Garry Kasparov. The *Communist Party* may also field a candidate, and Vladimir Zhirinovsky may run again as the candidate of the *Liberal Democrats*. The odds heavily favor the Putin-designated government candidate.

Foreign Policy

After independence, the various ex–Soviet republics agreed to honor the various arms agreements signed by the now defunct Soviet Union. President Yeltsin, who took control of the Soviet Union's nuclear missiles after Gorbachëv resigned, ordered that ICBMs be targeted away from American cities.

In his State of the Union speech in January 1992, President Bush proposed that the USA and the former republics of the Soviet Union eliminate all multiple–warhead missiles and reduce the number of permitted nuclear warheads to 4,500. President Yeltsin countered with an offer to end production of all new nuclear warheads and reduce the total number of long–range warheads to 2,500 on each side. In a speech at the United Nations a few days later, he suggested that the USA and Russia jointly construct a global anti–missile shield. In that same speech, Yeltsin proclaimed that he considered "the United States and the West not as mere partners but as allies."

This major change in foreign policy probably came about because Yeltsin recognized that the collapse of the Soviet Union threatened the unified Soviet armed forces, and might make them vulnerable to attack. Since that time, most of the republics have indeed opted for separate armed forces. In most cases, the new armed forces are only lightly armed and there is a real question whether they would be able to defend their borders if attacked. In 1992, however, the Russian Government was probably thinking about its long border with the People's Republic of China and so wanted the assurance of American and Western support should such a threat arise.

The United States Government also announced in early 1992 that the Peace Corps would begin operating in the area of the former Soviet Union. Peace Corpsmen were to be sent to Russia, Ukraine, Armenia and one Central Asian country. A separate program applied to the three Baltic republics. Those various programs are now in place.

Yeltsin paid an official visit to the United States in June 1992. The highlight was the signing of an agreement in principle setting a new limit of 3,000–3,500 nuclear warheads on each side. This agreement was then codified into the START–2 agreement, which the United States and Russia signed in Moscow in December 1992. START–2 remained in a state of limbo for the next three years, however, because of a problem with the Government of Ukraine over START–1. Although the United States and Russia had ratified

Secretary of State Rice in Moscow

START–1 and had begun implementing it, certain parts needed the cooperation of the Government of Ukraine. But the Ukrainian legislature refused to support implementation of the agreement, because, it was argued, there were no funds to commit to the cost of dismantling the nuclear missiles, estimated to cost at least $1.5 billion. The American Congress had already authorized $800 million to help defray the cost of dismantling nuclear missiles in the four ex–Soviet Republics that had them. Eventually the Ukrainian Government received a promise of an additional sum of money and then signed off on the agreement. With START–1 finally on its way, START–2 was ratified by the U.S. Congress in January 1966. President Yeltsin then committed himself to seek Russian ratification of START–2 by April of that year but, in fact, the Duma ratified the agreement in the spring of 2000 after new parliamentary elections in December 1999 had changed the composition of the Duma. Pushing ratification through the Duma was one of Vladimir Putin's first victories, and he accomplished it while still acting president.

Also during the Yeltsin visit in 1992, the U.S. and Russia worked out the broad outlines for an agreement for joint space flight beginning in 1993. Since then, a Russian cosmonaut participated in a U.S. shuttle flight in 1993 and a U.S. astronaut began a lengthy stay aboard the Russian space station *MIR* in March 1995. In January 1996, the U.S. Government announced that cooperation was continuing on a planned international space station. To facilitate cooperation and reduce Russian costs, NASA had agreed to add three space shuttle missions, two to ferry supplies to the existing space station Mir and one to place in orbit a Russian science module. These were nine such joint missions through 1998. With the space station completed and having received its first occupants, Mir was allowed to plunge to earth in a controlled descent in early 2001.

Another area of Russian–American cooperation until recently was that of ex–Yugoslavia. Russia originally supported sanctions against Serbia after war broke out in Bosnia, then adopted a rather ambivalent policy, sometimes refusing to support further actions against the Serbs. On the other hand, Russia played an important role in getting the Serbs to withdraw from the vicinity of Sarajevo in the spring of 1994 and it supported the effort that led to the agreement on Bosnia in December 1995. In addition, the Russian troops sent to Bosnia as a part of the implementation force take their operational orders from the American general who is the senior NATO military commander in Europe. The quirk is that the Russian troops come under his operational command as part of the American forces serving under him, not in his role as NATO commander.

Russia's relations with Japan remain somewhat cool. The issue between the two countries remains the four islands taken by the Soviet Union at the end of World War II which Japan insists on getting back.

An important part of Russia's foreign policy is concerned with that area which they refer to as the "near abroad," a term they apply to the ex–Soviet republics other than the three Baltic nations. Russia had negotiated individual agreements with a number of republics, but it became clear in 1993 that the Russian Government's policy toward these republics had changed. Essentially, Russia began placing its emphasis on the Commonwealth of Independent States, demanding that relations between the various republics take place within that context. Since that time, Georgia has joined the CIS, Azerbaijan has reactivated its membership, and a number of general agreements have been negotiated dealing with a customs union, currencies, and military assistance. A number of the ex–Soviet republics, in particular Kazakstan and Belarus, but most of the Central Asian republics as well, favor a much closer working relationship with Russia. These republics actively participate in the CIS's Inter–governmental Assembly and have also signed agreements establishing an economic union, a payments union, a customs union and CIS peacekeeping forces. Russia has always favored the CIS because it provided, in the Russian view, a framework for Russia's relations with the "near abroad."

Several of Russia's actions over the past two years suggest that that attitude is changing, partly because of the color revolutions that took place in Georgia in 2003 and Ukraine in 2004, plus a continuing disagreement that Russia has with Moldova over Russia's support for the breakaway area of Moldova east of the Dniestr River.

Until recently, Russia offered special economic concessions to the countries of the near abroad, in particular providing energy at or near the price inside Russia. But in December 2005, Gazprom, the government-controlled Russian natural gas company, informed the governments of Georgia, Ukraine, and Moldova that they would have to pay world market prices in 2006. Shortly afterwards, the Russian Government banned the importation of wines from Georgia and Moldova. Russia also instituted a visa requirement for Georgians entering Russia, though it specifically exempted residents from the breakaway regions of Abkhazia and South Ossetia from this requirement. Russia has since ended its ban on Moldovan wines and fresh fruits and vegetables and it announced in May 2007 that it would begin issuing visas to Georgian citizens again. It has not reversed his position on natural gas prices, however, and has, in fact, enlarged the policy by extending it to Belarus.

It should be emphasized that Russia will always have an independent foreign policy that sometimes puts it into competition with the United States on specific foreign policy issues. For instance, Russia objected to American threats to launch retaliatory bomb attacks against Iraq after Saddam Hussein blocked United Nations inspections. It also supported the Kofi Annan mission to Iraq, which defused the situation, and promised to act as an advocate for Iraq in the future. Russia's "pro-Iraq" position is understandable if one recalls that it was owed several billions dollars by Iraq and wanted to be repaid.

A second illustrative case relates to Serbia's actions in its province of Kosovo in the 1990s. The United States threatened additional sanctions against Serbia after Serbian paramilitary units carried out attacks on Kosovan villages in an effort to put down an independence movement in the province. Russia condemned the killings of Kosovan villagers, but opposed additional sanctions. Here Russia's position is explained by the cultural connection arising from the fact that both countries are Slavic and Orthodox.

In 1998, NATO launched a new attempt to get Serbia to grant the Kosovans renewed autonomy. It achieved agreement on a ceasefire in Kosovo in November, but outbreaks of violence began to grow again in early 1999. NATO then sponsored new peace talks in France, which included a demand that Serbia restore autonomy to Kosova. Serbia grudgingly agreed, but it was not willing to permit the stationing of NATO troops there to enforce the agreement. When NATO launched air strikes

Russia

against ex–Yugoslavia in March 1999, Russia threw its support to the Serbs and temporarily withdrew its representatives from NATO. After the fighting was over, however, Russia joined in sending troops to Kosovo and subsequently reestablished its contacts with NATO.

Russia still tends to support Serbia, however. The Russian Government has consistently opposed granting Kosovo during current United Nations discussions about the future of Kosovo.

President Putin placed his major emphasis on domestic problems during his first year or so in office, so little changed in the international arena. There were, however, internal discussions between various factions about the direction of Russian foreign policy, with the left and the nationalists pushing for reinvigoration of relations with old allies, while the more centrist and liberal parties urged greater engagement with the West. All of this changed almost completely after the terror attacks of September 11 against the United States and the subsequent American-led international campaign against terrorism.

This was largely President Putin's doing, for he quickly condemned the attacks and offered his government's fullest cooperation in Washington's war against terrorism. Putin set forth the position of the Russian Government in a speech given on September 24. "Russia," he said:

is supplying and intends to continue to supply all the information we have about the infrastructure and the location of international terrorists and their training bases. Second, we are ready to offer Russian airspace for airplanes with humanitarian aid for the region where the antiterrorist action will be carried out. Third, we have agreed on this position with our allies, including Central Asian states.

There was a great groundswell of sympathy for the United States among ordinary Russians after the attacks of September 11, so Putin's strong support for America's war against terrorism was well received at home. But it was also true, as the Putin administration pointed out, that Russia and the states of Central Asia had been struggling with terrorism launched by radical Islamists for a number of years, and the United States-led campaign would give a strong boost to that endeavor.

However, the government did come in for a lot of criticism in October when it announced that it intended to dismantle its electronic espionage center in Lourdes, Cuba, and close its naval base at Cam Ranh Bay, Vietnam. Mainly, the government was taken to task for voluntarily giving up a major source of intelligence

on the United States as part of a shift to a pro-U.S. point of view, presumably in connection with Russian support for the international war on terrorism. As the Russian Government was careful to point out, however, the decisions to close Lourdes and Cam Ranh Bay had been taken prior to September 11 and reflected a determination that these bases were no longer worth the money they cost to maintain.

Putin's strong support for the war against terrorism greatly improved relations between Russia and the United States. It also brought him an invitation to visit United States in November 2001. The several-day visit cemented a relationship between the two presidents, though the wide-ranging discussions highlighted differences between the two nations even as they resolved some of them.

President Bush announced, for example, that the United States would reduce its nuclear arsenal of strategic warheads from 7,000 to between 1,700 and 2,200 within ten years. Putin, in turn, advocated a mutual reduction to 1,500 warheads. President Bush originally preferred unilateral reductions by the two nations, but eventually he gave in when President Putin expressed a strong wish for a mutual agreement. START-3 negotiations in Geneva subsequently produced an agreed text which was initiated by Presidents Putin and Bush during the latter's visit to Moscow in May 2002. The final agreed text was extremely short. Article I, the operative clause, reads:

Each Party shall reduce and limit strategic nuclear warheads, as stated by the President of the United States of America on Novem-

ber 13, 2001 and as stated by the President of the Russian Federation on December 13, 2001 respectively, so that by December 31, 2012 the aggregate number of such warheads does not exceed 1700–2200 for each Party. Each Party shall determine for itself the composition and structure of its strategic offensive arms, based on the established aggregate limit for the number of such warheads.

The Bush administration's desire to build an anti-missile shield led to negotiations between the two nations in the summer and fall of 2001. Since the ABM treaty they had signed in 1972 banned any such defensive shield, the United States proposed revising the AMB treaty to permit work on such a missile shield. When negotiations made it clear that Russia opposed any change this major, however, the United States formally withdrew from the treaty. Though Russia had wanted to keep the treaty intact, the withdrawal was accepted calmly; as Prime Minister Kasyanov expressed it, "although we favor preservation of the treaty, U.S. withdrawal from it would pose no threat to Russian national security."

Russia's strong support for the war on terrorism raised the issue of its relationship to NATO in such a way that Russia could participate fully in formulating common policies on such subjects as terrorism and weapons proliferation. It was decided to replace the Joint Permanent Council, established in 1997 as a vehicle for Russian cooperation with NATO, with a new NATO-Russia Council where Russia would, in some respects, have rights equal to NATO's 19 member nations. The details were approved on May 28 at a Russia-

President Bush in Moscow

NATO summit meeting near Rome. In theory, the new organization allows for the full participation of Russia in the formulation of common policies outside the core mission of NATO.

War in Iraq 2003

An area of great concern and difference of opinion between Russia and the United States is the policy with regard to Iraq. Russia has a long history of close relations with Iraq going back to the time when the Soviet Union was a major source of military equipment for Iraq. One legacy of that relationship is the multibillion dollar debt owed by Iraq to Russia. More recently, a Russian consortium negotiated multibillion dollar contracts with the Iraqi Government to develop an oil field in southern Iraq. As late as September 2002, in fact, the Russian Government announced a proposed long–term trade agreement between the two countries that was estimated to be worth $40 billion. The Russian Government thus had a strong economic incentive to maintain good relations with the Iraq regime.

When the United States proposed a UN Security Council resolution to force Iraq to disarm or face military action, the Russian Government took the position that it would support requiring Iraq to allow UN weapons inspectors to resume their work, but would oppose any explicit endorsement of military action. UN Security Council Resolution 1441 was essentially drafted along those lines and it passed in November with Russia's full support.

Three months later, the United States began advocating for additional measures to be taken after it had become convinced that the Iraqis were not cooperating with the UN weapons inspectors. But Russia reacted to the argument by joining the French and German Governments in a statement supporting a continuation of the UN weapons inspection process.

A week later, President Putin explained the rationale for the Russian position. "The international community cannot interfere with the domestic affairs of any country in order to change its regime," he said, adding that "the only legitimate goal the United Nations can pursue in this situation is the disarmament of Iraq."

Russia condemned the invasion of Iraq in March 2003, and continued to oppose the war as major resistance continued. As the Iraqi regime collapsed, however, the Russian Government softened its position.

When Condoleezza Rice, the U.S. national security adviser, went to Moscow on April 7, it was clear that both sides were working to repair the frayed relationship. As President Putin said on April 11, "nobody liked the regime of Saddam Hussein, except Hussein himself."

Yet it should be pointed out that President Putin's statement was made during a joint press conference with French President Chirac and German Chancellor Schroeder and that President Putin also endorsed the French–German position that the administration of Iraq should be under the aegis of the United Nations rather than of the U.S.–led coalition.

The question of the United Nations role in post–war Iraq was resolved in May when the UN Security Council reworked, then passed, a draft resolution proposed by the United States and Britain. The resolution, which brought 13 years of Iraqi sanctions to an end, essentially recognized the U.S.–British role as occupiers and rulers of Iraq until such time as Iraq has an elected government of its own. In a gesture to Russia and France, both of whom have big contracts under the previous oil–for–food program, the resolution specified that the sanctions regime would be phased out over a period of six months, during which old contracts would continue to be honored.

The question of who should be responsible for the administration of Iraq until such time as it has its own reconstituted government was resolved by instructing the UN Secretary General to send a "special representative" to Iraq whose "independent responsibilities" would include, first, coordinating, promoting, and facilitating Iraq's reconstruction and, second, facilitating the "process leading to an internationally recognized, representative government." This gave a role for the United Nations in Iraq, a position already endorsed by the United States and Britain, while making it clear at the same time that the ultimate authority would rest with the occupying powers, the USA and Britain. In the end, Russia supported this formulation, as did France and Germany.

President Bush had been long scheduled to pay an official visit to Russia in June to participate in the 300th anniversary celebrations of the founding of St. Petersburg. To smooth the path for the visit, President Putin dispatched Defense Minister Sergei Ivanov to Washington on May 21 with a message stressing Putin's view that Russian–American cooperation benefited the entire world by enhancing global stability and security and expressing his further wish that the Bush visit to St. Petersburg would move forth the bilateral dialogue between the two countries. Back home, Putin also persuaded the Duma to ratify the arms reduction treaty signed by Bush and Putin a year earlier which pledges the two sides to reduce their nuclear arsenals by two–thirds over the next ten years.

In the end, the Bush visit went off smoothly, the one remaining issue of dis-

agreement being Russia's sales of nuclear technology to Iran. While President Putin defended the sales to Iran, he also stated his own opposition to Iran's obtaining nuclear weapons. Since that time, Russia has offered to enrich nuclear fuel inside Russia for Iran—-an offer Iran has spurned. In the end, Russia supported a United Nations Security Council resolution threatening Iran with sanctions unless it agreed to give up nuclear fuel reprocessing. Russia has also suspended sales of processed uranium fuel to Iran.

Russia's position with regard to North Korea nuclear program is similar. Russia has been participating in six nation talks on the issue, but it is unwilling to support more stringent actions against North Korea.

But even as the United States has found itself at odds with Russia on several issues over the past couple years, the two nations have continued to cooperate against the threat of terrorism, and this has kept relations at a sort of even pitch. President Bush's official visit to Russia in May 2005 to mark the 60th anniversary of the end of World War II in Europe also helped to create positive atmospherics. President Bush went to Moscow again in August 2006 to attend a meeting of the G-8 Countries, hosted that year by Russia.

Currently, three issues divide the United States and Russia. Two of these issues are long-standing: Iran and Kosovo. The third issue is the American plan to deploy missile defense systems in Eastern Europe. Related to that, Russia recently suspended its implementation of the 1998 revisions to the Conventional Forces in Europe treaty. These issues are likely to be some of the major topics discussed when the G-8 summit takes place in Germany in June.

Russia

A presidential bodyguard salutes Russian President Boris Yeltsin and Italian President Francesco Cossiga at the Quirinale Presidential Palace on December 19, 1991.

Reuters/Bettmann

Government of the Russian Federation

Under the new constitution approved in December 1993, Russia is a federation with a division of powers between the central government and the local governments. The federal government is delegated certain exclusive powers. Those powers which can be exercised concurrently by the federal government and the member units are specifically enumerated. The constitution then stipulates that the member units may exercise powers not mentioned in the constitution. The constitution thus achieved Yeltsin's intention to devolve considerable authority on the republics and regions.

The President of the Russian Federation, directly elected by popular vote, is the head of state and the guarantor of the constitution. He is commander–in–chief of the armed forces. He conducts foreign policy and provides the general guidelines for domestic policy. He also has wide powers of appointment. In addition to the prime minister (technically, chairman of the Government of the Russian Federation), he appoints and dismisses members of the cabinet, judges, the Prosecutor– General of the Russian Federation, top commanders of the armed forces and diplomatic representatives. He has the power to call elections and dissolve the State Duma (as specified in the constitution), submit bills to the State Duma, and sign federal laws. He decides questions of Russian citizenship and may grant political asylum.

The prime minister proposes the members of his cabinet to the president and pre-

sides over meetings of his cabinet. Neither the prime minister nor members of his cabinet may be members of the State Duma. In case of a vote of no confidence in the prime minister, the president decides whether to dismiss the government or dissolve the State Duma and call for new elections.

The Court System

The new constitution creates a court system modeled on western democracies. There is a Constitutional Court which reviews laws when requested to do so by the President of the Federation, the Supreme Court of the Russian Federation, the Supreme Arbitration Court of the Russian Federation and local legislative and executive bodies. The Constitutional Court will also accept original jurisdiction over cases of individuals who feel that their constitutional rights and freedoms have been violated.

What is Being Changed

One of the first things that Lenin did after coming to power in 1917 was to abolish the old Russian court system and create new people's courts staffed by communists and other revolutionaries. The Russian court system, created by Alexander II in the 1860s, was modeled on western judicial practices. It incorporated the concept of "equal justice under the law" and included an independent judiciary, trial by jury, public trials, and defense attorneys.

The Soviet court system was specifically created to defend the revolution. Judges

and prosecutors were required to be members of the *Communist Party* and to be loyal implementers of the party line. Trials by jury were abolished. Guilt or innocence was determined by a judge, assisted by two ordinary citizens who were referred to as lay assessors. Their function was to support the prosecution. Defense attorneys existed, though their role differed from that of attorneys in western countries. With no presumption of innocence, a long legal tradition developed against an acquittal–oriented defense. The function of the defense attorney was therefore to negotiate for the most lenient sentence rather than to get the client off. This was reinforced by the fact that, under the law, defense attorneys had a lesser status than representatives of the state. Acquittals were almost unknown.

Attitudes toward the law began to change after Gorbachëv came to power in 1985, particularly after he endorsed the concept of a "nation of laws." The first practical manifestation of this changed thinking came in December 1989, when a law on judicial procedure went into effect giving individual republics the authority to increase the number of lay assessors on the bench. This was viewed by some as a move toward creation of a jury system. Defense attorneys were also permitted to establish a national Union of Advocates and the number of acquittals began growing slightly.

Gorbachëv's main goal was to free the legal system from outside political interference. He wanted to create courts where fairness and objectivity were the rule and cases were decided exclusively on the basis of evidence presented in court. He made some progress, but most of the authoritarian system originally created in the 1920s and 1930s continued to exist even after his reforms.

The repudiation of communism and the emergence of an independent Russian Government created a new situation, however. Moscow was full of talk about reforming the entire legal system in 1992–93, but the quarrel between President Yeltsin and the Russian Supreme Soviet meant that little was resolved.

All of this began to change in December 1993 when a new Russian constitution was approved which made major modifications in the legal system. Under Article 120, judges are "independent and subject only to the Constitution of the Russian Federation and federal law." Article 121 makes them irremovable, while article 122 guarantees their inviolability. Article 123 reintroduced the concept of trial by jury. In addition, Chapter 2 of the constitution contains numerous individual legal rights, including "the right to have a case heard by a court with the participation of jurors in the cases provided for by federal law (Art. 47);" the right to receive qualified legal assistance (Art. 48); presumption of innocence (Art. 49); guarantees against double jeopardy (Art 50); and protection against self–incrimination (Art. 51).

The problem was that most of the changes and new rights required implementing legislation by the Duma before they took effect. In the case of trials by jury, the Duma authorized implementation on an experimental basis in nine of the 89 regional courts beginning in December 1993. In the first eight months of 1994, something over 5,000 trials were held in regional courts; of that number, 99 were trials by jury. The experiment continued, however, and, in July 2002, the Duma adopted a new legal code governing the prosecution of criminal cases which, among other things, authorized trials by jury throughout Russia beginning in January 2003. In addition, the new legal code guarantees habeas corpus (i.e., anyone accused of a crime must appear in court within 48 hours) and the presumption of innocence. It also changes the role of the judge to that of a neutral arbitrator, and authorizes defense lawyers to challenge the admissibility of evidence. Thus far, jury trials have been resumed formally in 61 Russian regions, but they will presumably be instituted in the remaining 28 regions in the near future. Separately, the Constitutional Court ruled in July 2002 that a former procedure that allowed prosecutors or courts to overturn acquittals or to increase sentences on appeal was unconstitutional.

In related developments, a new Arbitration Procedure Code came into force on July 29, 2002 which broadened the sphere of competence of arbitration courts and established a procedure for transferring cases to them from courts of general jurisdiction. In addition, a new Civil Procedure Code went into effect in February 2003 which establishes new procedures for settling civil disputes such as those in the workplace and among family members. Together, these new codes complete the transformation from the judicial system set up under communism. As Justice Minister Yurii Chaika expressed it,

with the introduction of the new Criminal Procedures Code, the Civil Procedures Code, and the Arbitration Procedures Code, the role of the legal profession in defending the rights, freedoms, and interests of citizens has radically changed and immeasurably grown.

Yet a series of reports coming out of Russia in 2005 make it clear that Justice Minister Chaika was wildly optimistic about the effect of the new laws on the actual operation of the legal system. As an October 2005 report by Peter Finn, reporter for *The Washington Post*, put it, "the jury system remains the object of suspicion, even contempt, among prosecutors and some judges in Russia." Finn points out that, under Russian law, prosecutors can appeal verdicts

Midnight, with the Russian tri–color floating over the Kremlin after 74 years. St. Basil's Church is in the foreground.   Courtesy: NOVOSTI

Russia

and almost all not-guilty jury verdicts are appealed. He then gave the example of a defendant who had been found non-guilty by three separate juries and then quoted the leader prosecutor in the third trial as saying afterwards: "He's guilty. We cannot leave an unlawful verdict in force."

The Supreme Court, which has the prerogative to propose legislation, called for a law restricting jury trials to murder cases. The Supreme Court's proposal was made in the fall of 2005. At about the same time, the Russian Department of Justice proposed legislation aimed at bringing defense attorneys under the control of the state. One part of its proposed legislation would give the state the right to demand "information which the lawyers obtain while providing legal assistance to their clients;" a second part would bring the self-governing bar under state control by giving the state "direct control, as well as control via its territorial branches, over the activities of lawyers, law firms, and bar associations. Neither of these proposed laws has been enacted yet, but they illustrate the hostility of many in the government to recent judicial reforms.

Criminality in the Russian Federation

Over the past few years, American newspapers have been full of stories about rising crime in Russia and the private security forces that have become necessary to cope with it. Many journalists seem to be at a loss to explain this new phenomenon, though they clearly tie it to the economic transformation currently underway there. There is no question but that crime has been increasing in Russia over the past several years. On the other hand, it should be remembered that the Soviet Union never permitted any reporting on crime until the last years of the Gorbachëv regime and the very existence of adequate reporting creates an image of a greater increase in crime than has been the case. Moscow is still, for most people, one of the safer cities of the world.

Another problem is that the police had been until recently responsible for suppressing the very sort of "economic crimes" which now constitute the emerging market system. Since many of those who arrested such "criminals" remain on the police force, it should not be surprising that they have been less than vigorous in enforcing the new legality.

A more serious problem is that corruption became endemic in the last years of the Brezhnev Era with many officials taking bribes to overlook black market activity. Payoffs became an important way to supplement salaries and the corruption reached high into the government and party. The minister of the interior, Shelokov, and his deputy, Chubanov, who

also happened to be the son–in–law of Brezhnev, were eventually accused of illegal transactions. Shelokov committed suicide before being brought to trial, but Chubanov was found guilty and sentenced to several years in prison. But the corruption was too pervasive for the arrests of these top people to put a stop to it. When, with the fall of communism, private economic activity became legal, many of these officials and ex–officials continued to demand protection money from the new capitalists in much the same way they had milked black marketeers earlier. For example, *Izvestia* reported on May 6, 1994 that a group of senior ministry of interior officials had been charged with operating a protection ring for well–connected gangsters (i.e. ex–black marketeers) which included intervening to help killers, kidnappers and thieves stay out of jail.

As a result of widespread police corruption or even, in some cases, antipathy to developing capitalism, most businessmen have felt that they could not depend on the police for protection. This spawned a whole new industry, private security companies, most of them started by retired Soviet soldiers, former members of *spetsnaz*, i.e., special interior ministry troops, or ex–policemen. The size of these security forces is sometimes enormous. Moreover, foreign businessmen wanting to establish a presence in Moscow have often found that one of the first things they had to deal with was the matter of security. One such American businessman reported that he had been accosted by five men with pistols and a print–out of his firm's worth. They demanded 7 percent of future earnings. In this case, the businessman took the first flight back to New York. In the late 1990s, it was estimated that three–fourth of all private firms were paying 10 percent or more of their earnings in protection money.

According to two recent reports out of Russia, the situation has improved little or not at all since that time. In May 2002, a two–year study of corruption by the INDEM think tank concluded that Russians pay about $37 billion each year in bribes and unoffial fees, a sum equal to 12 percent of the Russian GDP. About 90 percent of the bribes are paid by businesses, with roughly 75 percent going to low–level local officials. In February 2003, Mikhail Khodorkovskii, head of Yukos, one of Russia's larger oil companies, told President Putin that corruption costs Russia up to $30 billion annually and he gave an example of the sort of dislocations it causes. The prestigious Moscow Gubkin Oil Institute has only two applicants for each opening, even though the average starting salary for graduates is about $500 a month. At the same time, there are four or five applicants

for each slot at the state tax academies, even though starting salaries for their graduates range from $150–$200. His point was that graduates of the state tax academies expect to more than make up the salary difference through bribes. This is obviously a heavy tax on the new market system.

A number of Russian legislators, journalists and businessmen were killed in the period 1992–95, but the killing that brought the public to a frenzy of rage was that of Vladislav Listyev, the head of Russia's public television network, gunned down in his apartment stairwell on March 1, 1995. In the resulting political firestorm, President Yeltsin himself went on television to express his sorrow at the killing and to apologize for allowing crime to spiral out of control. In the end, of course, the things that President Yeltsin could do about crime were all long term.

Although rising crime has been, in part, a symptom of the disruptions and discontinuities arising out of Russia's transformation from a command system to a market economy, another factor was that, until recently, there was no pro–reform majority willing to pass legislation establishing clear and easily enforceable property rights in the Duma. That changed with the election of the current Duma in December 1999 but, even so, the Duma did not get around to passing a land code permitting the sale of non–agricultural land—thus making possible a resolution of who owns the land on which privatized enterprises and buildings are located—until March 2001. The Duma finally got around to passing legislation governing the sale of agricultural land in 2002, and it went into effect on January 27, 2003. Yet it will probably be years before any significant amount of land is sold, since most regions have neither land registers nor land–quality surveys. According to Ivan Starikov, chairman of the Federation Council Agricultural Policy Committee, not one region has yet adopted the corresponding local legislative acts required for the law to begin to operate.

**Hon. Yuri M. Luzhkov,
Mayor of Moscow**

The New Constitution

Article 1

1. The Russian Federation—Russia shall be a democratic, federative, law-based state with a republican form of government.

Article 3

1. The multi-ethnic people of the Russian Federation shall be the bearers of its sovereignty and the sole source of authority in the Russian Federation.

Article 5

1. The Russian Federation shall be made up of republics, territories, regions, cities with federal status, the autonomous region and autonomous areas, all of which are equal members of the Russian Federation.

Article 8

1. A unified economic space, the free movement of commodities, services and finances, and support for competition and freedom of economic activity shall be guaranteed in the Russian Federation.

2. Private, state, municipal and other forms of property shall be equally recognized and protected in the Russian Federation.

Article 12

Local self-government shall be recognized and guaranteed in the Russian Federation. Local self-government shall be independent within the limits of its powers. The bodies of local self-government shall not be part of the system of the bodies of state authority.

Article 13

1. Ideological pluralism shall be recognized in the Russian Federation.

2. No ideology shall be established as a state or compulsary ideology.

Article 15

4. Universally acknowledged principles and standards of international law and international treaties of the Russian Federation shall be a part of its legal system. Should an international treaty of the Russian Federation establish rules other than those established by law, the rules of the international treaty shall be applied.

Article 27

1. Each person who is legitimately within the territory of the Russian Federation shall have the right to move freely and to choose where to live temporarily or permanently.

Article 35

1. The right of private ownership shall be protected by law.

Article 38

3. Able-bodied children who have reached the age of eighteen years shall take care of parents who are unable to work.

Article 40

1. Each person shall have the right to housing. No person may be arbitrarily deprived of housing.

Article 41

1. Each person shall have the right to health protection and medical assistance.

Article 43

3. Each person shall be entitled on a competitive basis and free of charge to receive a higher education in a state or municipal educational institution or at an enterprise.

Article 47

1. 2. A person accused of committing a crime shall have the right to have a case heard by a court with the participation of jurors in the cases provided for by federal law.

Article 49

1. Each person accused of committing a crime shall be presumed innocent until his/her culpability is proved in the manner specified by federal law and established by a court sentence which has become effective.

2. Defendants shall not be obliged to prove their innocence.

Article 59

3. In cases where the performance of military service runs counter to a citizen's persuasions of religion, and also in other cases specified by federal law, a citizen of the Russian Federation shall have the right to replace military service with alternative civilian service.

Article 81

1. The President of the Russian Federation shall be elected to office for a term of four years by the citizens of the Russian Federation on the basis of universal, direct and equal suffrage by secret ballot.

3. The same individual shall not be elected to the office of President of the Russian Federation for more than two consecutive terms.

Article 83

The President of the Russian Federation shall:

a) appoint, with the consent of the State Duma, the Chairman of the Government of the Russian Federation;

b) be entitled to preside over sessions of the Government of the Russian Federation;

d) nominate for approval by the State Duma the Chairman of the Central Bank of the Russian Federation and bring before the State Duma the issue of removing the Chairman of the Central Bank of the Russian Federation from office;

f) nominate judges to the Constitutional Court, Supreme Court and Court of Arbitration of the Russian Federation and the Prosecutor-General of the Russian Federation; and appoint judges to other federal courts;

g) organize and chair the Security Council of the Russian Federation, the status of which shall be defined by federal legislation;

k) appoint and dismiss the top commanders of the Armed Forces of the Russian Federation;

Article 86

1. The President of the Russian Federation shall:

a) be in charge of the foreign policy of the Russian Federation;

Article 87

1. The President of the Russian Federation shall be Commander-in-Chief of the Armed Forces of the Russian Federation.

Article 90

1. The President of the Russian Federation shall issue decrees and directives.

2. Decrees and directives of the President of the Russian Federation shall be binding for execution throughout the territory of the Russian Federation.

Article 95

1. The Federal Assembly shall consist of two houses—a Federal Council and a State Duma.

Article 103

1. The State Duma shall have the power:

a) to approve the nominee of the President of the Russian Federation to the office of the Chairman of the Government of the Russian Federation;

c) to appoint the Chairman of the Central Bank of the Russian Federation and to remove him from office;

f) to declare amnesty;

g) to lodge accusations against the President of the Russian Federation for the purpose of removing him from office by impeachment;

Article 105

1. The federal laws shall be adopted by the State Duma.

3. The federal laws adopted by the State Duma shall be submitted for consideration by the Federation Council within a period of five days.

5. In case of the disagreement of the State Duma with the decision of the Federation Council, a federal law shall be considered adopted if in the repeat voting at least two-thirds of the total number of the State Duma deputies have voted for it.

Article 117

3. The State Duma may give the government of the Russian Federation a vote of no confidence . . . by majority vote of the total number of the State Duma deputies. . . The President of the Russian Federation may announce the resignation of the government of the Russian Federation or reject the decision of the State Duma. If within the next three months the State Duma again gives the government a vote of no confidence, the President of the Russian Federation shall announce the resignation of the government of the Russian Federation or dissolve the State Duma.

Article 120

1. Judges shall be independent and subject only to the Constitution of the Russian Federation and federal law.

Article 121

1. Judges shall be irremovable.

Article 123

4. Judicial proceedings shall be conducted with the participation of a jury in cases provided for by federal law.

Article 132

1. The bodies of local self-government shall independently manage municipal property; prepare, approve and execute the local budget; establish local taxes and levies; maintain public order; and decide other questions of local importance.

Russia

The grand staircase in the Winter Palace (now part of the Hermitage Museum in St. Petersburg.) In 1732 Tsarina Anna commanded Italian architect Bartolomeo Rastrelli to build a four–storied Winter Palace of extravagant design and furnishings; it was built during the reign of Tsarina Elizabeth (1741–62).

Photo by Miller B. Spangler

Culture

The failure of the August 1991 *coup* led to the repudiation of communism and the subsequent collapse of the Soviet Union, thereby giving birth to an independent Russian Federation committed to the goals of pluralism, democracy, privatization and a market economy. These events marked the end of an era of official culture, but seventy years of sloganistic indoctrination of the people with the philosophy of Marxism–Leninism cannot be overcome overnight. Proletarianism and socialism remain defining ideas for many people, and even terms like "socialist realism" have their supporters among conservatives. The old ideas live on, particularly among the old, among the peasants of the countryside, and among all segments of the population in the old industrial towns.

The greatest transformation has occurred in St. Petersburg and Moscow. Even in large cities, however, change is often resisted. In St. Petersburg, for example, the Kirov Ballet, which resumed the name of Marinsky in 1992, as it was known prior to the revolution, is once again known as the Kirov Ballet, though it has retained the name Marinsky for the theater. Even today, the battle continues over just how commercial the new Kirov needs to become to survive as a great ballet company.

That probably should not be surprising. Throughout the Soviet era, at least two other cultures co–existed with the official version of Soviet culture. The first of these was pre–revolutionary Russian culture; the second was non–official culture. To these must be added religious culture, which survived in spite of official disparagement by the state, and today again

flourishes. The meaning of the repudiation of communism is that these cultures have, once again, assumed their traditional role in defining Russian culture; now it is Soviet culture that is tolerated and lingers on.

How much of Soviet culture will persist? Some "proletarian" authors and artists will undoubtedly continue to write or paint, although the Russian people have very little taste for political art after a steady diet of it for 70 years. But the fact is that there never was very much purely "Soviet" art and what there was of it was usually tied to specific political campaigns that became outdated. Such art has a historical interest, of course, but it was by definition not made to transcend the age in which it was produced, and so it now lacks artistic interest.

Some of the work by revolutionary artists and novelists in the 1920s was an

mired were mostly pre–revolutionary. In effect, except for elements considered anti–revolutionary, the regime appropriated Russian culture to itself. Thus poets like Alexander Pushkin and Michael Lermontov continued to be published throughout the Soviet period, along with short story writers like Nikolai Gogol, novelists like Ivan Turgenev, Fedor Dostoyevsky, Leo Tolstoy and Maxim Gorky, and playwrights such as Anton Chekhov.

Russian ballet, one of the "glories" of Soviet culture, continued to be dominated by classical French choreography. There were some experiments with modern dance after Stalin's death but, because they usually expressed revolutionary themes, they seldom rose to the level of art. Most Russian operas performed throughout the Soviet era were pre–revolutionary. All of this gave Russian culture the eerie aspect of being a museum of the past.

Things did get better after Stalin's death, but artists had been repressed so long by that time that very few of them were capable of great art. Still, some of these works are interesting for historical purposes. Ilya Ehrenburg's novel, *The Thaw*, is not a very good book, but everyone read it because of its message of hope. To a certain extent, this period of liberalization was associated with the personal fortunes of Nikita Khrushchëv. Although vocal in his own dislike for modern, especially abstract, painting, he encouraged writers who wrote works critical of the "distortions" of the Stalin era. He personally defended the book *Not By Bread Alone* by Vladimir Dudintsev. It was also he who authorized the publication of Alexander Solzhenitzyn's *A Day in the Life of Ivan Denisovich*.

Cultural controls were tightened again after Khrushchëv's departure. This produced a great outpouring of unofficial Soviet culture. Some painters had always found their art to be unacceptable to the regime, so they had to find ways of supporting themselves by other means. The number of individuals able to afford paintings increased considerably after the death of Stalin, however, so artists, though shut out of official exhibits, were able to find customers for their unofficial art.

The situation for writers was somewhat different. Unable to get works published, some resorted to circulating them in manuscript form. This was referred to in Russian as *samizdat*—literally, self–publication. Others, seeking a wider circulation, contrived to have a manuscript smuggled abroad, where it would be published, usually in translation. Having an unapproved manuscript published abroad was legally an anti–Soviet act, however, and a number of writers were imprisoned for this offense. Because of the Soviet

Russian artist in his St. Petersburg studio.

exception to this, but even that period had its darker aspects. Many artists, stifled in the new conformity, fled abroad. Others, like the poets Vladimir Maiakovsky and Sergei Yessenin, committed suicide.

The Association of Proletarian Writers was an annoyance in the late 1920s because of its intolerant attitude toward those who did not share its "proletarian" outlook, but that period appeared mild in retrospect after Stalin had instituted his authoritarian cultural controls and enforced his "socialist realism." Most of the great works of the 1920s were banned as unproletarian in the 1930s. These included the novels of Mikhail Bulgakov, author of *The Master and Margarita and Heart of a*

Dog, and the paintings of Andrei Malevich, who even in the 1920s had been forced to give up his earlier, abstract style.

Dmitri Shostakovich, the composer, and Sergei Eisenstein, the film producer, were two exceptions who managed to produce great works in the 1930s, but both of them came under criticism in the periods of the 1940s and either had to revise their works or couldn't get them released at all.

But the fact is that most "Soviet" culture was actually pre–Soviet culture. There never were that many revolutionary artists, and most of these eventually found themselves stifled by the regime's tight controls. So the great novels that people continued to read or the great artists that they ad-

Russia

Union's policy of "socialist realism," nearly every great work of Soviet literature written after 1930 had to be published abroad and almost every Soviet Nobel Prize winner for literature was labeled a dissident.

In the early 1970s, the Brezhnev regime added a refinement when it began expelling Soviet artists or stripping them of their citizenship while abroad. The most famous of those was Alexander Solzhenitsyn, expelled from the Soviet Union in 1974. A number of other artists who had been given permission to travel chose to live and work abroad. The pianist Vladimir Ashkenazy chose to live in England. The renowned cellist–conductor Mstislav Rostropovich and his talented wife settled in the United States. Several top ballet performers defected while touring abroad, while others, like the Panovs, emigrated after long delays in waiting for permission to leave Russia.

The beginning of the Gorbachëv era, with its emphasis on *glasnost*, widened the area of the permissible and brought the publication of previously banned works. Thus writings of Anna Akhmatova, Boris Pasternak, Alexander Solzhenitsyn, Mikhail Bulgakov, Vladimir Nabokov, Osip Mandelshtam and Marina Tsvetaeva were all published. A selection of Akhmatova's poems was put out by the journal *Oktyabr*. Moscow's Taganka Theater brought a play about Pasternak and his novel, *Dr. Zhivago*, to the Soviet stage, and the novel itself, for which Pasternak received the 1958 Nobel Prize for literature, was published beginning in January 1988 by the journal *Novy Mir*.

Another example of greater freedom for the arts under Gorbachëv was the new play by Mikhail Shatrov, *The Brest Peace*. Shatrov's play gives a detailed and fairly sympathetic treatment of Lev Trotsky and Nikolai Bukharin. Trotsky's name had been anathema in the USSR ever since his expulsion by Stalin in 1929; Bukharin was executed in 1938 as part of the Stalinist purges. What is perhaps most interesting about the play is that it was written in 1962, but the author had previously been unable to get it performed or published. Gorbachëv eventually put his personal stamp of approval on this new trend:

There should be no forgotten names or blanks. We must not forget names and it is all the more immoral to forget or pass over in silence large periods in the life of the people."

As Gorbachëv apparently intended, part of this new "openness" turned into an attack on Stalin. Thus a novel by Anatoly Rybakov published in 1986, *Children of the Arbat*, depicts Stalin as pathologically suspicious and politically obtuse. Like Sha-

Performance of the Kuban Cossack Choir in Kranodar   Courtesy: NOVOSTI

trov's play, *The Brest Peace*, Rybakov's novel was written in the 1960's but he was not able to get it published earlier.

New plays with similar themes also began to appear by 1988. The best known was another play by Mikhail Shatrov, entitled "On, On, On," which was published in the January 1988 issue of the literary monthly *Znamya*. A controversial play, it is full of suppressed details of Soviet history and is harshly anti–Stalinist. Interviewed about the play, Shatrov commented that

If you read my plays you will see that all of them are in essence about one thing: Stalin is not Lenin's heir. Stalin is a criminal of the kind the world has never had. He is not a Communist for me, because if he is a Communist, I have to leave the party immediately.

102

Many Soviet intellectuals who shared Shatrov's point of view began pressing the party for a total repudiation of Stalin and a rehabilitation of his victims. Gorbachëv was, in general, sympathetic but other members of the leadership, including Ligachëv, Chebrikov and Yazov, spoke out against what they termed the "one–sided" evaluation of Stalin. While willing to condemn such things as the 1930s purges, they argued that Stalin should be given credit for such things as industrialization and collectivization and the USSR's victory in World War II. In essence, their view of Stalin was that he was a good Communist who had made mistakes.

The resulting division led to a battle in the Soviet media in which Shatrov, in particular, was accused of "inaccuracies," "juggling with the facts," and "departure from the truth." What more conservative reformers like Ligachëv apparently feared is that excessive criticism of the past would weaken popular faith in the party. In the summer of 1990, after the final defeat of Ligachëv at the 28th Party Congress, Gorbachëv ended the controversy by issuing a decree rehabilitating Stalin's victims.

After 1990, artists were basically free to write or compose or paint what they wanted, free of party tutelage. Thus, with few exceptions, Gorbachëv had brought an end to the long period of official supervision of the arts by the cultural affairs section of the Communist Party. These last few exceptions ended in August 1991 with the failure of the *coup* to unseat Gorbachëv and reinstate a new orthodoxy. The complicity of the *Communist Party* in the *coup* led to its repudiation and Boris Yeltsin subsequently issued a decree in effect banning the party.

The collapse of the Soviet Union and the emergence of an independent Russian Federation with Boris Yeltsin as President marked the beginning of a new era in which Russian culture, free finally of all state controls, was free to develop as Russians wished it. This has already brought changes, not all of them laudable, to be sure. Culture now has to be much more "commercial," since it needs customers to survive. As some artists are beginning to recall with nostalgia, the old Soviet regime subsidized art as well as controlled it.

Perhaps that is why the government's attitude toward culture began to change soon after Vladimir Putin took over as president in 2000. Many changes occurred as a result in the change in political leadership, but the most important difference is that Putin reversed the "hands off" attitude that was so dominant a theme under Yeltsin and he began talking about the need to encourage patriotism. He also publicly endorsed creation of a youth organization modeled along the lines of the *Komsomols*, the communist youth organization of the Soviet Union. As another gesture in that direction, Putin authorized the use of the old Soviet flag by units of the military. Finally, he threw out the national anthem approved under Yeltsin—actually a piece of music written by Glinka—and replaced it with the music from the Soviet anthem approved under Stalin. A contest held to provide new words for the music was won by Sergei Mikhaikov, the 87–year old poet who co– authored the original anthem during World War II. The new words to the Russian (and old Soviet) anthem are as follows:

Russia our sacred state!
Russia, our beloved country!
A mighty will, a great glory
[are] your inheritance for all time!

[Refrain]
May you be glorious, our free Fatherland.
An eternal union of fraternal peoples.
Popular wisdom given by our forebears.
May you be glorious, country! We are proud of you!

From the southern seas to the polar region
Extend our forests and meadows.
You are unique on earth! You are the only such!
Native land protected by God.

Faithful Moslems gather for Friday prayer at the central mosque in Kazan, capital of the Tatar autonomous region on the Volga River.

Photo by Steve Raymer © 1991 National Geographic Society

Russia

A broad space for dreams and for living,
The years open up the future to us.
Our loyalty gives strength to the Father-
land.
Thus it was, thus it is and thus it will be
forever!

Religion in the Russian Federation

Religion had a peculiar status in the now defunct Soviet Union. There was an officially declared separation of church and state, and Soviet citizens had a constitutionally guaranteed freedom of worship. But communism, the ideology of the only legal political party, was militantly atheistic, so the constitution guaranteed the right of anti–religious propaganda as well. Official opposition to religion had its roots in the basic materialistic philosophy of Marxism, which held that spiritual matters were merely a reflection of material things and conditions. Karl Marx, in a famous phrase, stated that religion was being used by the ruling classes as an opiate, or drug, which dulled the ability of the masses to know their real problems and find the solution for them. Claiming to derive their views from scientific knowledge, communists saw themselves as secular and "this world" minded and opposed religion as "unscientific" and false. Since communists held that their value system represented "truth," they were extremely intolerant of all religious teachings, because of their competing claims to truth. In fact, communism had a comprehensive world outlook and set of beliefs which made it a sort of "religion" itself. It even promised paradise, though it was to be here on earth rather than in another world.

Communist theory held that communism represented a new "consciousness" on the part of mankind. To reach the stage of communism, therefore, it was necessary to "transform" the thinking of the people through a process of consciousness–raising or indoctrination. This process was to result in the emergence of a "new man," conditioned to living in a communist society.

Communists attached particular importance to the "educational" functions of the party. They were especially concerned with shaping the basic beliefs of the younger generation, since young people were still untainted with the corruptions of the previous system. Religious bodies, since they represented the values of the previous system, were forbidden to proselytize or to carry on any public functions other than the worship service itself. Churches, synagogues, and mosques were barred from all areas of education, including Sunday schools and catechism classes. Organized acts of charity were also forbidden and religious marriage ceremonies were banned. For a time, even the ringing of bells was forbidden.

His Holiness Patriarch Aleksiy of Moscow and All Russia

Beyond that, the regime tended to differentiate in its treatment of individual religions depending on the total number of adherents and the role accorded it in pre–revolutionary Russia. The Orthodox Church, to which most Russians, Ukrainians and Byelorussians belonged, had been one of the mainstays of the old system and a loyal tool of the tsarist governments. Moreover, the Orthodox Church adopted a strongly anti–Bolshevik position during the revolutionary upheaval of 1917 and the civil war that followed. Thus the Orthodox Church became a particular target. During the civil war, many members of the clergy, including the Patriarch, were arrested and quite a number were executed. All church buildings were nationalized and many were closed. In the 1920s, the party created an organization known as the *League of Militant Atheists* to carry on the battle against religion. Members of the league, lavishly supported by the regime, engaged in all sorts of anti–religious propaganda. One of the things they did was to turn Kazan Cathedral in St. Petersburg, a beautiful, neoclassical church built in the 18th century, into the Museum of Atheism.

Islam came under similar restrictions. Islam was considered to be even more dangerous than Christianity in some respects, since it recognized no distinction between the secular and the religious. In addition, the Muslim clergy were strong defenders of the traditional way of life, and so opposed most of what the communists were trying to do. Communists therefore did their best to stamp out Islam in Central Asia. Religious schools and mosques were closed and many of the Islamic clergy were imprisoned.

Nor did this cease after the regime had consolidated its power. In the 1930s, Stalin ordered churches, synagogues and

mosques closed all over the country and he had a number of Moscow's historic churches torn down as a part of his re-building of the center of the city. Most of the remainder were turned into museums or converted to other secular uses.

As conditions became stabilized in the late 1930s, the Stalin regime adopted a somewhat less militant position toward religion. A dramatic turn occurred after the German invasion of the country in June 1941. The *League of Militant Atheists* was dissolved and its printing facilities were actually turned over to the Russian Orthodox Church. Stalin had come to the conclusion that, in a crisis, the communist regime could make use of the support of the Church with its deep roots among the masses.

The regime tightened its control again after the end of the war, but this was mainly to guarantee that the church continued to serve the goals of the state. Internationally, members of the higher Orthodox clergy were frequently used as delegates to various international peace congresses. Domestically, the Patriarch and other members of the hierarchy were expected periodically to speak out in support of Soviet policy. The Islamic clergy, by this time tamed, was also used occasionally for diplomatic missions, mainly to the Middle East.

Even so, about 10,000 additional churches were closed between 1959 and 1964—about half the remaining total in the Soviet Union. In 1960, the Archbishop of Kazan was tried and sentenced to prison. That same year, the Metropolitan Nicholas of Krutitsy was deprived of his offices. And in Central Asia, historic mosques, sitting unused, fell further into disrepair. This policy of repression, associated mainly with the regime of Nikita Khrushchëv, came to a partial end in 1964. The Brezhnev regime later permitted 500 of the closed churches to be reopened. Mosques were not reopened, but the most historic ones were given the classification of national treasures and the first efforts at restoration were begun.

The Brezhnev regime remained officially atheist, but it was a conservative regime that tended to accept religion as part of the *status quo*. Russian nationalism enjoyed something of a revival at this time as well, and that was often extended to include the Orthodox Church. As a result, it was the best–treated of all the organized religious groupings in the USSR under Brezhnev and saw even a modest growth in its nominal membership to more than 30 million. In the last years of the Brezhnev regime, church services were overflowing and, in a change from the past, many young people began attending services. Since most of this growth occurred

Russian school girls. School uniforms are no longer required attire.

Photo by Miller B. Spangler

in the period now known as "the era of stagnation," it was partly a symptom of the loss of faith in communism that was then only beginning to manifest itself.

Brezhnev died in November 1982, but the era of stagnation really lasted until March 1985, when Mikhail Gorbachëv was appointed General Secretary. Although it was not immediately apparent, Gorbachëv had an entirely different attitude toward religion than his predecessors as leader of the *Communist Party of the Soviet Union*. Although not a believer, his attitude may have been influenced by the fact that his mother was. But whatever the reason, Gorbachëv set out rather systematically to end the party's traditional hostility toward religion. One of the points he made in justifying this change of position was that people needed moral values and that religion had an important contribution to make in this area. In 1988, official celebrations marking the millennium of Russia's conversion to Christianity symbolized this changed attitude on the part of regime.

In September 1990, the USSR Supreme Soviet passed new legislation prohibiting the government from interfering in religious activities. Another law required the state to reopen a place of worship on receipt of a petition signed by at least 20 believers. Some 4,000 new parishes opened between 1985 and 1991.

In another indication of this change, when Patriarch Pimen died in May 1990, one of those who spoke a eulogy at his funeral service was Anatoliy Lukyanov, chairman of the USSR Supreme Soviet. And in 1991, Boris Yeltsin, the president of the Russian Federation, and Valentin Pavlov, the Soviet chairman of the Cabinet of Ministers, were among those attending

Easter services at Epiphany Cathedral in Moscow. Easter services were also held at St. Basil's Cathedral on Red Square, even though it was still officially a museum.

Gorbachëv's changed policy eventually came to be applied to Muslim areas as well, though somewhat later because the Iranian revolution and the war in Afghanistan had created fears of an Islamic fundamentalism sweeping through Central Asia. The Soviet troop pullout from Afghanistan and the death of Iran's Khomeini reduced that threat, and paved the way for a changed policy toward Islam.

This brought the beginnings of a religious revival. Mosques were reopened all over Central Asia. In 1990, fourteen new mosques were opened for services in Kokand, some while still under construction. For decades, a single mosque had served a Muslim population of 150,000 in that city. Elsewhere, mosques were being opened at the rate of almost one a day. In Uzbekistan, over 200 new mosques were opened in 1989–90. Hundreds of students were enrolled in theological colleges and millions of copies of the Koran were distributed. And more than 1,500 Soviet Muslims made the pilgrimage to Mecca in 1990, the largest number in recent memory. As Muhammad Yusuf, the grand mufti of Tashkent and Central Asia's senior Muslim leader said,

at first Muslims were rather passive and did not react quickly to what was happening elsewhere in the country. Now we are demanding the same privileges accorded to other religions.

Judaism represented a somewhat different situation because, under Soviet law, Jews were viewed as both a religious

group and a nationality. Various factors made the situation complex, including a pre–revolutionary tradition of anti–Semitism which Lenin combated as being a tool of reaction. Stalin reversed this position in the late 1940s with his campaigns against "rootless cosmopolitan writers," and his later "doctors' plot." Anti–Zionism survived Stalin and continued to justify anti–Semitism under his successors.

In the past, religious practices of Soviet Jews were limited by the government, but the Gorbachëv regime's changed attitude toward religion brought about a basic change of attitude toward Jews as well. In general, the restrictions on the practice of Judaism were abolished. Jews were authorized to set up religious schools and seminaries and to begin giving religious instruction to young people. One problem was the lack of trained rabbis. That was partially solved by bringing in rabbis from abroad. Hasidic organizations from the United States and Israel have also actively provided assistance of all sorts.

The failed *coup* of August 1991 created a new situation by bringing a repudiation of the *Communist Party* and a break up of the Soviet Union. The newly independent Russian Federation closed down the *Communist Party* and rejected its ideology. Religion is now considered to be a matter of conscience and as such beyond the purview of the state. In December 1991, President Yeltsin symbolized this new approach by issuing an appeal to heads of religious faiths and believers in which he condemned "the policy of spiritual genocide" of the previous regime and promised to

eliminate the consequences of the profoundly unjust policy of the many–year–

Russia

long communist dictatorship with regard to believers [and] to hand over religious shrines, churches, and cloisters to those to whom they should rightly belong.

Christian churches have a job of rebuilding and renovation after the years of repression, but they have already made a great deal of progress, including a major new Orthodox church on Red Square. Smaller Christian denominations have had greater problems since the government passed legislation aimed at restricting sects, partly at the behest of the Orthodox church. This has not stopped the growth of non–Orthodox Christianity, however.

The Muslims of the former Soviet Union, located mainly in the six republics of Central Asia, now have their own independent governments to look after their interests. There are also a fair number of Muslims living in the Russian Federation, though they constitute a tiny percentage of the population. Guaranteed the same rights as other believers, most live in one of the autonomous republics or other autonomous regions, and they are to be found mainly in the Volga River Valley or in the area of the north Caucasus. However, a sufficient number live in Moscow to support six mosques, and there are plans to construct several more. The growth in the number of mosques in Russia over the past decade or so has been phenomenal, in fact. In 1989, there were 98 mosques in all of Russia; by 2001 that number has grown to almost 6,600.

The greatest current threat to Jewish culture in the Russian Federation is probably the large emigration that has occurred in recent years. For example, approximately 400,000 Jews left the Soviet Union in the last two years of its existence, 1990–91. It then subsided for the next several years as Jews began to reconsider leaving. During this time, a number of new Jewish high schools, newspapers and theaters were opened, and an increasing number of individual Jews began speaking about the newly independent Russian Federation as a place that offered bright prospects for Jewish life. This trend was reversed after Russia's financial crisis began in August 1998. Emigration has since dropped again, but even at these reduced levels, there will soon be few Jews left in Russia. That is unfortunate, since the Jews have made many great contributions to Russian culture in the past.

Education

Russian education, like almost everything else in Russian society, is currently in a state of transition. The failure of the August 1991 *coup* brought about a repudiation of Communism and the subsequent collapse of the Soviet Union itself. As a result, the regimentation in the area of education enforced by that old system also disappeared. The Government of the Russian Federation has not rushed in to assume the authority of the old center, so individual school districts find themselves very much on their own. The result is that individual schools are beginning to make changes and institute programs that, increasingly, set them off from other schools. Some school authorities fear that this is producing a fragmented, localized system, but others see this as another example of increasing pluralism in the society.

A St. Petersburg school specializing in English. Russian students present Tom Sawyer, Becky Thatcher, and the fence painted white—with the dialogue all in English!

Photo by Miller B. Spangler

106

One of the changes already evident is an abandonment of the school uniforms worn by all school children under the old system. Most children continue to wear the uniforms, or parts of them, but they now also wear a variety of sweaters and jackets. Some schools have also begun offering classes in religious education. In other schools, educational reformers are asking how school systems can be changed to make them better able to serve the needs of a market economy.

An Historical Overview

Education in Russia saw many changes in the 74 years following the Russian Revolution of 1917. In the first years after the revolution, "progressive" methods were tried on all levels, with an almost total elimination of classroom discipline. Teachers were subjected to the rule of committees of pupils; there was much noisy activity and very little learning.

When the revolutionary fervor faded, education was reestablished along traditional lines, with uniform studies for all schools of the huge country and a strong emphasis on the sciences and mathematics. Elective courses were abolished in favor of a standard curriculum throughout the Soviet Union. Teaching was conducted in the native languages of the various Union Republics, but the content was centrally determined in Moscow.

A major problem of pre–revolutionary Russia was that more than 60 percent of the people could not read and write. This high illiteracy rate was vigorously attacked by the Soviet government and as a result, by 1928, more than half of the citizens were literate. The figure rose to 81 percent in 1939 and is now almost 100 percent.

For a while, the state–controlled school was looked upon as a counter–balance to the "reactionary" influences of traditional family ties; at the height of the purges in the 1930s, children were encouraged to report "subversive" activities of their own parents and other relatives. In the late 1930s, however, this approach was abandoned in favor of an emphasis on the Soviet family as the source of "correct" values. The events of August 1991 have reinforced this approach.

Because increasing numbers of Russian women were drawn into the work force in the 1930s, a wide network of nurseries and kindergartens—usually run by individual factories—was created to take care of children of working mothers. These facilities have often been crowded and not particularly well run, and in recent years privately–operated day care centers have come into existence. That trend has accelerated as the Russian privatization program was implemented over the past several years. In addition, many factories now run their day care centers as commercial ventures, meaning that they are available, at a fee, to anyone who wants to use them, not just their own employees.

Regular schooling lasts for 8, 10 or 11 years, depending on where the student lives and his or her academic achievement—though this is changing. In June 2000, the ministry of education proposed a 12–year educational program for Russian students. One thing holding up implementation of the plan is an objection by the ministry of defense, which fears a shortfall in the number of conscripts if students stay in secondary school for an additional year.

Children attend school six days a week, though the school day for primary students is relatively short, consisting of four 45–minute lessons. Additional after–school supervision is offered to children of working mothers. Such children are organized into "extended–day" groups and they remain at school until their parents come to take them home. After–school supervision is an area that has felt the pinch of tight budgets, which has led to a scaling back of the amount of money going into education.

There are basically two types of secondary schools—general and technical—but a movement began in the late 1970s to merge the two. In 1978, for instance, the time reserved in the school curriculum for machine–shop practice was doubled. Senior pupils were also required to spend four hours a week at a factory or on a farm, receiving on–the–job training.

A new reform decree, issued in early 1984, carried this evolution further. Beginning in 1986, children started school at age 6, one year earlier than previously, and they received greater vocational training as an integral part of their schooling. Each student was expected to master at least one basic mechanical skill before graduating, even though enrolled in an "academic course." Such compulsory vocation courses have largely disappeared under the new system, though vocational education may actually be more available for those who opt for it.

There were great fears even before August 1991 that Gorbachëv's move to a market economy would have an adverse effect on the university system. Thus far, the collapse of the union government has had no such effect, mainly because the Russian Government has taken over responsibility for institutions of higher education and continued to fund them.

The scarcity of funds over the past several years, plus the policy of the Russian Government that societal institutions should, to the maximum extent possible, be self–supporting, have brought about a number of changes. Universities have instituted tuition fees to cover part of the cost of education, for example. Further, a number of new schools and universities have been created over the past several years. These have included some church schools and private schools. Some current state universities have also proposed turning themselves into private institutions. Thus the growth of pluralism within the system is real, even if gradual.

The area of culture with the greatest freedom of expression under the old system was that of the natural sciences, mainly because the regime came to the conclusion that keeping scientists in a strait–jacket in harmony with official dogma hampered Russia's ability to compete with nations with superior technology. Scientists were some of the most independent people in the Soviet Union and some of them spoke out courageously against the official pressures and Party–imposed limitations. One has only to think of Andrei Sakharov as an example.

The life sciences such as biology always had to put up with greater tutelage than the natural sciences, but even here the party eventually withdrew as an arbiter. The social sciences remained under official tutelage until 1985, but gained almost total freedom under Gorbachëv. Sociology, not even recognized as a separate discipline until after Stalin's death, was also freed by Gorbachëv.

Even history, always the most controlled of the social sciences, underwent the beginnings of a renaissance when Gorbachëv called for new histories of the *Communist Party* and new school books that would restore names and historical periods that had been cloaked in official silence. "There should be no forgotten names or blanks either in history or literature," he said, adding that "history must be seen for what it is." In fact, Gorbachëv's policy of glasnost had brought about so many changes in this area by 1988 that the history exams had to be canceled that year, since all of the history books were completely out of date.

Thus the older system of control had been greatly weakened even before the attempted *coup* of August 1991 brought the system down completely. Still, much that existed down to August 1991 had nothing to do with Communist ideology as such, but rather reflected traditional Russian cultural mores. For that reason, society continues to look and operate the way it always did. The difference is that there is greater pluralism in the new system being created than there had been in the one being replaced.

Russia

Democratic groups march through Moscow in September 1990 to demand immediate steps towards a market economy

The Changing Economy

The old command economy created by Stalin in the 1930s had already been seriously undermined—though not eradicated—by Gorbachëv's policy of *perestroika* even before the failed *coup* in August 1991 brought about a repudiation of communism and a collapse of the Soviet Union. The end of the Union and the emergence of an independent Russian state transformed the situation completely. With the Union abolished, the old centralized bureaucracy—which had dominated the economy for so long—came under the control of the Russian Federation, which gradually phased it out. The Government of the Russian Federation retained some instruments of economic control, but it systematically set out to eradicate the old command system and replace it with a market economy based on private enterprise.

This process of transformation was not only painful; it was also even more difficult and challenging than anybody imagined as the process was launched at the end of the 1980s. Insofar as the economy was concerned, the last two years of Gorbachëv's *perestroika* were a disaster.

The Russian Federation therefore inherited a system that was basically in collapse. Some of the symptoms were a hy-

perinflation in which the ruble, officially valued at about $1.75, actually traded at about one cent; a state trading system which was unable to provide the public with any goods, because it could not obtain them at the low fixed prices it was authorized to pay—and much of what it did obtain was siphoned off for sale at a large mark-up on the black market; and a budget deficit that was over half the size of the overall budget. Overall industrial production was down approximately 10 percent over the preceding year as individual enterprises found it more and more difficult to obtain raw materials and component parts.

President Yeltsin launched his program to begin the transformation to a market economy and private enterprise on January 2, 1992 by abolishing state–set prices for most goods. Reflecting the hyperinflation of the preceding months, prices jumped an average of 300–350 percent by the end of January. More goods began to appear in the shops, however—and even more frequently in kiosks along the streets—and prices started to drift downward, reflecting the increased supply and resistance among consumers to the higher prices. In particular, the lively street vending in the cities and towns made more consumer goods available.

The price increases permitted the government to begin phasing out subsidies to industry and agriculture, and allowed it to draw up a budget for the first three

months of 1992 with a deficit reduced to 4.4 percent of the Gross Domestic Product. The government later lowered the Value Added Tax, which the Yeltsin Government had instituted to replace the old turnover and sales taxes, from 28 percent to 15 percent as a way to lower costs to consumers. The value of the ruble stabilized, and then actually began to increase in value as demand for the ruble grew—in effect a vote of confidence in the government's program.

Freeing prices and moving toward a balanced budget were necessary first steps. President Yeltsin's government was also committed to achieving ruble convertibility as soon as possible and had negotiated with the International Monetary Fund for a ruble stabilization fund, like the one created in 1990 to support the Polish currency. As an interim step, he announced that the Russian Central Bank would set a single official value for the ruble based on the results of weekly currency auctions. Yeltsin hoped that the stabilization process could begin in the summer of 1992, after Russia was admitted to the IMF and World Bank.

Yeltsin also moved forward on other aspects of his economic reform. In February 1992, he announced plans to privatize 25 percent of state property by the end of the year. Under the plan, 25 percent ownership in state firms would be turned over to current employees, while the remaining 75 percent would be sold at auction.

The government also decided that, in order to maintain a tightened fiscal policy, it would have to phase out most remaining subsidies. Even in this first stage of reform, however, approximately 90 percent of consumer goods and 80 percent of industrial goods were freed of direct administrative regulation. Controls were maintained over twelve basic food products, certain communal services, certain fuels and some semi–finished products. The government also announced that it would begin a liberalization of fuel prices after the winter heating season was over. Fuel prices were then to begin rising in steps until they reached world prices at the end of 1993. The government predicted that the economy would continue to decline until sometime in 1993, when a turnabout was expected.

In retrospect, the government's predictions on the amount of inflation that would be unleashed with the freeing of prices turned out to be unduly optimistic. By June 1992, the exchange rate for the ruble had declined to about 100+ to the dollar, there were money shortages throughout the country and many individuals had not been paid for weeks. Other disruptions were occurring as well. Many of the state stores had closed down, while others had almost nothing to sell. Overall, more goods were available, but they were mainly sold from kiosks erected along the sidewalks, since most of these new, private entrepreneurs operated on a small–scale and, in any case, the state–owned buildings were still not available for private entrepreneurs to rent. Many of the items sold were imported also, since the state companies continued to deal only with other state companies. Some private shops did manage to find local suppliers, but it wasn't easy. The result was that ordinary individuals were ambivalent in their attitudes. There was still support for Yeltsin, but almost everybody had their complaints.

In this atmosphere, the Supreme Soviet, which five months earlier had granted President Yeltsin the power to rule by decree for one year, emerged as a center of opposition to Yeltsin's reforms. Under the leadership of Arkady Volsky, Chairman of the *Union of Entrepreneurs of Russia*, and with the cooperation of Vice President Rutskoi and Ruslan Khasbulatov, Chairman of the Supreme Soviet, the Supreme Soviet became the forum for blistering attacks on President Yeltsin's economic policies.

During the month of June, the Supreme Soviet voted down two separate attempts to pass a bankruptcy law, rejected a land reform law permitting greater private ownership, and refused to consider the draft constitution submitted by President Yeltsin. It also began putting extreme pressure on the government to loosen up on credit to state enterprises. About 25 percent of the members of the Supreme Soviet and the larger parent body, the Congress of People's Deputies, were managers of state enterprises, but this was not viewed as a conflict of interest. In their rhetoric, in fact, the enterprise managers portrayed themselves as protectors of the workers' livelihoods.

By this time, industrial production had dropped by about 15 percent over the preceding year and President Yeltsin recognized that something would have to be done to prevent further declines. Accordingly, the government agreed to provide industry with an extra 320 billion rubles in credit. In addition, President Yeltsin issued a decree at the beginning of July canceling the accumulated debts of all state enterprises, a sum amounting to approximately 1.9 trillion rubles. The government also agreed to postpone scheduled increases in energy prices.

The conservative majority in the Supreme Soviet was not satisfied with these governmental actions. Moreover, Yeltsin continued to issue decrees that further implemented his program of economic reform. At the beginning of July, he issued a decree establishing a process for bankruptcy for enterprises defaulting on debts incurred after July 1. Another decree called for the privatization of all state–owned enterprises by July 1, 1995, exempting only state farms and certain defense and energy firms deemed vital to the country.

Coincidentally, the Supreme Soviet was presented with an opportunity to further undermine economic reform when Georgy Matyukhin, head of the Russian State Bank, resigned toward the end of June. Taking advantage of the fact that the old Communist Era constitution designated the parent Congress of People's Deputies as the highest authority within the system and made the chairman of the State Bank accountable to the Supreme Soviet, Speaker Khasbulatov and the Congress appointed Viktor Gerashchenko, former head of the USSR State Bank, as chairman of the Russian State Bank.

Gerashchenko immediately began issuing large amounts of credit to state enterprises. This policy, which Gerashchenko later said he had instituted at the behest of the Supreme Soviet leadership, had the full and vocal support of the members of the Supreme Soviet. The alternate, argued individual speakers, was massive layoffs of workers. Over the next five months, the chairman of the State Bank flooded the country with massive new credits, setting off an inflation that dropped the value of

President Yeltsin with alert bodyguards

Courtesy: NOVOSTI

Russia

the ruble from about 100+ to the dollar to about 750 to the dollar.

Then in December the leaders of the Supreme Soviet convened the parent Congress of People's Deputies and used this forum to challenge Yeltsin directly. Here they attempted to strip him of most of his powers; though they failed, they did manage to oust Yegor Gaidar as deputy prime minister and to force Yeltsin to accept a man of their choice, Viktor Chernomyrdin, as prime minister. In a surprise, Prime Minister Chernomyrdin turned out to be a disappointment to the parliamentary leadership, for he shortly became a convert to Yeltsin's overall economic reform.

Parliamentary opposition to Yeltsin and economic reform continued, however. In March 1993, the Congress of People's Delegates narrowly failed to impeach Yeltsin, then structured the referendum he had requested into a four question query designed to undermine him. But in that they were to be disappointed, for the April 25 referendum actually provided a vote of confidence in Yeltsin and his economic program. Meanwhile, the parliamentary attacks continued.

Yeltsin's political struggle with the legislature undoubtedly consumed a great deal of his time but, surprisingly, his overall reform remained more or less on track. Much of the credit for this properly goes to Anatoly Chubais, the minister in charge of privatization, who announced in March 1993 that his ministry had managed to privatize 46,815 firms in 1992. The 1992 privatizations were largely limited to small firms, mostly retail shops. The first privatizations of large industrial firms occurred in December 1992 when the government transformed 18 large firms into joint–stock companies, then began exchanging shares of stock for some of the 144 million priva-

tization vouchers which had been issued earlier to the general public.

This became the new pattern. In March 1993, another 249 large firms were privatized using this method, among them the automobile manufacturing company Zil. This industry, with 103,000 workers, was important not only because of it size, but because the privatization was supported by the management and employees. The voucher system of privatization continued over the next fifteen months. When it finally ended in July 1994, more than 100,000 state companies had been transformed. These included 15,779 medium–sized and large enterprises, representing 62 percent of gross domestic production and employing 60 percent of the industrial work force. In addition, the 85,000 shops represented 70 percent of the national total. Approximately 50,000–70,000 kiosks continued to operate in the major cities, but the more successful ones now began to buy or lease permanent shops. Perhaps the most interesting statistic of all is that approximately 40 million people had become shareholders in operating companies.

Privatization continued after July 1994, but enterprises were sold for cash, not vouchers. This led to significant infusions of foreign capital over the next couple years as investment firms began to pump money into the newly privatized Russian firms. Some 500–600 American firms had set up shop in Moscow by the end of 1997, sometimes alone and sometimes in joint ventures with Russian companies. The total amount of private American investment remained relatively small, however.

Although the privatization program was a success, general economic statistics for this period were more mixed. Overall production declined drastically in the first half of 1992, then leveled out in August

1992. Overall production began growing again after that, but sharp contractions in the military sector and a downturn in textile production, the latter caused mainly by a sharp increase in the cost of cotton imported from Central Asia, kept overall production figures below the December 1991 level. Subsequent government statistics seemed to indicate that the economy had taken a turn for the worse and that what was left of the state–run economy was collapsing.

That was probably misleading, however. First of all, as privatization was implemented, government statistics became less and less meaningful. As an article in *The New York Times* put it in August 1994, "Russian figures barely touch the growing private economy." A second point to take into consideration is that official retail trade turnover figures for this same period were actually stable. Finally, many of the remaining state–run firms, refusing to adjust or change, continued to turn out products that no one wanted to buy. Cutting out such production would actually be a help for the economy.

Still, statistics suggesting many firms in deep financial trouble were obviously a matter of concern for the government. President Yeltsin's response came in August 1994 when he signed a decree making available approximately $2 billion in state credits to firms, to use either for investment projects or to help them convert to other activities. Under the terms of the decree, enterprises were required to provide one–third of the money for conversion projects and half of the money for investment projects. Concurrently, the government announced that debts between companies totaled about $45 billion, and that a commission had been set up to deal with that problem.

The Russian Economy and Inflation

Inflation was the Russian economy's most persistent problem after prices were freed in January 1992. The problem was that, although the government was committed to a policy of relative fiscal austerity, political forces representing sectors of the economy hurt by the policy periodically managed to get the government to grant huge new credits to their ailing sectors. The argument used was always that such credits protected jobs that would be lost if the firms were forced out of business. Separate subsidies were also voted for agriculture each fall in response by threats by collective farmers that otherwise they would not harvest the crops.

The first flood of state credits began in June 1992, ordered by the Supreme Soviet and provided by the Russian State Bank. This brought a quick jump in inflation and a corresponding drop in the value of the

The ice cream vendor in St. Petersburg is a highly popular figure even in winter.

Photo by Miller B. Spangler

110

economy. Following publication of the 1994 budget and inflation figures for March indicating that inflation was running at 7.8 percent, the IMF agreed to release the requested funds.

Inflation dropped further to 6.4 percent in May, then to about 4 percent in June, and it began to appear that Russia was close to establishing a stable economy. In fact, however, the government was once again under extreme pressure from conservatives to come to the aid of the ailing defense industries and agriculture. Thus, beginning in July and continuing through September, the government made available an estimated 10 trillion rubles to these two sectors of the economy. Such a large influx of new money into the economy would normally have been accompanied by a downward drift in the value of the ruble. To counteract this trend, the Russian Central Bank spent some $2 billion between August and October to support and stabilize the ruble.

But the central bank's foreign reserves were not unlimited and it could not afford to dissipate all of its reserves. When it was forced to stop its support of the ruble in October 1994, the ruble all but collapsed, dropping in a single morning from 3,081 to the dollar to 3,926 to the dollar. Heavy intervention on the part of the Russian Central Bank brought the exchange rate down to 2,988 to the dollar, but Viktor Gerashchenko, president of the bank, coming under extreme criticism, submitted his resignation after President Yeltsin demanded his dismissal.

Following the events of October 1994, the government instituted a new stabilization policy. Furthermore, when it submitted its 1995 budget to the Federal Assembly, it indicated that it intended to utilize a new mechanism for financing the deficit. Instead of requesting credits from the central bank, the government pledged to finance the deficit through the issuance of government securities and/or external loans from the West. The government also reached an agreement with its 600 foreign bank creditors for the refinancing of $26 billion in loans. Finally, the ministry for privatization announced in October that foreign investment was coming into Russia at the rate of $400 million a month, four times what it had been at the beginning of 1994.

The Russian Government asked for loans totaling $6.2 billion from the IMF, but discussions held in February 1995 failed to produce an agreement. The two decisive factors were undoubtedly a January inflation rate of 17.8 percent, a 12–month high, plus the military campaign that started in December in Chechnya and was still continuing at the time of the meeting. Everyone recognized that the cost of the cam-

For a century, the GUM Department Store flanking Red Square has been the Macy's of Moscow (in importance, if not quality).   Photo by Miller B. Spangler

ruble. By January 1993, inflation was running at 27 percent a month. A renewed restraint on credit then caused it to drop to 21 percent by March, and it then continued downward throughout the summer. The Russian Government also got greater control over credit creation in April 1993 when the Russian State Bank agreed to work within restraints set by the government—though Gerashchenko, head of the State Bank, said that he agreed to the restraints because he believed that the government would find itself unable to live within them.

The government also received some psychological help when the industrial nations promised an additional $43 billion in the run–up to the April 25 referendum—even though a large part of that package included things such as loan facilities conditional on further reform, debt relief that would provide no new cash, and aid promised earlier and not yet delivered.

By September, however, the battle between reformers and conservatives had been renewed in full vigor. After rejecting the government's budget, the Supreme Soviet attempted to force a budget on the government which would have destroyed the government's program of reform. This brought on the confrontation between the

Supreme Soviet and President Yeltsin that ended with the legislature being disbanded with new elections set for December 1993.

Although inflation had dropped to 12 percent a month by December, reformers did badly in that month's elections to the new Federal Assembly. By January 1994, most reformers had withdrawn from or been forced out of the cabinet, with only Anatoly Chubais remaining on as minister for privatization. Although Chernomyrdin continued as prime minister, the policy statement of the new government stressed a need for cushions against market forces and for investment in export industries, while downgrading the fight against inflation.

When the new budget was presented in March 1994, however, it appeared that the fight against inflation was not dead after all. In his budget message, Chernomyrdin warned that hyperinflation "means death" and announced that he had trimmed the budget from an estimated 17 percent of GDP to just over 10 percent of GDP. Why the reason for the change of emphasis? As it happened, the Russian Government was in the middle of negotiations with the IMF for a $1.5 billion loan to help finance the continued transformation to a market

Russia

paign would inevitably increase the size of the budget deficit. The IMF position was that the Russian Government would have to make a greater effort to rein in inflation if it wanted any further credits. Perhaps in response, President Yeltsin signed several decrees which gave him unprecedented control over government spending. Meanwhile, inflation dropped in March to 9.9 percent, an encouraging sign.

Reacting to the government's new-found will to control its money supply, the IMF agreed to make $6.4 billion available to the Russian Government, with the restriction that the monies would be advanced on a monthly basis and would be subject to greater controls than previous loans. This worked. Inflation fell steadily throughout the year and had fallen to 3.2 percent per month by December 1995. Partly based on these results, economists predicted in early 1996 that the Russian economy would begin growing again for the first time since 1989.

These predictions, based on a continuation of the government's economic program, proved to be premature, for subsequent events changed the political, and therefore the economic, situation. First of all, the December 1995 Duma elections gave the *Communist Party* and their allies a plurality that was just 12 seats short of an absolute majority. Gennady Zyuganov, leader of the party, liked to point out when talking with non–Russians that his party was not the old *Communist Party of the Soviet Union*—that it was, in fact, founded during the last years of the Gorbachëv era as a reform party. He would then add that the party accepted a market economy and private property.

But some of Zyuganov's other position statements, while vague, were less reassuring. Thus he described the situation in Russia in January 1996—"in our country, it's the mafia and corrupt bureaucrats who have power," then suggested re-nationalization of major companies—"We believe in a regulated market where every type of ownership—state, collective, partial, private—is allowed to have its place in the sun." To make the point clear, he added that privatized companies could stay in private hands "if they work well and are being run properly."

The relatively weak Duma could not, of course, unilaterally force a change of economic policy. But President Yeltsin, a candidate for reelection in the June 1996 presidential race, began desperately trying to reposition himself to increase his chances of winning. Meanwhile, Vladimir Kadannikov, Anatoly Chubais's successor as first deputy prime minister for economic policy, began pushing for additional subsidies for industry. As he put it, "directors of state enterprises have exhausted all inner re-

sources that could help enterprises survive. Now the only thing left to do is deal with the financial and political environment."

Still, because most western economists continued to believe that Yeltsin's reelection would be preferable to a victory by Gennady Zyuganov, the IMF signed an agreement with Russia in February 1996 making available $10.2 billion in loans linked to a sweeping plan to proceed with privatization and trade liberalization, in the words of Michel Camdessus, the IMF's managing director, to make the economic reforms "truly irreversible."

Yeltsin did win reelection in 1996, but this was followed by a period of almost six months when he was incapacitated, first by a heart bypass operation, then by a bout of pneumonia. Then, in March 1997, Yeltsin took charge again and appointed Anatoly Chubais and Boris Nemtsov as first deputy prime ministers. These two reformers managed to carry out a series of reforms in 1997, but Chubais then discredited himself by agreeing to take a large advance from a book company for a book on privatization. Chubais subsequently quit government and was appointed chief executive of Unified Energy Systems, Russia's giant electricity company.

Yeltsin also got a new prime minister, Sergei Kirienko, in April 1998. Unfortunately, this new, young reformer proved unequal to the job and was dismissed by President Yeltsin in August 1998. Essentially, Kirienko and his economic team were overwhelmed by the Asian economic crisis which began driving oil prices lower about the time that Kirienko became prime minister. The government attempted to address the problem with a 25–point anti–crisis program, but the Duma voted down several parts of the plan that would have raised government revenues. In spite of this, the government managed to obtain a promise of a further

$17 billion in loans from the IMF in July, $12.6 billion of which was to be paid out to the Russian Government during the last half of 1998. That appeared to provide the government with some room to maneuver, but it turned out not to be enough.

On August 17, Prime Minister Kirienko announced that the Russian Government would discontinue support for the ruble, plus institute a whole series of measures which added up to a partial repudiation of outstanding Russian loans. These measures included freezing the repayment of state securities up to December 31, 1999, placing "temporary" restrictions for Russian residents on large–scale foreign currency operations, and prohibiting non–residents from investing funds in short–time ruble assets. The effect of these measures was to destroy confidence in the ruble which, in turn, brought rising prices and sharp cuts in the availability of imported goods. It even appeared that the government might default on up to $200 billion in foreign debt.

President Yeltsin reacted by dismissing the Kirienko cabinet and attempting to reinstate Chernomyrdin as prime minister. But the fall of the Kirienko government, only four months after Yeltsin had forced Kirienko on the Duma, weakened Yeltsin's position and he had to agree to a new prime minister acceptable to the Duma. That turned out to be Yevgeny Primakov, the foreign minister in the previous two governments and an old Soviet bureaucrat. Primakov was confirmed as prime minister in September, though he had some difficulty assembling a cabinet acceptable to the Duma.

Those appointments made it clear that economic reform was dead in Russia for the foreseeable future. For example, the new minister of economics was Yuri Maslyukov, a member of the *Communist Party*. It is true that Maslyukov actually

On Moscow's Arabat Street, models pose in some of the latest fashions

112

joined the Kirienko cabinet in July, but his portfolio at that time was trade, a far less sensitive position than that of minister of economics. In addition, Viktor Gerashchenko, who presided over the massive inflation in 1992, was reappointed Central Bank chairman.

Primakov remained prime minister for approximately nine months, but he never developed any clear economic policy that one could identify. However, the government did begin printing additional ruble notes under Primakov—apparently in order to be able to pay back wages to workers—ignoring the contribution this was likely to make to future inflation. Granted, the continuing fall in oil prices throughout the fall placed the government under sharp pressure as its revenues continued to fall. As a result, the government drew up a budget that included billions in IMF and other loans, even as it failed to come to any agreement with the IMF.

In retrospect, it appears that Primakov was attempting to take Russia in the direction of "state capitalism," a sort of market economy heavily supervised by the state. For example, prices of essential foods and medicines were re–regulated, exporters were required to deliver 75 percent of all hard currencies to the state, and plans were announced to restructure the entire commercial banking system and bring it under greater government control. All of these actions could possibly be justified on a temporary basis as a reaction to growing unemployment, a general decline in incomes, and, in general, increased domestic distress. But if they were to become permanent policy, Russia would find its economy increasingly isolated internationally, and declining domestically.

His successor, Sergei Stepashin, stressed his commitment to reforming the economy but, as he only remained prime minister for approximately two months, apparently because of a disagreement with Yeltsin over the developing situation in Chechnya, his only accomplishment was to finalize an agreement with the IMF whereby that organization agreed to provide a $4.5 billion financial package, the first $640 million of which became available to Russia in August.

Stepashin's successor, Vladimir Putin, was confirmed as prime minister on August 16, 1999. His support for the war in Chechnya—a popular policy in Russia— won him wide popularity within the country. This may also explain why pro-government political parties made such an improved showing in the December 1999 parliamentary elections. And these two factors, together, probably explain why Yeltsin resigned as president on December 31, thereby elevating Putin to the position of acting president.

George A. Cohon, Vice Chairman of Moscow–McDonald's and President/CEO of McDonald's Restaurants of Canada Ltd., with Russian crew members at McDonald's on Pushkin Square.

Program of the Putin Administration

Putin went on to win the presidency in March; he was inaugurated as president on May 7, 2000. Putin's economic views were largely unknown at this time. Of course, it was well known that he was not an economist but, rather, had made his career as a member of the KGB until 1994. He won the presidency largely on the basis of his dogged pursuit of the war in Chechnya and because he was perceived as a strong leader who would restore Russia's national pride.

Four years later, as his first term was coming to an end, it was clear that Putin had given the country its most united, effective government since the collapse of communism. He was therefore reelected by a huge majority.

On the negative side, it had also become clear that, politically, Putin favored what he called "managed democracy," which included considerable government oversight, and sometimes ownership, over television and the press. On the other hand, Putin supported a fairly coherent program of economic reform throughout his first term of office, and he managed to get most of it enacted by the Duma.

Putin's policies were certainly important, but it helped that he became president just when the Russian economy had begun growing at a remarkable pace for the first time since the 1970s. Since 2000, the Russian economy has averaged a seven percent growth rate and the economy has grown almost fivefold, from $200 billion in 2000 to $920 billion at the end of 2006. Predictions that GDP will triple by 2010 now seem quite plausible. At the same time, the growth in real incomes has

been even more impressive, averaging better than eight percent.

On the other hand, it is also true that the fairly high levels of industrial production since 2000 have been primarily—at least until recently—the result of high energy prices rather than any major growth in manufacturing. It is also true that much of that growth occurred—again, at least until recently—in the Moscow metropolitan area, while most of the rest of the country lagged significantly behind. Monthly salaries also reflect this trend; as of February 2007, the average monthly salary in Moscow was $1,000, while it was $640 in St. Petersburg, and $325 nationally.

Still, it is becoming more and more expensive to do business in Moscow and, as a result, capital has begun flowing to other areas, particularly regional capitals with a population of one million or more, such as Samara, Ekaterinburg, Novosibirsk and Krasnodarsk, where new malls, office buildings and apartment blocks are going up in large numbers. IKEA, the Swedish furniture maker, has spent $100 million to open a huge new mall in Kazan and has plans to open a number of other malls in other provincial cities.

Russia has had large trade surpluses over the past several years, most of which is attributable to higher world prices for petroleum and gas. Russia's trade surplus in 2005 was $120 billion. On April 1, 2006, the Russian Central Bank Chairman Ignatyev announced that Russia's gold and foreign currency reserves totaled $205.9 billion, giving Russia the fifth largest reserves in the world.

Because over half of all government revenues come from gas and oil exports,

Russia

the budget surpluses have been large enough to allow the government to set up a stabilization fund that reached $100 billion as of February 2007. The fund would have been even larger, but the Russian Government used $3.3 billion to pay off its debt to the IMF in 2006. Russia's debt to the Paris Club——$29.8 billion as of October 1, 2005——was also completely paid off in 2006.

On the negative side, the large cash inflows resulting from the high price of oil have contributed to an inflation rate which reached 11 percent in 2005 and remained at that same approximate rate thereafter, in spite of government efforts to lower it. The ruble has also gained considerably in value since 2005. These two developments, inflation and a more valuable ruble, have threatened the competitiveness of the non-energy sectors of the economy.

One area of particular concern to the Russian Government over the past several years was that of capital flight, estimates of which ranged between $200 and $300 billion for the period 1991–2001. The trend began to reverse in 2002–2003, dropping to $9–10 billion for 2002 and less than $3 billion in 2003. But capital flight grew fourfold in 2004, mainly as a result of the arrest of Mikhail Khodorkovsky and the government's largely successful campaign to dismantle Yukos, his oil company, through exorbitant tax liens that, for one year, were larger than the total revenues of the company.

According to the Economic Development and Trade Ministry, Russian businesses and banks took a record $19 billion out of the country in the first three months of 2005. Capital flight clearly grew after the Russian Government began using its tax laws to punish those deemed to be opponents of the government. Even so, much of this outflow was the result of the various Russian companies, and in particular those in the energy field, using their huge profits to buy productive facilities abroad. This trend actually grew in 2006, but with one important difference—the trend now has the support of the Russian Government.

Putin's Industrial Policy

The reason for the change is related to the Russian Government's new industrial policy, originally launched in the energy area, of bringing the "commanding heights" of the Russian economy back under government control. (For more on Russia's energy policy, see the section titled **Putin's Energy Policy** beginning on page 121.)

In February 2006, President Putin issued a decree setting up the United Aircraft Construction Corporation as a joint-stock company, three-quarters of whose shares would be owned by the Russian

Government. The purpose of the move was to merge all Russian civilian and military aircraft producers into a single, state-owned, holding company. A press release issued at the time described the move as a way

to preserve and develop the research and production potential of the Russian aviation construction industry, to ensure the state's security and defense capabilities, and to pool the intellectual, industrial, and financial resources for implementing prospective programs to create technical equipment used in aviation.

The government also began consolidating the Russian airline industry, using state-owned Aeroflot to take control of the largest privately-owned airline companies through a series of mergers. In July 2006, German Gref, minister of economic development, drafted a decree on the "consolidation of regional airlines." By that time, Aeroflot had already absorbed several of its major domestic competitors, including Pulkovo, Krasair, and Sibir (also known as S7) Airlines, obtaining control through a series of share swaps involving shares the Russian State held in the companies. Other airlines that have since been absorbed include two Siberian airlines, Omskavia and Sibaviatrans, Moscow's Domededovo Airlines, and Samafra, which serves the Volga region.

The program also has an international component. In the spring of 2006, the state-owned Vneshtorgbank purchased $1 billion in stock of the European Aeronautic Defense and Space Company (EADS), which owns Airbus. The payoff came in March 2007 when EADS agreed to outsource five percent of the design and manufacture of the A-350 frame to the newly-created United Aircraft Company; in return, Aeroflot signed an agreement to purchase 22 A350 aircraft from Airbus.

Another state-owned industrial sector which has extended its control over areas that had been privatized in the 1990s is the Russian arms industry. In September 2006, Rosboroneksport, the state arms trader, purchased a 66 percent share in VSMPO-Avisma, the world's largest titanium maker. Titanium has, of course, both civilian and military usages. In January 2007, however, President Putin issued a decree giving Rosboroneksport a monopoly of all arms exports. At the time, there were 22 joint-stock companies operating in the arms and military hardware field; all of their foreign sales will now be handled by Rosboroneksport. All of this is probably preliminary to their being absorbed by Rosboroneksport.

Similarly, the Russian Federal Ministry for Industry has drawn up plans to unite

20 of the leading heavy-machinery manufacturers and the leading tank and artillery manufacturing companies in a single new holding company controlled by the state. The Russian State is already a majority stockholder in a number of these companies; the state will purchase majority stock-holdings in the remainder of the companies.

A similar consolidation has also begun in the aluminum industry, though in this case the company taking over its rivals, RusAl, is owned by Russian billionaire Oleg Deripaska. RusAl took over its chief rival, Sual, in October 2006 with the blessing of President Putin. RusAl became the world's largest aluminum company at about this same time when Deripaska took over Swiss-owned Glencore—all of this with the blessing of the Russian Government.

Part of Putin's industrial policy also appears to be to permit and even encourage private investment in non-strategic sectors of the economy. Here the best example is probably the United Energy System (UES), the state-owned Russian company that provides electricity for the entire company. In March 2007, UES announced that it was hoping to raise $15 billion from the sale of 15 major asset sales.

Essentially, Russia's non-nuclear power generation stations have been parceled out into 21 new power generation companies, and all are now being privatized. All nuclear power generation stations will remain under control of the Atomic Energy Agency. (For more on Nuclear Power developments, see the section entitled **Nuclear Power**, beginning on page 124.)

The first of the sales occurred in March 2007 when Norilsk Nickel, the Russian nickel mining giant, paid $3.1 billion for a 38 percent share in OGK-3, which operates power plants in several parts of Russia. Norilsk's interest in obtaining power generation plants is obvious, considering the role that energy plays in the manufacture of nickel. In a separate deal with UES, Gazprom recently acquired a majority interest in Mosenergo, which operates electric power plants in the Moscow area.

Russia did not do well in attracting private direct capital investment when it opened up its economy after 1992, but that situation seems now to be changing. In January 2006, Deputy Prime Minister Zhukov announced that the inflow of private capital in 2005 exceeded Russian capital outflows for the first time since 1991. The net inflow was $300 million. Zhukov said that the private sector brought $77 billion into Russia in 2005; $39 billion—or just over half of that total—represented foreign loans by Russian companies. Five Russian companies were, in fact, responsible for $28 billion of this borrowing—

Rosneft and Transneft, two oil companies, plus Sovkomflot, Russian Railways, and Alrosa.

An additional $16.7 billion came into the country in the form of direct foreign investment. The foreign companies making investments included Coca Cola, which purchased the Russian juice-maker Multon for $600 million; the Dutch brewer Heineken, which made $750 million in acquisitions during the year; Nestlé's, which invested $120 million in an instant-coffee factory that opened in Krasnodar in November 2005; Whirlpool Corporation, which is building a plant to manufacture washing machines in Russia; American Express, which launched its first ruble credit cards in December 2005; Amway Corporation, which began selling cosmetics and detergents in Russia in March 2005; the Austrian Bank Raiffeisen, which purchased the Russian private bank Impexbank for $550 million; and the Deutsche Bank, which paid $420 million for UFG, a Moscow investment bank.

Boeing, which has invested $2.1 billion in Russia since 1991, announced in April 2005 that it planned to invest $2.5 to $3 billion in Russia's aviation sector over the next five years. That same month Toyota announced that it was planning to construct its first automobile plant in Russia. The plant, to be located in St. Petersburg, will represent an investment of $142 million; production is scheduled to begin in 2007. The remaining $21.9 billion mainly represented share issues of Russian companies floated on foreign exchanges.

Of course, there are also the companies who have been operating in Russia for a number of years. These include the Ford Motor Company, which sold 115,985 vehicles in Russia in 2006, and General Motors, which sold 111,458 vehicles in 2006. One should also mention Avon, which is the largest-selling cosmetics company in Russia.

As for non-energy parts of the Russian economy, industrial areas that have shown strong growth include microbiology firms, polygraph companies, and crystal and ceramic manufacturers. The advertising market is also booming, with television advertising reaching $900 million.

There have also been some turnarounds. For one, Russian banks, which have been notoriously weak, often operating primarily as conduits for channeling public funds to favored firms, have shown significant improvement as a result of a banking reform launched by President Putin in 2002. Even so, *The Economist* reported in May 2006 that "all but 100 or so of Russia's banks are tiny, or dormant, or are 'pocket' institutions serving the needs of at most one or two controlling shareholders."

The largest Russian bank is Sberbank, the government-controlled savings bank. Vneshtorgbank and Gazprombank, the second and third largest banks, are also state-controlled; together, these three banks account for approximately 40 percent of all bank-held assets.

There are 42 foreign-owned banks operating in Russia and collectively they control about 7 percent of the banking market. Because the Russian Government only allows foreign banks to operate branches through subsidiaries that must be registered in the country, nearly all foreign banks maintain a presence in a single city, usually Moscow.

The two largest are the U.S.-based Citibank and the Austria-based Raiffeisen International Bank. Raiffeisen, which has been operating in Russia since 1996, greatly expanded its operation in Russia in 2006 by purchasing the privately-owned Russian Impexbank for $550 million. By buying Impexbank and turning it into a subsidiary, Raiffeisen obtained 190 new branches across the country and 350 consumer-finance outlets in supermarkets and shopping centers. Other foreign banks could take this same route, but Russian bank assets are no longer cheap; Raiffeisen paid almost three times book value for Impexbank.

Russian Minister for Economic Development and Trade Gref announced in November 2006, however, that subsidiaries of foreign banks will be barred from Russia, but "100 percent companies are permitted to operate on the Russian market with a 50 percent stake in combined banking capital." It is not certain how this will affect the banking industry.

There are also continuing weaknesses. A major long–term problem is the scarcity of

small businesses in Russia. Currently, small and medium–sized companies employ only 22 percent of the labor market; in countries with longer–term market economies, the figure is usually closer to 65 percent. At President Putin's urging, the Duma passed legislation aimed at cutting red tape for small companies; indications thus far suggest that the new legislation has not solved the problem. Additional legislation calling for a three–year moratorium on inspections for small businesses is still pending in the Duma.

Health is another long–term problem. Russia reported 70,000 new cases of HIV infection in the first 10 months of 2001, which is 1.6 times as many as reported in 2000. A second problem is tuberculosis. The disease has spread rapidly throughout Russia over the past decade, particularly in prisons, and drug–resistant strains have been appearing in greater numbers. The Red Cross estimates that 130,000 new cases develop each year in Russia, and 30,000 people die annually from the disease. USAID and the International Federation of Red Cross and Red Crescent are currently supporting a 3–year, $3.4 million program in Russia to address this problem.

Finally, 20.8 million Russians, or about 14.6 percent of the population, live below the official poverty line—meaning that they have monthly incomes of less than 2,451 rubles ($81.70). Although there has been a sharp decrease in those living below the poverty line over the past five years or so, Russia still has a long way to go yet to reach the standard of living found even in neighboring countries to the west such as Poland and Hungary. The government did raise the minimum wage to 720 rubles on January 1, 2005; it then went up to 800 rubles on September 1 and to 1,100 rubles on May 1, 2006. Even the May 2006 minimum wage is considerably under the poverty line, however.

What is Being Changed: a Look Back at the Old Soviet Command Economy

The most distinctive feature of the now defunct Soviet economic organization was the reliance on a rigid central plan for the national economy. This is in contrast to a *market* economy, which relies on the independent or semi–independent decisions of many producers. In theory, a rigidly planned economy was supposed to avoid the ups and downs—inflation and depression—of a free market economy. Marx and Engels charged that a market economy amounted to "anarchy of production."

In practice, centralized planning proved to be difficult. For many years, economic targets and goals were met by lavish investments of capital and labor. Progress was identified with the rate of growth of

Russia

specific key industries—coal, steel and heavy industry in general—and a high percentage growth rate for overall industrial production. Quantity was stressed over quality.

Such a growth strategy produced an economy that led the world in the production of a long list of industrial products, including coal, steel, cement, manganese and chrome ores, locomotives, metal–cutting lathes and mineral fertilizer. Yet it also produced an economy that, from the point of view of the consumer, was an economy of scarcities. Some consumer goods were not manufactured at all while others were obtainable only after a long waiting period. Still, there were important improvements in the availability of consumer goods over the years. By the time Gorbachёv became General Secretary in 1985, for example, most Russian families had a color television set.

Although the Soviet standard of living improved between 1960 and 1985, it was still only about 37 percent of the level of the United States—and probably falling. Moreover, it was even below the level of the neighboring countries of Eastern Europe. From the point of view of the consumer, an even more important problem was that Soviet goods were of such poor quality that they could not be sold abroad.

Gorbachёv was already aware of the weaknesses in the system when he came to power in 1985. During his first year as General Secretary, he put together a team of younger and better–educated individuals and, at the 27th Party Congress in February 1986, he put the party on record as favoring economic reform. He then began to give substance to this commitment.

It soon became clear that many party members objected to any major modification of the economic system on ideological grounds, however. As Gorbachёv pointed out at the 27th Party Congress:

Unfortunately, there is a widespread view that any change in the economic mechanism is to be regarded as virtually a retreat from the principles of socialism.

Gorbachёv was faced with a major contradiction. Gorbachёv's own chief source of authority was his leadership of the party. Moreover, since the party controlled the levers of power, economic reform was possible only with the party's support. Yet how could he use the party to direct his program of economic reform if the party was itself the chief opponent of that reform? Gorbachёv's twofold answer was to remake the party in terms of personnel, organization and ideology while, at the same time, restructuring the system so that the party was no longer in direct control.

Russians line up in front of McDonald's in Moscow for a "Beeg Mak."

The process began in 1987 with the introduction of three slogans which came to symbolize his campaign for reform—openness (*glasnost*), restructuring (*perestroika*), and democracy. Unfortunately, his successes in political reform were not matched in the economic area.

In June 1987, Gorbachёv outlined future economic plans to a Central Committee Plenum. Here he called for "cardinal reform" in the *financing and credit systems*. He also spoke of the need for "development of self–management," and "fundamental change in the style and methods of work." Factories should, he urged, be "self–financing" and more efficient so as to reduce their work force.

That same Central Committee session approved a "Law on the Socialist Enterprise" which went into effect on January 1, 1988. Under the terms of the law, 60 percent of Soviet industrial and agricultural production began working under a new system of "economic accountability" in which individual enterprises became responsible for obtaining their own raw materials and fuel and were expected to compete with other enterprises for business.

While they now had the right to dispose of any profits earned by the enterprise, they also became responsible for replacing obsolete machinery and paying the wages of their employees. Subsidies to money–losing enterprises were supposed to be phased out and such enterprises were to be permitted to go bankrupt, if they could not begin turning a profit. Companies were also to be able to get rid

of surplus workers, so unemployment became another possibility. All of this was supposed to be in effect by the end of the 1986–90 Five Year Plan.

The system was never fully implemented, however. In 1988, 90 percent of the output of factories was still produced for "state orders." Two years later, state orders still controlled nearly 90 percent of industrial production. The state was also supposed to gradually withdraw from direct control of most economic activity, with GOSPLAN relinquishing its control over individual enterprises and concentrating on long–term planning. Some of that happened. In 1987, for example, the number of centrally planned indicators was reduced from 46,000 to 22,000. It was supposed to be further reduced to 3,500 indicators in 1988, though it cannot be verified that this second reduction took place. Ministries and departments were supposed to be reduced by approximately one–third and there was supposed to be a drop of approximately 100,000 in personnel. Again, reductions occurred but not in those magnitudes.

One problem was that the economic program had two major goals—a short–term goal of accelerating the growth rate of national income and a long–term one of promoting innovation and reconstruction—and they were in basic conflict with each other. The first goal required all out production, while the second goal could only be met by things like closing down assembly lines while obsolete machinery was being replaced by modern technology

BASKIN 31 ROBBINS

ПЕРЕЧЕНЬ ВКУСОВЫХ
СОРТОВ МОРОЖЕНОГО

САМОЕ ПОПУЛЯРНОЕ МОРОЖЕНОЕ В АМЕРИКЕ

ВАНИЛЛА	Сливочное ванильное мороженое.	П
СТРОБЕРРИ	Клубничное мороженое с кусочками клубники.	П
ЧОКЛАТ	Шоколадное мороженое.	П
ЧОКЛАТ АЛМОНД	Шоколадное мороженое с жареным миндалем.	П
ЧОКЛАТ ЧИП	Ванильное мороженое с шоколадной стружкой.	П

Times are changing! Baskin Robbin's offers Moscovites a "List of Ice Cream Flavors"— "The most popular ice cream in America" . . . beginning with Vanilla, Strawberry, Chocolate, Chocolate Almond, Chocolate Chip, etc. (Courtesy of David Hertzberg)

The result was well summed up in February 1990 by N. N. Slyunkov, a member of the Politburo, in remarks he made at the Central Committee Plenum:

The situation has deteriorated especially in the consumer market as regards both food and essential goods over the past two years.

A similar picture of the state of the Soviet economy is to be found in a poll published in the Moscow *Ogonek*, also in February 1990. Seventy–three percent of all respondents said that they "constantly or quite often" experienced difficulty in locating food that they needed, while 60 percent reported that they spent over half of their income on food.

All of this economic distress put the government under extreme pressure. Everybody agreed that *something* had to be done but there was no consensus on what that something should be. The radical reformers wanted to push forward rapidly, while conservatives urged pulling back; Gorbachëv fell somewhere in the middle. The draft Five Year Plan submitted in December 1989 by Nikolai Ryzhkov, Chairman of the Council of Ministers, represented a distinct pulling back, but there continued to be strong pressures to move more quickly.

Ryzhkov submitted a later version of his plan in May 1990. Saying that the state of the economy and the mood of the people did not permit any immediate changes, he proposed a continuation of the policy of state orders for another 18 months coupled with what he called price reform. They were, in fact, just price increases, since prices were not to be freed but simply raised. He characterized his program as "a transition to a regulated market economy." Radicals attacked his proposals and Gorbachëv called them absurd, though he added that people were unprepared for market economics.

Economic reform was on the agenda at the 28th Party Congress in July 1990. After heated discussions, the party adopted a document called "Toward humane, democratic socialism," one of whose major points was that private property did not contradict communist ideology. Reflecting this change, Ryzhkov, in a speech given on July 20, spoke of moving toward a market economy. All references to the word "regulated" were dropped.

Then in August came the Shatalin Plan for a 500 day transition to a market economy. It had the support of Boris Yeltsin and the other radicals and was actually accepted by the Russian Supreme Soviet in early September. Gorbachëv rather reluctantly endorsed the plan, but it came under attack by conservatives and Ryzhkov threatened to resign if the plan were adopted. Eventually the USSR Supreme

and enforcing higher quality standards by rejecting goods that failed to meet the new standards. That conflict, obvious by 1989, got considerably worse in 1990–91, with the result that neither goal was met.

A second problem had to do with decentralization of decision–making authority within the system. Essentially, enterprises were given authority to set wages but no responsibility for paying them. As a result, they granted wage increases far in excess of increases in productivity, and

the state had to make good the difference. It did this through the expedient of printing additional money. The increase in money in circulation first produced shortages as individuals used their higher wages to buy more goods. In a capitalist system, that would have led to inflation as prices increased to reflect additional demand. But all prices were controlled, and so could not increase. What happened instead was a loss of faith in the banking system and the currency itself.

Russia

Soviet turned it down. Essentially the Soviet Union had no plan for economic reform.

Ryzhkov suffered a heart attack at the end of December and was replaced by Valentin Pavlov in January 1991. Pavlov, who had been finance minister under Ryzhkov, was a conservative. One of his more notorious "reforms" was to attempt to reduce the fiscal overhang by withdrawing 50 and 100 ruble notes from circulation. Since individuals were limited in the amount of bills they could redeem, Pavlov in effect reduced the overhang by expropriating a portion of the public's wealth. Its most important effect was to further reduce faith in the currency.

Real GNP fell by ten percent in 1990 and shortages were even more pervasive than they were in 1989. Yet the stalemate continued. Conservatives were convinced that further moves in the direction of a market economy would disrupt the economy even more, while reform advocates argued that any action was better than no action. Gorbachëv, no economist, didn't know what to believe. A joke he told reporters in November 1990 illustrated his position.

They say that Mitterrand has 100 lovers. One has AIDS, but he doesn't know which one. Bush has 100 bodyguards. One is a terrorist, but he doesn't know which one. Gorbachëv has 100 economic advisers. One is smart, but he doesn't know which one.

By May 1991, Gorbachëv had lost confidence in Pavlov's economic program and he began seeking outside advice. Grigory A. Yavlinsky, who had helped draw up the Shatalin Plan, now proposed a new plan whereby the western nations would provide substantial aid to the Soviet Union to help in its economic transition. Gorbachëv endorsed this plan and used it as a basis for his meeting with the "Group of Seven" nations in July 1991. Though no specific overall sums were mentioned, Soviet economists talked about the need for $30 billion a year in grants and loans. The G–7 nations gave a cool reception to the general idea, though they promised assistance once transition to a market economy had begun. Before any further progress could happen, the August 1991 failed *coup* brought an end both to the Soviet Union and Gorbachëv's leadership.

Agriculture

The failure of the August 1991 *coup*, although it gave Mikhail Gorbachëv four more months as President, actually marked the beginning of the breakup of the Soviet Union and the emergence of Boris Yeltsin as head of an independent Russian Federation. What this meant in-

sofar as agriculture was concerned is that the reforms that Yeltsin had been demanding for two years could finally be implemented.

This had a two–fold significance. First of all, the demise of the Soviet Union definitively ended the various central control mechanisms of the old regime. For the first time since the early 1930s, Russian peasants were on their own. Amazingly, they managed to plant even more winter wheat following the collapse of the ministry of agriculture than they had when it was telling them what to plant and when.

Yet while the peasants welcomed the end of bureaucratic control, they very quickly realized that being on their own meant an end to supports, credits, loans and guidance. Moreover, although the reformers said that they wanted to break up the collective and state farms and create a private agriculture, the government offered almost no assistance to peasants who wanted to leave the collective and start on their own. It was in fact, another two years before President Yeltsin finally issued a historic decree granting Russians the right to buy and sell private land.

The reform of prices also turned out to be a negative factor insofar as agriculture was concerned. Two examples will illustrate this point. In 1991, one pound of wheat would buy two pounds of diesel fuel or fertilizer. By 1994, that same two pounds of fuel cost the equivalent of nine pounds of wheat, while a single pound of fertilizer sold for the equivalent of eight pounds of grain.

Although the government has been, on paper, largely successful in its campaign to break up the collective/state farm system—94 percent of the agrarian sector was officially classified as private by the end of 1994—the real situation is that, while collective/state farms are now "joint stock companies," they continue to operate in much the same way they always have. Moreover, the state continues to set the prices of many grains through Agroprom, its state buying agency, which still collects grain from the farms and delivers goods in return.

Farms are, to be sure, not obligated to sell to Agroprom, but the lack of alternative purchasing agents means that farms that do not want to sell to Agroprom have to find a way to market their goods on their own. At the Koltsovo joint agricultural enterprise, formerly the Suvorov Collective Farm, for example, all milk is still sold at fixed prices to the state. To the question, why not sell it elsewhere, the reply was:

Where will we get the fuel, the trucks? We did try once, but these thugs met us and suggested we go home.

According to the most recent figures, there are about 350,000 private farmers in Russia—out of 30 million people who depend on the land. Many of these private farms are, moreover, extremely small, and most lack adequate machinery to work their land. Most do not have access to credit, so they are unable to improve their holdings. They also control only about 4 percent of the agricultural land in the country.

One reason is that, although article 35 of the 1993 constitution promises that "the right of private property shall be protected by law," this remained only a theoretical right until January 2003, when a new law on agricultural land sales finally went into effect. Legislation permitting the sale of non–agricultural land was passed by the Duma in March 2001—but it explicitly exempted agricultural land sales. The new law remains controversial, however, and certain regions, including Krasnodar Krai, have indicated that the new law will not be implemented on their territories. In any case, most regions do not have land registers or land–quality surveys, so it will be some time before significant amounts of land will become available for sale.

On the other hand, approximately 40 regions had passed their own local land laws setting up procedures for the purchase of land even before the new law came into effect. One such region is Saratov province, which passed a local land law in 1997. Since then, the authorities have conducted 335 auctions of land, selling 1,202 plots that comprise a total of 20,485 acres. To put those sales figures into context, the total amount of agricultural land in Saratov province is 25 million acres.

There are several reasons why this should be so. First of all, demand for land is small, since farmers can lease land for less than $4 an acre. Second, land mortgages do not exist, so it is not possible to borrow money to buy land. In addition, most farmers do not have the capital to buy the farm equipment which would be needed to work a larger piece of land. Finally, without a viable legal system, no one can be certain that they can keep what they buy.

One farmer in Saratov province, who owns 316 acres and leases an additional 9,815 acres, explained why he remains an exception as a private farmer:

Today, basically, land doesn't belong to anybody, and so nobody is interested in working on nobody's land and increasing the productivity of nobody's land. It's like if you rent an apartment and you renovate it at your own expense; you can still be thrown out in a month.

Patrons buying drinking water at dispensers in St. Petersburg Photo by Miller B. Spangler

The transition to a genuinely privatized agriculture is likely to be long and arduous. In the first place, most ordinary peasants oppose change, fearing apparently that they will lose what they already have. Many are also older—the average age for collective farmers is over 50—and they don't want to start over. Thus real change may have to wait until the next generation of farmers takes over. In the meantime, the question appears to be whether the ex–collective farms can be turned into competitive enterprises. One sign of progress is that the central committee of the *Agrarian Party*, which had opposed privatization of land in the past, endorsed the concept of a new land code which would "guarantee the property rights of agricultural producers" in March 2000.

It helped that grain production began growing in 1999 and continued for the next three years. As a result, Russia exported about 3 million tons of grain in 2001 and over 6 millions in 2002. Part of the reason for rising agricultural production is that oil companies, awash in profits, began investing excess funds in cooperative farms, taking them over and then pouring money into them to modernize them. Unfortunately, Russia then had a partial grain failure in 2003; this led the government to ban all grain exports and begin making grain available from its reserves when the poor harvest began to translate into increased bread prices. But Russian farmers had a good year in 2004,

producing 45 million tons of grain, the largest harvest since 1991.

What is Being Changed: Collectivized Agriculture

When the Soviet Union introduced the collectivization of agriculture as part of its first Five Year Plan, it was considered to be the first step in the creation of a modern, scientifically–organized, mechanized agricultural system. Distinctions between city and the countryside were to be abolished and peasants were to become "proletarians in the fields." Until 1953, this remained largely a dream, although Khrushchëv's plan for the creation of *agrogoroda*—loosely, "agricultural cities"—which he first put forward in 1950, showed that the dream had only been postponed, not abandoned. Khrushchëv, as he consolidated his power after 1953, gave a great deal more emphasis to agriculture than had Stalin. Agriculture was placed much higher on the Soviet list of priorities and additional investments were directed into this area.

In addition, a program of consolidation of the collective farms, actually begun in 1950, continued under Khrushchëv and, in the process, many were transformed into state farms (*sovkhozy*). The Machine Tractor Stations were also phased-out beginning in 1958 and their agricultural equipment was sold to the *sovkhozy* and *kolkhozy*. As the process of transformation and consolidation continued over the next two decades, the number of agricultural

units shrank until, by 1987, the number had dwindled to 22,900 *sovkhozy* and 26,300 *kolkhozy*, with slightly over half of the land being organized as *sovkhozy*.

Another innovation in agricultural organization, introduced in the early 1970s, was the "agro–industrial complex." Always considered experimental, their numbers nevertheless increased over the next decade until there were more than 9,000 of them in existence. Most tended to specialize in the production of a single crop—for example, grapes, which they also further processed into wine or raisins.

One Khrushchëv policy innovation that was to have great consequences in later years was his decision, made in the late 1950s, to commit the country to a great increase in meat production. The large increases in the numbers of livestock and poultry that resulted from this policy led to a greatly increased demand for grain for use as animal feed. Between 1960 and 1980, the amount of feed grains used for livestock and poultry tripled, going from 40 million tons to 120 million tons.

Grain production also increased during this period, but it could not keep up with the constantly growing demand. In 1963, after a relatively poor harvest, the Soviet Union imported its first grain. It imported grain only intermittently during the remainder of the 1960's, but after 1972 it become a regular customer on the world grain market.

This concerned the Soviet leadership and under Brezhnev huge sums of money were poured into the agricultural sector. Capital investment in the 1970s was over 300 billion rubles, which was 2.3 times what had been invested in agriculture in the previous decade. Most of the investment went into creation of a large artificial fertilizer industry.

None of this did any good. Grain harvests from 1979–1985 were uniformly dismal, averaging between 40 and 50 million tons below annual targets specified in the Five Year Plan. As a result, the Soviet government stopped publishing overall grain production figures in 1980. No overall figures were published again until October 1986, when it was announced that the grain harvest for 1985 totaled 191.5 million tons. Although this figure was 47.4 million tons less than the target, it actually was an improvement over the trend for the period 1981–1985, when production averaged only 179.5 million tons.

Grain figures for 1987 and 1988 were higher, at 210 and 211.3 million tons, but dropped in 1989 to 195 million tons. The 1990 harvest, on the other hand, was magnificent, reaching 247 million tons, though a significant amount was lost before reaching the Soviet public. The 1991 grain harvest was a disappointing 180–185 million tons.

Russia

The important thing, however, is that the Soviet Union, year after year, imported an average of 40 million tons of grain because Soviet collective and state farms fell that much short in meeting the demands of the economy. Even in the bumper year of 1991, the government imported approximately 28 million tons of grain.

Western agricultural experts have believed for a long time that the basic problem was in the system itself—that a basic conflict existed "between a centrally planned and controlled agriculture and the evolution of a modern, highly productive agriculture." Before Gorbachëv, Soviet planners always rejected this point of view and tended to blame it on Russian weather.

Western experts also point out three other problems which they feel contributed to the failure of Soviet agriculture. The first is that Soviet farm equipment was always breaking down. This is partly because Soviet tractors didn't last very long and partly because there was never a sufficient supply of spare parts for them. This is still an unsolved problem. A February 1992 report indicated that 200,000 tractors were standing idle because of a lack of spare parts.

The second problem is the lack of adequately trained and motivated labor in the countryside. Young, better educated individuals have been leaving the collective and state farms and seeking work in the cities for a long time. In the 1970s, 15 million workers left for the cities and that trend, though diminished, continued in the 1980s. The reason is that young people could see no opportunity for advancement on the collective or state farm. A large number of persons are still employed in agriculture, but many of these persons are women (12% of the workforce) and lesser educated, older men, precisely those elements which are least productive and least amenable to change.

The third problem is related: there is a terrible shortage of food–carrying railroad cars and storage facilities. Because of this a substantial part of annual production fails to reach city markets, and simply rots. When properly used, food–carrying cars, refrigerated and unrefrigerated, properly become a place of storage as they move over large distances.

Gorbachëv had held the agriculture portfolio in the secretariat for a number of years before becoming General Secretary. There were some reforms he had been urging for a number of years, and he began implementing them after 1985. In his keynote speech to the 27th Party Congress, Gorbachëv spoke of the need to significantly extend "the independence of collective and state farms," and he proposed a two–fold plan for agriculture. State and collective farms would be assigned fixed annual quotas that would not be altered. All production in excess of the quotas could be used as the farms saw fit, including selling it "in fresh or processed form at the collective farm market or through cooperative trade."

Gorbachëv described his proposal as "the creative use of the Leninist idea of a tax in kind"—a reference to Lenin's *New Economic Policy*. The idea had great potential, for it could have been manipulated to create a major free market for agricultural produce if the level of fixed deliveries were set low enough. In addition, 100 percent of the production of state farms had traditionally gone to the state. Including them in the proposal was a departure from past practice and a genuine decentralization as far as state farms were concerned. Including them was also important because slightly over 50 percent of all agricultural land belonged to state farms. The potential was never reached, however, largely because so many people were opposed to any general loosening of control, and they managed to sabotage the reform.

Another of Gorbachëv's innovations was to suggest that the "brigade" or "team" system in agriculture might be extended by making them available at the level of families. Under this setup, a group of workers "contracted" to perform certain agricultural tasks as, for example, to cultivate a specified acreage or run a dairy. Remuneration, divided according to the individual contributions of the members of the brigade or team, was based on the productivity of the unit. Gorbachëv's innovation was approved, but the problem was in the implementation. Some family contracts were certainly written, but anecdotal reports indicate that the idea was not widely implemented.

This is the background that produced a Central Committee Plenum on Agriculture that took place in March 1989. In his speech to the Plenum, Gorbachëv argued that "the essence of economic change in the countryside should be in granting farmers broad opportunities for displaying independence, enterprise and initiative." To accomplish this, he proposed turning collective and state farms into "a supreme type of cooperative."

To accomplish this, he proposed that land, equipment and buildings be leased out to individual farmers for periods up to 50 years. The state and collective farms would continue to exist as some sort of coordinating agency, but would not directly control production.

Although conservatives such as Ligachëv spoke up for lesser reforms, Gorbachëv's plan was approved in principle.

The Plenum also voted, once again on Gorbachëv's initiative, to abolish *Gosagroprom*, the super–ministry for agriculture that Gorbachëv had created in 1985.

In April 1990, the Supreme Soviet actually passed a new law allowing the leasing of land, equipment, buildings and other property for 50 years. Private farms were now a possibility. A few braver peasants moved to take advantage of it. They often had difficulty with the management of their collective or state farm, but there were an estimated 100,000 private farmers in Russia by the beginning of 1992.

Natural Resources

The Russian Federation is well supplied with most of the raw materials necessary for industrial production, although the major source of minerals is Siberia. European Russia is less well supplied. The area of the Russian Plain has bauxite and lignite deposits, while anthracite and iron ore are found mainly along the western slopes of the Ural Mountains. The northern Caucasus has a petroleum field, an extension of the famous petroleum field centered on the city of Baku, in the Republic of Azerbaijan. Oil is also produced in the area between the Volga River and the Ural Mountains.

In Siberia, on the other hand, there are found some of the largest reserves of coal, petroleum and natural gas in the entire world, plus gold, silver, diamonds, platinum, copper, lead, zinc, chromium, cobalt, tungsten, manganese, and uranium. Beginning in the west, there are the iron ore and anthracite coal deposits of the eastern Urals that are exploited by the cities of Magnitogorsk and Yekaterinburg (Sverdlovsk).

To the northeast is Russia's largest oil field, centered on the city of Raduzhny, in Tyumen Province. The Tyumen Field, located in the southern part of the West Siberian Plain, produced 6.1 million barrels a day in 1992, more than any country other than the United States and Saudi Arabia. Small fields are found in the vicinity of Pechora, far to the north on the Barents Sea, and further to the east in an area known as the East Siberian Lowland. Both are extremely isolated areas and production costs are thus higher.

The rest of the Russian Federation produced another 2.13 million barrels a day in 1992, making Russian production 9.23 million barrels a day at that time. Daily production was approximately 1.3 million barrels a day higher in 1990. Production continued to decline after that time, dropping 11 percent in 1994 alone. A large part of the problem was the result of Russian Government policy. Until March 1992, the government continued to sell petroleum for the equivalent of a dollar a barrel, not

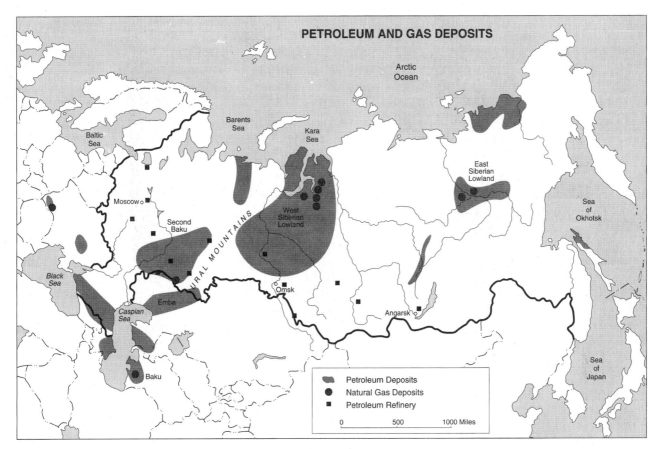

PETROLEUM AND GAS DEPOSITS

only domestically but to the former Soviet republics as well. Oil exported to Europe brought $18 a barrel, but oil companies got only 25 percent of the resulting revenues, the rest going to the government as a royalty.

At those prices, particularly with the virulent inflation raging in the country, the state companies producing the oil were not getting a sufficient return to replace worn out or broken equipment. Domestic petroleum prices were subsequently allowed to rise to 40 percent of world levels, but a new 50 percent royalty tax acted as a negative incentive.

Another disincentive was Russia's system of oil–export quotas, which required oil producers to sell 65 percent of their output at home, at prices 70 percent less than the world price. In an attempt to raise its own revenues, the government also instituted a $5 a barrel tax on oil exports. After strong pressure from the IMF and the World Bank, Russia ended quotas on oil exports as of January 1, 1995, though the new export tax of $3.75 a barrel instituted as an alternative depressed oil exports even further. Domestic oil prices then began to rise gradually toward world levels, and that produced some new investment in 1996–97. That trend was reversed in 1998, however, and new investment only began to grow again after 2000.

Putin's Energy Policy

Somewhere during his first term, President Putin decided that privatization of the energy sector had not served the best interests of the Russian people. In particular, he was disturbed by the new wealth being amassed in the privatized energy sector even as the government remained starved for funds. It also bothered him that some of the new oil barons were using their wealth to finance opposition political movements. Putin concluded from all of this that the "commanding heights" of the energy sector had to be brought back under government control.

This led to the move against Mikhail Khodorkovsky and the eventual destruction of Yukos, the best run energy company in Russia. It also led to the government's decision to regain majority ownership of Gazprom, then primarily a producer of natural gas, and—in the words of Dmitry Medvedev, its current chairman and concurrently a deputy prime minister—"to gradually transform it into a global energy company and a world market leader."

This was possible because a Gazprom-controlled subsidiary already controlled Russia's gas pipelines and Gazprom held a monopoly on gas exports—a sop given it in the 1990s when the government required it to provide gas domestically at low, controlled prices.

Most of Russia's reserves of natural gas are located in Siberia. Most of the natural gas is found in West Siberia, in the northern part of Tyumen Province. These are the Urengoi Fields. Some natural gas also comes from the area of the East Siberian Lowland. The production of natural gas has grown greatly in importance in recent years as new fields have been found and exploited. Production is down from a daily output in the 1980s of 1,000 million cubic meters—equivalent to 29 percent of total world output in 1981—but Russia remains the world's leading exporter of natural gas.

Gazprom, now Russia's main producer of natural gas, produces around 550 billion cubic meters (bcm) of gas a year. Gazprom could invest in developing untapped Arctic fields, but it has chosen not to do so. Instead, it has signed contracts to buy natural gas from Uzbekistan and Turkmenistan. This arrangement has been profitable for Gazprom because it has been able to obtain gas from these republics for about one-third of what it charges its customers in Central and Western Europe. Gazprom is increasing the capacity of the Central Asian pipeline to accommodate these increased amounts, and it has begun construction on another gas pipeline with a capacity of 30 bcm per year to connect Central Asia and Russia.

Russia

In June 2006, Gazprom used its wholly-owned subsidiary, Gazprombank, to purchase a 51 percent interest in Sibneftegaz, the owner of the large Beregovoye field in western Siberia. Sibneftegaz, a wholly-owned subsidiary of the gas production company Itera, had not developed the field because Gazprom's refusal to give it access to its gas pipeline network meant that it was unable to get the gas to market. Two other independent gas producers, North Gas and Novatek, were similarly denied access to Gazprom's pipelines until they allowed Gazprom to buy into their companies. Gazprom currently owns 19.4 percent of Novatek, while the state-owned Vneshtorgbank owns a further 5.6 percent.

It appears, however, that Gazprom may be willing to allow the Shell Oil Company to buy a 20 percent interest in Novatek as compensation for agreeing to sell Gazprom half of its interest in Sakhalin-2. As part of the deal on Gazprom's entry into Sakhalin-2, Gazprom signed a cooperation agreement with Shell allowing the lattter to expand its resource base in Sakhalin outside the Sakhalin-2 project.

Gazprom became a major oil producer when it paid Roman Abramovich $13 billion for 72 percent of Sibneft in September 2005. Prior to the acquisition, Gazprom had produced 12 million tons of oil a year; after its acquisition of Sibneft, its annual production became 46 million tons a year. This put in Gazprom third place among publicly traded oil and gas companies, with a market capitalization of the St. Petersburg Stock Exchange of $224.6 billion.

Gazprom recently put the squeeze on TNK-BP, a 50-50 joint venture between British Petroleum and three Russian tycoons, over a Siberian gas field called Kovykta. TNK-BP's license required it to produce 9 billion cubic meters of gas a year; however, TNK-BP was forbidden to export gas and domestic demand was perhaps a third of the required output. TNK-BP proposed a joint management agreement on Kovykta with Gazprom, but Gazprom refused. In June 2007, under threat that the Russian Government would revoke TNK-BP's license for the field, British Petroleum agreed to sell its stake to Gazprom. It is expected to get between $700 and $900 million for the field, somewhat more than the $500 million it spent developing the field.

In general, Gazprom has not spent significant sums to develop new fields, but has preferred to take over fields developed by other gas producers; most of its growth has been accomplished in this manner. As an exception, however, Gazprom is willing to develop new fields if foreign companies put up most of the basic capital in return for future deliveries of natural gas. One such current develop-

View of Lake Baikal

Courtesy: NOVOSTI

ment is in the area of Novy Urengoy, in western Siberia. Two German companies have put up $1.5 billion to finance development of the field; if all goes well, Gazprom will begin shipping natural gas to Germany in 2010.

Gazprom thus represents the new model of Russian capitalism that has emerged since Putin became president in 2000; at the same time, it represents the contradiction which is inherent in that new model. Gazprom is a huge, largely state-owned and wholly state-directed company; at the same time, it is a publicly traded company whose stock is available for purchase by private investors. Since 2005, several more such companies have come into existence in Russia.

Another part of the picture is provided by the history of Rosneft, a state-owned oil company which went from being a middling oil firm in 2004 to Russia's second largest oil producer in 2005. It then went on to become Russia's largest crude producer in May 2007 when it picked up Tomskneft, the last remaining Yugos subsidiary, at a bankruptcy sale. The sale included the Angarsk and Achinsk refineries plus the East Siberian Oil Company.

The secret behind Rosneft's growth is that 70 percent of its output comes from a subsidiary called Yuganskneftegaz, which until December 2004 was owned by Yukos. Rosneft therefore owes its growth to the destruction of the Yukos Oil Company. The Russian Government forced the sale of Yuganskneftegaz in 2004 to pay for several billion dollars in tax liens against Yugos, the mother company. Yuganskneftegaz was purchased for $9.4 billion by a fictitious company set up by the Russian Government; it was then immediately sold to Rosneft. After the sale, the Russian Government magically reduced the tax claims against Yuganskneftegaz by $3.9 billion.

According to newspaper reports at the time, President Putin originally intended Yuganskneftegaz to go to Gazprom; worries about possible civil lawsuits against Gazprom by disgruntled Yukos stockholders led the government to create the fictitious company and arrange the resale to Rosneft. To pay off money borrowed to finance the purchase of Yuganskneftegaz, Rosneft made an initial public offering of $10.4 billion of its stock in London and in Russia in July 2006. With the company's oil reserves larger than those of Exxon and its profits in 2005 almost five times higher than in 2004, many foreign investors were willing to forget how Rosneft got 70 percent of its assets.

The surprise, however, was that $1.1 billion of the shares were bought by Malaysia's state-run oil company, Petronas. The second government-run company to participate in the offering was the China National Petroleum Corporation, which took another $1.5 billion of the shares.

Although it is clearly the intent of the Russian Government to obtain control over the "commanding heights" of the energy sector, it does continue to permit individual private Russian oil companies to grow and prosper. The best example of this is Lukoil, the second largest producer of crude oil in Russia.

One of Lukoil's attractions to the Russian state is that it has aggressively expanded abroad, opening the American market for Russian gasoline sales. Over the past several years, Lukoil purchased the Getty Petroleum Marketing Company plus ConocoPhillips stations in New Jersey and Pennsylvania (Mobil brand); Lukoil now operates over 2,000 service stations in 13 eastern states, all of them supplied with gasoline shipped from its Vysotsk terminal on the Baltic Sea near St. Petersburg.

Although the general policy of the Russian Government is to bring energy production under state control, until recently it had continued to encourage foreign investment in technically challenging projects, particularly those offshore or in the Arctic. The largest of the projects being developed by foreign capital is the offshore drilling east of Sakhalin Island in Eastern Siberia.

Although Russian state companies pumped oil from wells on Sakhalin Island beginning in the 1930s, it was only in the 1970s that large pools of oil and gas were discovered off Sakhalin Island itself. The government mapped the offshore recoverable reserves at the time, but it then lacked the money and the technical expertise to develop the field itself.

In the 1990s, when the area was opened for foreign development, Exxon Mobil put together a consortium, Exxon-Neftegas Ltd., to develop the field; the two other participants were Mitsui & Company and the Mitsubishi Corporation. Somewhat later, Royal Dutch Shell set up the Sakhalin Energy Investment Company and began developing a second part of the field; in 2004, Gazprom became a shareholder through the mechanism of an asset swap. More recently, BP began developing a third section.

Oil production of 300,000 barrels a day began in October 2005; this is expected to grow to 550,000 barrels a day by 2008, when it will constitute 10 percent of Russia's total oil production.

Shell also began building two 400-mile pipelines, one for oil and one for gas, that begin at two huge offshore drilling platforms in the Sea of Othotsk off Sakhalin Island. The gas pipeline will end at Aniva, where a $2.5 billion liquefied gas plant is under construction. The oil pipeline will end at a deep-water loading terminal on a bay 90 miles northeast of Japan.

The plan of the private companies was to export the oil to China, Japan and South Korea, though Exxon intended to ship some of its oil through an existing Russian-owned pipeline. Much of the natural gas was to be shipped to a terminal being built in northern Mexico. From there, it was to be fed into a pipeline and shipped to California.

Now those plans are moot. In September 2006, Russia's Natural Resources Ministry wrote to the companies essentially demanding that the original agreements be rewritten. That same month, the Russian Government withdrew its environmental approval for the Sakhalin-2 liquefied natural gas project. After some months of negotiations, Royal Dutch Shell and its two Japanese partners were forced to cede control of their Sakhalin-2 venture to Gazprom.

Sakhalin-1 is still operating, but the Russian Government awarded a bid to a small oil field near Sakhalin-1 to Rosneft rather than Exxon in September 2006. Russia is now threatening to disallow $4.2 billion in cost overruns associated with Sakhalin-1. It appears clear that non-Russian companies will be limited to a minority—and probably diminishing—role in the development of Russian energy in the future.

One of the Soviet Union's larger and more controversial industrial projects in the 1980s was a 3,400 mile pipeline constructed from the Urengoi fields of Siberia to Western Europe. The pipeline was largely constructed with Western technology and credits, with the Western European countries that have financed it—Great Britain, France, Germany and Italy—receiving payment in future gas deliveries. The first gas began to flow to Western Europe in December 1983.

Russia is currently planning the construction of an oil pipeline to connect with Germany along the bottom of the Baltic Sea. It is also constructing an oil pipeline to the Pacific, which will allow it to export large quantities to oil to Japan. A spur may also be built which will connect the pipeline to China. In the meantime, Russia has contracted to begin exporting oil to China through a pipeline which Kazakhstan recent built which connects Kazakhstan's western oilfields and western China.

Russia's oil pipelines are controlled by Transneft, a state-owned joint-stock company which has a network of about 50,000 kilometers of pipelines that carry more than 95 percent of the crude oil produced in Russia. As with the case of Gazprom, Transneft's shares are traded on the Moscow Stock Exchange; again, like Gazprom, 75 percent of its shares are owned by the Russian Government, which actually owns 100 percent of the voting stock. Transneft is currently constructing the Baltic Pipeline System as a way of reducing Russian dependence on shipments through neighboring countries. It is also attempting to gain control of oil pipelines in other parts of the CIS and in Central and Western Europe for the same reason.

Until recently, a second state-owned company, Transnefteprodukt (TNP), controlled the pipelines which handled the export of refined oil products. In 2006, over 16 million tons of gas product was moved through TNP pipelines.

In April 2007, however, President Putin signed a decree transferring ownership of TNP to Transneft. As Putin's decree states, the purpose of the merger is "to create a unified system of transporting crude and products in order to protect the country's economic interests. Russia's long-term goal is to process more crude inside the country and thereby increase product exports, thereby diversifying away from dependence on exports of raw materials."

The Russian Federation, and the Republics of Kazakhstan and Ukraine together contain almost 20 percent of the world's known reserves of coal and lignite. The three republics today account for nearly a quarter of all coal mined in the world. Russia's two largest coal fields, which are both located in Siberia, were de-

Moscow's Arbat Street in summer

Courtesy: NOVOSTI

Russia

veloped by the Soviet Government after 1917. Pechora, the first Siberian field developed, is in the far north at the beginning of the Ural Mountains, along the Barents Sea. More interesting—and more challenging—is a major new coal field located in the southern part of the Republic of Yakutsk–Sakha (formerly the Yakutsk Autonomous Republic), which the Soviet Union began developing in 1974 in a joint project with Japan.

The Republic of Yakutsk–Sakha in eastern Siberia has large deposits of gold, diamonds, gas and tin, in addition to coal. But it is also one of the coldest inhabited places on earth, with temperatures known to plunge to –60°C (–108°F). It is also extremely remote from the major populated areas of Russia.

This provides a problem for any form of development, but presents a especially difficult one in the case of a low value, bulk item like coal. As early as the 1930s, Soviet scientists had identified deposits of high grade coking coal in the vicinity of the city of Neryungri, estimated to be as large as 300 million tons. It is an isolated area, however, and the Soviet government poured its limited development funds into more accessible areas. Then, in 1974, the Soviet Government negotiated a joint project with a number of Japanese companies to develop the coal field. The Japanese companies provided the necessary technology and equipment, while the Soviet Union built a spur rail line to connect Neryungri with the Baikal–Amur Railway (BAM), a new railway constructed in the 1980s that runs parallel to but north of the Trans–Siberian Railway. The Japanese

Religious procession in Moscow
Courtesy: NOVOSTI

payment was in the form of deliveries of coal.

The project was eventually completed, though capital costs turned out to be four times the level of European Russia, and the project took several years more to complete than originally planned. As a result of the development, however, Yakutsk, the regional capital, has grown from a small settlement to 200,000 people. The potential for further development in this area is very great, though costs remain a significant factor.

Russian deposits of iron ore are found, first of all, in the Ural Mountains and, secondly, in the mountains that form the southern border of Siberia, particularly in the area around Lake Baikal. There are vast deposits around Lake Baikal, but the iron mines of the Urals are extremely old and largely worked out, having been originally developed in the 18th century. But Russian iron ore deposits are lower in ore content than those of the Republic of Ukraine, particularly those of Krivoy Rog, where the pure iron content runs as high as 68 percent. Russia will continue to get much of its iron from the Ukraine for the next several years, but development of the iron deposits of the Lake Baikal area is a good possibility for the future.

With respect to other ferrous metals, the Russian Federation is remarkably endowed; it is the world's largest producer of manganese and chromium and has substantial reserves of nickel, titanium and vanadium. On the other hand, there is a relative shortage of such important metals as cobalt, molybdenum and tungsten, all of great importance in steel production.

Insofar as non–ferrous metals are concerned, copper mining resources, developed primarily since World War II, now produce about 12 percent of the world total. Tin is in relatively short supply; lead and zinc are available in relatively large quantities. Russia is the world's second–largest producer of gold, though production is down and the mines, at the moment still all state owned, have been having labor problems. The production of light metals such as aluminum is steadily growing; the known deposits of aluminum ore are estimated to be adequate for at least forty years.

In discussing the natural resources of this country, mention must be made of the extensive system of waterways. Because of the difficulty in building roads in some areas, waterways played an important role in past centuries. The network of navigable inland waterways, totaling some 75,000 miles, is still of importance in reaching certain otherwise almost inaccessible areas, but the total volume of goods now carried by water is no more than 10 percent of the total. Practically no rivers

remain open all year, and those that do suffer from seasonal shortages of rainfall which makes them too shallow.

The water resources of the Russian Federation have been used to construct hydroelectric power stations, including some of the largest in the world. An intricate system of canals, developed in the past, is still maintained and continues to play a significant economic role.

Paved roads continue to be scarce and the number of all–weather roads suitable for trucks is limited, so people and goods are still carried primarily by railroad. The Soviet Union was the first country to use jet airplanes for passenger traffic and certain remote areas can still be reached only by air; thus the network of air routes gets much use. Flights tend to be irregular and many times are simply cancelled. Railroads have been designated a "Commonwealth" interest, and the newly independent republics are committed to maintaining the integrated network that had existed under the now defunct Soviet Union.

Nuclear Power

Until the nuclear accident at Chernobyl in April 1986, the Soviet Union had been committed to nuclear power as a major source of electric power. At that time, the USSR had a capacity of 17.5 million kilowatts generated from this source and it had 18 more nuclear power stations under construction. In addition, Russia had produced two prototype industrial fast breeder–reactors, plus two nuclear heat supply stations, each of which was designed to produce enough heat for a city with a population of about 400,000. The most important reason for this ambitious program was the severe lack of alternate energy sources in the area of European Russia. The nuclear accident at Chernobyl changed all that. Under growing public

Source: *The Economist*

pressure, most of the nuclear power stations under construction were put on hold, and then later canceled entirely.

Chernobyl is a small town about 60 miles north of Kiev, in the now independent Republic of Ukraine. The plant had four reactors, two with "containment" buildings and two without. An experiment was underway using one of the unprotected devices when a sudden burst of power surged through the reactor, causing a steam leak. This led to the formation of hydrogen gas, which then exploded, demolishing the roof of the plant and killing two workers. Unrestrained by containment, the released radioactive gases quickly spread into the atmosphere, leading to widespread contamination not only of Soviet territory, but of neighboring nations as well.

The world found out about the accident two days later when the Swedes, detecting increased radiation in the atmosphere, began making inquiries. After first denying that anything untoward had occurred, the Soviets finally admitted the fact of the accident. It is now known that the reactor which got out of control was an unusual type that made use of graphite in its core. The graphite caught fire when overheating occurred. There was at least a partial "meltdown" and the reactor continued to spew out radiation for about two and a half weeks before it began to be controlled.

About 300 radiation victims were brought to Moscow hospitals; thirty five of these had suffered severe radiation exposure. Emergency bone marrow transplants were performed under the direction of an American surgeon. The death toll from radiation quickly reached 19 out of the 35; *The Times* of London later 1`reported that the figure had grown to 31 and that 209 others "remained in hospitals or sanatoria suffering from various degrees of radiation sickness." Dr. Gale, the American surgeon who performed the emergency bone marrow transplants gave as his own estimates that there were "about 50,000 to 100,000 individuals who have received at least some dose [of radiation] that may be of long–term concern. Twenty years later, an April 2006 *National Geographic* report lowered this estimate considerably; as the article put it, it is now estimated that "the cancer fuse lit by Chernobyl will claim 4,000 lives."

Even so, that does not alter the fact that Soviet handling of the Chernobyl disaster was, at best, shabby—both with its delay in reporting what happened and its subsequent failures of communication. Primary blame was placed on local officials who "didn't have a true assessment of the accident."

The Soviet Union did carry out major modifications of the 14 other graphite–core nuclear reactors which it operated. It also announced that future reactors would have containment buildings and would be pressurized. That was not enough for an increasing number of Soviet citizens, however. Protests grew around the Soviet Union and, increasingly, republic governments began putting pressure on the central government to cancel nuclear reactor building programs in their republics. The Soviet Government canceled the two reactors it had been planning to build at Chernobyl, and later stopped construction on a number of other plants in southern Russia, Armenia, and elsewhere, but it never abandoned its commitment to nuclear power.

The Russian people were not among the major protesters against nuclear power in the past, but there was an increasing movement in Russia in the 1990s urging that the government phase out nuclear energy. The government, concerned about the continuing energy shortages in the area of European Russia put the entire question on hold for the next several years.

The matter was reopened in November 2005 when President Putin appointed Sergei Kirienko as the new head of the Atomic Energy Agency. In his acceptance speech, Kirienko said that the government intended to build a new generation of nuclear power plants to replace the plants that would shortly have to be retired. Two months later, President Putin said that he wanted nuclear plants to provide one-quarter of Russia's energy needs to be provided by nuclear plants by 2030, up from the 16–17 percent derived from nuclear energy at that time. Kirienko, speaking two days later, said that Russia needed to build 40 new nuclear plants to meet the 25 percent figure. Russia currently has 31 nuclear reactors in operation.

In March 2006, Viktor Opekunov, who chairs the Duma's Atomic Energy Committee, said that the government intended "to consolidate the nuclear power industry and turn it into a 'vertically integrated holding" under state control." Two months later, TVEL was set up as a state holding company with control of all the enterprises that make up the country's nuclear power industry. The new head of TVEL is President Putin's own chief of staff, Sergei Sobyanin.

Another state-owned consortium, which may eventually become a part of TVEL, is Rosenergoatom. In June 2006, Rosenergoatom announced that it had begun constructing the world's first floating nuclear power plant to provide electric power to populations in the area of the White Sea; the consortium also indicated that the government planned to construct six additional floating nuclear power plants to provide power to other remote areas. These projects mirror other recent government actions to bring strategically important sectors of the economy under state control, as was done, for example, with oil and gas and the aircraft industry.

The government has also announced plans to bring all Russian uranium-producing enterprises together in a single holding company. The holding company also has plans for partnerships with partners from former Soviet republics. One such partnership already exists with the Republic of Kazakhstan. Inaugurated in December 2006, the joint venture will extract uranium for further processing in Russia. Two Russian companies, Tekhsnabexport and Atomredmetzoloto, have formed the joint venture with Kazakhstan's Kazakatomprom.

The Russian Government has the problem of disposing of tons of radioactive plutonium and enriched uranium from warheads now being disabled because of the CFE and START agreements. Disposing of the warheads alone will eventually cost billions of dollars. The U.S. Congress provided $400 million to help pay the cost of dismantling the missiles, but much more will be needed.

THE FUTURE

President Putin's overwhelming victory in the March 2004 presidential elections reflected the fact that he had done a good job as president during his first four years, but it signaled as nothing else could that he is the man who is totally in charge in Russia and that Russians like it that way.

Over his first four years, Putin established himself as an economic liberal with a strong authoritarian streak. As he began his second term, however, Putin instituted a series of programs whose purpose was to further centralize control in Moscow and reduce potential political opposition. In effect, Putin had gone from a program of "managed democracy," which characterized his first term, to an authoritarianism that is largely indistinguishable from a dictatorship. His decision to have the government take a commanding presence in the energy field, coupled with more recent decisions to reorganize and bring back under state control the aircraft industry, the airline industry, and the nuclear power industry, would indicate that he has abandoned his earlier flirtation with economic liberalism and intends to establish the same sort of control over the economy that he already exercised over political life.

If the lives of ordinary Russians continues to improve over the next several years—as is likely, considering the massive new wealth currently flowing into government coffers as a result of the recent great increase in energy prices—that is a trade-off that most Russians will probably gladly pay.

The Commonwealth of Independent States

Five of the plotters: Interior Minister Pugo and Vice President Yanayev
(third and fourth from left)

THE COLLAPSE OF THE SOVIET UNION

It was early in the morning in Moscow on Monday, August 19, 1991, when Soviet television issued its news bulletin. Mikhail Gorbachëv, alleged to be unable for health reasons to perform his duties, had been relieved as president. His powers had been transferred to his vice president, Gennadi Yanayev, who was to exercise them in consultation with an eight–member "State Committee for the State of Emergency," composed of himself, the prime minister, the ministers of defense and interior, head of the KGB, two individuals representing the military–industrial complex, and the chairman of the Farmers' Union of the USSR.

A state of emergency was announced throughout in the country, demonstrations and protest meetings were banned and independent newspapers were closed. Subsequently it was revealed that Gorbachëv had actually been in military custody since the preceding evening.

Although portrayed as an ordinary transfer of power resulting from the inability of the Soviet president to fulfill his duties, this was actually the beginning of an attempted *coup d'etat*, a fact that became clear as soon as one looked more closely at what was happening. First of all, if Gorbachëv had really been ill, his vice president could have temporarily assumed his duties without further ado. It was not necessary either to declare a state of emer-

gency or create a "State Committee for the State of Emergency" to supervise it.

Secondly, not only was every member of the "State Committee for the State of Emergency" a prominent conservative; this was the second attempt by four of them to assume Gorbachëv's powers. Two months earlier, the prime minister, Valentin Pavlov had asked the Supreme Soviet to give him the right to issue decrees that would not require Gorbachëv's signature; his request had been supported by the ministers of defense and interior plus the head of the KGB. Gorbachëv had to personally and energetically intervene to defeat this first maneuver of the conservatives. In retrospect, Gorbachëv should have dismissed Pavlov and the other plotters at that time, but he evidently thought he could continue to control them and he desired to rule by consensus without breaking with the more conservative members of his government.

Now the plotters were trying again. They decided to make their move because Gorbachëv, vacationing in the Crimea with his family, was due to return to Moscow that morning. A second consideration was that Gorbachëv was scheduled to sign a new union treaty the next day that would transfer considerable powers to the republics. Communist traditionalists opposed the new union treaty and were determined to stop it.

That the pending union treaty was a major factor in the timing of the *coup* was made clear by the plotters when they issued their first statement announcing the removal of Gorbachëv. Here they listed their aims as "overcoming the profound and comprehensive crisis, political, ethnic and civil strife, chaos and anarchy that threaten the . . . territorial integrity, freedom and independence of our fatherland" and referred specifically to the March 1991 "referendum on the preservation of the Union of Soviet Socialist Republics." Further, Yanayev's first action after assuming power was to cancel the treaty–signing ceremony. The question was, could the *coup* succeed?

In theory, it should have. The leaders controlled all of the traditional instruments of force within the country. Marshal Dmitri Yazov controlled the military as minister of defense; Vladimir Kryuchkov was head of the KGB and Boris K. Pugo controlled both security troops and the police as minister of the interior. They demonstrated this control by ordering tanks, troops and armored vehicles into the major cities at the beginning of the attempted *coup*, ringing republic government buildings with troops and tanks, and seizing control of television and radio facilities.

Moreover, the *coup* leaders included, in addition to the prime minister, the first

The Commonwealth of Independent States

deputy chairman of the defense council (Oleg Baklanov), the president of the Association of State Enterprises and Industrial, Construction, Transport and Communications Facilities of the USSR (V.A. Staradubtsev) and the chairman of the Farmers' Union of the USSR (A.I. Tizyakov). Further, they had the support of the *Communist Party* and a significant percentage of officials throughout the country.

It must be noted that the *coup* would probably have succeeded two or three years earlier. What the leaders overlooked, however, was the significant democratization that had taken place over the preceding years. These moves had produced new leaders such as Boris Yeltsin, elected president of the Russian Federation in June 1991, and Anatoly Sobchok, mayor of Leningrad. An order was actually issued for the arrest of Yeltsin, but no attempt was made to take other democratic leaders into custody or even to dismiss them from their positions.

The attempt to arrest Yeltsin was bungled. Eluding his would–be captors, Yeltsin made it to the Russian Republic Parliament building by 10:00 a.m. and immediately began organizing opposition to the *coup*. His first step was to call a press conference to question the authority of the "State Committee for the State of Emergency." He followed this up with a decree ordering all Russian Republic citizens to obey the orders of the Russian Republic Government, rather than the orders of the unconstitutional "Committee."

In perhaps his grandest gesture, he then went outside where tanks ringed the parliament building, climbed up on top of one of them, and called for an "unlimited general strike" and mass civil disobedience. The soldiers, apparently devoid of orders about what to do in case of opposition, allowed Yeltsin to then climb down and go back into the Parliament building. Subsequently, thousands of Yeltsin supporters gathered around the structure and, forming a human shield, made it impossible for the *coup* leaders to move against Yeltsin and his democratic supporters without inflicting major casualties.

The *coup* leaders overlooked many things, but perhaps their greatest failure was in communications. They took the traditional action of seizing control of the radio and television stations (which abruptly acquired an air of unreality) and they closed down opposition newspapers, but they never gained control of telephone lines or stopped foreign reporters from filing their dispatches with their home organizations. As a result, the democrats built up their own internal communications using computers and modems (a means for communication by telephone line from one computer to another). News of the *coup* and

growing opposition to it was broadcast to the Soviet Union by the BBC, Voice of America, and the rest of the international media. The Soviet people also learned thereby of the nearly universal condemnation of the attempted *coup* by world leaders. Western nations suspended aid programs and otherwise made it clear that its leaders would find themselves isolated internationally if they won.

What the leaders also forgot to take into account was the possibility that parts of the military and the KGB might be weaned away from loyalty to the attempted *coup*. In fact, however, as popular demonstrations grew, many individual commanders

adopted a passive stance or actively threw their support to Yeltsin and the forces of democracy. In Leningrad, 200,000 demonstrators gathered in the square outside the Winter Palace, while in Siberia coal miners announced a protest strike. Gradually, one after another of the Republic leaders came out against the *coup*.

When it became clear to the *coup* leaders that the Soviet people (1) would not accept their rule peacefully and (2) that they could win only through a ruthless use of force and a continuing regime of oppression that would leave the Soviet Union isolated internationally, one after another of the *coup* leaders lost his nerve

August 20: A heavily–armed bodyguard watches over Russian President Boris Yeltsin inside the Russian parliament.

Reuters/Bettmann

127

The Commonwealth of Independent States

and the movement began to collapse. After approximately 60 hours, Gorbachëv was freed, the troops were ordered out of Moscow, and an order went out for the arrest of the *coup* leaders.

Boris Pugo, minister of the interior, committed suicide as did, later, Marshal Sergei Akhromeyev, Gorbachëv's chief military adviser, who was implicated in the attempted *coup*. Aleksandr Bessmyrtnikh, the foreign minister, was fired because of questionable loyalty despite his protests of innocence which were even expressed by live satellite TV in the United States.

The Return of Gorbachëv and Collapse of the Union

Gorbachëv arrived back in Moscow Thursday morning to loud cheers but, though he claimed to be in complete control of the Soviet Union, it soon became clear that the three–day attempted *coup* had rung a death knell to the old system. Even as Gorbachëv defended the *Communist Party* and promised to work for its renewal, Yeltsin issued a decree banning party activities in the Russian Republic and specifically prohibited party cells in military units, police units of the ministry of interior and in the KGB.

Abruptly, on Friday, Gorbachëv, speaking to the Russian Parliament, abandoned his earlier defense of the party and referred to the Central Committee as "traitors." On Saturday, he followed this up by resigning as General Secretary and calling on the Central Committee to dissolve itself. He then issued a decree suspending the activities of the party and seizing all its property. This about–face created a serious problem of credibility.

The Soviet Union, which Gorbachëv still hoped to save, was crumbling around him. Estonia had declared itself independent on August 19 and Latvia followed the next day. In the week following the defeat of the *coup*, four more republics followed with their declarations of independence: the Ukraine on August 25; Byelorussia (now Belarus) on August 25; Uzbekistan on August 26; and Moldavia (now Moldova) on August 27. Armenia set a referendum for a vote on independence for September 16.

Several of the other republics also promised to hold plebiscites to confirm their declarations. The most important of those was the Ukraine, which set its referendum for December 1. Thus the situation was that, including Lithuania and Georgia, which had declared their independence even before the attempted *coup*, nine of the fifteen republics were committed to independence. If the republics really meant their declarations of independence, no viable union was possible. It was unclear whether their declarations of

independence were real or only bargaining tools in preparation for negotiations on a new union treaty.

The Rise of Boris Yeltsin and Attempts Toward Union

Crucially, Boris Yeltsin, president of the Russian Federation, still favored some form of union, and on August 28 he sent a delegation to the Ukraine to see what could be worked out. What he got was a provisional economic and military alliance which, the Russian and Ukrainian Governments announced, other "former subjects of the USSR" were welcome to join.

The next step came on September 2 when a special session of the Congress of People's Deputies met in Moscow, with the leaders of ten of the republics in attendance. Here Gorbachëv proposed the creation of a new interim government to replace the discredited one over which he presided. After three days of debate, the Congress voted, in effect, to dissolve itself and transfer authority to a new executive council and legislature controlled by the participating republics.

Gorbachëv remained president, but final executive authority was lodged in a State Council made up of Gorbachëv and the leaders of the participating republics. A separate Inter–republic Economic Committee, appointed by the State Council, assumed the functions of the former Council of Ministers. Finally, a two chamber legislature was established, the membership of the second chamber to be appointed by and represent the governments of the individual republics. In this chamber, voting would be by delegation, with each republic having one vote. This clearly interim government was to govern until a new union treaty could be signed by the individual republics bringing into being a proposed "Union of Sovereign States."

The first act of the State Council was to recognize the independence of Lithuania, Latvia and Estonia. It can be argued that recognition had become inevitable by this time, since most of the world, including the United States, had already recognized the independence of the Baltic Republics. Nevertheless, this was the first formal step in the breakup of the Soviet Empire. Even at this time, only ten of the twelve remaining republics were supporting the interim government. Moldavia refused to participate at all and Georgia sent only observers. Neither appeared likely to sign a new union treaty. In addition, over the next several days, all of the remaining republics other than the Russian Federation, Kazakhstan and Turkmenistan declared their independence. Later, even Kazakhstan and Turkmenistan would join the list.

The next three months were to prove decisive. Gorbachëv, determined to save

some form of union and, recognizing that Boris Yeltsin's support was absolutely vital, dismissed all of his former advisers and accepted Yeltsin's advice on the make–up of his new government, surrounding himself with liberals and even appointing Ivan Silayev, prime minister of the Russian Federation (i.e. the Russian state), as chairman of the Inter–republic Economic Committee, a post which effectively made him the caretaker prime minister of the union government. He then asked the reform economist Grigory Yavlinski to draw up a plan for economic union which he presented in draft form to the State Council in September.

The leaders of ten of the republics attended the meeting and gave their general approval to the plan. The two missing leaders were the presidents of Moldova (formerly Moldavia) and Georgia. Zviad Gamsakhurdia, then president of Georgia, had made it clear that his government was pursuing a policy of complete independence and wanted nothing to do, even economically, with a union. The Moldovan Government was undecided whether to participate in an economic union and so chose to abstain.

The other key republic was the Ukraine, led by Leonid Kravchuk, the former head of the Ukrainian *Communist Party*, who had repudiated the party and become a convert to democratization and a market economy. Kravchuk himself supported the idea of some form of continued union at first, but he came under increasing pressure from the Ukrainian parliament, which opposed supranational ties as a limitation on Ukrainian independence. In October 1991, the Ukrainian parliament drew up two pages of objections to the pending economic treaty, after which the Ukrainian Government announced that it would not sign the agreement without significant changes in the language. Among the changes that the parliament was demanding was the right for the Ukraine to set up its own national bank, issue its own currency and, in general, to control its fiscal policy.

The Ukrainian parliament then decided that the deputies selected to represent the Ukraine in the Union Supreme Soviet would participate only in the Council of the Republic and only as observers. It came as no surprise, therefore, when the Ukraine joined Georgia and Moldova in boycotting sessions of the State Council called to talk about a new union treaty.

Thus, only seven republics agreed, on November 14, to establish a new "Union of Sovereign States." The additional two republics not signing were Uzbekistan and Armenia. Two weeks later, when the State Council met again, supposedly to initial the draft agreement, seven republics were again present but, this time, Uzbekistan was represented while Azerbaijan was missing. And instead of initialing the treaty, they decided to submit it to their republic parliaments for approval, a process that put the proposed treaty into severe jeopardy.

By this time, Leonid Kravchuk had dropped his earlier general support for some continuation of the union. Having said on November 12 that the Ukraine would "never sign" a treaty which would contain "even the slightest hint of certain governing central bodies," because "the center has fully exhausted itself," he added two weeks later that he would "take no part in the . . . talks on signing a new Union Treaty" and "all allegations that I meant to join the treaty later are nothing but fiction."

All of that might have become more or less academic, had the December 1 referendum on Ukrainian independence gone differently. In fact, nearly 90 percent of all Ukrainians voted *yes* for independence. At the same time, Kravchuk proved himself to be in line with Ukrainian thinking and a popular politician by winning 61.5 percent of the vote in the concurrent race for the newly created office of Ukrainian president.

"The independence of the Ukraine is a new political reality," commented Boris Yeltsin upon receiving the results of the Ukrainian vote. And what Yeltsin meant when he used the phrase "new political reality" was that Gorbachëv's draft for a political union was now dead. The Ukraine would not join and, as Yeltsin had already said, he could not conceive of a political union that did not include the Ukraine. As far as that goes, Gorbachëv had said much the same thing, although he apparently still hoped that the Ukraine might still be persuaded to reverse its stand. Yeltsin had no such hopes.

Yet Kravchuk had said on a number of occasions that he favored some kind of co-ordinating mechanism to handle the many problems of the now-separating republics. The question was what sort of political structure the Ukraine was willing to accept to achieve that coordination. Yeltsin decided to find out. He contacted Kravchuk and Stanislav Shushkevich, president of Belarus, and suggested that the three presidents meet the following weekend to discuss the future of the union. Shushkevich agreed to host the meeting and offered the use of a hunting lodge located not far from the Belarus city of Brest. "We came to the conclusion," Shushkevich commented after the meeting, "that we had to sort out the concept of the kind of union we are capable of building."

So the three leaders talked for two days and, in the end, they produced the agreement, which they signed late in the day on December 8, 1991, in the Belarusian capital of Minsk, calling into being the "Commonwealth of Independent States."

COMMONWEALTH OF INDEPENDENT STATES

The suddenness of the December 8th agreement probably shocked a lot of people, but two aspects of the agreement caused some disquiet in the beginning. The first was that the three signatories were the heads of the three Slavic republics of the old union, suggesting to some that they were creating a "Slavic Commonwealth," even though the agreement specified that membership was open to "all member states of the former USSR," plus "other states that share the goals and principles of the present agreement." The second cause for concern was that the agreement also specified that "the USSR has ceased to exist as a subject of international law and as a geopolitical reality."

The first issue was defused rather quickly when the leaders of the five Central Asian Republics met in Ashkhabad, Turkmenistan, and there signed an agreement to become co-founders of the Commonwealth of Independent States. This led to a conference in Alma–Ata, Kazakhstan, on December 21, 1991 which was attended by the presidents of eleven of the republics, with President Gamsakhurdia of Georgia the sole hold out. Even Georgia sent an observer, however. The three Baltic Republics were not represented, having made it clear earlier that they would not join any new political union.

At Alma–Ata, the eleven presidents signed a protocol making all eleven republics co-founders of the Commonwealth of Independent States. An additional protocol and two accords were also signed dealing with subsidiary matters. They also signed a resolution supporting Russia's claim to the USSR's United Nations membership, including its permanent membership in the Security Council. They further agreed to meet again in Minsk on December 30.

The December 30 meeting was actually the first "session" of the executive bodies of the Commonwealth of Independent States and included separate meetings of the heads of state and heads of government. A total of 15 documents was negotiated and signed at these meetings, fleshing out the structures of the CIS and establishing certain forms of cooperation. Since the CIS was seen as a coordinating body, there was to be no "center" as such—no president or prime minister, no

ministries and no legislature. Instead, using to some extent the structure of the European Community (EC), the leaders drew up documents creating a Council of the Heads of States and a Council of Heads of Government.

Another agreement created a "working group" as a sort of secretariat to "prepare organically and technically the holding" of the meetings of the two councils. Unlike the EC, however, they did not create the presidential commission and cadre of bureaucrats that plays such an important role in Brussels. In fact, possibly to underline that point, the CIS Heads of State agreed that the job of drawing up proposals on how this working group should be structured would be handled by a conference of CIS foreign ministers meeting in Minsk in early January.

Perhaps the most important topic discussed at the Minsk meeting was the future status of the armed forces. Immediately prior to the meeting, the defense ministers and chairmen of the committees for defense questions of the 11 member states had met in Moscow with Air Marshal Yevgeniy Shaposhnikov, named Soviet defense minister following the August attempted *coup* and designated temporary commander of the union forces at the Alma–Ata meeting.

An earlier proposal to maintain a unified armed force became moot when it became clear that the Ukraine, Azerbaijan and Moldova wanted to have their own armies. Thus the agreement that actually came before the CIS heads of state was based on the concept of joint CIS armed forces. The signed agreement stipulated that each republic had the right to establish its own army; but it also provided for continuation of a unified army under CIS command which republics could participate in if they wished. National armies were to be limited to conventional forces, however; all 11 republic heads of state agreed that nuclear forces would remain under unified command. Nuclear weapons were at that time based in four different republics—the Russian Federation, Ukraine, Belarus and Kazakhstan. All except for the Russian Federation had stated that they intended to go "non–nuclear"—that is, eventually to get rid of all nuclear weapons on their soil. In the meanwhile, it was agreed that the president of the Russian Federation would have primary authority over nuclear weapons with the other three republican presidents having a veto power on their use.

The Ukrainian Government immediately set about creating its own armed forces, and also moved to extend its control over the Black Sea fleet as well. Azerbaijan also moved to take control of the Caspian Sea fleet.

The Commonwealth of Independent States

The presidents of Ukraine, Belarus, and Russia: (l. to r.) Leonid Kravchuk, Stanislav Shushkevich, and Boris Yeltsin in Minsk, Belarus, December 8, 1991.

Reuters/Bettmann

Marshall Shaposhnikov, who also participated in the military discussions at the Minsk meeting, was named commander–in–chief of the CIS armed forces. A council of republic defense ministers was also created and charged with elaborating a common defense policy.

The CIS Heads of States also touched on the subject of foreign policy. In addition to a general commitment to coordinate policy, they signed an agreement which provided for the division of the former USSR's property held abroad, including embassy and consulate buildings.

Other agreements signed in Minsk included one that called for joint activities in the exploration and use of space, plus several that dealt with a number of regional issues which the various heads of state agreed to treat as matters requiring CIS cooperation. These included the problems of the Aral Sea, the consequences of the Spital earthquake [centering in Armenia], preservation of fish stocks in the Caspian Sea, and elimination of the consequences of the Chernobyl nuclear power station disaster.

Though he had very little faith in the viability of the Commonwealth of Independent States, President Gorbachëv recognized it as a *fait accompli*. He therefore agreed to a wind up of the old union by December 31 and the transfer of the Kremlin and the state bank to Russian control. Yeltsin, meanwhile, issued a series of decrees taking control of all union ministries other than defense and atomic energy. Gorbachëv himself resigned as president of the USSR on December 25. Separately

the USSR Supreme Soviet held its own last session on December 26. The handful of deputies present, far less than a quorum since most of the republics had already withdrawn their deputies, recognized the Commonwealth of Independent States before voting itself out of existence.

Thus the Union of Soviet Socialist Republics officially disappeared and the Commonwealth of Independent States came into being. The CIS did not, if fact, replace the USSR, since the individual independent republics see themselves as the collective heirs to the USSR. The CIS was not established as a sovereign entity, but rather as a coordinating body for the independent republics which make up its membership. For that reason, its significance, and even its viability, came under question at the time. In addition to Gorbachëv, among those who publicly questioned whether the CIS had any chance for long–time survival were Edward Shevardnadze, a former Soviet foreign minister and former president of Georgia, James Baker and Henry Kissinger.

Their criticisms were to the point. The CIS had then, and still has, a weak structure. It is also true that the CIS has not been able to contribute much toward the solving the mammoth problems faced by the newly independent republics.

On the other hand, the CIS came into existence precisely because the apparatchiks of the old center acted as a major force holding back and frustrating necessary reforms. Creation of the CIS got rid of most of that particular countervailing force. There are still many people who

question the long-term viability of the CIS but it must be pointed out that the CIS does provide a structure that has facilitated the negotiation of a number of multilateral agreements among individual members of the CIS in recent years.

Perhaps the greatest weakness of the CIS has been the political position of the Republic of Ukraine which opted out of most of the multilateral agreements negotiated for the first decade or so after independence because it feared that Moscow could use the organization as an instrument for continued domination. That changed when Ukrainian President Kuchma was elected head of the CIS Heads of State Council at its Kiev summit in January 2003. After that time, President Kuchma committed himself to revitalizing the CIS.

President Yushchenko, who replaced Kuchma at the beginning of 2005, had a fairly favorable attitude toward the CIS when he first came to power but events since that time have changed his attitude. The first of those was Gazprom's decision to begin charging world prices for natural gas furnished to Ukraine, Georgia, and Moldova—but not Belarus. It has not escaped anyone's notice that the three states being charged much higher prices are precisely those states who have recently taken the most independent stances toward Russia. One can, of course, make the argument that Gazprom's decision to raise prices was economically justified, even if it is majority-owned and controlled by the Russian state. However, Russia's decision this past winter to ban the importation of wines from Georgia and Moldova appears

130

to be an even cruder attempt to put political pressure on these three governments. It is therefore no surprise that sentiment is increasing in all three countries to withdraw from the CIS. If Russia took these actions for other reasons and never intended them as political acts, then it blundered badly. Clearly the CIS is much weaker today than it was in 2004.

ECONOMY UNDER THE CIS

The economy of the old USSR was designed and built as a single economy, with all important decisions coming out of Moscow. In addition, the first principle of the planners was economies of scale which translated into "bigger is better." Since all enterprises were owned and run by the Soviet state, they deliberately set out to create monopoly situations in every part of the economy, since these were considered to be more efficient. Accordingly, all over the Soviet Union, single, large factories were built, designed to serve the needs of a large part of the country or even, sometimes, the entire Soviet economy.

Such factories, being part of the "union" economy, took their orders from their supervising ministry in Moscow; the republic government exercised no control whatsoever. This made for a highly integrated economic system, though it also made it highly vulnerable, since a single, badly-run factory could disrupt a complete sector by failing to deliver acceptable products in good time. Two further factors were possible time delays and added transportation costs.

All of these factors were magnified tremendously in 1991 in the situation of a collapsing Soviet Union. As the individual republics moved to establish their political independence, they also moved to take control of their own economies. But when they tried to do so, they found that, in many cases, a significant part of their industry was totally dependent on deliveries of raw materials and parts from other republics and could not operate without these continued deliveries. Moreover, the same was true with regard to factory output. Worst of all, in many cases, too, the customers were factories located in other republics.

Just how complicated this could get was explained in November 1991 by V. Razumov, deputy minister of the former USSR ministry of the chemical and petroleum refining industry, just after the ministry had been abolished on November 15. Razumov used the example of the plastic that goes into making refrigerators. "One of the

Air Marshal Shaposhnikov arrives in Alma Ata, Kazakhstan, December 20, 1991
Reuters/Bettmann

many things that could make our life a little easier today," commented Razumov,

is refrigerators. But you can't make them in, say, Belarus, if you have no polystyrene, which is made in Kazakhstan. Kazakhstan cannot produce polystyrene unless ethylbenzene is supplied from Tataria. They cannot make ethylbenzene in Tataria if they have no benzene. And benzene is made from petroleum, which is extracted mainly in [the] Tyumen [region]. That is roughly the system that is currently just [barely] managing to supply plastic for refrigerators. It could easily be destroyed. The people of Tyumen will sell independently a little more of their petroleum, the refinery workers a little more of the benzene produced from their supply of petroleum, and so on, with the quantities being reduced at each stage of the production of plastic. And it could easily turn out that the end result is that we get no refrigerators.

Razumov was dealing with a single example. Just how serious is this problem for the overall CIS economy? A Moscow Interfax "Soviet Business Report," issued on October 31, 1991, looked at the overall problem based on 1989 data, the latest obtainable. What the report established was that 20.3 percent of all domestic trade was inter–republic in 1989. What the report also pointed out, however, is that the smaller republics were most closely bound into the old command economic

system, while larger republics like Russia and Ukraine were far less dependent on inter–republic trade.

Soviet Republics' Individual Share in Inter–Republic Trade
(from 1989 data)

	Imports	Exports	Average
Russia	12.2%	13.0%	12.6%
Ukraine	26.2%	26.6%	26.4%
Kazakhstan	36.6%	20.6%	28.6%
Azerbaijan	23.6%	41.6%	32.6%
Uzbekistan	40.5%	28.8%	34.5%
Georgia	34.4%	40.3%	37.4%
Kyrgyzstan	42.8%	32.5%	37.7%
Turkmenistan	40.2%	35.5%	37.9%
Armenia	39.7%	37.2%	38.5%
Tajikistan	48.9%	32.8%	40.9%
Belarus	37.5%	46.3%	41.9%
Moldova	43.3%	43.3%	43.3%

There was clearly some deterioration in inter-republic trade in 1991, but the number of alternate producers in the USSR/CIS is so limited that there is almost no likelihood that these figures had changed significantly by that time. What they make clear is that, except for the Russian Federation, there was a high level of mutual economic dependence among the republics which would lead to an almost total disruption if they were unable to work

The Commonwealth of Independent States

out some form of continued economic co-operation. A number of republics did negotiate bilateral trade agreements, but these did not work out very well, since suppliers and customers were seldom from a single republic or even from the *same* republic. An even more important problem was the matter of prices.

In the old Soviet Union, prices were largely symbolic, set by the state for reasons such as to subsidize development of individual industries or to discourage consumption, and having little or nothing to do with the international value of the articles. All of this was possible because it was then a closed system. In general, the prices of food, fuel and raw materials were kept low, while the prices of most consumer goods were above world prices. The movement to world prices after 1992 tended to disrupt inter-republic trade; some of the poorer republics were unable to pay the greatly increased prices for food and fuel, while other republics did not want to pay world prices for merchandise that did not meet world standards.

An even more important factor was the failure of the plan that called for all of the republics to continue using the ruble as their common currency. The former union-wide banking system having collapsed, the individual republics were unable to come to an agreement at the CIS level on the transfer of funds between the

Russian sailor in St. Petersburg

republics. The result was a rapidly growing mountain of debt, much of it owed to Russia. In response, the Russian Government first restricted credit to the other republics, then effectively forced them off the ruble standard. The various republics later developed their own currencies, but the CIS was very slow in developing adequate mechanisms for the transferal of funds between republics. As a result, inter-republic trade dropped by as much as 70 percent in the period 1992–94.

This was a transitional problem, of course, related to the fact that most economic activity in the CIS was still state-run. The real, long-term solutions were to be found in privatization and movement to a market economy. The various republican leaders were theoretically committed to move in this direction but, with the exception of Russia and, since 1993, Ukraine, the movement was extremely slow. Of the 12 members of the CIS, only Russia, Ukraine and Kazakhstan have made a full transition to market economies. After significant progress in the first years, war and political instability slowed the process in Georgia and Armenia, a situation which is only now beginning to improve. Belarus abandoned the process in 1994 when Alexander Lukashenka was elected president and this likely to remain its position so long as Lukashenka remains president. Moldova put the process on hold in 2000 after the *Communist Party of Moldova* returned to power; there is still very little support for further privatization, but the party is, in theory, committed to moving toward a market economy. Kyrgyzstan made some progress in the 1990s, and even became the first ex-Soviet republic to become a member of the World Trade Organization. However, a near collapse of the economy in 1998 has limited progress since that time. The least amount of progress is to be found in the three remaining states of Tajikistan, Turkmenistan and Uzbekistan. Tajikistan was sidelined by a civil war for several years and it is one of the poorest of the Central Asian states. The government is committed to transforming the economy, but it has very little to work with. Turkmenistan and Uzbekistan both have authoritarian leaders who have tended to view significant societal change as a threat to their power. In the spring of 2002, Uzbekistan negotiated an agreement with the IMF which committed it to begin the process, however, and it has made some minimal progress since that time; that leaves only Turkmenistan among the Central Asian states that remains committed to maintaining the status quo.

Developments Since 1992

The CIS heads of state and heads of government have continued to meet on a reg-

ular basis since 1992 and a large number of agreements have been negotiated. In some cases, only a minority of the republics have implemented the agreements, however. In 1993–94, the Russian Government began pushing for greater military cooperation at the CIS level, particularly with regard to guarding the old borders of the USSR, and it was successful in encouraging cooperation in this limited area. By the beginning of 1995, all of the CIS members except Azerbaijan had negotiated agreements authorizing the use of Russian troops along the frontier. And even in Azerbaijan, where Soviet troops were withdrawn after the collapse of the Soviet Union, Russian troops later returned to police the truce line between Nagorno-Karabakh and Azerbaijan proper.

Russian forces are, in fact, still quite active in the ex-Soviet republics. Russian troops prop up the Tajik government and they run Turkmenistan's army and frontier forces. Russian-Georgian relations have been something of a special case, but the Russian Government did negotiate a cease fire in Abkhazia, in return for a Georgian promise to join the CIS. Georgia later signed an agreement authorizing the stationing of Russian troops within its borders, though it now wants the Russian bases closed. Armenia, which has good relations with Russia, has a military agreement whereby Russian troops guard the Armenian border with Turkey. Although Belarus and Kazakhstan maintain separate armies, they work in close tandem with the military forces of Russia. As one Russian colonel commented, "the Belarusian army is virtually an adjunct of the Russian army." In the case of Kazakhstan, almost all officers are ethnic Russians and Russian is the language of command. It is probably wiser to think in terms of "influence" rather than "control," however. Such officers would undoubtedly support and even advise close cooperation with Russia, but there is no reason to believe they would disobey contrary orders deriving from the political leadership of their republics.

Ukraine, the chief holdout, held its participation in the CIS to a minimum during its first decade of independence and rejected any suggestion of "jointly" monitoring of CIS borders or CIS peacekeeping forces. Even so, the Ukrainian and Russian Governments reached an agreement in early 1995 to divide the Black Sea fleet between the two countries, and the Ukrainian Government also agreed to share the Sevastopol naval base with Russia.

Economic cooperation has been much harder to accomplish, however. When a CIS joint economic zone was mandated in 1994, individual CIS members hesitated to implement it, so what cooperation has taken place has been in the form of a series of bilateral and multilateral agreements. One of those was the Eurasian Economic Community (EEC), formed by Russia, Kazakhstan, and Belarus in January 1995. Kyrgyzstan and Tajikistan joined later. Separately, Russia and Kazakhstan signed an agreement calling for increased economic and military links.

Kazakhstan, Uzbekistan, and Kyrgyzstan also joined to form the Central Asia Customs Union, to which Tajikistan adhered in 1998. This was replaced by a new organization, the Central Asian Cooperation (CAC) in December 2001. CAC was meant to be a broader organization than the one it replaced, promoting political, economic, and military cooperation among the four member states. It is too early to say whether CAC will meet those goals, although the four presidents have met on several occasions since that time. In October 2002, they discussed removing customs barriers, improving transport infrastructure, expanding cooperation in the energy sector, regional security and the Afghan situation, and the rational use of the region's water resources. Turkmen representatives sat in on the meeting as observers. The current chair of the CAC is Uzbek President Karimov.

In October 1999, all of the CIS members with the exception of Belarus discussed introduction of a CIS free trade zone at a CIS meeting at Yalta. They also signed preliminary documents that, among other things, reduced customs regulations. This proposal was a major topic of discussion at a CIS summit meeting that took place in Moscow in December 2001. President Putin told the other eleven presidents at that time that any kind of integration, political or military, must have a strong economic footing. He also promised that Russia would work on the regulations and legislation needed to establish a CIS free-trade zone.

The idea did not get very far as long as it was viewed as a concept being pushed by Russia. That seems to have changed somewhat after Ukrainian President Kuchma was elected head of the CIS Heads of State Council at its Kiev summit in January 2003. In his acceptance speech, Kuchma argued that the best way to revitalize the Commonwealth of Independent States was to shift the emphasis from the political to the economic and he pledged that all of his efforts as president of the Heads of State Council would be focused on expediting the creation of a CIS free-trade zone.

This led to a meeting of the presidents of Ukraine, Belarus, Kazakhstan and Russia in Moscow on February 22–23. Here, the four presidents designated their countries as "core" CIS states for the purpose of developing a CIS free-trade zone and

committed their governments to cooperate in creating a single economic space within the CIS, which the other eight CIS states were invited to join. It is too early to say what will come of this initiative, but the new role being played by Ukrainian President Kuchma gives this particular initiative a greater chance of success than earlier efforts.

One other form of regional cooperation is the organization known as GUAM, the name representing the four countries (Georgia, Ukraine, Azerbaijan, and Moldova) that were its founding members in 1996. Uzbekistan became the fifth member in 1999 and the organization then became known as GUUAM. Primarily a support group, and set up originally with the encouragement of the U.S. Government, GUUAM's main success has been in coordinating member states' positions in arms–control negotiations over the issue of Russian troop levels. One other area where GUUAM has played a role is in developing a coordinated position on east–west energy pipelines. In 2000, members began discussions on creation of a free trade zone, but the idea probably doesn't have much of a future now that Ukraine is putting all of its efforts into creation of a free–trade zone within the CIS.

The terror attacks of September 11, 2001 and the subsequent United States–led war on terrorism that began that fall also provided an organizational impetus to the member states of the CIS, as most of them soon became heavily involved through the granting of bases to the anti–terrorist coalition. But the Central Asian republics had already been dealing with the problem of terrorism prior to September 2001, and six of the states—Russia, Kazakhstan, Kyrgyzstan, Tajikistan, Armenia, and Belarus—had agreed in 1999 to create a CIS Collective Rapid Reaction Force under the auspices of the CIS Collective Security Treaty, signed in 1999. In September 2001, they signed a supplementary agreement calling for coordination of the work of their arms industries. The agreement is a significant one if implemented, since it would cover 1,500 firms in Russia and another 700 firms in the other five countries. In April 2002, the defense and foreign ministers of the six signatories met in Yerevan, Armenia, to discuss transforming the Collective Security Treaty into an international organization corresponding to the UN charter. On April 28, 2003, the six countries, meeting in Dushanbe, signed the final documents creating the Organization of the Treaty on Collective Security (ODKB). The ODKB will have its own budget, secretariat, military staff and rapid–reaction force. Its main military base will be the Kant airfield in Kyrgyzstan. Addressing the Dushanbe meeting,

President Putin said that, in addition to its main mission of combating terrorism, the ODKB would be used to deal with drug–trafficking, an increasing problem for the various Central Asian states.

In February 2002, at the CIS defense ministers meeting in St Petersburg, agreement was reached to restore an integrated CIS air–defense system. Colonel General Mikhailov, a Russian general, was placed in charge. Russia has been calling for greater coordination in the defense area and this may have been the result. As Russian Security Council Secretary Rushailo said to the assembled security chiefs on April 11,

the success of our economic cooperation will also depend on how effective our cooperative action will be in the fight against international terrorism.

Terrorism was on the agenda again at the October 2002 meeting of the CIS heads of state in Chisinau. All CIS presidents attended the meeting except for President Niyazov of Turkmenistan. The 11 presidents approved the establishment of a joint anti–terrorism center in Central Asia.

Some Regional Problems of the CIS

Aral Sea. Kazakhstan, Kyrgyzstan, Turkmenistan and Uzbekistan are members of the International Fund to Save the Aral Sea (IFAS), an organization which has been in existence since 1992. Following the CAC meeting in October 2002, the four presidents met to discuss the Aral Sea. Tajik radio, reporting on the meeting, said that the four countries had projects worth $300 million under way focusing on problems of water supply, irrigation, and land reclamation. As part of that, Kazakhstan indicated that it was currently implementing a $70 million project aimed as saving a section of the northern part of the Aral Sea. In spite of more than a decade of discussions, the four republics do not have a plan to replenish the Aral Sea, nor have they been able to agree on how to manage their shared water resources in a coordinated and rational manner. The inability to agree on a program aimed at replenishing the Aral Sea is understandable, since any solution would have to include reductions in the amount of water each republic would be permitted to use. However, floods along the middle reaches of the Syr Dar'ya near the Uzbek-Kazakh border in February 2004 made it plain that the problem is even more complicated than that. Essentially the floods were man-made and resulted from a breakdown in the system of regional water management that had been established during Soviet times. At that time, a series of dams or reservoirs was constructed along the Syr Dar'ya and its tributaries for the joint pur-

The Commonwealth of Independent States

pose of producing hydroelectricity and storing water for irrigation. With the disappearance of the Soviet Union, however, each republic took charge of dams or reservoirs on its territory and ran them to suit its own purposes. In the case of Kyrgyzstan, the primary purpose was to produce hydroelectricity, for which its greatest need was in the winter.

In years past, the Kazakh and Uzbek governments, whose need for water for irrigation comes during the spring and summer, had agreed to provide energy supplies to Kyrgyzstan during the winter

in order to reduce its need for hydroelectric power; however, those supplies were cut in 2003–4 because the Kazakh and Uzbek governments had had a reduced need for water in the previous summer. Faced with a shortage of energy, the government of Kyrgyzstan released water from its Toktogul Reservoir to generate hydroelectricity, and this led to flooding along the Syr Dar'ya downstream after the Chardara/Shardara Reservoir, jointly managed by the Uzbek and Kazakh government, reached its capacity. A temporary solution was reached when Kaza-

khstan agreed to provide Kyrgyzstan with coal and fuel oil so it could make greater use of its thermal plants. It is clear, however, that a permanent solution will require the creation of some kind of transnational water consortium or an expansion of the responsibilities of the current IFAS. Such a consortium, which would have to include Tajikistan since it controls one of the important upstream reservoirs, might then provide the impetus for cooperation on the larger problem of the continuing destruction of the Aral Sea.

Caucasian Regionalism. The continuing political instability of the area of the Caucasus can be explained largely by two factors, geography plus the astonishing ethnic diversity found throughout the area. Because of the extensive fighting that has taken place there over the past decade, Chechnya has come to symbolize this situation for the area of the north Caucasus, though in fact the neighboring Russian republics of Ingushia, North Ossetia, and Daghestan suffer from many of the same problems. To give just one example, a suicide bomber set off 66 to 132 pounds of explosives as he pulled next to the limousine of Ingush President Murat Zyazikov on April 6, 2004. The attack failed because it was an armored limousine. That same day, there were two bomb explosions in Daghestan, one outside a police station in Khasavyurt and the other a car bomb that exploded on a residential street in Makhachkala. The attempted assassination of President Zyazikov may have been related to events in Chechnya, since Zyazikov is a supporter of President Putin while the political opposition in Ingushia has close ties with former Chechen President Mashkhadov. Or both may have been carried out by Chechnyan radical Islamists committed to uniting the entire area of the north Caucasus under Muslim rule.

An additional factor is that all of the peoples of the northern slopes have close ties of culture and blood with peoples living on the southern slopes of the Caucasus Mountains in Georgia. The best example of this phenomenon is South Ossetia, which fervently wants to unite with North Ossetia. Although most of these populations are Muslim, ethnic ties appear to be the decisive factor in their political orientations. Except for the Chechnyans, in fact, most of the populations of the north Caucasus appear to be satisfied to remain a part of the Russian Federation. Moreover, two of the Georgian separatist areas, South Ossetia and Abkhazia, have made numerous requests to be allowed to join the Russian Federation. To be sure, all of the separatist movements on both the northern and southern slopes of the Caucasus arose at the time of the collapse of the Soviet

Uralmach, the biggest Russian machine–building plant, which makes equipment for both Russian and foreign nations. The plant is located in the city of Ekaterinburg.

Courtesy: NOVOSTI

134

Union, though the reason for the movements along the southern slopes appears to be related to the rise of an extreme Georgian nationalism at this same time which threatened the traditional autonomy of these ethnic non-Georgian areas. It also helped that the Russian military tended to encourage and support such movements, though an even more important factor was the political weakness of the Georgian Government in the 1990s and the almost total failure of the economy. Now President Saakashvili appears determined to recreate a strong central government and to revive the economy. Success in these two areas might well lead to an end to the dissident movements, particularly if their cultural differences with Tbilisi are adequately addressed.

Caspian Sea. The countries bordering on the Caspian have not been able to agree on how to divide the seabed of the Caspian. The main question under international law is whether the Caspian is a sea or a saltwater lake. If it is determined that the Caspian is a saltwater lake, then, according to international law, its various resources can only be exploited on the basis of an agreement signed by all bordering states. On the other hand, if the Caspian is a sea, its resources would be divided into national sectors that each country would have the right to exploit as it pleases. Russia and Iran had until recently contended that the Caspian is a saltwater lake. Azerbaijan and Kazakhstan, on the other hand, took the position that it is a sea. Turkmenistan, the last of the states bordering on the Caspian Sea, has been divided on the issue. It first sided with Kazakhstan and Azerbaijan, then switched its position in 1996 and until recently was supporting the Russian–Iranian position. In 1998, Russia and Iran indicated that they might be willing to agree that the Caspian is a sea if an appropriate division of the seabed could be worked out. However, Iran's recent claim to 20 percent of the seabed has been rejected by Azerbaijan. In spite of these disagreements Azerbaijan has signed agreements with a number of international oil companies for the development of what it considers its national sector. In September 2002, Azerbaijan signed an agreement with Russia delimiting the two countries' respective sectors of the Caspian Sea bed. Azerbaijan has also instituted talks with the Iranian Government concerning the Caspian Sea bed. Thus far, Iran has continued to insist on an equal division, though the Azerbaijani negotiator, Deputy Foreign Minister Khalafov, said in January 2003 that the two sides are drawing closer.

Radical Islam. Islam is the dominant religion of six of the 12 members of the CIS and together these six republics have a Muslim population of approximately 52 million. In addition, the Russian Federation is made up of several areas with large Muslim populations plus a few autonomous republics where the majority of the population is Muslim. In all, there are perhaps 20 million Muslims who are citizens of the Russian Federation. With approximately 72 million Muslims in the CIS, it would not be surprising if a certain percentage of them were fundamentalist Muslims and that among these fundamentalist Muslims one would find even more radical groups espousing some form of Islamic state.

And that is the case. On the other hand, it must be remembered that the Soviet Union was extremely intolerant of too overt religiosity and that this applied particularly to the adherents of Islam. Although the government became much more tolerant of religion under Gorbachëv, Islam was only beginning to recover somewhat when the Soviet Union collapsed.

All of the successor states were, and are, secular in their orientation and although they have been much more tolerant of religion than the old Soviet Union, all have tended to treat religion in a neutral way as a cultural phenomenon. On the other hand, their very neutralism meant that they were willing to allow the Saudis to provide money for the construction of new mosques and religious schools. Since there were very few trained religious leaders in any of the new states of the CIS, they for several years permitted religious leaders to be sent in from abroad, many from Saudi Arabia but also from other Muslim countries such as Jordan or Egypt.

Many of these teachers and religious leaders limited themselves to teaching the *Koran*, but some transmitted a political message that included a call for an Islamic government. In Russia, these movements were been largely limited to the area of the North Caucasus, and particularly associated with Chechnya—though it should be emphasized that radical Islam made its appearance in Chechnya only recently and was not responsible for the original Chechnyan War. Radical Islamists have also been active in neighboring Dagestan, though they have had little success in recruiting followers there. Even in Chechnya, where there are a significant number of radical Arabs fighting alongside the Chechnyans, their influence is still largely limited to such leaders as Shamil Basayev, while ordinary Chechnyans are more motivated by feelings of nationalism.

The situation is somewhat different in the Central Asian republics, and in particular in Uzbekistan, Kyrgyzstan, and Tajikistan. Here we find actual organizations and a growing number of new adherents who are carrying the message of radical Islam. The oldest of these organizations is the *Islamic Movement of Uzbekistan,* founded in the 1990s by an Uzbek who took the name of Juma Namangani. Namangani was killed in Afghanistan in 2001 but remnants of his organization continue to exist in Uzbekistan, Tajikistan and Kyrgyzstan. A second, even more pervasive organization is the *Hizb ut-Tahrir,* an organization that was founded in 1953 by Taqi al-Din al-Nabhani, a Palestinian who received an education in Islamic law in Egypt, and only recently introduced into Central Asia. In theory an organization that eschews violence, its main platform is the creation of a new emirate that would bring all Central Asians together under a new Islamic regime. Outlawed in every Central Asian republic, its followers have been arrested in every country of Central Asia and even in Russia.

Radical Islam is a worrisome phenomenon throughout Central Asia, but the Central Asian republics may be overreacting to its supposed threat. *Hizb ut-Tahrir* is indeed a potential threat to the secular governments throughout the area, but only a minor one at best. As for terror attacks, until recently they had been traced to members of the *Islamic Movement of Uzbekistan,* but it was believed that it had largely ceased to exist after Namangani's death. However the terrorist attacks that took place in Uzbekistan between March 28 and April 2, 2004 raise the issue whether the organization has been reconstituted. Uzbekistani officials are inclined to believe that the attacks, which involved at least two different female suicide bombers and resulted in the death of at least 44 persons, had to have been the work of the *IMU.* There are reputed to be about 800 active members in Uzbekistan, certainly sufficient to carry out this most recent series of terrorist attacks.

Russian student at College of Europe

WESTERN REPUBLICS

Showing principal cities (with Russian spellings)

The Republic of Belarus

Area: 80,150 sq. mi. (207,600 sq. km., about the size of Minnesota).

Population: 9.724 million (October 2006 estimate).

Capital City: Minsk.

Climate: Temperate.

Neighboring States: Russia (east), Latvia, Lithuania (northeast), Poland (west), Ukraine (south).

Languages: Belarusian, Russian.

Ethnic Composition: Belarusian (81.2%), Russian (11.4%), Polish, Ukrainian and other (7.4%).

Principal Religions: Russian Orthodox (80%). The government has extended legal recognition to 25 other religions, including Roman Catholicism, Lutheranism, Islam and Judaism but ascribes to the Russian Orthodox Church "a determining role" in national culture and government.

Chief Commercial Products: Grain, potatoes, cattle, agricultural machinery, motor vehicles, machine tools, oil, electricity, steel, coal and metal production.

Currency: Belarusian ruble. In a meeting of the Russia–Belarus Union Supreme Council in Minsk on 20 January 2003, it was reaffirmed that the Russian ruble would be introduced as the sole Russian–Belarusian currency as of 1 January 2005. This date was not met, however.

Per Capita Annual Income (Purchasing Power Parity): $7,700.

Recent Political Status: Part of the Russian Empire until 1917, became the Byelorussian SSR in 1919, part of the USSR (1922–1991).

Chief of State: Alexander Lukashenka, President (elected July 10, 1994).

Head of Government: Syarhey Sidorski, Prime Minister (appointed in December 2003).

National Flag: A broad red horizontal band fills in the upper two-thirds of the field, with a second, green stripe filling in the bottom third; a white vertical stripe on the hoist side bears Belarusian national ornamentation in red.

National Day: July 3 (1944), the date Minsk was liberated from German troops.

The Land

The Republic of Belarus is the ultimate independent successor state to the Byelorussian Soviet Socialist Republic, established on January 1, 1919. It is located in the northwestern portion of the Russian Plain, just southwest of the Valdai Hills. The northern part of the republic is made up mostly of low, rolling hills. Dzyarzhynskaya Mountain, the loftiest point in the republic, is only 1,135 feet high. Most of the southern part of the republic is covered by a lowland area known as the Prypyats (Pripet) Swamp. Much of this area is a mixture of swamp and forest with a very low population density.

Four major rivers flow through Belarus. In the north, the Western Dvina River, which begins in the Valdai Hills, enters from the east and then flows in a mainly northwestern direction until it crosses into Latvia, there becoming the Daugava. The Dnieper River also enters Belarus from the east, then flows in a southern direction a short distance west of the eastern border. It actually forms the eastern border for a short stretch before entering Ukraine. The third of the rivers is the Prypyats, which enters from the south from Ukraine, then flows eastward just north of the southern border. It crosses into Ukraine shortly before emptying into the Dnieper.

The last of the rivers is the Nyoman [Nemunas], which begins in northwestern Belarus, a short distance west of the capital city of Minsk, and flows west and then north before crossing the border into Lithuania. A tributary of the Nyoman, the Neris (Villia), starts in northwestern Belarus just north of Minsk. It flows in a meandering northwestern direction before crossing the border into Lithuania. Originally covered in forests and fens, today Belarus is a mixture of forests and fields. Reclamation projects in the south have reclaimed about 6.25 million acres of swampland, thereby increasing the agricultural potential of this area, particularly for pasturage, although hemp is another major crop. The south also has over six thousand peat deposits.

The People

According to an October 2006 report of the Belarusian Ministry of Statistics and Analysis, the country's population is 9,724,000, a drop of 321,200 since the 1999 census. According to the ministry, the population dropped by 26,500 persons in the first eight months of 2006. Belarusians constitute about 81.2 percent of this total. Russians, the largest minority group, are around 11.4 percent of the population. Other minorities include Poles, Ukrainians, Jews, and Lithuanians. Belarusian belongs to the eastern Slavic family of languages. It is fairly modern in origin and arose primarily for historical reasons. Its ancestor is Slavonic, which had been spoken by all eastern Slavs as late as the thirteenth century. This area became part of the Grand Principality of Lithuania in the fourteenth century. After the Lithuanian Union with Poland in 1569, the upper classes became heavily Polonized and this, plus the several centuries of separation, eventually produced a language that was different from either Russian or Ukrainian. As a result of the industrialization of the twentieth century, about half the population now lives in urban areas.

History

The area of the Prypyats (Pripet) Swamp, in southern Belarus, is believed to be the original home of the eastern Slavic peoples. Spreading out from that point, they eventually occupied most of the Russian Plain. The first organized Slavic state, Kievan Rus, came into existence as a trading state which controlled

Belarus

the "road from the Varangians (Vikings) to the Greeks." That "road" was the water system that permitted travel from the Baltic Sea in the north to the Black Sea and Constantinople in the south. The most important of those rivers was the Dnieper, which flows south through the eastern part of Belarus.

Kievan Rus was destroyed by an invasion of the Mongols in 1238–41. The collapse of that first Slavic state left the northwest in a state of anarchy which ended in the first half of the fourteenth century when Gedaminas founded the Grand Principality of Lithuania. It had its capital at Vilnius but the state extended southward as far as the Black Sea, including all of present–day Belarus. The majority of the people living in this state were Slavs and the language used at the court was old Slavonic, the language of Kievan Rus.

This situation continued until 1569 when Lithuania became part of the Polish Kingdom as a result of the Union of Lublin. From that time onward, the upper classes became increasingly Polonized. When an independent Patriarchate was established at Moscow a few years later, the Polish King separated the Orthodox Church in Lithuania from Moscow and forced it to recognize the Pope as the head of the church, thereby creating the Uniate Rite of the Church. That situation continued for over thirty years before the Orthodox Church was again allowed to begin operating again. After about 1625, therefore, you had a situation where the upper classes were Polonized and increasingly Roman Catholic and the peasants were Orthodox and enserfed.

The southern portion of the Orthodox lands broke away in 1654 and joined Russia; this became the Ukraine. But the northern Orthodox lands remained part of the Polish Kingdom until the three partitions of Poland in 1772, 1793 and 1795. These gave the area of present day Belarus to Russia. From 1795 to 1918, therefore, these lands were part of the Russian Empire. Russia did not recognize Belarusian as a separate language, however, so Russian became the language of government while Belarusian was merely the local dialect of the peasantry.

The Russian Revolution brought about a collapse of the old Imperial Government and the various parts of the empire began to set up autonomous governments. On March 25, 1918, anti–communist leftists established the independent Belarusian Democratic Republic. Lenin and his Bolsheviks in Moscow refused to recognize the new republic and it was later overthrown by the Red Army. On January 1, 1919, the communist victors set up the Byelorussian Soviet Socialist Republic.

The then Byelorussians accepted their inclusion in the new Soviet regime and they remained loyal and subservient citizens throughout the Soviet era. In return, Moscow transformed the country industrially over the years. In addition, the republic was greatly enlarged in November 1939 when significant territories taken from Poland as a result of the Nazi–Soviet Non–Aggression Pact were added to the republic.

Gorbachëv's program of *glasnost* and *perestroika* brought some changes in Byelorussia, but the majority of the communist leadership was conservative. A *Byelorussian Popular Front* was established but, harassed by the leadership of the republic, it found it difficult to build up support and it remained a minority movement. The Chernobyl nuclear accident in April 1986 created great fear throughout the republic, but the accident had actually occurred across the border in the Ukraine, so Belarusian officials were only blamed for not doing enough. They, in turn, blamed Moscow and otherwise helped keep a tight lid on news of the event.

When the attempted *coup* against Gorbachëv began in August 1991, Nikolas Dementei, the first secretary of the *Byelorussian Communist Party*, made the mistake of supporting the *coup* leaders. When the attempt collapsed, therefore, Dementei was ousted from his position as Chairman of the Supreme Soviet. On August 25, the Byelorussian Supreme Soviet also declared the republic's independence, adopting the name *Belarus* (initially spelled Belorus). It then suspended the activities of the communist party.

Stanislav Shushkevich was elected chairman of the Belarus Supreme Soviet

on September 20, 1991. He previously had held the position of first deputy chairman of the Supreme Soviet. He is a nuclear physicist by training, however, and "headed laboratories and departments of nuclear physics in various Minsk higher educational institutions." He was also a member of the USSR Supreme Soviet where he belonged to the liberal Interregional Deputies Group.

Shushkevich supported a continuation of some form of union as long as that appeared a viable option. After the December 1 referendum and elections in the Republic of Ukraine, however, Shushkevich joined with Presidents Yeltsin and Kravchuk in creation of the Commonwealth of Independent States on December 8. Shushkevich had hosted the meeting at his hunting lodge and the agreement was signed in Minsk, the capital of Belarus.

Once Belarus had opted for independence, Shushkevich pushed for "the speediest introduction of market relations and private ownership." However, the Belarus Supreme Soviet, still filled with ex-communists, was really controlled by Vyacheslav Kebich, who held the position of prime minister. Kebich, much more conservative, advocated a "go slow" policy. Because Shushkevich attempted to govern by consensus, he was never able to bring about very much economic change. Over time, however, his relations with Kebich grew worse. In January 1994, Shushkevich informally supported an attempt to oust Kebich. Kebich won the vote of confidence 175 to 101. The legislature then voted 209 to 36 to dismiss Shushkevich as chairman of the Supreme Soviet. Although Shushkevich had been an advocate of the need for economic reforms, the most important

One of the few buildings to survive World War II when most of the city of Minsk was destroyed, an Orthodox Church holds a lonely vigil as it stands surrounded by modern office and apartment buildings.

Photo by Miller B. Spangler

Marc Chagall's memory of his hometown Vitebsk (1922)

reason for his ouster was his nationalism. Kebich, feeling that the situation in Belarus had deteriorated after the collapse of the Soviet Union, wanted to rebuild economic ties to Russia. Shushkevich favored good political relations with Russia but opposed closer economic ties because he thought they would compromise Belarus's independence.

Following Shushkevich's ouster, the Supreme Soviet elected Myechyslaw Hryb as its new chairman in 1994. Under Hryb's leadership, the Supreme Soviet voted to adopt a presidential republic, and voted approval of a new constitution on March 4. This paved the way for new presidential elections in June. These elections were won by Alexander Lukashenka, a former collective farm director without previous political experience. Lukashenka's winning platform called for rebuilding ties with Russia with the ultimate goal of merging the two economies.

Three months earlier, in fact, Prime Minister Kebish had negotiated an agreement with Viktor Chernomyrdin, the Russian prime minister, under which Belarus would begin reintegrating itself into the Russian economy. According to the terms of the agreement, Belarus was to lift all customs barriers with Russia; Belarusian "coupons" would be replaced by Russian rubles; and military bases in Belarus being used by Russian troops were to be leased to Russia free of charge. As the July elections would later confirm, the major-

ity of the Belarusian population favored a policy of reintegration with Russia, particularly in light of its dismal experience running its own economy.

President Lukashenka continued to push the policy of reintegration with Russia after his election but, in fact, almost nothing changed because the Russian Government decided that it would be too expensive for Russia to exchange Belarusian coupons for rubles, and backed out of the deal. The "coupons" were eventually replaced by Belarusian rubles.

Meanwhile, the Belarusian economy continued to decline with no sign of a reversal in sight. A $300 million standby loan from the International Monetary Fund was approved in July 1995, based on a government promise to begin a program of reform. When the government did nothing, however, the loan was eventually suspended. Since that time, Belarus has rejected any movement toward privatizing its massive state sector.

Part of the problem is the lackluster attitude of the people of Belarus themselves. In the May 1995 elections, for example, a majority of eligible voters turned out to vote in only 119 out of the 260 electoral districts, thus invalidating the results in the remaining districts. Since the new constitution specified that 179 delegates constituted a quorum, the new parliament was unable to meet. The crisis continued until new elections took place in November, with President Lukashenka mean-

while ruling by decree. The electorate did manage to vote in a new parliament the second time around; however, they gave a majority of the seats to communists and agrarians, both opponents of reform.

But Mr. Lukashenka's authoritarian manner made it impossible for him to work with even this "ideal" parliament; in essence, Lukashenka was even unwilling to consult with people who agreed with him. In August 1996, therefore, Lukashenka called for a "vote of confidence" in his policies in the form of a constitutional referendum to take place on November 7 (not coincidently the anniversary of the November Revolution). Under the terms of the referendum, Lukashenka was to be given a fresh five year term of office, additional powers to rule by decree, authority to create an appointed upper house of parliament, and authority to appoint half of the members of the constitutional court.

Parliament, which opposed the referendum, tried to stop it but failed. When the vote finally took place, it did so under a general presumption that the outcome was rigged. Giving the charge added credence, Mr. Lukashenka's prime minister, Mikhail Chigir, resigned after the result was announced. Internationally, both the European Union and the United States refused to accept the validity of the referendum vote; in addition, Belarus's memberships in the Council of Europe and the OSCE Parliamentary Assembly were suspended at that time.

The IMF and the World Bank have also not approved new lending or projects since 1997. Most of the various members of the European Union suspended economic aid projects at the same time. Lukashenka's authoritarian style of governing was a factor, but an even more important reason is that these countries were convinced that foreign credits would just be wasted because Belarus had proved itself unwilling to introduce any real economic reforms. President Lukashenka's response to its international isolation was to announce that Belarus did not need foreign credits.

Meanwhile, Union with Russia continued to be Lukashenka's answer to all of Belarus's problems. A Union treaty negotiated by the Russian and Belarusian governments supposedly went into effect on June 11, 1997 but brought little change. President Lukashenka even told an assembly at Almaty State University in September 1997 that "speculation on the full merger of Belarus and Russia was dreamed up by politicos who have nothing better to do," adding that Belarus would never give up its sovereignty.

There was some tangible progress toward union eventually, however. In Octo-

Belarus

ber 1998, Russia and Belarus signed a military security agreement, described as a supplement to the Union Treaty, which led to some integration of the economic and political systems of the two countries during 1999. But Russian Foreign Minister Ivanov undercut the significance of this new Union Agreement by characterizing the documents as "a declaration, not a treaty of further unification." Blurring the situation further, Yugoslavia was formally invited to join the "union" after the beginning of NATO air strikes over Kosovo, though of course that did not happen.

In December 1999, a second Union Treaty was signed by Presidents Yeltsin and Lukashenka under which Belarus and Russia agreed in principle to form an economic and political union with its own separate executive and parliament, union citizenship, a single, common external tariff, and, by 2005 or so, a common currency and defense policy. Membership was also to be open to other republics that wanted to join.

This second Union Treaty has provided the theoretical framework for Russian–Belarusian relations since that time—though it is sometimes difficult to determine what has actually been implemented.

Although President Putin specifically endorsed the idea of a Russia–Belarus union after he became president, Russia has tended to be more hard–nosed toward Belarus under Putin. In April 2000, for example, the Russia Government sharply repudiated an assertion by Lukashenka that the two countries intended to create a joint 300,000-strong military force in response to NATO's expansion. The Russian government has also expressed uneasiness about Lukashenka's human rights record—in particular the fact that domestic political opponents suffer constant harassment and several have simply disappeared.

Another concern that sometimes surfaces is the economic cost of union to Russia. One factor is that, because of the state of Belarus's still unreformed economy, most of Belarus's manufactured products are uncompetitive in Russia. In fact, a couple of years ago, Belarus even had to subsidize the cost of bread in areas near the Russian border because cheaper Russian breads had begun to monopolize the local market. At that time, Russia was providing a subsidy of up to a billion dollars a year through such mechanisms as providing gas and oil at the Russian domestic price. By 2002, the subsidy had grown to at least $2 billion a year.

This may explain why President Putin characterized Minsk's proposals for a common Belarusian–Russian state as "legalistic nonsense" in June 2002. Two months later, he told President Lukashenka that

Hon. Stanislav Shushkevich

the two countries should establish equal market conditions and ensure the rights of both citizens and enterprises. He next proposed that unification of the two states proceed on the basis of the Russian constitution, with a single government and parliament. Pointing out that the Belarusian economy is only 3 percent of the Russian economy, Putin declared that "the future union state can only be a federation." Lukashenka rejected Putin's proposal, saying that it was tantamount to "dividing Belarus into seven parts, incorporating these parts into the Russian Federation, and granting these Belarusian parts equal rights with Russia's regions." Lukashenka then added that "to form union bodies on the basis of the Russian constitution—[that] is totally absurd."

The Russia–Belarus Union is not dead—the Parliamentary Assembly of the Russian–Belarus Union actually met for the first time in Moscow in January 2003 and it has met annually to approve a union budget since that time—but it appears to be at a dead-end. Although Moscow is supposedly still committed to allowing the Russian ruble to become the sole currency of the union (which was originally supposed to occur as of 1 January 2005), it has coupled it with a caveat—a single state bank—which Lukashenka has always found unacceptable. Yet Putin cannot just pull out of the Union, since polls indicate that over 80 percent of all Russians favor closer relations with Belarus. Nor can Lukashenka agree to become part of Russia, since only 5 percent of Belarusians favor that approach.

Meanwhile, President Lukashenka continues his authoritarian method of rule at home. In 2000, he made a sham of the parliamentary elections by pushing through a new electoral law which allowed him to disqualify dozens of candidates and rig the count.

Neither the United States nor the countries of the European Union recognized

the results of the 2000 parliamentary elections. Even so, Lukashenka pursued similar policies when he ran for reelection in September 2001. Months prior to the election, the government launched a series of attacks on the political opposition in an effort to have them seen as puppets of foreign interests. As part of this attack on the opposition, the Belarusian Government broadcast a television program in February 2001 which accused the U.S. Central Intelligence Agency of providing support to the political opposition. All television broadcasts are controlled by the state, as are almost all newspapers.

Although the political opposition managed to unite behind a single candidate—Trade Union Federation leader Hancharyk—it probably never had a chance in spite of Lukashenka's growing unpopularity with the public. In fact, President Lukashenka announced prior to the vote that he would be satisfied if he received 75 percent of the vote and that turned out, not coincidentally, to be the precise percentage he officially received. Again, neither the United States nor the various countries of the European Union recognized the validity of the voting. In addition, the U. S. and E. U. diplomats in Minsk boycotted Lukashenka's inauguration.

The situation with regard to Russia was more nuanced. President Putin called up Lukashenka to offer congratulations on his election, but Aleksandr Veshnyakov, the chairman of Russian Central Election Commission, characterized the election as "far from being an example to Russia and other countries that have embarked on the path toward democracy."

As if to further emphasize that point, Lukashenka continued his attacks on

President Lukashenka

Hancharyk and the Trade Union Federation after the election. Hancharyk was forced out as president and, then, out of the country. He eventually settled in Moscow. Frants Vitko, his successor as Trade Union Federation leader, then came under pressure and he was in turn forced to resign in July 2002.

Two months later, the government completed its takeover of the Trade Union Federation; an extraordinary congress of the union voted to change its name to the Trade Union Federation of Belarus (FPB) and elected Leanid Kozik, the former deputy chief of the presidential administration, as its head.

After the vote, President Lukashenka addressed the congress of the FPB. "I came to the conclusion," he said, "that we need to [place our society] on three powerful pillars; the renewed trade unions, the powerful youth organization, and the [system of] soviets." The government had created the Belarusian National Youth Organization approximately one month prior to Lukashenka's speech. Lukashenka has not yet spelled out what he meant by his reference to soviets. But even more interesting, Lukashenka made reference a little later in his speech to a fourth pillar: political parties. But society has not matured enough to handle having political parties, he added, characterizing current political parties as

something incomprehensible. If only I see— provided that I am still your president—or you let me know that such [comprehensible political parties] have crystallized themselves, we will make them the fourth pillar of our—as it is trendy to say nowadays— civic society.

With new legislative elections scheduled to take place in the fall of 2004, the government extended its control further by sponsoring new legislation giving itself the authority to ban political parties, trade unions or other organizations if found guilty of even a single violation of the law during rallies. To understand the significance of this legislation, it should be pointed out that the Belarusian High Court banned 54 nongovernmental organizations (NGOs) during the preceding year, almost all for technical violations of the law. The government also moved to restrict the influence of the few remaining independent newspapers at this time by making it difficult for them to distribute their newspapers. In January 2004, Belarus's national postal service cancelled a contract to distribute subscriptions of *Belorusskaya delovaya gazeta*, a prominent independent newspaper. Simultaneously, the Belarusian national press's retail-sales network refused to handle the newspaper

Dissident Alyaksandr Milinkevich

at its news stands. These moves came after the government had earlier suspended publication of the newspaper for three months.

Elections to the 110 seat Chamber of Representatives took place on October 17, 2004. In the lead-up to the elections, the government first denied registration to or disqualified nearly half of the opposition candidates, then harassed and intimated those it permitted to run. Since the ballot also included a referendum on lifting the two-term constitutional limit on the presidency, President Lukashenka had a personal interest in the outcome. In the end, supporters of the president won all but one of the 110 seats, while it was declared that the presidential referendum had won with an 86 percent majority—even though an independent poll had indicated less than 50 percent support among the voters. The OSCE and the European Union rejected both the elections and the vote for the referendum. In March 2005, the European Parliament adopted a resolution on Belarus calling on EU member nations to recognize Belarus as a dictatorship and President Lukashenka as a dictator. U.S. Secretary of State Rice echoed this position in April 2005 when she referred to Belarus as "the last dictatorship in Europe" during a visit to Lithuania.

This pattern has continued since that time. New presidential elections took place on March 19, 2006. Once again, the government carried out a program of intimidation against the few remaining independent newspapers, suspending one newspaper for three months, confiscating individual editions of other newspapers, and refusing to allow distribution through state-controlled kiosks in other cases. In addition, a new, tougher public-security

law was passed in December 2005 which made it a crime punishable by a jail term of up to two years for any public comment which would bring discredit to Belarus in the international arena. Candidates guilty of this offense would be "removed from the election process."

The opposition probably never had a chance to win the election, but it did not help that they were unable to unite behind a single opposition candidate. In the end, the official tally gave Lukashenka 82.6 percent of the vote, with his chief presidential rival, Alyaksandr Milinkevich, getting six percent of the vote. The other two presidential candidates together took 5.8 percent of the vote. The United States, the OSCE and the European Union refused to accept the results of the election. Since that time, they have coordinated on new sanctions against Belarus, including travel bans against those officials held responsible for the flawed voting process. There is, however, little more that these countries can do, since Belarus was already under sanctions for numerous acts of this nature in the past.

In May 2006, however Belarus got a rude shock when Energy Minister Azyarets was invited to Moscow for talks with Gazprom on a natural gas price for 2007. According to a Gazprom spokesman, the gas price charged Belarus would depend on Belarus's steps to "satisfy the economic demands" of Gazprom. In essence, Gazprom wanted to buy Beltranshaz, Belarus's gas-pipeline system; if Belarus wouldn't sell, the price for natural gas would go from $47 per 1,000 cubic meters to $200 per 1,000 cubic meters. Negotiations continued for the rest of the year. Belarus eventually agreed to sell a controlling interest in the pipeline to Gazprom, but it wanted to continue to receive gas at the Russian domestic price. There was also disagreement on the valuation of Beltranshaz, although the Dutch ABN AMRO Bank gave a valuation of $3.5 billion in December.

A new natural gas agreement was finally signed on December 31, 2006, but only after the Belarusian Government threatened to pull gas for its own use out of the pipelines that carry natural gas to Poland, Lithuania and Germany—much as the Ukrainian Government had done in 2006. In the end, the Belarus Government and Gazprom signed a five-year agreement on gas deliveries to Belarus. Under its terms, Belarus would pay $100 per 1,000 cubic meters of gas in 2007, with the price gradually rising to the European market level by 2011. Gazprom also agreed to pay $2.5 billion for a 50 percent stake in Beltranshaz, the gas pipeline company.

Even as the gas price argument was being resolved, the Russian Government an-

Belarus

Lukashenka Propaganda: "Always There For You" Courtesy: Maaike Göbel

nounced in December that it would begin charging a duty of $180 per ton on crude oil exported to Belarus. Here the problem was that Belarus had been importing Russian crude oil at the domestic Russian price for a number of years, refining it and then selling it abroad at world prices.

The Belarusian Government retaliated by placing a fee of $45 per metric ton on all crude oil shipped across Belarus enroute to Western Europe. Russia then retaliated by cutting off all shipments of crude oil to Belarus in the first week of January. The impasse was broken a week later as the result of a telephone call to President Lukashenka by President Putin. Lukashenka agreed to drop the export duties Minsk had imposed on Russian oil shipments, and the two presidents agreed that their prime ministers would meet the following week to discuss several related issues.

Business Week estimated in January 2007 that Belarus would "pay approximately $1 billion more for energy in 2007 than last year." On the other hand, President Putin said on Russian television on January 15 that his country would continue to support Belarus, but at a "significantly reduced" level. Putin argued that the deal amounted to a $5.8 billion subsidy by Moscow and "is a payment by Russia for a calm and smooth…method of transition to a market relationship." Russia subsequently lowered its export duty on oil to Belarus from $180 to $53 per ton; in return, Belarus pledged to pay 70 percent of the export duty it receives for refined products.

At the end of January, a new agreement was announced that appeared to wipe out the new export duty entirely. According to the Belarusian petrochemical concern Belnaftakhim, it had signed an accord with a number of Russian oil companies for oil at some $240 a ton, including the oil export

tax of $53 per ton. That was approximately what Belarus paid for oil in 2006.

In addition, the Belarusian Government announced on February 5 that it had increased its tariffs for Russian oil in transit via Belarusian pipelines from $2.60 a ton to $3.50, a 34.6 percent increase. It appears that, on this issue, it was the Russians who blinked.

While these disagreements were going on, President Lukashenka began making noises about wanting to settle his disagreements with the west. By April, he was still resentful at Russia's decision to "switch to market economic relations." "How can you build good, human, brotherly relations, when they have bled you dry under the guise of the establishment of market relationships? How could I respond to this and what relations could I build with Russia?" At the same time, Lukashenka rejected European Union overtures aimed at improving relations because, he said, of the preconditions set by the EU for talks; as he put it, Belarus would not tolerate dictation and pressure exerted by the EU.

Foreign Policy

The Government of Belarus adopted an official stance of international neutrality upon independence. To that end, it signed the Nuclear Non–Proliferation Treaty and, in February 1993, its legislature ratified the START–1 agreement. At that time, there were 81 nuclear–armed SS–25 missiles stationed in Belarus. Over the next two years, all but 18 mobile launchers were shipped to Russia for dismantling. President Lukashenka then canceled the remaining redeployments in July 1995, saying that the decision to withdraw the missiles had been a "major political mistake." Belarus remained in technical violation of the START–1 agreement for the next two years

before finally arranging for a transfer of the remaining missiles to Russia.

In general, Belarus has played a rather reticent role internationally, although it did negotiate agreements with the three Baltic Republics shortly after independence and made a point of establishing good relations with its western neighbors. All of that began to change after President Lukashenka was elected and began to reverse the reforms initiated by his predecessors. Things came to a head in September 1997 when the presidents of ten countries in the region sharply criticized Belarus for its retreat from democratic reforms. The meeting, hosted by the presidents of Poland and Lithuania and held in Vilnius, attracted the presidents of Belarus, Bulgaria, Estonia, Hungary, Latvia, Moldova, Romania and Ukraine, plus Prime Minister Chernomyrdin of Russia. The meeting underlined President Lukashenka's isolation, for virtually everyone present was outspokenly critical of Belarus's policies under his leadership, both in its retreat from a market economy and its abandonment of democracy.

Belarus's relations with his eastern neighbors are somewhat better. An active supporter of the Commonwealth of Independent States from the beginning, Belarus adopted a policy of favoring closer relations with Russia even before Lukashenka was elected president. For example, Belarus signed an agreement subordinating its military policy to that of Russia in December 1993. In 1994, it signed a second agreement with Russia which was supposed to result in a common customs and currency zone, though it was never implemented. President Lukashenka then negotiated an agreement for full economic and political union in the spring of 1996, during the Russian presidential campaign, but this was never implemented either. Finally, Russia and Belarus exchanged ratifications for a Union Treaty in June 1997 which once again called for the unification of the two peoples.

Little changed after that time, while relations between the two countries actually appeared to deteriorate when Belarus detained several TV journalists working for Russian Public Television (ORT) and charged them with entering the country illegally. Three of the journalists were released after Russia protested, but a fourth was detained for several months longer. In addition, two Belarusians working for ORT were arrested and put on trial. Relations turned even colder in October when Russia barred President Lukashenka from visiting two Russian regional cities. When Lukashenka protested, President Yeltsin replied that he would be happy to have Lukashenka visit—but only when the fourth Russian journalist was released.

Under President Putin, relations between the two countries have been outwardly cordial, though, increasingly, Russian politicians have complained that Russian support for Lukashenka is not only expensive but is actually detrimental to Russian interests in the long run. In addition, various individuals in the Russian Government have argued that Russia could maintain Belarus in its sphere of influence under another leader who would move Belarus toward economic reform and a market economy.

Instead, President Putin strongly supported his government's decision to cut its subsidies of Belarus by moving toward charging Belarus the world market price for natural gas and crude oil as of the beginning of 2007. Although the move angered Lukashenka, it did not represent a withdrawal of political support for Lukashenka. While nearly every other neighbor was appalled by the blatantly undemocratic nature of the 2006 presidential elections, President Putin congratulated Lukashenka and promised him support.

Belarus's relations with the United States were fairly good between 1991 and 1994, but began to deteriorate after Lukashenka took over as president. They suffered a severe setback in September 1995 when border guards shot down a hot air balloon, killing its two American pilots, and they were made even worse after President Lukashenka absolved the military from any wrongdoing. Relations suffered a further setback in the spring of 1997 when Belarus accused an American diplomat of spying and expelled him. The United States subsequently withdrew its ambassador for consultations, though he later returned.

Another irritant occurred in June 1998 when President Lukashenka decided that the presidential compound at Drozdy was too small. Since the presidential compound was located in the middle of the diplomatic compound, Lukashenka's solution was to evict the ambassadors from the residences surrounding his compound. The ambassadors were first asked to move to other residences in the vicinity and, when they objected, they were told that the entire compound had become the "residence of the President of the Republic of Belarus," that they would require passes to enter the territory, and they would "have to comply with the special security rules of a presidential residence."

Following this, several ambassadors were denied reentry to the compound when returning from offices elsewhere in the city. Next, Lukashenka ordered that water and electricity be cut off from the residences. At this point, nine countries withdrew their ambassadors from Minsk "for consultations."

The House of Government, Minsk

In addition, the European Union retaliated by placing severe travel restrictions on Belarusian state officials. A number of non–EU countries also adopted the travel ban—Bulgaria, Cyprus, the Czech Republic, Estonia, Hungary, Iceland, Norway, Romania, Slovakia, and Slovenia.

Among Belarus's western neighbors, only Poland and Lithuania continued to maintain diplomatic relations, and even these two countries publicly criticized Belarus's actions. Poland felt that it had to continue contacts with Belarus at this time because Bronislaw Geremek, the then Polish Foreign Minister, was also chairman of the OSCE, which maintained an important headquarters in Minsk. Lithuania declined to join the visa ban on Belarusian officials because it wanted to "soften the impact of [Belarus's] isolation on Lithuanian–Belarusian relations."

The controversy lasted until December 1998, when the Belarusian Government and the European Union reached a compromise of sorts. European Union ambassadors were to be given access to their old residences for a period of one month while they located and leased new apartments. In return, the government of Belarus agreed to compensate the countries for the expense and inconvenience that they had been put to. Essentially, the nations of the European Union largely yielded to Lukashenka's demands because of their belief that the political and economic situation in Belarus had worsened greatly in the second half of the year and it was advisable that their ambassadors return to Minsk in case of some sort of emergency.

A standoff between Belarus and the American government continued for several more months, but Ambassador Daniel Speckhard finally returned to his post in September 1999. According to the U.S. State Department, Speckhard was ordered back to Minsk in response to Belarus's pledge to abide by the Vienna Convention and to pay compensation for losses suffered by the U.S. embassy as a result of the ambassador's earlier eviction. "Having Ambassador Speckhard back in Minsk will enable us more effectively to promote democracy and human rights, help those who support and work for the restoration of democratic rule, and promote other interests that we have in Belarus."

Relations between the United States and Belarus did not improve, however. When Michael Kozak, Speckhard's successor as U.S. ambassador, arrived in Minsk on October 20, 2000, he was kept waiting for four months before being permitted to present his credentials to President Lukashenka on February 22. Lukashenka's refusal to meet Kozak for such a long time was widely viewed as a snub to the U.S. Government for its criticism of his regime and policies. Relations between the two countries deteriorated even further after the United States refused to recognize the validity of the September 2001 presidential elections.

Subsequently, Deputy Assistant Secretary of State Steven Pifer announced during a visit to Minsk that Belarus had made no progress in "key areas of democratization and that the human rights situation had actually deteriorated in previous months. "We see no progress toward democratic election reform. We see no evidence of steps to empower an independent Belarusian parliament or encourage functioning independent media." Pifer then added that the United States was willing to resume productive bilateral relations only if Belarus fulfilled the conditions it agreed to in joining such interna-

Belarus

A folk music ensemble of the Belarus Conservatory

Courtesy: NOVOSTI

tional organizations as the United Nations and the OSCE. What might be taken as Lukashenka's reply came the next month when the Belarusian Government refused to allow Eberhard Heyken, the OSCE's new head, into Belarus.

The Belarusian Government continued to pursue its intention to close the OSCE Advisory and Monitoring Group offices in Minsk through the expedient of refusing to renew visas for OSCE officials. That office officially closed as of December 31, 2002, but new discussions between the OSCE Parliamentary Council and the Belarusian Government resulted in an agreement for a new OSCE office in Minsk to open as of the beginning of the year. The greatly reduced mandate of the new office calls for it to "assist the Belarusian Government in further promoting institution building, in further consolidating the rule of law, and in developing relations with civil society in accordance with OSCE principles and commitments."

In November 2002, fourteen of the fifteen European Union states imposed a travel ban on President Lukashenka and seven other senior officials as a protest against human rights abuses in Belarus. In February 2003, the European Parliament passed a resolution condemning the Belarusian Government's "indiscriminate attacks on the media, journalists, members of the opposition, human rights activists, and any person who attempts freely to voice criticism of the president."

In March 2004, a joint U.S. and EU mission that had come to Minsk in order to meet with government officials and representatives of the Belarusian political opposition issued a statement afterwards in which it "noted with regret that Belarus has failed conspicuously to make progress toward meeting its OSCE commitments and thereby realizing an improvement in its relations with the European Union and the United States. The following month, the UN Human Rights Commission adopted a resolution condemning alleged human rights abuses by the government of Belarus. In November 2004, in response to "fraudulent legislative elections and presidential referendum" on October 17, the foreign ministers of the European Union voted to ban senior Belarusian officials from entering EU territory. This ban added 15 people to the list of four Belarusian officials banned in September 2004 in connection with the disappearance of political opponents.

Addition political sanctions were imposed by the United States, the European Union and the OSCE following the 2006 presidential elections. But they have not had any affect on the actions of the Belarusian Government.

Nature of the Regime

Belarus has been a presidential republic since March 1994, when the Supreme Soviet adopted a new constitution which called for creation of a new executive offi-

cial as head of state who would be called the president of the republic. Under the terms of the constitution, the president is the chief political figure within the new system. Charged with determining general policy, he is assisted by a prime minister who is responsible for day–to–day operations of the government.

President Lukashenka was elected under the terms of the 1994 constitution, but found that its terms constricted his actions. In November 1996, therefore, he sponsored a constitutional referendum which gave him an increased power to issue decrees, permitted him to create an upper house of parliament to be appointed directly or indirectly by him, gave him the right to appoint half of the members of the constitutional court, and extended his term of office to the year 2001. The government announced subsequently that the referendum had passed.

The constitutional referendum did not change the duties of the prime minister, who continues to be appointed by the president and must be confirmed by the legislature. He thus continues to preside over the cabinet, to oversee day–to–day operations of the government, and to be responsible for maintaining good relations with the legislature. Syarhey Sidroski, the current prime minister, has held that office since his confirmation by the Chamber of Representatives on December 19, 2003.

The new National Assembly, which replaced the old Supreme Soviet, is a bicameral legislature, consisting of a lower house, the 110 seat Chamber of Representatives, and an upper house, the 64 seat Council of the Republic. The Council of the Republic is not elective but, instead, is made up of senators proposed either by regional councils (56 members) or appointed by the president himself (8 members).

New elections to the Chamber of Representatives took place on October 17, 2004. With a single exception, all of the 110 members are supporters of the president. The OSCE, the European Union and the United States all refused to recognize the validity of the 2004 elections.

Culture

Belarus has one prominent architectural monument from the period of Kievan Rus, the Cathedral of St. Sophia in Polotsk, which dates from the eleventh century. There are also two church–fortresses dating from the period of the Lithuanian Grand Principality, Maloye Mazheykava and Synkavichy. The seventeenth century saw the introduction of the Baroque style. The Jesuit church at Grodno exemplifies this new style and also the growing presence of Roman Catholicism, officially fostered by the Polish Government at this particular juncture in time.

Polotsk was long a center of learning and there are a number of names associated with it. Frantsyk Skaryna produced the first Belarusian translation of the Bible in the first quarter of the sixteenth century. The two editions of the Bible were actually printed in Prague and Vilnius. Symeon of Polotsk was a seventeenth century poet who wrote in Belarusian.

Maksim Bahdanovich was an important poet of the late nineteenth century. Three poets of the early Soviet period are Ales Harun, Yanka Kupala, and Yakub Kolas. Kupala also produced a play, *Natives*, which was first produced in 1924. Kolas also produced a three volume novel, *On the Crossroads*. Maksim Haretski was a novelist who wrote *The Quiet Current*. His diary was also published under the title of *On the Imperialist War*.

There was, in fact, a great outpouring of literature in the period of the 1920s. These included poets (Uladzimir Dubouka and Yazep Pushcha) and writers of fiction (Kuzma Chorny and Kandrat Krapiva). Stalin's introduction of socialist realism in 1930 brought a decline in the level of Belarusian writing, although some writers continued to be published. After World War II, a number of good composers appeared in Belarus. Dzmitry Lukas produced his first opera, *Kastus Kalinouski*, in 1947. Ryhor Pukst produced three operas between 1947 and 1955. Yauhen Hlebau produced an opera, *Your Spring*, in 1963 and a ballet, *Alpine Ballad*, in 1967. Yauhen

Tsikotski and Yury Semyanyaka also wrote operas at this time. Belarus has both a conservatory of music and a philharmonic society. There is, in addition, the Belarusian State Theater of Opera and Ballet in Minsk, plus a state dramatic theater.

Belarus has a well–developed system of higher education. There are 33 institutes of higher education scattered throughout the republic, plus another 138 technical colleges. The Belarusian Academy of Sciences also has 32 scientific institutes in various parts of the republic. There is a comprehensive system of primary and secondary schools. In 1989, 71 percent of all eligible children were in preschool institutions.

In August 2006, Deputy Education Minister Faryno reported that 4,006 schools would open for the new school year. Faryno's report revealed that only 20.5 percent of Belarusian schoolchildren would be instructed in Belarusian; in Minsk, only four out of 234 general-education schools instruct children in Belarusian. Two years earlier, official statistics indicated that 57 percent of all schools had the status of instructing in Belarusian.

Russian was made an official language in Belarus in 1995 and, from that time, the government began cutting its subsidies to publishing houses and authors producing texts in Belarusian. All of this reflects President Lukashenka's comment, made in 1994, that:

The people who speak the Belarusian language cannot do anything else apart from speaking the Belarusian language, because it is impossible to express anything great in

Belarusian. Belarusian is a poor language. There are only two great languages in the world—Russian and English.

The republic also publishes approximately two hundred daily newspapers, 130 of which are in Belarusian and the rest in other languages. However, Belarus's state postal system, which holds a monopoly over the distribution of subscription periodicals, denied distribution in the first six months of 2007 to major nationwide independent newspapers and many local independent newspapers. While addressing the National Assembly, President Lukashenka said that he was ready to "solve" problems encountered by private newspapers. But, in fact, he took no action, and it was almost certainly his policy that the postal service was reflecting in its decision.

About 80 percent of Belarusians have at least a nominal connection with the Russian Orthodox faith. Even under communism, when religion was officially discouraged, the Russian Orthodox Church occupied a special position. For the first few years after the collapse of communism, the state took a completely neutral position, but this began to change after Lukashenka was elected president in 1994. Religious repression began increasing about three years ago, but it was not until October 31, 2002—when Lukashenka signed a new law, "About the Freedom of Confessions and Religious Organizations"—that the state took formal responsibility for determining what religions are legal in the country. Essentially, the new law makes it illegal for worshippers of

Wedding party at a public park in Minsk

Belarus

any faith to meet on a regular basis unless they are registered with the state. While it extends automatic legal recognition to 26 faiths, including Russian Orthodoxy, Roman Catholicism, Judaism, Islam and Lutheranism, it requires unrecognized faiths to be registered with the state before they can begin to hold regular meetings. In addition, any unrecognized faith must have been active in Belarus since 1982 and have at least 10 separate congregations in order to qualify for registration.

Although Vladimir Lameko, vice chairman of the Belarus Parliament's committee for religious affairs, claims that "all religions are equal before the law," the new religion law singles out the Russian Orthodox Church as playing "a determining role" in national culture and government. According to its authors, a major purpose of the law was to protect the leading role of the Russian Orthodox Church against dangerous sects. Government actions even before the law went into effect bear that out.

In August 2002, for example, the government bulldozed a western Belarus chapel of the Russian Autocephalous Orthodox Church, a splinter organization separate from the main Russian Orthodox Church. One month later, several Minsk branches of the Full Gospel Pentecostal Church received word that their prayer services were illegal. The Pentecostal Church, with 450 registered churches and 200 unregistered ones, is the largest Protestant group in Belarus. Other faiths which have come under harassment by the state include the Hare Krishna's and the New Life Protestant Church. In addition, a small 150–member Hindu community has been denied registration on technical grounds. Meanwhile, the apartment being used as a community temple by the Hindus was broken into and ransacked. The group has also been repeatedly denied the right to hold public meetings. Several members have also been arrested.

Economy

Belarus has a fairly well balanced economy, with an agricultural sector that is, in general, capable of feeding its population and a well developed industrial base. Agriculture in the northern part of the republic concentrates on raising beef and dairy cattle. The farms produce their own fodder and hay and otherwise, except for those areas set aside for growing flax, the land is in pasturage. In the center of the republic, the farms concentrate on pig breeding. The most important crop grown in this area is potatoes. In the south, there are once again many farms that specialize in the raising of cattle, either for milk or beef. Hemp is also grown in this area. Grain is grown throughout the republic.

Some grain is imported into the republic, but mainly to be used as cattle feed.

The problem with agriculture is that about two–thirds of the peasants are still organized into collective farms, with most of the remainder in state farms. A few private farms were set up after that became possible, but the treatment they received from the state sector discouraged others from trying. The first post–independence Belarusian Government favored a changeover to private agriculture, but that policy was repudiated by President Lukashenka after his election in July 1994.

Today, there are 2,381 state–run agricultural enterprises. In general, all production is sold to the state at low controlled prices which covers only part of the cost of production. To keep the farms operating, the state makes "loans" to cover part of the cost of planting and harvesting. In April 2004, Belarusian Television reported that more than 40 percent of all collective farms were losing money. Nor was Belarus's problem limited to grain production. The potato harvest was also down to one million tons, a drop of two–thirds from 1990. As Deputy Agricultural Minister Aleksandr Prakopau put it,

Our potato sector is facing what our sheep industry has already gone through and what our flax industry is going through right now. Our sheep breeding is dead. The flax industry is slowly dying.

According to Deputy Agriculture Minister Anatol Rubanik, the total debts of agricultural enterprises were the equivalent of $720 million in November 2001, up from $22.8 million at the beginning of 1999. Agricultural officials have been stressing for years that a radical change in the state's pricing policy was necessary if Belarus wanted to get agricultural production back to 1991 levels.

Agricultural leaders have advocated changes such as encouraging new technologies, upgrading farm equipment, and reforming farm collectives but President Lukashenka, who was a state farm manager before entering politics, does not favor such changes.

Lukashenka came up with his own program concerning collective farms in March 2004 when he issued a decree aimed at attracting investment from Belarusian companies in state-owned collective farms. Such firms would receive deferments on lingering debts, tax arrears, and overdue utility bills owed by the collective farm taken over. Perhaps this new policy has had some affect. Last September, Statistics Minister Zinouski reported that the 2006 grain harvest was some 6.5 million tons.

Belarus has very little heavy industry. In 1991, it was capable of producing about 1.1 million tons of steel a year, while it also

manufactured machine tools, agricultural machinery and motor vehicles. It also manufactured chemicals, paper and bricks. There was a branch of industry that manufactured consumer goods such as watches, radios, televisions and bicycles. Most of the rest of industry was associated either with textiles or processing of agricultural products. There was a flax–spinning industry and another that manufactured artificial silk. Shoes and boots were also made. Agricultural end products included sugar and preserves. Domestic energy supplies were limited mainly to peat, which was widely used in industry.

But Belarusian industry had two major weaknesses. It imported most of its raw materials from other republics and it was dependent on imports for most of its energy. As a result, industry came under severe economic pressure soon after independence and this so frightened the political leadership that economic reform never really got off the ground. Only about 5 percent of enterprises had been denationalized by July 1994 when President Lukashenka took office and halted the process completely.

In November 1997, President Lukashenka issued a decree giving the government the right to intervene in the affairs of private joint–stock companies, including forcing them to remain open even if they were unprofitable. Three months later, the government moved against what little private enterprise continued to exist by announcing that it was reestablishing state monopolies on oil, tobacco, and cars. The government denied that it was going back to "totalitarian planning" and characterized the new program as "indicative planning." The government also decided to turn to the printing presses to cover the shortfall in the budget.

If these moves were intended to shore up the failing economy, they did not work. By March 16, 1998, the *zaichik* was trading at 59,000 to the U.S. dollar, down some 25 percent from the previous week. By December 1998, the *zaichik* had virtually collapsed, with unofficial trading reaching nearly 400,000 to the U.S. dollar. That the financial collapse of Russia played an important role in this collapse cannot be denied, since Russia had been the recipient of 70 percent of Belarusian exports before the crisis, and the drop in sales to Russia forced Belarusian enterprises to reduce output or, in some cases, to cram storehouses full of unsold products.

But this is at best only a partial explanation. By the fall, there was also an acute shortage of foodstuffs and a number of regions began instituting rationing. In this case, one factor was that Belarus's grain harvest was down by about 1 million tons. Another factor was that Belarus exported

$250 million in foodstuffs to Russia in 1998 as payment for natural gas imports.

But it also did not help that state-controlled food prices were set so low that collective farmers were forced to sell their produce to the state at about 50 percent of what it cost to produce. Under those circumstances, no one had any incentive to raise any more food than they could consume themselves.

Even before the crisis, in fact, relatively little local produce was available in the stores. Almost all food for sale in stores was imported. And when the *zaichik* collapsed, Belarus could no longer afford to pay for imported food.

President Lukashenka appears not to understand what has been happening to the Belarusian economy. Speaking to the nation in February 1999, he blamed "mismanagement" for the country's economic decline in 1998. He also outlined the country's economic priorities as closing the trade deficit (over $1 billion in 1998), halting spiraling inflation, maintaining economic growth, and reducing the number of unprofitable companies. All these are laudable goals, to be sure.

But as he had asked his ministers at a televised cabinet meeting shortly before, "Why are our people becoming poorer and poorer every month while we are so dynamically developing industry and agriculture?" None of his ministers was able to give him an answer.

Over the next two years, Lukashenka intensified the command aspects of the economy. In May 1999, for example, he signed a decree regulating prices and service charges; he next ordered the government to bring the Belarusian Union of Consumer Cooperation and the consumer trade sector directly under government control, thus effectively nationalizing trade in the countryside.

As the slide in the economy continued, Belarusian workers organized a number of rallies protesting the government's economic policies. None of this had any effect on government policy, however, and the situation in the countryside worsened through the rest of 1999. In January 2000, therefore, the government announced a plan to increase the productivity of the agricultural sector. It turned out, however, that the government's "plan" merely consisted in raising the prices at which the government purchased meat and milk. Responding to an annual inflation rate of more than 200 percent, the government also decided in January to trim three zeroes off the currency.

President Lukashenka made no major changes in policy until after his reelection in September 2001. He then appointed Henadz Navitski as his new prime minister and, in introducing him, announced that the new cabinet had been tasked with ensuring macroeconomic and financial stability, reformation of the state economic sector, and the development of entrepreneurship in the country. Lukashenka promised to liberalize economic relations and support private businesses and he further promised that the government would reduce to the minimum direct interference in the activities of economic entities. Somewhat later, Lukashenka made it clear that it was the Chinese economic model that he had in mind as a model for Belarus. Prime Minister Navitski was dismissed in December 2003; his successor, Syarhey Sidorski, has had no greater success in his overseeing of the economy. But this is not surprising, since it is President Lukashenka who makes all important governmental decisions. Thus far, international organizations such as the IMF and the World Bank have indicated that they are willing to talk with officials of the Belarusian Government about reform but are not willing to resume loans.

According to official Belarusian statistics, GDP grew at an 11 percent rate in 2004; industrial output rose by 15.6 percent while agricultural production rose by 12.9 percent. There was also a 40 percent rise in foreign trade, with exports to Russia accounting for 46.6 percent of exports. Belarus has a $4.7 billion deficit in trade with Russia, partly explained by the fact that it obtains almost all of its energy supplies from Russia. Belarus had an overall trade deficit of $2.6 billion in 2004. The government also announced that the average before-tax monthly wage rose from 299,859 Belarusian rubles ($139 at the then exchange rate) in December 2003 to 434,900 Belarusian rubles ($200 at the current exchange rate) in December 2004. Based on these figures, Belarus is making good economic progress and life is improving for ordinary citizens. Outside observers tend to be skeptical about official Belarusian statistics, however.

In March 2006, Siarhej Karol, a financial manager at American International Group, wrote that the Belarusian economic model

seems to defy economic theory. An economy entirely consisting of the old, unreformed Soviet industrial base, manages to churn out high single digit growth in gross domestic product (GDP), provided guaranteed monthly income and full, if not always full-time, employment, even as it remains in a state of complete isolation from the modern world. That, indeed, is the puzzle of Belarus.

The decision of the Russian Government to introduce market pricing in its relations with Belarus as of the beginning of 2007 appears bound to further stress the Belarusian economic model. Under the new policy, Belarus pays $100 per 1,000 cubic meters of natural gas (versus $46.68 per 1,000 cubic meters in 2006), and the price will increase each year until 2011, when Belarus will pay the European market price. The price increase is expected to cost Belarus an extra $1 billion in 2007, though this will be offset by Gazprom's purchase of a 50 percent interest in Bentranshaz, Belarus's gas-distribution network, for $2.5 billion.

Russia was also upset that Belarus was importing and refining 17 million tons of oil from Russia, but exporting all but 4 million tons of the refined oil to Western Europe and selling it at world market prices. President Putin first threatened to place a duty on oil exported to Belarus of $180 per ton, though this was later reduced to $53. In fact, Belarus appears to be paying approximately the same price for oil in 2007 as it did in 2006. But that may change in the future. Belarus is economically and politically dependent on Russia; as Kremlin policymakers see it, President Lukashenka's policies are "bringing the country to a political and economic dead end. Russia only has to wait for 'the fruit to ripen and fall into its hands.'"

The Future

The independence bestowed on Belarus as a result of the collapse of the Union of Soviet Socialist Republics in 1991 turns out to have been an unhappy experience for most Belarusians. Belarus inherited a weak political leadership at independence that never managed to even begin the process of economic reform. The sharp economic decline that occurred led to an ousting of the post-independence political leadership in early 1994 and the election of Alexander Lukashenka, who argued during the campaign that the answer to Belarus's economic problems lay in a program of reintegrating Belarus with the Russian economy, a policy he has pursued ever since.

That policy seems to be paying off since the various "color" revolutions in Georgia, Ukraine, and Kyrgyzstan, for Russia has increased its economic and political support and there has recently been some improvement in economic conditions inside the country. Belarus is almost completely isolated internationally, but it has one friend, Russia, and for now that appears to be enough.

The Republic of Ukraine

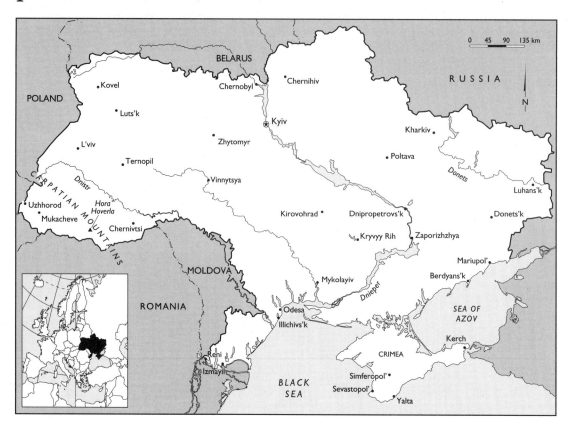

Area: 240,000 sq. mi. (621,840 sq. km.), twice the size of New Mexico.

Population: 46.646 million (December 2006 estimate).

Capital City: Kyiv (Pop. 2.6 million, estimated).

Climate: Temperate.

Neighboring States: Russia (east), Belarus (north), Poland (northwest), Slovakia, Hungary (west), Romania, Moldova (west).

Languages: Ukrainian (only official language), Russian.

Ethnic Composition: Ukrainian (77.8%), Russian (17.3%), Crimean Tatar (0.5%), Jewish (0.2%), other (4.2%).

Principal Religions: Ukrainian Orthodox (Moscow Patriarchate, Kyiv Patriarchate, and Autocephalous) and Ukrainian Greek Catholic (Uniate).

Chief Commercial Products: Grain, potatoes, fruit, vegetables. Ukraine has some of the richest land in the former USSR. Highly developed fuel and power resources, iron and manganese ore, metal production, engineering, chemical production, gas, processed food, building materials. The nation has 60% of the former USSR's coal reserves.

Currency: *hryvna* (issued summer of 1996).

Per Capita Annual Income (Purchasing Power Parity): $6,800.

Recent Political Status: Part of the Russian Empire until 1917, Ukrainian Republic (1917–1922), Ukrainian Soviet Socialist Republic (1922–1991).

Chief of State: Viktor Yushchenko (YOOSH-chen-kaw), President (inaugurated on January 23, 2005).

Head of Government: Viktor Yanukovych, Prime Minister (New parliamentary elections have been called for September 2007).

National Flag: Two horizontal stripes, the top a light blue, the bottom yellow; the blue represents the sky, yellow the wheat fields.

National Day: August 24 (1991), Independence Day.

The Land

The Republic of Ukraine is the independent successor to the Ukrainian Soviet Socialist Republic, a constituent republic of the Union of Soviet Socialist Republics. Ukraine declared its independence on August 24, 1991 and this was confirmed by a popular referendum that took place on December 1, 1991. The Republic of Ukraine also includes the Crimean Autonomous Republic (created in 1991).

The Republic of Ukraine lies in the southwestern part of the Russian Plain. The chief feature of the landscape is the Dnieper River, which flows down through the center of the republic. There are two upland regions, a series of rolling hills in the southeast and the Volyn–Podol Plateau, which stretches from the Polish to the Moldovan border in the west. The only large mountainous area is along the western border, where the northern ridges of the Carpathian Mountains cross the republic. The southern tip of the Crimean Peninsula also has a small mountainous area, a western extension of the Caucasus Mountains. Mountains make up only about five percent of the total land surface of the republic.

Because so much of the republic consists of a level plain, the differentiation between the various parts is based on the amount of rainfall that each gets. The most rainfall occurs in the north and diminishes to the south. The northern part of Ukraine is actually a large swampland, called the Pripet Marsh, the major part of which lies across the border in Belarus. The Dnieper Lowland dominates the central part of the republic. It is flat in the west and gently rolling in the east. Its chief feature is the Dnieper River and its tributaries. This is the traditional grain basket of the republic, which extends as far south as the city of Dnipropetrovs'k, on the Dnieper River. Here the rainfall is adequate to support wheat and other grains without irrigation. In the area south of Dnipropetrovs'k, on the other hand, irrigation becomes necessary.

The area immediately north of the Crimean Peninsula is known as the Nogai Steppe. This area, plus the northern part of the Crimean Peninsula—referred to as the Crimean Lowland—were once grassy steppes, homelands of the Nogai and Crimean Tatars and pasturelands for their animals. Today a huge artificial lake on the Dnieper provides water for irrigation.

The southern shore of the Crimean Peninsula has a mild Mediterranean–type climate, with average January temperatures of 39°F. Summers are hot and dry. The northern shore of the Black Sea is much colder, with average January temperatures of 26°F. Spring comes early, however, usually at the end of January. Average January temperatures in Kyiv are 18°F. Temperatures are also lower in winter and higher in summer in the eastern part of the republic.

Soils vary somewhat throughout the republic, but rich *chernozems* (black earth soils), which cover the entire central part of the republic, make up about 65 percent of the total. To the north of the *chernozems* area are found mixed gray *podsol* and black earth soils, and eventually pure, gray *podsol* soils, which are less fertile and also acidic. South of the *chernozems* belt is an area of chestnut soils, not as rich as *chernozems* and tending to be saline as one nears the Black Sea. The vegetation also reflects this soil division. Forests are found only in the north, in the area of the gray *podsols*. Mixed forest and grassy steppe cover the *chernozems* area. Desert and semi desert plants grow in the chestnut soils of the south.

The People

According to the State Statistics Committee, the estimated population of the Republic of Ukraine was 46.646 million as of December 2006, down several percentage points from 1991. The drop has been occurring because of rising death rates (16.4/1000 population) and falling birth

Ukrainian student at College of Europe

rates (9.59/1000 population). Experts believe that a major causative factor derives from the Chernobyl nuclear accident of 1986, which has contributed to male fertility problems, but other factors that have contributed to the decline in population would certainly include things like AIDS, tuberculosis, and even poverty.

Approximately 77.8 percent of the population speaks Ukrainian as their first language. Russian-speakers constitute the largest minority, making up 17.3 percent of the overall population; Russian-speakers are actually a majority in certain parts of eastern Ukraine and the Crimea. Reflecting this fact, Deputy Education Minister Viktor Ohnevyuk said in August 2005 that Russian is the language of instruction in 1,500 Ukrainian schools with a population of 1.2 million students, i.e., approximately 20 percent of the school population.

In addition, there are nearly a hundred smaller ethnic groups, including Belarusians, Moldovans, Crimean Tatars, Bulgarians, Hungarians, Romanians, Poles, and Jews.

Ukrainian belongs to the eastern Slavic family of languages, the other two of which are Russian and Belarusian. Ukrainian is derived from Old Slavonic, the language spoken by all eastern Slavs during the period of Kyivan Russian history. Ukrainian evolved after the split caused by the Mongol invasion in 1240. After 1240, the area that constitutes modern Ukraine was ruled directly by the Mongol Empire for a hundred years, before it was incorporated into the Grand Principality of Lithuania. The area east of the Dnieper River came under Russian control in 1654; the rest was added in the eighteenth century. It was this historic separation, and the connection with Lithuania and Poland between 1341 and the end of the eighteenth century, that resulted in the Ukrainian language.

The word Ukraine (no modifier) means "something that is on the edge or periphery" and describes Ukraine's position *vis-à-vis* Moscow. At various times in history, the land has also been referred to as Malorossiya, or "Little Russia."

History

Archaeological evidence indicates that the first settlement at the city of Kyiv, capital of modern–day Ukraine, was made in the seventh century (though there is a popular tradition that dates the founding to the fifth century). Kyiv, built on the bluffs above the Dnieper River, commanded traffic on the river and soon became a regional trading center. At the end of the ninth century, then, it became the capital of the first organized Slavic state—historically known as Kyivan Rus—when

Olaf the Norwegian conquered it and moved his headquarters there from Novgorod. Kyiv remained the capital of Kyivan Rus until 1169 when Yuri Dolgaruki, Prince of Vladimir, became Grand Prince and moved the capital to his own city of Riazan.

Although Kyiv lost its political preeminence at this time, it remained an important trading center until 1240, when it was sacked and virtually destroyed by the Mongols. All of southern Kyivan Rus was then incorporated into the new Mongol Empire and ruled from its regional capital of Sarai, located on the eastern bank of the Volga River, just north of the Caspian Sea. Kyiv itself became a ghost city when the craftsmen who had not been killed in the sack of the city in 1240 were rounded up and sent to Sarai.

The Golden Horde, as the Russians called the Mongol Government, appointed new Grand Princes to govern in the north, but the weight of the Mongol yoke brought a collapse of this line by the early fourteenth century. Slowly, then, Moscow rose in the northeast and built its leadership, all the time acting as agent for the Golden Horde.

In the northwest, however, a new leadership rose, based on freeing as much of the area as possible from the Mongol yoke. The leader of this new state was the Lithuanian Prince Gediminas (Gedymin in Russian), founder of the Jagellon dynasty; however, the majority of the subjects of this new Grand Principality of Lithuania were eastern Slavs and this was exemplified by the fact that their language, Old Slavonic, became the official language of the court. As Gediminas extended his control southward, he freed Kyiv and the western territories as far south as the Black Sea from Mongol control.

One effect of the Mongol control had been that most of the area of southwestern Kyivan Rus was virtually depopulated. Since this area remained subject to periodic attack from the Mongols, it remained a borderland for another two hundred years where only the brave or the desperate dared to live. Increasingly, however, communities of Slavic speakers fleeing from oppression in either Lithuania or Muscovy area settled this area, adopting many of the habits of nomadic neighbors, particularly the use of the horse and methods of fighting. These became the Cossack communities of the southern steppe, one of the most important of which was the Zaporozhian Cossacks, with their settlements south of the cataracts on the Dnieper River.

These Cossacks had to fight constantly for their freedom, against nomads to the east and against encroachments from governments to the north. After the Grand

Ukraine

Principality of Lithuania was merged with the Kingdom of Poland in the Union of Lublin in 1569, the combined Kingdom of Poland–Lithuania attempted to control this southern borderland area. The fighting prowess of the Cossacks was such, however, that the government was often willing to sign a treaty recognizing their status as Cossacks in return for military service to the Polish–Lithuanian state. At the same time, however, the government was giving out land to Polish noblemen and encouraging their settlement in this borderland area. These Polish noblemen brought the institution of serfdom with them—and there were constant efforts to enserf individual free peasants of the steppe.

A second issue, religion, arose at the end of the sixteenth century. The Cossacks were Orthodox, while the Polish nobility moving into the area were Roman Catholic. When the Patriarch of Constantinople recognized Moscow (Muscovy) as a separate Patriarchate at the end of the sixteenth century, he recognized the Russian Patriarch's jurisdiction over all Orthodox in the Slavic-speaking area, including those of the southwest under Polish–Lithuanian control. For political reasons, the Government of Poland–Lithuania refused to recognize this jurisdiction and outlawed the Orthodox Church within the area of its jurisdiction. Instead, it created the Uniate or Eastern Catholic Church, which used the traditional Orthodox service and the Old Slavonic language but recognized the spiritual leadership of the Pope.

Thus the free peasants of Ukraine found themselves under a three–pronged attack in the first half of the seventeenth century—encroaching serfdom, Polonization pushed by the increasing numbers of Polish nobility establishing estates in the area, and attempts to destroy the independent Orthodox Church. The man who now rose to the leadership of the Ukrainian forces was Bodgan Khmelnitsky, a Ukrainian landowner elected Hetman (head) of the Zaporozhian Cossacks. Khmelnitsky defeated the Polish forces a number of times (which contemporary Ukrainian history calls the "War of Independence) and for a while apparently dreamed of creating an independent Ukraine. But it soon became apparent to him that the Ukrainian forces were not strong enough to sustain an independent Ukraine. Believing that a victory by Poland would mean the end of the Orthodox Church and the enserfment of the free peasants of Ukraine, he turned to Muscovy and offered to bring Ukraine under Russian control.

Tsar Alexis, then ruler of Muscovy, hesitated for some time before accepting the offer because he recognized that it would mean war with Poland. He finally accepted in 1653, however. This led to a war between Poland and Muscovy that began in 1654 and ended with the Truce of Andrusovo in 1667. Under the terms of the truce, Poland recognized Moscow's control over all lands east of the Dnieper River, plus temporary control of the city of Kyiv. Russia never gave Kyiv back, however, and the terms of the truce were confirmed by a peace treaty signed in 1686. Russia got the remaining parts of the Ukraine during the partitions of Poland in 1772 and 1793. Thus the destinies of the Ukrainian people were tied to those of Russia primarily over the issue of religion (i.e., loyalty to the Orthodox Church).

Cossacks also retained their freedom from serfdom, though there was some encroachment in this area in the eighteenth century.

Russian–Ukrainian relations were not always smooth. Part of the problem was that Ukraine had been guaranteed its own autonomous government with its own Hetman or ruler under the treaty of 1654, but Ukrainian leaders were not always happy with Moscow's policies as they affected Ukraine. Perhaps the most extreme example of this occurred in 1708, when Ivan Mazepa, Hetman of the Zaporozhian Cossacks since 1687, signed an alliance with Charles XII of Sweden (then at war with Russia) under which Ukraine was to

Cossacks of yesteryear hunt on the open Ukrainian plains

150

become an independent nation under Mazepa's leadership. After Peter the Great's victory over Sweden at the battle of Poltova, he moved to curtail most of Ukraine's autonomy. There were three further Hetmans in the eighteenth century, all Russian nominees. The last Hetman was Kyrylo Razumovsky, younger brother of Empress Elizabeth's "Gentleman of the Bedchamber." Catherine the Great accepted his resignation in 1764.

Catherine the Great incorporated Ukraine directly into Russia by dissolving separate Cossack bodies and dividing the area into *guberniyi*. In 1793, when the remaining territories occupied by Ukrainians were taken from Poland in the second partition, the name Ukraine was dropped and all of the territory simply became part of Russia.

Ukrainian nationalism resurfaced in the nineteenth century when the secret Brotherhood of Saints Cyril and Methodius was founded in Kyiv in 1846. The membership of the Brotherhood included two historians, Mykola Kostomariv and Panteleimon Kulish, plus the Ukrainian poet Taras Shevchenko. It was suppressed in 1847 and its thirty members were exiled to other parts of the empire.

Tsar Alexander II authorized the publication of a journal, *Osnova* (The Outset) in Ukrainian in 1861. In 1876, however, Alexander II prohibited the publication of journals or books in the Ukrainian language and closed all Ukrainian language schools. Thereafter, Ukrainian nationalists migrated abroad, either to Lvov (L'viv) in Austrian Galicia or to Switzerland. The Austrian Government permitted a Shevchenko Scientific Society to be founded there in 1872 and in 1890 a chair in southeastern European history was established at the University of Lvov (L'viv).

The first man appointed to fill the position was Myhailo Hrushevsky, a Ukrainian historian. Hrushevsky eventually published a ten–volume *History of Ukraine–Rus*, whose major thesis was the continuation of Kyivan Rus–Ukrainian history and the separate development of the history of Muscovy–Russia. After the Revolution of 1905, when the Russian Government lifted its ban against the publication of journals and books in Ukrainian, Hrushevsky moved back to Kyiv.

After the Russian Revolution of 1917, Ukrainian nationalists held a National Ukrainian Congress in Kyiv in April and elected a Rada (Council) headed by Hrushevsky. The Ukrainian Rada proclaimed an autonomous Ukrainian republic in June with Hrushevsky as president, Volodymir Vinnichenko as premier, and Symon Petlyura as minister of war.

After the *Bolshevik* revolution in November, the Ukrainian Rada called for convocation of a freely elected Ukrainian Constituent Assembly. Opposing this, the *Bolsheviks* announced formation of a Ukrainian Soviet Government on December 26. On January 22, 1918, the Ukrainian Rada proclaimed a "free and sovereign" Ukrainian Republic. The Central Powers signed a separate peace treaty with this government at Brest–Litovsk on February 9, but the *Bolsheviks* managed to seize Kyiv on February 8. After the Rada fled to Zhitomir, German and Austrian troops occupied most of Ukraine. The Rada and the Central Powers now came into conflict, whereupon the Central Powers overthrew the Ukrainian Rada on April 24 and appointed Pavlo Skoropadsky as Hetman of Ukraine.

After the collapse of Germany in November 1918, a five–man directorate took over in Ukraine, with Volodymir Vinnichenko as chairman and Symon Petlyura as commander in chief. A separate Republic of the Western Ukraine was proclaimed in L'viv. The Poles occupied L'viv about three weeks later, however, so this government fled to Ivano–Frankovsk. In January 1919, a union of the two Ukraines was proclaimed, but a Red Army occupied Kyiv the same day. On March 14, 1919, a Ukrainian Soviet Socialist Republic was formed under the leadership of Khristian Rakovsky. However, the whole of Galicia remained in Polish hands. The Bolsheviks were then driven out of Kyiv by the anti–*Bolshevik* forces of General Denikin in September 1919. However, Denikin had a falling out with the Ukrainian nationalists because he was opposed to a separate Ukraine. After Denikin's defeat in December 1919, the Ukrainian Soviet Socialist Republic established its control over most of Ukraine.

Communist Control

In December 1919, Lenin, speaking of the equality of the Russian and Ukrainian peoples, proposed an alliance. The Ukrainian nationalists couldn't bring themselves to come to terms with the *Bolsheviks*, however. Instead, Petlyura allied himself with Pilsudski, the Polish leader, which led to a Polish invasion of the Ukraine in April 1920. The Poles occupied Kyiv on May 7. Pilsudski now began dreaming of a reconstructed Polish–Lithuanian–Ukrainian Commonwealth. But that vision was no more acceptable to Ukrainian nationalists than Lenin's offer had been, and the Polish forces were soon forced out of Ukraine. In December 1920, Lenin and Rakovsky, head of the Ukrainian Soviet Socialist Republic, signed an alliance uniting Soviet Russia and Ukraine. A peace treaty with Poland was signed on March 18, 1921. Under the terms of the treaty, Poland got to keep Eastern Galicia and Volhynia.

In December 1922, an All–Union Congress of Soviets representing the Russian, Ukrainian, Byelorussian and Transcaucasian Soviet Socialist Republics agreed to form the Union of Soviet Socialist Republics. A constitution for the new union was adopted in July 1923.

In Ukraine, a Language Act of August 1, 1923 established the priority of Ukrainian over Russian. Hrushevsky was appointed president of the Ukrainian Academy of Science, founded in 1918. This period of Ukrainization came to an end in 1928 when Stalin forced the government to introduce Russian as the second official language. Two years later, "nationalist deviation" became a crime punishable by death when 45 intellectual leaders were put on trial and charged with treason. Thirteen were sentenced to death and the rest were deported. Hrushevsky, though not one of the 45 accused, was also deported. As part of Stalin's grisly purges, additional trials were held in 1931 and 1933. Being a member of the *Communist Party* was no defense. Yury Kotsiubinsky, deputy premier, was shot in 1933; in 1937, Panas Lyubchenko, an ex–premier, was also shot; and in 1939, yet another premier, Vlas Chubar, was shot.

Collectivization and the Great Famine

The other program that was to wreck havoc on Ukraine was collectivization. Launched in 1929, the purpose of collectivization was to put an end to individual farming and organize all of the peasants into collectives controlled by the state. By mid-1932, 70 percent of all Ukrainian peasants were in kolkhozes. The origins of the Ukrainian famine of 1932–33 can be seen in the rising grain quotas enforced during the period 1930–33. In 1926, the best harvest year before collectivization, 3.3 million tons of grain were taken from Ukraine. In the good harvest of 1930, 7.7 million tons were taken. In 1931, the quota was again set at 7.7 million tons, but the harvest was poor and only 7 million tons were actually collected. But this marked the beginning of a famine in 1932, for only an average of 250 pounds per capita was left to feed the rural Ukrainian population until the next harvest. But even with widespread evidence of grain shortages throughout the republic, the quota was again set at 7.7 million tons for 1932—and this out of a harvest reduced by two-thirds by collectivization and poor weather. When local officials complained that the poor harvest made it impossible to meet the state quota, Moscow's response was to issue in August 1932 which spelled out the legal sanctions which were to be used to enforce the quota. The decree further specified that those guilty of offenses under the terms of the decree

Ukraine

President Leonid Kuchma

were to be considered enemies of the people and shot, unless there were extenuating circumstances. Over a fourth of the officials staffing agricultural middle management were arrested because of their opposition to the quota; the actual collections were carried out by gangs of thugs sent into the villages to root out the hidden grain.

As the collection process stripped the villages of food, many of the peasants attempted to flee elsewhere; lacking internal travel documents, they were stopped by guards at the border of the republic and prevented from entering Russia proper. In the end, most stayed in the villages and tried to find enough to survive on until the next harvest.

Although people had been dying all winter, death on a mass scale really began in March 1933. To keep the fact of the famine a secret, foreigners were forbidden to travel to Ukraine. The grain harvest collection in Ukraine was officially ended on March 15, 1933. Estimates of the total number of deaths vary greatly, but they certainly numbered in the millions. The famine served its purpose in a peculiar way, however, for it broke the will of the Ukrainian peasantry; never again would they dare to challenge the will of the Soviet government.

In November 2006, President Yushchenko submitted a bill to the *Verkhovna Rada* declaring the man-made famine an act of genocide against the Ukrainian people. Lawmakers from the *Party of Regions* and the *Communist Party* opposed the bill during the ensuing debate, arguing that it would only worsen relations with Russia. In the end, 233 deputies voted in favor of the bill.

The territory of Ukraine was considerably enlarged as a result of World War II. Those parts of Poland where Ukrainians lived, essentially eastern Galicia and Volhynia, were occupied by the Red Army beginning in September 1939 and incorporated into Ukraine later that year. Romania

ceded Bessarabia and northern Bukovina to the Union of Soviet Socialist Republics in June 1940. Northern Bukovina and the Bessarabian districts of Hotin and Izmail went to Ukraine. On June 29, 1945, Czechoslovakia ceded Sub–Carpathian Ruthenia to the USSR, and this area was also incorporated into Ukraine.

The last addition to Ukraine came in February 1954 when Nikita Khrushchëv marked the 300th anniversary of the Russo–Ukraine union by transferring the Crimea to Ukraine. In 1991, the Government of Ukraine granted the Crimea the status of an autonomous republic.

The Gorbachëv program of reform instituted after 1985 found no immediate response in Ukraine, for Vladimir Shcherbitsky, first secretary of the *Ukrainian Communist Party*, was a Brezhnev stalwart who was quick to slap down any signs of dissent. He was removed in September 1989 and died soon afterwards. His successor, Leonid Kravchuk, although also a product of the party apparatus, showed himself to be more "liberal" than his predecessor and more willing to make concessions on nationalism.

This made good political sense for *Rukh*, the national front movement, had come into existence by this time and it was challenging the communists for the political leadership of the republic. By stealing a number of their positions, Kravchuk managed to turn back the *Rukh* challenge in the March 1990 elections. After the communists had managed to hold on to 239 out of the 450 seats in the legislature, Kravchuk sponsored a declaration of republican sovereignty, which was adopted in July 1990.

In March 1991, Kravchuk agreed to hold a referendum on a new union treaty drawn up by Gorbachëv, but insisted on rewording it to make it clear that Ukraine was unwilling to give up its claim to sovereignty. As the same time, Kravchuk worked to insulate Ukraine from Gorbachëv's economic policies, suggesting in July, for example, that Ukraine intended to issue its own currency. The Ukrainian legislature also began taking more nationalistic stances, for example repealing a series of Soviet tax and foreign–trade laws.

When conservatives launched their *coup d'etat* to overthrow Gorbachëv in August 1991, Kravchuk compromised by refusing to recognize the authority of the leaders while, at the same time, not condemning them publicly. After the collapse of the *coup*, he resigned as first secretary of the *Ukrainian Communist Party* and banned the party from the republic. On August 24, he got the Ukrainian legislature to declare Ukraine independent, subject to a popular referendum scheduled to take place on December 1, 1991.

At this point, it appeared that Kravchuk favored some form of continued union, and Ukrainian delegates cooperated in creating the new interim government that the Supreme Soviet approved on September 5. Nationalist pressures continued to grow, however, and by October Kravchuk was beginning to sound as though he wanted a completely independent Ukrainian state. In November, the Ukrainian legislature voted to "decertify" the Ukrainian deputies to the USSR Supreme Soviet; henceforth they were to participate as observers only. Meanwhile, Kravchuk had stated that Ukraine also intended to create its own national army.

The December 1 referendum and popular election for the office of President of Ukraine became the culmination of this increasing trend. Over 90 percent of all voters cast their ballots in favor of Ukrainian independence, at the same time giving 61 percent of their votes to Kravchuk to make him the first president of an independent Ukraine. Eight days later, Kravchuk met with the presidents of Russia and Belarus to declare the Union of Soviet Socialist Republics dead and create the Commonwealth of Independent States. Eight other republics joined the CIS on December 21, and Gorbachëv resigned as president of the USSR on December 25.

The history of the CIS has been extremely uneven since its creation in December 1991 and Ukraine has contributed to that unevenness. Essentially, Ukraine, fearing a new domination by Russia, has mostly been only a half–hearted participant in CIS efforts to create independent structures that would permit continued cooperation between the ex–Soviet republics. For example, the Republic of Ukraine made it clear from the beginning that it intended to take control of all conventional forces stationed in Ukraine, including naval forces. There were no problems with the army, including nuclear forces, but a quarrel did arise with Russia over the Black Sea Fleet, headquartered in the Crimea. Ukraine first claimed the entire Black Sea Fleet, then only the conventional portion of it, while Russia took the position that dividing it would destroy it. The two countries worked out an arrangement for joint supervision of the Black Sea Fleet in 1992, but it wasn't until 1997 that they were able to reach an arrangement acceptable to both sides.

Another problem has been the status of the Autonomous Republic of Crimea. Crimea, which has a population of about 2.5 million, is about 67 percent Russian and 26 percent Crimean Tatar. Ukrainians actually make up only 26 percent of the population. A majority of the Crimea population voted for Ukrainian independence in December 1991, but Russian nationalists in the Crimean legislature subsequently pushed for a vote of independence from Ukraine, with the real aim of joining Russia. The Crimean legislature has actually been ambivalent on the issue, voting for independence and then modifying the vote to indicate that Crimea was a part of Ukraine. The issue has also been fueled by Russian nationalists in Russia, who argue that Crimea ought to be returned to Russia, to which it belonged until 1954. In May 1992, the Russian Supreme Soviet actually passed a resolution declaring the 1954 transfer to be invalid. The Yeltsin Government repudiated the resolution, but the Supreme Soviet's vote was seen by Ukrainian nationalists as another example of Russia's traditional tendency to bully and dominate. The Friendship Treaty between Russia and Ukraine, signed in May 1997, presumably put an end to this problem because it includes an explicit Russian recognition of Ukraine's borders.

Ukraine's main problems after independence were economic, however, partly because the leadership of the country remained in the hands of ex–communists opposed to significant economic change until 1994. President Kravchuk was, of course, first secretary of the Ukrainian Communist Party before 1991. His first prime minister, Vitold Fokin, was another old–line communist bureaucrat who found himself beyond his depth in the new circumstances of a collapse of the old communist system. Even as Ukraine's economic circumstances continued to grow worse over the next several months, the government did nothing to tackle the problems. By September 1992, inflation was outpacing even the Russian rate so Ukrainian coupons were trading at a ratio of 3 coupons to 2 rubles and, in spite of seemingly unlimited easy credit to industry, economic activity was down 18 percent over the preceding year. Faced with that situation, even the Supreme Soviet,

dominated though it was by ex–communists, was unwilling to continue to put up with Fokin's policies. On September 30, he and his cabinet were forced to resign.

President Kravchuk's first choice as his successor was another former communist boss, Valentin Simonenko, but he was unacceptable to the Supreme Soviet. President Kravchuk then settled on Leonid Kuchma, a member of the Supreme Soviet who had also been director of *Yuzhmash*, Ukraine's largest producer of nuclear missiles, since 1986. Although a long–time member of the *nomenklatera*, Kuchma had a reputation for being hard–driving and competent. Moreover, he took office with a mandate to step up the pace of economic reform if he so wished. In confirming him, the Supreme Soviet also gave him the power to rule by decree until May 1993.

Over the next year, Kuchma pushed a major economic reform—issuing decrees on privatizing land, reforming income tax and commercializing state–owned enterprises—that was supposed to address most of Ukraine's problems and move the country toward a market economy. But Kuchma's policies brought loud objections from the legislature, which made several attempts to revoke his right to rule by decree. Over the next several months, therefore, Kuchma spent his time quarreling with parliament and getting very little accomplished. Parliament then refused to renew his right to rule by decree in May 1993. Kuchma remained on as prime minister until September, apparently hoping to work out some accommodation with parliament. He then resigned and was replaced by Youhym Zviahilsky.

Zhiahilsky, an ex–Soviet enterprise director from the Donbass, never claimed to be a reformer and the policies he implemented as prime minister were in line with the hardliners in parliament. Not surprisingly, prices increased 30–fold in 1993 and the government's budget was almost 90 percent of GDP. Having a large

budget deficit to contend with, the government also instituted punitive taxes which suppressed economic activity. With company taxes levied on gross revenues instead of profits, it was not uncommon for companies to hand over more than 100 percent of their official profits as tax. This had the effect of driving most private economic activity underground. By the end of 1993, the "underground" category was estimated to encompass 60 percent of the economy.

The Government of Ukraine withdrew from the ruble block in November 1992, at the prompting of Russia. From that time until the summer of 1996, its currency consisted of "coupons" that the government had begun issuing in the spring of 1992. The government had a new currency, the *hryvna*, already printed up but, because of a virulent inflation, did not dare to release it.

New parliamentary elections took place in March 1994. 338 out of the 450 seats were filled, with the remainder to be filled in a second round of voting. Of the 338 seats filled, 163 were won by persons running without a party label. Most of these were prominent local people, usually ex–communists. Among parties, those associated with the old communist regime made the best showing. The *Ukrainian Communist Party* came in first with 86, followed by the *Peasant Party*, with 18 seats and the *Ukrainian Socialist Party* with 14 seats. *Rukh*, largest of the nationalist parties, won 20 seats while five other nationalist parties garnered 20 more seats among them. Six centrist parties won 17 seats. In general, communists and their allies did best in eastern Ukraine, while nationalists did best in western Ukraine. While most Ukrainians thus voted against change, Leonid Kuchma, leader of the centrist *Interregional Reform Bloc* won over 52 percent of the vote for president on July 10, 1994, defeating incumbent Leonid Kravchuk.

Kuchma had run as a reformer and he signaled this by meeting with Michel Camdessus, managing director of the IMF on July 28, ten days after taking office. This was, in effect, a follow–up of a meeting that Kuchma had had with Camdessus in Washington earlier that spring. During that meeting, Kuchma had invited Camdessus to come to Kyiv if Kuchma won the election and had concrete economic proposals ready. After the Kyiv meeting, Camdessus promised that the IMF would work with Kuchma to develop an economic program for the Ukraine aimed at keeping monthly inflation to single digits, reducing the budget deficit, and freeing prices.

This, in turn, would permit a start on implementation of the $4 billion aid package promised at the economic summit

Kyiv, capital of Ukraine, on the Dneiper River

Ukraine

meeting in Naples earlier in the month. That promise had been conditioned on the Ukrainian Government's moving forward on programs such as land redistribution, privatization of state enterprises, elimination of price controls, and drastic cuts in the budget. Kuchma subsequently pushed a far–reaching economic reform program through the legislature which promised large–scale privatization of state companies, cuts in the national budget and the removal of price controls on many goods.

Ukraine received its first IMF loan, for $371 million, in October 1994 and agreement was reached for a second loan for $1.5 billion in March 1995. With the payments deficit for 1995 expected to be $5.5 billion, however, the Ukrainian Government requested an additional $900 million from individual Western countries as well. The U.S. Government pledged $100 million, while additional funds eventually came from the members of the European Union. After some Western arm twisting, Russia also agreed to reschedule $2.5 billion in Ukrainian debts, and Turkmenistan took similar action on monies owed it for deliveries of natural gas.

Economic reform continued after that time, with the government gradually selling off state assets. With inflation slowly being brought under control, the Ukrainian Government was finally able to begin issuing its new currency, the *hryvna*, in the summer of 1996. However, the economy remained stagnant, the 1996 budget continued to run a large deficit, and the gross foreign debt at the end of 1996 stood at $8.5 billion.

The Ukrainian Government did have promises of loans totaling approximately $4 billion from the West, including the IMF, if it carried through with a promised structural reform. President Kuchma worked hard to do so, though he was not always been able to get his proposals through the legislature. A particular example of this occurred in 1997 when the legislature delayed passage of the budget for over six months, threatening up to $3 billion in credits from the IMF.

Kuchma's policies had considerable support within the country but they were by no means universally liked. Another problem was that, until 1997, Kuchma was unable to get parliament to accept a prime minister who was in agreement with his economic policies. His first prime minister, Vitaly Masol, an old communist bureaucrat, often opposed specific elements of Kuchma's policy of economic reform. Kuchma retained him as prime minister because it would have been difficult to get any more liberal successor approved by the communist–dominated parliament.

Masol stepped down in March 1995. He was replaced by Pavlo Lazarenko, a for-

St. Sofia Cathedral, Kyiv, the city's oldest structure dating back to the times of the Kievan Rus
Courtesy: NOVOSTI

mer state–farm boss from the Dnepropetrovsk region of eastern Ukraine. Lazarenko served from July 1995 to July 1997, then was replaced after a period of illness. His successor as prime minis-ter was Valery Pustovoitenko, a former Mayor of Dnepropetrovsk. A leading member of President Kuchma's *People's Democratic Party*, Pustovoitenko was as committed to radical economic reform as President Kuchma. Confirmed as prime minister in August 1997, Pustovoitenko attempted to win support for his policies from members of parliament by involving them earlier in the process as new policies were being developed. This technique allowed him to get more new legislation approved by the legislature than his predecessors had managed to do.

One example is the election law which parliament approved in September 1997. With new parliamentary elections scheduled for March 1998, Kuchma wanted to get a new electoral law enacted establishing single member constituencies throughout the country. Although the legislature rejected Kuchma's plan, the electoral law which it did approve provided for half of

the seats in the 450–seat legislature to be filled by ballots cast in single–member constituencies, while the other half were to be elected by party lists.

The stakes in those elections were raised in November 1997 when the parliament passed a resolution suspending privatization. Although the government adopted the position that privatization was already the law of the land so the parliamentary vote could not be binding, this was still a serious setback. The chief reason for the vote against privatization was that the parliament was controlled by individuals hostile to economic reform, but it is also true that the situation of the economy gave them an excuse. For example, GDP fell by 4 percent in 1997. This was an improvement over 1996, when the drop was 10 percent, but it still presented a negative picture. Moreover, the currency came under international pressure at this time and began dropping in value. The pressure on the currency was primarily a reaction to the economic collapse in Thailand, Korea and Indonesia, but it was easy for opponents to blame it on economic reform. The government countered with the argument that parliament's opposition was responsible for the continued fall of the currency. This argument, plus negotiations between the government and the legislature over the government's 1998 budget, persuaded the parliament to approve the budget and lift its ban on privatization in February 1998.

The results of the March 29, 1998 parliamentary elections were not encouraging, however; the *Communist Party of Ukraine* (*CPU*) and its left–wing allies increased their representation in the 450-seat parliament and now controlled a clear plurality of the seats. The *CPU* took 121 seats, while its left–wing allies, the *Peasants/Socialists Bloc* and the *Progressive Socialist Party*, took an additional 73 seats. Other parties in the parliament included the nationalist *Rukh* party (32 seats); the *Greens* (19 seats); the *Popular Democratic Party*, led by then Prime Minister Valery Pustovoitenko (17 seats); the *Hromada* party, led by former Prime Minister Pavlo Lazarenko (who in March 1999 went into exile in the United States) (16 seats); and the *United Social Democrats*, led by former President Leonid Kravchuk (14 seats). Independent candidates won 114 seats.

When the parliament met on May 12, however, it became clear that the *Communists* and their allies did not control an ideological majority in the legislature. Although only a simple majority of 226 votes was necessary for election, the *Communists* and their allies were only able to produce 176 votes for their candidate for the office of speaker. Meanwhile, several of the smaller political parties made a point

A young Ukrainian economist
Courtesy: NOVOSTI

of abstaining because they were pressing for the speaker and two deputy speakers to be elected on a single slate. That would have, of course, required some agreement in advance on the three candidates and given these parties some say in the selection. Since the left rejected this procedure, the legislature was unable to elect a speaker and so organize itself for nearly two months. The legislature finally elected Oleksandr Tkachenko, a member of the *Peasants/Socialists* parliamentary group, as its speaker on the 19th round of voting on July 7.

Although a member of the left, Tkachenko met with President Kuchma soon after his election; after the meeting, he joined the president in calling for "constructive cooperation and concerted action." In addition, he expressed his own support for recent presidential economic decrees. There was, in fact, considerable cooperation between the president and parliament after that time, with the speaker one of those pushing for decisive action. The legislature even managed to pass the 1999 budget on December 31 after a compromise with the *Communists* provided more money for education and health care.

With the beginning of 1999, however, most political activity began to focus on the presidential elections which were due in the fall. Parliament passed a new law on presidential elections in January which stipulated that presidential candidates could be nominated by political parties or a group of at least 500 voters but that each candidate had to collect a million signatures from among Ukraine's 35 million eligible voters. The legislation also stipulated that a candidate needed to be positively supported by more than half of the voters who cast their ballots in order to win in the first round of voting. If nobody won in the first round, a runoff would follow. Here a simple majority of votes cast was required to win.

Thirteen individuals contested the October 31 vote. President Kuchma came in first with 36.36 percent of the vote, followed by Petro Symonenko, candidate of the *Communist Party of Ukraine*, with 22.32 percent. Symonenko won the endorsement of six of the losing candidates, including Oleksandr Moroz, the *Socialist Party* leader, who came in third. He also received the endorsement of parliamentary speaker Oleksandr Tkachenko. However, Symonenko had openly acknowledged that he favored a return to Soviet–style government and intended to reverse those market reforms Kuchma had introduced. In the November 14 runoff, therefore, Kuchma won a convincing victory by obtaining 56.31 percent of the votes to Symonenko 37.76 percent.

President Kuchma took his victory as a popular mandate to speed up reform, something which would be very difficult if he continued to face a parliament controlled by the left–wing. Kuchma therefore took his victory as a mandate for parliamentary reform. This became even more compelling when the parliament rebuffed his attempt to reappoint Pustovoitenko as his prime minister. In the event, parliament did accept his second candidate, Viktor Yushchenko, confirming him by a vote of 296 to 12. Yushchenko, who was chairman of the National Bank of Ukraine at the time that he was appointed prime minister, was a pro–market reformer who argued for a reduction in government's role in the economy, massive privatization, and abolition of collective farms.

On January 15, 2000, Kuchma announced on national television that he had signed a decree to hold a nationwide referendum on April 16 involving six questions. The first was, in effect, a confidence vote in parliament; the second would give the president the right to disband parliament if it failed to form a majority within a month or adopt a budget within three months; the third abolished legislators' immunity from criminal prosecution; the fourth and fifth reduced the size of the legislature from 450 seats to 300 seats and split it into two houses; and the sixth provided for the possibility to adopt the constitution via referendum.

A week later, the center and rightist parties organized themselves into a new parliamentary majority consisting of 242 deputies and voted to oust Oleksandr Tkachenko from the post of parliamentary speaker. However, Tkachenko, supported by the caucuses of the *Communist Party, Socialist Party, Progressive Socialist Party,* and *Peasant Party*, refused to recognize the new majority. The majority then met again on February 1 and elected Ivan Plyushch as the new parliamentary speaker. Still refusing the validity of the vote or to relinquish control, the left occupied the parliamentary building and held its own session of the leftist minority on February 3. Proclaiming all decisions of the parliamentary majority to be illegal, the leftists called on the international community for support. Instead, a district court in Kyiv ruled on February 9 that former speaker Tkachenko and his supporters had taken illegal action by preventing the majority from entering the parliamentary building and by not allowing the newly elected parliamentary leadership to take its place in the parliamentary presidium. That brought an end to the confrontation, but the left, refusing to cooperate with the new parliamentary leadership, referred to the events of February 1 as a *coup*.

NORTHEAST HIGH SCHOOL MEDIA CENTER

Ukraine

Speaker Plyushch has said that the majority was formed "to end any confrontation, assume responsibility, and follow the path the people voted for." President Kuchma referred to the election of the parliament's new leadership as a "momentous" event and promised that the government would seek cooperation with the legislature to show Ukrainians that the "six–year confrontation" in the country was over.

Meanwhile, the political left brought a challenge to President Kuchma's referendum before the constitutional court, but lost when the court ruled that the referendum could go forward. President Kuchma did later revise the terms of the referendum somewhat, dropping points one and six. Voting took place over a period of ten days in April, with voters endorsing Kuchma's four referendum questions by margins of between 80 and 90 percent. In spite of this strong showing, none of the four proposed changes was ever implemented, since the amendments required a positive vote by two–thirds of the membership in parliament in order to go into effect.

In the spring of 2000, Prime Minister Yushchenko instituted a program that he described as "serious systemic reform." This included privatization of Ukraine's still largely state–owned industry plus a major campaign against corruption and inefficiency in the economy and in the government. During this period, the government managed to renegotiate its foreign debt, increase its foreign exchange reserves, and cut the annual rate of inflation to about 20 percent on an annual basis, still high but impressive if one recalls that the annual inflation rate five years earlier had been 377 percent. In addition, the economy grew by six percent in the first nine months of 2000 with industry growing at an even faster pace.

All of this progress was suddenly challenged by a political scandal that erupted on November 28 when *Socialist Party* leader Olexander Moroz accused President Kuchma and Interior Minister Yuriy Kravchenko of having organized the murder of a journalist by the name of Heorhiy Gongadze. Gongadze, editor of an independent internet newspaper called *Ukrainskaya Pravda*, disappeared on September 16. Six weeks later, a headless corpse turned up which relatives identified as being the missing journalist. But the real bombshell came from the fact that Moroz's "proof" was a number of tapes which, he said, had been made by a former member of the presidential security service by the name of Mykola Melnichenko. In one of the conversations on the tapes, two male voices, which Moroz identified as being President Kuchma and

A family dance group in Ukraine

Courtesy: NOVOSTI

Interior Minister Kravchenko, discuss getting rid of Gongadze.

Moroz's revelations led to a splintering of the government's parliamentary majority and an effective end to progress on the government's reform program. The government originally denounced the tapes as fakes; after some individuals heard on the tapes verified their conversations, however, the government changed its position, arguing that the tapes were genuine but that they had been doctored. Kuchma himself has flatly denied any role in the disappearance of Gongadze.

The Ukrainian Government subsequently invited FBI experts to come to Ukraine, presumably to give any assistance they could that would help solve Gongadze's murder. During the visit, which took place on April 8–15, 2002, the government arranged meetings with officials of the Prosecutor–General's Office, the Interior Ministry, and the Security Service, but refused to give the FBI experts access to the Gongadze file. The explanation given by Ukrainian law enforcement officials was that they were unable to discuss any aspects of the case, share evidence, or conduct a joint site inspection, because "Ukrainian law prohibits sharing any information that is not in the public domain." These actions clearly did not help to establish that the government was attempting to get at the truth of Gongadze's murder.

If the government appeared to be a little paranoid on the subject, it should be added that Gongadze's murder had become a major political issue, and those

leading the attack were mainly from those parties which have opposed Kuchma and his policies all along. After the attacks began, Kuchma was forced to dismiss Interior Minister Kravchenko; next, Prime Minister Yushchenko was ousted in April 2001 after the opposition called for a vote of confidence in his government. Yushchenko's defeat was a blow to Kuchma, since the president had called on parliament to support the prime minister prior to the vote. Essentially, the vote against Yushchenko was supported by the Communists and Socialists plus those pro-business parties that, prior to this time, had been allies of Kuchma. The fact that the pro–business parties voted against the prime minister was interpreted by many Ukrainians to mean that Kuchma wanted to get rid of Yushchenko and used this opportunity to do so. Although that is certainly a possibility, the argument is not convincing, since it was always a possibility that Yushchenko would join the political opposition if it became clear that the charge was true. In fact, it appears that the pro–business political parties—which are really controlled by the oligarchs who have emerged as a result of privatization—opposed Yushchenko because his efforts to stamp out corruption in the economic sphere had begun to affect their business activities negatively. In the short run they benefited from Yushchenko's fall, since President Kuchma named Anatoly Kinakh, leader of the *Ukrainian Union of Industrialists and Entrepreneurs*, as his new prime minister. Although, Kinakh promised to continue his predecessor's "market reforms and move to civil society," the government did little to move the program forward over the next year.

Instead, both the government and the opposition increasingly focused on the new parliamentary elections scheduled for March 2002. Kinakh's task here was to produce a parliamentary majority for the president. Although he ultimately failed in that endeavor, he did manage to hold the pro–Kuchma forces together and this, coupled with a lavish use of the prerogatives of the government during the campaign, allowed the pro–Kuchma forces to win a plurality of the seats in the new parliament.

There was also a fairly significant realignment of political forces during the year preceding the new parliamentary elections. It began when two prominent anti–Kuchma leaders, Yulia Tymoshenko, at that time leader of the *National Salvation Forum*, and Oleksandr Moroz, leader of the *Socialist Party*, proposed that Yushchenko join forces with them to create an anti–Kuchma electoral bloc. Instead, Yushchenko created his own *Our Ukraine* electoral bloc of reformers, liberals, and nationalists by bringing together Ukrainian nationalists associated with the two wings of *Rukh*, the *Christian Republican Party*, the Federation of Trade Unions, and a number of smaller liberal political parties. At the same time, Yushchenko was always careful to define his electoral bloc as an "alternative," not an opposition, to Kuchma, so as not to alienate those with whom he had worked as prime minister.

Fearful of the growing support for Yushchenko's electoral bloc and the threat this represented from the middle, President Kuchma sought to increase his own support on the left by appealing to the more Russified, urban, and industrialized populations of Eastern Ukraine. The chief competition for this vote was from the Communists—always among Kuchma's strongest opponents—whose principal platform advocated a return to the old Soviet way. The Communist program, which included a return to a socialist economy, nationalization of banks, introduction of a planned economy for state enterprises, official status for the Russian language, and a break of all relations with NATO, made Kuchma seem, by contrast, both more liberal and more western, so he was able to increase his support from among the more liberal elements in eastern Ukraine.

When the new parliamentary elections finally took place on March 31, 2002, Yushchenko's *Our Ukraine* bloc came in first in the popular vote with 23.52 percent (70 seats), followed by the *Communist Party* with 20.04 percent (59 seats). Kuchma's *For a United Ukraine* bloc came in third with 11.98 percent (36 seats).

Three other political parties surpassed the four percent barrier to obtain proportional representation seats—the *Yulia Tymoshenko* bloc with 7.21 percent (21 seats), the *Socialist Party* with 6.93 percent (21 seats), and the *Social Democratic Party–united*, which ran a separate slate as an ally of President Kuchma, with 6.24 percent (18 seats).

In the races for the 225 single–mandate constituencies, however, Kuchma's better organized *For a United Ukraine* bloc came in first, winning an additional 66 seats. His ally, the *Social Democratic Party–united*, won five single constituency seats, giving it a total of 26 seats. Since President Kuchma could count on the support of at least 56 of the 93 "independents" who won individual seats, the pro–government bloc consisted of 182 seats at this point, making it the largest political force in the new parliament. The *Our Ukraine* bloc of former Prime Minister Yushchenko won 42 individual mandates and was, in addition, joined by five independents, putting it second with 117 seats. The *Communist Party* won five single mandate seats, which made it the third strongest party in the parliament with 66 seats (down from 112 seats in the previous parliament). The *Yulia Tymoshenko* bloc came in next with 22 seats.

With no single party or bloc in a position to organize the new parliament on its own, maneuvering began to create a coalition that would have enough votes to organize the parliament. The first move came in early May when President Kuchma appointed Viktor Medvedchuk, leader of the *Social Democratic Party–united* as head of the presidential administration. It was Medvedchuk who then managed to get Volodymir Lytvyn, the former head of the presidential administration, elected as parliamentary speaker later in May. But Lytvyn received only 226 votes, one vote more than the required minimum, and that one vote was cast by Mykhayko Potebenko, who had been elected to the parliament on the *Communist Party* ticket—an action for which he was subsequently expelled from the *Communist Party*. A number of other yes votes had come from political independents, however, since the nine groups forming the pro–presidential coalition claimed only 201 members.

Political maneuvering continued over the summer but things came to a head in September when the leaders of the *Yulia Tymoshenko Bloc*, the *Communist Party*, and the *Socialist Party* called for massive demonstrations to demand the resignation of President Kuchma. Viktor Yushchenko, leader of *Our Ukraine*, was still attempting to form a majority centrist coalition at this time committed to creat-

ing a harmonious working relationship between the prime minister, the president and the parliament and, on August 15, he had actually met with President Kuchma. As he hesitated, parts of the *Our Ukraine* bloc decided to participate in the planned demonstrations. Fearing the collapse of his political support, Yushchenko announced his support for the protest demonstrations and, at the last minute, joined the 20,000 demonstrators gathered in Kyiv's main square on September 16. However, Yushchenko's fence–straddling exasperated both sides and several members of his bloc later left to join the pro–presidential grouping.

It was on October 8 that Parliamentary Speaker Lytvyn announced the creation of a 231–member pro–presidential majority—consisting of *Labor Ukraine–Party Entrepreneurs* (42 deputies), *Ukraine's Regions* (37), the *Social Democratic Party–United* (37), *Democratic Initiatives* (20), *Power of the People* (18), *European Choice* (18), *Popular Democratic Party* (17), *Ukraine's Agrarians* (16), *People's Choice* (13), and *United Ukraine* (7), plus six deputies who left opposition caucuses. Three of those came from the *Yulia Tymoshenko* bloc, two came from the *Communist Party*, and one came from *Our Ukraine*.

Now that the pro–presidential forces were in control of parliament, President Kuchma decided that the time was ripe to change prime ministers. He therefore announced Kinakh's dismissal and in the accompanying official decree explained that he was taking this action in order to boost "cooperation" with parliament and "implement the proclaimed course of reforming the political system in the country." Kuchma's choice for the new prime minister was Donetsk Oblast Governor Viktor Yanukovych, who had close ties to the *Ukraine Regions* parliamentary caucus. Yanukovych was confirmed as prime minister on November 21, receiving 234 votes, eight more than the minimum required. The four opposition parties—*Our Ukraine*, the *Communist Party*, the *Socialist Party*, and the *Yulia Tymoshenko* bloc—refused to take part in the voting, though one member each from *Our Ukraine* and the *Socialist Party* cast yes votes for Yanukovych.

During the confirmation process, Yanukovych had explained that he saw his most important task as "strengthening the positive dynamic and the tempo of economic growth. This progress must give the signal to the world that Ukraine is a country which is developing quickly and transforming into a democratic country." Less than a month later, however, Yanukovych found himself involved in a major quarrel with the political opposition when the pro–presidential majority moved to dismiss National Bank of

Ukraine

Ukraine Governor Volodymyr Stelmakh and to replace him with Serhiy Tyhypko, leader of the *Labor Ukraine–Party of Industrialists and Entrepreneurs* parliamentary caucus. The political opposition now threw their support behind Stelmakh and managed to defeat two attempts to replace him. Declaring that the political opposition would do everything in their power to prevent the dismissal of Stelmakh, Yushchenko declared that Stelmakh "is our last bastion, and we will not move away."

Responding to the opposition's attempts to obstruct the vote, the majority created an ad hoc commission for tabulating the vote made up solely of its own deputies. In addition, the majority held the roll call vote in the office of the permanent presidential representative to parliament rather than in the session hall itself. In a move to consolidate its control, the 229 majority deputies also voted to remove all opposition party members as chairs of parliamentary committees.

Declaring the two votes to be illegal, the four opposition parties began to block parliamentary proceedings and promised to continue to do so until the two votes were annulled. In the end, the government had the votes, however, and so got its way. It also helped that Yanukovych was willing to hold talks with the po-litical opposition concerning President Kuchma's program of constitutional changes aimed at transforming Ukraine into a parliamentary–presidential republic. Kuchma's proposed reforms would have transferred some presidential authority to parliament and enhanced the role of the prime minister; one important clause specified that all parliamentary seats would be allocated on a proportional basis. After a year of further debate, the legislature approved a separate bill mandating a fully proportional system of parliamentary elections in March 2004. However, the separate constitutional reform bill required a minimum of 300 votes to pass, and it received only 294.

In March, parliament passed legislation setting the presidential election for October 31, 2004. Although 24 candidates managed to qualify for the ballot, it was always understood that the race was between Prime Minister Viktor Yanukovych, leader of the pro-presidential coalition, and former Prime Minister Viktor Yushchenko, leader of the opposition coalition.

The campaign, which became rather vicious, perhaps reached its nadir on September 6 when Viktor Yushchenko disappeared for a week, and it turned out later that he was in Austria, being treated for a mysterious illness which—three months later—was diagnosed as dioxin poisoning. Yushchenko would later make the accusation that he had been poisoned by the Ukrainian authorities, but, in fact, the Ukrainian Government is still attempting to discover how he was poisoned or by whom. Nevertheless, the poison weakened him physically and caused his face to be covered by swellings; even months later, he bears the scars of the poisoning.

Because there were so many candidates on the ballot, the October 31 elections proved to be inconclusive. According to the Central Election Commission, Yushchenko and Yanukovych each had slightly more than 39 percent of the votes. Since neither candidate had won anywhere close to 50 percent of the vote needed to avoid a run-off, a second round of voting was set for November 21.

In the period leading up to the run-off, several of the other presidential candidates threw their support to Yushchenko. Two important endorsements came from Oleksandr Moroz, leader of the *Socialist Party of Ukraine*, and former Prime Minister Kinakh, leader of *the Party of Industrialists and Entrepreneurs.*

Nevertheless, the Central Election Commission announced on November 22 that Viktor Yanukovych had won the run-off election, taking 49.42 percent of the vote to Yushchenko's 46.69 percent.

Yushchenko and the Orange Revolution

Yushchenko's supporters were particularly incensed because two separate exit polls had shown Yushchenko winning comfortably over his opponent. On November 22, a crowd estimated to be at least 100,000 gathered on Kyiv's Independence Square to protest, as they said, the government's falsification of the previous day's run-off vote. Pitching tents in the center of the city, the protesters vowed to remain until Yushchenko was declared president. As the "Orange Revolution," as it came to be called, spread throughout the nation, city councils of various Ukrainian cities began adopting resolutions declaring Yushchenko to be the legal president. Later, the demonstrators also began a blockade of the parliament so that it was unable to meet.

Finally, roundtable talks to resolve the dispute took place in Kyiv on December 1; attending were the two contenders, President Kuchma, EU High Representative Javier Solana, OSCE Secretary-General Jan Kubis, Polish President Aleksander Kwasniewski, Lithuanian President Valdas Adamkus, and Russian State Duma Chairman Boris Gryzlov. The resulting document bound the two sides to eliminate the use of force in resolving the election crisis; unblock government offices that were being surrounded by pro-Yushchenko supporters; prepare proposals for concluding the presidential election in line with the ruling of the Supreme Court; prepare a new presidential election law, draw up a constitutional reform bill which would shift the balance of power from president to the parliament and prime minister; and work toward preventing an economic crisis in Ukraine.

On December 6, the Supreme Court invalidated a decision of the Central Election Commission certifying Yanukovych as the winner of the November 21 run-off; simultaneously, the court ruled that the second round of voting take place by De-

President Yushchenko, before and after his dioxin poisoning

158

cember 26. Two days later, the parliament adopted a constitutional reform bill conforming to the December 1 roundtable guidelines plus amendments to the presidential election law aimed at eliminating election abuse and fraud. The two pieces of legislation, passed by an overwhelming vote of 402–21, were signed into law by President Kuchma that evening. That same day, the parliament dissolved the old Central Election Commission and then appointed a new Central Election Commission, which was sworn in immediately. The next day, President Kuchma sent Prime Minister Yanukovych on leave to campaign for the presidential runoff election, set for December 26.

That election was won convincingly by Viktor Yushchenko, who got 51.99 percent of the vote to Yanukovych's 44.19 percent. Reflecting the political geographic divide, Yushchenko won in 19 western and central oblasts and Kyiv, while Yanukovych won in nine eastern and southern oblasts and Sevastopol.

Yushchenko was sworn in as president on January 23, 2005; one day later, he appointed Yulia Tymoshenko as his prime minister. Tymoshenko, a recent political ally of Yushchenko, had served as energy minister when Yushchenko was prime minister. She was confirmed by parliament on February 4. The 373 votes to confirm constituted a strong vote of support for the new government's policies.

The new government passed a budget law in March 2005 which eliminated most tax and customs privileges, which had the effect of bringing more economic activity out of Ukraine's large shadow economy. But a 50 percent increase in crude oil prices during the first three months of 2005 caused gasoline prices to begin to rise in early April; and as the price of gasoline rose, confidence in the government fell.

Ex-Prime Minister Yulia Tymoshenko

Prime Minister Tymoshenko, who publicly charged that the fuel price increase was a "plot" by Russian oil traders—who control 75 percent of fuel supplies to Ukraine—to destabilize the government, attempted to deal with the fuel crisis using administrative and non-market levers. In mid-April, she ordered prices for gasoline to be stabilized at a level below 3 *hryvnyas* a liter. Simultaneously, the economics ministry informed Russian oil traders that the government would not guarantee their property rights for Ukraine's refineries unless they agreed to cut fuel prices.

The Russian traders did cut fuel prices—but Russian-owned oil refineries in Ukraine then either significantly decreased their daily output or halted it altogether because of "planned repairs." As a result, long lines began to appear at gasoline stations. President Yushchenko then accused Prime Minister Tymoshenko of incompetence in dealing with the fuel crisis and went on to suggest that she might consider resigning. Instead, the differences between president and prime minister were papered over after Tymoshenko agreed to try a more market-oriented solution. Parliament then abolished import duties on fuel in May, which temporarily resolved the fuel crisis.

However, a larger policy difference soon arose between the president and prime minister concerning how to investigate alleged corruption in past privatizations of state industries. Tymoshenko, arguing the corruptness of the entire system of privatizations under Kuchma, wanted thousands of companies to be investigated and renationalized; Yushchenko, arguing for the need to build a market-oriented system that would encourage international investment, wanted a much narrower examination of past privatizations.

Ultimately the battle centered on two past privatizations, the Nikopol Ferroalloy Plant and the formerly bankrupt Severodonetsk Azot. A consortium controlled by Viktor Pinchuk, son-in-law to President Kuchma, acquired a controlling interest in the Nikopol Ferroalloy Plant in 2003; Worldwide Chemical, a subsidiary of New York-based IBE Trade, obtained 60 percent of the shares of Severodonetsk Azot in return for a promise to invest $180 million in the new company.

In August, the Kyiv appellate court nullified the Pinchuk consortium's 50 percent plus one share stake in the Nikopol Ferroalloy Plant and returned it to the state. A week later, the private industrial group Privat, which is allegedly supported by Prime Minister Tymoshenko, attempted a takeover of the company. President Yushchenko had no problem with the court's nullification of the Pinchuk consortium's

stake in the Nikopol Ferroalloy Plant; however, he did intervene at this point, ordering the government to "resolve the conflict according to the law" and get the plant back into operation.

A lawsuit challenging the Severodonetsk Azot privatization was filed in a district court in Kyiv in March 2005. The court ruled against the privatization without permitting either the new investors or the state to testify. In August, the minister of industrial policy signed an order returning control of Severodonetsk Azot to the state. Armed with this order, dozens of men dressed in camouflage and body armor stormed and seized the headquarters of the company on September 2. According to a senior government official, "the order was based on a court case filed by a fictitious company, on behalf of a politician who stood to gain from the seizure."

On September 6, President Yushchenko ordered that Severodonetsk Azot be returned to its new investors until the matter was resolved in court. President Yushchenko's interventions in the two cases set off a whole series of charges and countercharges that led to several high-level resignations and, on September 8, to President Yushchenko's dismissal of Prime Minister Tymoshenko and her cabinet. At the same time, the president accepted the resignation of Petro Poroshenko, his national security and defense council secretary.

Tymoshenko's successor as prime minister was Yuriy Yekhanurov (yeh-kay-NOOR-awf). Yekhanurov served as head of the state property fund between 1994 and 1997, in that position overseeing the initial stage of Ukraine's privatization. Elected to parliament in 2002 as a member of Yushchenko's *Our Ukraine* bloc, Yekhanurov was appointed governor of Dnipropetrovs'k Oblast in April 2005.

Yekhanurov was confirmed as prime minister on September 22, after President Yushchenko signed a memorandum of understanding with *Party of Regions* leader Viktor Yanukovych.

However, the government had been declining in popularity even before Tymoshenko's dismissal and this only accelerated afterwards. A public opinion poll taken just before the first anniversary of the beginning of the Orange Revolution showed that more than half of all Ukrainians felt the new government had failed to keep the promises made a year earlier. The poll also indicated that one in seven Ukrainians fully supported President Yushchenko.

Matters got even worse in December as gas prices continued to rise, especially after Gazprom announced that the price of natural gas sold to Ukraine would go

Ukraine

A Kiev newspaper (June 9, 1995) reports on Presidents Kuchma and Yeltsin signing the treaty which permits the Russian Black Sea fleet to berth at Sevastopol on the Crimean peninsula.

from $50 per 1,000 cubic meters to $220-230 per 1,000 cubic meters. After Ukraine rejected Gazprom's demand for a price hike, Gazprom cut off gas supplies to Ukraine as of January 1, 2006. Since Russian gas exports to Western Europe go by way of the Ukrainian pipeline, however, a half dozen Western European countries quickly complained of sharp drops in the gas they were receiving; Gazprom restored gas to the Ukrainian pipeline on January 2. The following day, Ukraine and Gazprom announced a face-saving compromise. Gazprom would set up a new trading company, RosUkrEnergo, as a Swiss-based joint venture of Gazprom and Austria's Raiffeisen Zentralbank. RosUkrEnergo would purchase natural gas from Gazprom for $230 per 1,000 cubic meters and mix it with cheaper gas from Central Asia. The end result is that Ukraine would pay $95 per 1,000 cubic meters of natural gas.

From the beginning, the political opposition—led by Yulia Tymoshenko—condemned the gas deal and there were calls for the president's impeachment and the prime minister's resignation. On January 10, parliament actually voted to dismiss

Prime Minister Yekhanurov, though President Yushchenko refused to recognize the vote as legal.

This was the background to the March 29 parliamentary elections, the first in independent Ukraine to be contested under a fully proportional, party-list system. Under this system, voters would no longer get to vote for individual representatives; instead they would have a choice between political parties. Voters would determine the number of representatives awarded to each party; each party's leadership would choose the candidates and determine their placement on the candidate list. Only parties that obtained at least 3 percent of the national vote would be represented in parliament. This new parliament would serve for five years instead of four years previously. Most importantly, the constitutional changes adopted in December 2004 reduced the power of the presidency and increased the power of the prime minister and parliament.

Four electoral blocs won seats in the new parliament. The *Party of Regions*, led by Viktor Yanukovych, came in first with 32.14 percent of the vote (186 seats). The *Yulia Tymoshenko Bloc* came in second with

22.29 percent of the vote (129 seats). *Our Ukraine* came third with 13.95 percent of the vote (81 seats). The *Socialist Party* came fourth with 5.69 percent of the vote (33 seats, followed by the *Communist Party* with 3.66 percent of the vote (21 seats).

In mid-April the three parties of the Orange Coalition signed a protocol pledging to work toward creating a parliamentary majority. When the new parliament convened on May 25, however, the country remained in a state of political stalemate.

The chief stumbling block in the coalition talks was the question of who would become prime minister. Yulia Tymoshenko insisted that she was entitled to become prime minister again.

After three months of negotiation, an agreement by the three parties of the Orange Coalition was signed on June 22. Tymoshenko was to become prime minister, while *Our Ukraine* was given the right to name the parliamentary speaker and deputy prime minister. But Oleksander Moroz, leader of the *Socialist Party*, felt that he was entitled to the office of parliamentary speaker so, when the *Communists* and the *Party of Regions* agreed to support him for that position, he abandoned the newly reconstituted Orange Coalition and signed a new "anti-crisis" agreement with the *Communists* and the *Party of Regions*. Those three parties then elected Moroz to the office of parliamentary speaker. The same coalition then went on to nominate Viktor Yanukovych, leader of the *Party of Regions*, as prime minister.

Political Coexistence:
Yushchenko and Yanukovych

Ukraine's experiment in political coexistence had a rather acrimonious beginning with Yulia Tymoshenko calling for the two remaining parties of the Orange Coalition to give up their seats in order to force new elections. President Yushchenko's party, *Our Ukraine*, announced, however, that it accepted the legitimacy of the "anti-crisis" coalition and would go into the opposition.

Although President Yushchenko waited the constitutionally-permitted 15 days before he announced that he would formally propose Yanukovych as prime minister, Yanukovych easily won confirmation as prime minister, receiving the positive votes of 271 of the 296 deputies that were present. What that vote masked, however, is that the *Verkhovna Rada* has 450 members and 154 deputies belonging to the *Yulia Tymoshenko Bloc* and *Our Ukraine* boycotted the meeting. In the end, Yanukovych won with the support of the *Party of Regions*, the *Socialists*, and the *Communists*; only 30 *Our Ukraine* bloc deputies and six deputies from the *Yulia Tymoshenko Bloc* voted for the new prime minister.

President Yushchenko with Prime Minister Yanukovych

Thus, although President Yushchenko signed a declaration of national unity with the "anti-crisis" coalition and nominated five members of the *Our* Ukraine bloc for seats in the cabinet, the majority of the *Our Ukraine* bloc considered themselves to be in the opposition.

Discussions went on for another two months on whether the *Our Ukraine* bloc would formally join the government coalition; in September, however, one of the members of the *Our Ukraine* bloc, the *Reforms and Order Party*, announced that it was switching alliances and going into the opposition. This was the beginning of a split that eventually led most of the deputies belonging to the *Our Ukraine* bloc to reject an alliance with the governing coalition and formally join the opposition. Coalition talks ended on October 19 when the five *Our Ukraine* deputies in the Yanukovych cabinet tendered their resignations. One of the five, Interior Minister Lutsenko, later withdrew his resignation and remained in the cabinet; he later resigned his membership in the *Our Ukraine* bloc.

The formal withdrawal of *Our Ukraine* exacerbated problems in relations that already existed between the president and prime minister. According to the constitution, two of the members of the cabinet, the defense and foreign ministers, are appointed by the president; in November, Prime Minister Yanukovych called on the president to dismiss them, saying:

How can I react to a minister who says he is in opposition to the government? What does this mean? This means he disagrees with the program the government is fulfilling. If you are a man, if you have principles, resign.

When the president took no action, the *Verkhovna Rada* voted to dismiss Foreign Minister Tarasyuk on December 1. Shortly thereafter, the *Verkhovna Rada* voted to dismiss Interior Minister Lutsenko as well. The *Verkhovna Rada* then voted to install Vasyl Tsushko, head of the *Socialist Party* parliamentary caucus, as interior minister.

President Yushchenko refused to accept Tarasyuk's dismissal and appealed to the Constitutional Court, but Tarasyuk, a career diplomat, submitted his own resignation on January 30, saying that he refused to allow the foreign ministry to become hostage to unlawful actions of the government. The *Verkhovna Rada* then twice rejected President Yushchenko's next candidate for foreign minister, Volodymyr Ohryzko, another career diplomatic official. After the second rejection, *Our Ukraine* and the *Yulia Tymoshenko Bloc* walked out of the parliamentary session and announced that they would return only after the ruling coalition complied with demands their representatives had signed in President Yushchenko's presence the previous day.

Prime Minister Yanukovych then requested that the president propose a new candidate for the post of foreign minister. President Yushchenko nominated Arzseniy Yatsenyuk and he was confirmed as foreign minister on March 21. Members of *Our Ukraine* and the *Yulia Tymoshenko Bloc* attended the session and cast their votes for Yatsenyuk, but they left the session hall immediately after the vote.

But by now the political opposition had begun to crumble. That same day, Anatoliy Kinakh, leader of the *Party of Industrialists and Entrepreneurs*, whose party was part of the *United Ukraine* bloc, joined the government as economy minister. The next day, it was announced that five deputies from the *Yulia Tymoshenko Bloc* and six deputies from Kinakh's party had changed sides and joined the ruling coalition, which then renamed itself the national-unity coalition.

President Yushchenko believed that the government had acted unconstitutionally when it accepted individual opposition deputies into its ruling majority; according to the constitution, a government is put together by enlisting party factions, not individual members. On the other hand, the constitution gives the president only four circumstances when he may dissolve parliament and call for new elections and none of those circumstances appears to apply to this situation.

President Yushchenko therefore met with Yanukovych in an attempt to get him to adhere to constitutional procedure; when he was rebuffed, he ordered the dissolution of parliament, accusing Prime Minister Yanukovych of usurping power. Mr. Yanukovych's supporters replied by calling an emergency session of parliament and passing a resolution declaring President Yushchenko's decree unconstitutional. Both sides then appealed to the Constitutional Court to resolve the matter, thus thrusting the Constitutional Court into the middle of the on-going political battle.

One of the first acts of the Yanukovych government—carried out on August 4, 2006—had been to reconstitute the Constitutional Court, which had been inoper-

US and Ukrainian officers in front of bomber earmarked for dismantling

Ukraine

ative since the preceding November when the terms of nine of the judges had come to an end. As prescribed by the constitution, the *Verkhovna Rada* had elected five judges, who then joined eight others already on the court. Five of the incumbents had been elected earlier by the Congress of Judges, while three other members had been named to the court by President Yushchenko in November 2005. Five judges were added later, bringing the court to its full complement of 18.

The newly reconstituted Constitutional Court soon came under attack from both sides; on April 10, five Constitutional Court judges asked the state to provide them with bodyguard services because of pressure being exerted on them.

More seriously, the Security Service announced on April 16 that it was investigating Syuzanna Stanik, the deputy head of the Constitutional Court, on a charge of possible corruption. She was charged after the Security Service had established that $12 million in property had been transferred to an unemployed close relative of Judge Stanik. Volodymyr Lytvyn, former *Verkhovna Rada* speaker, probably summed up the public reaction when he said on April 20 that "I think we all acknowledge that the Constitutional Court does not exist in Ukraine. People are frankly saying [about the Constitutional Court]: You are all scoundrels."

On May 2, President Yushchenko dismissed Judge Stanik and a second judge, Valeriy Pshenichnyy. Yushchenko then appointed Vasyl Kostytskyy and Stepan Havrysh to replace the two dismissed justices. Judge Pshenichnyy refused to accept his dismissal, however, and he was reinstated on the court after a district judge in Donetsk suspended the president's decree dismissing him and Judge Stanik. Two weeks later, Ivan Dombrovskyy, the head of the Constitutional Court, resigned and his duties were entrusted to Judge Pshenichnyy. Constitutional Court Judge Dmytro Lylak then tendered his resignation on May 21. Three days later, the *Verkhovna Rada* dismissed Constitutional Court Judge Petro Stetsyuk. The next day, Judge Pshenichnyy announced that he had been able to assemble only ten judges of the 18-judge panel; 12 judges are necessary for legally binding rulings. "The court has been paralyzed and demoralized," President Yushchenko announced on May 23;

I am forced to admit that the Constitutional Court is losing its constitutional legitimacy and, under the existing circumstances, cannot perform its function of ensuring the supremacy of the Basic Law in the country.

When it became clear that the Constitutional Court would be unable to resolve the

A country wedding day—complete with troubadours

constitutional situation, Yushchenko and Yanukovych attempted to resolve their differences in a series of meetings which also included Parliamentary Speaker Moroz. On May 27, the three announced that they had reached a deal on holding early parliamentary elections on September 30. President Yushchenko also agreed to suspend his decrees dissolving parliament so it could legally meet to adopt the necessary legislation.

This is not the last word on the crisis. But it appears likely that new parliamentary elections will be held some time in the fall of 2007.

Foreign Policy

When it declared its independence at the end of 1991, the Ukrainian Government expressed the idea that it wanted to become part of Central Europe, and to that end expressed an interest in joining NATO and the European Union. Although it was one of the founding members of the Commonwealth of Independent States, it was extremely fearful of a continued Russian domination. As a result, its participation in the CIS was often nominal, and it several times refused to support CIS initiatives, even when it might have been in its economic interest to do so. Thus Ukraine failed to sign agreements on payments and a customs union, it opted for "observer" status at the CIS's Intergovernmental Assembly, and it has refused to provide troops for CIS peacekeeping.

This fear of Russian domination has also affected Ukraine's ability to develop

ties with the west. For example, the Ukrainian Government agreed to foreswear nuclear weapons but then balked at turning the weapons over to Russia. The legislature also refused to ratify the Nonproliferation Treaty, apparently because of a fear that Ukraine might become subject to Russian nuclear blackmail at some time in the future. The stalemate was resolved in January 1994 when the Ukrainian Government signed a trilateral agreement with the United States and Russia, under which it stipulated that it would dismantle all missiles on its territory and deliver the warheads to the Russian Government for destruction. Even so, Ukrainian legislators waited until November 1994 to ratify the Nonproliferation Treaty (NPT), and then coupled it with a stipulation that it would go into effect only after the United States, Russia, and Great Britain had provided assurances that they would respect Ukraine's borders and never use nuclear weapons against it. Ukraine was the last of the ex–Soviet republics to ratify the NPT.

These changes in foreign policy came about because of the election of Leonid Kuchma in July 1994. Kuchma personally lobbied the Ukrainian legislature for several weeks before the vote, insisting that the legislature's attempt to use the nuclear warheads as a bargaining chip was counterproductive and that Ukraine would get nothing from the west until it had foresworn nuclear weapons. As Kuchma told the legislature, "Ukraine today has no choice between being nuclear or nonnuclear. The process of world disarmament depends on our decision today." Ultimately his argument prevailed, with the final vote being a lopsided 301 to 8.

After his election, the U.S. Government signaled its support by sending Vice President Gore to Kyiv following his visit to Poland to commemorate the 50th anniversary of the Warsaw uprising. Kuchma received a warm welcome when he visited the United States in November 1994, which was coupled with a promise of $200 million in addition to the $700 million that the United States had promised earlier.

In addition, President Clinton extended the security assurances that the Ukrainian legislature had asked for in ratifying the NPT. Essentially, the United States Government decided that political stability in Ukraine was a critical element for peace in Europe and that economic aid was essential for the success of President Kuchma and his program of reform, a position that had strong support in Congress from both Republicans and Democrats. In May 1995, President Clinton paid an official visit to Ukraine after participating in ceremonies in Moscow commemorating the end of World War II in Europe.

During his visit to the United States in September 1996, Prime Minister Lazarenko was quoted as saying that "integration with the West is the main thrust of our foreign policy." The Republic of Ukraine pursued that policy with regard to Western Europe and this brought membership in both the Council of Europe and the Central European Initiative, a regional trade forum, in 1996. Ukraine is also a member of NATO's Partnership for Peace. President Kuchma also favored Ukrainian membership in both the EU and NATO. His successor, Viktor Yushchenko, is perhaps an even greater supporter of membership in the EU and in NATO. On the other hand, Prime Minister Yanukovych, while he supports ties with the west, has said that there should be a popular referendum on the question of whether Ukraine should join NATO; at the moment, a majority of Ukrainians are opposed to NATO membership.

Ukraine has also cultivated good relations with Poland, Germany and Greece. Among other things, this produced a five–year military cooperation agreement with Germany and a pledge that the Greek government would support Ukraine's eventual entry into the European Union.

As it built up its relations with the West, Ukraine began to allow its relations with Russia to become warmer as well. Perhaps this reflected an increased sense of self–confidence in its own ability to deal on a level of equality with its much larger Slavic neighbor. In any case, a Ukrainian–Russian Friendship Treaty and an agree-

ment on the disposition of the Black Sea Fleet were signed during President Yeltsin's May 1997 visit to Kyiv. The Friendship Treaty included a mutual recognition of borders, thus affirming that the Crimea, with its large Russian population, was an integral part of Ukraine.

While Russia agreed to cancel part of the debt that Ukraine owed to Russia for past oil deliveries, Ukraine ceded most of the Black Sea Fleet to Russia and also gave Russia a long–term lease on the naval base at Sevastopol. Both agreed that neither could reach an accord with a third party that would threaten the other.

Although the Friendship Treaty and agreement are important in themselves, of greater long–term significance for Ukraine is the fact that Russia has recognized its borders. Of even greater importance is the fact that the Russian government was willing to treat with Ukraine as a sovereign equal.

Ukraine ratified the Friendship Treaty in early 1998; the Russian Federation Council finally got around to ratifying it in February 1999, but only after adding the proviso that it would not go into effect until Ukraine ratified three agreements on the Russian Sevastopol Black Sea Fleet. Kuchma hailed the Russian ratification and added, "I think it won't take long for the Ukrainian parliament to ratify the [agreements] accompanying the pact."

Ukraine voted to join the CIS Interparliamentary Assembly in March 1999. Originally sponsored by the *Communists*, the resolution eventually won 230 votes and passage.

Ukraine's relations with the West tended to suffer during President Kuchma's last years in office, particularly after the release of the Melnichenko tapes. As a result, President Kuchma turned increasingly toward Russia in 2001, a situation that continued even after the events of September 11 brought a partial reversal of Ukraine's isolation after Ukraine signed on to the United States-led coalition against terrorism.

Thus while Kuchma spoke about enhancing Ukraine's relations with NATO and filling Ukraine's strategic partnership with the United States with specific content, he signed a series of agreements with Russia during this same time period; these included an agreement on a parallel operation of their power grids which will allow Russia to export electricity to the West, an agreement on Ukrainian debts for Russian gas, an agreement on the joint production of a new AN–148 passenger jet aircraft, and continuing talks concerning broad cooperation between Ukrainian and Russian military–industrial companies. Most of these agreements are economic in nature, of course, and are likely to be ben-

eficial to the Ukrainian economy. They also fitted in well with Kuchma's political strategy leading up to the 2002 parliamentary elections.

U.S.–Ukrainian relations deteriorated further in 2002 over a charge that Ukraine had illegally sold highly sophisticated Kolchuga radar system to Iraq in 2000. Ukraine denied the allegations, but the United States blocked $55 million in previously approved aid to Kyiv in September. The basis for the charge was an audio recording made by Mykola Melnychenko in which a Ukrainian arms dealer tells President Kuchma that Iraq was seeking to buy four Kolchuga systems. In October, the United States sent investigators to Ukraine to probe the charges.

While this was going on, President Kuchma was discouraged from attending the November NATO conference in Prague and, when he insisted on coming, he was ostracized by the American delegation. Kuchma told a press conference in February 2003 that he regretted the state of poor relations with Washington. Asserting that Ukraine had proven its innocence to U.S. and British experts probing allegations that Kyiv sold Kolchuga radar systems to Iraq, Kuchma added that "On my word, I do not know what else we need to do to change the mind of the United States."

Later in the month, the Ukrainian Government announced that it was sending a radiation and chemical battalion to Kuwait in support of United States objectives there. The Ukrainian government also contributed troops to the occupation after Iraq's defeat in the subsequent U.S.–Iraqi war. These two actions largely restored Ukraine's relations to the United States.

The United States strongly supports President Yushchenko, both because he is perceived as a democrat and because there is a pro-western orientation to his foreign policy. But the United States has also been willing to work with Prime Minister Viktor Yanukovych, who took office in 2006, even though Yanukovych is perceived as being more pro-Russian than Yushchenko. Yanukovych is, in fact, somewhat cooler toward the idea of NATO membership than Yushchenko, but Ukraine is not likely to be considered for membership in NATO in the near future in any case.

The Republic of Ukraine's relations with the Commonwealth of Independent States showed a sharp improvement after President Kuchma was elected to head the CIS Council at the beginning of 2003. After that time, Ukraine took the lead in pushing for the creation of a free–trade zone for the CIS. In another sign of increasing cooperation with its neighbors, the Republic of Ukraine signed a defense

Ukraine

cooperation agreement with Azerbaijan in January 2003. Ukraine has also expressed its willingness to provide troops to guard the planned Baku–Tbilisi–Ceyhan pipeline. Ukraine's relations with the CIS have cooled since Yushchenko became president, however; Yushchenko places a strong emphasis on eventual membership in the EU and is unwilling to sign any agreements which might get in the way of eventual EU membership.

Ukraine's continuing quarrel with Russia over the price of imported energy supplied by Gazprom has also caused some Ukrainian politicians to question the value of the CIS; Ukraine is not yet ready to leave the CIS, but it may come to that if the quarrel grows worse.

Nature of the Regime

The Republic of Ukraine has a presidential–parliamentary system with a popularly elected president who until recently has acted as spokesman for the nation and set general policy. However, a series of constitutional amendments adopted in December 2004 strips the president of much of his former authority. Under the constitutional reform, the majority in parliament appoints the prime minister and most of the cabinet. The president retains the right to appoint the foreign minister, defense minister, the prosecutor-general, the head of the Security Service, and all regional governors. The president retains the right to dissolve parliament if it fails to form a majority within 60 days of the resignation or dismissal of the previous government. Only parliament can dismiss the prime minister, however.

The Ukrainian legislature, the *Verkhovna Rada*, has its own internal organization which is independent of either the president or the prime minister. In 2006, for the first time all 450 members were elected under a fully proportional party-list system. Under this system, voters cast their ballots for a political party or electoral bloc rather than for individual representatives. The total number of votes for a party determines the number of representatives awarded to that party; each party's leadership draws up the party-list and so determines which candidates are placed on the candidate list and where they will be placed on the list. The higher up a name appears on the list, the greater is the likelihood that the individual will be elected. Two other changes found in the 2004 legislation are that, first, only those parties or blocs obtaining at least 3 percent of the national vote will receive any representation in parliament and, second, the parliament elected in 2006 will serve five years, instead of four years as previously.

Four electoral blocs won seats in the new parliament. The *Party of Regions*, led

Even in Kyiv . . .

by Viktor Yanukovych, came in first with 32.14 percent of the vote (186 seats). The *Yulia Tymoshenko Bloc* came in second with 22.29 percent of the vote (129 seats). *Our Ukraine* came third with 13.95 percent of the vote (81 seats). The *Socialist Party* came fourth with 5.69 percent of the vote (33 seats, followed by the *Communist Party* with 3.66 percent of the vote (21 seats).

An abortive attempt by the *Yulia Tymoshenko Bloc*, the *Socialist Party*, and the *Our Ukraine* bloc to reconstitute the Orange Coalition failed after Oleksander Moroz, leader of the *Socialist Party*, signed a new "anti-crisis" agreement with the *Communists* and the *Party of Regions*; in return, they agreed to support him for the office of parliamentary speaker. Viktor Yanukovych, leader of the *Party of Regions*, was named prime minister in August 2006.

The experiment in political coexistence has not worked out well, however. In April 2007, President Yushchenko issued a decree dissolving the *Verkhovna Rada* after he became convinced that Yanukovych was using unconstitutional means to create a super majority which would allow him to strip the president of most of his powers. Yushchenko and Yanukovych have since agreed to hold new parliamentary elections in the fall of 2007, possibly at the end of September.

Culture

There is a rich cultural life in the Republic of Ukraine, but most of it belongs to a larger Slavic culture, except for a traditional Ukrainian folk culture. Ukrainians are different from Russians, but it is a matter of degree. Ukrainian houses tend to be painted or whitewashed with traditional decorations worked into the wood trim and around the windows. Ukrainians plant many more flowers in their yards. The Ukrainian folk costume is often highly embroidered, with bright colors worked over white or black. Ukrainian villages also tend to be more prosperous looking and better cared for, reflecting the richer soil found in most of the Ukraine.

Historically, the Ukrainian Orthodox clergy has had greater contacts with the Greek Orthodox Church and so is closer to the Greek original. Church music of the Ukraine was patterned on Byzantine and Bulgarian models, which set it off from the music of Russia. The Ukraine also developed its own distinct choral music, which also came to influence Russian music in the seventeenth century.

The Ukraine has produced many writers, poets and historians over the years, a number of whom were mentioned in the historical section above. On the other hand, Ukrainian intellectuals were always getting into trouble because of their Ukrainian nationalism, and often found themselves unable to get their works published. This has been true in the Soviet period as well.

The Ukraine began to develop a secular music in the nineteenth century. There are a number of nineteenth century operas with specific Ukrainian themes, such as Semen Hulak–Artemovsky's *A Cossack Beyond the Danube*. Mykola Lysenko was an early twentieth century composer who wrote the opera *Taras Bulba*. Two other composers of this period were Kyrylo Stetsenko and Mykola Leontovych. Lev Revutsky and Borys Lyatoshynsky were two composers of the early Soviet period. The cultural regimentation of the 1930s led to a cultural decline, but there was a revival of sorts after Stalin's death. Contemporary composers include Kostyantyn Dankevych, Yuliy Meytus, and the brothers Yuriy and Platon Maiboroda.

The Ukrainian theater is primarily a twentieth century phenomenon, primarily because censorship laws would not allow works in the Ukrainian language before 1905. Three pre–Soviet Ukrainian playwrights are Lesya Ukrainka, Volodymyr Vynnychenko and Oleksandr Oles. All wrote before 1905, but their works were not available in the Ukraine until after that time.

There was a flowering of Ukrainian theater in the period of the 1920s, the so-called period of Ukrainization. Mykola Kulish, who used expressionist techniques, was perhaps the most famous. As in opera, the introduction of socialist realism led to a decline in drama. A contemporary Ukrainian playwright of some fame is Oleksandr Korniychuk.

The Ukraine has great cultural potential for the future, however, since the Soviet era left it with plenty of facilities. There are currently six opera theaters, numerous symphony orchestras, 60 professional theaters, plus a Ukrainian motion picture industry.

One interesting development since Ukraine became an independent republic is the matter of language. While it was a soviet republic, Ukrainian nationalism was discouraged and the Russian language was used as the language of instruction in all of the schools throughout the republic. Changing this situation has been difficult, since Russians probably make up a majority of the population in the eastern part of the republic plus the area of the Crimea. Even in Kyiv, perhaps a third of the people use Russian while a second third use Russian and Ukrainian interchangeably. Still, Ukrainian has been introduced as the language of instruction in over 1,300 schools in the past decade so that, today, only about ten percent of all schools conduct their classes in Russian. In the media, on the other hand, Russian continues to be the dominant language, with 57 percent of all publications printed in Russian.

Economy

The Ukraine has been the historical "bread basket" of Russia and, although industry today plays a larger role in the economy, agriculture continues to play an extremely important role. In recent years, the Ukraine produced about 20 percent of all Soviet food. Grain, in the form of wheat and corn, is the most important crop, but others include potatoes, vegetables, fodder crops, fruits and grapes. Sugar beets are the most important industrial crop. Cattle are raised for both milk and meat. Other important animals raised include pigs, sheep and goats. Honey is another important product, as are silkworms.

Most of the land had been organized as joint–stock cooperative farms since a 1993 government decree breaking up the collective farms and turning the land over to private farmers created such a storm of protest in the legislature that the government retreated and took this step instead. The government did manage to distribute 11 million garden plots among approximately two–thirds of the population. Although these garden–plots constituted only 14 percent of farmland, they accounted for 95 percent of the potato crop in 1996 and 82 percent of all vegetables. They also produced more than one–half of the country's meat and milk and two–thirds of its eggs.

The large, poorly managed cooperatives had been in decline for several years, however, producing even less than the collective farms did under communism. Grain production in 1997 was approximately 37 million tons, lower than any year since 1985, and sugar beet production was the smallest in 30 years. Although farm privatization was the logical longer–term solution to these problems, the improved showing of the *Communist Party* and the *Socialist/Peasants' Bloc* in the March 29, 1998 parliamentary elections convinced the government that it would be unable to get such a program through the *Verkhovna Rada*.

However, Kuchma decided that his re-election victory in November 1999 had given him a window of opportunity to take action if he chose. In addition, his advisers informed him that Ukraine needed to import 1.5 million metric tons of grain between then and September 2000 if the country were to be guaranteed a continuous supply of bread. These two things, the opportunity and the threat, convinced Kuchma that it was time to act.

After several months of preparation, President Kuchma issued a decree in December 2000 that divided the land of the country's 11,000 cooperative farms into plots which were to be distributed among the country's 6.4 million farm workers. By October 2001, approximately 1.8 million Ukrainian farmers had received certificates documenting the private ownership of their plots. To help complete the process, the World Bank agreed to loan the Ukrainian Government $120 million. This was later supplemented by a $14.5 million grant from the United States Government. The money has been used to finance the issuance of another 5 million documents certifying property rights on land lots and to create a registration system for real estate rights.

The Ukrainian parliament also passed a Land Code in October 2001 specifically authorizing the buying and selling of farmland after 2004, though this legislation never went into effect. In October 2004, parliament passed new legislation extending an earlier moratorium on land sales until January 1, 2008. President Kuchma vetoed the legislation, but it was passed over his veto the following month. The moratorium has since been extended to 2009.

Ukraine's grain harvest was 39.7 million tons in 2001, the best crop in the past ten years. That allowed Ukraine to export about 7 million tons of grain, mainly to the Middle East and North Korea. Overall food exports in 2001 were valued at $1.8 billion, a 34 percent rise from 2000 and accounting for 12 percent of total exports. The 2002 harvest, at 36.7 million tons, was down slightly but still very good. This had a down side for farmers, however, since the increased production tended to drive down grain prices. Since meat and milk prices also declined in 2002, many cooperative farms were reported to have lost money. The news for 2003 was even worse; the total grain harvest dropped to 20 million tons after severe frosts destroyed more than 60 percent of the winter grain crop. When rising grain prices began to drive up the price of bread in the cities, the government intervened and began buying grain abroad. Fortunately, Ukraine had a bountiful grain harvest of 45 million tons in 2004, the largest grain harvest since independence.

The development of industry in the Ukraine goes back to the end of the nineteenth century when fourteen steel mills were built on the steppe north of the Black Sea. Even today, the center of Ukraine's heavy industry is a belt that stretches from Krivoi Rog in the west to the border of the republic in the east. Here the republic produces cast iron, steel and rolled steel, and steel pipe. Other allied manufactures include diesel locomotives, freight cars, automobiles, giant airliners, seagoing vessels, electric generators, thermal and gas turbines, metallurgical equipment, and tractors.

Another major Ukrainian industry is coal–mining, with huge reserves of anthracite and bituminous coal in the Donets Basin and brown coal in the Dnieper

Ukraine

Basin. Originally developed in the nineteenth century and then greatly expanded under the Soviets, the industry is now a dead weight on the economy. With only seven of 176 mines able to operate without government subsidies, the mines cost the government about $500 million a year to keep going. Nor can the government just close down the mines, for this would lead to mass unemployment. It did close down 90 mines using a $300 million loan from the World Bank in the period 1997–2002, but then put on the brakes. Although the World Bank expressed its willingness to provide another $100 million to finance the closure of an additional 40 to 50 mines, the government demurred after strong protests from local communities. Current plans still call for the closure of an additional 30 mines by 2011, but that will leave a lot of uncompetitive mines, all requiring government subsidies. The government would like to privatize the industry but, thus far, only two mines have been privatized.

The Republic of Ukraine produces a small amount of oil and gas, and it is very interested in expanding the industry as much as possible. Ukraine's state oil-and gas producing company, *Ukrnafta*—which produces 93 percent of Ukraine's crude oil—produced almost 3 million tons in 2004, or about 62,800 barrels a day. Ukraine's current consumption is 290,000 barrels a day. According to the CIA *World Fact Book*, Ukraine has proven reserves of 197.5 million barrels, so it could increase production further but probably not by very much. Natural gas production reached 3.3 billion cubic meters in 2003 but, again, the Republic of Ukraine consumed 74.1 billion cubic meters of natural gas in 2001. Ukraine will obviously remain an importer of natural gas in the future. The recent large increases in the price of oil and natural gas have therefore had a fairly significant effect on the Ukrainian economy.

The Ukrainian food–processing industry includes the processing of granulated sugar, vegetable oils, and wine. Light industry includes textiles, the manufacture of ready–to–wear garments, and shoes.

The preponderant weight of heavy industry in the Ukraine's industry meant that a large percentage of its production was shipped to other republics—amounting to approximately 25 percent of the republic's gross domestic product. In return, it imported oil and natural gas, some raw materials, and a good percentage of its consumer goods. It was unable to maintain many of those markets after independence and lost, in fact, a fifth of its export market in the first year.

For the first ten months after achieving independence, very little was done about

the economy and the result was a disaster. By October 1992, inflation was running at 30 percent monthly, economic activity was down 18 percent over the preceding year, and the budget deficit was running at 44 percent of GDP. Prime Minister Fokin was forced out at the end of September and replaced by Leonid Kuchma.

Kuchma turned out to be a reformer. One of his first acts was to raise the central bank lending rate to 80 percent and to announce that the government would no longer provide inefficient state enterprises with soft credit. In November, he submitted an ambitious, market–oriented reform program to the Supreme Soviet which called for a tight budget, a temporary wage freeze in state–owned enterprises, cuts in social welfare payments, a law forbidding the government to finance the budget deficit by printing money, and a commitment to begin large–scale privatization. Kuchma also wanted to break up inefficient enterprises and sell their pieces on the auction block.

However, Kuchma's program was opposed by the communist-dominated majority in the Supreme Soviet, and it began passing legislation negating what Kuchma was trying to do. It also imposed controls over wages and prices. Kuchma lost his power to rule by decree in May 1993 and resigned in September. After that, everything was put on hold.

New parliamentary elections in March 1994 reconfirmed communist control of the legislature, but Kuchma's victory in the July 1994 presidential elections brought in a whole new equation. Kuchma quickly announced concrete proposals for reform and arranged a quick meeting with Michael Camdessus, head of the IMF, to win the support of that organization. Kuchma subsequently pushed a far reaching economic reform program through the legislature which promised large–scale privatization of state companies, cuts in the national budget and the removal of price controls on many goods.

As a result, Ukraine got its first IMF loan in October 1994 and began receiving loans from individual western countries as well. As economic reform continued, some 11,000 state–owned enterprises were privatized through March 1995 and a further 8,000 large and medium–sized firms privatized in 1996 and 1997. Inflation was brought under control and this allowed the issuance of a new currency, the *hryvna*, in the summer of 1996.

Foreign investment also began to grow, though the amounts were still minimal. Ukraine received $335.5 million in foreign investment during the first half of 1997. The United States was the largest foreign investor (with $315 million), followed by Germany ($165.9 million), the Nether-

lands ($160.2 million), Great Britain ($130.9 million), Cyprus ($116.4 million), Russia ($114.2 million) and Liechtenstein ($103.1 million). Investments were mainly in the food industry, machine building, metal processing, finance and insurance, construction and construction materials, and the chemical and petrochemical industries.

Although the overall economy had not yet achieved positive growth by the end of 1997, the government was predicting a 0.5 percent growth rate in 1998. Some positive growth (0.1) was actually achieved during the first five months of 1998, but international economic events overtook the Ukrainian economy soon after. The economic crisis in Russia in September then came on top of that and threatened Ukraine with the same events that were already occurring in Russia. But President Kuchma was determined that it not happen. As early as June, in fact, he had issued a package of economic decrees to steer the country past its economic crisis. He had little choice; at that time, he was faced with a paralyzed parliament unable to elect its own leadership. These decrees—whose purpose was to raise additional government revenue—lowered the value–added tax, simplified tax procedures for small businesses, and introduced a fixed rate tax on agricultural products.

Even so, the Ukrainian National Bank was forced to devalue the national currency, the *hryvna*, in July in order to stop the drain on foreign currency reserves. The *hryvna* continued to be gradually devalued in steps throughout the rest of the year, so there never was a collapse in the currency. It also helped that the IMF approved a new $2.2 billion loan to Ukraine in September, while the World Bank granted a $900 million loan that same month.

Because Russia was responsible for 44 percent of Ukraine's general trade turnover, however, there was no way that the Ukrainian economy could be unaffected by the Russian economic collapse. Thus the Ukrainian economy shrank as Russian customers canceled orders for Ukrainian goods and Russian suppliers of key components shut down their production lines, leaving Ukrainian companies without the means to continue production. Metallurgical products, heavy machinery and chemicals were particularly affected, for it was products of these industries that made up most of the trade with Russia. Other sectors were less affected. Ukraine thus suffered tremendous economic distress, but it escaped the general collapse that occurred in Russia.

The situation began to turn around in 2000. The economy began growing again for the first time since 1990, managing an impressive 6 percent growth during the year. The government also renegotiated its foreign debt and cut its annual rate of inflation to 20 percent. The economy grew at an even faster 9 percent in 2001, while inflation dropped to 6.1 percent; industrial production was, in fact, up a whopping 14.2 percent over 2000. This spurt in growth was possible because there was still a great deal of unused capacity within the system. Wages have also remained low. According to the Ukrainian Government, the average worker earned the equivalent of $61.50 in October 2001. Lower–paid workers such as farmers, medical workers and teachers earned even less than this minimum.

The economy slowed to a 4.1 percent growth rate in 2002, though industry continued to expand at a 7 percent rate and inflation had dropped to practically zero. Growth reached the torrid rate of 9.3 percent in 2003, in spite of the extremely poor grain harvest, fueled by a 15.8 percent growth in industrial production. Another factor is that exports grew by 28 percent during the year. Helped by a bountiful grain harvest, Ukraine's GDP grew at a 12 percent rate in 2004.

The "Orange Revolution," which occurred toward the end of 2004, introduced an element of political instability that had a temporary negative effect on the economy. However the significant increase in energy prices in 2005 probably had a more significant effect. GDP growth decreased significantly as the year progressed, dropping to 3 percent by November.

The quarrel between President Yushchenko's and Prime Minister Tymoshenko, which became public in May 2005, was another negative factor; her dismissal in September 2005 further shook the political system. Gazprom's decision to begin charging Ukraine world market prices for natural gas, announced in December 2005, was a further blow whose consequences are still reverberating today. Russia's subsequent decision to ban the importation of Ukrainian wines has also created a situation which has also not been resolved. Finally, the March 2006 parliamentary elections represented a partial repudiation of President Yushchenko and rehabilitated Yulia Tymoshenko.

After hard negotiations, the Orange Coalition was reconstituted on June 22 with Yulia Tymoshenko set to become prime minister. One week later, however, the coalition fell apart after Oleksander Moroz, leader of the *Socialist Party*, signed a new "anti-crisis" agreement with the *Communists* and the *Party of Regions* after these two parties agreed to support him for the office of parliamentary speaker. Moroz has since been elected parliamentary speaker; Viktor Yanukovych, leader of the *Party of Regions*, became prime minister in August. In April 2007, however, President Yushchenko dissolved parliament and called for new elections; they are currently scheduled for September 30, 2007.

Ukraine's recent economic progress has also made it eligible for international loans once again. In September 2001, the European Bank for Reconstruction and Development extended $600 million worth of credits, to be used to finance various projects in the country's food industry, financial sector, industrial sector, and in its transportation, telecommunications, and municipal infrastructures. At about the same time, the IMF issued Ukraine a credit tranche of $377 million, while the World Bank approved a $250 million loan to support the government's economic program. The World Bank made another $100 million available to the Ukrainian Government in December 2001, again in support of the government's program of reforms. The World Bank made two further loans to Ukraine in December 2003, one for $30 million and another for $250 million. Finally, the IMF approved a one-year $605 million credit facility to Ukraine in March 2004. The Ukrainian government has used this latter loan to cover high-interest government bonds issued during the economic crisis of the late 1990s.

The Future

The Ukrainian economy grew at an accelerating pace between 2000 and 2004, largely through the use of already existing industrial capacities; it faltered in 2005, with GDP growth dropping to 3 percent, but recovered in 2006. That growth is now threatened by the current quarrel between President Yushchenko and Prime Minister Yanukovych. New parliamentary elections are supposed to occur on September 30. Yanukovych's *Party of Regions* is likely to get a plurality of the votes, but he will still have to put together a governing majority in order to retain his position as prime minister.

Moldovans visiting "White Fortress" (Belgorod), once Modova's capital, but in Ukraine since 1939 Molotov-Ribbentrop Pact.

Courtesy: Olesea Kovali

The Republic of Moldova

Area: 13,000 sq. mi. (33,843 sq. km., a little larger than Maryland).

Population: 4.4 million (July 2006 estimated).

Capital City: Chisinau (pronounced *Kee–shee–nau*, Pop. 716,000).

Climate: Moderate winters, warm summers.

Neighboring States: Romania (west). Ukraine surrounds the country on the other sides.

Official Languages: Moldovan/Romanian and Russian.

Ethnic Composition: Moldovan/Romanian (78.2%), Ukrainian (8.4%), Russian (5.8%), Gagauz (4.4%), Bulgarian (1.9%), others (1.3%).

Principal Religion: Eastern Orthodox.

Chief Commercial Products: Grain, livestock, silk, honey, processed foods, wine and cognac. Over 70 percent of exports still go to other members of the Commonwealth of Independent States and Moldova is heavily dependent on energy supplies from these same republics.

Currency: *leu/lei* (singular/plural); adopted in December 1993.

Per Capita Annual Income (Purchasing Power Parity): $2,100.

Recent Political Status: Formed in 1940 by union of the Moldavian SSR, previously only an autonomous republic within the Ukrainian SSR, and most of Bessarabia, transferred to the USSR by Romania in 1940.

National Day: August 27 (Independence Day 1991).

Chief of State: Vladimir Voronin, President (re-elected on April 4, 2005).

Head of Government: Vasile Tarlev, Prime Minister (since April 2001).

National Flag: three vertical stripes, sky blue, yellow and red. A right–facing golden Roman eagle, outlined in black with a red beak, is centered on the yellow. The eagle holds a yellow cross in its beak, in its right claw a green olive branch and in its left claw a yellow scepter. A heraldic device forming the body of the eagle pictures a bullhead, star, rose and crescent, all in yellow outlined in black.

The Land

The Republic of Moldova is the independent successor state to the Moldavian Soviet Socialist Republic. The Moldavian SSR was created in August 1940 when Stalin merged Bessarabia, which he had forced the Romanian Government to cede to the Soviet Union in June 1940, with the autonomous republic of Moldavia, which was then part of the Ukrainian SSR. He gave it constituent republic status. In 1941, after Nazi Germany invaded the Soviet Union, Romania (then an ally of Nazi Germany) reclaimed Bessarabia. Soviet troops retook

the territory in 1944 and the Moldavian SSR was reestablished. The republic was renamed Moldova in 1990. Moldova declared its independence on August 27, 1991.

The Prut River, a tributary of the Danube, forms the western border with Romania. The area immediately east of the Prut is somewhat elevated, with a flat highland in the north and rolling hills interspersed with deep flat valleys further south. The highest elevations are about 1400 feet. The southern part of the republic is a low plain.

The chief feature of the eastern part of the republic is the Nistru (Dniestr) River, which originates in the Carpathian Mountains to the northwest and flows southward across western Ukraine, then forms

the border between Moldova and Ukraine for some distance. At this point, the border shifts eastward, while the Nistru continues south and into Moldova. A major feature of the river is the 60-mile-long Lake Dubossary, created when a dam for producing hydroelectric power was built on the Nistru. The Nistru crosses back into Ukraine again shortly before it empties into the Black Sea. On its western side, the Nistru has a high bank, formed by the eastern slope of the Nistru uplands. Trans-Nistria, the small strip of territory east of the Nistru, is a low plain.

Rainfall in the republic varies considerably but averages between 18 and 22 inches. Most of it falls in summer. Moldovan soils are mostly rich, black *chernozem* soils. About 40 percent of the land is covered by forest, most of it in the uplands.

The People

According to the National Bureau of Statistics, the estimated population of Moldova as of July 2005 was 3.4 million. Moldovan/Romanian speakers make up 64.5 percent of the population, followed by Ukrainians (13.8%) and Russians (13%). The Gagauz (3.5%), who come next, are a Turkic-speaking people who converted to Orthodox Christianity. Bulgarian-speakers make up a further two percent of the population, while other ethnic groupings make up the remaining 3.2 percent.

History

Moldova's modern history is really the history of Bessarabia, the name bestowed on the area between the Prut and Nistru (Dniestr) Rivers by the Russians at the beginning of the nineteenth century. But Moldova's history begins long before that. At the beginning of the second century A.D., this area, and the area of present-day Romania, became the province of Dacia in the Roman Empire after being conquered by the Emperor Trajan. Although Rome soon lost control, 70 percent of the roots of the modern language—whether called Moldovan or Romanian—derive from the Latin language carried to the region by the Roman conquerors. Over the following centuries, the area was to know many masters. The eastern part came within the sphere of influence of Kievan Rus in the tenth century. Later, independent Galician princes ruled. After 1240, it became part of the Mongol Empire for about one hundred years. The Genoese built fortified commercial outposts on the Nistru (Dniestr) in the fourteenth century, though they never attempted to rule the area.

In the fifteenth century, an independent Principality of Moldavia came into existence which included the northern part of present-day Romania and all of Bessarabia. The Ottoman Empire soon extended its control over most of the area, however, along with the second Romanian Principality of Wallachia. In 1711, Peter the Great occupied part of Bessarabia during a short war with Turkey. He was forced to abandon the territory after his army fell into an ambush, however. Russia occupied the territory three more times in the eighteenth century, each time relinquishing it to the Turks. In 1812, Russian forces again occupied Moldavia and Wallachia after a new war broke out between the two countries; Russia won and forced Turkey to cede the territory (which it called Bessarabia) in the Treaty of Bucharest.

After Russia's defeat in the Crimean War, it was forced to cede Bessarabia to Moldavia, at that time an autonomous principality under the Ottoman Empire, in 1856. After its victory in the Turkish War of 1877–78, Russia took Bessarabia back and kept it until 1918. After the overthrow of the Tsar in 1917, a National Moldavian Committee was organized in Bessarabia in April. Its program included autonomy, use of the Romanian language, and land reform. After the Bolshevik *coup d'etat* in November, a government was established in Bessarabia, called the *Sfatul Tarei*. On December 2, 1917, the government proclaimed Bessarabia to be an autonomous constituent republic of the Federation of Russian Republics. The Bolsheviks occupied the capital, Chisinau (Kishinev) on January 5, 1918. Two weeks later, they were driven out and the Bessarabian Government then proclaimed itself an independent Moldavian Republic. Two months later, it voted for a conditional union with Romania. Unconditional union was voted on December 9, 1918. The Union of Bessarabia with Romania was recognized by the Treaty of Paris, signed by Great Britain, France, Italy, and Japan, on October 28, 1920.

The Union of Soviet Socialist Republics never recognized Romania's right to the province and refused to establish diplomatic relations with Romania until 1934. In the meantime, the frontier along the Nistru (Dniestr) was closed.

Under the terms of the Nazi–Soviet Non–Aggression Pact of August 23, 1939, Hitler recognized Bessarabia as being in the Soviet sphere of influence. The Soviet Union revived its claim to Bessarabia, but Romania rejected the claim until after the fall of France in June 1940. On June 27, the Soviet Union demanded the immediate cession of Bessarabia, plus the additional territory of northern Bukovina as "compensation for Romanian misrule in Bessarabia." Without an ally, Romania had to submit. Troops of the Red Army entered Bessarabia on June 28.

The central districts of Bessarabia were merged with part of the Moldavian Autonomous Republic, which then became the Moldavian Soviet Socialist Republic in August 1940. Ukraine was compensated for the loss of the Trans-Nistria territory by receiving the Khotin district in the north and the Cetatea Alba and Izmail districts in the south.

Romania declared war against the Soviet Union in July 1941. Its war goal was to reclaim Bessarabia and to reincorporate it into Romania. This was accomplished by December 1942. Soviet forces reentered Bessarabia in 1944 and its forces occupied all of Romania as well. Bessarabia was formally ceded back to the Soviet Union by the peace treaty signed between the two countries on February 10, 1947.

After Gorbachëv launched his programs of *glasnost* and *perestroika*, a nationalist movement arose, which called itself the *Popular Front of Moldavia*. The ultimate goal of the front was union with Romania. In 1989, the legislature abolished use of the Cyrillic alphabet (see Russia), and restored the Latin alphabet which had been used prior to the republic's incorporation into the Soviet Union. On July 29, 1989, Mircea Snegur was elected president of the presidium of the Moldavian Supreme Soviet. Snegur was at that time first secretary of the *Moldavian Communist Party*, but he represented the democratic–nationalist faction of the party. In June 1990, the legislature adopted a declaration of republic sovereignty and changed the name of the republic to Moldova.

In March 1991, the Government of Moldova refused to participate in a referendum on continuation of the Soviet Union. It also refused to take part in subsequent discussions on a new union treaty. When conservatives launched their attempted *coup* against Gorbachëv in August 1991, Moldova became a target also. The local military commander surrounded the capital of Chisinau (Kishinev) with troops and threatened to use them against the republic government. President Mircea Snegur refused to recognize the *coup* committee, however, and called on the people of Moldova to demonstrate in support of democracy and freedom; over 100,000 persons demonstrated in the capital. Following the collapse of the Russian *coup*, Moldova declared its independence on August 27. It also formally outlawed the *Communist Party*.

Moldova now began to have its problems with the area east of the Nistru (Dniestr) region after it declared its independence as a separate state in August 1991, motivated by its fear that the rest of Moldova intended to reunite with Romania.

Some violence occurred when the Moldovan Government tried to reestablish its control east of the Nistru. The situation only calmed down after President Snegur threatened to resign if the Moldova Supreme Soviet insisted on using force to restore control. The government also repudiated the idea of immediate union with Romania.

This led to the opening of talks between the two sides. At first, the situation appeared to be hopeful, particularly after Igor Smirnov, the "Dniestr Moldavian" leader, said in October that he would be willing to join a federal Moldova, together with Moldova and Gagauzia. The Gagauz, a Turkic-speaking but Orthodox Christian people, had proclaimed a separate republic in southern Moldova in 1990. Like

Moldova

The "Republic of Transnistria"

Dniestr-Moldova, the area east of the Nistru ((Dniestr) River, proclaimed itself the "Republic of Transnistria" in August 1991, more or less simultaneously with Moldova's own declaration of independence.

The population of the area in 1991 was an estimated 600,000; according to the 2004 census, the population has since decreased and is now about 555,000. Moldovans/Romanians account for only 31.9 percent of the population; another 30.3 percent speak Russian while 28.9 percent speak Ukrainian. The Russian and Ukrainian speakers rejected Moldovan independence because they felt independence was merely the first step to merging with Romania. In fact, a separatist movement was organized in this area in 1989 in response to the republic government's declared intention to move toward independence.

A September 2 referendum that followed its declaration of independence showed that a majority of people of the area supported the policies of the breakaway republic. The region's capital is Tiraspol, which has 131,000 inhabitants. The region's other major cities are Bendery, with 76,500 inhabitants, and Rybnitsa, with 62,000 inhabitants.

Igor Smirnov was elected to the position of president of the new republic in December 1991, a position he has retained ever since. There is also a 43-member elected legislature, called the Supreme Soviet. The chairman of the Supreme Soviet is Grigorii Marakutsa, who has also held that position since December 1991.

In 1991, the Russian 14th Army was stationed here and at least some elements of the army actively supported the area's separation from Moldova. Most of the Russian forces and part of their equipment were later removed from the area, though some Russian forces are still stationed here.

In November 2003, the Russian Government proposed that the problem of Transnistria's separatism be settled by creating a new federal government with Moldova and Transnistria as equal partners. The proposal, known as the Kozak memorandum, further proposed that Russian troops would remain in Transnistria for another 20 years.

Relations between Moldova and Russia deteriorated after President Voronin rejected the Kozak memorandum. Moscow's present position is that the Moldovan Government is holding up a settlement by its insistence that Russian troops leave Transnistria. In April 2006, Nikolai Ryabov, the Russian Ambassador to Moldova, publicly announced that Russia "would never give up its interests" in Transnistria "where it has been present for more than a century." Ryabov was responding to a March 2006 Moldovan-Ukrainian customs agreement that required all cargo on the Transnistrian stretch of the Ukrainian border to be cleared by Moldovan customs. The new customs regulations, which are aimed at curbing illegal trade, are supported by the European Union but strongly opposed by Russia.

Although the area is somewhat more industrialized than the rest of Moldova, it has always been clear to outside observers that the Transnistrian enclave is not viable as a separate entity without political and economic support from Russia. The Moldovan Government has always stood ready to grant the region autonomous status with the broadest rights, but it has always insisted on the eventual withdrawal of Russian troops. But a Russian troop withdrawal has always been opposed by the Transnistrian leadership, which might not survive without the Russian presence.

"Dniestr Moldavia," the Gagauz objected to the idea of merging with Romania.

Another favorable development occurred in October when President Snegur, breaking with the leadership of the *Popular Front of Moldova*, publicly pledged his support to the concept of an independent Moldova. "A union with another state is out of question," he was quoted as saying, adding "at present, Moldova promotes a policy pursuing the assertion of our independence internationally." Snegur also supported continued economic ties with the former Soviet republics.

The Moldovan presidential elections were scheduled to take place on December 8, 1991; the major issue in the campaign was the question of independence versus merging with Romania. There were originally two other candidates in addition to President Snegur—Grigori Eremei, the former first secretary of the *Moldovan Communist Party* and Gheorghe Malarciuc, a writer—but both candidates withdrew in the middle of November. *The Popular Front of Moldova* did not nominate a candidate since Mircea Druc, the head of the *Front*, did not meet the residence requirements; instead, the *Front* urged voters to boycott the election. The leadership of "Dniestr Moldavia" adopted the same position. "Dniestr Moldavia" and the "Republic of Gagauzia" held their own separate elections on December 1. Smirnov was confirmed as president of "Dniestr Moldavia" and Stepan Topal was elected president of Gagauzia. Neither area permitted voting in the December 8 republican elections.

Because President Snegur was running unopposed in the December 8 elections, the fact that he got 98 percent of the vote came as no surprise. On the other hand, the results showed that 83 percent of all registered voters participated in the election, meaning that they rejected the *Popular Front of Moldova's* call for a boycott of the election. This gave President Snegur a great deal more leeway in dealing with the *Front* than he had had before.

Unable to resolve its differences with either "Dniestr Moldavia" or Gagauzia, the Moldovan Government formally nullified the results of the December 1 elections in the two breakaway republics on December 11. Later, President Snegur offered to establish a free economic zone in "Dniestr Moldavia," if it would withdraw its declaration of independence. Neither carrot nor stick worked. The main issue remained the question of Moldova's merging with Romania. Even though President Snegur publicly supported an independent Moldova, the leaders of "Dniestr Moldavia" and Gagauzia remained convinced that union with Romania was still on the agenda.

Later in the month, President Snegur went to Alma–Ata and took Moldova into the Commonwealth of Independent States. Moldova did not agree to maintain a CIS military command, however, and began to create its own national army. The plan called for it to be a cadre army of about 12,000 persons, with a larger number of citizens serving in an army reserve.

In March 1992, a weekend of clashes that left 23 dead caused President Snegur to issue an ultimatum to "Dniestr Moldavia" to lay down their arms or face the use of force against them. Igor Smirnov, leader of "Dniestr Moldavia," then declared a state of emergency, closing the enclave to outside contact. According to reports, "Dniestr Moldavia" had by this time created its own 10,000 man militia to defend the enclave.

Meanwhile, the unstable political situation was contributing to a deteriorating economic situation. This led on June 1 to the resignations of the prime minister, Valeriu Muravschi, and his cabinet. President Snegur then nominated Andre Sangheli, outgoing agriculture minister, as the new prime minister.

President Snegur was more concerned about establishing political control throughout all of Moldova than about the economy. Fighting with "Dniestr Moldavia" flared up again in June 1992 when President Snegur's troops tried to take control of the city of Tighina (Bendery). It appeared for a while that Moldova might find itself involved in a confrontation with Russia when elements of Russia's 14th Army, stationed in eastern Moldova, supported the "Dniestr Moldavia" forces. It turned out that it was only rogue elements of the 14th Army that were involved, however.

Moldova held its first parliamentary elections since independence on February 27, 1994; a week later, it held a referendum on whether Moldova should remain independent or seek unification with Romania. More than 90 percent of all voters supported the option of remaining an independent state within current borders. In the parliamentary elections, most of the parties that did well favored closer relations with Russia and reconciliation with the breakaway region of "Dniestr Moldavia." The *Agrarian–Democratic Party* got about 45 percent of the vote, while the pro–Russian *Socialist Bloc* got 25 percent. Andre Sangheli, the prime minister, was the leader of the *Agrarian–Democratic Party.*

Subsequent Moldovan-Russian discussions resulted in an agreement, signed in October 1994, calling for a three-year phased withdrawal of the troops of the 14th Russian Army from the region of the self–declared "Transnistrian Republic." This agreement has never been fully im-

An aerial view of Chisinau　　　　　　Courtesy: NOVOSTI

plemented, however. Although some elements of the 14th Russian Army were removed, significant Russian forces remained. The Russians claimed that the problem was logistical—how to get the 14th Russian Army's arms and equipment to Russia; this position was contradicted by Petru Lucinschi, the chairman of the Parliament, who claimed to have obtained the Government of Ukraine's agreement to allow everything to be shipped across its territory.

Periodic talks continued to take place between the Moldovan Government and the leadership of the "Dniestr Moldavian Republic," but no agreement proved possible; the "Dniestr Moldavian" leadership did agree to allow the circulation of the leu, Moldova's official currency, along with Transdnistria's own largely worthless coupons, however. For its part, the Moldovan Government offered autonomous republic status with its own parliament to the "Dniestr Moldavian Republic;" even more important, the Moldovan Government agreed that the area east of the Nistru had the right to opt out should Moldova ever decide to merge with Romania. There was also an agreement not to use force against each other.

The issue apparently holding up final agreement was Moldova's insistence that defense remain the exclusive prerogative of the Moldovan Government. "They can have their own symbols and parliament—an autonomous republic," said Ion Gutsu, a deputy prime minister; "but Moldova must have a single domestic policy and army."

The Moldovan Government also reached an agreement with the Gagauz in August 1995. The Gagauz separatists, who had hitherto refused to recognize the authority of the government, had demanded

autonomous republic status for their own area but agreed to lay down their arms in return for a broad measure of autonomy.

New presidential elections were held on November 17, 1996. President Snegur stood for reelection but was opposed by several candidates. President Snegur and Petru Lucinschi, who at that time held the position of chairman of the Parliament, were the two highest vote–getters, but no candidate obtained a majority of the votes. In the run-off, Lucinschi won with approximately 53 percent of the vote.

Lucinschi, a Central Committee Secretary of the Communist Party of the Soviet Union in its final days, had by this time become a social democrat and as a centrist. It appears that Snegur lost because of a falling out earlier in the year with Andre Sangheli, his prime minister. In April 1996, Snegur accused the Sangheli Government of incompetence and corruption and urged the parliament to dismiss it. Although there may have been other issues involved, the quarrel between Snegur and Sangheli began in March 1996 when Snegur accused the defense minister of corruption and attempted to have him dismissed; Sangheli, opposing the dismissal, carried the issue to the Constitutional Court and won. Sangheli then formed a tacit alliance with Lucinschi. A bitter presidential campaign followed, won in the end by Lucinschi.

Lucinschi appointed Ion Ciubuc as his new prime minister in January 1997. Because of the political make up of the legislature, the Ciubuc cabinet contained representatives of several parties and even two communists serving as individuals. The cabinet was essentially centrist—supportive of reform but aware that the reforms, although necessary, were hurting many individual Moldovans.

Moldova

President Vladimir Voronin

New parliamentary elections took place on March 22, 1998. The political situation in Moldova was still rather fluid, however, so the political parties that competed in these elections were rather different from those that competed in the 1994 elections. Fifteen political parties and electoral blocs—plus some 70 independents—competed in the parliamentary elections. Only four of the contesting parties or blocs won representation in the parliament, however.

The largest winner was the *Party of Moldovan Communists (PCM)*, which won approximately 30 percent of the vote and 40 seats. Although there were communists in the previous parliament and two of them even held portfolios in the previous cabinet, the *PCM* was a new party to the parliament, for it was still banned at the time of the 1994 elections. The center-right but pro-reform *Democratic Convention of Moldova (CDM)*, led by former President Snegur, came in second with approximately 20 percent of the vote and 26 seats. The pro-presidential *For a Democratic and Prosperous Moldova (PMPD)* bloc, led by Prime Minister Ciubuc, came in third with approximately 18 percent of the vote and 24 seats. The *Party of Democratic Forces (PFD)* won some 9 percent of the vote and 11 seats. The *Agrarian–Democratic Party*, the dominant party in the previous parliament (with 56 seats), fell below the minimum 4 percent barrier and so was eliminated from the new parliament.

Since no single party had a majority in the 101-seat parliament, negotiations began in early April for creation of a coalition government. The *PCM* opened negotiations by announcing its willingness to set up a coalition with the *PMPD* and the *PFD*; it rejected cooperation with the *CDM*.

Since such a coalition would have meant the end of reform, the *PMPD* did not respond to the overture of the *PCM* but, instead, opened discussions with the

PFD and the *CDM*. These discussions were successful and resulted in an agreement on a coalition government which was announced on April 21. Under the terms of the agreement, each party was to receive government representation proportional to the number of votes each received in the March elections. The agreement also stipulated that the *PMPD* would have the chairmanship of the parliament, while the prime minister would be a member of the *CDM*. In addition, the three parties agreed to form a joint faction in the parliament, to be called the *Alliance for Democracy and Reform*, and elected former President Mircea Snegur as the joint faction leader. Dumitru Diacov was elected to the position of chairman of the parliament.

Although it appeared that Mircea Snegur, the leader of the *CDM*, would become prime minister, he opted, in the end, to remain in the parliament, so the incumbent, Ion Ciubuc, was reappointed as prime minister. In compensation, the *CDM* got one deputy prime minister slot plus the interior portfolio.

Moldova was badly affected by Russia's financial crisis which began in August 1998, however, and this led to increased inflation, a growing trade deficit, dropping foreign currency reserves and, finally, a sharp drop in the value of the currency unit, the *leu*. In the resulting crisis, the several parties were unable to agree on a single policy and this led to the resignation of Prime Minister Ciubuc and his cabinet on February 3, 1999. Mircea Snegur also resigned as leader of the governing *Alliance for Democracy and Reform* at the same time.

On February 5, President Lucinschi named Serafim Urecheanu, the mayor of Chisinau, as the new prime minister. Urecheanu attempted to set up a cabinet of "experts" not tied to the relative strength of the individual parties in the parliament, and he also called on the parliament to grant the government the right to rule by decree for at least two years. This attempt to curtail the power of parliament brought a negative reaction and Urecheanu was forced to give up his attempts to form a cabinet on February 17.

Two days later, President Lucinschi appointed Ion Sturza, a member of the pro–presidential *For a Prosperous and Democratic Moldova (PMPD)* as the new prime minister–designate. Sturza, taking an opposite tack to that of the unsuccessful Urecheanu, promised that his government's structure would "reflect the expectations of the parliamentary majority." He also promised a "continuation of economic and democratic reforms." But Sturza got only 51 votes when parliament was asked to approve his government on March 3,

one vote short of the 52 votes necessary to win approval. Sturza lost because one of the parties of the government coalition, the *Christian Democratic Popular Front (FPCD)*, refused to vote for the cabinet unless it was given two additional cabinet seats. President Lucinschi renominated Sturza as prime minister on March 9; this time, Sturza got 52 votes and was installed as prime minister, though that vote was also challenged, since the 52nd vote was an absentee ballot cast by a member of parliament detained in Transnistria.

In spite of his promise to reflect the "expectations of the parliamentary majority," Sturza's government was no more stable than its predecessor; however, the sharpest blow came in late October when four parliamentary deputies resigned from his political grouping, *For a Prosperous and Democratic Moldova*. Sturza submitted his resignation on November 9, shortly after losing a confidence vote in parliament. At issue was an agreement the government has signed with the IMF promising to privatize Moldova's wine and tobacco industries.

After Sturza's fall, the IMF froze all loans to Moldova and it appeared that the World Bank and the European Union would do the same. This led to six weeks of political maneuvering, during which parliament rejected two candidates as prime minister, before finally voting to confirm Dumitru Braghis on December 21, 1999. This represented a victory for the government, for Braghis had participated in drafting the program of the Sturza cabinet which had been rejected in November; moreover, the prime minister announced after his confirmation that he would not change the program drawn up by Sturza's outgoing cabinet. Braghis put together a cabinet of non–political technicians—in Braghis's words, "competent people, selected on the basis of professionalism"—with the expressed purpose of reducing the role of parliament in the government. In spite of that, 57 deputies voted for confirmation. Support came from the *Party of Moldovan Communists* (40 votes), the *Christian Democratic Popular Party* (9 votes), plus eight independent deputies. Braghis, an engineer by training, headed the Moldovan Komsomol organization when the republic was still part of the Soviet Union.

Three and a half months later, Braghis managed to get his new budget through parliament—but only after he had threatened to resign if his program were not enacted. Parliament refused to pass the remainder of the government's program, however—in particular privatization of the wine and tobacco industries—even though the IMF had stipulated this as a prerequisite for additional funding. In ret-

Prime Minister Vasile Tarlev

rospect, that should have been expected, since the *Party of Moldovan Communists*, parliament's strongest block, opposed privatization.

By the summer of 2000, the economic situation in Moldova had become desperate. By IMF estimates, the economy had declined by 60 percent since independence in 1991. In Soviet days, a quarter of the country's earnings had come from high–tech plants serving space and submarine programs. Those had collapsed, leaving the country dependent on subsistence farming, some wine sales, and money sent home by emigrants. Average salaries, when paid, were $30 a month. Most rural people were destitute. Statistics showed that Moldova had become the poorest country in Europe, edging out Albania and Romania for that honor.

The essential problem was the stalemate in parliament. Responding to this situation, President Petru Lucinschi proposed creation of a "presidential" regime which would allow him to rule by decree. But parliament saw this proposal as a threat to its prerogatives; instead, it moved to reduce the power of the president, abolishing direct presidential elections and providing for the president to be elected by parliament.

President Lucinschi's term of office was scheduled to end in December; parliament held its first in a series of votes to elect his successor beginning on December 1. Vladimir Voronin, leader of the *Party of Moldovan Communists*, won 48 votes during this first round, and he continued to fall short in subsequent rounds of voting. Pavel Barbalat, candidate of the center–right, received 37 votes. When it had become clear that no candidate would win the necessary 61 votes, President Lucin-

schi dissolved parliament in mid–January and scheduled new parliamentary elections for February 25.

Those elections were won by the *Party of Moldovan Communists* with 50.7 percent of the popular vote and 71 seats of the 101 seats in parliament. Only two other parties cleared the 6 percent barrier for representation in parliament—the *Braghis Alliance*, headed by Prime Minister Braghis, which got 13.3 percent (and 19 deputies)—and the *Christian Democratic People's Party*, which got 8.24 percent (and 11 deputies). Two prominent political parties—the *Party of Revival and Accord*, led by former President Mircea Snegur, and the *For a Prosperous and Democratic Moldova*, led by outgoing speaker Dumitru Diakov and former Prime Minister Ion Sturza—fell below the 6 percent barrier and so failed to win any representation in parliament.

Vladimir Voronin was elected as the country's new president on April 4, 2001 and took the oath of office three days later. Four days later, he named Vasile Tarlev as prime minister. Tarlev, an ethnic Bulgarian and a political independent, had served a stint as chairman of the Supreme Economic Council. He was also a businessman who served as chairman of the Moldovan Association of Producers. Essentially a technician, Tarlev's job has been to implement the large political decisions made by President Voronin.

At the time of his inauguration, Voronin indicated that Moldova's foreign policy would "undergo some modifications," but he saw "no serious obstacles" hindering the "continuation of reforms" domestically. He probably meant it when he promised to pursue a foreign policy "oriented toward the West, toward the East, and toward the international organizations;" however, his first foreign policy initiative was to propose to Russia that the two nations negotiate a new basic treaty to replace a treaty negotiated in 1990 but never ratified by the Russian Duma because it lacked provisions for safeguarding Russian interests of Transnistria. To deal with this problem, Voronin proposed that the new treaty specifically designate Russia as mediator in negotiations between the Moldovan Government and the Dniestr Moldova authorities. At the time, it appeared that Voronin had gotten even more for Russia specifically condemned "separatism in all its forms" in the new treaty, signed by the two presidents on November 19, 2001. To reciprocate, President Voronin gave a promise, which was also written into the treaty, that "measures will be taken to satisfy the need for Russian language instruction" in Moldova.

This was, in fact, a major foreign policy coup. Russia subsequently shipped out about two-thirds of the ammunition and

equipment held by the Russian 14th Army in Transnistria and afterwards it consistently supported the principle of Moldova's territorial integrity in its communications with the Transnistrian authorities. This did not produce a settlement to the conflict, however.

President Voronin had two other foreign policy successes in the summer of 2001, though they appeared at the time to be less significant that his treaty with Russia. Moldova was admitted to the Stability Pact for Southeastern Europe in June and entered the World Trade Organization in July. Both of these initiatives had their origins under the previous government, of course, so they were not really the result of actions by the current government.

Voronin's domestic policy initiatives were less successful; in addition, his promise to Putin that he would satisfy the need for Russian language instruction in Moldova got him into trouble later. In September 2001, the government announced its intention to make the teaching of Russian language mandatory in all primary schools. The following month, the government announced that it was replacing a course in the "History of the Romanians" with a course in the "History of Moldovans."

In December, the Ministry of Education issued an order introducing mandatory Russian language classes in schools. Almost simultaneously, the leader of the *Party of Moldovan Communists* parliamentary group put forth an initiative at the Constitutional Court to introduce Russian as the country's second official language.

In response, the smaller of the two oppositional parties in the parliament, the *Christian Democratic People's Party (CDPP)*, organized a series of anti-Russification demonstrations. As the protests continued, the government suspended the *CDPP* for one month; however, it was forced to rescind the suspension after international protests. After two months of protest, the government annulled its decision to introduce mandatory Russian language classes and introduced a "moratorium" on its earlier decision to replace the "History of the Romanians." President Voronin then sacked his minister of education after he told protesters that he had "made a mistake" in deciding to introduce mandatory Russian language classes. Two days later, the president accepted the resignation of his interior minister because, according to local analysts, he had refused to crack down on protesters.

Another issue which reflected badly on President Voronin was the government's handling of an application by the Bessarabian Metropolitan Church for registration in Moldova. The Bessarabian Metropolitan Church, which existed in Moldova be-

Moldova

A wheat–growing area of Moldova

tween 1918 and 1940, is under the jurisdiction of the Bucharest Patriarchate. When it annexed the territory in 1940, Moscow created the Moldovan Metropolitan Church under the jurisdiction of the Moscow Patriarchate. After previous Moldovan Governments had refused to register the Bessarabian Church, it had filed an appeal with the European Court of Human Rights (ECHR). In December 2001, the ECHR ruled in favor of the Bessarabian Church, stating that the Moldovan Government had breached ECHR provisions on religious freedoms and the right of association when it refused to register the church. The Moldovan Government appealed the ruling but a five-judge panel ruled against the appeal on March 25, 2002. The Bessarabian Church then applied for re-registration.

When the government stalled on the issue, the Council of Europe's Parliamentary Assembly issued a new order on April 24; two weeks later, the Council of Europe's Committee of Ministers approved a resolution calling upon the Moldovan Government to report by July 31 on measures it had taken to register the Bessarabian Metropolitan Church. Most Moldovan officials still opposed registra-

tion of the Bessarabian Metropolitan Church, but the government, realizing that it had no choice, hastily drew up a draft law modifying procedures for registering religious organizations and submitted it to the parliament on July 11. On July 30, one day before the Council of Europe's deadline, the government announced that it had registered the Bessarabian Metropolitan Church. Since that time, the Bessarabian Church has managed to open several dozen parishes in Moldova. By way of comparison, there are 1,200 Russian Orthodox parishes in Moldova.

The government's relations with the political opposition remained poor throughout its entire first term in office, both from those represented in the parliament and from within the general population. For instance, none of the opposition political parties was happy when the government proposed new legislation requiring political formations to reregister and prove that membership had not dropped below 5,000 members after the initial registration.

Press freedom also became an issue in the fall of 2002 after the Audiovisual Council withdrew the broadcasting licenses of several radio stations for violating broadcasting regulations. Three weeks

later, the government ordered that the independent Voice of Bessarabia private radio station be closed down, despite the fact that the station is politically independent and had received support from the U.S. Embassy in Chisinau.

A related issue was new legislation concerning the state-owned Teleradio Moldova. The original government plan would have transformed Teleradio Moldova into a public company but the government would have controlled the Board of Observers. After protests—and an appeal to the Council of Europe by opponents of the government plan—the government modified the legislation so that only five of the 15 members of the Board of Observers are appointed directly by the government.

In spite of all of the political bickering, however, the *Party of Moldovan Communists* managed to retain most of its popularity. A poll taken in December 2003 indicated that President Voronin was the country's most popular politician and that 64.4 percent supported the *Party of Moldovan Communists*.

However, an important part of President Voronin's program—his espousal of a pro-Russian foreign policy in return for

Russia's support on "Dniestr Moldavia" issue—fell apart in November 2003 when the Russian side put forth a proposal for resolving the matter in the so-called Kozak memorandum. Essentially, the Russians proposed that Transnistria be given the status of a separate republic under a federal government with Russian troops remaining in Transnistria for another 20 years. Relations with Russia deteriorated after Voronin's rejection of the Kozak Memorandum; this, in turn, convinced Voronin that his foreign policy up to this time had been based on a false premise.

As a result, the past three years have seen a reorientation in Voronin's foreign policy. The first step came in June 2004, when Voronin submitted a Declaration on Stability and Security Pact requesting the various nations to recognize Moldova's territorial integrity, to the OSCE. The declaration has been under discussion at the OSCE, but it has been opposed by the Russian Government. Among other things, the document called for the removal of Russian troops from Dniestr Moldova. In October 2004, Moldova formally proposed that U.S. and the E.U. representatives be added as observers to the Dniestr Moldova negotiations.

Relations with Romania have also improved, partly because the government has begun to look toward of eventual membership in the European Union and Romania is a little further along that same road. In connection with this, the government has also approved a blueprint for a series of reforms designed to bring the country closer to EU standards. The European Commission approved the action plan in January 2004.

New parliamentary elections were scheduled to take place on March 6, 2005. Nine political parties, two voting blocs, and 12 independent candidates were registered to run in the elections. To win representation in parliament, independents had to win three percent of the overall vote, while parties had to garner six percent, blocs of two parties nine percent, and blocs of three parties or more 12 percent.

The *Party of Moldovan Communists (PCM)* took 46.1 percent of the vote (56 seats), the *Democratic Moldova Bloc (BMD)* drew 28.1 percent (34 seats), and the *Popular Party Christian Democratic (PPCD)* won 9.07 percent (11 seats).

One of the first responsibilities of the new parliament was to elect a president. It takes 61 votes to win the presidency. This became a problem for Voronin, when the leaders of the *BMD* and the *PPCD* announced that they planned to boycott the presidential vote. In fact, the *BMD* split over the issue when Dumitru Diacov and

seven followers left the party to form a new group, called the *Democratic Party (PD)*. When the vote for the presidency took place on April 4, Voronin won with 75 votes. He got not only the eight votes of the *PD* but also the 11 votes of the *PPCD*. This never became a formal government coalition, but most of the parties that supported Voronin's reelection tend to cooperate with the government on most issues.

The *Democratic Moldova Bloc* has since broken up; the main opposition is now known as *Our Moldova Alliance*, though there is a second opposition party which split off from the *Our Moldova Alliance* in October 2005 which is led by former Prime Minister Dumitru Braghis.

An IMAS-INC poll published in April 2007 shows some interesting things about the Moldovan population. While 53 percent expressed the view that the direction of economic policy was wrong, 49 percent expressed confidence in the government. President Voronin remains the country's most trusted politician and the Communist Party the most popular party. Publication of the poll came as the government was discussing a reform of the Moldovan economy proposed by President Voronin which included tax advantages to companies that reinvest their profits, a tax amnesty, and the legalization of previ-

Moldovan school children supporting the economy

Moldova

Moldovan family celebrating a special day

ously undeclared assets at a cost of five percent of their value. That may indicate that a majority of the population is opposed to President Voronin's economic reforms, but dislikes every other Moldovan political figure even more.

Foreign Policy

Moldova, when it achieved independence in 1991, adopted a policy of neutrality and it has adhered to that stance ever since. Although it became a member of the Commonwealth of Independent States, it has kept its membership at the nominal level and it has eschewed other regional organizations that have come into existence in recent years. Moldova has been active in world organizations such as the United Nations and it has had good working relations with the IMF and World Bank. President Voronin met with the president of both organizations in October 2002 while paying an official visit to Washington. In return, Voronin received World Bank President Wolfensohn's promise of support for the reform process in Moldova. Most recently, Moldova has been working to improve relations with the European Union, In April 2005, the European Commission gave Moldova a grant of $11.77 million to im-

prove public finance management, social services, and for projects in the agricultural sector.

Relations with Russia were correct but cool until the current government came to power as a result of the 2000 elections. One reason for this was Russia's support for the breakaway government in the area east of the Nistru (Dniestr) River. However, the current government postulated that it was necessary to improve relations with Russia in order to win its support and this paid off handsomely for a while. Russia committed itself to supporting Moldova's territorial integrity and it began pulling its military equipment, though not all of its troops, out of the area of Dniestr Moldova.

Things began to fall apart in November 2003 when Russia submitted its plan for unification of the two parts of Moldova. The plan, called the Kozak Memorandum, called for the creation of a federal state with Moldova and Transnistria as equal partners, each with its own government. The Memorandum would have also legalized the presence of Russian troops in Transnistria for another 20 years. President Voronin rejected the plan and Russo-Moldovan relations have deteriorated since that time.

By February 2005, the situation had gotten so bad that the Moldovan Government expelled 11 Russian citizens who had come to Moldova as observers for the parliamentary elections—according to the Moldovan Government because the Russians were interfering in the election campaign and spreading disinformation. In response, the Russian Duma adopted a resolution calling for a boycott of Moldovan wine and tobacco and an increase in the price of energy exports to Moldova.

The Russian Government did temporarily ban the importation of Moldovan wines and fruits and vegetables in May 2005. This ban was lifted, but it was then re-imposed on March 27, 2006. The ban on the import of Moldovan wines was lifted in November 2006; it was lifted on fruits and vegetables in March 2007, along with the ban on Moldovan meat. Moldova's total exports fell by 3.6 percent in 2006; however, Moldova's exports to CIS states (including Russia) accounted for only 40.3 percent of total exports, down from 50.5 percent in 2005.

Three agreements, reached in December 2006, show the current state of Moldovan-Russian relations. In early December, Russia and Moldova signed an agreement on resumption of passenger rail traffic between their two republics via the Transdniester region. Russia also agreed to accept rail traffic through the Moldovan-Ukrainian checkpoint; it was the March 2006 agreement with Ukraine on a common border checkpoint that brought the original Russian ban on rail traffic from Moldova. A few days later, Gazprom agreed to provide natural gas to Moldova for $170 per 1,000 cubic meters in 2007, an increase of only $10 from what Moldova paid in 2006—though the agreement does state that the natural gas price would continue to increase until it reached the average European level in 2011. Eight days later, Moldova signed a bilateral agreement on Moscow's accession to the World Trade Organization. After the signing, President Voronin described Russia as Moldova's strategic partner; "Russia is our main economic partner, the main market for our goods and a supplier of energy carriers."

The United States Government gave its blessing to an independent Moldova from the beginning, but relations between the two countries have never been extensive. Yet the United States has supported IMF and World Bank loans to Moldova, a policy it has continued under the current government. The United States also supports the reintegration of the area east of the Nistru (Dniest) River in a new federal framework. After an official four-day visit to Washington in December 2002, President Voronin commented that Moldova "counts on U.S. backing" in its efforts to shape a "unified, neutral, and demilitarized country." During his meeting with President Bush, Voronin told him that Moldova would be sending five members of the Moldovan military-engineering corps to participate in de-mining operations in Afghanistan. Relations warmed further in 2004, particularly after President Voronin proposed in October that the United States join the talks on Dniestr Moldova as an observer, along with representatives of the European Union.

Moldova's relations with Romania have been at the center of its politics since achieving independence in 1991. It was, in fact, the existence of political leaders arguing for union with Romania that led pro-Russian leaders in the area east of the Nistru (Dniestr) River to create their separate mini-state. Most Moldovan political figures long ago gave up any thought of merging with Romania, but the fact that the two countries share both a language and a religion means that relations with Romania are different than they are with any other country. In recent years, Romanian politicians have gone out of their way to respect Moldova's separate identity, and this has helped smooth relations somewhat, but there continue to be issues.

One of the more important is the decade-long struggle of the Bessarabian Metropolitan Church to receive permission to operate legally in Moldova. This church, which operated in Bessarabia between 1918 and 1940, was banned when Bessarabia was incorporated into the Soviet Union because it operates under the jurisdiction of the Bucharest Patriarchate. After the collapse of the Soviet Union, it applied to operate in Moldova, but previous governments refused to give it permission. As it continued to press its request for permission to operate in Moldova, the Moldovan Government came to believe that the Romanian Government was behind the actions of the Bessarabian Church.

The present government escalated the matter further when it accused Romania of interfering in Moldovan politics through its support of such things as the demonstrations against mandatory Russian language instruction and dropping the course on the "History of the Romanians" from the school curriculum. Relations reached their nadir in March 2002 when Moldova expelled the Romanian military attaché and Romania retaliated by expelling the Moldovan military attaché in Bucharest. The breach was partially healed when Romania appointed a new military attaché to its embassy in Chisinau in August.

In October 2002, President Voronin met with Romanian President Iliescu in Beirut, and the two presidents discussed measures they could take to improve relations. Three months later, President Voronin gave an interview with Romania Radio in which he again took up the subject of how to improve Moldovan-Romanian relations. The main thing that Bucharest could do to improve relations, he said, was to renounce talk of the existence of "two Romanian states." A second condition for improving relations would be for the two

countries to concentrate on economic rather than "all sorts of political or national problems."

In the past year, however, relations between the two countries have improved enormously. This was partly due to a new foreign policy orientation on the part of Moldova, which turned westward after relations with Russia deteriorated toward the end of 2003. Today, Moldova is looking forward to eventual membership in the European Union, and it looks to Romania for assistance in achieving that goal.

Nature of the Regime

The Republic of Moldova has a presidential–parliamentary system, with the president recognized as spokesman for the nation and also responsible for setting general policy. The president was popularly elected until the fall of 2000, when, in reaction to President Lucinschi's attempt to increase the powers of the office, the legislature amended the constitution to give itself the power to elect the president, thus creating in theory a parliamentary republic. However, the *Party of Moldovan Communists (PCM)* won the February 2001 parliamentary elections, so it was Vladimir Voronin, the *PCM* leader, who got to interpret and implement the constitutional reform. He chose the office of president (while retaining the position of head of the *PCM)*, and he has given the office a much more powerful mandate than his constitutionally reserved ceremonial role.

The president appoints a prime minister who must be confirmed by the legislature. The president also appoints members of the council of ministers on recommendation of the prime minister. The prime minister and members of the council of ministers must be approved by the legislature before they can take office, and the prime minister must retain the support of a ma-

Moldova

jority in the legislature in order to remain in office. The prime minister handles day–to–day policy and presides over meetings of the council of ministers.

Moldova has a unicameral parliament of 101 members. Formerly known as the Supreme Soviet, it is now referred to as the Supreme Council or parliament. The latest parliamentary elections took place on March 6, 2005. The *Party of Moldovan Communists (PCM)* took 46.1 percent of the vote (56 seats), the *Democratic Moldova Bloc (PCM)* drew 28.1 percent (34 seats), and the *Popular Party Christian Democratic (PPCD)* won 9.07 percent (11 seats).

Moldova's current constitution was approved in July 1994. The new constitution made some changes in the administrative divisions of the state, but otherwise mainly codified changes adopted after Moldova's declaration of independence in 1991. On one interesting point, however, the constitution created a Supreme Court but gave it no judicial review of legislative acts; instead, it created a separate Constitutional Court, which has sole authority for constitutional judicature.

Culture

The Republic of Moldova is primarily an agricultural society, with about 60 percent of the population still living in the countryside. On the other hand, Moldovan villages are large, averaging over a thousand inhabitants, and fairly modern. All have electricity, for example, and most are supplied with natural gas as well. Because of the ethnic identity of most Moldovans, the culture of Moldova is similar to that found in Romania. Most people think of themselves as members of the Orthodox Church and that has become more important since all restraints on religion were lifted. The border with Romania is also now open, so that reinforces the connection.

Most Moldovans are literate, and there is a comprehensive system of primary and secondary schools throughout the republic. Around 70 percent of the children go to preschool before entering primary school.

The most prestigious institutes of higher education are the State University, the Nicolae Testimiteanu University of Medicine, and the Academy of Economic Studies, all located in Chisinau (Kishinev), plus the Aleco Russo Pedagogic University at Bain. There are several other institutions of higher education in other parts of the republic, including ten private institutions of higher education founded since 1992. Two of the better known ones are the Free University of Moldova and the Cooperative Commercial University. There are also 51 technical schools scattered throughout the republic.

The Moldovan Academy of Sciences was established in 1961. It has 17 research institutes under its jurisdiction.

Economy

The Moldovan economy is still predominantly agricultural, with approximately 40 percent of the people still employed on the land. Its mild climate and fertile soil, plus the extensive mechanization that has taken place since 1940, mean that agriculture is fairly productive, in spite of the fact that most land is still organized into successor organizations of the old collective or state farms.

President Lucinschi said in March 1998 that some 700,000 land titles had been distributed, though the titles were for parcels of land varying in size from one to three hectares (2½ to 7½ acres). Saying that it was "high time to end the useless debates about land privatization," Lucinschi urged the country to accelerate reforms in the villages. His personal choice, he said, would be a model where peasants would work their land in "well–equipped peasant associations." The overwhelming victory of the *Party of Moldovan Communists* in the February 2001 parliamentary elections put the entire question of land tenure on hold for the foreseeable future, however.

Winter wheat and corn are the main grain crops grown. Wheat is consumed within the republic, while some of the corn is exported to other republics. The 2005 grain harvest was 1.4 million tons, including 1.1 million tons of wheat, "the largest crop in recent years." Other crops that have traditionally produced surpluses for export include sugar beets, tobacco, and sunflower seeds. Moldova also produces significant quantities of fruits, vegetables, berries, grapes and walnuts, all of which have been exported to other republics in the past.

Moldova has a diversified industry, though the most significant branch is food processing. These include sugar refining, wine making (including champagne and brandy), oil pressing, canning and the processing of essential oils. All of these branches have traditionally exported to other parts of the Soviet Union, though a March 2006 ban by the Russian Government on the importation of Moldovan wine is causing the Moldovan Government to rethink future export markets. Flour mills, dairies, meat processing and candy making industries also exist, but these serve the domestic market.

Other light industry includes things such as the processing of pelts for fur coats, footwear, and textiles, particularly knitting and the processing of silk. There is relatively little heavy industry, though

the republic does have some machine–building, including tractors, and it also manufactures building supplies, including bricks, tiles, cement, slate, and concrete blocks. In 2005, Industry accounted for 23.9 percent of GDP and 14 percent of the labor force.

A draft privatization program submitted in January 1992 by the department for privatization to the Supreme Economic Council was rejected as being too narrow in scope. Cabinet members who participated in the discussion favored an alternate program drawn up by government experts. The disagreement appeared to be more political than economic. Parliament had set up the department for privatization as an agency separate from the cabinet, but several cabinet members wanted the cabinet to be in charge of privatization. Parliament, which wanted privatization to start immediately, opposed this. The disagreement caused privatization to be put on hold for the next year.

Another factor was the bad economic situation. By some estimates, real income dropped by two–thirds between 1990 and 1994. The first privatizations finally occurred in 1994, when the government finally began to implement a voucher program which privatized 940 companies; some new private companies also began to appear at this time. Currently, around 50 percent of the national economy is in private hands.

GDP growth, which had increased by 1.3 percent in 1997, turned negative again in 1998. The Russian financial crisis which began in August 1998 hit the Moldovan economy perhaps harder than any other former Soviet republic, probably because Moldova had continued to maintain most of its trade with Russia. Thus even as the parliament was calling for a speed up in privatization of state enterprises and of the energy sector in September 1998, the government was reporting that the budget would no longer stand the effects of the Russian financial crisis and would have to be revised.

After three years of decline, the Moldovan economy began growing again in 2000, though by a pallid 1.9 percent; the trend continued in 2001, however, and has remained at or above the 6 percent level every year since. In 2005, the economy grew by 6.9 percent.

These growth figures are somewhat misleading, however. Moldova always has great difficulty finding markets for its exports, since they are mainly agricultural—mainly wine, fruit and vegetables—and the European Union's Common Agricultural Policy keeps products out. Even worse, the European Union is undercutting Moldovan products in the Russian market with subsidized products of its own. The latest blow came in March 2006, when the Russian Government banned the importation of Moldovan wines, fruits and vegetables and meat. The ban lasted for only about 9 months, but industrial production actually decreased by six percent during the first half of 2006.

The situation might have been far worse but—according to a report of the International Organization of Migration Moldovan—migrant workers sent home a record $1 billion in 2006. According to the report, one-third of Moldova's working-age population is employed abroad, and cash remittances account for 30 percent of the country's gross domestic product.

Most Moldovan men find work either in Ukraine or Russia, mainly in the construction industry or agriculture. The city with the largest number of Moldovans is Moscow, where an estimated 136,000 work. Moldovan women are found mainly in Western Europe, Turkey or Israel, where they work as domestics, as agricultural workers, or in the sex industry.

About 80 percent of all Moldovans still live below the poverty line. For those employed, the average wage is only $70 a month.

Moldova has received some outside assistance from international organizations such as the IMF. But the relationship has not been smooth because of the Moldovan government's inability to follow a consistent policy of reform.

To give one example, the IMF suspended a $190 million loan in the fall of 1997 because of the stalled reform process; it then agreed to unfreeze a $35 million tranche in January 1999, in view of the impact of the Russian crisis on Moldova's economy. It froze lending again in the summer of 2000 when the legislature deadlocked over privatization. After the *Party of Moldovan Communists* won an overwhelming majority in the February 2001 parliamentary elections, however, the IMF offered to open talks with Moldova; under an agreement reached in the summer of 2001, the IMF resumed its external financing for Moldova.

The World Bank also renewed its support to Moldova in 2001, providing $20 million for budget stabilization. Moldova was also admitted to the World Trade Organization in 2001.

In 2006, the Paris Club agreed to restructure the foreign loans Moldova received before December 31, 2000—worth about $150 million. In addition, the International Trade Committee of the European Parliament approved $58 million in economic aid to Moldova in January 2007. The European Union has also pledged to double aid to Moldova over the next four years. It has pledged $336 million for the period through 2010.

The Future

Moldova's economic difficulties since independence have caused many Moldovans to lose any faith they ever had in reform. In addition, Moldovans have struggled with a whole series of political questions—most of which remain unanswered.

Moldova is still the poorest country in Europe, but the economy did show positive growth of about 6 percent for the period 2000–2005. Industrial production fell by 6 percent in the first half of 2006 after Russia banned the importation of Moldovan wines, fruits and vegetables and meat. The ban was lifted in December 2006, but it had a strong negative effect on the economy.

The *Party of Moldovan Communists* eked out a new majority in the March 2005 parliamentary elections, though with a slightly diminished mandate. The years in power have changed the communists, who now are evolving into a western-style social democratic party. President Voronin still remains the most trusted politician in the country, and the Communist Party remains the most popular party.

The government's foreign policy orientation has turned westward in the past two years or so, partly because of disappointments with the Russian Government over Dniestr Moldova. Although President Voronin patched up his relationship with Russia recently, he still appears to want good relations with the west, in particular with the European Union.

Panel in Chisinau on European Integration, sponsored by Soros Open Society

Courtesy: Olesea Kovali

TRANSCAUCASIAN REPUBLICS

Due to their shared histories as well as frequent geographical and cultural similarities, there is necessarily some repetition from one entry to the other.

Showing only capital cities and political boundaries

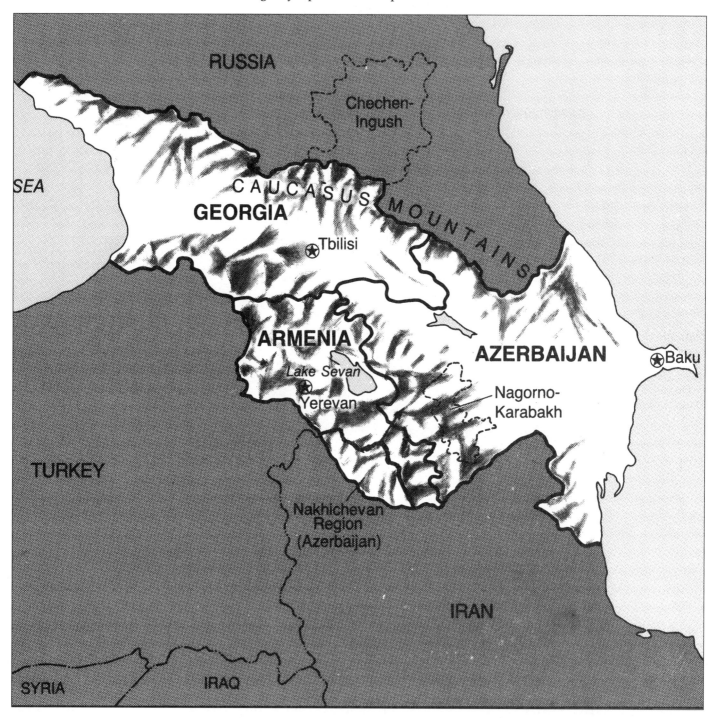

The Republic of Armenia

Area: 11,503 sq. mi. (29,800 sq. km.), slightly smaller than Maryland.

Population: 3.22 million (July 2006 est.).

Capital City: Yerevan (Pop. 1.2 million, estimated).

Climate: Dry and highland continental.

Neighboring States: Georgia (north), Turkey (west), Nakhichevan Region of Azerbaijani (southwest), Azerbaijan (east), a slender border with Iran (southeast).

Language: Armenian.

Ethnic Composition: Armenian (97.9%), Yezidi (Kurd) (1.3%), Russian (0.5%), others (0.3%) (2001 census).

Principal Religion: Armenian Apostolic.

Chief Commercial Products: Livestock, chemicals, textiles, wine, grain, footwear.

Currency: *dram* (introduced in Nov. 1993).

Per Capita Annual Income (Purchasing Power Parity): $5,300.

Recent Political Status: The Armenian S.S.R. was established in 1920; from 1922 to 1936 it was joined with Georgia and Azerbaijan into the Trancaucasian S.S.R., but reverted to status as a constituent republic of the former USSR. It declared independence on August 23, 1990.

National Day: September 21 (1991), Independence Day.

Chief of State: Robert Kocharian, President (re–elected March 5, 2003).

Head of Government: Serzh Sarkisian, Prime Minister (April 2007).

National Flag: Three equal horizontal stripes, red, blue, and orange.

The Land

The Republic of Armenia (Hayastani Hanrapetut'yun), which emerged as an independent state as a result of the collapse of the Union of Soviet Socialist Republics in 1991, is located in a landlocked area south of the Caucasus Mountains. The ancient empire of which it is a remnant included Western Armenia, an area of about 57,999 square miles (147,000 sq. km.) across the western border in present–day Azerbaijan.

Today, it consists of 11,503 square miles (29,800 sq. km.). It borders on Turkey to the west, Iran to the south, Georgia to the north and Azerbaijan to the east. Yerevan, the capital, is the largest city. The second big city is Gyumri (formerly Leninakan), which was one of the cities badly damaged by the earthquake of 1988.

All except about ten percent of Armenia is extremely mountainous. Its "lowlands" are over 3,000 feet high, while the average height above sea level for the entire country is slightly over a mile high; its highest mountains are in the northwestern part of the country. Mt. Aragats, the highest peak, is 13,418 feet high. The northern part of Armenia consists of a series of ranges and elevated volcanic plateaus, into which deep river valleys have been cut.

In the east, the dominant feature is a high mountain lake surrounded by mountains. Lake Sevan, which is 525 square miles in size, lies at 6,200 feet, while the surrounding mountains soar to 11,800 feet. In the south is the Ararat Plain, only the northern half of which belongs to Armenia. The Ararat Plain is divided by the Aras River, which forms Armenia's southern border.

Armenia's rainfall varies considerably, with over 300 inches in the high mountains and an average of 80 inches on the Ararat Plain. Most of this precipitation falls in the form of heavy rains in the autumn and as snow in the winter.

Armenia's many rivers arise in the mountains in the north and west. Because of the sharp drop in elevation, they tend to be short and turbulent, with many waterfalls and rapids. Armenia accordingly has great hydroelectric power potential, estimated at nearly 22 billion kilowatt–hours a year. Four of these rivers—the Akhuryan, the Hrazdan (which flows out of Lake Sevan), the Arpa, and the Bargushat—provide water to irrigate the Armenian half of the Ararat Plain before emptying into the Aras River, itself a tributary of the Kura River, which flows into the Caspian Sea.

Since it lies at the northern edge of the subtropical zone, Armenia has long, dry, hot summers with long, mild, sunny autumns. Because of the elevation of most of the land, it also has a winter with average temperatures below freezing, though only the plateau and mountains in the north have really inclement weather.

In spite of its small size, Armenia has an unusually large variety of landscapes. Because of a combination of location and variation in altitudes, it possesses five different vegetation zones: semi desert, steppe, forest, alpine meadows, and high–altitude tundra. The semi desert landscape is found in the south at altitudes below 4,600 feet. This region, unless irrigated, produces only a scanty vegetation of mostly sagebrush and similar drought–resistant plants.

The land between 4,600 and 6,600 feet is mostly steppe, and here, if not watered, mainly drought–resistant grasses grow. The forest zone is found mostly in the southeast at altitudes between 6,200 and 6,600 feet, and in the northeast, at altitudes between 7,200 and 7,900 feet. Oak grows mainly in the southeast, while beech grows in the northeast.

The alpine zone lies above 6,600 feet, where thinning forests give way to mountain meadows. Such meadows are used as summer pastures for goats and sheep. Finally, above the alpine zone is the area of tundra, where little grows other than cushion plants such as moss.

The Ararat Plain produces fruits such as figs, grapes, pomegranates, apricots, peaches and melons. The plateau and the mountain valleys produce cereals and grains, tobacco, vegetables, and orchard crops such as cherries, apples, pears, almonds, and hazelnuts. Higher altitudes produce potatoes, grain and fodder grasses.

Armenia

The People

The estimated population of Armenia as of July 1, 2006 was 3.22 million, a decrease of 60,000 since the 1989 census. That figure does not include the out–migration of young, educated Armenians leaving to seek jobs elsewhere that has occurred over the past 15 years, however; it is estimated that at least 900,000-1,000,000 people have left Armenia since 1992.

Armenians constitute 93 percent of the population, with Russians, the largest minority, about 2 percent. Azerbaijani, Ukrainians and Kurds make up most of the remaining five percent.

History

Armenians, who refer to themselves as the *Hayk*, are an Indo–European people who, it was traditionally considered, migrated into the area in the 7th century B.C., overrunning and conquering an earlier, high civilization. More recently, some Armenians have suggested that Armenians did not move into the area but were simply the successors of the same civilization that lived there. Whichever version is correct, they subsequently came under the influence of the Medes, Persians and Greeks as they became part of these empires. The first Armenian Empire came into existence during the period of the rise of the Roman Empire. As the Roman Empire became ever more powerful, however, this empire disintegrated and Armenia became a sort of buffer zone between Rome and the Parthian Empire.

The people of Armenia converted to Christianity about 301 A.D., the first country to establish Christianity as a state religion. Not surprisingly, the Armenian Orthodox Church is known for its ancient and rich liturgy. Under communism, the role of the Church was severely limited but today the Church is playing an important role, particularly in the cultural sphere.

An independent Armenian state first emerged around 190 B.C., but it was not until the middle of the first century B.C. that a united Armenian state was created under Tigranes I the Great (c.94–c.55 B.C.). The first capital of this state was Artaxata, located on the Aras River not far from modern–day Yerevan. This kingdom lasted for almost 500 years and it reached its pinnacle under Tigranes, who extended his kingdom eastward to include parts of modern–day Iran and westward to encompass Syria. His conquests brought him to the attention of the Roman General Pompey, who defeated him in battle in 66 B.C. Tigranes was forced to relinquish Syria and become an ally of Rome.

For the next 120 years, Armenia remained a buffer state between Rome and Parthia, each manipulating Armenia to achieve its ends. The area was annexed by the Emperor Trajan in 114, but abandoned by his successor, Hadrian. An army of Marcus Aurelius destroyed Artaxata in 163. Caracalla attempted to annex Armenia in 216, but his successor, Macrinus, abandoned the attempt and recognized Tiridates II as King of Armenia. The resurgent Persian Empire then began pressing Armenia from the east. In 238, it conquered Armenia and established it as a vassal state holding it for fifty–some years later before another Roman Emperor, Diocletian, intervened and restored Tiridates III, son of Tiridates II, to the throne.

The reign of Tiridates III is extremely important for Armenian history, for this is when Armenia was converted to Christianity. Tiridates III was himself converted by St. Gregory the Illuminator and he made Christianity the official religion of the realm in 300 A.D. From this time onward, the Armenian patriarchate also became an important symbol of Armenian unity, holding the people together in periods of political instability.

Tiridates was later assassinated by his own court chamberlain in league with local nobles and Armenia split into two parts, with the smaller part gradually being absorbed into the Byzantine Empire. The larger part came under Persian domination in 428 when the Armenian nobility deposed their king and requested a Persian governor.

The religion of Persia at this time was Zoroastrianism and the Persian ruler made the mistake of attempting to impose it on the Armenians. An Armenian revolt in 451 caused the Persians to declare that they would not attempt to impose Zoroastrianism by force; a second revolt in 481–484 won Persian recognition of a native Armenian ruler and a Persian promise to honor Armenia's political and religious freedom in return for Armenia's agreement to provide military assistance to Persia when called upon.

The Armenians asserted their religious freedom even further in 554 when an Armenian Church Council got into a quarrel with the rest of the Christian Church over a minor point of dogma, the dyophysite formula enunciated by the Council of Chalcedon in 451. The Armenian Church, by rejecting this formula, isolated itself from the rest of Christianity and turned the Byzantine Empire into an enemy.

Armenia came under attack from the Arabs beginning in 640. Thirteen years later, Armenia came under Arab control as an autonomous region under its own native ruler. This situation continued for the next three hundred years.

In the tenth century, however, a resurgent Byzantine Empire invaded from the west, effectively destroying Armenia politically. The final blow came in the 11th century when Armenia was invaded from the east by the Seljuk Turks. The Seljuk Turk conquest was complete by 1071, although a few minor Armenian kingdoms survived for a time in the more remote mountains. In the 12th century, part of northern Armenia was annexed to the Georgian Kingdom. However, Armenia was overrun again in 1236–42 by the Mongols.

Most of Armenia eventually became part of the Ottoman Empire and, after the fall of Constantinople in 1453, the Armenian bishop of Bursa was transferred to Constantinople and appointed leader of the Armenian Church in the Ottoman Empire. The eastern area fell to the Ottoman Empire in 1516, but it soon became a battlefield as Persia and the Ottoman Empire fought for control. Persia gained control of the regions of Yerevan, Karabakh, and Nakhichevan as a result of the peace of 1620. In the mountainous region of Karabakh, however, five Armenian princes managed to assert their independence at the beginning of the 18th century. Forces of the Ottoman Empire occupied the area in the 1730s, but were driven out by the Persians.

Amid the swirling events that ultimately resulted in the end of the Ottoman Empire, Armenians claim that 1.5 million of their people were mercilessly slaughtered by the Turks in the late 19th and early 20th centuries. Many fled, and a substantial number were admitted to the U.S.

Armenia under Russian–Soviet Rule

The Russians began to focus their attention on the area of the Caucasus at the beginning of the 19th century. A war be-

President Robert Kocharian

tween Russia and Persia beginning in 1809 gave Russia Georgia, northern Azerbaijan and Karabakh. In 1828, Yerevan and Nakhichevan were added. A large part of traditional Armenia still remained under Ottoman control, but the area that was to become modern Armenia had become part of the Russian Empire.

The Russian Government tended to treat Armenians as co–religionists throughout most of the 19th century and being part of the Russian Empire meant that Armenians had greater access to western ideas than before. The 19th century therefore ushered in a cultural renaissance in Armenia.

This changed toward the end of the century, however, when the government of Nicholas II began to get worried about Armenian nationalism and introduced repressive measures to stamp it out. In 1897, hundreds of schools and libraries were closed and Armenian newspapers were banned. And since the Armenian Orthodox Church was closely associated in people's minds with Armenian nationalism, the government moved in 1903 to confiscate all property of the Armenian Church.

Armenian nationalists joined with Georgians and Azerbaijani to form the Transcaucasus Federal Republic in April 1918, but the new state collapsed in just over a month. An independent Armenia was then declared on May 26, 1918. The republic, which lasted until March 1922, had a bumpy independent existence as it attempted to secure as much of the lands occupied by Armenians as it could. It fought short wars with Georgia and Azerbaijan—the latter over the area of Nagorno–Karabakh—and a war in 1920 with Turkey. The loss to Turkey in 1920 led to a change in government and the creation of the Soviet Republic of Armenia in December 1920.

The new government was established as a coalition of communists and nationalists, but the nationalists were soon eliminated and it became a purely communist government. In March 1922, this new government joined with Georgia and Azerbaijan to form the Transcaucasian Soviet Federated Socialist Republic. On December 30, 1922, it became a part of the Union of Soviet Socialist Republics.

The Transcaucasian Soviet Federated Socialist Republic was dissolved in 1936 when a new Soviet constitution was adopted and Armenia at that time became the Armenian Soviet Socialist Republic. Armenia did relatively well as a part of the Soviet Union. Quite a bit of industry grew up around Armenia's chief cities, and individual Armenians held important positions in industry and the professions in major cities throughout the Soviet Union.

Yet Armenia was one of the first republics to "explode" after Gorbachëv launched his program of *glasnost*. The most important reason for this was the Nagorno–Karabakh Autonomous Republic, the Armenian enclave in the neighboring republic of Azerbaijan. The situation in Nagorno–Karabakh is treated in greater detail under the Republic of Azerbaijan (See section on Nagorno–Karabakh immediately after the discussion of Azerbaijan's foreign policy). Suffice to say here that this became a galvanizing issue for the vast majority of Armenians when the Nagorno– Karabakh regional council petitioned in February 1988 to become part of Armenia.

Within weeks, the Armenian political leadership had endorsed the Nagorno–Karabakh position. The Azerbaijani leadership angrily rejected Armenia's claims on Nagorno–Karabakh and began to encourage popular demonstrations in support of its position. The demonstrations got out of control, however, and turned into an anti–Armenian move in the Azerbaijani city of Sumgait. Within weeks, an incipient state of war existed between Armenia and Azerbaijan.

Gorbachëv dismissed the *Communist Party* leaders of both Azerbaijan and Armenia in May 1988, on the grounds that they had not acted quickly enough to control the situation. The new first secretary of the *Armenian Communist Party* leader was Suren Arutunyan, a Gorbachëv loyalist who had spent the previous several years working in Moscow. He tried his best, but he was constantly caught between Moscow loyalists on the one side and nationalists organized as the Karabakh Committee on the other. In the process, the *Armenian Communist Party* lost much of its authority.

Armenians fleeing Turkish lands in the early 20th century

Armenia

Armenia was hit by a natural disaster in December 1988, when a major earthquake killed over 25,000 persons and injured thousands more. Other thousands were left homeless. International aid poured in, but Armenians lost further faith in both the Armenian and union leadership when help was slow in coming.

The people applauded in January 1989 when Gorbachëv announced that he had decided to suspend Azerbaijan's control over Nagorno–Karabakh and put the autonomous republic under Moscow's direct control. They suffered when the *Azerbaijan Popular Front* instituted its road and rail blockade against Armenia, but they refused to give in. They were, therefore, extremely angry when Gorbachëv gave in to the *Azerbaijan Popular Front's* blackmail and requested the USSR Supreme Soviet to relinquish control back to Azerbaijan. Armenian delegates refused to participate in that vote.

Armenians now turned conclusively against the Communist Party. By the spring of 1990, there were an increasing number of armed clashes between Armenian nationalists and Soviet troops. In July, Gorbachëv ordered all such vigilante groups to be disbanded, but then the Armenian Supreme Soviet defied Gorbachëv, declaring that his order "contradicts the Armenian people's natural right to self–defense." In August 1990, the Armenian Supreme Soviet elected Levan Ter–Petrossian to the top post in the republic, chairman of the Supreme Soviet. Ter–Petrossian, a leader of the Karabakh Committee, was Armenia's first post–communist leader. On August 23, 1990, the Armenian Supreme Soviet followed this up by passing a declaration of Armenian independence.

Ter–Petrossian turned out to be a cautious leader in practice. He did not attempt to challenge Moscow but, again, his quarrel was not really with Moscow. The confrontation with Azerbaijan continued and Armenia continued to suffer from an Azerbaijani blockade of fuel and most other supplies, but it would not cede on the political question. In the spring of 1991, it boycotted discussions about a new union treaty. Armenia took advantage of the *coup* attempt against Gorbachëv in August 1991 to reiterate its declaration of independence. This was followed by a popular referendum that received overwhelming approval. The Armenian Supreme Soviet also created the office of president to be elected by popular vote. The election took place on October 16 and Ter–Petrossian won 83 percent of the votes. He formally assumed the office in December 1991.

Armenia accepted Russian–Kazakh mediation of the Nagorno–Karabakh dispute with Azerbaijan in September 1991 and

agreed to yield its claims over Nagorno–Karabakh at this time. It subsequently recognized the independence of the Republic of Nagorno–Karabakh, however, so its confrontation with Azerbaijan continued.

Armenia agreed to join the Commonwealth of Independent States at the December 1991 founding meeting. Unlike Azerbaijan, it opted to not establish a separate republic army at that time, even though large numbers of Armenian "freedom fighters" were already involved in the fighting in Nagorno–Karabakh. Partly this was because it hoped to win CIS backing for its position on Nagorno–Karabakh; partly it was because the Azerbaijani blockade had been successful and its economy was in terrible shape.

As a result of strains between individual CIS members and a continuing fear of being dominated by Moscow, however, most CIS members began to create national armies in 1992. Armenia created a ministry of defense and an Armenian army and began to equip these forces with heavier equipment such as tanks, transferred mainly from Soviet forces.

The war between Azerbaijan and Armenia widened somewhat in the spring of 1992, when forces within Nagorno–Karabakh extended their control over areas

formerly occupied by Azerbaijani forces. These same forces then overran Azerbaijani territory lying between Nagorno–Karabakh and Armenia, creating a corridor connecting the enclave with Armenia at the point where the two territories are the closest together. This had a military significance, since Armenia, which had been shifting supplies in by air up to this point, could begin bringing supplies in by truck.

Azerbaijan was going through a great deal of domestic political turmoil at this point, at least partly because of its military defeats. Azerbaijani forces in the enclave of Nakhichevan (cut off from Azerbaijan by a strip of Armenian territory), then began shelling Armenian villages across the border. This led to an Armenian attack on the enclave city of Sadarak, and so the war widened further. Fighting continued intermittently over the summer and into the fall, in spite of a series of truces negotiated with the assistance of international third parties; however, no further significant changes in the military situation occurred. But Azerbaijan maintained its blockade of Armenia, so the economic situation within Armenia deteriorated further.

The situation within Armenia became desperate in January 1993 when the sole gas pipeline leading into the country through Georgia was blown up. A new temporary pipeline was opened in February, however, and gas began flowing again from Georgia. But even with almost all Armenian factories closed because of a lack of energy, there was no sign that Armenians were ready to compromise or lessen their support for fellow Armenians in Nagorno–Karabakh. Demonstrations in Yerevan calling for President Ter–Petrossian's resignation and for new parliamentary elections did occur in February 1993, but many of the demonstrators were critical of the president precisely because he had not pursued the war against Azerbaijan firmly enough.

Russia brokered another cease–fire between Armenia and Azerbaijan in March 1994. Under the agreement, Russian troops were to be stationed around the borders of Nagorno–Karabakh and both sides were to withdraw troops, heavy guns and aircraft. The ceasefire lasted approximately six weeks before heavy fighting erupted in April. A new cease–fire eventually set in, however. With no solution to the problem of Nagorno–Karabakh in sight, however, Armenia remained cut off from its traditional energy supplies and its industries continued to operate only at an extremely low level.

Parliamentary elections, carried out in 1995, were won by President Ter–Petrossian's political party, but only after the government had moved to ban one of the opposition political parties. International observers later reported that the elections were unfair.

New presidential elections took place in September 1996, with President Ter–Petrossian a candidate for reelection. The president's chief opponent in the election was Vazgen Manukian, a former prime minister. The other candidates were Sergei Badalian, leader of the *Communist Party*, and Ashot Manucharian, the president's former national security adviser. The two chief issues in the campaign were the continuing stalemate with Azerbaijan over Nagorno–Karabakh and the state of the economy. A cease–fire with Azerbaijan had largely held since 1994 and the economy, which had grown by 7 percent in 1995—albeit from an extremely low level—continued to expand at about the same rate in 1996.

President Ter–Petrossian won with just under 52 percent of the vote, but the results were tainted by widespread charges of voting irregularities during the election. In consequence, his opponents protested the result and thousands of demonstrators gathered near the presidential palace to demand that the president step down. After three days of demonstrations, the government called in the armed forces

to break them up. Most of the opposition political leaders were jailed or went underground. All serious opposition was then banned.

Concerned about his growing unpopularity, President Ter–Petrossian dismissed his prime minister, Hrant Bagratian, in November 1996, supposedly because Bagratian, who had been prime minister since February 1993, had become increasingly unpopular because of his close identification with painful economic reforms. He then appointed Armen V. Sarkisyan as his new prime minister. It was certainly true that conditions for most Armenians remained severe, in large part because of the trade embargoes put into effect by both Azerbaijan and Turkey. Most outside observers were also convinced that Armenia could expect no significant longtime economic improvement unless it were able to reach a settlement of the conflict with Azerbaijan over Nagorno–Karabakh.

The Organization for Security and Cooperation in Europe (OSCE) put forth its terms for peace in November 1996. These terms, which became known as the Lisbon principles, essentially called for the restoration of Soviet era borders, broad autonomy for ethnic Armenians in the disputed region of Nagorno–Karabakh, and international guarantees of such a settlement.

The leaderships of both Armenia and Nagorno–Karabakh rejected the OSCE terms, but President Ter–Petrossian found himself coming under increasing international pressure to accede to the Lisbon principles in succeeding months. Recognizing that these demands from abroad threatened to weaken domestic support from among top military leaders as well as hardliners within his own party,

Ter–Petrossian, in March 1997, asked Robert Kocharian, then president of the unrecognized Republic of Nagorno–Karabakh, to become his prime minister.

The president and his prime minister worked closely together over the next several months, drawing up plans for economic reform. Then President Ter–Petrossian dropped a bombshell in September 1997 when he gave a press conference in which he admitted publicly for the first time that the status quo was untenable. He then went on effectively to endorse the OSCE Lisbon principles, suggesting that Nagorno–Karabakh could retain effective independence, but would technically have to remain part of Azerbaijan. The president had apparently become persuaded that all of his plans for economic reform would fail without peace.

But this was the beginning of the end for Ter–Petrossian. Not only did his opponents call him a traitor; he also came under severe attack from members of his own party and of the government, particularly from his military allies. One of his severest critics was his prime minister, Robert Kocharian, who essentially argued that Ter–Petrossian was wrong and that Armenia could rebuild its economy while continuing its support for Nagorno–Karabakh.

President Ter–Petrossian's resignation came on February 3, 1998. Speaking on national television, he said that he was resigning in response to demands by "state bodies well known to you." Although he characterized his resignation as "the defeat of the honorable party of peace in Armenia," he argued that differences over Nagorno–Karabakh were just a pretext

Looking down the main boulevard in Yerevan   Courtesy: NOVOSTI

Armenia

that hard-line forces were using to make him resign.

In line with the Armenian constitution, Robert Kocharian then became prime minister and acting president. He also became a candidate for election to a full term as president, in spite of the fact that, as a former president of Nagorno–Karabakh, he could hardly claim to have been a citizen of Armenia for ten years as required by the constitution. Kocharian had the support of several political parties, organized as the *Justice and Unity Bloc*.

In the first round of voting, which took place on March 16, 1998, Kocharian won 38.82 percent of the vote, followed by Karen Demirchian, candidate of the *Armenian Communist Party*, with 30.62 percent. Vazgen Manukian, head of the *National Democratic Union*, came third with 12.22 percent and Sergei Baldalian came fourth with 11.02 percent. Since no candidate won a majority, a second round of voting took place on March 30. Here Robert Kocharian came in first with 59.7 percent of the vote.

Eleven days later, he chose Armen Darbinian, his 33–year old finance and economy minister, as his new prime minister. Darbinian, who also served as first deputy chairman of the Armenian Central Bank from 1994 until May 1997, when he became finance minister, was known internationally as an economic reformer. After becoming prime minister, he concentrated on domestic economic policy, with an emphasis on encouraging private enterprise. In June 1998, for example, he announced that the Armenian state airline company would be put up for international sale, arguing that "privatization is the only way to guarantee its efficient and competitive work."

This emphasis on privatization brought in $98 million in direct foreign investment during the first six months of 1998 and contributed to an annual growth rate of 6.7 percent during this period. Although this was impressive, the IMF resident representative cautioned that the growth took place from a "very low base."

The Armenian economy suffered something of a setback during the last half of the year, reflecting Russia's financial collapse in September. In particular, Russian investors sold off Armenian government bonds, thus causing a drop in value of the *dram*, Armenia's national currency. Armenia's tight fiscal and monetary policies saved the country from most of the effects of the Russian collapse, though economic growth was slowing as 1998 ended. In December 1998, the parliament passed a 1999 budget which had the approval of the IMF and the World Bank. Although it included a budget deficit of 5.3 percent of GDP, 95 percent of this deficit was covered by foreign loans.

Elections to the 131–member National Assembly, which took place on May 30, 1999, were won by the *Miasnutyun* (Unity) alliance, which took 41.67 percent of the vote. The *Miasnutyun* alliance was comprised of the *Republican Party of Armenia*, headed by then Defense Minister Vazgen Sargsian, and the *People's Party of Armenia*, led by Karen Demirchian, former first secretary of the *Communist Party of Armenia*. The *Miasnutyun* alliance won 29 of the 56 seats allocated under the proportional system plus 28 of the 75 seats allocated in single–mandate constituencies, giving it a total of 57 seats. By contrast, the former ruling *Armenian Pan–National Movement* squeaked into the National Assembly with a single seat. Since 32 deputies ran and won as independents, it was not difficult for the *Miasnutyun* alliance to put together a majority in the National Assembly. After the electoral results were in, Armen Darbinian submitted his resignation as prime minister. President Kocharian then named Vazgen Sargsian as the new prime minister on June 10. Karen Demirchian was elected to the position of parliamentary speaker.

Prime Minister Sargsian pledged to continue the liberal reforms begun by his predecessor, though he indicated that he would attempt to minimize the economic hardships they had caused for much of the population. He also promised to crack down on corruption and tighten the government's supervision of investment policy. International financial organizations liked Sargsian's policies; in October 1999, the World Bank pledged a further $238 million to fund development projects in Armenia over the following three years while, at the same time, agreeing to disburse a third and final structural adjustment credit worth $23.5 million to help offset the country's budget deficit.

However, tragedy struck on October 27 when five gunmen burst into the parliament and began shooting. They killed Prime Minister Sargsian, parliamentary speaker Karen Demirchian and his two deputies, a government minister, and two parliamentary deputies. Six other parliamentary deputies were seriously wounded.

The gunmen held about 40 persons hostage overnight, then surrendered to the authorities the following morning. Three of the men were charged with terrorism aimed at undermining authority, but the reason for the attack never became clear. Although Nairi Hunanian, the leader of the assault, had earlier been associated with the Armenian Revolutionary Federation, a radical nationalist party, the party itself denied any connection with the attack. Hunanian, who had worked as a journalist, first said that the group was staging a *coup*, but later said that they only

wanted to protest the country's economic collapse, for which they held Sargsian responsible.

Shocked by the events, the Armenian parliament met in emergency session on November 2 and elected *People's Party* member Armen Khachatrian as parliamentary speaker. Gagik Aslanian, also a member of the *People's Party*, and Tigran Torosian, of the *Republican Party*, were elected deputy speakers. Those two parties constituted the majority *Miasnutyun* parliament faction.

One day later, President Kocharian appointed Aram Sargsian to succeed his murdered elder brother as prime minister. The 38–year old Sargsian had been elected a deputy to the parliament in May 1999 but had no other political experience. He turned out to be a disappointment as prime minister and lasted only six months. Within weeks of taking office, he became embroiled in a series of political assaults on the presidency; he was finally dismissed as prime minister on May 2, 2000.

His successor, appointed ten days later, was Andranik Markarian, chairman of the *Republican Party of Armenia*, the larger of the two parties in the ruling *Unity* alliance. Markarian, a computer specialist, served a three–year term in prison in the 1970s for his membership in an underground nationalist party called the *National Unity Party*.

Markarian, in his first speech as prime minister, promised that "reform should be the main essence of economic change;" however, little changed under him. One reason is that the ruling *Unity* alliance largely disintegrated in September 2001 after the leader of the *People's Party of Armenia (HZhK)*, the junior partner in the coalition, declared the *Unity* alliance to be defunct, called Markarian a stooge of President Kocharian, and called for new parliamentary elections. Following these events, over half of the membership of the *HZhK* defected to the opposition. Even the *Republican Party of Armenia* lost 11 of its members, reducing it to 46 deputies. Having lost its majority, the government only remained in power because the 20 member *Kaynutyun* (Stability) parliament group agreed to support the government without becoming part of the government coalition.

Intending to stand for reelection but without a party structure or organization of his own to back him, President Kocharian was dependent on the support of the oligarchs and power elites of the country. Two of the most important of his supporters were Prime Minister Andranik Markarian, leader of the *Republican Party of Armenia,* and Defense Minister Serzh Sarkisian. To widen his support, President Kocharian proposed a series of constitutional amendments—favored by most of the opposition political parties, particularly those on the left—whose effect would be to somewhat reduce the powers of the president. Although these amendments did not go as far as the left wanted—most argued for the replacement of the presidential system with a parliamentary system—it did increase Kocharian's popular support.

When the Armenian local elections took place on October 20, 2002, Prime Minister Andranik Markarian's *Republican Party of Armenia* won the post of mayor in 30 of Armenia's 37 towns and cities. Since Markarian was supporting President Kocharian for re–election, this indicated that he would be difficult to beat.

Realizing this, the political opposition began discussions aimed at uniting behind a single presidential candidate. In November, Stepan Demirchian, chairman of the *People's Party of Armenia (HZhK)*, won the support of 15 other opposition political parties, but this opposition unity began to unravel in November when the *National Accord Party*, the *Communist Party*, and the *Socialist Armenia* bloc formed a separate alliance to field joint candidates in both the presidential and parliamentary elections. By the time the presidential voting took place on February 19, there were nine candidates vying for the presidency.

President Kocharian came in first but, because he won only 49.5 percent of the vote, he was forced into a run–off with Stepan Demirchian, who placed second with 28.2 percent of the vote. President Kocharian easily won the run–off on March 5 with 65.5 percent of the vote, but there were numerous irregularities which were reported on by outside observers. Charging that the election was marred by legal, constitutional, and procedural violations, Demirchian requested the Constitutional Court to void the election. The Constitutional Court ruled against Demirchian, but it did order the Prosecutor General's Office to launch a criminal investigation into those irregularities.

With new parliamentary elections scheduled to take place on May 25, 2003, the political opposition made those irregularities the basis of its campaign as it attempted to discredit the pro–presidential parties. The opposition also gave a great deal of publicity to the fact that the Constitutional Court had recommended a "referendum of confidence" in the country's leadership.

Because the parties and blocs contesting the election were in basic agreement on all policy issues, the major issue became whether a candidate was a supporter or opponent of President Kocharian. Opponents were organized as the *Artarutiun*

(Justice) bloc, which brought together the parties that had supported Stepan Demirchian in the presidential elections. The *National Unity Party*, headed by Artashes Geghamian, campaigned as part of the opposition, though its only major platform issue was its demand that the elections themselves be free, fair, and democratic. That put it in the opposition precisely because so many Armenians questioned whether Kocharian and his supporters were prepared to ensure that the ballot was truly free and fair.

In the end, the opposition won an impressive share of the votes, but failed to gain control of parliament. The three pro–presidential parties—the *Republican Party of Armenia (HHK)*, the *Armenian Revolutionary Federation*, and the *Orinats Yerkir*—came in first, third, and fourth with 26.4 percent, 12.1 percent and 11.1 percent of the votes, giving them a majority of the seats in the parliament. The *Artarutiun* bloc pulled 14.3 percent, while the *National Unity Party* got 9.7 percent. The *Communist Party of Armenia* drew less than five percent and so failed to win any proportional seats. In addition to the proportional seats, the *HHK* won 12 single–mandate constituencies, and *Orinats Yerkir* six; the opposition *Artarutiun* bloc won three.

In a joint statement released after the election, the OSCE and the Council of Europe characterized the voting as "a marked improvement" over the February–March presidential election, but it still "failed to meet international standards in several key areas."

After several relatively quiet months, the opposition, led by Stepan Demirchian, began organizing demonstrations demanding a referendum on President Kocharian's rule. These political attacks escalated after the so-called "Rose Revolution" in neighboring Georgia led to the resignation of President Shevardnadze.

Hoping for a similar result, the Armenian opposition demanded that President Kocharian step down and permit new elections. As the demonstrations continued, the opposition bloc announced a boycott of parliament. The boycott was not total, however; the two dozen deputies from the *Artarutiun* bloc and the *National Accord party* continued to attend debates on "crucial" issues such as constitutional reform and amending election legislation.

In 2005, the Armenian Government submitted a set of draft constitutional amendments to the Parliamentary Assembly of the Council of Europe for its approval prior to bringing them up for discussion and vote in the legislature. The Council of Europe's Venice Commission endorsed the changes—as did both the European Union and the U. S. Government—but the

political opposition was not mollified. When the constitutional amendments came up to a vote in the Armenian legislature, the opposition quit the chamber prior to the vote and thereafter urged a boycott of the November 27 referendum on the amendments.

In the end, the boycott was unsuccessful. According to the government, there was a 65.3 percent turnout for the referendum and a 93 percent positive vote for the amendments. The opposition claimed massive fraud, however, and began to organize mass rallies and demonstrations in an effort to overturn the result. The protests had no sustained mass participation, however, so Stepan Demirchian withdrew his support for the mass rallies in December 2005. Things then quieted down, though the opposition continued to boycott parliament.

With new parliamentary elections scheduled to take place in May 2007, signs of a political realignment began surfacing in 2006 in both the government coalition and in the opposition *Artarutiun* bloc. In May 2006, the *Orinats Yerkir* party pulled out of the government coalition after its leader, then parliament speaker Artur Baghdasarian, gave an interview to a German newspaper advocating future membership for Armenia in the EU and NATO. Baghdasarian was forced to resign as parliamentary speaker after being verbally abused by President Kocharian, presumably because Kocharian saw the parliament speaker's statement as a challenge to the president's pro-Russian foreign policy.

As it turned out, this did not affect the government majority because ten *Orinats Yerkir* party members left to form a new party pledged to continued cooperation with the government, while the six-member *United Labor Party* joined the government coalition at this time. And, in another development, Defense Minister Serzh Sarkisian formally joined the *Republican Party of Armenia (HHK)*; he subsequently was appointed chairman of its governing council.

As for the political opposition, Stepan Demirchian, nominal leader of the nine-party opposition *Artarutiun* bloc, announced in April 2006 that his *People's Party of Armenia* was considering contesting the next elections on its own. His statement was probably triggered by rumors that at least three parties belonging to the opposition bloc had threatened to leave the bloc.

In fact, several oppositional politicians formally joined pro-government political parties over the next several months. Another prominent opposition figure, Victor Dallakian, left the *Artarutiun (Justice)* bloc and joined the *Prosperous Armenia* party,

Armenia

the party of millionaire businessman Gagik Tsarukian, a close associate of President Kocharian. These defections reduced the size of the *Artarutiun* bloc to 12 seats.

The next change came in March 2007 when Prime Minister Andranik Markarian died suddenly of a heart attack. His successor is Serzh Sarkisian, the former Defense Minister. It is also expected that Sarkisian will be the candidate of the ruling *Republican Party of Armenia (HHK)* for president in 2008.

In the May 12 parliamentary elections, Prime Minister Sarkisian's *Republican Party of Armenia (HHK)* came in first with 33.8 percent of the proportional vote; the *Prosperous Armenia* party, headed by wealthy businessman Gagik Tsarukian, came in second with 15.1 percent of the vote. The *Armenian Revolutionary Federation-Dashnaktsutiun (HHD)* came in third with 13.1 percent of the vote. The other two parties to garner the minimum 5 percent of the vote needed to win proportional representation were the opposition *Orinats Yerkir (Law-based State)* party, which pulled 6.8 percent of the vote, and the *Zharangutiun (Heritage)* party of former U.S.-born Foreign Minister Raffi Hovannisian, which got 6 percent. Factoring in wins in the 41 single-mandate seats, the final parliamentary distribution is expected to be *HHK* 57 seats; *Prosperous Armenia* 24 seats; the *HHD* 16 seats; the *Orinats Yerkin* 10 seats; *Zharangutiun* 7 seats; and the *Dashink (Alliance)* party one seat.

Foreign Policy

Armenia is technically at war with its eastern neighbor, Azerbaijan. Though there has been only sporadic fighting since a ceasefire signed in 1994, this continues to be a major factor in Armenia's domestic and foreign policies, since it colors its relationships with all of its neighbors. This situation got even more complicated in 1998 when Robert Kocharian, the former president of Nagorno–Karabakh, was elected president of Armenia. Kocharian's official position at that time was that Nagorno–Karabakh had to have the right to decide its own future status *vis–à–vis* the Azerbaijani Government; at the same time, he also made it clear that he would not support any proposed settlement that would directly subordinate Nagorno–Karabakh to Azerbaijan. Kocharian's preferred solution was a "horizontal" arrangement between Nagorno–Karabakh and Azerbaijan based on "federative or confederative relations." It is not clear how such an arrangement would work out in practice but, in any case, Azerbaijan has always opposed granting Nagorno–Karabakh anything more than autonomy.

Armenian Prime Minister Serzh Sarkisian

Azerbaijani President Aliyev and President Kocharian met for the first time in 2000 and continued to meet periodically down through 2003. Although these conversations produced no breakthrough, they did indicate that both leaders favored a resolution to the situation if one could be found that was minimally acceptable to their own peoples. The OSCE Minsk Group became involved in 2002. The OSCE had been working on a draft of a modified version of its peace plan and the OSCE Minsk Group arranged meetings with the deputy foreign ministers of Armenia and Azerbaijan. These talks were inconclusive but they did lead to a four–hour meeting of the two presidents, which took place in the village of Sadarak on the border between Armenia and Naxcivan (Nakhichevan). The two presidents met again on November 22 on the sidelines of the NATO summit in Prague, which led to speculations about a proposal that might prove acceptable to both sides. Two weeks later, however, President Kocharian harshly criticized Azerbaijan's approach to resolving the Karabakh conflict when he addressed the OSCE Ministerial Council meeting in Porto, Portugal.

Foreign matters were largely put on hold during Armenia's 2003 presidential and parliamentary elections; by the time they were out of the way, President Aliyev was already ill and in a hospital in the United States. His subsequent death left relations between the two neighbors in limbo. When Ilham Aliyev, the son, won the presidency in November 2003, he retained most of his father's advisers, but spent the next year or so consolidating his control domestically. The two presidents did meet in Warsaw in May 2005 and again in February 2006 in France. They have continued to meet periodically since that time, but there has been no breakthrough. Both presidents remain committed to a peaceful resolution to the Karabakh conflict, but they cannot

agree on basic principles for resolving their differences.

Armenia has fairly good relations with Georgia and Iran, but its relations with Turkey are cold, partly because Armenia refuses to renounce its traditional claim to Armenian Turkey and partly because Turkey tends to favor Azerbaijan in its war with Armenia. Although Turkey did recognize Armenia's independence in 1991, it has refused to establish diplomatic relations with Armenia and it has maintained an embargo on Armenian goods since 1993.

It appeared for a while that a breakthrough in Turkish–Armenian relations might have occurred when Suleiman Demirel, the Turkish president, invited President Kocharian to attend the 75th anniversary celebrations of the founding of the Republic of Turkey on October 29–30, 1998. Kocharian accepted the invitation, and this led to an improvement in the atmospherics, but there was no breakthrough. Then the atmosphere cooled once again when President Kocharian, in remarks made during ceremonies commemorating the 91st anniversary of the 1915 genocide of Armenians in Ottoman Turkey (in April 2006), publicly declared that "Ottoman Turkey and its legal successor bear full responsibility for this crime."

In March 2007, the Turkish Government invited Hasmik Poghosian, the Armenian Minister of Culture, to attend the inauguration of a recently restored tenth century Armenian church, located on an island in Lake Van. Poghosian accepted the invitation, but he was criticized harshly inside Armenia by individuals who charged that Turkey was using its restoration of the church for propaganda purposes.

Armenia has always favored good relations with Russia and has seen active participation in the Commonwealth of Independent States as part of that policy. Russia and Armenia have signed a series of bilateral agreements in recent years whose purpose was to boost military cooperation. The most significant such document, signed in August 1997, was a treaty "on friendship, cooperation, and mutual assistance" under which Russia, for the first time, committed itself in an accord to defend an ally militarily in the event that the ally was attacked by a foreign country. The treaty also calls for coordination of military–technical policy, mutual development of defense industries, standardization of military hardware, and joint financing of military projects. This treaty was supplemented in 2001 by a bilateral agreement on the common use of Armenian and Russian forces for "ensuring common security." There are currently two Russian military bases in Armenia. Russia and Armenia have also discussed setting up a joint military unit whose primary focus would be terrorism.

Russia and Armenia have negotiated a number of economic accords, including one that established a joint venture for the re–export of Russian gas to Turkey. Another, signed in March 2002, provided for the transfer of five state–run Armenian companies to Russia in payment of a $94 million debt that Armenia owed the Russian Government. The Armenian parliament ratified this particular agreement in December 2002. In their joint statement after President Kocharian's three–day visit to Moscow in January 2003, Presidents Putin and Kocharian praised the level of bilateral political, economic, and military cooperation between their countries. Separately, President Kocharian characterized the relations as "close to ideal." In 2006, the Russian state-owned Unified Energy Systems purchased the Armenian power-distribution system for $73 million from British-registered Midland Resources Holding.

Americans tend to be sympathetic to Armenia and this is reflected in the aid program that the U.S. Government instituted in 1993. In 2006, the U. S. Government announced that $236 million had been allocated to Armenia under the Millennium Challenge program.

The events of September 11 and America's subsequent worldwide campaign against terrorism affected Armenia directly because the United States decided to partially waive Section 907 of the Freedom Support Act (that barred direct U.S. Government aid to Azerbaijan as long as that country maintained its embargo against Armenia and Nagorno–Karabakh) because of Azerbaijan's assistance in the war against terrorism. During two days of talks during a visit to Washington in October 2001, Foreign Minister Oskanian expressed Armenia's disquiet at the partial lifting of Section 907, but said that Armenia understood the U.S. Government's need for flexibility in dealing with Azerbaijan for an effective fight against terrorism. Armenia's own commitment to the war against terrorism brought an invitation to Defense Minister Sarkisian to visit the United States in March 2002. During this visit, which Sarkisian described as marking "the beginning of American–Armenian military consultations," the United States offered training to Armenian military personnel and assistance in upgrading Armenian communications facilities.

Armenia has excellent relations with Iran, and Iran is, in fact, Armenia's chief trading partner. The reason for cultivating good relations with Iran is not difficult to discover, however. At war with Azerbai-

Presidential candidate Robert Kocharian campaigns in Yerevan

jan and with Turkey enforcing an embargo against Armenian products, only Iran and Georgia remain. And Georgia has been nearly as badly off economically as Armenia. What has given Armenia the opportunity to develop such relations is that Iran has poor relations with Azerbaijan, partly because it fears Azerbaijani influences on Azeris within Iran, partly because Azerbaijan has welcomed American companies and their billions of dollars of investment.

Armenia has also made major efforts to counteract its lack of relations with Azerbaijan and Turkey by building up its relations with other countries in the area.

President Kocharian paid an official visit to Tajikistan in April 2002. Four bilateral documents were signed that included an Agreement on Friendship and Cooperation. The talks also covered bilateral military cooperation and regional security.

In March 2002, President Kocharian had negotiations with President Niyazov of Turkmenistan which resulted in an agreement for Armenia to purchase two billion cubic meters of Turkmen gas annually. Because the gas has to be shipped by way of Iran, a new gas pipeline connecting Armenia and Iran had to be built; it was completed in March 2007.

Armenia was admitted to the United Nations at the same time as the other members of the Commonwealth of Independent States. It is also a member of the Council for Security and Cooperation in Europe, the IMF and World Bank, and a full member of the Council of Europe.

Armenia's long–term goal of joining the European Union received a boost in September 2002 when the Armenia–EU parliamentary commission expressed its support. The following month, the Arme-

nia– EU coordinating council announced an agreement on creating "new mechanisms for broader EU engagement and political consultation." Already, the EU countries are collectively Armenia's largest trading partner. Armenia's application for membership in the World Trade Organization was approved in December 2002. Armenia had applied for membership six years earlier, but its membership was held up while the government worked to draw up and pass a new customs code plus other legislation required by the WTO dealing with matters such as VAT and excise taxes.

Armenia was also granted observer status in the NATO Parliamentary Assembly in May 2002. In November, Armenia hosted a three–day NATO conference in Yerevan, a sort of preparatory conference to discuss military exercises scheduled to take place in Armenia in June 2003 under the Partnership for Peace program. The following month, a NATO delegation headed by former Supreme Allied Commander Europe General Joseph Ralston arrived in Yerevan for meetings with President Kocharian, Foreign Minister Oskanian, and Defense Minister Sarkisian. Ralston and Kocharian also discussed Armenia's participation in the Kosovo peace-keeping operation.

Armenia signed an individual Partnership Action Plan with NATO in 2005. President Kocharian has made it clear however that, while he values the individual Partnership Action Plan, his government "is not going to join NATO."

The Nature of the Regime

The National Assembly instituted a modified proportional system prior to the 1999 legislative elections. At that time, 56 of the 131 seats were to be apportioned proportionally with the remainder elected in single mandate seats. In July 2002, the National Assembly raised the number of proportional seats to 75 and that system was used for the 2003 legislative elections. Since the new law kept the number of deputies at 131, the total number of single–mandate constituencies was reduced from 75 to 56.

In May 2005, parliament amended the electoral law again, to take effect at the 2007 parliamentary elections. Under this latest legislation, the proportion of parliamentary mandates distributed under the proportional system was raised to 90 and the number of single-mandate constituencies was reduced to 41.

The legislation also reduced from three to one the number of members which the president was empowered to name to the electoral commissions, and it transferred responsibility for maintaining accurate voter lists from the local authorities to the

Armenia

police. The changes, which were endorsed by the Council of Europe, were supposed to help minimize electoral fraud.

According to international observers, the May 12, 2007, elections largely complied with international standards. In the lead-up to the elections, opposition political parties held public rallies without police harassment, and they were allowed free air time on public television. In the end, however, neither the *People's Party of Armenia* nor the radical opposition *Hanrapetutiun* party (headed by former Prime Minister Aram Sargsian) won any representation.

The big winner in the 2007 elections was Prime Minister Sarkisian's *Republican Party of Armenia (HHK)*, which came in first with 33.8 percent of the proportional vote; the *Prosperous Armenia* party, headed by wealthy businessman Gagik Tsarukian, came in second with 15.1 percent of the vote. The *Armenian Revolutionary Federation-Dashnaktsutiun (HHD)* came in third with 13.1 percent of the vote. The other two parties to garner the minimum 5 percent of the vote needed to win proportional representation were the opposition *Orinats Yerkir (Law-based State)* party (6.8 percent of the vote), and the *Zharangutiun (Heritage)* party of former U.S.-born Foreign Minister Raffi Hovannisian (6 percent).

Factoring in wins in the 41 single-mandate seats, the final parliamentary distribution is expected to be *HHK* 57 seats; *Prosperous Armenia* 24 seats; the *HHD* 16 seats; the *Orinats Yerkin* 10 seats; *Zharangutiun* 7 seats; and the *Dashink (Alliance)* party one seat.

Culture

Traditional Armenian culture has deep historic roots that reach back as far as the 5th century when the first written literature began. Two works that date from that period are Movses Khorenatsi's *History of Armenia* and Eznik Koghbatsi's *Refutation of the Sects*. The two themes represented by the works, history and religion, continued to be important in subsequent centuries, but they gradually began to be expressed in new forms.

Grigor Narekatsi, who lived in the 10th century, was Armenia's first great poet. A deeply religious man, his mystical poems and hymns heavily influenced the Armenian Orthodox Church and led to his canonization after his death.

A secular tradition began to emerge in the 16th–18th centuries with the appearance of popular bards (troubadours). Known as *ashugh*, they produced numerous love songs which are now known by the people. The 19th century saw the emergence of both the novel and the short story. Famous Armenian novelists include

Hakob Paronian, Ervand Otian and Hakob Maliq–Hakobian, whose pen name is "Raffi." Paronian also wrote plays, as did Gabriel Sundukian.

The communist era had a negative effect on Armenian culture; it rejected nearly every theme associated with traditional literature. Pre–revolutionary novelists and playwrights continued to be read and performed, but modern writers were required to conform to communism's "socialist realism," a requirement which turned them into party hacks.

There were some good Armenian writers during the 20th century, and these include Hovhannes Tumanian, Paruir Sevak, Avetik Isahakian, and Eghishe Charents. If none of these writers ever became known outside of Armenia, it is nevertheless true that the 20th century did produce Armenia's first great composer, Aram Katchaturian, probably because it was hard for Moscow authorities to apply "socialist realism" to classical music. Two lesser known composers of this period were Komitas and Alexander Spendiarian.

ՍԱ ԵՐԵՎԱՆՆ Է

Ինչ գով գիշեր է. մեկն ինչ հիշել է.
Նա ինչ հուշել է անհուշելին.
Նա է իմ հույսր, անպարապկույար
Նա է իմ լույսր՝ մութ գիշերին:

Նա, ով եկել էր. կյանքս պեկել էր.
Բախտս պեկել էր ինքն իր բախտին.
Բայց արդեն ուշ է. հուշր մշուշ է.
Սերր քրքուշ էր կեսգիշերին:

Ներս արի. ներս արի. ի°նչ ես կանգնել.
ի°նչ ես հիմար ժպիտով քարացել:

Սա Երևանն է. այստեղ դու պանն ես.
Ուր քեզ սպասում են դեռ կեսգիշերին:
Ուր կամ սիրում են. կամ քունդ հայհոյում են.
Երբ հիշեցնում են անհիշելին:

Ներս արի. ներս արի. ի°նչ ես կանգնել.
ի°նչ ես հիմար ժպիտով քարացել:

Սա քո փողոցն է. կյանքիդ դպրոցը.
Ուր քեզ հիշում են. դեռ չեն մոռացել:
Սա քո փողոցն է. կյանքիդ դպրոցը.
Ուր քեզ հիշում են. դեռ չեն մոռացել:

Ինչ գով գիշեր է. մեկն ինչ հիշել է.
Նա ինչ հուշել է անհուշելին.
Բայց արդեն ուշ է. հուշր մշուշ է.
Սերր քրքուշ էր. կեսգիշերին:

1995

Sa Erevann e (This is Yerevan), the lyrics of a song by Rouben Hakhverdian, a famous contemporary Armenian singer and song-writer.

Armenian student with her Estonian friend

Two famous artists from this period were Martiros Saryan and Minas Avetisian. Armenia also has its famous actors, including V. Papazian and H. Nersisyan.

Famous Armenians living abroad who were considered to be part of Armenian culture included Charles Aznavour, a popular singer who lived in France; William Saroyan, a playwright who lived in the United States; and Atom Egoyan, a film director who lived in Canada.

Communism did leave behind an established society which will help Armenian culture to develop further in the future. There is both a state radio and television broadcasting system with studios in Yerevan. The city is also the site of a State Academic Theater of Opera and Ballet. Several drama theaters also exist, a national dance company, several orchestras and a film studio.

Old folk arts such as dancing, singing and artistic crafts were left undisturbed by communism. Thus, the new non–communist government has a firm basis on which to build. An Armenian Academy of Sciences runs a number of research institutes throughout the country.

Economy

Armenia today is overwhelmingly an urban and industrial society, with agriculture perhaps accounting for a fifth of the national income. Three fifths of the country's industries are located in and around the city of Yerevan, however, and because so many of them are types of heavy industry which heavily pollute, Yerevan today is one of the most polluted cities of the former Soviet Union. These include factories which produce synthetic rubber, fertilizers, chemicals, nonferrous metals, machines and equipment. It also produces other polluting minerals; all of these have badly polluted large areas of the countryside. The government will probably deal with this problem in the coming years.

It also has light industry—textiles, carpet–weaving, food processing, wine–making, fruit, meat–canning and creameries. Medium industries include electrical equipment, precision instruments and machine tools. It is also a large producer of cement, marble, pumice, volcanic basalt and fireproof clay.

Industry, which makes up about 41 percent of the economy, suffered a sharp collapse between 1991 and 1993 and only began to recover in 1994. Essentially, this occurred largely as a result of Armenia's political quarrel with Azerbaijan over the Armenian–populated enclave of Nagorno-Karabakh. From the beginning of the fighting, Azerbaijan maintained an embargo against Armenia; as the war continued, it was joined by Turkey, which instituted a blockade against Armenian goods in 1993. As a result, Armenian industry had great difficulty obtaining energy supplies and raw materials. Petroleum and gas, which formerly came from Azerbaijan and Turkmenistan, remained in short supply until Armenia negotiated a deal with Iran for the delivery of petroleum. A similar agreement was signed with Turkmenistan for the purchase of natural gas. In December 2004, construction began on a gas pipeline connecting Armenia to Iran in December 2004;

the line was completed in March 2007. The Iranian pipeline provides (Iranian and Turkmenistani) natural gas to the thermal power plant in Hrazdan, recently modernized by a state-owned Iranian company.

A high-voltage transmission line connecting Armenia to Iran was constructed three years ago; a second such line went into operation at the beginning of 2007. In this instance, energy is actually exchanged between the two countries on a seasonal basis with Armenia exporting excess electricity in the spring and summer and importing it in the winter. Also, Armenia reopened the Medzamor nuclear plant in 1995; it now relies on that source for much of its electricity, though it is under continuing pressure from the European Union to close the plant. Armenia also signed a trilateral agreement on energy with Georgia and Iran in late 2006, under which the three countries agreed to "synchronize" and link their power grids.

As a direct result of its conflict with Azerbaijan, the Armenian economy suffered a 63 percent drop in GDP between 1991 and 1993. The economy gradually stabilized in 1993, then began growing again. GDP grew by 5.4 percent in 1994, by 6.9 percent in 1995, and by 5.8 percent in 1996. Inflation, which has been in four

Ultra-modern Zvartnots Airport in Yerevan

Armenia

figures in 1993, dropped to 5.7 percent in 1996.

In a reversal of this trend, GDP grew by only 2.7 percent in 1997, while inflation hit 21 percent. GDP growth reached nearly 6 percent in 1998, however, and industrial output, which had stagnated in 1997, grew by 4.3 percent.

Armenia launched a program of privatization based on vouchers in 1994, but the program was not very successful because it failed to inject new capital into enterprises or change the way that they were managed. Accordingly, the government launched a new program in 1997 which involved a shift toward market capital. Examples of that approach, which was further expanded in 1998, include the sale of a 90 percent interest in Armentel, the national telecommunications company, to a Greek consortium, and the Canadian company that invested $200 million in gold mining.

Total direct foreign investment reached $98 million in the first half of 1998, though it dropped off in the latter part of the year after the Russian market collapse. On the other hand, General Motors announced in January 1999 that it planned to begin manufacturing minibuses, small tractors, and trucks in Armenia, and planned to sell its products throughout the region.

Growth was slower in 1999 and 2000, but picked up again in 2001 when GDP growth was a torrid 9.1 percent. The Armenian Government launched another round of privatization in 2001 when it put 300 large and medium state–owned industries up for sale. Many of the firms were loss–making, however, so buyers were scarce. In the end, the government managed to sell about 225 of the firms, earning a total of about $4.5 million. As an example, one of the firms put up for sale was the Armenian power grid which was crippled by losses of $50 million a year and a debt of some $100 million. The government accepted an offer to buy a 81.1 percent stake in the company for $40 million in August 2002. However the buyer, a Canadian citizen whose company was registered in the Channel Islands, reneged on the deal. The Armenian Government then negotiated a deal with the Daewoo Engineering group of South Korea, which assumed full management of the energy distribution network in December 2002. In September 2005, the Armenian Government agreed to sell the network to Unified Energy Systems (EES), the Russian Government-owned company. EES took final control of the network in September 2006.

Foreign investment has been growing for several years, though it remains at a fairly low level, perhaps $300 million a year. The economy has now been growing at double digits for six years, since 2001. It grew at a 12 percent rate in 2002; a 15 percent rate in 2003; 10.1 percent in 2004; 13.9 percent in 2005; and 13.2 percent in the first 11 months of 2006. Agriculture and capital construction were two areas of consistently faster growth, with industrial growth consistently much lower. Industry grew at a 2.1 percent rate in 2004, though the rate increased to 7.5 percent in 2005.

Small and medium-sized firms now account for more than 40 percent of total GDP. One factor that inhibits industrial growth is that interest rates for small businesses average 20 percent or more. The government began addressing this problem in December 2002 when it created a new state fund of 250 million drams ($430,000) which is being used to provide credit guarantees for small and medium–sized businesses.

While the economy is making progress, Armenia continues to run budget deficits of 2–3 percent of GDP which must be covered by foreign loans. The 2007 budget, which is 16 percent larger than the previous year's budget, envisages revenues of 490 billion drams ($1.32 billion) and expenditures of 558.7 ($1.51 billion) drams. The 68.7 billion dram deficit is to be largely financed by domestic borrowing. Although defense spending makes up almost 19 percent of the budget, more than one-third of expenditures are earmarked for education, health care, social security, and other public services.

The country continues to have the support of both the IMF and World Bank for its economic policies. When Jerome Kremers, a senior IMF official, visited Yerevan in October 2005, he commended Armenia for its double-digit economic growth over the proceeding five years. He then announced a three-year $33 million credit which is to be used to increase tax collection and customs revenues and reduce poverty. Roger Robinson, head of the World Bank's office in Armenia 2001–2006, stated this previous October as he was leaving that he had witnessed "a significant change in the quality of life" in Armenia over those five years and added that he believed economic growth could continue over the next five to ten years, though he warned that it would require deeper "institutional reforms" dealing with governance, tax and customs administration, as well as the overall business environment.

The European Union signed an agreement with Armenia in March 2004 providing Armenia with $25 million in the years 2004–2007. The EU would like Armenia to decommission the Medzamor nuclear-power plant and has offered Armenia 100 million euros as an inducement to set a concrete date for doing so. Since Armenia receives 30 percent of its electricity from the plant, its position is that it can not do so until alternative energy sources are available. Since 2003, the Medzamor plant has been managed by RAO Unified Energy Systems, the Russian state electricity monopoly.

The United States Government announced in December 2005 that it had awarded Armenia a Millennium Challenge Grant worth $236 million which was to be made available over the next five years. $67 million is being spent to rehabilitate almost 600 miles of rural roads, while the remainder is to be used to finance irrigation projects and the introduction of higher-yield crops.

Agriculture contributes only about 19.8 percent of GDP to the economy than industry, but it continues to provide employment for almost half the population, either in agriculture itself or in related industries. Armenia began replacing the republic's state and collective farms with private agriculture even before it achieved its independence in 1991. The government has also set up regional scientific centers to offer consulting services to farmers and engage in long–term agricultural planning, but growth has been hindered by a weak market infrastructure and a lack of machines.

Armenia's most valuable agricultural product is probably grapes, from which famous wines, brandies and champagnes are made. Orchard crops are next in importance—peaches, apricots, apples, cherries, pears, pomegranates, walnuts, hazelnuts and almonds are abundant. Tobacco is another important cash crop. Extensive mountain pastures support a significant dairy industry, plus many sheep for wool and meat. Pigs and poultry are also raised.

The Future

Armenia's future is still clouded by its continuing quarrel with the Republic of Azerbaijan over Nagorno–Karabakh. So long as this situation remains unsettled, the Armenian economy will suffer from the embargoes maintained by Azerbaijan and Turkey. However, the economy has been growing since 1994, and the country has enjoyed double-digit growth since 2001. According to the World Bank, the quality of life within the country has improved greatly over the past five years.

Presidents Kocharian and Aliyev have publicly committed their two countries to a peaceful settlement of the Nagorno-Karabakh quarrel—and have met on a number of occasions in the past three years in an attempt to find such a solution—but there has been no breakthrough and no sign that one is likely in the near future.

The Republic of Azerbaijan

Area: 33,428 sq. mi. (86,600 sq. km.), about the size of Maine.

Population: 7.96 (July 2006 estimate).

Capital City: Baku (Pop. 1,782,000).

Climate: Generally dry, sub–tropical.

Neighboring States: Russia (north); Georgia (northwest); Armenia (west and east, where the Naxcivan (Nakhichevan) Region is separated from the rest of the country); Iran (south).

Language: Azerbaijani (Azeri).

Ethnic Background: Azeri (90%); Dagestani (3.2%); Russian (2.5%); Armenian, mainly within the enclave of Nagorno–Karabakh which lies within its borders (2%); others (2.3%).

Principal Religion: Islam, principally Shi'a.

Chief Commercial Products: Agriculture—grain, cotton, rice, grapes. Industry—oil, natural gas, concrete, nonferrous metals, alumina, carpets, processed food (fish, caviar, and meat), wine, cheese.

Currency: *manat.*

Per Capita Annual Income: $2,400.

Recent Political Status: Democratic Republic of Azerbaijan (May 28, 1918–April 1920); Azerbaijan S.S.R., founded in 1920; part of Transcaucasian Federation (1922–1936); Constituent republic of the USSR (1936–1991).

Chief of State: Ilham Aliyev, President (elected October 15, 2003).

Head of Government: Artur Rasizade, Prime Minister (re-appointed October 2003).

National Flag: Three equal horizontal stripes, sky blue, red and green, with a crescent moon and star superimposed in the center of the red.

National Day: May 28, (founding of the Democratic Republic of Azerbaijan).

The Land

The Republic of Azerbaijan (Azarbaycan Respublikasi), which was one of the 15 Soviet republics before the collapse of the Union of Soviet Socialist Republics in 1991, is located in an area south of the Caucasus Mountains along the western shores of the Caspian Sea. It covers an area of 33,428 square miles (86,600 sq. km.). Iran lies to the south, Armenia and Georgia to the west, and the Russian Federation to the north. It also includes the Naxcivan (Nakhichevan) Autonomous Republic, occupied mainly by Azeri but separated from the rest of Azerbaijan by the southeastern part of Armenia, and the Nagorno–Karabakh Region—which had the status of an autonomous republic until the Azerbaijani Supreme Soviet abolished it in November 1991—mainly occupied by Armenians.

More than 40 percent of Azerbaijan is lowlands, most of which are in the Kur River valley, which runs in a northwest direction beginning at the Caspian Sea and ending in the mountains of Georgia. The Kur River actually originates in the Small Caucasus Mountains, which stretch along the border between Georgia and Turkey. It flows down through the high valley of central Georgia before crossing the border into Azerbaijan.

The Aras River, a southern branch of the Kur, originates in the Aras Mountains of Turkey. It forms the southern boundary between Armenia and Turkey, between the Naxcivan (Nakhichevan) Autonomous Republic and Turkey and Iran, and between Azerbaijan and the Iranian province of Azerbaijan. It then turns northeast and joins the Kur River.

The remaining lowland areas include the Lenkoran Lowland in the south–east, plus a strip of land beginning at the Apsheron Peninsula, which juts out into the Caspian Sea to the north of the mouth of the Kur River, and then running north along the western shores of the Caspian.

To the northeast of the Kur River Valley, the chain of the Great Caucasus Mountains runs southeast, ending just before the Apsheron Peninsula. Here the highest mountains are over 14,000 feet, though most of the territory is covered by foothills running perpendicular to the line of the higher mountain ridge and varying in height from 1,300 to 4,900 feet.

Southward across the Kur River Valley, the ground again flows upward, becoming foothills then rising to become the Small Caucasus Mountains, which mark the border between Azerbaijan and Armenia. The Karabakh upland, where the Nagorno–Karabakh Region is situated, is also in this area.

The annual rainfall of the Kur–Aras Lowland varies from 8 to 16 inches and so has the plant life of the steppe and the semi–desert. A well–developed system of dams and canals means that most of the lowland is irrigated, however, and today most of the area is devoted to the cultiva-

Azerbaijan

tion of cotton. The largest of these dams is the Mingechaur, built in 1953 along the Kur River in northwestern Azerbaijan. Mingechaur Dam, which is also a major hydroelectric station, forms a lake that covers an area of 234 square miles and has a storage capacity of 565 trillion cubic feet.

The Kur River Valley has a dry, subtropical climate with hot summers and mild winters. Southeast Azerbaijan, which receives the most rainfall of any part of the republic, has a humid, subtropical climate. Here the annual rainfall is about 50 inches, which falls mainly in the winter. The Naxcivan (Nakhichevan) Autonomous Republic, with altitudes between 2,300 and 3,300 feet, has a dry, continental climate, with cold winters and dry summers.

The Caspian Sea shoreline has a Mediterranean type climate, cool in winter and dry in summer. Forests are found on the upper slopes of the Great Caucasus and Small Caucasus Mountains. The main trees are beech, oak and pine.

The People

The estimated population of Azerbaijan as of July 2002 is 7,798,497. Azeris or Azerbaijani, who make up about 90 percent of the population of the republic, are a Turkic–speaking people. They migrated into the area in the 11th century as part of the Oguz Seljuk migrations. There are another 16.5 million Azeris living across the border in northern Iran, an important factor in Azerbaijani–Iranian relations.

Dagestani, the largest minority, make up about 3.2 percent, followed by Russians (2.5%), and Armenians (2%). Iranians, Ukrainians and Kurds make up the remaining 2.3 percent. Most Russians reside in the major cities, particularly Baku, the capital and largest city, and Sumgait, an industrial city located 22 miles to the north.

History

After the Bolsheviks came to power in Moscow, national groups in Azerbaijan, Armenia and Georgia got together and established the Transcaucasian Federal Republic on April 22, 1918. It collapsed after one month. In Azerbaijan, a National Council of the Tatars, dominated by the Mussavat (Nationalist) Party, announced the birth of the Democratic Republic of Azerbaidzhan on May 28, 1918. This government continued to exist until April 1920, when it was overthrown by the Red Army. The communists established the Azerbaijan Soviet Socialist Republic on April 28, 1920.

This was the beginning of Azerbaijani political history. Prior to that time, the Azeri were an undifferentiated Islamic people, first under Persian then under Russian rule, of the area of the Transcaucasus.

Peter the Great was the first Russian ruler to take an interest in the area, when he occupied Baku in 1723. The coastal region actually became Russian in 1813 by the Treaty of Gulistan, under which Persia ceded the lands bordering the western shores of the Caspian Sea from the Lenkoran Lowland northward to Derbent. The interior was annexed by Russia in 1829.

Although Azerbaijan came under communist control in 1920, it remained theoretically independent until March 1922. It was then merged with Armenia and Georgia to form the Transcaucasian Soviet Federated Socialist Republic. The Transcaucasian SFSR became a formal part of the Union of Soviet Socialist Republics in December 1922. Fourteen years later, under the terms of Stalin's 1936 Constitution, the Transcaucasian SFSR was dissolved and the Azerbaijan Soviet Socialist Republic reemerged.

Azerbaijan was a pliant republic under the communists until Gorbachëv's policy of *glasnost* began to challenge the old *status quo*. The situation had been building up over a number of years, however, in connection with jobs in the modern, industrial sector. Azeris were traditionally either nomads or farmers, so when the Baku oil industry was developed, most of the jobs went to Armenians or Russians. After the Russian Revolution, literacy campaigns gradually carried education to the countryside where most Azeris lived.

As more and more Azeris became educated, they began to be recruited for positions in industry and government. For a long time this was nominal, but the Brezhnev leadership, in particular, encouraged the development of native elites in the republics. This new Azerbaijani leadership founded numerous institutes of higher education and, increasingly, favored a policy of edging out non–Azeris and replacing them with Azeris. Thus there was a very distinct bias among the Azerbaijani political leadership to favor Azeri speakers. Armenians were a particular target of this policy.

Many Armenians from Armenia had taken jobs in the Baku area in the past. When they found themselves edged out of a job, however, they could always return to Armenia. This presented a different problem for the Armenians of the Nagorno–Karabakh Autonomous Republic, however, since this was a relatively

The fortress at Baku (ca. 1300)

194

poor area without significant industry. The Armenians of Nagorno–Karabakh also felt that the leadership at the republic level ignored needs of the autonomous republic. Thus they formally requested to be transferred to Armenian jurisdiction in February 1988.

When the Armenian Republic leadership supported Nagorno–Karabakh's request two weeks later, apparently spontaneous riots broke out in the Azerbaijani city of Sumgait which turned into a slaughter of Armenians. When this was followed by retaliatory moves against Azeris living in Armenia, the result was a dual stream of refugees, Armenians fleeing to Armenia and Azeris fleeing to Azerbaijan.

This first, open manifestation of Azerbaijani nationalism was exacerbated when Gorbachëv dismissed the first secretaries of the Azerbaijani and Armenian *Communist Parties* in May 1988 for allowing the situation to get out of hand. The Azerbaijani educated classes, up to this time loyal supporters of the party, now began to think of the party as Moscow–dominated. Gorbachëv aggravated the situation even further when he announced in January 1989 that he was suspending Azerbaijan's authority over Nagorno–Karabakh and putting the autonomous republic under direct Muscovite control.

That summer the *Azerbaijan Popular Front* was founded for the specific goal of safeguarding Azeri national interests. And the national interest was defined as meaning the territorial integrity of Azerbaijan. In a challenge to the *Communist Party*, the front launched a series of mass demonstrations and labor strikes in August.

In September 1989, the front organized a road and railroad blockade of Armenia. With 85 percent of Armenia's freight entering the country by way of Azerbaijan, this action brought Armenian industry almost to a halt. The success of the blockade also brought the front a political victory over the *Azerbaijan Communist Party*. On September 13, Abdul Vezirov, the first secretary, signed a protocol with the front in which he agreed to call a special session of the Supreme Soviet to pass a law on sovereignty. The law was passed ten days later. Meanwhile the front threatened to maintain its blockade of Armenia until Moscow dissolved its special commission and allowed control over Nagorno–Karabakh to revert back to Azerbaijan. On November 28, the USSR Supreme Soviet voted to end Moscow's direct rule over Nagorno–Karabakh. The rail blockade was eased, but not lifted entirely.

In January 1990, a new series of killings of Armenians broke out in Baku, the Azerbaijani capital. The government declared a state of emergency to handle the matter. Gorbachëv then sent in Soviet troops to re-store order and to forestall a *coup* by the *Azerbaijani Popular Front* against the Azerbaijan Government. Soviet Defense Minister Yazov later said that the Soviet troops were sent in "to destroy the organizational structure" of the *Azerbaijan Popular Front*. The *Azerbaijan Communist Party* leadership was changed as well. Ayaz Mutalibov, who had been prime minister up to this time, was installed as the new party leader and head of state.

Azeris were extremely angered by Gorbachëv's actions. Elmira Kafarova, chairman of the Azerbaijani Supreme Soviet, referred to the events of January 1990 as "a gross violation of Azerbaijani sovereignty." More than a million people turned out for the funeral of the approximately one hundred Azerbaijanis killed when Soviet troops entered Baku.

There were also rallies when *Communist Party* membership cards were burned, but Gorbachëv kept the troops in Baku and eventually order was restored. Mutalibov survived as party first secretary, though he never dared to lift the state of emergency declared in January 1990.

Independent Azerbaijan

Mutalibov was abroad on a visit to Iran while an attempted *coup* against Gorbachëv was going on. He never condemned the attempt, but, after it failed, he resigned as head of the party and issued a decree banning party cells in government and industry. The party later dissolved itself.

Mutalibov announced Azerbaijan's independence on August 30. He then had the Azerbaijan Supreme Soviet modify the constitution by creating a popularly elected, executive presidency. He was later elected president in an uncontested election.

Mutalibov remained under intense pressure from a growing political opposition, however. In September 1991, he created an 8–member Defense Council and appointed members of the *Social Democratic Party*, the *National Independence Party*, and the *Popular Front* to it. By this time, Tamerlan Karayev, leader of the *Azerbaijan Popular Front*, had been elected deputy head of the Supreme Soviet.

The front demanded that the Supreme Soviet be replaced by a temporary "National Council" which would prepare for new elections. When Karayev threatened to resign his post as deputy leader in October, Mutalibov agreed to the creation of a National Council and to a second demand that Azerbaijan establish its own army.

On October 18, 1991, the Supreme Soviet passed a law formally reestablishing Azerbaijan's independence. It declared the present government the legitimate successor to the Azerbaijan Democratic Government, overthrown by the communists in April 1920. The law further declared that "all acts and treaties concluded by the republic since April 1920" were considered invalid.

In early November, Mutalibov closed down the gas line to Armenia, cutting off the delivery of gas. Later in the month, when an Azerbaijani helicopter was downed over Nagorno–Karabakh, Mutalibov announced that he was calling an extraordinary session of the Supreme Soviet and would request them to dissolve the Nagorno–Karabakh government. At the same time, he cut all railway links with

At prayer in the Mashtagin mosque　　　Courtesy: NOVOSTI

Azerbaijan

Armenia. The Azerbaijani Supreme Soviet endorsed Mutalibov's actions on November 26. By this time, Azerbaijan had its own defense minister and had created a military force of about 25,000. Mutabilov ordered his defense minister to restore order in Nagorno–Karabakh. Something approaching full–scale war existed in the area.

The Azerbaijan National Council met for the first time on November 29. Its first act was to pass a law putting all of Azerbaijan's borders under state control, to be guarded by Azerbaijani border guard troops. The purpose of the legislation was to give Azerbaijan control of its border with Armenia.

Meanwhile, the Armenian political leadership in Nagorno–Karabakh had declared the area to be an independent republic. A referendum, held on December 10, brought overwhelming popular approval.

The war between Azerbaijan and Nagorno–Karabakh continued for the next two months. All of Nagorno–Karabakh's connections with the outside were cut off and Azerbaijani troops carried out raids into the area from the east. There were reports that the city of Stepanakert had been virtually destroyed, but the Armenian leadership of Nagorno–Karabakh refused to give in. They were also being assisted by elements of the Armenian National Army, which had opened a corridor between Armenia and Nagorno–Karabakh.

When Mutalibov said that he was still seeking a political solution to the problem, the *Azerbaijan Popular Front* demanded his resignation on February 20, 1992, charging that the course of military actions in Nagorno–Karabakh was detrimental to Azerbaijan. As Azerbaijani nationalists continued to press the government to step up the fighting against the Armenians in Nagorno–Karabakh, Mutalibov resigned as President on March 6.

The *Azerbaijan Popular Front* never accepted Mutalibov's conversion to nationalism, and they never forgot that he was installed by Moscow after Soviet armed forces had been used against the front. Under their prodding, an Azerbaijani legislative commission, appointed to investigate the events of January 1990, had concluded that Moscow had deliberately chosen Azerbaijan as a test case to see whether an independence movement could be crushed through the massive use of force. Forcing Mutalibov's resignation was therefore part of their revenge for the events of January 1990. They did not take any personal revenge against him, however. In addition to a grant of immunity against prosecution and a 10–man bodyguard, the legislature provided him with a pension of 10,000 rubles a month and a villa in the countryside.

View of the port area of Baku

Courtesy: NOVOSTI

Following his resignation, the legislature transferred presidential authority to the newly elected chairman of the legislature, Yagub Mamedov. One of the first acts of the new government was to launch new attacks against Nagorno–Karabakh. Their target was the city of Askeran, located not far from the capital city of Stepanakert. They were driven back by Armenian forces, however.

Ordinary Azerbaijanis reacted by calling for greater efforts to reclaim Nagorno–Karabakh. Mamedov, however, called for diplomatic efforts to get negotiations under way.

In March, Prime Minister Hasan Hasanov, said that

the chance of the conflict erupting into an all–out war and the chance of a political solution are 50–50. This depends on how much world public opinion realizes that the Armenian state terrorist army must immediately leave the occupied territory of Azerbaijan. If it continues its occupation of Nagorno–Karabakh, the chances of a military outcome will greatly increase.

In fact, Azerbaijani attempts to extend their control in Nagorno–Karabakh were unsuccessful. In May, forces of the Nagorno–Karabakh Defense Council managed to capture the Azerbaijani stronghold of Shusha and drive most Azerbaijani forces out of the enclave. Even as the Armenian and Azerbaijani Governments continued discussions aimed at bringing an end to the fighting, the Nagorno–Karabakh Defense Council forces captured a corridor across the Azeri territory separating Nagorno–Karabakh and Armenia, thereby creating a ground connection with Armenia.

Later in May, the war widened when fighting broke out along the border between Armenia and the Azerbaijani enclave of Nakhichevan, separated from the rest of Azerbaijan by a strip of Armenian territory. According to Armenian reports, the fighting began after Armenian villages were shelled from across the border. Armenians retaliated by launching attacks on the Azeri villages of Sadarak and Lachin. Both Turkey and Iran protested the Armenian "aggression" at this point, however, and a sort of quasi–truce settled in along the border.

The next development came on June 7, when the Azerbaijani population went to the polls to elect a new president. There were five candidates, but the easy winner was Abulfaz Elchibey, leader of the *Azerbaijan Popular Front*, who won 60 percent of the vote. Elchibey was 53 years old at the time of his election and a noted historian. He was also one of the founders of the *Azerbaijan Popular Front*.

Though the *Popular Front* came into existence as part of a popular response to Nagorno–Karabakh's demand that it be permitted to become part of Armenia, it claimed democratic credentials and was determined to break the old–line Communist leadership's hold on power. Strongly nationalist, it also opposed cooperation with the other former Soviet republics in the CIS. One of Elchibey's first acts as president was to announce that Azerbaijan would withdraw from the Commonwealth of Independent States and that Azerbaijan would deal with the other republics only on a bilateral basis. Elchibey was particularly incensed that several of the CIS members had negotiated a mutual security pact which included Armenia, though he had been cool to the CIS from its first inception.

Aside from that, however, Elchibey was relatively moderate in his actions after becoming president. This may be partly because he looked to Turkey as a model for his own government and the Turkish Government was urging that course on him. He was committed to an economic reform based on free market principles, but did little in that direction, partly because of his continued preoccupation with Nagorno–Karabakh.

The struggle over Nagorno–Karabakh did not cause the bad economic effects in Azerbaijan that it did in Armenia, but it did appear to preclude Azerbaijani leaders from thinking about anything else. Unfortunately for Elchibey, however, Armenian forces overran the northern part of the strip separating Nagorno–Karabakh from Armenia in April 1993, capturing the Azerbaijani regional town of Kelbajar and in the process bringing about ten percent of Azerbaijan's territory under Armenian control. The defeat at Kelbajar also produced an estimated 100,000 new refugees for the Azerbaijani Government to cope with.

This was a severe setback for President Elchibey, made worse by the fact that the Azerbaijani forces suffered a series of humiliating defeats when they attempted to regain control of the overrun territories in subsequent fighting.

President Elchibey then found himself challenged by his own forces when he tried to discipline one of the regional commanders, a 35-year old army colonel by the name of Suret Guseinov. Instead, Guseinov rebelled and ordered his troops to march on Baku. As Guseinov's troops approached the capital, Elchibey fled to his home base in the Nakhichevan enclave, leaving a political vacuum in Baku.

The Azerbaijani parliament now elected Geidar Aliyev to the position of chairman of parliament and acting head of state, and then called on Guseinov to negotiate an end to his uprising. After discussions, the matter was resolved when Aliyev agreed to nominate Guseinov as prime minister, and the parliament confirmed him in this position on July 1.

Although Aliyev and his allies had now taken effective control of the government, there remained the problem that Elchibey was still legally president. To remedy that situation, parliament voted to strip Elchibey of his authority; it then set a referendum for August 29 on the question whether he should remain president. More than 90 percent of those going to the polls cast their ballots against Elchibey. This cleared the way for Geidar Aliyev to be elected president in new elections that took place on October 3, 1993.

President Aliyev continued to consolidate his power over the next year, but this threatened the position of Guseinov and led to a falling out between the two leaders. In October 1994, Aliyev fired Guseinov as prime minister and named Fuad Quliyev as his successor. Quliyev lasted for two years; he was then replaced by Artur Rasizade in November 1996.

New presidential elections took place in October 1998. Aliyev was heavily favored to win reelection from the beginning because the man considered the main oppositional leader, Rasul Guliev, had lived in exile in the United States after he was ousted as speaker of the Azerbaijani parliament in September 1996. Although Guliev announced his intention of running for president in January 1998, he eventually did not do so because he risked arrest if he returned to Azerbaijan. In the end, six candidates entered the race but, because all were second rank candidates, Aliyev swept the race with 76.1 percent of the vote. Etibar Mamedov, the runner-up, got 11.6 percent of the vote.

Although several candidates protested the poll results, Aliyev was sworn in as president on October 18, 1998. He then reappointed Artur Rasizade as prime minister, and the appointment was confirmed by the parliament on October 23. Since a large majority of the seats in the parliament were held by *Yeni Azerbaycan*, the political party founded by Aliyev in late 1992 as his personal power base, it was fairly clear that President Aliyev was thoroughly in political control of the country.

Yet, one should not forget that Aliyev twice had to put down armed rebellions and there were a number of attempts on his life. Azerbaijan was still a badly divided country where regional loyalties are strong and a significant percentage of the people live below the poverty line. Although Azerbaijan has the promise of significant future revenues as foreign consortiums develop Azerbaijan's oil wealth, very little of that money has trickled down to the level of the ordinary citizen as yet.

There is also the continuing problem of Nagorno–Karabakh. Although there have been only occasional, and usually isolated, skirmishes since a cease-fire signed in 1994, the Armenian and Nagorno–Karabakh Governments still control not only the entire territory of Nagorno– Karabakh, but, also, all Azerbaijani territory lying between Armenia and Nagorno– Karabakh. The Organization for Security and Cooperation in Europe (OSCE) continues to mediate the situation, but no plan has been capable of winning the support of either side. President Ter–Petrossian of Armenia was, in fact, forced out of office in February 1998 after he indicated his willingness to consider a 1997 OSCE plan. President Aliyev was in a similar situation. He said that he would be willing to consider a corridor linking Armenia and Nagorno–Karabakh but he could not go further without losing domestic support. Meanwhile, the war created up to 750,000 refugees and internally displaced persons that the Azerbaijani Government has had to take care of.

President Ilham Aliyev

President Aliyev underwent heart bypass surgery in the United States in April 1999 and he spent the next couple months recuperating. In spite of that, he met with Armenian President Kocharian later in the year to discuss a possible Nagorno–Karabakh settlement. The two presidents met again at the OSCE summit in Istanbul in November. None of these talks produced any significant progress, though the atmospherics improved somewhat. Meanwhile the Nagorno–Karabakh ceasefire continued to hold, except for a three-hour exchange of fire in June 1999 in which two Azerbaijanis were killed and four injured near Mardakert.

President Aliyev paid a visit to the United States in February 2000 with the major purpose to persuade the United States to end the 1992 Congressional ban on United States government aid to Azerbaijan. Although the Clinton White House supported lifting the ban, it was never able to persuade the Senate of the merit of its argument. It took the events of September 11, 2001 and Azerbaijan's offer to the United States of the use of its airspace during the anti–terrorism campaign to get the Senate to reverse itself and partially waive the ban on aid. The waiver, signed into law on January 25, 2002, allowed Azerbaijan to receive some $50 million in aid in 2002. The chief benefit to Azerbaijan has probably been political, however.

Presidents Aliyev and Kocharian met once in August and again in November of 2002, the second time on the sidelines of the NATO summit. Both characterized the August talks as "useful" and Armenia even confirmed the existence of a new Karabakh peace proposal after the November meeting. Only days later, however, Armenia accused Azerbaijan of backtracking on Karabakh and two weeks later the Armenian Foreign Minister con-

Azerbaijan

The "Independent" Republic of Nagorno–Karabakh

Nagorno–Karabakh, which declared itself an independent republic in December 1991, was for many years an Armenian enclave located in Azerbaijan with the status of an autonomous republic. The majority of the population of the enclave has always been Armenian, but not overwhelmingly so. However, today, as a result of refugee movements caused by the armed conflict that raged between 1992 and 1994, around 180,000 Armenians live here and make up approximately 90 percent of the population.

Nagorno–Karabakh's current problems began in February 1988 when the Nagorno–Karabakh regional council, feeling itself discriminated against by the Azerbaijani Government, asked that the region become part of the Armenian SSR. The matter became an interrepublic dispute when Armenia endorsed Nagorno–Karabakh's request. While the two republics were still discussing the issue, nationalist demonstrations in Azerbaijan and Armenia turned to violence, producing hundreds of thousands of refugees on both sides. In January 1989, with the situation as bad as ever, Moscow suspended both the local provincial committee and Azerbaijan's control over Nagorno–Karabakh and instituted "a special form of administration" for the rebellious autonomous republic, thus putting it under Moscow's direct control.

This led to the birth of the *Azerbaijan Popular Front*, a political organization with a single plank that was at the same time a demand—that Moscow return Nagorno–Karabakh to Azerbaijani jurisdiction. The *Front* backed up its demand by organizing a blockade of railway traffic going into Armenia. Moscow, fearing further popular demonstrations, gave in to the demand and returned Nagorno–Karabakh to Azerbaijani control in November 1989.

In September 1991, Russia and Kazakhstan offered to mediate the dispute between Azerbaijan and Armenia. This produced a ceasefire agreement between the two republics and Armenia also agreed to give up its claim to the enclave in return for a promise by the Azerbaijani leadership that it would allow free elections in Nagorno–Karabakh and bestow additional autonomy on the enclave. The agreement also called for disarming illegal local militias and the right of Armenian and Azeri refugees to return to their homes.

But President Mutalibov of Azerbaijan never implemented the agreement, probably because of his fear of the nationalist opposition. Mutalibov, with little popular support of his own, deliberately appealed to nationalism in an attempt to outflank his nationalist opposition. When an Azerbaijani helicopter was downed in November 1991, Mutalibov suspended talks with Armenia, then called an emergency session of the Azerbaijani legislature and got it to abolish Nagorno–Karabakh's autonomous republic status.

In December 1991, Nagorno–Karabakh responded by holding a referendum on the question of independence, then declaring itself an independent republic after the referendum received overwhelming approval. It also set up a new governmental structure at that time, essentially a presidential–parliamentary system of government with a 81 seat legislature (with 11 seats reserved for Azeris).

Nagorno–Karabakh remained under siege by Azerbaijani forces for the next two years. Turkey and Iran attempted to mediate the dispute and at least six truce agreements were actually signed, though none held. In 1992, after both Azerbaijan and Armenia had been admitted as members of the Conference on Security and Cooperation in Europe (now the Organization for Security and Cooperation in Europe), that group agreed to sponsor new negotiations. Although the talks initiated at that time failed to produce a breakthrough, the OSCE has continued to play the leading role in negotiations since that time.

In 1993, the nature of the conflict changed when forces from Nagorno–Karabakh (with covert assistance by forces from Armenia) overran significant parts of Azerbaijan. As Armenian and Karabakh forces continued to advance during the summer and fall, a large part of western Azerbaijan was overrun and occupied. This brought a rebuke from the United Nations and a demand that Karabakh pull back from its occupied territories. Negotiations now reopened. Once again, a number of ceasefires were negotiated but it was not until 1994 that a ceasefire held. Technically, a state of war continues, though there have been only occasional outbreaks of violence along the ceasefire line since 1994.

Meanwhile, the military forces of Armenia and Nagorno–Karabakh continue to occupy approximately 20 percent of Azerbaijani territory and the OSCE has continued its mediation efforts. In 1997, its Minsk Group, co–chaired by the United States, Russia and France, produced a peace plan that called for a "phased" approach. Armenia would first withdraw from all occupied territory outside of Nagorno–Karabakh, then discussions would follow on the final status of Nagorno–Karabakh. The government of Azerbaijan accepted the proposal, not difficult to understand since the proposal essentially endorsed the Azerbaijani position. Surprisingly, President Ter–Petrossian of Armenia agreed to accept the proposal "as a basis for further talks." However, the leadership in Nagorno–Karabakh rejected the peace plan because it would have required Karabakh to withdraw all of its forces from Azerbaijani territory before any talks took place on Nagorno–Karabakh's final status.

The leadership of Nagorno–Karabakh has publicly stated that it is willing to trade territory for an assurance that Azerbaijan will not again invade the enclave. But Azerbaijan refuses to negotiate directly with Nagorno–Karabakh because it is unwilling to concede a separate status. President Aliyev did indicate, in July 1997, that Azerbaijan would agree to continued use of the Lachin transit corridor linking Nagorno–Karabakh and Armenia, but he made it clear that he would never accept an independent Nagorno–Karabakh.

A new twist came in March 1998 when Robert Kocharian, a former president of Nagorno–Karabakh who had been made prime minister of Armenia by President Ter–Petrossian, was elected president of Armenia. Kocharian argues that Armenia can never abandon its fellow Armenians in Nagorno–Karabakh. He has called for direct talks between the Azerbaijani and Nagorno–Karabakh leaderships (something Azerbaijan has always rejected). Although he does not call for recognition of Nagorno–Karabakh's independence, he does argue that any solution would have to exclude the possibility of "any direct subordination of Nagorno–Karabakh to Azerbaijan.

The current president of Nagorno–Karabakh is Arkadi Ghukasyan, elected in September 1997 with 89.3 percent of the vote. He had previously held the office of foreign minister. His position is that Nagorno–Karabakh is an independent state entity.

The political stalemate thus continues.

---

demned Azerbaijan at the OSCE Ministerial Council meeting in Porto, Portugal. As the situation deteriorated, there was a military skirmish between Armenian and Azerbaijani forces in which one Azerbaijani soldier was wounded and another taken prisoner. The following week, President Kocharian reaffirmed his commitment to a peaceful solution to the Karabakh conflict in a speech he gave during the presidential campaign, though he reiterated his position that it was impossible for the Armenian population of Karabakh to live within an Azerbaijani state. President Kocharian won his campaign for re-election in March 2003, but nothing

changed with regard to Karabakh. Four years later, that is still true.

In April 2003, President Aliyev collapsed during a speech at a military academy in Baku one month after returning from the United States where he had been operated on for an inguinal hernia. On May 3, President Aliyev flew to Turkey for specialized medical care at the Gulhane Military Medical Academy in Ankara. In July, he traveled to the United States for further medical treatment. At the beginning of August, he appointed his son, Ilham, as prime minister, while the *Yeni Azerbaycan* nominated both father and son to run in the October 15 presidential elec-

tions. President Aliyev pulled out of the presidential race on October 2. His death came shortly after the election.

There were eight presidential hopefuls, including the leaders of three of Azerbaijan's most influential political parties. In the final tally, Ilham Aliyev polled 76.84 percent of the vote. *Musavat Party* Chairman Isa Qambar came second with 13.97 percent, followed by independent candidate Lala Shovket Gadjieva with 3.63 percent and *Azerbaijan National Independence Party* Chairman Etibar Mammedov with 2.92 percent. Word of Aliyev's victory brought several thousand Qambar supporters into the streets on October 16.

Azerbaijan

When police and Interior Ministry forces attempted to disperse them, they resisted; fighting continued for three hours in and around the main square in Baku. At least two persons were trampled to death and several hundred persons were injured, including over 60 policemen. 174 of the participants in the clashes were arrested, among them four deputy chairmen of the opposition *Musavat Party* and *Umid Party* Chairman Iqbal Agazade.

President-elect Aliyev placed special blame for the rioting on *Musavat Party* Chairman Isa Qambar who, according to Aliyev, urged his supporters to resort to violence. Qambar's reply was that "people would not have protested if the elections had not been falsified."

The evaluation of the OSCE election observation mission was that the

voting had been "generally well administered in most polling stations but the overall election process still fell short of international standards in several respects. International observers noted a number of irregularities in the counting and tabulation."

That mild reproof was undoubtedly welcomed by the Azerbaijan Government, even though the OSCE issued a later statement deploring the arrests and detentions that followed the rioting.

As the government and the opposition faced off against each other in subsequent weeks, the government launched a crack down that eventually led to the arrest of up to a thousand persons, including opposition party leaders and members, democracy activists, journalists and election officials.

One year later, seven of the leading opposition politicians were found guilty of inciting clashes between police and protesters following the 2003 presidential election. Rauf Arifoglu and Arif Hadjili,

both deputy chairmen of the opposition party *Musavat*, were sentenced to five years in prison. Panakh Huseinov, chairman of the *People's Party of Azerbaijan and Serdar Djalaloglu, secretary general of the* People's Party of Azerbaijan each got four years. *Musavat* Party Deputy Chairman Ibrahim Ibrahimli and *Unmid Party* Chairman Igbal Agazade were sentenced to three years. Lastly, Etimad Asadov, head of an organization representing veterans of the Nagorno-Karabakh war, got two years. Six months later, in March 2005, all were pardoned by President Aliyev in response to a representation made by a visiting delegation of the Council of Europe Parliamentary Assembly.

With new parliamentary elections scheduled to take place in the fall of 2005, the level of rhetoric between the government and the opposition escalated over the next several months. As part of the preparation for the elections, a new electoral alliance called *Solidarity and Trust*, was set up in January 2005, bringing together 26 non-governmental organizations and movements plus individual figures from both the ruling *Yeni Azerbaycan* party and the opposition *Musavat* and *Democratic* parties. The stated purpose of *Solidarity and Trust* was to ensure that the November parliamentary elections would be free and fair.

A second, more specifically political bloc of three opposition political parties was also set up in March 2005. This new bloc, called the *Ugur Bloc* (Forum for Free Elections), brought together *Musavat*, the *Democratic Party of Azerbaijan* and the progressive wing of the divided *Azerbaijan Popular Front Party*. A month later, the *New Policy* bloc was formed by a group of prominent political and civic figures, under the leadership of Lala-Shovket Gadjieva, leader of the *National Unity Liberation Movement*. The group included former

Deputy Prime Minister Ali Masimov, who was also the main opposition candidate in the 1998 elections. Two weeks later, the seven Azerbaijani oppositionists who had had their prison sentences annulled by President Aliyev a month earlier announced that they were establishing a political movement called *16 October*. The group did not intend to field candidates for the November parliamentary elections but said, rather, that the purpose of the group was to further democracy based on free and fair elections. However, Rauf Arifoglu, one of the members of the new group, who is also editor of the opposition newspaper *Yeni Musavat*, was quoted as saying that, "if the people want a revolution, we shall bring one about."

Responding to these developments, the Council of Europe released a statement on April 25 which called the situation in Azerbaijan alarming. Decrying the almost total lack of dialogue between the authorities and the opposition, the restrictions on the freedom of assembly and expression, and the lack of pluralism on television channels, the report urged the government to ensure that the November parliamentary ballot is free, fair, and democratic.

Two weeks later, talks took place involving the ruling *Yeni Azerbaycan Party*, two other pro-government parties, and four opposition parties, which produced consensus on some issues and questions on others. Following the meeting, President Aliyev issued a decree setting forth measures intended to preclude violations and falsification during the parliamentary election. The decree promised that all candidates would be provided with equal access to the media and freedom to conduct their electoral campaigns.

Yet the campaign did not go smoothly. Candidates sometimes had difficulty getting permission to hold rallies. On at least one occasion, the regional office of one of the opposition parties was attacked by persons wielding iron bars. In addition, only those parties and blocs that had registered candidates in no fewer than 60 constituencies qualified for three hours of free airtime per week on Azerbaijani State Television and the recently launched Public Television channel. The situation was further complicated by the fact that there were over 1500 candidates vying for the 125 parliamentary seats.

After the voting, it was reported that *Yeni Azerbaycan* had won 63 of the 125 mandates, with independent candidates filling a further 44 seats. The *Musavat Party* was awarded 4 seats, *Civil Solidarity* three, two each went to *Ana Veten* and the progressive wing of the *Azerbaijan Popular Front* Party and one each went to the *Umid Party, Civic Unity, Civic Welfare,* the *Demo-*

Azerbaijan

cratic Reforms Party, the Unified National Front Party, and the Great Creation Party.

After monitors from both the United States and the European Union complained about "major irregularities and fraud", however, the Azerbaijan Government was forced to backtrack. In the end, ten of the results were annulled, with new elections scheduled for May 2006. In December, the Constitutional Court endorsed the election results in 115 of the 125 constituencies. The ruling Yeni Azerbaycan held 58 of the 115 filled seats, while an additional 42 seats went to independent candidates—most of whom support the government. The opposition originally held ten seats, but the Musavat Party—which controlled four seats—quit the opposition bloc in February 2006 after it voted to participate in the parliament and field candidates for the ten parliamentary seats to be filled in the May 13 elections. Later that same month, a sixth member of the opposition—Djamil Gasanli, deputy chairman of the progressive wing of the Azerbaijan Popular Front Party—announced that he would take up his mandate and participate in parliament.

In the end, Musavat, Adolat, and Civic Solidarity all fielded candidates in the May 13 elections. Eight of the seats went either to members of Yeni Azerbaycan or nominally independent candidates. Opposition Adolit Party Chairman Ilyas Ismailov won a seat in the rural constituency of Tovuz; the tenth seat was won by a candidate from the opposition Civic Solidarity Party. None of Musavat's seven candidates won. The 13-person team from the OSCE reported afterwards that there has been "improvement in some aspects of the process," but that there has also been "instances of interference by local authorities in the election process."

One year later, the political opposition remains dispirited and divided. As oppositional parliamentary deputy Panah Huseynov put it in December 2006, "Mutual distrust, insincerity, and fundamental disagreements continue to preclude closer cooperation between the various opposition forces." Nothing better illustrates that point than the fact that Prime Minister Rasizade's annual report to parliament, made in March 2007, was endorsed by a vote of 103 to five, with five abstentions.

Foreign Policy

Azerbaijan's foreign policy since independence has been held hostage by the state of war that exists with Armenia over the status of Nagorno–Karabakh, the enclave located in Western Azerbaijan which is inhabited by ethnic Armenians. That situation was further complicated when Robert Kocharian, a former president of Nagorno–Karabakh, was elected president of Armenia in March 1998. However, President Aliyev arranged to meet with President Kocharian in 2000, and they held several meetings thereafter. While these discussions did not lead to a breakthrough on Nagorno–Karabakh, both presidents believed them to be valuable enough that they should be continued.

President Aliyev's son and successor, Ilham, did very little during his first several months as president as he first of all focused on consolidating his power. His first initiative on Nagorno-Karabakh came in the fall of 2004 when his government submitted a request to the UN General Assembly to debate the issue. At issue were four UN Security Council resolutions adopted in 1993 calling for the withdrawal of "Armenian forces" from occupied Azerbaijani territory. Azerbaijan's permanent representative to the UN, Yashar Aliev, also accused Armenia of colonizing occupied territory by building permanent settlements there.

Separately, President Aliyev told journalists in Baku that he wanted the OSCE Minsk Group to continue to mediate a solution to the Karabakh conflict. He merely wanted the conflict to be debated more widely by international organizations, including the United Nations and the Council of Europe. Armenian Foreign Minister Vartan Oskanian responded to President Aliyev's comments to the press by reaffirming Armenia's willingness to resume Karabakh talks. He also pointed out that the "Armenian forces" referred to in the UN resolutions were troops of Nagorno-Karabakh and that no troops from Armenia were in occupied Azerbaijan. Arkadi Ghukasian, president of the unrecognized Nagorno-Karabakh Republic, interviewed on Armenian television, also reiterated his government's position that it was "ready to negotiate with Azerbaijan in any format, with or without Armenia."

The foreign ministers of Azerbaijan and Armenia met in Sofia and Brussels in December 2004 in what was actually their fifth meeting in 2004.; the Armenian foreign minister commented afterwards that his meeting with the Azerbaijan foreign minister had yielded "a framework of issues that can serve as a basis" for a future peace deal. President Aliyev, taking up the issue in a New Year's address, called 2004 "a turning point" in talks over the unresolved Nagorno-Karabakh conflict, though he did add that Azerbaijan would "never make any concessions in question of its territorial integrity."

The Parliamentary Assembly of the Council of Europe did take up Nagorno-Karabakh in January 2005, though the outcome was not particularly pleasing to either side in the conflict. Although the resolution called for the withdrawal of un-named occupying forces from districts of Azerbaijan bordering on Nagorno-Karabakh, it also called on the Azerbaijani leadership to "embark immediately and unconditionally on talks with the leadership of the unrecognized Nagorno-Karabakh Republic on the region's future status. Azerbaijan got some further bad news in March when the OSCE Minsk Group published its conclusions following an extensive tour of the occupied territories in February. Essentially, the fact-finding mission concluded that resettlement is "quite limited" and that most of the Armenian settlers involved were displaced persons from other regions of Azerbaijan.

Although the presidents of Azerbaijan and Armenia, as well as each country's foreign ministers, have met several times since that time, the situation with regard to Nagorno-Karabakh remains unchanged.

Azerbaijan had very poor relations with Russia under the government of President Elchibey, partly because of Elchibey's nationalism and partly because he believed that Russia was pro-Armenian. Elchibey also pulled Azerbaijan out of the Commonwealth of Independent States (CIS). Geidar Aliyev reversed this policy when he came to power in 1993. Under Aliyev, Azerbaijan rejoined the CIS, and began building better relations with Russia. The ceasefire signed by Azerbaijan and Armenia in 1994 was one of the first fruits of his new policy.

Throughout the nineties, Azerbaijan's relations with the United States were always cool, largely because of the influence on U.S. foreign policy of the significant Armenian Diaspora in the United States. Under this influence, the U.S. Congress instituted a ban on U.S. assistance to Azerbaijan in 1992, even as Armenia was becoming the second largest recipient of American assistance, on a per capita basis, among ex–Soviet republics.

Azerbaijanis interpreted this to mean that the United States had allied itself with Armenia, and this limited the influence of the U.S. Government on Azerbaijan. Accordingly, the United States played no significant role in outside attempts to bring a peaceful resolution to the conflict over Nagorno–Karabakh until 1997 when, at the urging of both Armenia and Azerbaijan, the United States agreed to accept one of the three co–chairs of the Minsk peace talks.

This situation began to change in July 1998 when the U.S. State Department asked Congress to lift sanctions on Azerbaijan, arguing that this would benefit American companies involved in developing energy resources in the Caspian Sea region. Although the U.S. Senate rejected the recommendation, relations began to improve from this time onward.

After the September 11 terrorist attacks against the United States, Azerbaijan was among the first of the CIS states to offer the use of its airspace for the United States–led war on terrorism. Wishing to include Azerbaijan in its war on terrorism, the United States Government recommended to Congress that it waive the appropriate section of U.S. law that banned all assistance to Azerbaijan. Congress quickly responded and President Bush signed the waiver in January 2002. Since that time, military talks have resulted in a number of agreements between the two countries, with the United States making specific commitments to provide training for the armed forces, the navy, and the air force. Perhaps most important, Mira Ricardeli, deputy assistant to Secretary of Defense Rumsfeld, told a press conference in Baku in March 2002 that the United States attached great importance to Azerbaijan's national security, sovereignty, and territorial integrity.

President Aliyev paid a formal visit to the United States in February 2003. Azerbaijan supported the United States on Iraq and Azerbaijan agreed to send a contingent of 150 Azerbaijani troops to Iraq following the collapse of Saddam Hussein to guard Muslim holy sites in the cities of Karbala, Kirkuk, and Mosul. In April 2003, President Aliyev formally announced Azerbaijan's intention to join NATO.

Azerbaijan's relations with its other neighbors are for the most part correct but not cordial. Its relations with Iran, its southern neighbor, were poor until recently because Iran has refused to support Azerbaijan's attempts to isolate Armenia and, in fact, has been Armenia's largest trading partner since 1991. Religious rivalries also play a role in this relationship. Although, as in Iran, the majority of the population of Azerbaijan is Shi'a Muslim, the Azerbaijani Government fears and distrusts the religious fundamentalism currently dominant in Iran. In turn, Iran worries about the fact that it has millions of its own Azeris living along the border with Azerbaijan. However, the two countries signed a cooperation agreement in 2002 on the joint struggle against terrorism, drug smuggling, and organized crime and followed this up in April 2003 with a second bilateral agreement that added border security and arms proliferation to the list. There have also been a number of economic agreements for Iranian financing of several transportation projects and a $40 million Iranian credit package for a natural–gas project in Azerbaijan.

Azerbaijan's best relations are with Turkey, which has closed its borders with Armenia in support of the Azerbaijani position on Nagorno–Karabakh and in other ways continues to cultivate good relations with Azerbaijan. Some recent signs of that close connection include a new bilateral military agreement between the two countries, signed in May 2002, under which military aid is being provided to the Azerbaijan armed forces; somewhat related to that, the Azerbaijan Government decided in November 2002 to provide a small military contingent to serve as part of the Turkish forces in Afghanistan. The decision also enhanced the American connection, since the United States Government is providing $1 million toward the expenses involved.

Nature of the Regime

Azerbaijan has completed its transition to a pluralistic political system in principle, but the political situation associated with Nagorno–Karabakh has tended to polarize the society and to make moderate political stances suspect. Although a political opposition is permitted, a number of opposition politicians have been forced into exile and several more are serving terms in prison for various offenses.

After several opposition politicians called for hunger strikes and demonstrations against the government after the 1998 presidential elections, the parliament passed legislation limiting the right to hold public demonstrations and imposing a sentence of up to three years for organizing or participating in an unsanctioned demonstration. The government has also used libel suits on several occasions to bankrupt newspapers owned by the opposition. The ruling party, *Yeni Azerbaycan*—founded by President Aliyev in 1992 as his personal power base—controls a majority of seats in the parliament. His son, Ilham, who succeeded his father in 2003, continues to use the *Yeni Azerbaycan* as his chief instrument for controlling the country. During the lead-up to the 2005 parliamentary elections, however, he took a number of actions aimed at facilitating a somewhat greater pluralism. Most of these actions were in response to international pressure on his government to allow fair and free elections, but the new president does appear to be somewhat more democratically oriented than his father.

One problem President Aliyev has had to contend with is the fact that Azerbaijan political parties tend to be organized around the leadership of a single individual whose following is recruited from among the numerous clans that dominate Azerbaijan society. Because they lack a coherent political agenda, political alliances and clan relationships become the dominant factor in determining friends or enemies. Governmental officials, themselves part of this system of clan relationships, are seldom able to set aside these relationships in their official actions. For example, President Aliyev issued a decree in 2005 instructing local officials to maintain a neutral position toward all candidates; one of the larger complaints among election monitors was that governmental officials frequently ignored this particular instruction in actual practice.

The Azerbaijan Government

Azerbaijan's government resembles that of Russia. There is a popularly elected president who is considered to be the spokesman for the nation. He is responsible for general policy, but has a prime minister who handles day–to–day affairs of government. The president is commander–in–chief of the armed forces. He also presides over the State Council and the Defense Council.

The prime minister and members of the cabinet are appointed by the president, but must be confirmed by the legislature, formally known as the *Milli Mejlis* or National Assembly.

New elections to the National Assembly took place on November 7, 2005, with a second round of voting on May 13, 2006 in ten constituencies where the result was annulled because of charges of voting irregularities. Technically, the National Assembly contains 125 seats, but there was no election for the seat reserved for Nagorno– Karabakh. The final result gave the *Yeni Azerbaycan party* 58 seats, with an additional 42 seats won by independent candidates, many of them supporters of the ruling party. Three opposition political parties took ten seats, with the remaining seats held by individuals who were the sole representative of their political party.

The current president is Ilham Aliyev, who was elected in October 2003 after his father withdrew as a candidate because of illness. Aliyev's prime minister is Artur Rasizade, who had held that office from 1996 to August 2003; he was reappointed after Ilham Aliyev won his own election as president.

Azerbaijan has no office of the vicepresident. Until 2002, the constitution had specified that the speaker of the parliament became acting president in the case of the death or incapacity of the president. Under a constitutional amendment approved by national referendum in 2002, however, the prime minister becomes acting president under any circumstances in which the president is unable to serve. Since the prime minister is appointed, this gives the president virtually unlimited authority to name his successor and Ilham Aliyev held that office from August to October before being elected president. Azerbaijan's system of proportional representation was abolished at the same time. All

Azerbaijan

A view of Baku with the Adjarbek Mosque

Courtesy: NOVOSTI

125 parliamentary seats have therefore become single–seat constituencies.

Culture

Most Azeribaijani are Shi'a Muslims, unlike their Muslim neighbors in Central Asia, who are mostly Sunni. This probably results from the fact that the area of Azerbaijan was part of the Persian Empire for several centuries. When it became a part of the Russian Empire at the beginning of the 19th century, however, the Azeris became merely one of the Muslim peoples of Russia.

There was no sense of national Azerbaijani identity until fairly recently, but there have been a number of famous Azeri thinkers, poets and scientists. Abul Hasan Bakhmanyar, who lived in the 11th century, wrote a number of books on mathematics and philosophy. Abul Hasan Shirvani, a later contemporary, left behind a book on astronomy. Nezami was a later poet and philosopher.

The Azeris have an ancient musical tradition which has survived. Musicians improvise the words to songs as they play a stringed instrument called a *kobuz*. There are also vocal and instrumental compositions that have been kept alive in a folk tradition.

They also have modern composers with international reputations. Two of these are Uzeir Hajjibekov, author of a number of operas, and Kara Karayev, who writes ballets. The Baku Film Studio also has an international reputation. *Little Vera*, a fairly recent film, tells a depressing story of a young girl growing up as a member of a working–class family in Baku.

Although a large part of the population was still illiterate in 1917, modern Azerbaijan now has 16 institutes of higher education with a student population of over 100,000. The largest of these is the Azerbaijan Institute of Petroleum and Chemistry.

In January 1992, the Azerbaijan National Council passed a law adopting the Latin script for the Azeri language. It acted on the basis of a recommendation from a special commission, appointed two years earlier, to look into the question. The commission, made up of a number of linguists, historians, and literary specialists, concluded that the Azeri language's phonetic "peculiarities are best 'superimposed' on the Latin script." Azerbaijan had used the Latin script in the 1920s but, under pressure from Moscow, went over to the Cyrillic script at the end of the thirties.

Economy

Baku, now the capital and largest city, was the center of the oil industry of Imperial Russia. In 1901, the Baku fields produced over 11 million tons of oil, which was 50 percent of the world's oil production at the time. The fields lost much of

their earlier significance after World War II, but the region still produced three percent of the Soviet Union's oil in 1991. Even then, Baku was still surrounded by oil derricks, though natural gas came to rival petroleum in significance in the last years of the Soviet Union.

Once a beautiful city that spread out along natural terraces running down to a gulf of the Caspian Sea, Baku was, by 1991, a grimy industrial city with terrible pollution problems. The emergence of Azerbaijan as an independent country has given the city new life, however. Today, it is the center of a boom associated with new oil fields that are being opened up on the seabed of the Caspian Sea. Recent drilling by international companies has proven oil reserves of between 15 and 20 billion barrels beneath the Caspian Sea, with the possibility that the basin might hold between 40 and 178 billion barrels. Azerbaijan's share of this treasure trove is estimated to be worth $100 billion over the next 30 years. International companies have already signed contracts with Azerbaijan worth an estimated $60 billion.

Most of this wealth is still years off, but the first oil from the Chirag Caspian field began flowing in November 1997. The Chirag field was developed between 1994 and 1997 by a consortium of Western oil companies plus Russia's Lukoil. Yet another milestone was reached in December

1998 when the first oil was pumped into the new 930–kilometer pipeline connecting Baku with the Georgian Black Sea port of Supsa. The new pipeline has an annual capacity of 2.5 million metric tons. Crude oil production—9 million metric tons in 1997—rose to 11.4 million metric tons in 1998; oil production has gone up every year since that time. In early 2006, Azerbaijan began pumping oil through the newly completed Baku-Ceyhan pipeline, which added another million tons a day to Azerbaijan's export capacity.

Azerbaijan's ability to move crude oil to world markets remained a major bottleneck until the summer of 2006 when the first oil began flowing through the 1,091-mile Baku–Tbilisi–Ceyhan export pipeline, which was constructed by an international consortium including British Petroleum, STATOIL, and UNOCAL, with Azerbaijan's state oil company, SOCAR, holding a 25 percent equity stake. Since the pipeline has a throughput capacity of 50 million metric tons per year, Kazakhstan will use some of this capacity for its own oil exports, though that use is limited by the lack of a pipeline connecting the Kazakh oil fields with Baku.

A second, parallel 690-kilometer gas pipeline has also recently been completed. Azerbaijan produced about 5 billion cubic meters of natural gas in 2006, but it had to import an additional 4.5 billion meters from Russia to meet domestic demand. However, the government cut its natural

gas imports in early 2007 after Gazprom raised the price to $230 per 1,000 cubic meters. It could do so because the Shah Deniz gas field began producing its first gas in November 2006. Shah Deniz has estimated reserves of 1 trillion cubic meters of gas; production is expected to be 5-6 billion cubic meters in 2007 and 8 billion meters in 2008. Because the government is also using domestic oil to replace some natural gas, it is estimated that about half of the production of the Shah Deniz field will be available for export.

There are still diplomatic problems that need to be solved before Azerbaijan can feel free to develop all of its potential wealth, however. The problem is that the countries bordering on the Caspian have not been able to agree on how to divide the seabed of the Caspian. The main question under international law is whether the Caspian is a sea or a saltwater lake. If the Caspian is determined to be a saltwater lake, then, according to international law, its various resources can only be exploited on the basis of an agreement signed by all bordering states. On the other hand, if the Caspian is a sea, its resources would be divided into national sectors that each country would have the right to exploit as it pleases.

Russia and Iran had until recently contended that the Caspian is a saltwater lake. Azerbaijan and Kazakhstan, on the other hand, took the position that it is a sea. Turkmenistan, the last of the states bordering on the Caspian Sea, has been

divided on the issue. It first sided with Kazakhstan and Azerbaijan, then switched its position in 1996 and until recently was supporting the Russian–Iranian position. The recent death of President Niyazov is likely to change that stance once again. His successor, President Berdymukhammedov, has shown some interest in finding a way around Turkmenistan's oil dependency on Russia.

Russia and Iran indicated in 1998 that they might be willing to agree that the Caspian is a sea if an appropriate division of the seabed could be worked out. However, Iran continues to claim 20 percent of the seabed, a position rejected by Azerbaijan. Partially ignoring these disagreements, Azerbaijan has signed agreements with a number of international oil companies for the development of what it considers its national sector. In addition, Azerbaijan signed an agreement with Russia in September 2002 delimiting the two countries' respective sectors of the Caspian Sea bed. Azerbaijan has also continued talks with the Iranian Government concerning the Caspian Sea bed.

Sumgait, a city located 22 miles north of Baku, is Azerbaijan's second most important industrial center. Major chemical and oil–drilling industries are located here. In fact, Sumgait was the primary manufacturer of oil–drilling equipment in the now defunct Soviet Union. Since 95 percent of its customers for oil–drilling equip-ment were located in other parts of the Soviet Union, the area is currently suffering badly. Three other cities with significant industry are Mingechaur, Gyanja (formerly Kirovabad), and Stepanakert. Mingechaur manufactures appliances and instruments and electrical equipment of all kinds, plus textiles, shoes and other consumer goods. Gyanja and Stepanakert manufacture consumer goods, including textiles, and things like knitwear and souvenirs. All have suffered with the loss of customers in other parts of the ex–Soviet Union but certain industries, in particular those manufacturing consumer goods, have begun to recover somewhat.

Most of Azerbaijan's industry was developed to process its petroleum and natural gas supplies. Thus it has refineries producing gasoline, herbicides, industrial oils and kerosene and it also manufactures chemical fertilizers, synthetic rubber and plastics. Although many of these industries suffer from obsolete or outdated technology, they have been given a new life as Azerbaijan begins to rebuild its petroleum production.

Another issue is privatization. Azerbaijan was slow to begin the process of privatization, but it did initiate the privatization of companies with fewer than 50 employees after 1991. Approximately 15,000 such

The Museum of Azerbaijan Literature at Baku

Azerbaijan

companies were sold between then and 1997, most of them to the managers who had run them under communism.

Finally, in March 1997, Azerbaijan launched a mass privatization program that was supposed to result in the privatization of 70 percent of all enterprises by the end of 1998. This is a voucher program in which each citizen is issued a coupon book of four vouchers. (War veterans received eight vouchers.)

All enterprises that were to be privatized were turned into joint–stock companies and 55 percent of their shares were then auctioned off for vouchers. The vouchers were distributed between March and August 1997 and voucher auctions were held regularly after that time. By December 1997, approximately 400 large enterprises had been privatized.

The state is committed to privatizing all medium–scale enterprises, but many large–scale enterprises are to remain in state hands. For example, the state oil company will not be privatized. Other companies that will remain in the state sector include railroads, water facilities, pension funds and the state bank. In addition, companies involved in fuel and energy production, petrochemicals, and telecommunications, plus bakeries and wineries, can only be privatized by presidential decree.

In March 2001, President Aliyev gave approval for the privatization of over 100 state–owned enterprises in the chemical, machine–building, and fuel and energy sectors. While he ordered the government to determine how enterprises in the fuel and energy sectors are to be privatized, he approved the privatization of the remainder of the companies using public auctions. In a few cases, 15 percent of the shares were offered in closed subscriptions to staff of the enterprises concerned.

Azerbaijan is also a major producer of electric power and traditionally has exported electricity to neighboring republics. There is a handicraft industry in the south along the border with Iran. Here the Talysh, an Iranian people, live in their mountainous villages and support themselves by weaving rugs and carpets by hand in the traditional way.

Fishing is another industry that makes a major contribution to the gross domestic product, though it has declined in importance in recent years. The Caspian Sea is famous for its sturgeon, and Azerbaijan is a major source of caviar. But the sea is being rapidly polluted and the caviar supplies are quickly diminishing.

Agriculture is less significant than industry insofar as total value is concerned, but it still provides employment to over a third of the population. Cotton is the most valuable crop, followed by tobacco, grapes, vegetables, fruits and nuts. Most of the grapes are used to produce wine. There is also a small silk industry. In 1998, semi–processed cotton was the second most important export good after crude oil.

The Lenkoren region in southern Azerbaijan produces subtropical crops such as citrus and tea. It also produces rice and to-bacco and is a major source for winter and spring vegetables.

The Naxcivan (Nakhichevan) Autonomous Republic has a semi–desert climate, but irrigation allows it to raise grapes, cotton and grain. It is also famous for its mineral water from local springs, which is bottled and sold as far away as Moscow.

The economy has been growing for a number of years, but the growth has been uneven. Much of the recent growth has been in the construction, transport and communications sectors.

Economic Development Minister Farkhad Aliev, speaking to an international investment conference meeting in Baku in May 2003, announced that total foreign investment in Azerbaijan for the period 1996–2002 was $9.6 billion. Projected foreign investment for the following three years was expected to reach $10 billion. A World Bank official at the conference then announced that Azerbaijan would be receiving $235 million in aid during the period 2003–05.

The 2007 budget, passed in November 2006, envisages a 39.1 percent increase in revenues, to $6.13 billion. Expenditures are projected to grow by 42 percent, reaching $6.6 billion. GDP is expected to grow by 26.3 percent to 22 billion manats (ca. $25.2 billion). There is some concern, particularly on the part of the IMF, that this great growth in government expenditures could lead to runaway inflation. In fact, the Azerbaijani Government is aware of the problem, and it has been funneling part of its energy revenues into the State Oil Fund (SOFAR) since 2001. SOFAR held around $1.6 billion in deposits by September 2006, and that figure has presumably grown since that time.

The Future

Geidar Aliyev's death in 2003 raised the specter of a new period of political instability, but Aliyev recognized the danger and managed to have his son, Ilham, installed as prime minister in August. When it became clear that the father was too ill to stand for reelection, Ilham stepped in, replaced his father on the ballot, and went on to win the presidency in October 2003. The political opposition was not happy with this new variation on dynastic succession, but the various oppositional political parties also did poorly in the November 2005 parliamentary elections, eventually ending up with ten seats. Since then, internal quarrelling and mutual distrust has reduced their significance further. The significant economic growth of the last several years has probably convinced most ordinary Azeris that their lives are improving; yet many remain uneasy about the future.

Fountain near the President's Office

The Republic of Georgia

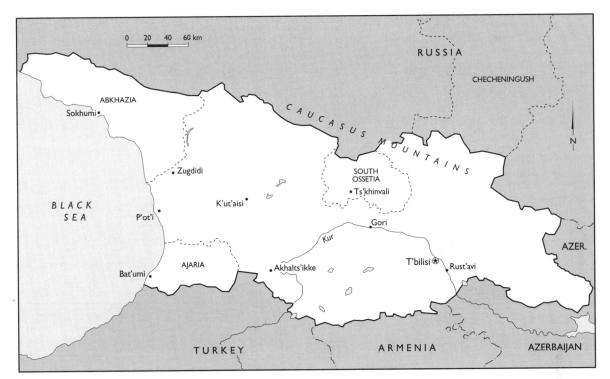

Area: 26,903 sq. mi. (69,700 sq. km), slightly smaller than South Carolina.

Population: 4.63 million (May 2003).

Capital City: Tbilisi (Pop. 1,260,000).

Climate: Humid, subtropical in the Kolkhida Lowland (along the eastern shore of the Black Sea) and on the interior, high plateau known as the Kartalinian Plain; temperate in the high mountains to either side of the Kartalinian Plain.

Neighboring States: Russia (north), Turkey, Armenia (south), and Azerbaijan (southeast).

Official Language: Georgian; Abkhaz is the official language of Abkhazia.

Ethnic Composition: Georgian (78.6%), Azeri (6.5%), Armenian (5.7%), Ossetian (3.2%), Abkhazian (2%), Russian (1.5%), others (2.5%).

Principal Religions: Orthodox Christian (83.9%); Muslim (9.9 %).

Chief Commercial Products: Hydroelectric power, mining, electrical equipment, metals and alloys, automobiles, electrical manufactures, instruments, wines, fruits, tea, vegetables, livestock.

Currency: *lari* (introduced on October 2, 1995).

Per Capita Annual Income (Purchasing Power Parity): $3,300.

Recent Political Status: Soviet Republic (1921), part of Transcaucasian SSR (1922–1936), Republic of the USSR (1936–1991).

Chief of State: Mikheil Saakashvili, President (elected January 2004).

Chief of Government: Zurab Nogaideli, Prime Minister (February 2005).

National Flag: Large red cross superimposed on a white background with four small red crosses centered on the four fields created by the large cross. The flag had been the banner of President Saakashvili's *National Movement* prior to his taking power.

National Holiday: May 26 (1918), date of independence from Soviet Russia.

The Land

The Republic of Georgia (Sak'art'veld) is the independent successor state to the Georgian Soviet Socialist Republic, which was one of the fifteen republics of the Union of Soviet Socialist Republics. The Georgia Supreme Soviet announced the republic's intention to separate from the Soviet Union in November 1990, but it was the August 1991 failed *coup* against Mikhail Gorbachëv that created a situation of *de facto* independence for Georgia. Georgia covers an area of 26,903 square miles (69,700 sq. km.). It includes the Abkhazian and Adjarian Autonomous Republics, plus the South Ossetian Autonomous Region. Of the three, only the Adjarian Autonomous Republic recognizes the authority of the central government, however; the other two have declared themselves to be independent republics.

Georgia lies at the eastern end of the Black Sea, just to the south of the Great Caucasus Mountains. Eighty-five percent of the country is mountainous, the exception being a small area in the west bordering on the Black Sea known as the Kolkhida Lowland. This is the site of ancient Colchis, where Jason and the Argonauts sought the Golden Fleece. The Kolkhida Lowland is a delta region formed by the deposits of three rivers that flow through the area, the Inguri, Rioni, and Kodori. It was once mostly swampland, but drainage projects have turned it into a major producer of subtropical crops and winter vegetables. Here winter temperatures average 41°F and there is a plentiful year-round rainfall.

Behind Kolkhida, the land rises until it reaches two saddle ridges which connect the Great Caucasus and the Little Caucasus Mountains. Beyond that is a high plateau which runs eastward to the border of Azerbaijan. This high plateau, known as the Kartalinian Plain, is the heartland of Georgia.

Most of it is covered by a loess type soil. Drier than the western coast, it nevertheless gets sufficient rainfall to sustain agriculture. In addition, the Mtkvari (formerly Kur or Kura) River flows down out of the Little Caucasus in the southwest and then eastward across the plateau, providing plenty of water for irrigation.

Open to the warm, moist air from the Black Sea and protected on the north by the wall of the Great Caucasus Mountains, the Kartalinian Plain has winters warm enough for citrus groves to thrive. The high mountains to the north and south of this plateau are covered with forests of oak, chestnut, beech, ash, linden, alder, and Caucasian fir. Fruit trees also abound, including apples, pears, and various kinds of nuts. Dairying is practiced on the lower slopes of the mountains and on parts of the plateau. Vineyards are also widely cultivated. Grapes are sold fresh or turned into wine, brandy, or champagne.

Georgia

The eastern part of the country consists of the Alasari River Valley plus a saddle land to the south between that valley and the Kara River Valley. This area receives only between 16 and 28 inches of rainfall and therefore makes use of the water from the Alasari River for irrigation.

The People

According to new figures released by the Georgia Statistics Department, Georgia's population as of May 2003 was 4.63 million, a decline of about 870,000 since the 1989 census. According to the Statistics Department, the primary reason for the decrease is the out-migration of young people seeking employment. Another 300,000 Georgians are expected to leave the country over the next year. Georgians make up approximately 78.6 percent of the population. The two largest minorities are Azeris (6.5%) and Armenians (5.7%), followed by Ossetians (3.2%), Abkhazians (2%), Russians (1.5%), and others (2.5%).

Georgia is an ancient center of civilization. Archaeological excavations place the beginning of the Bronze Age here as early as 3,000 B.C. The ancestors of the Georgian people emerged for the first time in the first millennium B.C. in the annals of the Assyrian Empire. The Georgian language itself is classified as one of the Caucasian languages, meaning that, as far as it known, the Georgians originated here.

Among the Georgian tribes were the Kulkha (Colchians), who once dominated most of the eastern shores of the Black Sea. Their city, Colchis, was known for its fabulous wealth and gave rise to the legend of Medea and the Golden Fleece. Colchis was later colonized by Greeks and still later incorporated into the Roman Empire.

History

Georgia converted to Christianity in the year 337. Over the next three centuries, it became a battlefield between the Byzantine Empire and Persia. In 654, however, it was conquered by the Arqab caliphs, who established an emirate in Tbilisi. In reaction to the Arab presence, the various Georgian tribes united around a princely family long prominent in the affairs of Armenia, and this family eventually brought most of Georgia under its sway. King Bagrat III (975–1014) ruled all of Georgia except for the Tbilisi emirate, and that was conquered in the year 1122 by one of his descendants, King David II ("the Builder"). The Georgian Kingdom reached its zenith under Queen Tamara (1184–1213), when it included most of the Caucasus.

The end came in 1220 with the appearance of the Mongols from the east. Eastern Georgia became part of the Mongol Empire, with only the area west of the mountains along the Black Sea maintaining its independence. The decline of the Mongol Empire brought part of the high central plateau back under Georgian control, but the new kingdom was destroyed by a fresh onslaught by Tamerlane, who created a great empire stretching across Central Asia.

The fall of Constantinople to the Ottoman Turks in 1453 isolated Georgia. In the sixteenth century, it, too, was incorporated into the Turkish Empire. The Turks were in turn driven out by Shah Abba I (1587–1629), ruler of the Persian Empire. In the process, thousands of Georgian Christians were transported to distant parts of the Persian Empire. There was a brief respite after 1658, when the Persians installed the House of Mukhran as viceroys at Tbilisi, but this was brought to an end by a fresh Turkish invasion in 1722. The Persians expelled the Turks twenty-two years later. Another kingdom based on Georgia was installed by the Persians and lasted until near the end of the eighteenth century.

In 1783, Erekle, the Georgian king, signed the Treaty of Georgievsk with Catherine the Great, whereby Russia guaranteed Georgia's independence and territorial integrity in return for Erekle's acceptance of Russian authority. When Georgia was invaded by Persia in 1795, however, Russia offered no assistance. Tbilisi was sacked in 1795 and Erekle died three years later. His son, George XII, offered the kingdom to Paul, the Russian Tsar. Paul died before the treaty could be signed, so it was Alexander I who incorporated Georgia into the Russian Empire. In spite of the

An artist's concept of the medieval fortress of Queen Tamara in the towering Caucasus Mountains

treaty of 1783, Alexander I then deposed George XII and replaced him with Russian military governors. Erekle's kingdom had included only the areas of Kartalinia and Kakhetia, so other parts of Georgia were incorporated in the Russian Empire between 1810 and 1864. The Black Sea ports of Poti and Batumi were added at the time of the Russo–Turkish War of 1877–78.

Georgia's incorporation into the Russian Empire provoked a number of popular uprisings at various times, but it did have the merit of ensuring the corporate survival of the Georgian nation. Georgia also benefited economically and culturally from its connection with Russia. A railroad connecting Tbilisi with Poti on the Black Sea opened in 1872 and mines, factories and commercial farms were established with Russian and foreign capital. Alexander II's reforms also included the end of serfdom and the spread of education. Alexander III's policy of Russification fostered nationalism among the middle-class intelligentsia, however, and marked the beginning of a national revival.

A number of illegal nationalist groups were founded in the 1890s, the most important of which was the "Third Group," a Marxist group affiliated with the *Russian Social Democratic Party*. In 1898, the Third Group recruited Joseph Dzhugashvili, better known by his later revolutionary name, Joseph Stalin. Five years later, Stalin became a Bolshevik when the *Russian Social Democratic Party* separated into *Bolshevik* and *Menshevik* factions at its second congress. The Georgian Marxist party, on the other hand, was controlled by *Mensheviks*.

Georgia saw widespread disturbances and guerrilla fighting during the 1905 Russian uprising, but these were put down by Cossacks in 1906. After the 1917 Revolution, an autonomous Transcaucasian committee was established under the authority of the Provisional Government. After the *Bolshevik* Revolution in the fall, however, this Transcaucasian committee, which was dominated by *Mensheviks*, broke with the national government and established the Transcaucasian Federal Republic on April 22, 1918. When this collapsed a month later, the Georgian National Council set up the Georgian Social Democratic Republic. The republic was under German protection for a while, but then was occupied by the British. The Georgians refused to cooperate with the British, however, and the latter departed Batumi in July 1920.

Georgia signed a treaty with the Russian Soviet Government in May 1920; Moscow then dispatched S. M. Kirov, a Georgian Bolshevik, to Tbilisi. Kirov's task was to undermine the *Menshevik* regime and prepare for a *Bolshevik* seizure of power. In February 1921, a Red Army

under the control of two Georgian *Bolshevik* leaders, Joseph Stalin and G. K. Ordzhonikidze, entered Georgia. A Soviet regime was installed on February 25.

Georgia was incorporated into the Transcaucasian Soviet Federated Socialist Republic in March 1922 which, in turn, became a part of the Union of Soviet Socialist Republics on December 30, 1922. Stalin, who was people's commissar for nationalities in the Moscow government, carried out a purge of active nationalists, including even members of the *Georgian Communist Party*. In December 1936, the Transcaucasian SFSR was formally dissolved and the Georgian Soviet Socialist Republic became one of the constituent republics in its own right.

Georgia certainly derived some benefits from its participation in the Union of Soviet Socialist Republics. Illiteracy was wiped out, schools of higher education were set up, a Georgian Academy of Sciences was established, and a great deal of industry was built. Yet the price was conformity to Marxist-Leninist ideology and a suppression of traditional Georgian culture.

When Gorbachëv launched his policy of *glasnost* after he took over in 1985, therefore, one of his early supporters was Eduard Shevardnadze, first secretary of the *Georgian Communist Party* from 1972 to 1985. Shevardnadze, made a full member of the Politburo and minister of foreign affairs, became a strong voice at the center urging on Gorbachëv the necessity for further reforms.

Gorbachëv's reforms were endorsed and exploited as much in Georgia as any part of the Soviet Union and the *Georgia Communist Party* soon found itself outbid by Georgian nationalists, who did not have to worry about loyalty to Moscow. When Gorbachëv decided to permit real elections in 1989, the nationalists were given their chance. A seven party coalition called *Round Table-Free Georgia* won 62 percent of the seats in the October 1990 republic elections. They then proceeded to elect Zviad Gamsakhurdia, a long-time nationalist dissident and anti-Communist, as Georgia's head of state. The name of the country was also changed to the Republic of Georgia.

In April 1991, the Supreme Soviet declared Georgia's independence and amended the constitution to create a popularly elected, executive president. Gamsakhurdia swept the subsequent May 26, 1991 presidential elections with 86.5 percent of the vote.

Shortly after assuming the presidency, Gamsakhurdia began to show rather authoritarian tendencies. For example, he signed a law which made "maligning" the president a crime punishable by six years in prison. He also accused reporters of ly-

ing and had them thrown out of a news conference. And he began to attack the political autonomy enjoyed by Muslim South Ossetians in the north of the country.

When the attempted *coup* against Gorbachëv began in August 1991, Gamsakhurdia opted for a policy of neutrality. This led to a split in the government coalition because Tengiz Sigua, the prime minister, and Gyorghi Khoshtaria, the foreign minister, publicly opposed the *coup*. Gamsakhurdia dismissed both of them in the days following collapse of the *coup* and, when the dismissals led to popular demonstrations in the main square of Tbilisi, Gamsakhurdia ordered the National Guard to fire on the demonstrators.

When Gamsakhurdia ordered Tengiz Ketovani, the commander of the National Guard, to use force against a subsequent demonstration, the latter refused. Gamsakhurdia then fired him also, thereby driving him into the opposition.

Gamsakhurdia also abolished South Ossetia's autonomous status; in the resulting unrest, over a hundred persons were killed and 50,000 Ossetians sought refuge over the mountains in North Ossetia, in the Russian Federation.

As daily demonstrations continued in Tbilisi against Gamsakhurdia, members of the government coalition began to go over to the opposition. When Gamsakhurdia ordered the arrest of Georgi Chanturia, the leader of the opposition *National Democratic Party*, Tengiz Sigua and Tengiz Ketovani led a series of demonstrations demanding that Gamsakhurdia resign. After anti-Gamsakhurdia demonstrators seized control of the government radio and television station on September 22, they were joined by members of the Georgia National Guard and more than ten thousand demonstrators marched on government house to demand President Gamsakhurdia's resignation

Gamsakhurdia spent the next three months penned up in the parliament building as, outside, riots, shootings and demonstrations took place in the streets. Gamsakhurdia fled Tbilisi on January 6, making his way first to Azerbaijan and then to Chechnya. Eventually he made his way to western Georgia. Here he rallied his supporters and attempted to force his way back to power; but his remaining support was just too small.

Meanwhile the victorious opposition set up a Military Council to govern the country, with Tengiz Sigua taking the office of provisional prime minister while Tengiz Ketovani continued as commander of the National Guard. Rumors soon began to spread that Eduard Shevardnadze would return to Georgia and reenter Georgia politics. In February, Shevardnadze announced that he had agreed to

Georgia

serve as honorary chairman of an umbrella group called the *Democratic Union*. The Military Council immediately welcomed Shevardnadze's return.

In March, the Military Council relinquished power to the legislature, which set up a governing State Council to run the country until elections could take place. Shevardnadze was elected chairman of the State Council on March 10.

In October 1992, a new legislature was elected and Shevardnadze was elected to the office of speaker of the State Council. In spite of his new title, Shevardnadze had to share power with his prime minister, Tengiz Sigua, and his defense minister, Tengiz Ketovani, the two men who arranged for his installation as chairman of the State Council in the first place.

Meanwhile, the political situation remained unstable. In June, Gamsakhurdia's supporters launched a coup to overthrow the new government. They managed to seize the television tower but were easily routed by Georgia National Guard troops. A second coup attempt, launched in November 1992, was more serious and was put down only after Russian troops were deployed on the railway running through the area. Gamsakhurdia died in Samegrelo in the western part of Georgia, an apparent suicide.

Georgia's Secessionist Movements

Shevardnadze inherited two secessionist movements from his predecessor. The first of these, South Ossetia, was set off when Gamsakhurdia attacked its autonomy, though it later became tied in with the wish to unite with neighboring North Ossetia. Tengiz Ketovani, defense minister and head of the Georgian National Guard, carried out an attack on Tskhinvali, the capital of South Ossetia in May 1992. Shevardnadze preferred a negotiated settlement, however, and responded favorably when President Yeltsin offered to mediate the dispute. The two sides eventually agreed to a negotiated ceasefire which was to be policed by a joint Russian-Georgian-Ossetian force. The government of South Ossetia had declared its independence during the confrontation, however, and has since referred to itself as the Republic of South Ossetia. A 2000 conference, organized by the Russian Government brought together officials from Georgia, South Ossetia, North Ossetia and the OSCE. The sticking point was South Ossetia's unwillingness to give up its claim to independence. In spite of subsequent talks, that is still the situation today.

The Abkhazian secessionist movement can be traced back to 1990 when Abkhazian nationalists began to demand greater local autonomy. In August 1992, the Abkhazian legislature voted to reinstate the

Centenarian dancers of *Narta'a* go to give a concert   Courtesy: NOVOSTI

region's 1925 constitution, in effect asserting its independence.

In response, Shevardnadze sent in a force of 3,000 men armed with tanks and helicopter gun ships in an attempt to take control of the capital city of Sukhumi. The Abkhazian Government, headed by Vladislav Ardzinba, fled the capital, and Georgia was facing the possibility of a long period of guerrilla warfare. When President Yeltsin offered to mediate this dispute, therefore, Shevardnadze accepted and he and Ardzinba signed a cease-fire agreement in September.

The cease-fire did not hold. More fighting broke out again in October and the Abkhazians, this time supported by other mountain tribes of the Caucasus plus some Russian Cossacks, managed to gain control over a large part of northwest Abkhazia.

Russia mediated a new cease-fire in the summer of 1993 which required heavy weapons and most of the soldiers to be withdrawn from both sides. The Georgian Government complied, but the Abkhazians did not. After the Georgian troops had been withdrawn from the area, the Abkhazians launched an attack on Sukhumi, the regional capital. Sukhumi fell on September 27.

In February 1994, President Yeltsin flew to Tbilisi, accompanied by General Grachev, to sign a treaty, under whose terms Georgia not only joined the CIS but also granted Russia the right to establish military bases within the country; in turn, Russia agreed to train and arm the Georgian army and to provide Georgia with 40 billion rubles ($25 million) in trade credits. A CIS peacekeeping force was to be stationed along a 13 km. stretch of the Inguri River, which marks the internal border between Abkhazia and the rest of Georgia. This force, which consists entirely of Russian soldiers, was installed in July 1994.

Later in the year, the United Nations brokered a peace agreement whereby refugees from the fighting in 1993 and early 1994 were to be permitted to return to their homes and talks were to begin on a political settlement. The resulting talks broke down when the Abkhazian parliament adopted a constitution declaring the Abkhazia to be a "sovereign democratic state." Vladislav Ardzinba was also inaugurated as president on December 6.

In March 1997, Russia backed a resolution at the CIS heads of state summit that extended the geographical area in which the CIS peacekeeping force operated and gave them more extensive powers to protect refugees attempting to return to their homes in Abkhazia. The Abkhazian leadership refused to recognize the legitimacy of the 1997 CIS resolution, however, so almost no refugees returned to their homes.

Angered, President Shevardnadze threatened to veto the extension of the mandate of the CIS peacekeeping force when it came up for renewal in July. The Georgian parliament also passed a resolution in May 1997 suggesting that Georgia leave the CIS if the 1997 CIS resolution were not implemented. Alarmed, President Yeltsin invited Shevardnadze and Abkhazian President Vladislav Ardzinba to meet with him in Moscow on August 2 for "one last serious talk." Russia announced, at the same time, that only the CIS could cancel the mandate of the CIS peacekeeping force, so that meant that the force would remain in place at least until the next CIS meeting in October. Shevardnadze accepted Yeltsin's invitation to come to Moscow, as did the Abkhazian leadership. Although Russia attempted to get the two sides to sign a peace protocol at the talks, both sides refused, so the meeting was essentially a failure.

The United Nations became actively involved in the Georgia-Abkhaz dispute during the summer of 1997. In July, the UN Secretary-General asked the United States, Germany, France and the U.K. to form a Friends of Georgia group (Russia was invited as an observer) to provide a new venue for talks. This group sponsored a series of meetings between Georgia and Abkhazia which at least got the two sides to promise not to use violence or the threat of violence against each other. Georgia refused to lift its economic sanctions against Abkhazia, however, and Abkhazia refused to allow the repatriation of refugees.

The Friends of Georgia group then arranged for another round of talks in Geneva on November 17–19. Here, the Georgian and Abkhaz delegations agreed to create a coordinating commission with three working groups that would focus on security issues, repatriation, and economic and social issues. Nothing else was accomplished, however.

Abkhazia carried out new presidential elections in October 1999 which resulted in the reelection of Vladislav Ardzinba for a second term. In that same election, the people approved a referendum on the 1994 constitution which defined Abkhazia as an independent sovereign state. A few days later, the Abkhazian parliament formally adopted a statute reaffirming the region's status as an independent state.

In the summer of 2001, there was a flare-up in relations between the Georgian Government and the Abkhazian authorities, but it was defused after President Shevardnadze met several times with Anri Djergenia, the prime minister of Abkhazia. At the time, Djergenia expressed his admiration for Shevardnadze, though other Abkhaz leaders were skeptical about Shevardnadze's intentions and wary of his peace proposal.

Two months later, a new crisis erupted when several hundred Georgian and Chechen fighters entered the Kodori Gorge, an area of divided control between Georgia and the Abkhazia, and began launching attacks against Abkhaz troops. The Georgian Government responded by sending in 350 of its own troops to restore order. Abkhazia immediately demanded that Georgia withdraw its troops, and a similar request came from Russia. In the end, Georgia agreed to withdraw its troops in return for a UN promise that the UN Observer Mission, which had pulled out of the area in 2000 after one of its patrols was abducted, would resume patrols of the upper reaches of the Kodori Gorge. It also helped that the UN released its latest peace settlement document at this time which, while allowing Abkhazia to retain its constitution and state bodies, required

it to acknowledge that it is a constituent part of Georgia.

The UN Observer Mission resumed its patrols in conjunction with the Russian peacekeeping force deployed under the CIS aegis on March 25, 2002. In return, the Georgian Government promised to remove its troops from the Kodori Gorge. Even as the last Georgian troops were withdrawn, however, a series of attacks were launched against the CIS peacekeepers. Blaming Georgia, the Russian Government sent some 200 troops into the Kodori Gorge on April 12, but pulled them out two days later after President Shevardnadze personally intervened with President Putin.

Meanwhile, the UN Security Council, in renewing the mandate of the UN Observer Mission in Georgia at the end of July, called on both sides to work for a durable political solution to the conflict which would define Abkhazia's status within Georgia, based on concessions and mutual understanding. Addressing this latter point, the Georgian parliament amended the constitution in October to designate Abkhazia as an autonomous republic within Georgia. Abkhaz Prime Minister Djergenia rejected the Georgia parliament's action, however, saying that the Abkhaz would not discuss the option of autonomy within Georgia. The Abkhaz political leadership has also refused to begin talks on the UN-drafted document "Basic Principles for the Distribution of Competencies between Tbilisi and Sukhumi."

In March 2003, in a new initiative launched under UN auspices, the ambassadors in Tbilisi of the five member countries of the Friends of the UN Secretary-General group tasked with mediating a solution to the Abkhaz conflict—the United States, Russia, France, Germany and Great

Britain—met with the Abkhaz leadership to present a new proposal for solving the crisis. The Abkhaz leadership rejected the new proposals, characterizing them as an attempt to force Abkhazia to renounce its independence and revert to being an integral part of Georgia. However, a breakthrough of sorts did occur at about this same time when the Georgian and Russian presidents arranged a meeting with Abkhaz Prime Minister Gennadii Gagulia (who had replaced Djergenia as prime minister in late 2002) in Sochi, Russia, on March 7. Here, agreement was reached to allow those Georgian displaced persons who fled their homes during the 1992–93 war to be repatriated, in the first instance to Abkhazia's southernmost Gali Region and then to other districts. After the repatriation is complete, railway communication will be restored between Sochi via Abkhazia to Tbilisi and modernization will begin at the Iguri Hydroelectric Power Station. In addition, a joint Russian–Georgian–Abkhaz police force and administration is to be created for Gali, which the Abkhaz side had previously rejected. These small steps appear to be the result of Russian pressure on the Abkhaz leadership.

There was a change in the political leadership of Abkhazia in January 2004 when Sergei Bagapsh was elected president. The new prime minister is Aleksandr Ankvab. Although Russia originally supported Bagapsh's opponent for the presidency, it does not appear that Bagapsh's election will bring any significant change in Abkhazia's relations with the Georgian central government.

Shevardnadze Consolidates His Power

By 1995, Shevardnadze had begun to assert a greater leadership role in the

The Metekhi Bridge across the Mtkvari (Kura) River, Tbilisi   Courtesy: NOVOSTI

Georgia

country. It also helped that Georgia was beginning to turn around again economically. That summer, Shevardnadze and his supporters pushed through a new constitution which established a presidential system. Elections for the presidency and a new legislature were set for November.

In August 1995, several persons attempted to assassinate Shevardnadze by throwing bombs at his vehicle. Although the instigators were never definitely identified, the Georgian Government accused Igor Giorgadze, a former minister of security, of being behind the attempt on Shevardnadze's life. After the assassination attempt, Shevardnadze won the presidency with approximately 70 percent of the vote; in addition, the *Union of Citizens* party, the political party Shevardnadze had founded, won a dominant position in the new parliament as well. Shevardnadze was now the dominant voice in Georgian politics.

Perhaps that explains the new attempt on President Shevardnadze's life that occurred on February 9, 1998, the second attempt within 2½ years. President Shevardnadze was returning to his residence in his limousine, a bullet-proof Mercedes provided by the German Government, when his vehicle was fired on by a several-man hit team armed with high caliber weaponry. In the battle that ensued, two presidential guards and one attacker were killed.

Five suspects arrested six days later were identified as supporters of ex-President Gamsakhurdia. The government eventually identified approximately fifteen possible plotters, most of them Gamsakhurdia supporters. But it is still not clear what the motives of the assailants might have been or who they might have been working for. Gamsakhurdia is, of course, dead, so killing Shevardnadze would not have brought their faction back to power.

Nevertheless, a group of approximately 20 individuals who identified themselves as Gamsakhurdia supporters abducted four members of the UN observer mission in Zugdidi on February 19 and demanded the release of seven men arrested in connection with the assassination attempt. The UN hostages were released six days later.

Two months later, it became clear that the two years of stability that Georgia had enjoyed in 1996–97 had come to an end. This time, it was renewed fighting between Georgian guerrillas and Abkhaz Interior Ministry forces in Abkhazia's southernmost province of Gali, which produced an additional 35,000 Georgian refugees.

The last event occurred in October 1998 when Georgian army units stationed in the west sector of the country mutinied,

seizing several high-ranking Georgian officials as hostages. Although the insurrection failed almost immediately, it was yet another sign that political opposition to Shevardnadze continued to exist. In this case, the young officer responsible for the mutiny was later identified as a former supporter of the late President Gamsakhurdia.

New parliamentary elections took place on October 31, 1999 with several dozen parties and blocs competing for seats. Four parties/blocs surmounted the seven percent barrier to participate in the division of the 150 seats distributed on a proportional basis. The pro-Shevardnadze *Union of Citizens* took 44 percent of these seats, followed by the *All-Georgia Union of Revival*, the vehicle of Adjar Supreme Council chairman Aslan Abashidze, came second with 23 percent. The other parties/blocs that surmounted the seven percent barrier were the *Labor Party* and the bloc *Industry Will Save Georgia*, led by beer magnate Gogi Topadze.

New presidential elections took place on April 9, 2000. Seven candidates entered the race but Adjar Supreme Council Chairman Aslan Abashidze, who was expected to give Shevardnadze the greatest amount of competition, withdrew from the race two days before the balloting. As a result, President Shevardnadze won an easy reelection victory, receiving over 80 percent of the vote. Dzhumber Patiashvili, Shevardnadze's successor as first secretary of the *Georgian Communist Party*, came in second with 16 percent.

What should have been a triumph for Shevardnadze actually sullied his record, however. Although most observers agree that Shevardnadze would have won in any fair election, his local officials apparently worried about a poor showing and so turned to ballot-stuffing and tampering with the results. "Local governors showed too much zeal "was the way Mikheil Saakashvili, parliamentary leader of the Shevardnadze-founded *Union of Citizens* party, phrased it. From that time onward, Shevardnadze came under increasing attack from the political opposition, in particular the leaders of the *Georgian Communist Party*, the *Socialist Party*, the *Labor Party*, plus supporters of deceased former President Gamsakhurdia. These attacks by the political opposition were probably not very important.

In the summer of 2001, however, the pro–government majority split over the question of fighting corruption and began to disintegrate. By all accounts, corruption has become a very real problem with Georgia's huge shadow economy accounting, by some estimates, for 30 percent or more of GDP. Moreover, leading government officials have been accused of cor-

ruptly protecting important individuals in this shadow economy in return for pay–offs. Mikheil Saakashvili, an energetic young reformer who became justice minister in October 2000, made corruption an important issue when he proposed requiring government officials to reveal the source of their wealth. When senior officials criticized Saakashvili's proposal, President Shevardnadze rejected Saakashvili's proposal. Shevardnadze later pushed through a requirement that all government officials file a formal statement of their assets with the government, but this did not satisfy Saakashvili, who resigned as justice minister and subsequently went over to the opposition.

In the bitter struggle that erupted over the issue of government corruption, the *Union of Citizens* party first split into quarreling factions and then began to disintegrate. The *Union of Citizens* party had always been a curious amalgam of former Soviet–era bureaucrats–now turned businessmen—who worked with Shevardnadze in the 1970s and 1980s; environmentalists who had formerly been organized into a separate, *Green Party*; plus a group of energetic young reformers recruited into government by Shevardnadze beginning in 1995. One of those young reformers was Mikheil Saakashvili, a lawyer who became chairman of the parliamentary faction in August 1998 at the age of 28; at the same time, he served as chairman of the parliamentary anti–corruption committee. When Saakashvili resigned as justice minister and subsequently left the party, most of the young reformers in the party left with him.

Shevardnadze resigned as chairman of the *Union of Citizens* in September, apparently hoping that the party might be able to hold together if he severed his connection with it. However, the opposite happened. Over the following two weeks, up to 50 deputies quit the party. It lost its majority on October 8 when the *Majoritarian–Georgia's Regions* faction formally withdrew its 21 deputies from the parliamentary majority bloc.

On November 1, Shevardnadze was forced to dismiss his government after a longtime ally, Zurab Zhvania, resigned his position as speaker of the parliament. The immediate issue that brought down the government was a controversial raid by state security agents against an independent television station, but the underlying issue was government abuse and corruption. The raid on the television station, Rustavi 2, was ostensibly for a tax investigation, but it was widely viewed as an attack on the independent press and it brought thousands of demonstrators into the streets. The crowds demanded the resignations of the minister for state security and the interior minister, but Shevard-

Georgia

Tea leaves are harvested from tea–bush fields

Courtesy: NOVOSTI

nadze chose to dismiss his entire cabinet instead.

In December 2001, Mikheil Saakashvili and nine other former members of the *Union of Citizens* formed a new faction called *For Democratic Reforms*. Saakashvili subsequently joined with other opposition parties to create the umbrella opposition *National Movement*. As a final blow, several members of the parliament faction of the *Union of Citizens* joined the parliamentary opposition in March 2002. Shortly afterwards, a second faction led by Zurab Zhvania, former speaker of the parliament, moved into open opposition; this breakaway faction later became the *United Democrats*. A core section of the party continued to support Shevardnadze, however, and it was reinforced when the *Tanadgoma (Support)* parliamentary faction, which split from the *Union of Citizens* in the fall of 2001, joined the pro-government coalition.

In January 2003, a new pro–presidential majority was formed when eight parliament factions and 15 independent deputies informally aligned to support the government. The new majority consisted of the *Union of Citizens of Georgia*, the *Alliance for a New Georgia, Tanadgoma*, the *Socialists, Abkhazeti, New Abkhazia–Christian Democrats*, the *Majoritarians*, and the *Industrialists*. The goals of the new majority were relatively limited—to ensure passage of the 2003 budget, to adopt the planned reform of the territorial–administrative system, and pass a new electoral law. The latter was necessary because new parliamentary elections were scheduled to take place on November 2, 2003.

As the time for the parliamentary elections approached, it became clear that the main opponents of the pro-government *For a New Georgia* bloc would be former allies of Shevardnadze. The most important of these was Mikheil Saakashvili, whose *National Movement* was contesting the

elections, but nearly as important was the allied *Burdjanadze-Democrats* bloc, a merger of Zurab Zhvania's *United Democrats* with Nino Burdjanadze's separate political organization. In all, nine blocks contested the November 2 elections. Five of the remaining six blocs ran in opposition to the government. The sixth, the *Revival Party*, threw its support to Shevardnadze at the last moment.

The trouble began shortly after the November 2 voting when early reports indicated that the pro-government political parties were gaining enough votes to rob Saakashvili and his allies of their hoped for electoral victory. From the beginning, Saakashvili made it clear that he and his supporters would accept nothing less than victory and he accused the government of rigging the vote. When the Central Election Commission announced the official outcome of the elections on November 19—Mr. Shevardnadze's party *For a New Georgia* came in first with 21.32 percent of the vote, the *Revival Party* came second with 18.84 percent—the opposition refused to accept the results.

Charging that the result had been manipulated, Mikheil Saakashvili immediately demanded that President Shevardnadze step down and that the election results be annulled. What came next was four days of demonstrations that came to be referred to as the "Rose Revolution." Shevardnadze resigned as president on November 23, and Nina Burdjanadze, speaker of the parliament, then became acting president until new presidential elections could be held. These elections were set for January 4, 2004. Separately, Georgia's highest court annulled the results of the November 2 parliamentary elections for the 150 proportional representation seats, and these elections were to take place on March 28.

Mikheil Saakashvili swept the January 4 presidential elections with 96 percent of

the vote. Shortly after his inauguration on January 25, he had the parliament reestablish the office of prime minister. He then appointed Zurab Zhvania to this post. Since Nina Burdjanadze already held the position of speaker of the parliament, Saakashvili and his allies controlled all of the top executive and legislative posts in the state. To guarantee that they would retain these posts, Saakashvili, Zhvania and Burdjanadze drew up a common list for the March 28 parliamentary elections, which ran under the name of the *National Movement-United Democrats*. Four other blocs and 14 individual parties registered for the March 28 contest, but none of them represented the discredited Shevardnadze forces.

When the votes were tabulated, the *National Movement-United Democrats* took 67.2 percent of the vote. The only other party to surmount the seven percent minimum required for parliamentary representation was the *Industrialists-New Rightists* alignment, an allied party. The only opposition in the new parliament is from among deputies who won in single member constituencies on November 2, not more than 13 deputies.

However, the results of the voting deepened a quarrel between Saakashvili and Aslan Abashidze, chairman of the Supreme Council of the Adjar Autonomous Republic and a former ally of President Shevardnadze. It had begun the previous November but escalated shortly after Saakashvili's inauguration as president. It got even worse when Saakashvili announced in March that he intended to bring the Adjar Autonomous Republic, together with the breakaway republics of Abkhazia and South Ossetia back under control of the central government.

Taking this as a challenge, Abashidze had his border police deny President Saakashvili entry at the border; Saakashvili could enter Adjaria, Abashidze said, but only if he came alone, unaccompanied by armed men. After a telephone conversation failed to resolve the differences, Saakashvili presented Abashidze with an ultimatum, in effect giving him 24 hours to accede to Saakashvili's demands. Abashidze's reply was to blow up the bridges connecting Adjaria with the rest of Georgia; thereupon Saakashvili declared a blockade of Adjaria. Moscow Mayor Yuri Luzhkov managed to defuse the quarrel temporarily after he flew to Adjaria for talks with Abashidze. This led to Saakashvili coming to Batumi, capital of Adjaria, on March 18.

When the parliamentary elections took place 10 days later, Abashidze's party, the *Union for Democratic Revival (DAK)*, won only 6.2 percent of the vote. Abashidze charged that Saakashvili and his allies had

211

Georgia

President Mikheil Saakashvili

manipulated the vote in order to keep the *DAK* out of the national parliament.

The quarrel went on for another month, with President Saakashvili insisting that Adjaria had to come back under central government control. Saakashvili secured a promise from Russia that its troops stationed in Adjaria would not support Abashidze. As the noose tightened, Abashidze finally realized that he could not win, and he fled into exile in Russia on May 6. Saakashvili immediately flew to Batumi, where he took charge of the autonomous republic. The next day, he dissolved the local parliament and established direct rule from Tbilisi. New parliamentary elections were then scheduled for June 15.

Saakashvili has made it clear that reestablishing central control over Adjaria is only the first step, He fully intends to bring Abkhazia and South Ossetia back under central government control, though he realizes that that will be a longer process, and he will probably have to use other measures than those used in Adjaria. Saakashvili has therefore established himself as a Georgian nationalist, a point he emphasized when he arranged for the body of former President Gamsakhurdia to be brought to Tbilisi from Chechnya for honorable burial.

In February 2005, Prime Minister Zhvaniya was killed by carbon monoxide leaking from a faulty gas heater while staying at the apartment of a political colleague in Tbilisi. His successor is Zurab Noghaideli, who had previously held the post of finance minister. Zoghaideli, a political ally of Zhvaniya's faction in the ruling political party, has placed his major emphasis on job creation and economic growth since becoming prime minister.

Foreign Policy

Under Gamsakhurdia, Georgia refused to join the Commonwealth of Independent States and attempted to sever all ties with the other former Soviet republics.

Since Gamsakhurdia also began to act in an authoritarian manner domestically, the United States withheld diplomatic recognition and it was only after Shevardnadze was installed as chairman of the State Council that the United States formally recognized Georgia. An embassy was opened in April 1992 and Secretary of State Baker paid an official visit to Tbilisi in May. Relations have been good ever since.

Shevardnadze began working for a better working relationship with Russia from the moment he returned to power in Georgia. A new treaty signed in February 1994 gave Georgia membership in the Commonwealth of Independent States and tied her to Russia militarily.

Georgia's continued struggles with its breakaway province of Abkhazia have also played an important role in its relations with Russia. Prior to 1994, Russia was inclined to support Abkhazia's attempts to break away. When Georgia agreed to join the CIS and to allow Russia to establish military bases within the country, however, Russia's position changed and, in early 1996, Russia even agreed, at the urging of the Georgian Government, to impose economic sanctions on Abkhazia. Since then, Russia has generally supported the Georgian position on Abkhazia.

The existence of four Russian military bases in the country has also had a negative effect on Georgia's relations with Russia. After negotiations, Russia agreed to close two of the bases. One of the two, the Gudauta base in Abkhazia, has been turned into a recreation facility for the Russian peacekeeping force deployed under CIS aegis in the Abkhaz conflict zone.

In May 2005, the foreign ministers of the Georgian and Russian Governments reached agreement on a timetable for the closure of Russia's two remaining bases at Akhalkalaki and Batumi. Sergei Lavrov, the Russian Foreign Minister, promised that Russia would complete the phased withdrawal of 3,000 troops by 2008. The announcement closed out one of the several issues straining relations between the two countries.

Another factor negatively affecting Georgian–Russian relations is the continuing conflict in neighboring Chechnya. Russia was particularly disturbed that Georgia had permitted as many as 8,000 Chechen refugees and perhaps 1,500 Chechen rebels to find refuge in the area of the Pankisi Gorge, an area of Georgia just south of the Chechen border where the local population speaks a language related to Chechen and is mainly Muslim. Georgia had always refused to extradite any Chechens or to allow Russia to send troops across the border into the area. In

December 2000, Russia instituted a visa requirement for Georgian citizens as a form of retaliation, for Georgia is the only CIS country whose citizens need a Russian visa to enter the country. Moreover, Russia exempted residents of Abkhazia and South Ossetia—the two areas that reject the authority of the Georgian Government—from this visa requirement.

The Pankisi Gorge was, however, only a minor irritant in Russian–Georgian relations until after the terror attacks launched against the United States on September 11, 2001. As the United States began to organize its war against terrorism, Russia—concerned about the long-time presence of foreign radical Muslim fighters involved in the fighting in Chechnya—was among the first nations to sign on. As Russia and the United States began sharing intelligence on terrorism and, in particular, Osama Ben Laden's Al Qaeda organization, the piece of information that particularly stood out was the large number of Chechens who had gone to Afghanistan for training and then became part of the Al Qaeda organization. By January 2002, both the Russians and Americans had information indicating that some of these radical fighters were present in the Pankisi Gorge.

Russia's first reaction was to suggest a combined Russian–Georgian force to clear the area of the Pankisi Gorge of all such individuals. But Georgia demurred, arguing that any military operation in the Pankisi Gorge would endanger civilians and risk bringing Russia's war in Chechnya to Georgia.

As it happens, Shevardnadze had made an official visit to the United States in October 2001, where the continuing conflict in Chechnya and Georgia's need for assistance in guarding its borders were two of the topics discussed. At the time, the United States had made a general offer of military assistance. After intelligence indicated the possible presence of Al Qaeda fighters in the Pankisi Gorge, however, the United States offered to train four battalions of Georgian troops—approximately 1,200 men—plus provide light weapons, vehicles and communications equipment, in all a military assistance program with a cost of $64 million. The package also included deploying 200 special operations forces to Georgia to provide the training for the four Georgian battalions. These U.S. forces, the first of whom arrived in Georgia in May 2002, conducted four stages of antiterrorist training, each of which took approximately six months. In March 2005, the program was essentially renewed when the United States agreed to fund a further two-year training program for the Georgian military forces at a cost of approximately $65 million.

Although this is the first time that U.S. military forces have been stationed in Georgia, it is actually only an intensification of a military relationship going back several years. Georgia has received a significant amount of military equipment, training, and financial aid from the United States over the past several years, and many members of Georgia's senior officer corps have received training in the United States. The United States has also provided indirect military assistance by encouraging Turkey to aid the Georgian military and to carry out military construction projects such as the rebuilding of Georgian airfields and military facilities.

This is not only related to the United State's current war against terrorism. In March 2001, David Tevzadze, the Georgian defense minister, and Irakli Menagharishvili, the foreign minister, paid official visits to Washington, D.C. The defense minister's talks with Defense Secretary Rumsfeld focused on an expansion of bilateral military cooperation; the foreign minister, who met with Secretary of State Powell, received American assurances of support in the face of Russian pressure plus a statement of the U.S. Government's commitment to the Baku–Ceyhan export pipeline.

In December 2002, Georgia and the United States signed a defense cooperation agreement which among other things allowed American military personnel to enter the country without a visa and to carry personal weapons. Implementation of the agreement was delayed by opposition in parliament, however; it then became an issue between Georgia and Russia when Russian officials attacked the agreement, charging that it "seriously upsets the balance of forces in the region and poses a threat to international security."

U.S.–Georgian relations continue to expand in spite of Russian objections, however. Georgia approved the opening of a FBI office in the country in February 2003. In April, Georgia offered to participate in the reconstruction of Iraq. Georgia was an early supporter of the United States over Iraq and it is now offering to provide construction materials and qualified specialists. In 2005, Georgia increased the number of troops it has in Iraq to 850, up from 156 previously.

President Bush made an official visit to Georgia in May 2005 where he hailed the Rose Revolution as a model for democracy movements everywhere. Bush's visit was a big boost for President Saakashvili, but it irritated the Russian Government enough that Russian Foreign Minister Lavrov wrote a letter of complaint to Secretary of State Rice about it.

President Saakashvili paid an official visit to the United States in July 2006, where he received a warm welcome from President Bush. In September 2006, a dozen U.S. military officers and officials visited Tbilisi to discuss an expansion of U.S.-Georgian military cooperation in 2007. The group also reviewed the Georgian NATO Individual Partnership Action Plan.

Georgia's relations with Russia have been in a downward spiral since the latter part of 2005. In December 2005, Gazprom, Russia's natural gas monopoly, announced that it was increasing the price it charged Georgia for natural gas to $110 per 1,000 cubic meters. Gazprom's explanation for the increase was that it represented a movement toward market pricing for natural gas and it was careful to point out that the price increase applied to Armenia, Moldova, and Ukraine as well; however, the news was not well received in Georgia—perhaps because the price increase did not apply in Abkhazia and South Ossetia, the two breakaway regions of Georgia.

Next, on January 23, 2006, two explosions in Northern Ossetia in southern Russia damaged both strands of the gas pipeline that supplies gas to Georgia, thereby cutting off gas supplies to Georgia (and Armenia) for several days. A third explosion damaged the main power line supplying electricity from Russia to Georgia. Although the breakages were almost certainly the result of sabotage, many Georgians were ready to believe that the Russian Government arranged the explosions in order to put economic pressure on Georgia.

The third event came at the end of January when President Putin, citing a need for "universal principles," seemed to endorse independence for the Georgian breakaway provinces of Abkhazia and South Ossetia. Putin's concern was actually with a United Nations discussion with regard to the future of Kosovo, but the argument he used was that "if people believe that Kosovo can be granted full independence, why then should we deny it to Abkhazia and South Ossetia?" He went on to add that Russia would not immediately recognize Abkhazia and South Ossetia as independent states, "but such a precedent does exist." Needless to say, the Georgian Government was not pleased.

The next development came on March 27, when the Russian Government banned the importation of Georgian wines—claiming that the Georgian Government was not maintaining adequate sanitary standards. A similar ban was applied to Moldovan wines at the same time. In April, Russia's State Health Directorate offered to lift its ban if Georgia would agree to a system of joint control over wine production in Georgia. Tbilisi considered the

Prime Minister Nogaideli

ban to be a form of political intimidation, however, and rejected the any system of joint control. Russia then banned the importation of Georgian mineral water in May.

Two months later, with feelings running high, the Georgian parliament passed a resolution demanding the removal of all Russian peacekeeping troops from Abkhazia and South Ossetia. The Russian foreign ministry responded by calling the resolution "a provocative step directed at fuelling tension, undermining the existing format for negotiations, and demolishing the legal foundations for resolving the Georgian-Abkhaz and Georgian-Ossetian conflicts peacefully."

Continuing the downward spiral, the Georgian Government arrested four Russian military officers on spying charges and police surrounded a Russian military headquarters in Tbilisi demanding that a fifth Russian officer be handed over to local authorities. Russia then recalled its ambassador from Georgia. President Putin, in his first comments on the crisis, accused Georgia of "state terrorism with hostage taking." At this point, The Russian Government then severed all transportation links with Georgia, including commercial flights and train service, and cut all mail delivery. At this point, President Saakashvili turned over the four Russian military officers to Karel De Gucht, the foreign minister of Belgium, who was also chairman of the OSCE. De Gucht delivered the four officers to a Russian Emergencies Ministry plane, waiting at Tbilisi airport.

But Russia continued its economic blockade even after the four Russian officers were returned and, domestically, began moving against Georgians living in Russia. Approximately 500 Georgians were deported during the first week of October and many Georgian shops, restaurants and businesses were closed because of alleged tax violations. Gazprom also announced that future natural gas sales to Georgian would cost $230 per 1,000 cubic meters—though it indicated that might offer a lower price if Georgia

Georgia

would sell Gazprom a stake in its energy sector.

In retaliation, the Georgian Government stated that it would oppose further meetings dealing with Russian accession to the WTO. Two months later, Georgia reversed its position. Foreign Minister Bezhuashvili announced on December 26, 2006, that "Georgia is interested in Russia's admission to the WTO, as we need to have a reliable and civilized trade partner." He did point out, however, that it is "illogical that Georgia, a full-fledged member of WTO, is blockaded by a country that is a candidate for admission in this organization." Russia sent its ambassador back to Georgia in January 2007, and since that time the two countries have taken steps to normalize relations. However, Russia continues its support for the separatist movements in both Abkhazia and South Ossetia, in November 2006 even submitting a petition on their behalf to the United Nations.

Georgia has been a member of the Council of Europe since January 1999, the first of the Caucasus republics to be so honored. Georgia became a full member of the World Trade Organization in June 2000. Georgia would also like to become a member of NATO. In May 2003, a NATO delegation of four military delegates arrived in Tbilisi to conduct an inspection of Georgian military facilities and to review the state of Georgia's military re-

Picking citrus fruit on a state farm near Batum, Georgia   Courtesy: NOVOSTI

forms. The North Atlantic Council formally endorsed the Georgia Membership Action Plan in October 2004. However, Sergei Lavrov, the Russian foreign minister, gave an interview in February 2007 in which he said that "we have warned Georgia, and those…who actively encourage Georgia to join NATO, that we shall not permit this."

Nature of the Regime

Georgia adopted a new constitution in 1995 which established a presidential system of government. It also created a 250-seat unicameral legislature, called the *Umaghiesi Sabcho* (Supreme Council). Since February 2004, Georgia has also had a prime minister who presides over the cabinet and oversees day-to-day operation of the government. The new prime minister is Zurab Zhvania.

Eduard Shevardnadze was forced to resign as president on November 23, 2003 after the opposition had accused him of fixing the November 2 parliamentary elections. Mikheil Saakashvili won the new presidential elections which took place on January 2, 2004, winning 96 percent of the vote. Meanwhile, the Constitutional Court had voided the November 2 elections to the *Umaghiesi Sabcho* as they pertained to the 150 seats to be distributed on a proportional basis to those parties/blocs that won over seven percent of the overall vote in the elections. These elections took place on March 28.

President Saakashvili, Prime Minister Zhvania and Speaker of the *Umaghiesi Sabcho* Burdjanadze drew up a common list for the March 28 parliamentary elections, which ran under the name of the *National Movement-United Democrats*. Four other blocs and 14 individual parties registered for the March 28 contest, but none of them represented the discredited Shevardnadze forces.

When the votes were tabulated, the *National Movement-United Democrats* took 67.2 percent of the vote. The only other party to surmount the seven percent minimum required for parliamentary representation was the *Industrialists-New Rightists* alignment, an allied party. The only opposition in the new parliament was from among deputies who won in single member constituencies on November 2, not more than 13 deputies. A small number of deputies have left the parliamentary majority faction since that time, however, and there is now an opposition within the parliament. Several opposition parties have also been created within the past year, though they have no way to get into the parliament before the 2008 elections.

In February 2005, the parliament approved a constitutional amendment which reduces the number of deputies from 235 to 150, Under the new rules, which will take effect at the time of the 2008 parliamentary elections, 100 deputies will be elected from party lists and 50 from single-seat constituencies.

Culture

Georgia is a land of ancient culture, a surprising amount of which has survived, considering that it was for centuries a battleground between the Persian and Byzantine Empires and, later, the Ottoman Empire. Georgian architecture is particularly interesting because of the role it played in the development of the Byzantine style of architecture.

Georgia has also had a written language since the fifth century A.D., and there are a number of great works which have survived. The earliest of these is an epic masterpiece by the poet Shota Rustaveli, called *The Knight in the Tiger's Skin*. A cultural renaissance at the end of the nineteenth century produced a number of poets, including Ilia Chavchavadze, Akaki Tsereteli, Vazha Pshavela, novelists such as Alexander Qazbegi, and writers like Mikhail Javakhishvili, Paolo Iashvili, Titsian Tabidze, Giorgi Leonidze and Irakli Abashidze.

Most of these artists were later executed by Stalin when he decided in the 1930s to stamp out Georgian nationalism in his native state. Georgia has also produced important painters (Niko Pirosmanashvili, Irikli Toidze) and composers (Zakaria Paliashvili, Meliton Balanchivadze). Vakhtang Chabukiani was the founder of the Georgian national ballet. There is also a vibrant Georgian theater and film industry. *Resurrection*, a recent surrealistic film about a Stalin-like dictator, was one specifically Georgian contribution to *glasnost*.

Nor should one forget Zviad Gamsakhurdia, the first anti-communist leader of the country, elected in 1990 and forced out as president at the beginning of 1992. Gamsakhurdia, the son of Georgia's best-known modern novelist, was a leading Georgian author in his own right, as well as a translator. Among the authors he translated are Shakespeare and Baudelaire. Tengiz Sigua, the former prime minister, was a professor before he entered politics, while Tengiz Ketovani is a sculptor.

Georgia has one major university, Tbilisi State University, which was founded in 1918. In addition, the Georgia Academy of Sciences, established in 1941, consists of a number of scientific institutions which conduct research throughout the republic. There is also an extensive library system.

Most citizens are nominal members of the Georgian Orthodox Church but the Georgian Orthodox Church does not play an important role in people's lives. Eleven

MEET PRESIDENT BUSH

TBILISI, GEORGIA

years after the fall of communism, President Shevardnadze took the first step to begin reversing that condition when he and Georgian Patriarch Ilia II signed a constitutional agreement between the state and the church in October 2002. In the document, the government confirms the church's ownership of all churches and monasteries on Georgian territory except for those now privately owned. It also acknowledges the material damage inflicted on the church since the loss of autocephaly in 1811 and pledges to recompense at least part of it. Parliament is reportedly currently working on legislation which will implement the promises contained in the constitutional agreement.

Economy

Georgian industry has four main branches—mineral extraction, machine-building, chemicals and textiles. Extensive coal deposits have been developed along the southern slopes of the Great Caucasus Mountains, particularly at Tkvarcheli and Tkibuli. Georgia also has petroleum and some natural gas. Other minerals include manganese and talc.

The machine-building industry produces railway locomotives, heavy vehicles, several types of planes, and earth moving equipment, but it also produces things like lathes and precision instruments. The chemical industry produces pharmaceuticals, synthetic fibers and mineral fertilizers. The textile industry produces cotton, woolen and silk fabrics and some clothing.

Agriculture contributes importantly to the economy, in spite of the fact that agricultural land is in short supply and much of it is located along mountain slopes. Major crops tend, therefore, to be labor intensive—and with a higher cash value—such as citrus fruits, tea and nuts. Georgia produced 97 percent of the citrus fruits and 92 percent of the tea of the now defunct Soviet Union. Georgia was also a major exporter of wines, brandy and champagne

to other parts of the Soviet Union, though here Armenia is a major competitor and Azerbaijan produces wines as well. Georgia was also a significant exporter of dairy products and canned foods. Other major agricultural products include sugar beets, tobacco, perfume oils, poultry, bees and silkworms.

This state has great potential for tourism. It already has several resorts and sanatoria located on the Black Sea coast, some of which are famous for their mineral springs. In the interior, there are many monasteries and churches which qualify as architectural monuments.

The Georgian economy suffered terribly in the first years after independence, however. The gross domestic product (GDP) dropped by nearly 73 percent between 1991 and 1994 and inflation soared to 1,500 percent. Georgia was forced out of the ruble zone in late 1992 and for the next three years they made do with "coupons" issued by the state.

During those years, anecdotal evidence portrayed an economy in deep collapse. In Tbilisi, the subway didn't run most of the time because of a lack of electricity. Buildings also remained unheated for the same reason. A female computer operator, earning the equivalent of $12 a month, commented that "that's a very good salary." Yet she also reported that butter was selling for the equivalent of $5 a pound. An academic at the Institute of Philosophy at the Georgian Academy of Sciences reported that his monthly salary was the equivalent of $3.

When Shevardnadze first took over, his government was tied down by a civil war so it was not immediately able to launch a program of reform. The economy stabilized in 1995, then grew by 11 percent in 1996, by 11.3 percent in 1997, and by 7.9 percent in the first eight months of 1998. Inflation showed the same trend, dropping from 13.8 percent in 1996 to 7.9 percent in 1997, then by 3.6 percent in the first eight months of 1998. The average monthly

wage, although still low, had begun to climb and stood at about $50 a month by the end of 1997. The currency, the *lari*, introduced in October 1995, also remained stable.

On the financial front, the banking system had been strengthened. Privatization, begun in 1995 then temporarily halted by a presidential decree in 1966, was restarted in July 1997 when 266 enterprises were sold. Foreign direct investment, still small, had reached $105.3 million as of October 1997. Among the firms that foreign investors bought were a brewery, a bottler, and a producer of sparkling wine.

Still there were more weaknesses than strengths. Georgia was still running budget deficits every year, though the trend was downward. More serious was the trade deficit, caused by the fact that imports were running 3.7 times the level of exports. Still, the Georgian Government had the support of the IMF and the World Bank, along with the EU and the United States, and their loans financed Georgia's current account deficit. Georgia's foreign debt stood at about $1.485 billion as of October 1997.

Then came the economic collapse of Russia in September 1998 and it was not long before the Georgian economy also came under attack. The government was forced to abandon support of the currency in December 1998, resulting in a 30 percent loss in value within a week. It later stabilized at a little less than 2 to the $1, but the effect was to bring a sharp rise in consumer goods. The *lari* managed to stabilize at this level, however, and as late as the beginning of 2001 it was trading at just over 2 to the dollar. Then the political instability resulting from the collapse of the government coalition in the fall of 2001 brought the currency under renewed downward pressure and by March 2002 it had fallen to 2.35 to the dollar.

The currency might actually have fallen even further but for two actions favorable to Georgia that occurred in early 2001. The first was the U.S. Government's decision to grant Georgia most favored nation status, an action that gives Georgia greater access to U.S. markets. The second was a decision by the Paris Club to grant Georgia a moratorium on debt repayment. This latter action, announced in March, rescheduled $921.9 million of Georgian debts. Repayment was postponed until the beginning of 2004 and would then extend over a period of 15 years.

The Georgian economy started growing again in 2000, though at an anemic 1.9 percent. Georgia's GDP increased by 5.4 percent in the first six months of 2001, though it faltered in the latter part of the year after the government coalition began to fall apart in the late summer. It also did

Georgia

not help that fighting broke out again in the Kodori Gorge in eastern Abkhazia after the area was infiltrated by a military force made up of Georgian guerillas and Chechen rebels. But there were other factors affecting the economy as witness the fact that industrial output actually dropped by 2.6 percent in the first half of 2001, i.e., before any of these events occurred.

Meanwhile, the Georgian Government was so strapped for funds that it failed to pay its dues for membership in international organizations. This led to Georgia's being stripped of its voting rights at UNESCO in November 2001. It was about to lose its voting rights in the United Nations in February 2003 when President Shevardnadze ordered the Georgian Foreign and Finance ministries to expedite payment of at least an initial installment of the $7 million it owed in back dues.

The economic situation showed some improvement over the next year, though things remained bleak for ordinary Georgians. In January 2005, the minimum monthly pension was raised from $7 to $15 and there are indications that the amounts of pension arrears has diminished as well. Government revenues have increased considerably, with the result that the 2005 budget called for revenues of $1.08 billion, approximately three times what the government was collecting just two years earlier.

The government has also taken a number of steps which help economic growth in the longer run. In January 2005, the government privatized the Georgian merchant fleet by selling it to a British-Australian consortium for $161 million. The new owners have pledged to increase the size of the fleet from 15 to 30 vessels, while all Georgian seamen are promised their jobs for 12 years. The government also passed a new amnesty law as a way to get rid of the "grey" market. Under its terms, businessmen who declared their previously undeclared assets and paid a 1 percent tax on them could not be pursued by the tax authorities for tax debts incurred prior to 1 January 2004.

The news in 2005 was even better. First of all, the United States Government approved a grant of $295.3 million in financial aid over the next five years under the Millennium Challenge Account. Some two-thirds of the money will go to four projects focused on the development and modernization of the infrastructure of the poorest regions of Georgia. The World Bank also approved a $13.5 million grant to support Georgia's poverty reduction program. Thirdly, the Georgian section of the Baku-Tbilisi-Ceyhan oil pipeline was completed in October 2005, and the entire pipeline was completed by the end of the year. Azerbaijan has begun filling the pipeline and the first deliveries to Ceyhan came in 2006. Next, the Georgian Govern-

ment reported that foreign investment increased by nearly 47 percent in 2004. Almost 87 percent was concentrated in Georgia's service sector, with industry a distant second. Lastly, Georgia regained its voting rights at the United Nations after it paid nearly $6 million to cover the country's UN membership dues arrears.

The Future

Independent Georgia's greatest problem has always been its lack of political stability. Mikheil Saakashvili's election as president has provided ordinary Georgians with the hope that they now have a strong president who will be able to enforce order and extend the writ of the government throughout the entire country. His actions with regard to Adjaria were a good beginning, though there is serious doubt that Abkhazia, for one, will peacefully return to Georgian central control unless Russia drops its position of support for the Abkhazian regime.

Saakashvili has also begun to address the problems of the economy, but they are so great that it may take years before significant progress occurs. Still, Saakashvili has begun to give the country a new political stability, which is indeed an important first step. As everybody says, Georgia has great potential as an independent country, provided it can work out its political problems.

The Village of Ushguli, Svaneti in the Georgian Mountains

Photo by: Giorgi Sulamanidze

The Republic of Kazakhstan

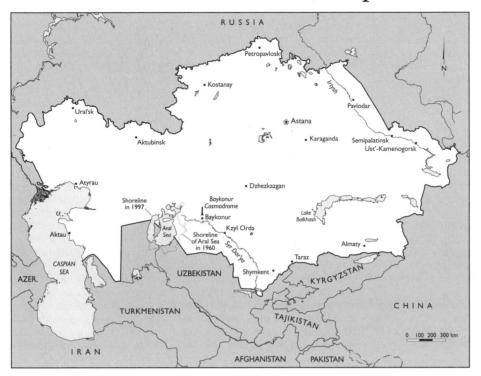

Area: 1,049,155 sq. mi. (2,717,300 sq. km., almost twice the size of Alaska, second largest state in the former USSR).

Population: 15.233 million (July 2006 estimate).

Capital City: Astana (Pop. 500,000). Astana (then Asmola) was designated the new capital in 1995 and the government formally moved to the new capital in December 1997. The name was changed to Astana in 1998. Most of the government ministries, as well as most foreign embassies, remain in Almaty.

Climate: Continental, with very hot summers and extremely cold winters.

Neighboring States: Russia (west and north), China (east), Kyrgyzstan, Uzbekistan, and Turkmenistan (south).

Principal Languages: Kazak (Qazaq), the state language; and Russian, official: used in everyday business, designated the "language of interethnic communication."

Ethnic Composition: Kazakh (Qazaq) (53.4%); Russian (30%); Ukrainian (3.7%); Uzbek (2.5%); German (2.4%); Uighur (1.4%); Other (6.6%).

Principal Religion: Islam (47%); Russian Orthodox (44%); Protestant (2%); Other (7%).

Chief Commercial Products: Agriculture—grain, livestock, cotton, wool. Industry—oil, coal, iron ore, mineral extraction (manganese, chromite, lead, zinc, copper, titanium, bauxite, gold, silver), tractors and other agricultural machinery, electric motors, construction materials.

Currency: tenge (issued November 1993).

Annual Per Capita Income: $5,100.

Recent Political Status: The Kazakh SSR was formally a part of the Russian Soviet Federative Republic (RSFR) but in December 1936 it was proclaimed a separate constituent republic of the former USSR, remaining in that status until 1991.

Chief of State: Nursultan Nazarbayev, President (reelected on December 4, 2005).

Head of Government: Karim Masimov, Prime Minister (January 2007).

National Day: December 16 (1991), independence from the Soviet Union).

National Flag: A golden sun rising above mountains superimposed upon a sky–blue background, with the left edge showing a stylized pattern in worked gold.

The Land

The Republic of Kazakhstan (Qazaqstan Respublikasy), successor government to the Kazakh Soviet Socialist Republic, declared its independence on December 16, 1991. The Kazakh Soviet Socialist Republic had existed only since December 1936. Its predecessor was the Kirghiz (later renamed Kazakh) Autonomous Soviet Socialist Republic, which had been founded in August 1920 as an autonomous republic of the Russian SFSR.

In spite of its size, Kazakhstan is geographically rather homogeneous. Essentially it is a great tableland, with lowlands, plains and plateaus making up approximately 80 percent of the landscape. Mountainous regions in the east and southeast make up the remaining parts of the land.

Kazakhstan is actually a Eurasian land, with its western border beginning at the northern end of the Caspian Sea, just east of the mouth of the Volga River. It then turns slightly west and runs northward just east of the Volga River before bending northeast and skirting the southern edges of the Ural Mountains. East of the Urals, it zig–zags north until it passes the Russian city of Magnitogorsk before turning eastward. After passing just south of the city of Omsk, it turns southeastward and pushes to the top ridge of the Altai Mountains. It then turns at a sharp angle and runs in a southwestern direction along the ridges of the Tarbagatay Range and the Ulu–Tau Mountains until it passes just south of the republic's former capital of Almaty. Here it turns westward and runs along the foothills, crossing the Syr Dar'ya River, until just north of Samarkand. It then crosses the Kyzylkum Desert and passes through the center of the Aral Sea, bending from there southward to reach the center of the Caspian Sea.

The western portion of the republic is dominated by the Caspian Depression. The Mogodzhar Hills, a southern extension of the Ural Mountains, separates the Caspian Depression from the Turan Plain, which stretches west–east just north of the Aral Sea. To the east of the Aral Sea is the

217

Kazakhstan

Kyzylkum Desert. To the northeast of that, separated by the valley of the Syr Dar'ya River, is an area called the Hunger Steppe. These areas in the south are all desert and only the presence of the Syr Dar'ya River makes any agriculture possible. The northern part of Kazakhstan is known as the Kazakh Steppe, however, and here there is sufficient rainfall to support grasses. The northern part of Kazakhstan is an area of farms that concentrate on growing wheat and other cereal crops.

Some irrigation is also possible in this northern area, using water from the Ural River in the west and the Irtysh River in the east. Two smaller rivers, the Ishim and Tobol, also provide water for irrigation. Overall, the republic has over 7,000 streams and rivers, plus about 48,000 small lakes. Kazakhstan also has 1,450 miles of coastline along the Caspian Sea.

The weather is sharply continental, with cold winters and hot summers. Temperatures in the southern part of Kazakhstan are much milder, however, with January temperatures averaging 23°–29°F. Average July temperatures are 68° in the north and 84° in the south. The area of the North had rich, black soils; south of that the soils are chestnut–brown, but still fertile. In the extreme South, soils tend to be infertile and alkaline, or sandy desert. Woodlands, found most in the mountains, make up only 3 percent of the total land surface.

The People

The population of Kazakhstan, which was an estimated 15.233 million as of July 2006, began shrinking and becoming more rural after the republic became independent at the end of 1991. The urban population dropped by 8.4 percent between 1989 (when the last Soviet census was taken) and 1999, while rural population dropped by a smaller 6.8 percent. Overall, there was a population drop of about 1.5 million in the past decade. That trend was reversed over the past couple years, however, and the population is once again growing. One factor may be the increasing number of migrants from Central Asia, drawn in by increase in available jobs as a result of the significant growth that has taken place over the past several years. Kazakhstan's Labor Ministry estimates that there were 300,000 illegal immigrants employed in the country in 2005; the vast majority of them were Kyrgyz, Tajiks, or Uzbeks.

According to an announcement by the director of the Migration and Immigration Agency in January 1999, 2.17 million persons left Kazakhstan during its first seven years of independence, while 590,000 entered the country. Approximately one million Russians, 600,000 ethnic Germans, 300,000 Ukrainians, and 70,000 Tatars em-

igrated during this period. Most Germans migrated to Germany, encouraged by free flights paid for by the German government. According to German government estimates, only about 170,000 ethnic Germans continue to live in Kazakhstan.

Meanwhile, ethnic Kazakhs increased by approximately 1.5 million. Natural population increase accounted for most of that growth, though approximately 170,000 ethnic Kazakhs migrated to Kazakhstan from other republics. Ethnic Kazakhs now constitute 53.4 percent of the population, making them the majority group in Kazakhstan for the first time since the 1950s.

Next come Russians, who dropped from 40 percent of the population in the 1989 census to 30 percent today. Percentage–wise an even greater drop occurred among ethnic Germans, from 6 percent of the population in 1989 to 2.4 percent today. The remaining larger minorities include Ukrainians (3.7%), Uzbeks (2.5%) and Uighurs (1.4%) The remaining 6.6 percent are divided among nearly a hundred nationalities, but the majority of them are Tatars, Belarusians, Dungans, and Koreans. The Kazakh people, who are mainly Muslim, speak a Turkic language, but are Mongol in physical appearance.

History

The first reference to Kazakhs living in Central Asia is found in a Russian source dated 1534. Subsequently, the Russians referred to these people as Kaisak–Kirgiz or simply Kirgiz. Undoubtedly, the reason for this is that the Russian word *Kazaky* means Cossacks and it describes Russian peasants living on the frontier. It appears, in fact, that modern Kazakhs are descendants of the old Kipchak tribes, which

were part of the East–Central Asian "Golden Horde."

In the fifteenth century, there was a Kazakh Empire that controlled the steppe land to the east of the Caspian Sea and north of the Aral Sea stretching as far east as the western approaches of the Altai Mountains. This empire lasted until the beginning of the eighteenth century, but then was weakened by attacks from a revived Oyrat Empire to the east. The Kazakhs were at this time organized into three principalities, the "Little Horde," "Middle Horde" and Great Horde.

When the Russians began their advance into this area in the eighteenth century, the Kazakhs decided to accept Russian protection against their enemies to the east. The "Little Horde" accepted Russian protection in 1731, followed by the Middle Horde in 1740 and the Great Horde in 1742.

The Kazakhs began to fear Russian control, however, and this led to a series of uprisings toward the end of the eighteenth century. As a result, Russia began to suppress the autonomy of the Kazakh Khans. The Khanate of the "Middle Horde" was suppressed in 1822, the "Little Horde" in 1824; and the "Great Horde" in 1848. In 1854, the Russians founded the fortress of Verna, which eventually became the modern city of Almaty. The area was administratively divided into four areas. In the latter part of the nineteenth century, there were large–scale settlements of Russian peasants established in the northern part of the territory.

A small Kazakh nationalist movement came into existence at the beginning of the twentieth century, and a number of Kazakh deputies were elected to the first and second legislatures. The first Kazakh

Kazakhstan's former capital of Almaty as seen from Mt. Kok Tyube   Courtesy: NOVOSTI

218

The dam in the Maly Almaatinsky Gorge at Medeo Courtesy: NOVOSTI

newspaper began publication in 1910. In 1916, a revolt broke out when the Russian Government ordered the mobilization of all persons between the age of 19 and 43. It was put down harshly.

After the *Bolshevik* seizure of power in November 1917 in Moscow, Kazakh nationalists demanded full autonomy for Kazakhstan. A Kazakh nationalist government was formed, but was suppressed in 1919–20 when the Red Army occupied the area. The Bolsheviks did sponsor creation of the Kirgiz Autonomous Soviet Socialist Republic in August 1920, however. In 1925, the name was changed to Kazakh; in 1929, the capital was established at Almaty (formerly Alma–Ata). Kazakhstan became a Soviet Socialist Republic in December 1936.

The *Kazakh Communist Party* was established in 1937; Zhumabay Shayakhmetov became its first ethnic Kazakh head during World War II. He was replaced in 1954 by P. K. Ponomarenko, a Slav, because he showed insufficient support for the Moscow–sponsored newly–launched Virgin Lands campaign. Ponomarenko was replaced by Leonid Brezhnev, who remained first secretary of the *Kazakh Communist Party* until 1956. After he became General Secretary, Brezhnev appointed an ethnic Kazakh, Dinmukhamed Kunaev, as first secretary of the *Kazakh Communist Party*. He held that position until December 1986, when he was removed by Gorbachëv and replaced by another Slav, Gennady Kolbin.

When word reached Almaty that Kunaev had been dismissed and was being replaced by an ethnic Russian, violent rioting broke out and several persons were killed. Gorbachëv, recognizing that he had to be more sensitive to nationalist sentiments, later reassigned Kolbin and replaced him with another ethnic Kazakh.

When hardliners launched their *coup* against President Gorbachëv on August 19, 1991, Nursultan Nazarbayev, the Kazakh president, condemned the action and called for Gorbachëv's return. After the *coup* failed, Nazarbayev severed all ties with the *Kazakh Communist Party*, then banned all political activity in government, the courts and police. The *Kazakh Communist Party* disbanded, then subsequently reconstituted itself as a *Socialist Party*. The *Socialists* held their first congress at Almaty in December 1991. They do not have much influence, however.

Even as the USSR began to disintegrate in late 1991, Nazarbayev strongly supported some form of continued union of the republics and, almost alone among the republic leaders, he did not press for a declaration of independence until it became clear that the old union was dead. This made sense from the point of view of Kazakhstan, for it is a large republic with a relatively small population and its economy was heavily tied to Russia. Most people still lived in the countryside and worked the land. The main industry was mineral extraction, most of which was traditionally shipped to other republics for further processing. In addition, a significant percentage of the population had ethnic ties to Russia or one of the other republics.

The Kazakh government carried out fairly extensive changes after Kazakhstan declared its independence in 1991, but the pace of change began to slow thereafter. The government still encouraged foreign investment, but there was some retrenchment on market–oriented economic changes introduced in 1991 and early 1992. In addition, terms like "pluralism" and "moving toward democracy" lost their earlier currency. The best characterization for Nazarbayev is that he is an "authoritarian modernizer" who is putting economic development before political liberalism.

On the other hand, Nazarbayev is in many ways rather pragmatic. Aware of growing nationalist currents within the country and sensitive to those feelings, he is also aware that Russian speakers still constitute 32 percent of the overall population. Moves to increase the use of the Kazakh language have accordingly been moderate. For example, the amount of instruction in the Kazakh language has been increased in the schools, but Russian is still the medium of instruction.

Kazakhstan's constitution designates Kazakh as the national language, but Russian is described as the language of inter–ethnic communication. The constitution also requires the president to have a good command of the Kazakh language, but does not stipulate that he be an ethnic Kazakh.

One of the strange things about Kazakhstan after 1992 was the almost total lack of any political opposition to Nazarbayev. Nobody challenged him at the executive level and the legislature remained compliant to his wishes. Yet Nazarbayev did not act in a particularly dictatorial manner and appeared to favor the development of at least some political pluralism. The ethnic split in the republic may have been part of the explanation. Nazarbayev was one of the few individuals who had significant support from both Kazakhs and Russians.

That began to change in late 1994. On the one side, ethnic Russians began to agitate for greater recognition within the state, including the designation of Russian as the second official language, and they also began demanding the right to dual Russian–Kazakh nationality. Nazarbayev's efforts to placate them brought a reaction from ethnic Kazakhs. For the first time, voices of criticism were heard in the Kazakh parliament. In early 1995, a majority rejected the president's proposals to give the Russian language equal status with Kazakh. The parliament also rejected a proposed law establishing procedures for the privatization of land.

The Constitutional Court then offered Nazarbayev an unusual opportunity when it declared the March 1994 elections to be illegal on the basis that they offended the "one man, one vote" principle. Nazarbayev immediately disbanded the parliament and accepted the resignation of the government. He then announced that he would rule by decree until a new parliament was elected. Parliamentarians protested, and some threatened to form an alternative assembly. Nazarbayev, however, used the interregnum to push ahead with measures he had been unable to get through the parliament, such as privatization, enhancement of the status of the Russian language, and streamlining the tax system.

New parliamentary elections took place in December 1995. There were multiple

Kazakhstan

candidates for most of the 67 seats, with the result that only 43 candidates won a majority of the votes in the first round of voting. A second election then followed to fill the remaining seats. Although many of the winners ran without a party affiliation, most were, effectively, supporters of government policies.

In 1999, President Nazarbayev established a new political party, *Otan,* as his support base. Within a short while, 44 of the 67 members of the lower house joined *Otan.*

Nazarbayev has been much concerned by the out–migration of ethnic Russians since 1991. In an attempt to address their concerns and encourage them to remain, he has made a number of gestures toward the Russian community. In 1994, he extended the time when residents would have to decide whether to opt for Kazakh citizenship; when it became clear that many Russians were hesitant to relinquish their Russian citizenship, he endorsed the concept of dual Russian and Kazakh citizenship. The migration of ethnic Russians to Russia and elsewhere continues, however.

Another of Nazarbayev's concerns is the possibility of a separatist movement in the northern part of the country where most Russian speakers live. Attempting to address that problem, he decided in 1995 to move the capital from Almaty in the extreme southeastern part of the republic to Akmola (or Aqmola), a town of 270,000 located near the center of the country. Akmola had the advantage that it was nearer the main population and industrial centers. Moreover, the northern half of the country contains most of the country's natural resources, including oil, gas, gold, chrome and copper, as well as much of its best farmland.

On the other hand, Akmola was only a provincial town in 1995 and it lacked the facilities to house a government. Over the past several years, therefore, whole new districts have been constructed to house the government, the parliament, the foreign embassies and the governmental workers. This also involved constructing new luxury hotels, new residential areas, an additional business center, and an enlarged airport.

The formal move to Akmola took place in December 1997 when President Nazarbayev sent state symbols, including the flag, coat of arms, and the presidential banner, to the new capital. In fact, much of the construction ordered in 1995 remained incomplete, so most of the government ministries remained in Almaty, as did most foreign embassies. Those government officials actually transferred to Akmola have had to be housed in temporary quarters for the most extent. Parliamentary deputies have been assigned to hotel rooms, while government officials have been put up in hostels or even kindergartens.

Although estimates of the amount of government funds invested in the new capital by this time stood at $1.5 billion, in one sense the task of constructing a new capital had only just begun. This was also reflected in the fact that the government decided to give the capital a new name. "Akmola," it turns out, means "white tomb," and it was too much of a reminder that Akmola was the site of a Stalin–era forced labor camp for the wives of political prisoners during the period 1937–1945. The new name of the capital is Astana.

In October 1998, the Kazakh Government officially selected the Japanese architect Kise Kurokawa to produce an overall design for the new capital. The basic plan is still Kurokawa's, but there have been a number of additions to the plan as other architects have been hired for particular projects. Manfredi Nicoletti of Italy has designed a concert hall, described by those who have seen it as having the basic form of a boat, but with folds like origami. Lord Foster, a British architect, has designed another new project, known as the Khan's Pavilion; it is "a giant conical structure, bent as though blown by the harsh winds that are notorious here;" when finished, it will contain stores, a theater, a water park and seven acres of terraced gardens. In 2006, Astana's population was just under 600,000.

Presidential elections, originally scheduled to take place in December 2000, were moved up to January 1999 by the Kazakh legislature in October 1998. President Nazarbayev probably requested the legislature to take this action because he felt that, with the economy already suffering from a sharp drop in the prices of oil and steel, Kazakhstan's two chief exports, the economic situation was only likely to decline further before it got better. Nazarbayev would thus have a better chance of winning reelection if the date were moved up.

Nazarbayev did win reelection, and with an impressive 79.78 percent of the vote. The election nevertheless tarnished Nazarbayev's reputation when the government refused to allow Akezhan Kazhegeldin—prime minister between 1994 and 1997—to run as one of the candidates for the presidency. As a result, the OSCE refused to send official international observers to the election and refused to recognize its results. The United States Government also expressed its displeasure, saying in part that "the conduct of these elections has set back the process of democratization in Kazakhstan and has made more difficult the development of the important relations between our two countries."

New parliamentary elections took place in October 1999. Under a new procedure, 10 of the 67 seats in the lower chamber of the legislature (the *Majilis*) were allocated on a proportional basis to those political parties polling a minimum of seven percent of the vote. Four parties qualified for proportional seats, the pro–presidential *Otan Party* with 30.5 percent; the *Communist Party* with 17.8 percent; the *Agrarian Party* with 12.6 percent; and the *Civic Party* with 10.9 percent. The *Otan Party* was the largest party in the legislature with 23 seats, down from 44 seats in the previous legislature. However, the government still had a clear majority since the *Civic Party,* which also supported the government, took 12 seats. The *Communist Party* had three seats; the *Agrarian Party* two; and the *Republican People's Party* had one. The remaining seats were held by independents, most of whom supported the government.

President Nazarbayev has changed prime ministers six times since he appointed Akezhan Kazhegeldin as prime minister in 1994. Although Kazhegeldin was in Switzerland for medical treatment when he tendered his resignation in October 1997 "for health reasons," it is more likely that he stepped down because of policy disagreements between himself and President Nazarbayev. On the same day that Kazhegeldin submitted his resignation, President Nazarbayev told the parliament that "reforms had been insufficient and in some aspects have not produced the desired results." Kazhegeldin later became a harsh critic of the president's policies and subsequently founded his own opposition party, the *Republican People's Party of Kazakhstan.*

Nurlan Balgimbayev, named prime minister in October 1997, had been head of the Kazakhstan National Petroleum Company prior to being named prime minister. An engineer by training, he spent the years from 1986 to 1992 in the

President Nursultan Nazarbayev of Kazakhstan

Sazgen, the folk music quintet, shown at the Old Instruments Museum in Almaty

Courtesy: NOVOSTI

we intend to mobilize public opinion and force the parliament and above all the president to accept [our program].

At first, it appeared that President Nazarbayev might attempt to co–opt his more moderate critics, but that possibility evaporated when the government ordered the arrest of two of the leaders of *Democratic Choice for Kazakhstan,* former Governor Zhaqiyanov and former Energy, Industry, and Trade Minister Mukhtar Abliyazov, in March. Zhaqiyanov actually took refuge in the French Embassy in Almaty to avoid arrest, which introduced an international component into the situation.

A statement issued by the political opposition after the arrest warrants were issued makes a very important point about Kazakhstan, however. As the statement pointed out, the only senior Kazakh officials to have been charged with corruption in the decade after Kazakhstan became independent were individuals whom the government considered to be members of the political opposition— Zhaqiyanov, Abliyazov, and Kazhegeldin. Kazhegeldin, charged with corruption, was sentenced to prison in absentia. He resides abroad in self-exile and may not return to Kazakhstan.

When the trials of the two leaders of *Democratic Choice for Kazakhstan* took place in July 2002, therefore, the verdicts were expected to be harsh and they were. Former Energy, Industry, and Trade Minister Mukhtar Abliyazov was sentenced to six years in prison with confiscation of all property, plus he was ordered to pay a fine of $3.6 million. Former Governor Zhaqiyanov was sentenced to seven years in jail.

Even as the trials were taking place, President Nazarbayev signed a new law on political parties which had been passed by the parliament at his request. Under the terms of the law, the number of signatures required for registration went from 3,000 to 50,000. In addition, any party that failed to enter parliament in two tries would lose its registration and be dissolved.

When the party registration program ended in April 2003, only six of the 19 parties that had existed up to that time had survived. Two of the parties had merged with *Otan,* the main government party. Six opposition parties never filed to reregister at all, while the remaining four parties were refused re-registration. Three of the four did not, indeed, qualify under the law, since they had fewer than 50,000 members.

However, the *Compatriots* (formerly the *Russian Party*) were refused registration even though they claimed 58,000 members. The government first challenged that figure, then ordered the party to amend

former USSR oil and gas industry ministry in Moscow. He then spent two years in the United States, first at MIT, then at Chevron's headquarters. He was appointed Kazakh gas and oil minister in October 1994, then head of the state oil company that replaced the ministry in March 1997. Balgimbayev's term as prime minister was not smooth, however, and he submitted his resignation in October 1999 after harsh criticism of his policies by Marat Ospanov, the speaker of the legislature. He was subsequently named head of KazakhOil, as the Kazakhstan National Petroleum Company is now called.

Qasymhomart Toqaev, Balgimbayev's successor as prime minister, had previously served as deputy prime minister and foreign minister. An important factor in his selection is that he was a trained diplomat with excellent international contacts, since President Nazarbayev was, at this time, particularly interested in increasing foreign investment in the country. Toqaev served as prime minister until January 2002, when he resigned and was reappointed foreign minister. His successor was Imangali Tasmagambetov who, as a former governor of the oil–rich Atrau region in western Kazakhstan, brought first–hand knowledge of the petroleum industry to the job.

It is likely that he was selected as prime minister by President Nazarbayev because of his previous portfolio as deputy prime minister of social issues and interethnic relations. Over the previous year or so, there had been increasing political

criticism of the government because of its increasing cronyism and insularity. One form this dissatisfaction took was the creation of new political parties and the merging of others to create a stronger opposition presence. President Nazarbayev's immediate reaction to these developments was to lash out against these new political entities and to treat them all as enemies. In the case of the *Forum of Democratic Forces* an umbrella organization of 16 opposition political parties, including the *Republican Party of Kazakhstan,* headed by former Prime Minister Kazhegeldin, this was probably an accurate characterization. Kazhegeldin, who subsequently merged his party with two other parties to form the *United Democratic Party,* was one of the drafters of a 15–point "National Plan of Political Transformations" in January 2002 which had as its first demand that "the president must resign."

On the other hand, the young reformers who founded *Democratic Choice for Kazakhstan* in November 2001 held various positions in the government at the time—positions they subsequently lost—and they saw themselves as advocates of a gradual political liberalization which they believed was necessary to provide the economic basis for the emergence of a middle class. They never criticized Nazarbayev personally but instead expressed the hope that their goals could be achieved through the current leadership. As one of the founders of *Democratic Choice for Kazakhstan,* former Pavlodar Region Governor Zhaqiyanov, put it in December 2001,

Kazakhstan

its political program when it filed again. The party filed yet a third time, but never achieved registration.

Thus when the re-registration process came to an end, four of the seven surviving political parties were loyal supporters of President Nazarbayev. They were *Otan*, the *Civic Party*, the *Agrarian Party*, and the *Aul* (Village) *Social Democratic Party*. The surviving opposition parties were the moderate opposition *Ak Zhol* (Bright Path) *Democratic Party*, and the *Communist Party*.

Imanghali Tasmagambetov resigned as prime minister on June 11, 2003, after he had failed to persuade parliament to pass land privatization legislation in the form desired by President Nazarbayev. His successor, Daniyal Akhmetov, governor of Pavlodar Oblast, was appointed two days later.

Akhmetov had previously been deputy prime minister for industry, transport, and communications. Akhmetov has degrees in construction engineering and economics. Stressing the need for continuity even when governments change, Akhmetov said that he intended few ministerial changes. As his previous job would indicate, Akhmetov had a particular interest in economic development. The government's first priority would continue to be on exploitation of hydrocarbon reserves, Akhmetov stated, but the agricultural sector would need greater assistance and the government would also have to provide more support for small and medium-sized businesses and domestic manufacturers.

Elections to the lower house of parliament took place on September 19, 2004, with a run-off election in 17 single-constituency seats on October 3. Twelve political parties were registered to participate in the elections and they put forth over 600 candidates for the 67 open single-constituency seats.

In the first round of voting, the pro-presidential *Otan Party* took seven of the ten proportional seats and 37 of the single-constituency seats. Its ally, the *AIST* bloc of the *Civic* and *Agrarian Parties* won two of the proportional seats plus nine of the single-constituency seats. *Asar (Mutual Help)*, the party created in 2003 by Nazarbayev's eldest daughter, Darigha Nazarbayeva, won one proportional seat and three single-constituency seats.

The only opposition party to win a seat in the parliament was *Ak Zhol*, which was awarded one proportional seat. Seventeen single-constituency seats were won by individuals running as independents, but ten independents joined *Otan* after the election, which means that the president's party actually controlled 53 of the 77 seats in the lower house.

Moreover, *Ak Zhol* announced that it was challenging the results of the elec-

tions by boycotting parliament, a position it maintained until September 2006, when the *Ak Zhol* deputy finally took his seat. Moreover, *Ak Zhol* broke up into two feuding factions after the elections, so the opposition is even further divided than it was before the elections.

New Senate elections took place on August 19, 2005. Sixteen seats were up for election; ten seats were won by *Otan* while three additional seats went to independents. The remaining three seats were won by *Auyl, Asar*, and the *Civic Party*, all allies of the pro-presidential *Otan Party*.

New presidential elections took place on December 4, 2005. Four candidates challenged President Nazarbayev for the post. Nazarbayev's main opponents were Zharmakhan Tuyakbai, head of the opposition bloc *For a Just Kazakhstan*, and Alikhan Baimenov, nominated by the opposition *Ak Zhol*. The other two candidates represented the old *Communist Party* and an environmental movement. In the end, President Nazarbayev won reelection with 91.1 percent of the vote. Tuyakbai came second with 6.6 percent, followed by Baimenov with 1.6 percent.

No one gave Nazarbayev's opponents a real chance to win, but there were problems during the campaign which reduced their chances further, in particular pressure on opposition newspapers. In the end, however, the OSCE issued a rather mild report which concluded that:

despite some improvements in the administration of this election in the pre-election period, the presidential election did not meet a number of OSCE commitments and other international standards for democratic elections.

The unmet international standards the OSCE referred to included pro-government bias in the state media, voter intimidation, and restrictions on freedom of press and assembly during the campaign. It also made reference to charges of ballot stuffing, multiple voting, putting pressure on students to vote for Nazarbayev, and irregularities in the vote counting.

It should be added that Kazakhstan has never held an election that met international standards. On the other hand, a pre-election poll by the U.S.-based survey group Intermedia showed 70 percent support for Nazarbayev; in other words, Nazarbayev would have won a fully free and fair election, though perhaps not with as many votes as he got.

Even so, the political system was severely shaken when Altynbek Sarsenbayev, an opposition leader, was found bound and shot outside the city of Almaty on February 13, 2006. Sarsenbayev, a former Kazakh ambassador to Russia, had

been co-chairman of the opposition party *Naghyz Ak Zhol* (True Bright Path), an unregistered splinter group that had split off from the *Ak Zhol*.

According to the official investigation that followed, he, his driver, and his bodyguard were victims of a contract killing carried out by five members of a special elite unit of the National Security Committee and the man who arranged for the killing was Erzhan Utembaev, a former deputy prime minister; at the time, he was serving as the administrative head of the Senate.

Even though Utembaev claimed that Sarsenbayev had been killed for private reasons—he had impugned Utembaev's honor—his killing shook the Kazakh political system and brought about the resignation of the head of the National Security Committee.

Perhaps more importantly, the killing brought a number of moves on the part of the government that point in the direction of greater political pluralism in the country. In March 2006, President Nazarbayev issued a decree creating a state commission to develop a program of democratic reforms in Kazakhstan. Nazarbayev commented with regard to the work of the state commission that "I do not rule out that it may be necessary to conduct constitutional reform as well."

The government also agreed to cooperate with the OSCE to develop "amendments and changes" to the electoral law in line with the OSCE's December 2005 criticisms of the presidential elections. In line with this trend, the government also registered Sarsenbayev's political party, the *Naghyz Ak Zhol*, in March.

In September 2006, the pro-presidential parties *Otan* and *Asar*, formally merged. *Azar* had been the party established by President Nazarbayev's daughter, Darigha Nazarbayeva. Since *Otan* already controlled a majority of the seats in the legislature, the merger may have been carried out in order to provide a larger political forum for Darigha Nazarbayeva. It will not necessarily give her any greater standing as a potential successor to her father, however.

That same month, a new opposition party, the *National Social Democratic Party (NSDP)*, was established under the leadership of Zharmakhan Tuyakbai, who ran against President Nazarbayev in the December 2005 presidential election, coming in second with 6.6 percent of the vote. The *NSDP's* platform calls for an end to the government's privatization program, a lowering of the retirement age, and free universal higher education.

In January 2007, Daniyal Akhmetov resigned as prime minister and was appointed the new defense minister; his suc-

Kazakhstan

Prime Minister Karim Masimov of Kazakhstan

cessor as prime minister is Karim Masimov, a 41-year old economist who previously had been deputy prime minister. Masimov, describing himself as President Nazarbayev's "faithful assistant," committed himself to continuity in the principles of government, "one of the most important conditions of sustained economic and social development." Masimov—who speaks Arabic, Chinese, English, Kazakh and Russian—appears to be well qualified for the position.

Foreign Policy

After the Presidents of Russia, Ukraine and Belarus agreed to formation of the Commonwealth of Independent States in December 1991, Nazarbayev was active in getting other republics to join and actually hosted the Almaty meeting where the general agreement was signed. Kazakhstan has since been an active participant in the CIS. At the same time, President Nazarbayev has been at the forefront in encouraging cooperation among the Central Asian republics. He was, for example, one of the early proponents of the Central Asian Customs Union. Uzbekistan and Kyrgyzstan were the other two original members. Tajikistan has been a member since March 1998, while Russia has observer status. The presidents and prime ministers of the Central Asian Customs Union meet periodically to work out economic differences and to discuss economic matters. The organization has facilitated economic agreements between the individual members, but its significance in terms of actual increases in trade has not yet been great.

At independence, President Nazarbayev said that he wanted Kazakhstan to become nuclear–free. In May 1993, however, he reversed himself and asked for security guarantees from the United States, Russia, and China in return for agreeing to give up Kazakhstan's nuclear weapons. He was, he said, asking for the pledge because some Chinese textbooks showed parts of Kazakhstan as being part of China. There

was also other evidence to show that at least some Kazakh officials were having second thoughts about the merits of going nuclear–free. As one of Nazarbayev's advisers pointed out, Kazakhstan would not be receiving the attentions of Secretary of State Baker and high–ranking officials of other countries, if it didn't have nuclear weapons.

Nazarbayev paid an official visit to Washington later that same month, however, and here he agreed to the withdrawal of nuclear weapons from Kazakhstan within seven years. Kazakhstan subsequently signed both the START–1 agreement and the Non–Proliferation Treaty.

Nazarbayev visited the United States again in February 1994. A major purpose of this visit was, according to his advisers, to get American help in reducing Kazakhstan's dependence on Russia. It appeared that Nazarbayev was uneasy about the rise to prominence in Russia of Vladimir Zhirinovsky, an ethnic Russian from Kazakhstan. Kazakhstan was also at that time under pressure from the Russian Government to regularize Russian control of the Baikonur space launch facility and several military bases.

During the visit, President Clinton promised to increase U.S. aid to Kazakhstan from the previous year's $91 million to $311 million in 1994–95. A number of agreements were signed, including one by President Nazarbayev formalizing Kazakhstan's adhesion to the nuclear non–proliferation treaty. Kazakhstan has since become a member of the NATO–sponsored "Partners for Peace" and has participated in military maneuvers in Central Asia.

Nazarbayev has always supported close relations with Russia but these relations were expanded in January 1995 when Kazakhstan and Russia signed an agreement calling for closer economic and military links. This was followed, a few days later, by a second agreement establishing a customs union between Kazakhstan, Russia and Belarus. President Nazarbayev also signed a key accord with Russia during a visit to Moscow in July 1998 which provided for the division of the northern sector of the Caspian Sea bed between the two countries.

The five states bordering on the Caspian Sea have been unable to agree on an overall legal demarcation of the Caspian Sea bed, considered to be a precondition for the exploitation of Caspian hydrocarbon reserves. But the 1998 agreement, which applied only to areas not claimed by the other three littoral states, allowed Russia and Kazakhstan to proceed with exploitation of the northern part of the Caspian Sea. This agreement was augmented in May 2002 when the Kazakh and Russian

presidents signed a protocol on the division of the Kurmangazy, Tsentralnoe, and Khvalynskoe oil and natural–gas fields in the northern Caspian. Under the protocol, Kazakhstan will get the Kurmangazy field while the other two fields will go to Russia. The protocol also defined the median line dividing the Kazakh and Russian sectors of the Caspian Sea.

Presidents Nazarbayev and Putin have met regularly over the past several years for wide–ranging discussions on topics such as the CIS Collective Security Treaty, energy cooperation, economic integration, and the weapons trade. In July 2006, the two presidents announced an agreement to create a joint venture to expand capacity of the Soviet-built Orenburg refinery in order to process natural gas from Kazakhstan's Karachaganak gas field.

In November 2006, Kazakh Defense Minister Akhmetov told a news conference in Astana that the top priority in Kazakhstan's new defense doctrine was participation in the Collective Security Treaty Organization (CSTO). CSTO brings together Armenia, Belarus, Kazakhstan, Kyrgyzstan, Russia, and Uzbekistan. Akhmetov then added that China and Russia "remain Kazakhstan's strategic partners under the new doctrine." He did add, however, that the doctrine accorded "serious attention to the strengthening and perfecting of cooperation with the United States and NATO."

President Nazarbayev also signed an important agreement with the Vatican during a visit there in September 1998. Essentially, the agreement grants the Roman Catholic Church full religious freedom and access to the media in Kazakhstan. This, the first such agreement that the Vatican has signed with a former Soviet republic, then provided the background for a visit which Pope John Paul II paid to Kazakhstan in September 2001. The pope celebrated a mass in Astana for some 50,000 pilgrims, then met later that same day with President Nazarbayev. There are an estimated 350,000 Roman Catholics living in Kazakhstan

U.S.–Kazakh relations deteriorated somewhat in 2000–2001 in response to U.S. criticisms of Kazakhstan's human rights record, particularly the U.S. world human rights report for 2001, which was critical of the Kazakh government's treatment of the political opposition. That changed somewhat after the terror attacks against the United States on September 11 when President Nazarbayev became one of the first among world leaders to join the American war against terrorism, declaring soon after September 11 that Kazakhstan was prepared to allow the use of Kazakh military bases by foreign troops involved in the war on terrorism. Nazarbayev also paid a

Kazakhstan

Drying astrakhan pelts of the new–born Persian lambs, used like fur for garments
Courtesy: NOVOSTI

four–day visit to the United States in December which included a 30–minute meeting at the White House. After the meeting, Nazarbayev and President Bush signed a joint statement calling for a

long–term strategic partnership and cooperation between our nations.

Military cooperation continued to expand in 2002, symbolized by the visit of General Tommy Franks, U.S. Forces commander in chief for the Middle East and Central Asia, to Astana in August. The United States received emergency landing permission for the airport at Almaty, Chimkent, and Lugovoi, while it promised to provide Kazakhstan with helicopters and humvees. Military assistance to Kazakhstan for 2003 was set at $270 million.

Yet there was another side to the relationship as well. The United States has been extremely critical of the Kazakh Government's harassment and arrest of political opponents and its actions to restrict press freedom. The Kazakh Government was also very unhappy when U.S. Justice Department prosecutors raised the issue of possible bribes paid to President Nazarbayev during the 1990s in connection with dispensing of oil concessions in Kazakhstan.

Still, the U.S. Government has made it clear that it favors continued cooperation in the military sphere. In November 2004, it offered $36 million to Kazakhstan to set up biological laboratories to track dangerous pathogens and diseases. The U.S. Government has also spoken favorably about the "excellent business opportunities" that exist in Kazakhstan, though it warned that corruption remained a hazard in the local business environment.

President Nazarbayev paid an official visit to the United States in September 2006. In Washington, he called for closer

relations with the United States, adding that "the time is coming when our relations can be raised to an absolutely different level." In a press release, the White House said that the visit had affirmed the 2001 strategic partnership agreement between Kazakhstan and the United States. The United States also expressed its support for Kazakhstan's entry into the World Trade Organization.

Nature of the Regime

Kazakhstan adopted a new constitution in 1993 which only slightly modified the presidential–parliamentary system (modeled rather closely on that of Russia) which had been set up after independence. The popularly elected, executive presidency was retained, but the new constitution created a 177–member parliament, with 42 seats to be filled by direct presidential appointees and another 11 by the official trade unions. In early 1995, the Constitutional Court ruled this system to be illegal because it violated the principle of "one man, one vote."

President Nazarbayev disbanded the legislature and ruled by decree while he had the electoral law redrafted to bring it into line with the decision of the Constitutional Court. The new electoral law created a bicameral parliament, made up of a completely elective lower house (or *Majilis*) and a partly appointed upper house (or Senate). Under the terms of the decree, seven of the Senate seats were to be filled by presidential appointment, while the remaining 32 seats were to be indirectly elected at a joint session of the representative bodies of all local government units, on the basis of two deputies from each *oblast* and major city.

Although a decision was made to postpone creation of the Senate until a later time, the first parliamentary elections for the lower house under the new system took place in December 1995. Many of the winning candidates ran as independents, since Kazakhstan was only beginning to create political parties at this time. When President Nazarbayev launched a new political party called *Otan* in 1999 as his own political platform, however, 44 deputies signed on as members.

Shortly before the 1999 parliamentary elections, new legislation was passed specifying that ten of the 67 seats in the lower house would be allocated on a proportional basis to those political parties drawing a minimum of seven percent of the national vote. In 2002, the total number of seats in the lower house was raised to 77 as of the 2004 elections, with, again, ten of the seats to be awarded to party slates on a proportional basis.

In October 2002, elections were held for 16 seats in the Senate. A total of 33 candidates—31 men and two women—competed for the seats. The majority of the candidates were members of pro– presidential parties and in six of the districts the candidate ran unopposed. Since the regional councils both nominate and elect the senators, there were few surprises. For example, The Almaty city council elected the man who had been the council's secretary for the preceding eight years. Neither woman was elected. The remaining 16 senators were elected on August 19, 2005. Ten seats were won by *Otan* while three additional seats went to independents. The remaining three seats were won by *Auyl, Asar,* and the *Civic Party,* all allies of the pro-presidential *Otan Party.*

Elections to the lower house of parliament took place on September 19, 2004. Twelve political parties nominated over 600 candidates for the 67 single-constituency seats plus separate slates for the ten proportional seats. First-round winners emerged in 45 of the 67 single-constituency seats, so run-offs were held in 22 constituencies on October 3. The pro-presidential *Otan Party* took seven of the ten proportional seats and 37 of the single-constituency seats. The pro-presidential *AIST* bloc of the *Civic* and *Agrarian Parties* won two of the proportional seats plus nine of the single-constituency seats. *Asar (Mutual Help),* the party created in 2003 by Nazarbayev's eldest daughter, Darigha Nazarbayeva, won one proportional seat and three single-constituency seats. One proportional seat was won by *Ak Zhol,* a moderate opposition party, while the remaining 17 single-constituency seats were won by individuals running as independents. Subsequently, ten of the 17 independents joined *Otan,* giving the party 53 of the 77 seats in the lower house. Since *Ak Zhol,* charging fraud, refused to take up its single proportional seat, the entire lower house is currently composed of supporters of the president.

A series of constitutional amendments passed in May 2007 specified that the size of the lower-house Majilis be 107 seats at the time of the next legislative elections; 98 Majilis seats are to be elected on the basis of proportional representation using party slates; the remaining 9 seats will be elected by the Assembly of Kazakhstan Nations. The Majilis will be organized on the basis of party factions, with the prime minister representing the majority party in the Majilis. The Senate will increase to 47, with 15 deputies to be appointed by the president. Party factions will not exist in the Senate. These same constitutional amendments reduced the term of office of the president to five years beginning at the end of President Nazarbayev's current term in 2012. The amendments also give the president the right to run for the office indefinitely; his successor will, however, be limited to two five-year terms.

Kazakhstan has had seven prime ministers since independence. The latest is Karim Masimov, appointed in January 2007 after Daniyal Akhmetov resigned. Masimov, 41, had been deputy prime minister under Akhmetov.

In October 1998, the constitution was amended to extend the term of president from five to seven years and move the time of election from December 2000 to January 1999. In July 2000, parliament passed a law bestowing on the incumbent president special powers for life. Under the terms of this law, Nazarbayev will retain a permanent seat on the Security Council after retirement; he will also retain the right to address the people, parliament, and future presidents. President Nazarbayev was reelected on December 4, 2005, winning 91 percent of the vote.

Culture

It is difficult to identify a separate culture for Kazakhstan. Kazakhs are basically a rural people who, until recently, played very little public role. Nearly all are Muslims, but there never has been a major center such as can be found in the Central Asian republics to the south, such as Tashkent, Samarkand, or Bukhara. Thus it affects the lives of the people, but in an easy–going way. There is a specific Kazakh style of clothing or interior decoration but there are no specifically Kazakh foods. Women still tend to wear a long, wide dress with a stand–up collar and bloomers gathered at the ankle, particularly in the countryside. Elderly men wear wide, white shirts, wide trousers and woolen or cotton robes. Young people of both sexes tend to wear European–style clothing. Kazakh homes exhibit specific Kazakh designs in stucco work and wall facings, while floors are covered with carpets.

There is a small national literature as well, most of it recent in origin. Abay Ibragim Kunanbayev, a 19th century humanist and poet, is usually considered to be the father of Kazakh written literature. Early twentieth century writers include Aqmet Baytursinuli, an author and newspaper editor, and Jambil Jabayev, a folk poet. The best known of the Kazakh literary figures of the Soviet period is Mukhtar Auezov, a playwright and novelist; his long novel, *Abay*, deals with Kazakh steppe life in the 19th century. It has been translated into English.

The population of the northern part of the republic is mostly Russian or Ukrainian and the culture here doesn't differ significantly from Russian areas across the border. The presence of significant numbers of Koreans and "Volga" Germans does introduce a greater element of cultural diversity, but these are mostly rural peoples who practice mainly a village culture.

Almaty is the largest city and the center for most higher education. The Kazakh S. M. Kirov State University is located here, as is the Abay Teachers College. Almaty also has polytechnic, agricultural and veterinary institutes. Karaganda has a medical institute and a teachers training college. Other institutes of higher learning are also found in regional centers.

There is a Kazakh Academy of Sciences, founded in 1945. This has particularly encouraged scholarship in ethnographic studies of the Kazakh language and the history of Kazakh literature. It also finances industrial and agricultural research.

In October 2006, President Nazarbayev told a session of the Assembly of the Peoples of Kazakhstan that the country should consider switching the alphabet for the Kazakh language from Cyrillic to Latin. He then appointed a panel of experts to produce specific proposals on the issue. At the same time, Nazarbayev expressed the hope that the next generation of Kazakh citizens would be trilingual— "they should fluently speak the Kazakh, Russian, and English languages."

Economy

About 20 percent of the residents of the republic support themselves from agriculture or stock-raising. The northern part of Kazakhstan is a major grain growing area, with supplemental crops like fruits, vegetables, grapes, sugar beets and potatoes grown. Stock-raising is concentrated in the dryer area to the south of the grain belt, in the area of the grassy steppe. Cotton, tobacco, grapes, and mustard are grown in the Syr–Dar'ya and Ili River Valleys.

Kazakhstan had already instituted a number of reforms in agriculture during the Gorbachëv era which began to break down the old system of command control. For example, a 1987 law abolished all restrictions on the number of animals that a farmer could have. This led to an increase of about 2.5 million in the sheep and goat population and about a million additional cattle. Meat sales in the cooperative sector also quadrupled in that time. In addition, 890,000 families received plots of land in 1991 and 46,000 private houses were constructed with state assistance.

In February 1992, Nazarbayev signed a decree on privatizing the property of enterprises in the agro–industrial complex, apparently intending to end the collective and state farm system. At the time, Nazarbayev commented that Kazakhstan did not need loss–making farms. "Private farming works because it is private," he was quoted as saying. There was bitter resistance to this approach at the local level, however, and as a result parliament refused to endorse any major changes. However, the government continued to pursue policies aimed at breaking up the old agricultural units with the result that, by 1999, 75 percent of agricultural land was held in leasehold by individual farmers. President Nazarbayev still favored the complete privatization of farmland, but he could not get a majority of the parliament to support him on this issue. In February 2000, therefore, Nazarbayev asked parliament to give private farmers the right to use the land they lease as a pledge on the land market.

In August 2002, President Nazarbayev took up the issue again while touring grain fields outside Almaty. Promising to submit a land law to the parliament, he said that he wanted to give farmers the right to purchase agricultural land directly, or on a 10–year installment plan. Nazarbayev next submitted the issue to Kazakhstan's National Council—which comprises representatives from the government, parliament, trade unions, presidential administration, and business community. The National Council approved a draft Land Code and ordered the government to submit the final version to parliament. Discussion of the Land Code began in parliament in March 2003. Many deputies objected and over 500 amendments were added to the bill. Two months later, the bill was still under discussion. Parliament eventually passed a privatization bill, though only after passing a number of amendments. Because he was unable to persuade parliament to pass the privatization bill in the form desired by the president, Prime Minister Tasmagambetov submitted his resignation in June 2003.

The grain harvest is usually between 14 and 15 million tons, though there can be a great variance from year to year. For example, the grain harvest went from 6.9 million tons in 1998—a year of drought—to 15 million tons in 1999 and 14 million tons in 2000, then climbed to 18 million tons in 2001. Kazakhstan produces a grain surplus for export in most years; it exported close to 6 million tons in 2001. However, Agriculture Minister Akhmetzhan Yesimov reported in August 2002 that the country had more than 4 million tons of grain in reserve, half of which was left over from harvests prior to 2001. The quality of the grain must be improved, he said, if the country wants to export all of its surplus grain. Kazakhstan produced a near record grain harvest of 17.1 million tons in 2003. Because of smaller grain harvests in the neighboring republics of Russia, Ukraine and Belarus, about half of the harvest was sold abroad. When this produced shortages at home and increases in the price of break, the government was

Kazakhstan

forced to institute an informal ban on the export of grain in January 2004.

Kazakh industry is mainly of the extractive variety. Most industry is located in the northeastern part of the republic, in and around the cities of Karaganda, Zelinograd and Semipalatinsk. It has large deposits of coal and iron ore. It also produces lead, zinc, copper, chromite, nickel, molybdenum, tin, antimony, cadmium, bauxite, gold, silver, phosphates, and oil. In addition to the processing of ferrous and nonferrous metals, it has chemical, machine–building, cement, and textile industries. Light industries associated with agriculture include food processing and leather. Overall, about 30 percent of the people are employed in industry, while approximately 50 percent are employed in services.

In September 1991, the government approved a program for the "first stage of destatization and privatization" of state property. The program, which included a coupon mechanism, promoted privatization in trade, public catering, construction, motor transport, agriculture, consumer services and small enterprises. Medium and large enterprises were to be converted to joint–stock companies, collective enterprises or partnerships. In a speech to the legislature in January 1993, however, Nazarbayev spoke of mistakes associated with free–market reform in Russia and Kazakhstan and declared that a significant decree of state control and regulation would be necessary in the future. He indicated that major enterprises would be run along commercial principles, but most would remain in state hands. Most small and medium–scale industries have been privatized since that time, but plans to extend privatization into the areas of gas and oil have been stalled. Prime Minister Balgimbaev announced in February 1998 that privatization could not proceed in these areas until the government had selected a "strategic partner." Private international companies are active in this sector, but essentially as partners of Kazakh state companies.

One colonial leftover that the Kazakhs are somewhat ambivalent about is the massive space complex at Baikonur Cosmodrone. There is no question but that the space program has given tremendous stimulus to the advancement of hi–tech education, but it has been almost exclusively Russians, not ethnic Kazakhs, that have benefited from the program. This has bothered the Government of Kazakhstan, which would like ethnic Kazakhs to be able to benefit more from its presence. A new agreement, signed in January 2004 during a visit of President Putin to Kazakhstan, extends Russia's lease to 2050. Subsidiary clauses make reference to bi-

lateral and international use of the spaceport and provide for the presence of Kazakh police, tax authorities, and customs officers in Baikonur City.

Kazakhstan is one of the few ex–Soviet republics to have attracted significant interest among foreign investors since independence. The reason for this is that Kazakhstan has some of the largest unexplored oil, gas and mineral deposits on earth. By the end of 1999, foreign direct investment in the oil, gas and mining sectors had grown to $3 billion, with an addition $1.2 billion on extraction expenditures, $1 billion invested in the construction or renovation of subsurface use facilities, and $213.7 million expended on geological surveys. In addition, Kazakhstan has commitments from foreign companies to invest more than $60 billion in the coming years. The 1998 decline in petroleum prices slowed this process, but Kazakhstan nevertheless received $1.3 billion in foreign direct investment in 1999, over one–half in the energy sector.

For example, the Chevron Corporation and the Government of Kazakhstan signed an agreement in April 1993 establishing a 40–year, $20 billion joint venture (Tengizchevroil) to develop the Tengiz and Korolev oil fields on the northeastern coast of the Caspian Sea. By June 1997, Chevron had invested $800 million in Kazakhstan and had committed itself to invest another $500 million over the next three years, with plans to invest $20 billion in the Tengiz oil field over the next 40 years. The Tengizchevroil joint venture was producing 160,000 barrels of oil a day as of June 1997 and planned to increase this to 700,000 barrels a day by 2003.

Things turned darker for Kazakhstan in 1998, however. The Asian economic crisis began affecting Kazakh steel exports first. Next, there was a 40 percent drop in oil prices which drove the price of oil below $10 a barrel. At that price, it no longer paid to invest in the relatively expensive Caspian oil. Although Petroleum prices quickly recovered, oil companies remained cautious about new investments. As an exception, Japan's Marubeni Company announced in February 2000 that it would invest $450 million to rebuild the Atyrau oil refinery over the next five years. Kazakhstan's three refineries were all in need of new capital to finance modernization.

Kazakhstan's oil production rose in 1999 to 26.6 million metric tons, an increase of 12 percent over the previous year. In addition, gas condensate production, at 3.39 million metric tons, was 60 percent higher than 1998. Kazakhstan exported 25 million tons of crude in 1999, slightly up from 24.1 million in 1998.

Oil production reached 30 million tons in 2000; the government hoped for a fur-

ther rise to between 37 and 40 million tons for 2001, though this was contingent on increasing the throughput capacity of the Atyrau–Samara pipeline to 15 million tons. Another necessary component, the new Caspian Pipeline, which runs 948 miles from Atyrau to the Russian port of Novorossiysk, was completed in March 2001.

But the greatest breakthrough occurred when the 1,580 kilometer Caspian Pipeline Consortium pipeline went on–line in November 2001. This pipeline, which runs from the Tengiz oil field in western Kazakhstan to Novorossiysk, a Russian seaport on the Black Sea, had an initial capacity of 28.2 million tons a year, which was scheduled to increase to 67 million tons. Chevron Texaco Oil, which owns a 15 percent stake in the Caspian Pipeline Consortium, announced afterwards that it would increase its production of Kazakh oil from 13 million tons per year to 20 million tons per year by 2005, and that this would involve an investment of some $1.5 billion over the following three years in the Tengizchevronoil joint venture.

In another change which occurred in February 2002, the Kazakhstan Government merged its largest oil–producing company, KazakhOil, with its largest oil–transporting company, Transport Nefti i Gaza [Oil and Gas Transportation], to produce a new closed joint–stock company, KazMuayGaz [Kazakh Oil and Gas]. The new entity will control 15 percent of the country's oil production capacity and over 6,400 kilometers of oil pipelines which deliver 80 percent of the country's oil. The government also indicated that it would retain a 51 percent stake in all new gas and oil contracts. The government anticipates that concentration of control over oil extraction and transportation will improve the coordination of operations in the sector.

Tengizchevroil cancelled plans to invest a further $3 billion into the project in November 2002 after a disagreement the Kazakh Government over funding of the planned second stage of development. The company wanted to fund the expansion out of revenues, while the government worried over the loss of taxes. Under a compromise reached in January 2003, the consortium agreed to pay $810 million to the government, of which $600 million was taxes to be paid in installments from 2003–05. In addition, the consortium agreed to take out a loan to finance the government's share of the cost of pushing ahead with development.

Direct foreign investment in the country between 1991 and 2002 was about $13 billion. However, an October 2002 government announcement that KazMunayGaz, the national oil–and–gas company, had discovered new reserves in the Caspian Sea some 80 kilometers south of the giant Kashagan field may soon make that sum seem small. In February 2004, it was announced that a consortium of international oil companies had formally agreed to invest $29 billion in developing the new oil field. Total oil reserves are now estimated to be 13 billion barrels. The oil companies involved are ENI, Royal Dutch Shell, Exxon-Mobil, Total of France, Conoco Phillips, and Impex of Japan. The Kazakh Foreign Ministry put U.S. investment in Kazakhstan at $11.43 billion as of the first quarter of 2005. In March 2006, U.S. Energy Secretary Samuel Bodman announced during a visit to Astana that U.S. investment in Kazakhstan "could double in the next five years."

The United States Government strongly supports continued American investment in Kazakhstan; in September 2006, during President Nazarbayev's visit to Washington, it issued a press release pointing out that the United States has accounted for 30 percent of foreign direct investment in Kazakhstan.

Kazakhstan's export potential is still limited by the lack of pipelines to transport energy to ports, however. The Caspian Pipeline Consortium pipeline was pumping 12 million tons per year as of October 2002, so the government is pinning great hopes on the Baku–Tbilisi–Ceyhan pipeline, which began its first oil shipments in early 2006. Kazakhstan is currently committed to build an undersea oil pipeline across the Caspian Sea that would connect Aktau in Kazakhstan with Baku in Azerbaijan. The project is timed to coincide with the beginning of production of production at Kazakhstan's Kashagan oil field in 2008. Production at Kashagan is expected to be only 75,000 barrels a day at first, but it will eventually climb to 1.2 million barrels a day. Kazakhstan is currently shipping 10 million tons of oil to Baku by boat, where it is then fed into the Baku-Tbilisi-Ceyhan pipeline.

The Kazakh Government also completed the 988-kilometer Atasu-Alashankou oil pipeline linking western Kazakh oil fields with China in December 2005. Deliveries to China began in mid-2006. The initial annual capacity of the pipeline is 10 million tons. Russia's state-owned Rosneft has also begun using the pipeline to ship oil to China. The pipeline will eventually transport 20 million ton of oil a year.

Kazakhstan's economy grew at an annual rate of 9.3 percent in 2004, with both its retail and financial sectors showing significant growth. Agricultural production jumped 6 percent in the first quarter of 2004, but that was dwarfed by a 21.5 per-

cent growth in capital investments. People are obviously much poorer in the countryside; to address this disparity, the government launched a three-year program in late 2003 aimed at providing $1 billion in new investment in agriculture over the following three years.

GDP growth in 2005 was 9.4 percent and 10 percent in 2006. Exports rose 36.3 percent to $28 billion. Industrial growth slowed to 4.6 percent in 2005, but the construction and service sectors grew so fast in 2006 that general unemployment declined. Inflation has been a problem in the economy, reaching 7.6 percent in 2005. In February 2007, Prime Minister Masimov presented an action plan to parliament with the aim of achieving an inflation of 7.5–8 percent in 2007–09. In addition, the government decided in 2006 to take some money out of the economy by paying off $849 million of the country's sovereign debt ahead of schedule, reducing it to $3.9 billion or 7.8 percent of GDP. In addition, the National Fund, created to set aside surplus energy-sector revenues, had grown to $8 billion by 2005; current figures are not available but are almost certainly larger today.

Also on the negative side, President Nazarbayev recently pointed out that "about ten mega holdings control almost 80 percent of Kazakhstan's total GDP. "We should work to transfer the secondary functions of mega holdings to medium and small business," he argued. A spokesman later explained that "what the president has in mind is that the ten financial and oligarchic groups in Kazakhstan that control 80 percent of the economy should in no way influence decision making in the government and in parliament." He also suggested that parliament would consider new laws to reduce the current economic concentration, but that such laws would take two to five years to enact.

Kazakhstan also has the second largest reserves of uranium ore in the world. In 2006, total production was 5,000 tons. At that time, the government announced a plan to raise production to 15,000 tons by 2010. In December 2006, the government celebrated the opening of the Zarechnoye mine, a joint uranium venture set up by Russia's Teksnabexport and Kazakhstan's Kazatomprom. The mine is expected to produce 1,000 tons of ore a year, all of which will be processed in Russia. In October 2006, The European Commission recommended that the European Union conclude a 10-year, $500 million agreement for Kazakhstan to supply Europe's nuclear industry; that agreement is probably years off, however.

One of Kazakhstan's problems which it inherited at the time of independence was

the situation with regard to the Aral Sea. For the first ten years or so of independence, Kazakhstan attempted to arrive at a common agreement with Uzbekistan, the other republic heavily affected by the drying up sea, but nothing was ever decided.

By 2000, the Aral Sea had split into two sections, with the larger sea largely in Uzbekistan and a small sea in Kazakhstan. Kazakhstan then turned to the World Bank, which agreed to help finance the Kok-Aral Dam and a series of dikes designed to create spillways to allow the flushing of excess salt from the sea while improving the overall water levels. The project began in 2001.

The project is still on-going, with plans to repair a second dam, dig a channel to connect the two Arals, and provide additional water management structures. However, the dam has already raised the level of the small Aral from 98 to 125 feet and it has expanded the Aral's surface area by 30 percent. The small Aral has recovered enough that commercial fishing is now once again occurring. Government experts warn that the process has only begun and it will take decades for the small Aral to recover. No one holds out any hope for the large Aral. Some water from the small Aral already makes its way to the large Aral, but it is only the excess water from a sluice on top of the dam. The Kazakh Government estimates that the small Aral will have to reach a depth of 138 feet before it will become minimally viable. When that occurs, a greater flow into the large Aral will be possible.

The Future

Overall, the Kazakh economy looks very good at the moment. Oil revenues are pouring in at a constantly increasing rate, and the government is using these revenues to finance a program aimed at spreading the wealth to the other sectors of the economy.

On the other hand, Kazakhstan has never held a national election that has met international standards for openness and fairness. President Nazarbayev has often pledged his support for political pluralism—and the OSCE did find some improvements in the latest presidential elections—but Kazakhstan still has some distance to go before it can qualify as democratic. Still, the increasing prosperity of the country has resulted in a major growth in the middle class over the past several years, so it may eventually move in that direction. If so, that would set it off from its neighbors, all of whom still adhere to more authoritarian political systems.

Kyrgyzstan

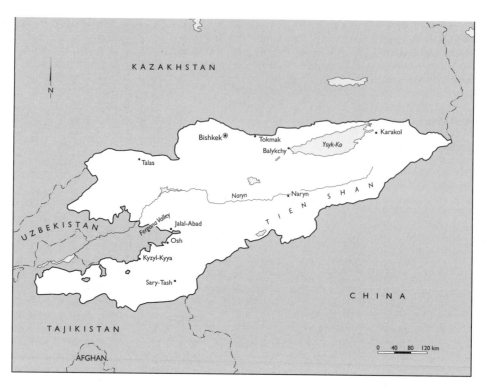

Area: 76,640 sq. mi. (198,500 sq. km., slightly smaller than Nebraska).

Population: 5.2 million (July 2006 estimate).

Capital City: Bishtek (formerly Frunze); Pop. 631,000.

Climate: Temperate in the northern foothill region; subtropical in the Fergana Valley; alpine in the high southwestern plateau; and high desert in the Tien Shan Mountains along the southeastern border with China.

Neighboring States: Kazakhstan (north), Uzbekistan (west), Tajikistan (west, southwest), China (southeast).

Languages: Kyrgyz, Russian.

Ethnic Composition: Kyrgyz (64.9%), Uzbek (13.8%), Russian (12.5%), Dungan (1.1%), Ukrainian (1%), Uygur (1%), Others (5.7%).

Principal Religion: Islam. About 20 percent of the people are nominally Orthodox Christian.

Chief Commercial Products: Cotton and cottonseed oil, tobacco, livestock, wool, hides, vegetables, sugar beets, refined sugar, flour, mining enterprises, metals, textiles.

Currency: *som* (May 1993).

Annual Per Capita Income (Purchasing Power Parity): $1,800.

Recent Political Status: Autonomous Republic within the USSR (1926), Constituent Republic of the USSR (1936–1991).

Chief of State: Kurmanbek Bakiev, President (elected July 10, 2005).

Head of Government: Almaz Atambayev, Prime Minister (confirmed by parliament on March 30, 2007).

National Day: August 31 (1991), independence from the Soviet Union.

National Flag: Red field with a yellow sun in the center having 40 rays representing the 40 Kyrgyz tribes; on the center of the sun is a red ring crossed by two sets of three lines, a stylized representation of the roof of the traditional Kyrgyz yurt.

The Land

The Republic of Kyrgyzstan (Kyrgyz Respublikasy) is the independent successor state to the Kirghiz Soviet Socialist Republic. Situated on a western spur of the Tien Shan Mountains, it is a mountainous country surrounded by more mountains; most of its borders run along mountain crests. Thus it is separated from Tajikistan by the Turkistan and Zaalay Ranges. The Kokshaal–Tau Range, a part of the Tien Shan, forms the border with the People's Republic of China.

The exception is in the southwest, where the border dips down to cross the upper reaches of the Fergana River Valley. Apart from the Fergana Valley, the only lowland areas are the downstream parts of the Chu and Talas River Valleys along the northern border. The capital, Bishtek, is located in the Chu River Valley. These lowland areas make up about 15 percent of the total surface of the republic.

Kyrgyzstan's most unusual geographical feature is Lake Ysykköl (Ysyk-ko), a high mountain lake found in the eastern part of the country. Set in a massive hollow much like the Fergana Valley in western Kyrgyzstan, it is surrounded by mountains with a high, alpine plateau to the west. A deep clear lake, it is rich in fish and supports fishing communities around its edges.

The People

The population of Kyrgyzstan is very mixed, with Kyrgyz speakers constituting only 64.9 percent of the population. Uzbeks, the largest minority, are 13.8 percent of the population, with Russians a close third at 12.5 percent. Other minorities found in the republic include Dungans (1.1%), Ukrainians (1%), Uygurs (Chinese Muslims) (1%), plus smaller numbers of Ukrainians, Germans, and other miscellaneous peoples. The Kyrgyz language belongs to the Turkic group of languages. The two official languages of the country are Kyrgyz and Russian.

History

The Kyrgyz have lived in the Tien Shan Mountains at least since the sixteenth century and some Soviet ethnographers postulate that they arrived as early as the twelfth century. Since they had no written language until recently and continued to live as a nomadic people until modern times, archaeological evidence provides most of what we know of them.

They came under the nominal control of the Kokand Khanate until about 1850, when this area became a major region of

Russian colonization. Since the Kyrgyz, as nomads, had no permanent claims on the land, the Russian colonists moved in and took most of the best land, leading to an uprising in 1916, which was put down with great force.

After the Russian Revolution, this area became a part of Soviet Turkistan. In 1921, it then became part of the Turkistan Autonomous SSR of the Russian SFSR. In 1924, it was separated from the Turkistan ASSR and given the status of an autonomous *oblast* (area) of the Russian SFSR. Two years later, it became the Kirgiz Autonomous SSR of the Russian SFSR. It was not until December 1936 that it became a constituent republic of the USSR as the Kirgiz Soviet Socialist Republic.

Much changed during the Soviet years. The nomadic life of the people ended when they were settled on collective and state farms. Some mechanization was also introduced in the countryside, and irrigation projects increased cultivated land in the lowlands. The exploitation of minerals found in the mountains has increased the number of jobs in industry and drawn more of the Kyrgyz people into cities and modern life. Most have preferred to remain in stock raising or farming, however, so the overwhelming majority of people in industry and in the urban areas are non–Kyrgyz.

Gorbachëv's *perestroika* left the republic untouched until 1990, when ethnic riots broke out in the Fergana Valley along the border with Uzbekistan. The riots left 200 people dead and damaged the reputation of Absamat Masaliev, the *Kyrgyz Communist Party* leader. Masaliev tried to repair the damage by calling on the republic's Supreme Soviet to create the office of president, to be elected by that body.

Masaliev's political opposition in the Supreme Soviet organized themselves into a new party, called *Democratic Kyrgyzstan*, and elected Askar Akayev instead. Akayev, who is a physicist by training, worked for twenty years in St. Petersburg (then Leningrad) before returning to Kyrgyzstan.

In August 1991, there was an organized attempt to depose President Akayev as part of the attempted *coup* against Gorbachëv. The local military commander threatened to send tanks into the street and the local KGB chief attempted to arrest Akayev. The president's loyal troops surrounded the *Communist Party* headquarters and then had the KGB chief arrested. He subsequently banned the *Communist Party* from government offices. When the *coup* failed, the *Kyrgyz Communist Party* dissolved itself. After his own return to power, Gorbachëv asked Akayev to come to Moscow to become his vice president. He turned it down, saying that he wanted to stay in Kyrgyzstan.

Kirgiz student at the College of Europe

As part of the further democratization of the country, the Kyrgyz Supreme Soviet modified the constitution to create an elective presidency and set new elections on October 12. Akayev's position was so strong by this time that no candidate bothered to oppose him.

Over the next two years, Akayev pushed democratic reforms and the creation of a market economy, but he was frustrated by opposition in the legislature. This led him, in February 1994, to call for a referendum in which the people were asked whether they supported his policies and wanted him to finish his term ending in 1996. Ninety–six percent of those voting answered yes. Acting on this vote of confidence, Akayev dismissed the old 350 member Supreme Soviet, elected during the Soviet era in 1990, and submitted a

229

Kyrgyzstan

Deposed President Akayev at dinner with his wife and children

second referendum to the people proposing a new, two–chamber "Assembly of the People of Kyrgyzstan," composed of 105 members. When the electorate approved his proposal, Akayev set new elections for February 5, 1995. Over a thousand candidates vied for the 105 seats, about 80 percent of them running as independents. This produced a cooperative legislature for Akayev to work with.

Following that, Akayev pushed through a whole sheaf of constitutional amendments, many of which significantly increased his powers. New constitutional amendments in 1999 changed the make–up of the legislature and created 15 seats to be elected by proportional voting on the basis of party lists.

Akayev also pushed through legislation authorizing some forms of privatization, including land. Some 61 percent of state–owned industrial enterprises had been privatized by May 1997 when President Akayev ended all forms of privatization after he became convinced that state–owned facilities were being sold at unjustifiably low prices. The ban lasted just under a year. In April 1998, the legislature approved a further privatization which included individual companies in telecommunications, mining and energy. Opposition to privatization has continued to grow, however, and calls have been made for an investigation into whether members of parliament have been making personal profit from the privatization process. Unfortunately, corruption is widespread enough to suggest that some of them probably are.

Kyrgyzstan was badly hurt by the collapse of the Russian ruble in 1998 and this had a negative effect on President Akayev's standing among the Kyrgyz people. As the government prepared for new parliamentary elections in February– March 2000, therefore, a major effort was made to minimize the vote for the political opposition. In the end, the actions of the authorities were so blatant that the Organization for Security and Co–operation in Europe declared the parliamentary elections so flawed that they had failed to meet international standards. Attempting to deal with the criticism, President Akayev called for a roundtable discussion with the political opposition which took place in June. Here, President Akayev solicited suggestions on measures to stabilize the political and economic situation. He also admitted that irregularities were registered in a number of court cases with regard to the parliamentary elections.

Presidential elections were scheduled to take place in October 2000. As a result of worsening economic conditions, President Akayev's popularity had declined greatly in the previous two years and many thought he could be defeated. Feliks Kulov, who had earlier held the post of vice-president, was seen by those same observers as the individual most likely to be able to defeat Akayev.

Kulov, who had also served as minister of national security and mayor of Bishkek, had earlier broken with Akayev and then founded the *Ar–Namys Party*. When Kulov was suddenly arrested on what most people considered to be trumped up charges, there was therefore some disquiet. This disquiet only grew when a military court reinstated the charges after Kulov had been acquitted. Kulov eventually pulled out of the presidential race—supposedly because he refused to take a required exam in the Kyrgyz language—but it probably was also because of the charges pending against him.

President Akayev eventually faced five challengers in the presidential race, none of any great stature; even so, any chance that one of them might win against Akayev was negated by the press coverage of the campaign on the part of a media almost entirely controlled by the government. In the end, Akayev won reelection with 74.47 percent of the vote; however, the OSCE once again declared that the presidential election had failed to comply with its standards for democratic elections.

After the results were in, Feliks Kulov, calling for cooperation with the government, told journalists that his party would avoid a confrontation with the government authorities at all costs, and added that he intended to participate in an upcoming dialogue between the authorities and political parties. In spite of his offer of cooperation, a court found him guilty in his retrial and he was sentenced to prison in January 2001. Apparently the authorities continued to fear him even after the elections were over.

If the authorities thought that sending Kulov to prison would negatively affect his political reputation, they were plainly wrong, however. In November 2001, the leaders of the opposition *Ar-Namys*, *Ata-Meken*, *Erkindik*, and *People's* parties organized a "People's Congress" in Bishkek and symbolically elected Feliks Kulov as chairman. The "Congress" then adopted a resolution condemning the country's "authoritarian" leadership and "thoroughly corrupt" government. In addition to demanding Kulov's release from prison, they called for constitutional changes that would transfer some of the president's powers to parliament.

In January 2002, the focus of the opposition changed after the arrest of Azimbek Beknazarov, a parliament deputy from Aksy Rayon of Djalalabad Region in southern Kyrgyzstan. Beknazarov's constituents became convinced that the criminal charges brought against him were a sham and that the real cause of the government's actions was Beknazarov's opposition to the ratification of a border treaty with China, which ceded some 95,000 hectares of disputed territory to China. His constituents therefore began organizing demonstrations demanding Beknazarov's release. These demonstrations continued until March, when they led to a clash with the government authorities in the Aksy Rayon which resulted in the death of six individuals when policemen fired on the demonstrators.

A state commission set up in April to investigate the Aksy incidents blamed government authorities on all levels and law–enforcement bodies for "political short-sightedness," and it criticized the Aksy authorities for refusing to permit pro–Beknazarov rallies. By the middle of May, when the state commission released its report, demonstrations were taking place all over Kyrgyzstan and demands were beginning to be heard for the resignation of President Akayev. Meanwhile, the border treaty with China was ratified by the lower house of parliament on May 10 and by the Senate a week later.

Hoping to calm the situation, the government issued arrest warrants for several local Aksy Rayon officials and ordered the release of Beknazarov. President Akayev followed these actions up with a national address to the Kyrgyz people. When none of these things defused the situation, Prime Minister Bakiev resigned on May 22. His replacement as prime minister, named the same day by President Akayev, was Nikolay Tanayev.

Demonstrations continued throughout the summer, with an increasing number of voices calling for President Akayev's resignation. In July, the president made another attempt to defuse the situation; calling on all political factions to engage in a dialogue with the government, he cautioned opposition politicians against exploiting current tensions for their personal political aims. He also hinted that he might be willing to cede some powers to parliament if the relevant constitutional amendments were endorsed in a nationwide referendum. In another concession, he also signed six laws recently passed by parliament, the most significant of which guaranteed the right of peaceable assembly. Prior official permission to hold rallies was no longer required, except in the vicinity of schools and hospitals.

A Constitutional Council charged with drawing up possible constitutional amendments was established by presidential decree on August 26. The first session, which took place on September 4, was presided over by President Akayev, but the Council then elected Absamat Masaliev, leader of the opposition *Communist Party of Kyrgyzstan*, as co–chairman three days later. Originally, the Council had 40 members, which included the prime minister, foreign minister, the speakers of the upper and lower chambers of parliament, the leaders and deputies of several opposition political parties, the chairs of the Constitutional and Supreme Courts, plus some NGO representatives. The Council later added two more opposition politicians, bringing the number to 42.

The series of constitutional amendments recommended by the Constitu-

Kyrgyz woman in traditional head–dress of a married woman making a felt rug ("shirdak")
Photo by Hermine Dreyfuss

tional Council was somewhat modified in January 2003, then submitted as a national referendum on February 6. Because there had been so many calls for President Akayev's resignation, the referendum also asked the public to indicate whether they wanted the president to serve to the end of his present term in 2005. Although 12 opposition parties called for a boycott of the referendum, the final vote showed participation by 86.36 percent of the electorate. The referendum received a 75.5 percent favorable vote.

The newly approved constitutional amendments created a new 75-member unicameral parliament—all elected in single-seat constituencies—to replace the bicameral parliament as of the 2005 elections. While President Akayev was con-

firmed in office until the end of his term in December 2005, another amendment stripped former presidents and their families of immunity from prosecution.

Elections to the new unicameral parliament took place on February 27, 2005, with approximately 400 candidates vying for the 75 seats. Although the political opposition was not entirely united, five major political parties did come together to form an electoral bloc under the leadership of Kurmanbek Bakiev, former prime minister and leader of the *People's Movement of Kyrgyzstan*. Since a candidate needed 50 percent of the votes to win in the first round, 44 of the seats went into a second round of voting, which took place on March 13. In the end, the opposition won only seven of the seats, with supporters of

Kyrgyzstan

President Bakiev

the government taking the rest. Perhaps the greatest blow was the fact that Kurmanbek Bakiev failed to win his seat in the run-off.

From the beginning, the opposition was unwilling to accept the results of the parliamentary elections and they were helped in this position by the statement by the Organization for Security and Cooperation in Europe (OSCE) that there were "significant shortcomings" in the electoral process. The OSCE statement went on to state that the areas of concern included "lack of effective voter access to diverse sources of information, bias in the media, continued de-registration of candidates on minor grounds, and inaccurate and poorly maintained voter lists."

Although President Akayev had announced on several occasions that he intended to step down at the end of his current term as president, the opposition was convinced that, with a two-thirds pro-government majority in parliament, Akayev would amend the constitution and run for a third term. They were, no doubt, reinforced in this belief by the fact that four members of the Akayev family—the president's son and daughter and his wife's two sisters—were originally awarded seats in the new parliament.

Ex-Prime Minister Feliks Kulov

The first protest rallies took place on March 14 with opponents of the government occupying government offices in several towns across the country. The largest, and most significant, of the protest demonstrations took place in the city of Jalalabad, located in the south of the country in the crowded and impoverished Fergana Valley. By March 22, protesters had completed their takeover of the south, occupying all three regional capitals. The next day, the protests spread to Bishkek, the capital. One day later, President Akayev and his family fled Bishkek, having decided to seek sanctuary in Kazakhstan.

The next day, the Supreme Court revoked the mandate of the newly elected parliament. Hours later, Kurmanbek Bakiev, an economics-oriented technocrat, was named prime minister by the old parliament and given the power to issue decrees as acting president, even though President Akayev had not resigned the presidency. That evening, as looters took to the streets, ransacking shopping centers and targeting bank machines and currency-exchange places, Bakiev began to put together a provisional government. He asked Feliks Kulov, who had been released from prison on March 24, to accept the position of coordinator of security services. Kulov's job was essentially to restore order in the country, putting an end to the looting which had broken out in the wake of the uprising. Kulov held this position for only a few days. In his letter of resignation, he stated that he had accomplished what he had been asked to do; it is likely, however, that he was positioning himself to run against Bakiev in the upcoming presidential elections.

In another twist, Acting President Bakiev decided to recognize the legitimacy of the new parliament. This was partly because the mandate of the old parliament was due to run out on April 15,

and he was concerned about the legitimacy of the revolutionary government. After Bakiev's action, the new parliament voted 54-0 to recognize Bakiev as prime minister and acting president. Since the Central Election Commission had, in the meantime, decided to annul the results in 13 constituencies, those elections would be rerun. The next step came on April 4, when President Akayev formally resigned his office.

New presidential elections were set for July 10, and it appeared that Bakiev and Kulov would be the two chief candidates. Instead, the two candidates met privately and then announced that Kulov had decided to withdraw from the campaign and to support Bakiev's run for the presidency; in return, Bakiev promised that he would appoint Kulov as prime minister if elected. Bakiev actually appointed Kulov to the post of acting deputy prime minister a few days later. According to reports, a major factor in Kulov's withdrawal was his fear that he would be unable to pass a fluency test in the Kyrgyz language, one of the requirements for all presidential candidates. Kulov's education had been primarily in Russian language schools, and he is said to have a limited fluency in Kyrgyz.

Bakiev won the July 10 presidential elections with 88.9 percent of the votes; he was formally sworn in as president on August 14. Since parliament was not scheduled to meet in its opening session until September 1, Bakiev appointed Kulov as acting prime minister while formally nominating him for the office prime minister. Kulov was confirmed in office on September 1 when parliament met in its opening session; he received the support of 55 of the 66 deputies present.

This overwhelming vote of confidence in the new prime minister was somewhat misleading, however. When Bakiev formally presented his new government to parliament on September 26, parliament

Prime Minister Almaz Atambayev

rejected six of the 16 cabinet nominees. Not wanting a confrontation with parliament, Bakiev submitted six new nominations for the vacant positions.

Parliament eventually confirmed his new appointees, but the political situation has remained extremely fluid ever since. Part of the problem is that, although everyone claims to support an expansion of democracy and political freedoms, there is a great deal of disagreement about what that means. Another part of the problem is that many people expected the situation to improve greatly with the departure of President Akayev; yet corruption and poverty have not been alleviated and have perhaps gotten worse, aggravated by the very political instability that continues to plague the country. It also did not help that three members of parliament were murdered in the six months following collapse of the Akayev regime.

Another part of the problem may be President Bakiev himself; although he has a reputation as a wily politician and a survivor, he does not appear to be capable of maintaining a consistent political position, For example, Bakiev opposed the expansion of presidential authority which Akayev pushed through in 2003, only to reverse his position after assuming that office himself. Currently, his position is that the presidential powers are necessary to put an end to the disorders and destabilization in the country. In November 2005, in fact, he proposed that the office of prime minister be abolished and the president made head of government. Many in parliament, on the other hand, have argued for a parliamentary system with a figurehead president.

Meanwhile, this infighting has resulted in to a great deal of frustration within the country and some loss of confidence in the new political leadership. Omurbek Tekebaev, the speaker of parliament, was forced to resign in February 2006 after he said of President Bakiev "he's become a disgrace, a dog; if he's a man, he should hang himself." Nor did the quarrel benefit Bakiev; a poll take at about that same time showed that 74 percent of those polled expressed a lack of trust in the president.

The discussions concerning the future form of government originally took place under the auspices of the Constitutional Council, a 114-member body set up by parliament in April 2005. In March 2006, President Bakiev took control of the discussions by forming a working group on constitutional reform with a mandate to take the materials produced by the Constitutional Council and use them to create draft constitutions; the task force delivered three drafts to President Bakiev and Prime Minister Kulov in July 2006, prescribing presidential, parliamentary, and

Kyrgyz family waiting at typical mosaic bus stop which dot the countryside. Man wears a "kalpak" hat
Photo by Hermine Dreyfuss

mixed presidential-parliamentary forms of government. All three drafts envisaged a 75-member parliament with 50 deputies elected on party slates and 25 in single-member constituencies; formerly all deputies were elected in single-member constituencies.

Bakiev also set up a new governmental body, the State Council, in April 2006. The membership of the State Council includes the president, prime minister, speaker of parliament, chairpersons of the Constitutional and Supreme Courts, state secretary, head of the presidential administration, prosecutor-general, defense minister, chairman of the National Security Service, and mayor of Bishkek.

The purpose of the State Council was to bring all of the leading political personalities together and provide them with a common forum where political differences could be discussed and resolved. It didn't work out that way. Instead, parliament passed a resolution in September 2006 which declared the "tandem" arrangement between President Bakiev and Prime Minister Kulov to be unconstitutional. Lawmakers also provided President Bakiev with a number of demands: to form a coalition government; conduct rapid constitutional reforms; place the National Security Service (SNB) under governmental, rather than presidential, control; replace the director of Manas airport; remove the head of the state broadcasting corporation; open a criminal case against Janysh Bakiev, the president's brother (and former head of the SNB) in connection with the arrest of Omurbek Tekebaev (former parliamentary speaker); and give the parliamentary commission on the Tekebaev affair more powers.

This was, as it turned out, the beginning of a season of additional demands. In October, a civic forum that took place under the auspices of the opposition *For Reforms* presented President Bakiev with a list of nine demands. Calling for the creation of a national unity government, this list included demands that Bakiev remove all relatives from government posts; withdraw his veto of a parliamentary act transforming state television into public television; and reject participation in the

Kyrgyzstan

The tunduk is the dome of the yert, the traditional Kyrgyz nomadic dwelling

Courtesy: Hermine Dreyfuss

Two months later, on December 30, parliament reversed itself and passed a new constitution with amendments that broadened the power of the presidency—giving the president the right to appoint cabinet members without parliamentary approval and giving the president control over law-enforcement and security organs. The new constitution gave the president the authority to nominate a new prime minister, though he would have to be confirmed by parliament.

Meanwhile, a schism occurred in Prime Minister Kulov's political party, *Ar-Namys*, and this led him to resign his office on December 19. President Bakiev prevailed on Kulov once again to accept the office, but when he sent Kulov's name to parliament, parliament rejected the nomination twice in succession. An important reason for parliament's rejection of Kulov was that the prime minister had strongly supported the Heavily Indebted Poor Countries debt-relief program. Although about half of Kyrgyzstan's $2 billion in international debt would have been forgiven if it joined the program, a majority of parliament opposed the program, fearing it would give international financial institutions too much authority over domestic policy. Reflecting this position, the government decided in February 2007 against participation in the program.

President Bakiev's choice as Kulov's successor was Azim Isabekov, at that time minister for agriculture. Isabekov was easily confirmed, but he held the office for only two months. He resigned on March 29 after President Bakiev blocked his attempt to sack five members of his cabinet.

When President Bakiev named Isabekov as Kulov's successor, he offered Kulov "any position" in government that was not subordinate to parliament. Kulov refused and, instead, set up a new opposition movement called the *United Front For a Worthy Future for Kyrgyzstan (UFFWFK)*. In March, Kulov announced that the *UFFWFK* would begin holding demonstrations calling for new presidential elections. Meanwhile, the rest of the political opposition, which was organized as the *For Reforms Movement*, had drawn up its own plans for demonstrations beginning in April. When Isabekov resigned as prime minister on March 29, therefore, President Bakiev turned to Almazbek Atambaev, co-chairman of the *For Reforms* movement, and offered to nominate him for the office of prime minister. Atambaev accepted, and he was confirmed as prime minister on March 30.

In his maiden speech as prime minister, Atambaev harshly condemned the policies of the government over the preceding two years—"over the past two years, necessary, cardinal, steps were not taken in the

Heavily Indebted Poor Countries debt-reduction initiative of the World Bank/IMF.

One month later, parliament adopted a new constitution significantly curtailing the powers of the presidency and increasing the powers of the legislature—though the curb on presidential powers was not go take effect until after the next presidential elections in 2010. Perhaps the most important change was to place the National Security Service under government, not presidential, control.

economy, corruption was not vanquished, and concrete measures were not taken to raise the living standards of ordinary citizens." However, he spoke against the demands of the rest of the opposition for early presidential elections which, he said, could "provoke a split in the country."

President Bakiev has given in to some of the demands of the opposition. In addition to rejecting participation in the Heavily Indebted Poor Countries debt-relief program, he agreed to legislation turning state television into public television. Yet the demonstrations called by Kulov have gone on as planned and they have begun to have a political affect. On April 17, for example, Kalyk Imankulov, the former head of the National Security Service, joined the Kulov opposition. Moreover, the opposition has raised its rhetoric by demanding the immediate resignation of President Bakiev. After some of the demonstrators began throwing stones at the police, the police retaliated by using tear gas and wielding batons. The government had originally ordered the police to take every action to avoid confronting the demonstrators, but as the demonstrations became more violent, the government authorized the arrest of some of the demonstration leaders. In particular, Kyrgyz prosecutors have charged two opposition leaders—but not Kulov—with "organizing mass arrest." The police also raided the offices of two Kyrgyz newspapers and seized entire press runs, plus the offices of Kulov's *Ar-Namys* party—acts which brought swift condemnation by organizations such as Freedom House in America.

The current state of unrest threatens the stability of the entire Kyrgyz State. President Bakiev has shown, again and again, that he is willing to bend when put under sufficient pressure. The only problem is whether he can bend enough to survive and, if not, whether any successor would be any more successful in restoring stability to Kyrgyz society.

Foreign Policy

In his early years after taking power, Akayev's reputation as a genuine democrat caused some problems with his neighbors, all of whose rulers are much more conservative and still attuned to the traditional communist ways of doing things. The partial exception is Kazakhstan, whose President, Nursultan Nazarbayev, although an ex–communist, has gained a reputation for pragmatism.

The U.S. Government showed its own support for Akayev when it opened the first U.S. Embassy in Central Asia in Bishkek on February 1, 1992. In 1993, Kyrgyzstan received the highest amount of U.S aid on per capita basis of any of the ex–Soviet republics.

President Akayev made an unofficial seven–day visit to the United States in July 1997. Among those he met with were George Soros, who has invested several million dollars in Kyrgyzstan, UN Secretary–General Kofi Annan, and IMF Deputy Managing Director Alassane Outtara.

Kyrgyzstan was also the first ex–Soviet republic to meet World Bank and IMF requirements for obtaining finance assistance. It has received loans from the World Bank and has negotiated a full standby agreement with the IMF. In 1997, the IMF increased its credits to Kyrgyzstan. Kyrgyzstan was also the first CIS state to be invited to join the World Trade Organization, the WTO having issued the invitation to Kyrgyzstan in October 1998. Kyrgyzstan still has to ratify the accession protocols, which require it to open the country's markets to foreign goods and services.

The government of Kyrgyzstan has established fairly extensive relations with the other states of Central Asia in recent years, but it has also worked to improve relations with Russia. Kyrgyzstan's decision in May 2000 to reestablish Russian as an official language in the republic was taken partly to stem the outflow of its Russian population, but it was an act that was also welcomed in Moscow. There are also signs that many in Kyrgyzstan view President Putin as a potentially more reliable partner and ally.

The September 11 terror attacks against the United States, followed by America's subsequent war on terrorism, have had a major effect on international Kyrgyzstan's relations. Kyrgyzstan has had its own problems with radical Islam in the form of periodic incursions into the country by units of the Islamic Movement of Uzbekistan, a group with ties to the Taliban in Afghanistan and to Al Qaeda. But the government had to take into consideration its close association with Russia, so President Akayev consulted with the Russian Government before the country offered the use of its air space and airfields to the United States.

On December 6, Kyrgyzstan's Legislative Assembly voted to allow U.S. military aircraft to use Bishkek's Manas international airport; the first American military aircraft arrived on December 19. By the middle of January, there were 250 U.S. military personnel in residence—the first contingent of as many as 5,000 troops who would be coming from the United States, France, Italy, and Canada. A reporter who visited the air base at the end of April reported close to 2,000 soldiers there, all living in air-conditioned tents. About half were American; most of the rest were French, though there were also some South Korean servicemen. The main func-

tion of the air base at the time was to service the FA–18 fighter jets and French Mirages that were flying daily sorties over Afghanistan, plus the two KC–135 tankers that provided in–flight refueling for the combat jets. The personnel also serviced the Spanish, Dutch, and Danish cargo planes ferrying supplies in from western Europe. The 420–person French contingent at Manas was replaced by an equivalent number of Danish, Dutch, and Norwegian airmen and troops in October 2002. With the departure of the French, the Mirages were replaced by 19 F–16 fighter jets.

A two–year U.S.–Kyrgyz military cooperation agreement signed in January 2002 authorized exchange visits and joint training. The Kyrgyzstan Government was also granted $50 million in American aid for various economic and social programs; that figure was expected to double for 2003. A U.S. Congressional delegation that visited Bishkek in March focused on such things as how the United States might help Kyrgyzstan to strengthen its borders and fight drug smuggling. The Kyrgyz prime minister raised the issue of rescheduling the country's foreign debt at the same meeting.

Secretary of Defense Rumsfeld visited Kyrgyzstan in May 2002. Secretary of Treasury O'Neill arrived in the middle of July. President Akayev then made an official visit to Washington in September. Although cooperation on antiterrorism was the focus of Rumsfeld's visit, both the O'Neill visit and President Akayev's own visit to Washington focused primarily on poverty–reduction strategies and Kyrgyzstan's own economic–recovery plan.

In December 2002, Kyrgyzstan signed a new security pact with Russia which authorized the stationing of an air squadron consisting of 10 SU–25 and SU–27 attack jets, five training aircraft, two transport planes, and two multipurpose MI–8 helicopters plus approximately 1,000 Russian troops at the Kant military airfield near Bishkek. The air squadron is intended to support a 5,000–member rapid–reaction force that is being created under the auspices of the Collective Security Treaty Organization by Russia, Kyrgyzstan, Kazakhstan, Armenia, Belarus, and Tajikistan. The first Russian forces began arriving that same month.

The revolutionary events of March 2005 have produced a new leadership, but they have not had any significant influence on Kyrgyz foreign policy. The United States did agree to increase the amount of money it pays the Kyrgyz Government for the lease of the Kyrgyzstan military base it has been using to support its military forces in Afghanistan. The U. S. Government has not confirmed the exact amount

Kyrgyzstan

it pays, but the Kyrgyz Finance Minister said in February 2007 that the government was receiving $17 million a year for the base. The U. S. Government has made it clear that it is not interested in having a permanent base in Kyrgyzstan.

The Kyrgyz Government expelled two American diplomats in August 2006 on the basis that the diplomats interfered "in the country's internal affairs." According to the American Embassy, the two diplomats had been accused of improper contacts with local NGOs. The U. S. Government denied the charges; when the Kyrgyz Government insisted on their departure, the U. S. Government declared two members of the Kyrgyz Embassy to the United States *persona non grata*. This does not seem to have affected relations between the two countries. In fact, the agreement on compensation for the military base was signed shortly after the expulsions. In addition, the Kyrgyz Foreign Ministry announced in March 2007 that Kyrgyzstan would be joining NATO's Planning and Review Program. Kyrgyzstan was already an active member of NATO's Partnership for Peace program.

Nature of the Regime

Kyrgyzstan currently has a presidential–parliamentary form of government with the president responsible for general policy and a prime minister, responsible to the legislature, formally known as the Jorgorku Kenesh (Supreme Council), handling implementation of policy. The president is advised by a State Council, while the prime minister presides over his cabinet. The prime minister is responsible to the Supreme Council and must be confirmed by that body in order to hold office. The new president is Kurmanbek Bakiev, who was overwhelmingly elected to that office on July 10, 2005. The new prime minister is Almaz Atambayev, confirmed in that office on March 30, 2007.

The Supreme Council is a newly created unicameral legislature. Its members were elected in elections that took place on February 26 and March 13, 2005. The parliament has 75 seats, all of which are elected in single constituency elections.

Culture

Most Kyrgyz are Muslims, and continue to live a largely traditional life within the context of changes forced on them during the Soviet period. An oral tradition among the people has kept alive epic cycles and lyric poetry. This has saved much that would otherwise have been lost, for the written language has been in three different forms in the twentieth century. The first written language used the Arabic script, but that was abandoned after World War I and the Roman script was introduced. In 1940, Stalin forced all of the Central Asian republics to adopt the Cyrillic alphabet. Now it is likely that they will switch back to the Roman script.

Kyrgyzstan has produced two writers of note in modern times, the playwright and novelist Chingiz Aytmatov and the playwright Kaltay Muhamedjanov. Aytmatov is the author of *Tales of the Mountains and Steppes*, which has been translated into English. It won the Lenin Prize in 1963. The two collaborated on the play *The Ascent of Mt. Fuji*, which has also been translated into English and was performed on stage in Washington, D.C. in 1973. Its theme is the moral compromises that people had to make under Stalin.

Newspapers and magazines are published in both Russian and Kyrgyz and radio and television broadcasts are made in both languages. National broadcasts are also received from Moscow by way of relay lines. The Russian cultural influence is, therefore, very strong. The State University of Kyrgyzstan is located in Bishtek; in December 1991, it opened a business school, support for which came partly

from IBM, which donated a roomful of personal computers.

Since its emergence as an independent republic in 1991, Kyrgyzstan has seen a resurgence in interest in the old epic poems and, in particular, a poem of over a million verses called "Manas," parts of which may date back a thousand years. A story of a wise folk hero who unites the Kyrgyz nomads against foreign enemies, the poem has become the center of a nationalistic up swelling throughout the country, plus something more. "This is our Bible," Jenishbek Sydykov, director of linguistics and literature at the Kyrgyz National Academy of Sciences, said of it. "As a people, we are one with this poem. In our eyes, the hero Manas is just below God—and higher than Lenin ever was to us." The United Nations was impressed enough to declare 1995 the International Year of Manas, commemorating the poem's thousand year anniversary.

Economy

The Kyrgyz were once mainly nomads who pastured their herds in summer on the alpine–like slopes of the mountains where 30–40 inches of rainfall annually provide lush meadows for grazing. During the Soviet period, they were settled into villages and made part of collective or state farms. Livestock includes sheep, goats, cattle and horses. Mare's milk is the source for *koumiss*, the local fermented drink. Pigs, bees and rabbits are also raised in the mountains. Agriculture, practiced mainly in the lowland areas, is dependent on irrigation, since these areas receive an average of 7 inches of rainfall a year. The main crops include sugar beets, cotton, tobacco, opium poppies and cereal grains. Agriculture contributes approximately 37 percent of the Gross Domestic Production (GDP). Of the main agricultural crops, only cotton and tobacco are exported in significant quantities.

Although there is, as yet, no general law permitting the privatization of agricultural land, approximately 700,000 Kyrgyz citizens have received plots of land free of charge. President Akayev proposed a constitutional amendment legalizing the private ownership of land in September 1998, but a majority of the legislature opposed such action.

The number of people involved in industry has grown greatly in recent years, and now makes up 21.9 percent of GDP. Extractive industries are important; Kyrgyzstan has significant deposits of gold and rare earth minerals and is a major source of antimony and mercury ores. It also has significant deposits of lead, nepheline, mercury, bismuth, and zinc. It also has large coal reserves, which have begun to be exploited. Hydroelectric

Traditional Kyrgyz Graves

power provides about half the energy needs of the republic. It also produces petroleum and natural gas. Kyrgyzstan has approximately 6 billion cubic meters of proven natural gas reserves, but its annual production is only about 30 million cubic meters. Food processing and light industry have been developed, and the republic also manufactures machinery and instruments.

Kyrgyzstan still has a predominantly agrarian economy, however, and many of the industries developed while it was still part of the Soviet Union, such as processing cotton brought from other republics or uranium mining, were heavily dependent on trade with the other republics for survival. Thus the break up of the Soviet Union had a particularly devastating impact on the standard of living. One effect has been that Russians, who make up Kyrgyzstan's professional elite, have been leaving in large numbers for Russia. In addition, there were about 100,000 ethnic Germans living in the republic in 1991, only about 11,000 of which remain. The effect has been to leave the economy even more profoundly agrarian than it was before.

Kyrgyzstan has religiously followed the prescriptions of the World Bank and IMF since independence, liberalizing the economy and privatizing shops and some enterprises. The results, satisfactory in the beginning, earned Kyrgyzstan an invitation to join the World Trade Organization in October 1998, the first CIS state to receive such an invitation.

However, Kyrgyzstan was badly affected by the economic collapse in Russia beginning in September 1998. Russia is Kyrgyzstan's chief trading partner, accounting for 25 percent of Kyrgyzstan's foreign trade. As Marat Sultanov, chairman of Kyrgyzstan's National Bank, put it in October 1998, "we were prepared for the Russian crisis in Kyrgyzstan, but not on such a scale." The *som*, Kyrgyzstan's national currency, continued to lose value through the fall, dropping from 17 to the $1 to 25, and it continued to drop thereafter. In spite of these negative factors, there was no economic collapse and the government was able to continue to pay interest on treasury bills and meet its foreign debt obligations. By revising the budget to reflect the new economic situation, making greater efforts to collect taxes from enterprises, and strengthening its controls over the country's banks, it somehow made it through.

The economic situation has improved since that time, but the weakest link remains the industrial sector. For example a 0.5 percent drop in GDP for 2002 was entirely attributed to a fall in industrial production, since agricultural output actually

increased by 3.5 percent while turnover trade increased by 8.2 percent. Imports increased by 31.7 percent and exports by 6.1 percent, which gave Kyrgyzstan a negative trade balance of $33.7 million. The economy improved again the next year, reaching a 9.6 percent annual rate of growth for the first nine months of 2003. Speaking in November 2004, President Akayev said that Kyrgyzstan had "managed to reduce poverty by 15 percent" over the preceding five years.

The revolution of 2005 brought in a new, democratic government, but it also has led to a lot of political instability. As a result, GDP grew by only about 1.4 percent and 2.7 percent in 2006. On the other hand, foreign direct investment for the first nine months of 2005 totaled $136.4 million, a 33 percent increase over 2004. In addition, Russian companies have begun to take a renewed interest in Kyrgyzstan and investment from Russia has been increasing. Russia's Renova Group purchased a 72.28 percent interest in the Kara Balta uranium-production facility in February 2007.

Kyrgyzstan is getting some international assistance. In May 2002, the IMF released the second tranche of a $93 million loan approved in 2001; it also agreed to write off or reschedule a portion of Kyrgyzstan's foreign debt. In March 2002, the Paris Club rescheduled $94.5 million in loans that would have come due during the period 2002–2004. Meeting in Bishkek in October 2002, the third annual Kyrgyzstan donor's conference pledged loans and grants worth $700 million for the period 2003–05. The World Bank granted a $5 million loan to rehabilitate uranium-tailings dumps in September 2003 and made two grants of $370,000 each for feasibility studies on renovating other nuclear dumps. In August 2006, it provided a further $15 million to be used for rural reform.

The government launched a new round of large–scale privatization in December 2002, though it was not very successful. For example, an electric–lamp company being offered for $3.2 million attracted no bids at all. Other enterprises being offered for sale included the Haydarken mercury factory, a cotton plant in Osh, and a semiconductor plant in Tash–Kumyr. A Russian metals company did purchase a controlling interest in tin and tungsten mines along the southern shore of Lake Issuk–Kul, however. Kyrgyzstan has never had great success attracting foreign investment, but that seems to be changing. In August 2004, Russia's Unified Energy Systems signed an agreement with the Kyrgyz Government to finish two massive hydropower plants in Kyrgyz at a cost of $2 billion.

Kyrgyzstan did receive two separate loans from the Asian Development Bank in 2004, the first for $40 million for each of the two years 2005–6 to reduce poverty by encouraging economic growth, a $32.8 million loan for road rebuilding, and $16.5 million for several smaller projects. Perhaps the best news it got came in March 2005 when the Paris Club decided to write off $124 million of Kyrgyzstan's debt and to reschedule an additional $431 million. Kyrgyzstan's total foreign debt stood at $1.44 billion as of December 2005, with $680 million of that owed to the World Bank. Kyrgyzstan also owes $239 million to Japan; in 2005, the Japanese Government rescheduled this debt, granting a 13-year grace period at 1.3 percent interest and a total of 40 years to retire the debt.

Kyrgyzstan was promised $105 million in economic assistance in 2006. Forty percent of this has been designated for agricultural and industrial development projects, 20 percent to transportation and communications, 13 percent to health, and the remainder to social projects.

It also appears that Russia is considering investing significant sums in the Kyrgyz economy. In April 2006, Russian Security Council Secretary Igor Ivanov visited Bishkek; while there, he told a press conference that Russian investment in Kyrgyzstan could reach several billion dollars in a few years. The most promising sectors, he added, were energy, gas and metallurgy. Meeting later with President Bakiev, he said that Russia was prepared to invest up to $3 billion in Kyrgyzstan. In March 2007, the Kyrgyz Government signed an agreement with the Russian and Kazakhstan Governments for construction of two Kambar-Ata hydroelectric power stations at a cost of about $2 billion.

The Future

Kyrgyzstan's revolution of March 2005 gave it a new and untried political leadership, and the period since that time has been one of almost continuous political challenges to the government. Kyrgyzstan has had three different prime ministers over the past year, and demonstrations took place in the capital demanding the resignation of President Bakiev.

The past five years did show some economic progress, but the current political instability is threatening that achievement. Current official employment figures show a 16.8 percent unemployment rate. Perhaps more significant, a report by the Committee on Migration and Employment determined that 547,000 persons had gone abroad seeking work. At home, 40 percent of the people earn incomes that put them below the poverty line.

The Republic of Tajikistan

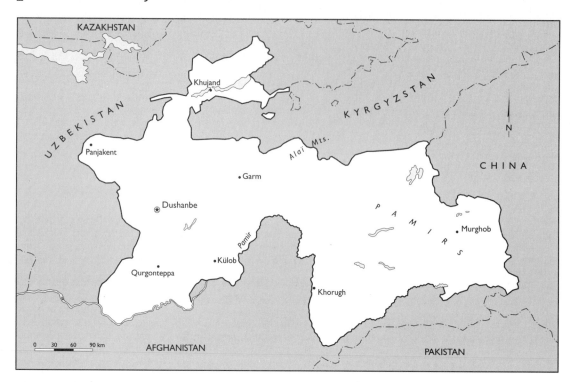

Area: 57,250 sq. mi. (143,000 sq. km., slightly smaller than Illinois).

Population: 7.32 million (July 2006 estimate).

Capital City: Dushanbe (Pop. 602,000).

Climate: Continental, with sharp changes depending upon altitude.

Neighboring Countries: China (east), Afghanistan (south), Uzbekistan (west and north), Kyrgyzstan (north).

Principal Language: Tajik.

Ethnic Composition: Tajik (80%), Uzbek (15.3%), Russian (1.1%), other (3.6%).

Principal Religion: Islam.

Chief Commercial Products: Mining, food processing, textiles, clothing and silk; fruit and livestock. The Ghissar sheep is famous for its meat and Karakul sheep produce wool and glossy, curly lamb pelts. The Republic has tremendous existing and potential hydroelectric resources.

Currency: *somoni* (introduced on October 30, 2000).

Per Capita Annual Income (Purchasing Power Parity): $1,200.

Recent Political Status: Autonomous Republic within the former USSR (1924) as part of Uzbek S.S.R.; Constituent Republic of the former USSR (1929–1991).

Chief of State: Emomalii Rahmon [prior to March 2007 Imamali Rakhmonov], President (reelected in November 2006).

National Day: September 9 (independence from Soviet Union).

National Flag: Three horizontal stripes; on top a narrow red and on the bottom a narrow green, with a broader white stripe across the center. Superimposed on the white a golden stylized mountain peak topped with a flag and surrounded by a semicircle of stars (a representation of Communism Peak, highest peak in the old USSR).

The Land

The Republic of Tajikistan is the independent successor state to the Tadzhik Soviet Socialist Republic. It declared its independence in September 1991.

Tajikistan is a small land, which includes the autonomous region of Gorno–Badakhshan. It is located in the extreme southern part of Central Asia.

It is also a mountainous land, with more than half of its territory lying above 10,000 feet. The northern border forms a loop around the western part of the Fergana Valley, running along the top ridges of the Kuramin Range in the north before turning south, crossing the valley, and then tracing its way westward along the foothills of the Zeravshan Range. Here the western and eastern borders almost meet before turning south. The western border continues south, turning somewhat westward, while the eastern border bends sharply eastward and runs along the northern slopes of the Zeravshan Range, continuing until it reaches the China border.

The center of the republic is dominated by the Turkistan Range and the slightly lower Zevavshan and Gissar Ranges. In the east are the Pamirs, which contain the highest peaks found anywhere in Central Asia. In the south, a series of transverse ridges and river valleys slope down to the Pyandzh River in Afghanistan.

Valleys make up about ten percent of the land of the republic. In addition to the western part of the Fergana Valley, there are the smaller Gissar, Vakhsh, Yavansu, Obikiik, Lower Kafirnigan and Pyandzh valleys in the south. There are also a number of small lakes in the eastern part of the country, in the Pamir Mountains. There is a dense river network. These include the stretch of the Syr Dar'ya that flows through the western part of the Fergana Valley and the upper reaches of the Amu Dar'ya. Most rivers flow northward into Central Asia.

Tajikistan has two climatic zones. The valleys are subtropical, with average July temperatures in the eighties and January temperatures hovering around freezing. Annual rainfall in the valleys is only 6–10 inches, so agriculture depends entirely on irrigation. In the highlands, average January temperatures are 0ºF or below. The mountains get very little precipitation in the summer, but the high ranges get 30–60 inches in the form of snow in the winter. In the highest ranges, there are also huge glaciers that partially melt in the summer, only to be replenished in the winter. The spring and summer runoff from the mountains provides water for irrigation on the lower slopes and in the valleys.

The People

Tajikistan's population as of May 2002 was 6.25 million, an increase of 750,000 over the past 10 years. Tajiks comprise approximately 80 percent of that figure. Uzbekis, found mainly in the northwestern part of the republic, come next with

15.3 percent. Russians, found mainly in urban areas and formerly about 7 percent of the population, today make up another 1.1 percent, while Ukrainians, Tatars, Germans, Kyrgyz, and Jews make up the remaining 3.6 percent.

Tajik belongs to the southwest group of Iranian languages, which set the Tajiks off from the rest of their Central Asian neighbors. It is also spoken in the Hindu Kush area of northeast Afghanistan, where it is called Farsi. Because of the nature of the terrain, Tajiks actually speak a variety of dialects, depending on which part of Tajikistan they live in. The two most important sub–groups are Pamir Tajik, which also includes Bartang, the language spoken in the Gorno–Badakhshan Autonomous Region, and Yaghnabi, the modern version of the language spoken in the ancient Kingdom of Sogdiana.

History

The Tajiks are the descendants of Iranian– speaking people who entered Central Asia as early as 2,000 B.C. They were incorporated into the Persian Empire and the subsequent Empire of Alexander the Great. The ancient kingdom of Sogdiana, conquered by the Arabs in the eighth century, was Tajik–speaking. In the tenth century, an invasion of Turkic–speaking peoples overran Central Asia. Many Tajiks were assimilated at this time, with Tajik culture surviving mainly in the mountains.

The Tajiks were later brought under the control of the Emirate of Bukhara. In the eighteenth century, Afghanistan extended its control over the area. The Russian Empire gained control in the 1860s. Bukhara became a Russian protectorate in 1868.

After the Russian Revolution, part of the area occupied by the Tajik people was incorporated into the Turkistan Autonomous Soviet Socialist Republic, established in April 1918. When the Red Army took over Bukhara in 1920, it also claimed most of the territory of modern Tajikistan. The Red Army captured Dushanbe early in 1921. The Basmachi revolt, which began in 1922 and lasted to the summer of 1923, was an attempt to throw off communist control, but it was ultimately unsuccessful. In 1924, the communist authorities decided to divide up Central Asia along ethnic lines. This led to the creation of the Tadzhik Autonomous Soviet Socialist Republic, at the time part of the Uzbek SSR. In December 1929, the Tadzhik Autonomous SSR was separated from the Uzbek SSR and made a constituent republic in its own right.

Mountainous and isolated and divided into different tribes that had a long history of rivalry, the Tadzhik SSR was run throughout most of the Soviet period by officials sent out by Moscow. Even as late as 1990, Tajiks were a minority in the *Tajik Communist Party*. Gorbachëv's programs of *glasnost* and *perestroika* changed that. By 1988, Tajik officials had recognized the opportunity offered by the Gorbachëv reform program and had begun to implement Tajik solutions to local problems. This led the Tajik Supreme Soviet to assert Tajikistan sovereignty in August 1990.

After the attempted *coup* against Gorbachëv collapsed in August 1991, Kakhar Makhkamov, who had supported the *coup*, resigned as party leader and Chairman of the Supreme Soviet. He was replaced by Kadriddin Aslonov. Upon taking office, Aslonov resigned his membership on the Politburo of the *Tajik Communist Party* and issued a decree banning the *Communist Party of the Soviet Union* on Tajik territory.

This irritated a majority of the members of the Tajik Supreme Soviet, 95 percent of whom were communists. Accusing him of "unconstitutional actions," they ousted him as chairman of the Supreme Soviet. In his stead, they elected Rakhmon Nabiyev, who had been first secretary of the *Tajik Communist Party* before Makhkamov. At about this time also, the Dushanbe party leader gave permission for a statue of Lenin to be torn down. He, too, was ousted and a state of emergency was declared in Dushanbe. In a related development, a hastily called congress of the *Tajik Communist Party* "dissolved" the party and established a new *Socialist Party* in its stead.

This combined set of developments appeared to political opponents to prove that the communists were determined to retain power. They organized a series of protest rallies in Dushanbe where they demanded that the state of emergency be lifted, the Supreme Soviet be dissolved and new elections called, and that Nabiyev resign as Chairman of the Supreme Soviet.

On September 30, after the rallies had continued for several days, the Supreme Soviet voted to lift the state of emergency in Dushanbe. Two days later, the Supreme Soviet suspended the activities of the officially dissolved *Tajik Communist Party* and its successor, the *Socialist Party*, "until the party's participation in the *coup* attempt is estimated." Finally, Nabiyev submitted his resignation as Supreme Soviet chairman on October 6. Akbarsho Iskandarov took over as acting chairman. The opposition had won every one of their points.

In September, the Supreme Soviet had created a new popularly elected presidency. That election had been set for October 27 but it was then postponed until November 24. As the presidential contest began, there were ten candidates, including Rakhman Nabiyev. Three later withdrew. There were also a number of politi-cal parties active, some registered and some not. Registered parties included the *Democratic Party of Tajikistan* and the *Popular Movement "Rastokhez"* (Revival). The *Islamic Revival Party* was still in limbo at this point.

The government banned all religious–oriented parties at first but then lifted the ban on October 22. At this point, a number of organizations had nominated Akbar Turadzhonzoda, head of the Spiritual Administration of Muslims of Tajikistan, for president. Turadzhonzoda's subsequent statement was therefore significant:

I support a secular parliamentary state with a free economy. Religion should be separated from the state so the sins of society cannot be attributed to Islam, which is what happened to the Communist Party.

Turadzhonzoda did not stand as a candidate for the presidency. When the election was finally held on November 24, 1991, Rakhman Nabiyev won with 56.9 percent of the vote. His chief opponent, Davlat Khudonazarov, who had been supported by the united opposition, won 30.7 percent of the vote.

Nabiyev's victory in the elections did not put an end to the struggle, however. In the early spring, the Islamic–led opposition, organized as the *Union of Popular Forces*, launched a campaign demanding multi–party elections and more freedom of religion, though their real purpose was to drive Nabiyev from office. Responding to the threat, the Tajik parliament attempted to strengthen Nabiyev's hand by giving him the power to rule by decree. As demonstrations continued, Nabiyev declared a state of emergency. Instead of calming the situation, this brought calls for Nabiyev's resignation. In early May, opposition forces seized control of Dushanbe, the capital, and declared the creation of a revolutionary council. In a compromise, Nabiyev then lifted the state of emergency and agreed to form a "government of national reconciliation." In the new government, eight seats were assigned to an opposition coalition consisting of democrats and moderate Islamists, plus the *Islamic Revival Party*, whose program at that time called for the creation of an Islamic state.

Nabiyev's compromise calmed the situation briefly, but there was no reconciliation. Not only did the two disparate groupings find it difficult to work with each other; Nabiyev also found himself under attack from ex–communist allies in the northern part of the country who accused him of ceding too much power to the opposition. In addition, the government began to lose control of the country as ex–communists took control of local

Tajikistan

governments in the north and Islamists took control of local governments in the south and east. Fighting then broke out between regions, eventually resulting in about one thousand deaths.

In an attempt to restore order, Nabiyev asked the Commonwealth of Independent States to dispatch peacekeeping troops to the country. The opposition now declared open rebellion and seized control of Dushanbe. Nabiyev, taken prisoner by demonstrators as he fled to the Dushanbe airport, was forced at gunpoint to resign as president. The Islamic–democratic coalition then declared itself to be the new government and named Akbarsho Iskandarov as acting president.

The Islamic–democratic coalition was unable to consolidate its control over the country, however. The northern, and most developed, part of the country was controlled by ex–communists associated with Nabiyev and they would have nothing to do with the new government. Meanwhile the situation in Dushanbe remained so unstable that the new government was unable to convene a new session of the parliament. This government lasted two months and then resigned on November 12, 1992, turning power over to an interim council. Meanwhile the parliament, meeting in the northern town of Khojand, elected Imamali Rakhmonov, an ex–communist, as chairman of the legislature after accepting President Nabiyev's voluntary resignation. On December 10, forces loyal to the former president took control of Dushanbe and at this time Rakhmonov was designated acting president. Islamists fled to their strongholds in the mountains of eastern Tajikistan, pursued by elements of the Tajik army. Other Islamists sought refuge across the border in Afghanistan.

As the civil war continued, the Tajik Government received more assistance from Russia. By the fall of 1993, there were more than 20,000 Russian troops in the country and Russia was providing subsidies amounting to 50 percent of the budget. Russia's interest was apparently its fear that the Islamic forces, allied with Afghan Islamic militants, would seize control of the government and establish a militant Islamic regime in Tajikistan. The Tajik Government received significant assistance from the Uzbekistani Government as well, partly for the same reason.

The government's control remained fragile, however. A reporter who visited Dushanbe in May 1994 reported that it was calm there during the day but that the streets were deserted at night and, in the distance, one heard a "chorus of automatic rifle shots. With daybreak come reports of assassinations of public figures or of men disappearing from sight."

Russian soldiers have guarded Tajikistan's border with Afghanistan since 1994. Eleven Russian soldiers were killed in skirmishes over that summer before government and opposition forces reached agreement on a ceasefire. The two sides later held talks in Islamabad which produced a ceasefire between government forces and guerillas based in the eastern mountains. From this time onward, the Russian foreign ministry supported a settlement that would reintegrate the rebels into the society.

In November 1994, the Tajik Government held a combined presidential election and referendum on a new constitution. With the real opposition excluded from participating, the presidential contest was between the acting president, Imamali Rakhmonov, and Abdumalik Abdulajanov, a former prime minister. Though not democratic by western standards, election observers said that the voting itself was free and fair. Rakhmonov won with about 60 percent of the vote and the new constitution was approved as well. At this time, Rakhmonov appointed Jamshed Karimov as his prime minister and announced that the government would launch a new privatization initiative. This resulted in some small–scale privatization of firms having fewer than 20 employees, mainly firms providing cater-

Spectators watch horses and riders at a popular equestrian event

Courtesy: NOVOSTI

ing and consumer services, but the economy continued to be basically state–run.

In the early part of 1996, a split among the forces supporting the government produced a new crisis. Two regional leaders who had been supporters of President Rakhmonov charged his government with incompetence and corruption and demanded its dismissal. They also demanded that he do something to improve the state of the economy. One of them, Colonel Makhmoud Khudoyberdyev, moved his troops within 10 miles from the capital, though no actual battle took place. Faced with the possibility of another civil war and informed by the Russian Government that it would not intervene again to save his government, Rakhmonov opened negotiations with the rebels. During the discussions, he agreed to dismiss several officials, including his first deputy prime minister, his chief of staff and a southern governor. In return, the rebels agreed to return to their barracks.

A few days later, Rakhmonov dismissed his prime minister, replacing him with Yakhyo Azimov, a little–known northerner who up to this time had been a carpet factory manager. It appears that this change was made because of the poor performance of the economy. In a news conference which he called after assuming office, Azimov announced that he favored market reforms and would cooperate with international donor organizations to rebuild the economy.

President Rakhmonov's greater, long–term problem was how to deal with the Islamic–democratic opposition, however. No real political stability could be achieved until he either came to terms with them or found some way to defeat them or deprive them of their popular political support. Many of Rakhmonov's supporters pushed for the second alternative, but this looked increasingly unrealistic to outside observers, in particular the Russians. According to Russian estimates, Rakhmonov's forces controlled, at best, a third of the republic, and the war would already have been lost but for the presence of 25,000 Russian troops.

Under strong pressure from the Russian Government to come to an understanding with the opposition, Rakhmonov traveled to Moscow in December 1996 to meet with Sayed Abdullo Nuri, leader of the *Islamic Renaissance Party*, largest of the parties in the *United Tajik Opposition (UTO)*. The talks went well and a peace agreement was signed which provided for a general amnesty and called for creation of a Reconciliation Council. When President Rakhmonov got back to Dushanbe, however, he found that he was unable to sell the peace agreement to his political supporters.

Under continuing pressure from the Russian Government, Rakhmonov traveled to Moscow again in March 1997 for new talks with the *UTO*. Here, Rakhmonov signed an agreement which called for integration of opposition troops into the regular Tajik armed forces. No agreement for a political reconciliation had been reached, however, so another round of talks was scheduled to begin in Tehran on April 9, 1997. No break–through occurred at this point, but the two sides did agree to meet again in Moscow in June. It was in Moscow that President Rakhmonov, under pressure from a Russian Government that had grown tired of the war and the continuing death of Russian soldiers, signed a final accord with Sayed

President Emomalii Rahmon

Abdullo Nuri on June 27, aimed at ending the years of fighting in the country.

The accord created a power–sharing arrangement and legalized the parties of the *United Tajik Opposition (UTO)*, including the *Islamic Renaissance Party*, the *Democratic Party*, the *Rastokhez People's Movement*, and the *Laadi Badakhshan*. The accord also created a National Reconciliation Commission which was charged with laying the groundwork for elections by the end of 1998, including recommending amendments to election laws. The interim power–sharing arrangement provided that the *UTO* was to obtain 30 percent of the ministerial posts in the government. It also specified that members of the *UTO* were to be allowed to return to Tajikistan accompanied by their own armed guards. After the accord was signed, the two par-

ties supporting the government—the *People's Party* and the *Political and Economic Renewal Party*—merged themselves into the *National Unity Movement*.

Thus the stage was set for Tajik politics to be dominated by two large political groupings, one representing President Rakhmonov and his allies and the other representing the political opposition. To the extent that these two political groupings represent most of the people of Tajikistan, they create the circumstances whereby disagreements may be transferred from the battlefield to the political stage.

Implementation did not go entirely smoothly, but it appears that one major reason for this was the Tajik Government's desire to assert greater control over subordinate commanders inclined to operate rather too independently of the government. This appears to have been the case with regard to Colonel Mahmud Khudaberiyev, commander of the Tajik army's First Brigade, who was accused of launching a military coup to overthrow the government in August 1997. According to Colonel Khudaberiyev, whose First Brigade was the rapid reaction force of the presidential guard, his unit was attacked by another unit of the presidential guard, led by its commander General Gafar Mirzoyev, and he and his unit only defended themselves. Two other outbreaks of military violence seem to have had similar roots. In each case, military forces loyal to the Tajik Government were able to assert their control.

A great deal of distrust continued to exist between the two sides, though they gradually managed to build a working relationship. Sayed Abdullo Nuri, head of the *UTO*, returned to Dushanbe in September 1997. Akbar Turadzhonzoda, deputy leader of the *UTO* (and former head of the Spiritual Administration of Muslims of Tajikistan), finally returned to Tajikistan in March 1998 and took up his post as deputy prime minister. Turadzhonzoda's position put him in charge of economic and trade relations with other CIS countries.

Instances of violence continued to occur on a fairly frequent basis, though it was often caused by renegade groups who flaunted the authority of the *UTO*. In fact, after the killing of a number of policemen at road checkpoints in March 1998, the government issued a statement accusing the leadership of the *UTO* of being "either unable to control its armed formations or insincere when it makes statements on its intention to establish a final peace."

It appears that, indeed, they often were not able to control these forces. In July 1998, for example, fighting even broke out between the followers of two different

Tajikistan

Grandfather shows his newly-fashioned whistles to his grandson and friend
Courtesy: NOVOSTI

UTO field commanders. Deputy Prime Minister Turadzhonzoda managed to mediate an end to that fighting after two days. Periodic gunshots were even heard in the capital itself, with the result that almost no one went out-of-doors after dark.

Assassinations also continued to occur. In September 1998, Otakhon Latifi, a leading Tajik opposition figure who was also head of the National Reconciliation Commission sub-committee on legal issues, was shot dead by unidentified attackers as he left his home in Dushanbe. In January 1999, Tolib Boboyev, the former prosecutor-general of Leninabad Oblast, was killed by masked gunmen while visiting the home of his son.

Implementation of the terms of the peace accord was painfully slow. For example, the president acknowledged in January 1999—eighteen months after the signing of the final accord—that the Commission on National Reconciliation had only just begun discussions on drafting necessary amendments to the country's constitution. Progress in disarming opposition and maverick armed formations was also both tedious and slow.

The 1997 agreement ending the civil war had specified that new parliamentary elections should take place by December 1998, but a ban on religious-oriented parties—instituted in 1993—remained a major impediment. In 1999, the government finally submitted three constitutional amendments to the people for their approval. The first authorized the formation of Islamic political parties; the second added an upper chamber to the parliament; and the third created a single seven

years term of office for the president. All three amendments were approved in a September 26 referendum. Elections to the lower chamber of the parliament were then scheduled for February 27, 2000.

Meanwhile, new presidential elections had to occur by November 6, 1999, the day President Rakhmonov's term was set to expire. That proved to be no simple matter. When three would-be candidates were denied registration after failing to obtain the number of signatures required by the Central Electoral Commission, they appealed their case to the Supreme Court on the grounds that local officials were actively preventing them from collecting signatures. They then demanded that the presidential elections be postponed until their appeals had been heard. When Ali Akbar Turadzhonzoda, deputy head of the UTO, criticized the demands of the three candidates for a postponement, the UTO presidium expelled him from the party and demanded that he be removed from his post as first deputy opposition leader and his government position as deputy prime minister. As it turned out, Turadzhonzoda kept his government position.

When the three would-be candidates lost their appeal to the Supreme Court, the Islamic Renaissance Party, senior partner in the umbrella UTO, called for a boycott of the presidential election. When the election went off as planned on November 6, however, the Central Electoral Commission announced that 98 percent of the electoral had participated in the polling. President Rakhmonov, with only nominal opposition from a candidate who had

asked that his name be withdrawn from the ballot, was reelected with 96 percent of the vote.

The lead-up to the parliamentary elections was equally rough. First of all, the Supreme Court banned the *Agrarian Party* and the *Party of National Unity* and annulled the registration of the *Justice and Development Party*, the *Renaissance of Tajikistan Party*, and the *Democratic Party of Tajikistan (Tehran Platform)*. In addition, the Justice Ministry refused to register the *Party of the National Movement of Tajikistan* and the *Social Democratic Party "Adolat Va Tarakkiyot."*

In the end, six parties participated in the February 27 parliamentary elections, the ruling *People's Democratic Party* (64.5%), the *Communist Party* (20.6%), the *Islamic Renaissance Party* (7.48%), the *Democratic Party (Almaty Platform)* (3.52%), the *Adolatkhoh (Justice) Party* (1.35%), and the *Socialist Party* (1.24%). As the percentages indicate, only the first three parties surmounted the five percent minimum needed to gain proportional representation seats. A run-off election was then held on March 12 in 12 constituencies where no candidate won an overall majority in the first round of voting. A second round of voting was also scheduled in two of the 36 single-mandate constituencies where the first-round poll was declared invalid. The results of these votes showed the same pattern of the first round of voting. The ruling *People's Democratic Party* won a total of 30 seats, giving them just short of a majority in the lower house of parliament. This actually gave the *People's Democratic Party* secure control, since 15 seats were won by independents allied with the party. The remaining seats were won by the *Communist Party* (13 seats) and the *Islamic Renaissance Party* (2 seats). Three seats were unfilled.

Elections to the 33-seat *Majlisi Milliy* (senate), the newly created upper body of the legislature, took place on March 23, 2000. Twenty-five of the senate members were chosen by five regional assemblies, with each regional assembly selecting five members. The remaining eight senators were nominated by the president. The senate is supposed to act as a stabilizing factor on the country's politics by guaranteeing representation to each of the individual regions.

With parliamentary elections out of the way, the government turned to another problem that had been growing in importance in the country—Islamic radicalism. The government was particularly concerned about *Hizb ut-Tahrir*, an Islamic extremist party whose program calls for the creation of a single Islamic state for all of Central Asia. Although banned by every Central Asian country, it is active throughout the region. Another Islamic extremist party that is worrisome to the government is the *Islamic Movement of Uzbekistan (IMU)*, which is also active throughout the region. The headquarters of the *IMU* are believed to be in Afghanistan, but it launched excursions into Kyrgyzstan from Tajikistan in 1999 and again in 2000.

About a hundred members of *Hizb ut-Tahrir* were arrested In Tajikistan in 2001. Two of those arrested in Tajikistan's Sughd region were found with a cache of several thousands of books and pamphlets calling for the overthrow of the Tajik Government. With evidence that the movement was growing in northern Tajikistan, President Rakhmonov launched a new campaign against militant Islamic groups in 2002. In July, a schoolteacher named Vakhob Khalilov was sentenced to five years imprisonment for heading a local cell of *Hisb ut-Tahrir*. That same month, police detained another *Hisb* activist in Dushanbe. In January 2003, two *Hisb ut-Tahrir* members were arrested while distributing leaflets and brochures calling for the establishment of an Islamic caliphate. The following month, police uncovered an extensive illicit publishing operation in Sughd Oblast. The police announced at the time that this arrest brought to 130 the number of *Hisb ut-Tahrir* members arrested in Sughd Oblast. As the anti–Islamic extremist campaign continued, police announced in April that they had discovered another clandestine print shop set up by *Hisb ut-Tahrir*, and that this was the third such printing shop they had discovered in 2003. Periodic arrests of *Hisb ut-Tahrir* members have continued since that time.

Concerned about the increased evidence of extremist Islamic activity, the government stepped up its surveillance of Islamic activity in general. Every year, the government's Committee for Religious Affairs and the Council of Religious Scholars examine Muslim cleric and lecturers at Islamic schools and universities on their knowledge of the canons and rituals of Islam. In 2002, the government decided that it would require imams, Friday preachers, and muezzins to sit the tests as well. In addition, the government began more strenuously enforcing the constitutional provision that prohibits clergy from participating in political organizations. In Tajikistan's northern Isfara Rayon, ten clerics were banned from preaching on the grounds that they were members of the *Islamic Renaissance Party*.

The problem of Islamic extremism seems to have waned of late, however. *Hizb ut-Tahrir* is probably still active but, if so, they have been more cautious in their actions. At the last reported trial involving *Hizb ut-Tahrir* members, which took place in Au-

gust 2005, nine individuals were given prison terms ranging from three to 15 years.

Police arrested 42 individuals, including 20 women, as suspected members of *Hizb ut-Tahrir* in the first half of 2006. And in July 2006, ten members of the *Islamic Movement of Uzbekistan* were arrested in the northern city of Khujand; three of the ten were Uzbek citizens. Another problem which the Tajik Government has given increasing attention to since 2002 is the drug trade. According to a 2002 report of the UN drug control office, 90 percent of all heroin consumed in Europe originated in Afghanistan and most of it passed through Tajikistan on its way to market. Tajikistan itself has as many as 20,000 drug addicts, at least partly because drug couriers are often paid off in illegal drugs. This has also been an increase in corruption as government officials accept bribes to look the other way and allow drugs through. To help fight the trafficking, the United Nations helped Tajikistan create an independent drug control agency and, to keep its 350 officers honest, arranged to pay them salaries equivalent to 17 times the average wage in the country. According to the International Narcotics Control Board, 9.6 tons of drugs were seized in Tajikistan in 2003, 5.6 tons of which was heroin.

The program has had some success; according to a 2006 report of the United Nations, "19 percent of the total volume of Afghanistan's drug production is smuggled north through Tajikistan, Turkmenistan, and Uzbekistan." Total seizures had also dropped to 2.5 tons, including 1.2 tons of heroin, with half of the drugs

seized on the Afghan border and half seized elsewhere in Tajikistan. Police also announced that they had broken up four drug-smuggling rings in August 2006.

New elections to the 63-member lower chamber of parliament took place on February 27, 2005. Six political parties ran candidates, but only three parties—the ruling People's Democratic Party of Tajikistan (PDPT) (17 seats), the Communist Party (3 seats), and the Islamic Renaissance Party (IRP) (2 seats)—cleared the 5 percent barrier to win party slate seats. The PDPT won 32 of the 41 single mandate seats, with an additional seat going to the *Communist Party*. Five additional seats were won by independent candidates, while the remaining three seats went to a second round. The *PDPT* thus controls a majority of the seats even without the support of the allied *Communist Party*.

New presidential elections took place on November 6, 2006. President Rakhmonov stood for reelection, but the election was largely pro forma, since most of the oppositional political parties were in disarray at the time. In particular, the *Islamic Renaissance Party (HNIT)* was hit hard when its leader, Said Abdullo Nuri, died on August 9. The new leader of the party, 42-year old Mohiedin Kasbiri, decided that the party would field no candidate for the election. The leader of the second opposition party, the *Democratic Party of Tajikistan (HDT)*, Mahmadruzi Iskandarov, is currently in prison, so the party has only an acting leader. Iskandarov, who had exiled himself in Russia, was sent back to Tajikistan under murky circumstances. Arrested on charges of terrorism,

Famous woodcarver Sirodzhitdin Nuritdinov in his studio Courtesy: NOVOSTI

243

Tajikistan

the embezzlement of state funds, and the illegal storage of weapons, he was sentenced to 23 years prison in October 2005. In addition, the party split in early 2006 when part of its membership left to form a new party, *Vatan*, which announced it would work with the government.

Rahmatullo Zoirov, leader of the *Social Democratic Party of Tajikistan,* would have been a good opposition candidate, but he suffered a stroke in August 2006. In the end, there were five candidates for the presidency, but all of the parties that put up candidates were actually part of the government coalition. These included the *Socialist Party,* the *Economic Reform Party,* the *Agrarian Party,* and the *Communist Party.* President Rakhmonov would probably have won reelection anyway, but against such weak candidates he managed to take 79.3 percent of the popular vote. After the vote, European Union monitors announced that they had seen some progress, though the election still fell short of "OSCE commitments and other international standards for democratic elections." The EU monitors were particularly concerned about the lack of meaningful competition.

Following the election, President Rakhmonov reappointed Oqil Oqilov as his prime minister. The decree reappointing Oqilov also announced a restructuring of government, including abolition of 26 ministries and committees. In April 2007, three parliamentary by-elections were held; all three seats were won by the ruling *People's Democratic Party.*

The other development occurred in March 2007 when the president announced that he was removing the "ov" ending from his name and that, henceforth, he would use the more Tajik spelling of "Emomalii Rahmon." Addressing a meeting of Tajik intellectuals on the traditional spring celebration of Norouz, he called on others to change their names in similar fashion. There does not appear to be any legal compulsion for adult Tajiks to change their names, but a decree issued by President Rahmon in March 2007 requires that the names of babies born to Tajik parents incorporate this change. The change has also caused speculation as to whether the next step would be to drop the Cyrillic alphabet and revert to the use of the Arabic script at some time in the future. Thus far, all of this is mere speculation.

Foreign Policy

Because of the civil war that ravaged the country between 1992 and 1997, the leaders of the Tajik Government turned to the Russian government for support in order to remain in power. For several years, therefore, Tajikistan's dependence on Russia meant that it was not really able to maintain an independent foreign policy. The civil war came to an end in June 1997 when an agreement was reached with the *United Tajik Opposition,* but Tajikistan continued to be dependent on Russia for military assistance. Currently, Russian troops guard its thousand mile border with Afghanistan. And a new treaty was signed by the two nations in February 2001 which regulates the status of Russian military bases in Tajikistan. As President Rakhmonov commented at the time, "Russia is our chief strategic ally." Currently, Russia keeps 10,000 troops stationed in the country. President Putin paid a visit to Tajikistan in April 2003 which included a visit to a Russian military base along the Afghan border. Here Putin announced that Russia would soon bolster its military presence in Tajikistan.

Tajikistan never recognized the Taliban government in neighboring Afghanistan, partly because it feared the threat which its extremist Islamic leadership represented. Tajikistan gave asylum to the Afghan opposition government and even permitted an ethnic Tajik commander from Afghanistan to bring his armed forces into the country. However, it refused to accept several thousand refugees who attempted to cross the border in the fall of 2000, and it was particularly concerned that about 12,000 of those who had been refused entry remained camped along the border for months.

When Islamic terrorists launched their attacks against the United States on September 11, 2001, therefore, the government of Tajikistan was among the first to express its willingness to cooperate with the United States in the fight against international terrorism, though it was hesitant about committing itself further because it feared for its own vulnerability. It also felt that it had to consult with the Russian Government before making any specific commitments, since Tajikistan's border with Afghanistan had been guarded for years by several thousand Russian troops.

As it happened, it was Russian Defense Minister Sergei Ivanov who announced on September 25 that the Dushanbe airport would be made available to the American military "if such a necessity arises." In October, the Tajik Government opened its air space to the use of American military planes, but it was not until U.S. Defense Secretary Rumsfeld visited Dushanbe in November that President Rakhmonov formally agreed to allow U.S. troops to be based in Tajikistan. Eventually, Kulyab air base, located about 200 miles south of Dushanbe, was made available for the international war against terrorism. The first Western military aircraft began arriving in December and the first use of the base was for delivering humanitarian cargos under UN colors to towns in northern Afghanistan.

Thus far, the base has been used primarily by a French military contingent, stationed in Tajikistan as part of the international coalition operating in Afghanistan. There had been discussions in 2001 about an American base in Tajikistan, but these talks were broken off when the United States opted for the Manas Airbase in northern Kyrgyzstan instead. However, the United States Government launched new talks with the Tajik Government in March 2003 about leasing three airbases in Tajikistan. Nothing has been settled yet, but there has been discussion of stationing some 1,500 troops from the United States, France, Great Britain and Italy there, along with F–18 bombers, C–130 transports, and French Mirage jets.

France currently has about 400 service personnel in Dushanbe. They service three Mirage fighters and three transport planes which provide support for International Security Assistance Force operations in Afghanistan.

The expansion in U.S.–Tajik relations since September 2001 has, in fact, been rather impressive. Relations were minimal for several years prior to September 2001, and the American Embassy was actually closed in 1998 following the embassy bombings in Africa. There has always been an ambassador accredited to Tajikistan, but he was based in Almaty, Kazakhstan and only paid periodic visits to Dushanbe. After the events of September 11, high–level American delegations visited Dushanbe on a number of occasions. In addition to granting the United States permission to use the Kulyab air base about 200 miles south of Dushanbe, the Tajik Government also formally joined NATO's Partnership for Peace program, the last of the CIS states to do so. President Rakhmonov paid an official visit to the United States in December 2002 where he had separate meetings with President Bush, Secretary of State Powell, and CIA Director Tenet. The talks focused on the war on international terrorism, combating drug trafficking, and economic reforms and poverty reduction in Tajikistan.

U.S. Secretary of State Rice paid a one day visit to Tajikistan in October 2005. While there, she stated explicitly that the United States did not seek a "permanent military presence in Tajikistan." That same day, Tajik Foreign Minister Talbak Nazarov committed his country to continued cooperation with the United States in international efforts to combat terrorism, extremism, and drug trafficking. As part of this cooperation, the United States Government carried out an airlift of winter supplies to Tajik border guards in January 2006. In addition to about $3 million in supplies and equipment delivered directly to Tajik border guards, the United States has a second assistance program, given under the auspices of the U.S. Export Control and Related Border Security Program, which has furnished over $7.5 million in equipment and training to Tajikistan since 2002. Lastly, in March 2006, the United States Government pledged $7.75 million to build facilities around a bridge linking Afghanistan and Tajikistan, plus another $800,000 to train Tajik security personnel with an eye to improving border security.

President Rakhmonov paid a three–day visit China in May 2002 and while there signed a border agreement resolving border issues between the two countries. Essentially, Tajikistan relinquished claims to approximately 1,000 square kilometers of mountainous terrain which the Tajik Government characterized as "of no great value to Tajikistan." As a result of the agreement, Russian troops who had been guarding the Sino–Tajik border turned the responsibility over to Tajik guards as of June 2002.

In May 2006, the Government of Tajikistan formally joined the Asian Cooperation Dialogue at a meeting of member state in Doha, Qatar. The ACD brings together 30 countries for discussion of topics such as energy cooperation.

Nature of the Regime

Tajikistan established a presidential–parliamentary form of government with a popularly elected president and a multiparty system in September 1991, shortly after it emerged as an independent republic. The subsequent struggles between the various factions that emerged led to parts of this system being changed or suppressed, but the new constitution that was approved in a popular referendum in November 1994 largely rebuilt the system put into effect in 1991.

Under this constitution, the key political figure in the system is the popularly elected president, who acts as the spokesman for the nation and establishes general policy. Next in line comes the prime minister, who is appointed by the president but must be confirmed in office by the lower chamber of the parliament. The prime minister and his cabinet are responsible for the day–to–day operation of government.

The new two–chamber parliament, created as a result of a constitutional amendment approved in 1999, represents the sovereignty of the nation. The *Majilisi Namoyandagon* or lower chamber has 63 members, 22 elected by party slate and 41 in single member constituencies. As the more popular, and therefore more powerful chamber, it is responsible for all legislation and has final authority over the budget. Most top government officials must also be confirmed in office by the lower chamber of the parliament.

In the case of the *Majilisi Milli* or upper chamber, five regional assemblies representing Tajikistan's five electoral districts each elect five deputies. An additional eight deputies are appointed by the president, bringing the total number of deputies to 33. Election or appointment to the upper chamber is considered an honor, so several of its deputies were selected because of their prominence in Tajik society rather than their politics. These elections took place on March 24, 2005.

President Rakhmonov and most of the people allied with him were formerly leaders in the now disbanded *Tajik Communist Party*. In June 1997, a power-sharing agreement was reached which brought the *United Tajik Opposition* into the government with thirty percent of the seats in the cabinet plus a similar representation in other government and local administrative posts. This legalized two political groupings in the country, the *National Unity Movement* (made up of the *People's Democratic Party* and the *Political and Economic Renewal Party*), representing the old communist elites, and the *United Tajik Opposition* (which brought together the *Islamic Renaissance Party*, the *Democratic Party*, the *Rastokhez People's Movement*, and the *Laali Badakhshan*).

This interim arrangement was supposed to last until new, free elections (originally stipulated as occurring before the end of 1998). Implementation of the agreement took much longer than anyone anticipated, however, so the power-sharing arrangement was renewed for three years in 1999. New parliamentary elections finally took place in February/March 2000—and resulted in a victory by the ruling *Democratic People's Party*. Because of the power-sharing arrangement, however, the government continued to be a coalition of the two major political forces in the country.

Before the series of *coups* and counter-*coups* of 1992, Tajikistan appeared to be evolving toward an institutionalized pluralism. Some experts speculated that this was because the *Tajik Communist Party* had always had its organized political factions, based on differences between regional clans, and this was now coming out in the open. That trend suffered a severe setback in 1992 as first one side, then the other, resorted to force to get its way. Then the coalition of democrats and Islamists that held power briefly in 1992 was overthrown and many of its members fled into hiding, either in the mountains to the east or in Afghanistan.

After that, the new government in Dushanbe went about systematically eliminating the opposition. "It was a real blood bath," said one Western diplomat.

During the period of the civil war—between 1992 and 1996—the government was essentially an alliance of the Leninabad and Kulyab areas. Excluded were other important areas such as Garm and Badakhshan. The power-sharing arrangement set up in 1997 and renewed in 1999, which guaranteed the opposition 30 percent of all government and local administrative posts, also provided representation to most of those other parts of the country which had been excluded from decision-making during the period of the civil war.

By March 2002, when the power-sharing arrangement was due to expire, the country's power structure had come to realize that the power-sharing arrangement, by institutionalizing political pluralism, had made a major contribution to political stability. Shortly before it was due to expire, therefore, the original signatories got together and renewed it for an indefinite period in March 2002.

Culture

Traditional Tajik festivals have always featured songs and dances and there is also a long tradition of theatrical and circus performances. Tajik circuses specialize in tightrope walkers, conjurers, singers and musicians. There is also a vigorous folk literature which is still being collected.

The Tajik National Theater was founded in 1929. It has nine separate theaters, performing operas, ballet, musical comedy and puppetry. There is also a Tajik film studio which makes both feature films and documentaries. Dushanbe has had its own television center since 1960.

Two pre–Soviet Tajik cultural figures are Abdalrauf Fitrat, author of *Last Judgment*, and Sadriddin *Ayni*, famous for two novels, *Slaves* and *Dokhunda*. His autobiography is titled *Bukhara*. Tajik writers of the Soviet period include the poets Abu ol–Qasem Lahuti and Mirzo Tursunzade. Tursunzade won the Lenin Prize in 1960 for his poem *The Voice of Asia*.

The Tajik State University, located in Dushanbe, is the largest of ten institutes of higher education. There are also 41 technical colleges. A Tajik Academy of Sciences was established in 1951. It now has sixteen institutions and oversees 61 research institutions located in various parts of the republic. The Pamir research station, located in the Pamir Mountains in the eastern part of the country, is a major regional meteorological observatory.

Most Tajiks are Sunni Muslims of the Hanafi School, although there are some Shiite communities among the Mountain Tajiks. Throughout the Soviet era, Islam

Tajikistan

was a barely tolerated religion and there were few mosques. But Islam is as much a way of life and a culture as it is a belief, so it survived in the villages in spite of official hostility. There has been a clear revival of Islam since about 1989, with many mosques being built, but it does not appear to have a great political significance.

Economy

Tajikistan is primarily an agricultural economy and its most significant crop is long–staple cotton. Cattle-raising (including sheep and goats) is also important, as is the growing of fruits, grain and vegetables. Fruits grown include apricots, pears, apples, plums, quinces, cherries, pomegranates and figs. Grapes and almonds are other major crops.

Tajikistan's light industry mainly involves processing agricultural products, such as cotton and silk processing, fruit canning and wine making. Related industries include knitted goods, shoes, leather working and carpet making. Light industry manufacturing plants tend to be small.

Its larger industry is either ore extraction or non–ferrous metallurgy. Tajikistan is rich in mineral deposits. It mines coal, iron, lead, zinc, antimony, mercury, gold, tin, and tungsten. Its mountains are the source of a number of non–metals, including salt, carbonates, fluorite, arsenic, quartz sand, asbestos and precious and semiprecious stones. Petroleum and natural gas have also been discovered and are beginning to be exploited, though it still imports natural gas from Afghanistan by means of a pipeline constructed in 1974. There are a number of large hydroelectric stations plus a number of thermal electric stations. Tajikistan exports some of its electricity to other republics.

Gold is mined at two sites in the northern part of the republic. Current production is fairly small, only 3.79 tons in 1991. A major new gold combine is currently under construction, however, and gold production is expected to double after it becomes operational.

Tajikistan manufactures a number of engineering or metalworking products, including looms, power transformers, cables, and agricultural and household equipment. There is also a nitrogen fertilizer plant, built in 1967. Most workers in industry are non–Tajiks.

The 1992–1997 civil war left Tajikistan with a badly damaged infrastructure and continued distrust among the political elites, but the March 2002 decision of the government to extend the power-sharing agreement with the opposition for an indefinite period may indicate that the country is moving toward greater political pluralism and, if so, that can only be good for the economy.

Tajikistan's economy has actually been growing since 1998, with the rate of growth increasing lately. After a growth in GDP of 3.7 percent in 1999, it spurted to over 9 percent in 2000. Although Tajikistan suffered a severe drought in 2001 which partially reversed the gains of the preceding two years, the economy has been growing again at an average of 10 percent since that time. In November 2004, President Rakhmonov told a gathering of international donors in Dushanbe that GDP had risen 50 percent over the preceding five years. GDP Growth in 2005 was just over nine percent. It dropped slightly, to 7.6 percent in 2006. The largest increases in growth were in agriculture and consumer products; industrial output grew by 6.2 percent. Inflation increased somewhat, growing to 9.8 percent from a 2005 inflation rate of 7.1 percent. The 2007 budget, adopted in November 2006, lists revenues of 3.195 somonis ($926 million) and expenditures of 3.290 billion somonis. Some 40 percent of expenditures are earmarked for spending in the energy, transport, and agricultural sectors. The budget also increases spending on education and health care. In July 2006, the World Bank approved $20 million for three projects for Tajikistan in the areas of poverty reduction, state sector reform, and health. The European Union has also pledged $80 million to Tajikistan during the period 2007-2010 for poverty reduction and economic development.

Over the past year or so, there have been a number of new foreign investments. However, one such project, a commitment by Russian Aluminum to invest over $1 billion to help construct the Roghun hydroelectric power station, fell through in 2006; the Tajik Government has now announced that it would complete the project on its own. In early 2007, the Tajik Government opened talks with the U.S.-based AES Corporation concerning investment in the Rogyun and Sangtuda-1 hydroelectric power stations, plus construction of electric transmission lines linking Tajikistan and Afghanistan. A related project to permit power exports to Afghanistan, the construction of a 220-kilovolt power line connecting Tajikistan's Vakhsh power state with cities in Afghanistan, involved financial backing from OPEC, the Islamic Development Bank, and Tajikistan's Vakhsh power station.

China has offered Tajikistan a $200 million loan to cover construction of a hydroelectric power station in northern Tajikistan; it is also providing a $267 million loan to build the North-South electrical transmission line, and a $55 million loan to build the Lolazor-Khatlon electric transmission line. In addition, China is financing the Dushanbe-Chanak road construction project.

However, Tajikistan has one of the highest rates of population growth in Central Asia, which means that the *per capita* growth rate is extremely low. Even after several years of fairly rapid growth, nearly 64 percent of the population continues to live in poverty and the government is often in arrears in paying wages and retirement benefits.

One side effect of the high level of poverty in the country is that up to a million men have left the country to seek work abroad, mainly in Russia or Kazakhstan. Though as labor migrants they are limited to the lowest–paying jobs, they manage to send somewhere between $480 and $840 million a year back to their families, a figure that is equal to between 42 and 75 percent of total GDP. To understand why remittances can constitute such a high percentage of GDP, one must be reminded that average wages inside the country are the equivalent of less than $10 a month. Yet the significance of these remittances cannot be underestimated. As a department head at the Economic Research Institute of the Tajik Economics and Trade Ministry put it, "these migrant workers are the reason why there is no mass hunger in the country."

Both the World Bank and the IMF are active in the country, and they sponsor a number of valuable programs; however, Tajikistan's foreign debt is $905 million, or 40 percent of GDP, and the country has some difficulty servicing its loans. One of the World Bank projects promotes economic structural reform. In June 2005, the World Bank announced that it was allocating $50 million for projects in Tajikistan. Most of the money was to help develop the country's agricultural sector, develop water resources in the Ferghana Valley, and to manage losses in the electrical power and gas sectors. In February 2006, the World Bank announced $32.5 million in grants to Tajikistan. Most of this money was to be used to improve health care and improve municipal services. The IMF also announced a new three-year program for Tajikistan which will provide up to $99 million in aid.

The Asian Development Bank and the European Bank for Reconstruction and Development (EBRD) also approved loans to the Tajik Government in 2005. The Asian Development Bank approved $145 million in projects to be carried out during the period 2006-2008. The EBRD agreed to loan $5 million to the Tajik air carrier Tojikiston to permit it to lease two new planes.

Individual foreign countries have also been very generous recently. Germany agreed to provide $33 million in technical and financial assistance to the Tajik Government, $7 million of which was in the form of a grant. In January 2006, seven donor countries announced that they had agreed to write off Tajikistan's $99 million debt to the IMF.

In March 2006, China announced that it had agreed to loan $172 million to Tajikistan for investment projects, in connection with Tajikistan's membership in the Shanghai Cooperation Organization. Two weeks later, it announced that it would loan the Tajik Government $269 million at two percent interest, to be used for the construction of a road between Dushanbe and the Uzbek border.

Foreign investment has been practically nonexistent until recently but that is now changing. In November 2004, RUSAL (Russian Aluminum) announced that it intended to invest $600 million to build an aluminum smelter in southern Tajikistan. RUSAL will also invest $150 million to modernize the Tajik Aluminum Plant, plus another $550 to finance construction of the Rogun hydropower plant. And in January 2005, the Russian, Iranian and Tajik Governments signed protocols to complete the construction of Tajikistan's Sangtuda-1 and Sangtuda-2 hydropower stations. Russia's Unified Energy Systems will provide most of the financing for Sangtuda-1 while Iran will provide almost all of the financing for Sangtuda-2. The two stations are scheduled for completion in 2009.

In April 2007, the Murodali Alimardonov, chairman of Tajikistan's National Bank announced that it was opening up the banking sector to foreign banks. Alimardonov commented that

Our banks have grown quite strong to stand up to the competition with the new banks that will enter our market, therefore we will gladly welcome them to our republic.

Alimardonov said that five foreign banks would soon receive licenses to operate in Tajikistan; one of those will be Kazakhstan's Kazkommertsbank. No other banks were named, but according to reports several foreign banks have signaled interest in working in Tajikistan.

The Future

Tajikistan's first five years after independence were characterized by a civil war and a collapse of most of the urban economy. The end of the civil war in 1997 has been followed by a fragile, but growing, political stability which allowed the economy to begin growing again in 1998. A decision, taken in March 2002, to extend the power–sharing arrangement indefinitely, holds out the promise that this new–found political stability can continue. The economy has been growing again since 1998, but total GDP is still below what it was prior to 1991. Since 64 percent of the people still live below the poverty line, progress will be slow, but things appear to be moving in the right direction.

In Tajikistan, mountains dominate the landscape

247

The Republic of Turkmenistan

Area: 186,400 sq. mi. (488,100. sq. km., as large as California and half of Oregon).

Population: 5.043 million (July 2006 estimate).

Capital City: Ashgabat (formerly Ashkabad) (Pop. 407,000).

Climate: Hot and dry summers, very cold in winter.

Neighboring Countries: Kazakhstan (north), Uzbekistan (north and east), Iran, Afghanistan (south).

Language: Turkmen.

Ethnic Composition: Turkmen (77%), Uzbek (9.2%), Russian (6.7%), Kazakh (2%), others (5.1%).

Principal Religion: Islam.

Chief Commercial Products: Oil, natural gas minerals, cotton, jute, fruits (grapes), vegetables, sheep, goats.

Currency: *manat* (issued November 1993).

Per Capita Annual Income (Purchasing Power Parity): $6,100.

Recent Political Status: A republic was formed in 1924, but in 1925 it was incorporated into the former USSR and remained so until 1991.

Chief of State: Gurbanguly Berdymukhammedov, President. He is also head of the Government Cabinet of Ministers (Elected in February 2007).

National Day: October 27 (1991), independence from USSR.

National Flag: A solid green background; superimposed against the green on the left, a red–brown fabric pattern consisting of five medallions runs slightly indented from top to bottom; to the right of that in the upper left, a crescent moon with five stars.

The Land

The Republic of Turkmenistan, independent successor state to the Turkmen Soviet Socialist Republic, declared its independence following the collapse of the attempted *coup* against the USSR's Gorbachëv in August 1991. October 27 has been established as the official Independence Day.

Although it borders on the Caspian Sea in the west, Turkmenistan is almost entirely a land of deserts and passes. The entire central part of the republic is occupied by the largest of these, the Kara Kum, or Black Sand Desert. Topographically, it is also the southern part of the Turan Plain. Only in the south are there foothills and mountains. The Kopet–Dag forms the border with eastern Iran, while northern–reaching spurs of the Pamir Alay Mountain Ranges form the border with Afghanistan and the south part of the border with Uzbekistan. On the northeast, the Amu Dar'ya River flows along the border with Uzbekistan. It borders on the Caspian Sea in the west.

Three other rivers, the Tedzhen, Murgab and Atrek, flow north out of the southern mountains and provide water for irrigation. In the 1950s, the Kara Kum Canal was constructed from Kerki on the Amu Dar'ya northwestward across the southern part of the Kara Kum to the city of Merv and Ashgabat, the capital. It is the world's largest irrigation and shipping canal. Oases exist along the rivers plus in the foothills of the Kopet–Dag Mountains. The rest of the country is desert.

Turkmenistan has a strongly continental climate, extremely hot in summer (average of 95°F), and bitterly cold in winter (temperatures as low as –27°F). Precipitation averages 3 inches a year in the northwestern desert and 12 inches in the southern mountains. Except in oases areas, only desert vegetation grows.

The People

Turkmen make up 77 percent of the republic's population. The two largest minorities are Uzbeks (9.2%) and Russians (6.7%). Kazaks make up a further two percent, while there are smaller numbers of Tatars, Ukrainians, Armenians, Kara Kalpaks and Azeris. Russians, found mainly in urban areas, have been leaving the country in large numbers since independence; at the time of the 1989 census, they constituted 13 percent of the population. About half the people live in urban areas, the rest in rural settlements and villages. Turkmen is, as the name implies, a Turkic language.

History

The Turkmens were mostly nomads up to the time of the Russian Revolution, though some had settled in oases and taken up agriculture. Divided up into a number of tribes, their main loyalty was to their tribe or clan, with almost no sense of a Turkmen identity. The creation of the Turkmen Soviet Socialist Republic in October 1924 provided a strong impetus toward creation of a Turkmen nation. Turkmens are the most distinctive of the Turkic peoples of Central Asia. Their language is closer to that of the Ottoman Turks and Azerbaijani than it is to the other Turkic peoples of Central Asia. Their origins are disputed, however. They have apparently been Muslims since the tenth century but, because they were desert tribes, the only record of their past is oral. Their main tribes were the Tekes, Ersaris, and Yomut. There were bitter rivalries between the tribes. Thus when the Tekes were fighting a struggle to drive back the Russians in the 1860s and 1870s, the other tribes offered no assistance whatsoever.

In 1869, a Russian military force landed on the eastern shore of the Caspian Sea and founded a settlement at the location of present–day Krasnovodsk. Five years later, the Transcaspian military district was established. This became the Transcaspian *oblast* in 1881. There was fierce resistance to the Russian advance, but it was broken at the battle of Geok–Tepe in 1881. In 1899, the area was incorporated into the Governor Generalship of Turkistan.

Turkmenistan was the scene of intermittent fighting during the Russian civil war that followed the *Bolshevik* Revolution. Red Army troops conquered Ashgabat in July 1919 and Krasnovoksk in February 1920. The *Bolsheviks* organized the western part of present–day Turkmenistan as a separate *oblast* of the Turkistan Autonomous SSR. The remaining parts were included in the Bukharan and Khorezmian Soviet Socialist Republics. In 1924, a Turkmen Soviet Socialist Republic was formed, which took in all three Turkmen–inhabited areas. The Turkmen SSR was formally incorporated into the USSR in May 1925.

The life of the Turkmen people changed almost completely during the seventy years of the Soviet period but, through it all, the Turkmen SSR remained one of the most obedient of the constituent republics of the USSR. This began to change somewhat after Gorbachëv became General Secretary in 1985 and launched his program of *glasnost and perestroika*. In August 1990, the Turkmen Supreme Soviet passed a declaration of sovereignty, though there was still no real challenge to Soviet authority. However, Saparmurad Niyazov, first secretary of the *Turkmen Communist Party*, had the Supreme Soviet create the office of president and he was elected to that office in October 1990.

The attempted *coup* against Gorbachëv in August 1991 changed this situation again. Following the collapse of the USSR President Niyazov issued a declaration of Turkmen independence and called for a referendum on the question, which took place on October 26. When the referendum received a 94 percent favorable vote, President Niyazov declared October 27 Turkmen independence day.

He confiscated all assets held by the *Communist Party of the Soviet Union* within the republic, but he remained first secretary of the *Turkmen Communist Party*, and on November 18–19, the Central Committee of the party held a plenum to consider the future. It called a party congress for

President Saparmurad Niyazov

December 16 and recommended that the party be renamed the *Turkmen Democratic Party*. This recommendation was implemented by the party congress when it met in December. President Niyazov was elected chairman. According to the program of the *Democratic Party*, it is "oriented towards market reforms, sale of the state's property and support of all forms of property."

On November 15, Niyazov, who had appointed his prime minister as the chief of a newly formed Turkmen Railroad, decided to take on direct leadership of the government himself. His assumption of the duties of the prime minister was temporary, according to a government spokesman. There was no question of abolishing the office of prime minister. By January 1992, it appeared that the deputy prime minister, Nazar Suyunov, had become the *de facto* head of government.

In April 1993, President Niyazov signed a decree approving a new alphabet of the Turkmen language based on Latin. This change marks the third alphabetic reform for the Turkmen language since the beginning of the century. The switch to the new Latin alphabet took place on January 1, 2000.

Over the past several years, President Niyazov has been increasingly referred to in the press and in public announcements as "Turkmenbashi," or "Leader of the Turkmen." His portrait is ubiquitous, appearing in every parade float, office build-

ing and hotel. Every park in the country has a statue of him. The purpose is apparently to increase his popularity among the people by portraying him as a traditional tribal leader and it appears to be working. In a referendum held in January 1994, the people were asked whether they approved extending his term of office until 2002. The final result of the vote was 1,959,408 votes for, 212 against and 17 spoiled ballots.

Talking to a Western reporter in December 1995, Niyazov admitted that the new cult of personality had gone too far. "I admit it, there are too many portraits, pictures and monuments. I don't find any pleasure in it, but the people demand it because of their mentality."

Elections to the newly created Majlis (legislature) took place in December 1994. Since no oppositional party managed to gain official registration, the candidates were almost all members of the *Democratic Party of Turkmenistan*. All ran unopposed.

President Niyazov had cardiac surgery in Germany on September 1, 1997. The operation was a success and there were no complications. Five weeks later, he chaired his first cabinet meeting since the operation and later attended a ceremony commemorating the victims of the 1948 earthquake that destroyed Ashgabat. President Niyazov's mother and brothers were among the victims.

President Niyazov paid an official visit to the United States in April 1998. One agreement signed during the visit provided for Export–Import Bank credit for purchasing U.S.–made goods, while a second provided $750,000 for a feasibility study of Trans–Caspian oil and gas lines on the Caspian Sea bed. In addition, Niyazov signed agreements with Mobil and Exxon on the exploration and extraction of oil in western Turkmenistan.

New parliamentary elections took place on December 12, 1999. A total of 102 candidates competed for the 50 mandates in the new parliament but, except for a few independents, all were members of the *Democratic Party of Turkmenistan*. After the elections, the new parliament approved an amendment to the constitution allowing Niyazov to serve as president for life. The next day, Niyazov announced that no alternatives to the *Democratic Party of Turkmenistan* would be allowed to exist during the next decade. Niyazov modified that position slightly in February 2001 when he announced that he would leave office no later than 2010, when he will turn 70. He promised that open elections for the presidency would be held at that time. Parliament duly passed a law setting presidential elections for 2010.

The matter came up again in August 2002 when the 3,000 delegates to the *Khalk*

Turkmenistan

Maslakhaty enthusiastically endorsed a proposal making Niyazov president for life. President Niyazov rejected the proposal the next day, but he then instructed the *Khalk Maslakhaty* to rename the months and days of the week. The *Khalk Maslakhaty* proceeded to rename January as Turkmenbashi (one of Niyazov's titles), April after Niyazov's mother, and September after the *Rukhname*, Niyazov's volume of spiritual writings.

Niyazov may not be permitted the quiet enjoyment of his remaining years in power, however. The political situation in the country has been deteriorating since the summer of 2001 when President Niyazov launched what looked like a political purge when he summarily sacked four government officials, five deputy governors of provinces, and the mayor of Ashgabat.

Three months later, he called the members of the Turkmen diplomatic corps to a meeting on October 30, 2001. Since the meeting was carried live on Turkmen television, the general population saw Niyazov chastise nearly every one of Turkmenistan's ambassadors and fire two of

them, the ambassadors to the United Arab Emirates and China. Two days later, Boris Shikhmuradov, the fired ambassador to China—who prior to becoming ambassador had served from 1995 to 2000 as deputy prime minister and foreign minister—arrived in Moscow where he issued a press statement denouncing President Niyazov's regime as "a primitive police state" which had isolated the country, and he accused Niyazov of having committed crimes, allowed crimes to be committed, and persecuted people on religious and ethnic bases. The press statement also included the information that Shikhmuradov had created an anti–Niyazov political organization, the *People's Democratic Movement of Turkmenistan*. One day later, the Turkmen Prosecutor–General's office in Ashgabat issued an indictment against Shikmuradov accusing him, among other things, of stealing $25 million worth of equipment from the state, 9,000 Kalashnikov assault rifles, and $2.5 million worth of ammunition. The Turkmenistan Government later requested Shikhmuradov's extradition, but the Russian Government demurred.

As it turned out, Shikhmuradov was the *second* high government official to break with Niyazov and then go on to form an anti–Niyazov political organization. The first, Avdy Kuliev, had served as foreign minister from 1990 until July 1992 and left after policy disagreements with his boss. He moved to Moscow in 1997, but when he attempted to return to Ashgabat for a visit in 1998, he was stopped upon his arrival at the airport, and then detained for five days before being sent back to Moscow. It was after his return to Moscow that he formed the *Committee for National Salvation* and began campaigning for Niyazov's resignation and for free and democratic elections.

In February 2002, a third former government official showed up in Moscow as a recruit to the anti–Niyazov opposition. This was Hudaiberdi Orazov, a former chairman of the Turkmen Central Bank, who was serving as a deputy prime minister when he was fired by Niyazov in 2000. Orazov also billed himself as a reformer—"all my attempts to change the situation in the country for the better came to nothing"—but his reputation suf-

Inside a typical Turkmen home in Ashgabat

Turkomen carpets for sale in a bazaar outside of Ashgabat

Photo by Hermine Dreyfuss

fered when, after being indicted by the Prosecutor General's office for embezzlement, he partially admitted the charge and returned $100,000 to the state.

It was never likely that a group of opposition figures living in Moscow could threaten Niyazov's hold on power, but it appears that Niyazov was nevertheless shaken by the nature of the charges made against him. But what has probably bothered him the most is the fact that all three of these individuals seemed to be loyal subordinates while in office. Now he could only wonder how many of his other "loyal subordinates" were secretly sympathetic to one or more of the Moscow opposition. This would explain another recent development—a purge of the National Security Committee (Turkmenistan's successor to the KGB)—which began in March 2002. More than two dozen top officials were fired outright while Mukhammed Nazarov, the head of the National Security Committee, was demoted from four–star general to lieutenant general. Perhaps even more significant, Nazarov, who had been very close to Niyazov, lost his other post as the president's chief legal adviser. Within days, Niyazov also fired Defense Minister Kurbandurdy Begendjev.

A few days later, Niyazov pushed the purge further down the ranks, dismissing two National Security Committee colonels, three lieutenant colonels, and two captains. In April, the purges spread out to other sections of the society when Niyazov dismissed another governor as the chairman of the Food Industry Association.

At the beginning of May, criminal charges were filed against Mukhammed Nazarov and 21 of his subordinates in the KBG. Nazarov was accused of 11 crimes, including murder, procuring prostitutes, bribe taking, and fraud. That same day, ex–Defense Minister Begendjev was charged with four counts of corruption. The trials followed quickly afterwards— ex–Defense Minister Begendjev was sentenced to 10 years in prison on May 23. Nazarov, whose sentencing came on June 15, got 15 years in prison.

As the purges continued, the chairman of the National Bank and the head of the country's main television channel lost their jobs on May 6. Deputy Foreign Minister Batyr Khadykuliev was fired on June 19. The chairman of the Council for Television and Radio Broadcasting and the rector of the Institute of Culture were fired on July 29. The firings and arrests then tailed off.

On November 25, there was apparently an attempt to assassinate President Niyazov. According to the initial story, the president's motorcade came under fire about 7 a.m. at an intersection in downtown Ashgabat as he was traveling to his office. The gunman or gunmen jumped out of a KamAZ truck—in later versions from the truck, a BMW, and a Gazel automobile— and began raking the motorcade with machine–gun fire. By the next day, the story involved the truck, two minibuses and a BMW, while more assailants ran out of nearby residential buildings and opened fire. In spite of the confusion about details, the one constant was that President Niyazov's car was untouched and he was, as he himself later reported, not even aware of the attack at the time.

From the beginning, some political opponents claimed that the attack was either staged or fabricated. Another theory propounded by Saparmurat Iklymov, former Turkmen deputy agriculture minister was that the assassination attempt had been carried out by the Turkmen National Security Committee, which had been the target of a Niyazov purge in the spring. Iklymov's evidence was that the KamAZ truck used in the attempt had been confiscated in 1999 from his brother Parakhat, who left Turkmenistan the following year.

Whatever the truth about the alleged assassination attempt, President Niyazov used it to justify a renewed attack on his political opponents, a further purge of the top echelons of Turkmen society, and a

Turkmenistan

general tightening up of the controls over Turkmen society. Hundreds of persons were arrested after November 25, including visitors in the country from several foreign countries, including one from the United States. Security officials even went so far as to raid the Uzbek Embassy in Ashgabat on December 16, during which they searched the ambassador's residence. The excuse was that they had information that Turkmen citizens involved in the attempted assassination had taken refuge in the building. When they failed to find anyone hiding there, the officers filmed a Turkmen man who had accompanied them into the building as he testified on camera to having been living in the embassy for some time. When the Uzbek Ambassador protested the violation of diplomatic immunity, the Turkmen Government declared him *persona non-grata* and expelled him from the country.

The Turkmen Government did capture former Foreign Minister Boris Shikhmuradov, who had secretly reentered Turkmenistan from Uzbekistan shortly before the assassination attempt. Shikhmuradov was sentenced to life imprisonment on December 30, six days after he gave himself up to Turkmen authorities. Shikhmuradov's public confession, with its description of the president as "a gift given to the people from on high" and the characterization of his policies as "absolutely correct," reminded one forcefully of the Stalinist trials of the 1930s.

Over fifty more men were sentenced to long prison terms during the third week in January. These included former parliament speaker Tagandurdy Khallyev, Konstantin Shikhmuradov, brother of Boris Shikhmuradov and former Foreign Minister Batyr Berdyev. And just as in the 1930s, President Niyazov ordered publication of the proceedings of the trials of those charged in the alleged assassination attempt.

International reaction has been rather uniformly negative. In its annual human rights report issued on March 31, the United States State Department described Turkmenistan as "a one–party state dominated by its president, who continues to exercise power in a Soviet–era authoritarian style." On April 16, the UN Commission on Human Rights adopted a resolution expressing its concern about limitations and violations of human rights in Turkmenistan and calling for an immediate end to mass repressions, the extrajudicial harassment of opposition figures and their families, the fabrication of evidence against people suspected of involvement in the assassination attempt, and the use of torture by law enforcement officials. The resolution also censured Turkmenistan for its lack of cooperation with international organizations. But

**President
Gurbanguly Berdymukhammedov**

Turkmenistan did have some support on the commission—Russia, Ukraine, Armenia and 13 other countries all voted against the resolution.

Since that time, there have been periodic reports of further purges, though in most cases these have been nothing more than dismissals. These involved, in particular, law enforcement and security officials and employees of the Turkmen foreign intelligence system. In addition, a special section has been created in the maximum–security prison in Turkmenbashi for people found guilty of participating in the original alleged assassination attempt.

President Niyazov died unexpectedly on December 21, 2006, apparently of a massive heart attack. That same day, it was announced that the new acting leader of Turkmenistan was Deputy Prime Minister Gurbanguly Berdymukhammedov, who also made a nationally televised address explaining that his selection was confirmed by his fellow ministers and members of the Turkmen State Security Council. The explanation was necessary because, according to the constitution, President Niyazov's successor was supposed to be the speaker of the parliament, Ovezgeldy Atayev.

As Marina Kozlova, writer for *Business Week* magazine, wrote in January 2007, "the inner workings of Niyazov's secretive regime are difficult to decipher." So we don't know why the speaker of parliament was placed under arrest and later sentenced to five years in prison, while a relatively little known junior minister in Niyazov's cabinet became Acting President. But he did. Moreover, parliament quickly passed legislation making Berdymukhammedov eligible to run for the presidency.

Parliament set the presidential election for February 11, then picked six candidates, including Berdymukhammedov, for the presidential poll. No actual opposition candidates were considered. All six presidential candidates said that they would

continue the political course set out by President Niyazov. Berdymukhammedov announced that the election would be conducted "in accordance with the concept of democracy as understood by Niyazov. On Election Day, Berdymukhammedov was elected with over 89 percent of the vote. He was sworn in as president three days later, on February 14.

With such a beginning for an administration, there could be little basis to expect that the new leadership would introduce significant changes. Yet there have been a number of surprising reversals of policy subsequently.

It is true that Berdymukhammedov had said during the electoral campaign that he wanted to improve education and that, internationally, he wanted to keep Turkmenistan neutral but engaged with its neighbors. Nevertheless, it came as a surprise when he almost immediately ordered the restoration of the 10th year of secondary education and replaced vocational training in secondary schools with physical education and social studies. In addition, he reduced teachers' work schedules and limited classroom size to 25 for secondary schools with lower ratios for primary grades. He also announced that young people would be permitted to study in foreign universities; that teachers would be sent abroad for professional training; that foreign diplomas would again be recognized; and that the two-year work requirement for university students would be dropped.

Another presidential decree called for the opening of the first Internet cafes in Ashgabat, with more Internet cafes to be opened later in other parts of the country. The news is not all good; the fees charged in the new Internet cafes will mean that few individuals will be able to afford to use them, but that could change.

In another change, President Berdymukhammedov instructed government officials to attend conferences and meetings abroad. This was a 180-degree change from the situation under President Niyazov, who forbade all but senior government officials from representing their country abroad.

All in all, it marks a good beginning for a new administration.

Foreign Policy

Since emerging as an independent nation in 1991, Turkmenistan has pursued an official policy of neutrality and nonintervention in the affairs of other nations. Except for its membership in the Commonwealth of Independent States, therefore, it has refused to join any of the supranational organizations that have come into existence in the region over the past decade, and its relations with its neighbors have been mainly economic where they have existed at all.

Turkmenistan's relations with Russia represent a partial exception, however, for the Government of Turkmenistan signed a agreement with Russia in December 1995 under which Russian troops guard Turkmenistan's borders with Iran and Afghanistan. The agreement was signed by the two presidents during a CIS meeting being hosted by the Turkmenistan Government at Ashgabat and an accord on dual citizenship was signed by the two nations at the same time.

Even with Russia, Turkmenistan's relations are mainly economic and revolve around the fact that Turkmenistan is a major producer of natural gas but is almost totally dependent on Russian-controlled pipelines to get its gas to world markets. This was made clear to the Government of Turkmenistan in 1994 when Gazprom, the Russian energy company that controls the pipelines, raised its transit fees to a level where Turkmenistan could no longer make a profit shipping to western Europe, and so it lost its western European markets. Over the next several years, Turkmenistan worked to reduce its dependency on Russia by supporting projects to construct pipelines to carry its gas south through Afghanistan and Iran. Taliban control of Afghanistan ruled out use of that route in the 1990s, but a pipeline to Iran was completed in 1998. There have also been discussions about building a new railroad between Turkmenistan and Iran which could serve the same purpose.

Having had little success in finding alternate markets for its natural gas, Turkmenistan signed an agreement with Gasprom in 2005 under which the latter agreed to import between 60 and 70 billion cubic meters of natural gas a year by 2007. Gasprom has been paying $44 per 1,000 cubic meters for this gas, but the Turkmenistan Government wants to raise the price to $100 per 1,000 cubic meters.

Turkmenistan probably has the best relations with Iran of any of his neighbors, and economic connections between the two states continue to grow. President Khatami of Iran was in Ashgabat in April 2002 to attend a Turkmenistan sponsored conference of the countries bordering on the Caspian Sea. The conference produced no agreement, but the two leaders did discuss raising the throughput capacity of the Korpedzhe–Kurt–Kui gas pipeline to thirteen billion cubic meters per year. The talks came to fruition in April 2006 with the announcement that Iran will purchase 8 billion cubic meters of natural gas in 2006 and 14 billion cubic meters in 2007. The price was set at $65 per 1,000 cubic meters of gas.

Turkmenistan has recently upgraded its relations with the People's Republic of China, particularly in the economic sphere. In April 2006, President Niyazov paid an official visit to China. While there, he signed an agreement with the Chinese Government on building a pipeline to export natural gas from Turkmenistan to China. This appears to be an agreement in principle thus far, since there was no indication in the announcement that the terms of financing have been worked out. On the other hand, with China's increased demand for energy, the pipeline looks like a good possibility for the future. According to the preliminary agreement, China will begin importing natural gas from Turkmenistan in 2009.

Relations between Turkmenistan and the United States had been cool for a number of years, as the United States has been critical of President Niyazov's government on issues such as the regime's authoritarianism and its human rights record. That changed to some extent after the terror attacks of September 11, but particularly after the United States launched its war on terrorism. Although the United States remains critical of certain policies of the government, it has also expressed its gratitude for President Niyazov's early condemnation of the terror attacks and for Turkmenistan's willingness to make its airspace and territory available for humanitarian aid flights to Afghanistan. In fact, almost all humanitarian aid going to Afghanistan prior to January 2002 passed through Turkmenistan. During a single week in November, nine planes carrying humanitarian cargo for Afghanistan landed at Ashgabat airport. In addition, the Government of Turkmenistan used its own jets to carry consignments of humanitarian aid from Ashgabat to an airport along the Afghan border.

This cooperation also brought a host of U.S. official visitors to Ashgabat. Lynn Pascoe, U.S. deputy assistant secretary of state, visited Ashgabat on November 9, followed three days later by Andrew Natsios, the director of the USAID. Two months later, a Senatorial delegation headed by Majority Leader Tom Daschle visited Ashgabat in January 2002, where they met with Foreign Minister Meredov and National Security Council Chairman Nazarov.

President Niyazov also moved to establish cordial relations with the new Government of Afghanistan. Hamid Karzai, the head of Afghanistan's interim government, was welcomed to Ashgabat in

A catch of wild carp is hauled from the Kara Kum Canal   Courtesy: NOVOSTI

Turkmenistan

March 2002. President Niyazov used the opportunity to bring up once again the possibility of a gas pipeline through Afghanistan. The two leaders signed a series of agreements for such things as construction of new roads between their countries and linking their power grids so Turkmenistan could begin providing electricity to Afghanistan. The Government of Turkmenistan also announced that it would be opening an embassy in Kabul.

In April 2002, James Wolfensohn, president of the World Bank, visited Ashgabat and was received by President Niyazov. Wolfensohn offered World Bank assistance in helping Turkmenistan speed up market reforms and also expressed an interest in investing in oil and gas infrastructure as well as projects contributing to the rational use of the country's water resources.

Most of this new international openness was put on hold after the alleged attempted assassination of President Niyazov, particularly after the widespread purges that he instituted at this time. The various "color" revolutions that took place in Georgia, Ukraine and Kyrgyzstan in 2003–2005 created a sort of siege mentality in Turkmenistan among the political elites and a further withdrawal from international involvement. Turkmenistan currently cultivates good relations only with Russia, Iran and China.

Turkmenistan's relations with Azerbaijan, its neighbor across the Baltic, were placed in a deep freeze in the late 1990s because of a disagreement over demarcation of the boundary between the two republics on the seabed of the Baltic that involved a potential oil field. For eight years, therefore, diplomatic relations had been suspended. The death of President Niyazov in December 2006, followed by the election of President Berdymukhammedov in February, has brought the beginning of a change in this relationship.

In March 2007, Berdymukhammedov proposed to President Aliyev that the two republics end the official eight-year boycott that has existed between them and begin talking again. For his part, Berdymukhammedov ordered the Turkmen Embassy to be reopened in Baku. This particular opening is especially important because it may lead to unfreezing the stalemate that has kept the Caspian littoral states from reaching an agreement on the demarcation of the Caspian seabed. This could, in turn, launch a new wave of foreign investment in Turkmenistan as well as in Azerbaijan, and it could also lead to construction of a pipeline connecting Turkmenistan and Azerbaijan, with the gas then flowing into the recently opened gas pipeline to Turkey.

Nature of the Regime

In December 1994, Turkmenistan replaced the governmental system inherited from the Soviet era with a new system, under which the president acts as both head of state and head of government. There is no separate prime minister. The presidential term was originally set for five years, but in 1999 the legislature amended the constitution to allow Niyazov to serve for life. Niyazov announced in 2000 that he intended to serve only until he reached the age of 70, i.e., until 2010, and parliament subsequently passed a law to that effect.

President Niyazov's death in December 2006 has created a new situation entirely. The new president is Gurbanguly Berdymukhammedov, who began his five-year term as president on February 14, 2007. Berdymukhammedov also assumed the second position as head of government.

The Majlis (legislature) consists of 50 members, elected for a term of five years. It is totally dominated by the executive. There is also a constitutional court and a supreme court.

The constitution specifies an additional entity, referred to as the *Khalk Maslakhaty* (People's Supreme Council) which is defined as the country's supreme consultative body. It is supposed to meet annually, but met for the first time in three years in August 2002. Turkmen television explained at the time that, although it was commonly referred to as the *Khalk Maslakhaty*, it was more accurately referred to as the 12th joint forum of three bodies: the Congress of Elders, intended to be an advisory group to the president; the National Revival Movement of Turkmenistan, a coalition of political parties and public associations in the country; and the People's Council proper, consisting of parliamentary deputies and Niyazov's appointees. Interfax added that, according to the Turkmen constitution, the council included cabinet members, heads of local executive bodies, judges, and representatives of nongovernmental organizations.

When the *Khalk Maslakhaty* met for its annual session in August 2003, President Niyazov presented a series of constitutional amendments to it which it duly passed. The most important of these amendments stipulated that the *Khalk Maslakhaty* would remain in permanent session and absorb many of the functions hitherto carried out by the *Majlis*, the 50-member legislature. According to a new edition of the national constitution published after the session, the *Khalk Maslakhaty* is described as the "supreme permanent representative body of authority."

In April 2007, President Berdymukhammedov was elected chairman of the *Halk Maslahaty* (People's Council).

Culture

Prior to the Russian Revolution, most educated Turkmens were graduates of one of the several seminaries located in Bukhara. Perhaps the most famous of these was Abdulhekim Qulmuhammed-oghli, a writer, editor, researcher and cultural organizer, who eventually joined the *Communist Party*. He was killed in 1937 at the time of the great Soviet purge. The level of literacy increased greatly during the Soviet era, but the strait-jacket of socialist realism, instituted by Stalin in 1930, has meant that most work has been written "for the masses." In addition, many Turkmen writers' works were in Russian. This is true also of films, television, radio and theater, which appear in Russian.

Since the fall of communism, there has been a concerted effort to revive traditional Turkmen culture. Mosques have been reopened, various ancient customs and rituals have been revived, and some old taboos are once again observed. Since 1999, even polygamy is now legal. Most Turkmens are Sunni Muslims, but religion, though important, often is less important than tribal loyalties. Turkmenistan is still essentially a tribal culture, dominated by its five major tribes. Tribal ties, officially suppressed under communism, have once again come to the fore.

The government has also taken efforts to reduce the influence of Russian culture since independence. The local publication of Russian-language newspapers stopped in 1992. Five years later, the government began to place restrictions on the importation of periodicals from Russia. Then in July 2002 it became illegal to import any publication from Russia. The motivation for this latest governmental action was probably more political than cultural, however, since Russian publications had recently become very critical of President Niyazov.

Still, the move to ban all Russian publications fits into a larger pattern of governmental actions taken recently to isolate Turkmen citizens from foreign influence. For example, President Niyazov issued a decree in February 2003 whose effect will be to severely restrict opportunities of Turkmen citizens to study abroad. Essentially, the decree stipulates that only students chosen by the Education Ministry may legally exchange *manats*, the national currency, for convertible currencies. Two months later, the government began dismissing all teachers who had earned their degrees from foreign institutions of higher or specialized secondary education after 1993.

Turkmenistan has no great literary tradition and in recent years the most important Turkmen author has been President Niyazov, who is famous for his published writings. His latest work, *Mahribanlarim*

(My Dear All), a mixture of prose and poetry, was published in October 2005. A perhaps more typical Turkmen writer is Rahim Esenov, author of more than 20 novels. The 79-year old Esenov was awarded the 2006 PEN/Barbara Goldsmith Freedom to Write Award in April 2006. Esenov was permitted to travel to New York City to receive the award, but he had been held in confinement in Ashgasbat for two years prior to that time, and his novels are banned in Turkmenistan. Esenov's most important novel is *The Crowned Wanderer*, which tells the life of Bayram Khan, a military general and man of letters from earlier Turkmen history.

The government tended to take a hands-off attitude toward religion during the first years of independence, but that changed when the number of Protestant Christians began to grow in the country. In 1997, the government began taking coercive actions against individual Protestant churches. Government police and security officers raided three Protestant churches in September–October 2000; congregation members had their passports confiscated, and members were warned not to attend services in the future. In February 2001, the government arrested and imprisoned a Baptist minister by the name of Shageldy Atakov. He had been serving his four year sentence at the Seydy labor camp in northeastern Turkmenistan but, according to the latest reports, he has been moved to a closed prison in the town of Turkmenbashi, on the Caspian coast. Atakov's wife and children were reportedly ordered to convert from Christianity or Islam with the proviso that, if they did not, their home would be confiscated. In March, the last open Baptist church in Ashgabat was seized and closed. City officials said afterwards that the congregation had not complied with a 1997 requirement to re-register with the Turkmen ministry of justice.

Arranged marriages are still the norm in the society, particularly in rural areas. Traditionally, the bride and groom must belong to the same tribe. This causes problems for young people of different tribes who fall in love. Occasionally, a young man will "steal away" the girl he favors, hoping thereby to force the parents to agree. This doesn't always work, however. As one Turkmen commented, "it's no joke. Some parents sue the husband in court. Others kill the bride."

Economy

The Soviet era brought about major changes in the lives of the Turkmen people. Prior to the Russian Revolution, most Turkmens were nomads who constantly moved from place to place in search of forage for their herds. Beginning in the 1930s, great engineering projects were launched to increase the irrigated areas. These irrigated lands were organized into state farms and the Turkmen people were settled on them, their nomadic life at an end.

Cotton became the chief crop grown throughout the area. New engineering projects in the 1950s and 1960s, in particular the Kara Kum Canal, brought additional lands under cultivation and increased Turkmenistan production of cotton even further. Local reports of increasing salinity in the soil or the constant drop in the level of the Aral Sea as a result of the new engineering projects were ignored by the central planners in Moscow.

After 1985, however, Gorbachëv's reforms allowed for greater local autonomy. Beginning about 1987, Turkmenistan began an attempt to restructure its agricultural economy. Moscow was asked to lower its cotton quota somewhat, and some land was removed from cotton production and switched to other crops. Turkmenistan began to grow more grain and feed, and the number of livestock grown also increased. The government has continued and expanded on this emphasis since independence. This improved the situation somewhat, but the republic is only beginning to think about restructuring its agriculture. When it does, some degree of centralization will almost certainly continue to exist, since all farming depends on irrigation, which must remain centralized.

President Niyazov has endorsed the idea of private property, but he has said that he favors transforming money-losing state farms into smaller collective farms and then allowing leasing and creation of rural cooperatives. He began this process in December 1996 when he issued a decree giving farmers the right to lease land for up to 15 years free of charge. The decree requires the leaser to grow certain specified crops for the first two years. At the end of the two years, if the leaser has achieved the minimum yields contracted for, he is then free to plant whatever crops he wants, and may even lease the land to someone else if he chooses, though he is not free to sell it. This is the likely direction for agriculture in the future.

In February 1998, President Niyazov addressed the Majlis on the need to improve agriculture. He reported that the country had met only half of the target for grain in 1997, while cotton production was only 41 percent of the expected total. The production figures for 1998 were somewhat better. Grain production actually reached the target figure of 1.2 million tons, while overall agricultural production was up by 20 percent over the preceding year. On the other hand, the cotton harvest of 690,000 tons was slightly less than half of what had been targeted.

These figures were evidently not good enough for President Niyazov, for he fired his agriculture minister in January 1999 and named his deputy to succeed him. Some days later, the government announced a six-year program for the partial privatization of farms, plus industrial and construction companies belonging to the agro-industrial complex. The announcement did not provide many details, but it did say that the government would retain a 51 percent stake in the newly privatized companies.

The agricultural sector did very well in 2002 with a record grain harvest of 2.3 million tons. The cotton crop was a failure, however, with production under 500,000 metric tons. The 2003 cotton harvest totaled 713,200 tons, an improvement but far below the 2.2 million ton target set by the state. That 2.2 million ton target was undoubtedly unrealistic, but it remained the target for 2004. When the harvest came in at 700,000 tons, President Niyazov dismissed Enebai Ataeva from the posts of deputy prime minister and governor of Ahal province. Ataeva's replacement is Murat Atagarriyev, formerly chairman of the Food Industry Association of Turkmenistan.

Currently, agriculture accounts for 26.9 percent of GDP. Even more importantly, 48.2 percent of all workers are employed in this sector.

Turkmenistan is the least industrialized of all the Central Asian republics, and industry is mainly extractive, essentially gas and oil production. According to recent estimates, Turkmenistan has the third-largest gas reserves in the world, while its estimated oil reserves in the Caspian Basin are second only to those of Kazakhstan. Unlike Kazakhstan and Azerbaijan, however, foreign investment is only now beginning to flow into the country.

Turkmenistan's natural gas reserves may actually be great than earlier estimated. In March 2007, the government announced the discovery of a massive new natural gas field in the Serhetabat district of Mary Province in southeastern Turkmenistan. Official sources claimed that the gas field was 10 times the size of its previously known reserves.

The petroleum industry first began to be developed in the 1930s; Turkmenistan now ranks fourth in production among CIS republics after Russia, Kazakhstan, and Azerbaijan. Turkmenistan exported about 7 billion cubic meters of gas annually before independence. Some of this gas went to other republics, but much of it was exported to Western Europe. In 1994, however, Gazprom, the newly privatized Russian gas company which controlled the pipelines to Western Europe, greatly increased transit fees for Turkmen gas and

Turkmenistan

cut off the government of Turkmenistan when it refused to pay the higher fees.

Turkmenistan continued to export gas to other members of the CIS for another two years, but it cut off most of these countries at the beginning of 1997 when they were unable to pay the large arrears that they had built up. This is the main explanation why gas export revenues fell to $275 million in 1997 (down from $674 million in 1996).

The situation began to change again in 1998 when construction was completed on a pipeline connecting Turkmenistan's Korpedzhe gas field and the Iranian town of Kord Kuy. This allowed Turkmenistan to export 4 billion cubic meters of natural gas to Iran in 1998. Natural gas exports to Iran remained stagnant for several years, but as new agreement, signed in April 2006, calls for exports to Iran of 8 billion cubic meters in 2006 and 14 billion cubic meters in 2007.

President Niyazov also announced in January 2006 that he had reached a verbal agreement with Ukrainian President Yushchenko to furnish Ukraine with 40 billion cubic meters of natural gas in 2006 at a price of $50 per 1.000 cubic meters. Turkmenistan also exports some gas to both Kazakhstan and Azerbaijan, but these quantities are much smaller.

In April 2003, President Niyazov personally negotiated a gas deal with the Russian natural–gas company Gazprom under which Gazprom agreed to purchase 10 billion cubic meters of Turkmen gas starting in 2005. The contract, which will continue until 2025, allows for purchases of up to 50 billion cubic meters of gas a year. This will essentially require a doubling of gas production plus a significant expansion of its pipeline system. In 2005, Turkmenistan exported 45.5 billion cubic meters of natural gas. According to Gurbanmurat Ataev, the country's Oil and Gas Minister, Turkmenistan's export capacity for natural gas is 100 billion cubic meters a year.

Although the role of the government in the economy has not diminished very much, there has been some restructuring of industry since independence. First of all, the production of gas was made the responsibility of *Turkmengaz*, a separately organized but still state–owned company. The rest of the energy sector was partially privatized (but still controlled by the state). Under this system, five separate joint–stock companies were set up with shared responsibility for energy. The first of these, *Turkmenrosgaz*, was responsible for gas exports. It is 51 percent owned by *Turkmengaz*, 45 percent by Gazprom, and 4 percent by a Russian trading company. The other four companies were *Turkmenneft* (oil production), *Turkmenneftegaz* (oil and gas marketing), *Turkmenneftgazstroy* (construction), and *Turkmengeologia* (exploration). In December 2005, President Niyazov abolished *Turkmenneftegaz*. Responsibility for gas sales was transferred to *Turkmengaz*, while responsibility for sales of oil and liquefied natural gas were assigned to the Turkmenbashi refinery complex. Perhaps coincidentally, these changes were initiated after it was announced that there had been a shortfall in oil production in 2005.

Little has changed in the rest of the industrial sector thus far. Some privatization of small enterprises was carried out in 1992, mostly purchased by employees, but everything else remained in state hands. According to an announcement made in November 1997, by President Niyazov, 50 state–owned enterprises were auctioned off in March 1998. Half of these companies were in the textile sector, with the remainder in the energy, industry, construction, and food and fruit sectors. The government has said that it will eventually auction off 350 such companies. Turkmenistan also permits joint ventures with foreign companies and a number of such companies have been set up, particularly in textiles.

The Future

The Death of President Niyazov in December 2006 and the inauguration of President Gulbanguly Berdymukhammedov on February 14, 2007 mark the beginning of a new era for Turkmenistan. Already, President Berdymukhammedov has instituted a number of changes which portent well for the future.

President Berdymukhammedov does not profess to be a democrat who will change all of Turkmenistan society. In fact, he has publically committed himself to continue the Niyazov tradition. But his actions thus far indicate that his vision for Turkmenistan differs greatly from that of Niyazov. As Berdymukhammedov has said, Turkmenistan is not yet ready for democracy; but he believes that it is ready for some changes, and he has begun to carry them out. Only the future will tell whether these changes will improve the lot of the ordinary people.

A scene in Ashgabat

The Republic of Uzbekistan

Area: 186,400 sq. mi. (447,400 sq. km.; slightly larger than California).

Population: 27.3 million (July 2006 estimate).

Capital City: Tashkent (Pop. 2,073,000).

Climate: Very hot and dry with average annual rainfall of only 8 inches.

Neighboring Countries: Kazakhstan (west and north); Kyrgyzstan and Tajikistan (east); Afghanistan (south); Turkmenistan (south and southwest).

Principal Languages: Uzbek and Russian.

Ethnic Composition: Uzbek (80%), Russian (5.5%), Tajik (5%), Kazakh (3%), Karakalpak (2.5%), Tatar (1.5%), others (2.5%).

Principal Religion: Islam.

Chief Commercial Products: Agriculture—cotton, livestock, melons, fruit, vegetables, wheat and rice, all due to vast irrigation. Industry—natural gas, petroleum, gold, chemicals, machinery, textiles, food processing and construction materials.

Currency: *sum* (Issued November 1993).

Annual Per Capita Income (Purchasing Power Parity): $2,000.

Recent Political Status: The republic was proclaimed in 1924 and became part of the USSR in 1925, which it remained until 1991.

Chief of State: Islam Karimov, President.

National Day: September 1 (1991), Independence Day.

National Flag: Three equal, horizontal stripes, sky blue, white, green, separated by narrow red stripes. In the upper left against the blue, a crescent moon and to the right of it three rows of stars (3, 4, and 5), aligned on the right.

The Land

The Republic of Uzbekistan (Ozbekiston Respublikasi) is the independent successor of the Uzbek Soviet Socialist Republic, which until August 1991 was part of the USSR. Its large area stretches from west of the Aral Sea to the Fergana Valley in the east.

Uzbekistan takes in parts of the Amu Dar'ya River Valley plus the southern half of the Kysyl–Kum Desert. In the east, the republic includes the Fergana River Valley up to the foothills of the Tien Shan Mountain Range, which surrounds the valley on three sides. A landscape of little populated deserts and dry steppes, most of the population live in the fertile oases along rivers flowing of the mountains to the south and southeast.

That part of Uzbekistan which lies west of the Aral Sea is known as the Ust–Urt Flatland. This area is a dry steppe land, flat and sun–baked and useful only for certain types of grazing. The Aral Sea, which Uzbekistan shares with Kazakhstan, was once the world's fourth–largest body of inland water and supported a large fishing industry. In the last 30–45 years, however, the sea and the land bordering on it have become an ecological disaster area. Since 1960, the Aral Sea has lost 60 percent of its water by volume and the level of the water has dropped nearly 50 feet. Each year, it drops another 9–10 inches.

The problem is that it receives its water from two main rivers, the Amu Dar'ya and the Syr Dar'ya, and those two rivers flow through 600 miles of desert and semi–desert before emptying into the Aral Sea. They form natural oases along their banks, but these cultivated areas were greatly extended in the Soviet era through new irrigation projects. Uzbekistan today has 10.75 million acres of land under irrigation, mainly along the lower reaches of the Amu Dar'ya. There are another 8.25 million acres of irrigated land in Turkmenistan, the Fergana River Valley of Kyrgyzstan and Kazakhstan. To stabilize the Aral Sea at its present level, the republics would have to agree to cut water usage sufficiently to allow the annual flow into it to grow from 11 million cubic kilometers to 35 million cubic kilometers per year. To raise it to its 1960 level, the republics would have to agree to cut out all water usage for three decades. Neither alternative is practical, so the Aral Sea will continue to shrink. Its salinity is steadily increasing.

The People

Uzbekistan is the largest of the Central Asian republics in terms of population. Uzbeks make up about 80 percent of the population of the country. Russians, who constitute another 5.5 percent, are the largest minority, followed by Tajiks (5%), Kazakhs (3%), Karakalpak (2.5%), and Tatars (1.5%). Since 1936, Uzbekistan has also included the Kara–Kalpakia Autonomous Republic, located along the southern shores of the Aral Sea in the delta region of the Amu Dar'ya River. Kara–Kalpakia has a population of about 1.2 million, with Kara–Kalpakians, Uzbeks and Kazakhs each constituting a little less than a third of the population. Both Uzbek and Kara–Kalpakian are Turkic languages.

Uzbekistan

Tashkent, the ancient capital of Uzbekistan shows its modern face

Courtesy: NOVOSTI

History

Uzbekistan has been a center of civilization since ancient times, beginning with the early states of Bactria and Sogdiana. It was incorporated into the Persian Empire of Darius the Great and the Empire of Alexander the Great. Islam was introduced in the eighth century when the area was invaded by Arab forces. Incorporated into the Mongol Empire in the thirteenth century, it next gave birth to the Empire of Tamerlane.

The Uzbek people were late–comers to the area, however, arriving probably sometime in the fifteenth century. They are believed to be subordinate tribes of the Kipchak Khanate who called themselves Uzbeks in honor of the greatest Kipchak Khans, Uzbek or *Uzbeg*. Originally settled in the area of the Irtysh River, they began to move southeastward in the fifteenth century under their ruler Abu al–Khayr Khan. His grandson, Muhammad Shaybani, conquered Samarkand and most of the Syr–Dar'ya River Valley and the land south of it up to the Amu Dar'ya.

The Shaybani dynasty ruled at Samarkand until 1598, with a collateral branch ruling in Khiva (called Khwarezm until the eighteenth century). Another dynasty, the Janids, ruled a portion of the country until the eighteenth century, when a reinvigorated Persia invaded and conquered Bukhara and Khiva.

The area between the Amu Dar'ya and Syr–Dar'ya was dominated by three khanates by the beginning of the nineteenth century—Bukhara, Khiva and Kokand. More city–states than empires, they exercised very little control over the nomadic tribes of the desert and semi–desert. These tribes subsisted by raids on settlements to the north.

As Russian settlers pushed into the area, raids became more frequent and a problem for the Russian military which was charged with protecting the area. Building first a line of forts along the frontier, they then began retaliatory raids. Finally they began annexing the border areas. Kokand was attacked in 1864–65 and the emir was forced to cede Chimkent and Tashkent. In 1868, Bukhara was forced to accept the status of Russian vassal. Khiva fell in 1873. Kokand was formally annexed in 1876.

The Imperial Russian Government referred to the areas it had annexed as Russian Turkistan. Bukhara and Khiva continued to be semi–independent khanates.

At the time of the Russian Revolution, a Turkistan Committee of the Provisional Government was set up in Tashkent, but it was replaced in April 1918 by the Autonomous Soviet Socialist Republic of Turkistan. Lenin extended his direct control over this organization in the fall of 1919. In 1920, the semi–independent Khanates of Khiva and Bokhara were conquered by the Red Army and made into People's Republics. Khiva was transformed into a Soviet Socialist Republic in 1923, Bokhara in 1924.

A fundamental redrawing of Central Asian boundaries along ethnic lines took place in 1924. The republics of Khiva, Turkistan, and Bukhara were abolished and five new republics were created. The Uzbekistan Soviet Socialist Republic created in October 1924 included a large part of the Samarkand region, a large part of the Fergana Valley, part of the upper reaches of the Syr–Dar'ya River, including

258

Gur-Emir Mausoleum 15th century Samarkand

Tashkent and the surrounding area, plus the western plains of Bukhara. It also included the Tadzhikistan Autonomous SSR until 1929 when Tadzhikistan became a Soviet Socialist Republic in its own right.

Soviet rule imposed many changes on Uzbekistan; perhaps the greatest change came in the 1950s when the development of huge state farms using irrigation made Uzbekistan one of the principal producers of Central Asian cotton and turned most people into state employees. Throughout the entire Soviet era, the *Communist Party* monopolized political power, so there was little chance for a political opposition to grow. The *Uzbek Communist Party* did begin making nationalist noises after several years of Gorbachëv's *perestroika* and in June 1990 the Uzbek Supreme Soviet adopted a resolution of sovereignty.

Islam Karimov, the leader of the *Uzbek Communist Party*, sat out the August 1991 *coup* against Gorbachëv until it became clear that it was failing. He then joined in condemning it and banned communist party cells in the armed forces, police and civil service. Uzbekistan declared its independence on August 31. In mid-September, Karimov called a congress of the *Uzbek Communist Party* and had it change its name to the *People's Democratic* Party.

Karimov adopted Uzbek nationalist slogans, but he publicly argued that Uzbek-istan was not ready for democracy or a market economy. Later, he took on some democratic trappings when he had the Uzbek Supreme Soviet create a popularly elected presidency and set elections for December 29, 1991. Other political parties became legal but they were not permitted to operate freely. The Uzbek popular front *Birlik*, potentially the largest opposition grouping, was not permitted to field a candidate. The *Islamic Renaissance Movement*, which advocated an Islamic state, was banned. Only the *Erk Democratic Party*, which split from *Birlik* in 1990, was permitted to field a candidate. Karimov won 86 percent of the popular vote. His opponent, Muhammed Salih, got 12.4 percent. In a separate referendum, 98.2 percent cast their votes in favor of Uzbek independence. The following year, the *Erk Democratic Party* was also banned and Salih left Uzbekistan for Turkey to go into self-imposed exile.

U.S. Secretary of State James Baker met with Abdurahmin Pulatov, co-chairman of *Birlik* when he visited Tashkent in January 1992. Pulatov urged Baker to recognize Uzbekistan independence but added that there was no democracy in Uzbekistan. "Politically, we have no freedom at all. The totalitarian regime has been destroyed in Moscow, but in Tashkent it continues to exist."

Current reports out of Uzbekistan indicate that the government still tolerates very little dissent. One reason given is the volatile nature of the Uzbeki people. In January 1992, for example, riots broke out in Uzbekistan after price increases, and calls were heard for the resignation of President Karimov. The 1993–97 civil wars in Tajikistan were another factor; Karimov feared that a similar situation could develop in Uzbekistan. For that reason, the government banned political demonstrations and religious–oriented political parties, and it arrested and imprisoned numerous members of the political opposition. The activities of *Birlik* were suspended in January 1993 and a number of its leaders were later arrested. Even the registered opposition party, *Erk* (Freedom), suffered tremendous harassment from the government, its newspaper shut and its bank accounts seized.

Parliamentary elections took place in December 1994 under the terms of a new constitution that reduced the number of deputies from 500 to 250. The governing *People's Democratic Party* won 205 seats. Real oppositional political parties were not permitted to participate in the elections, but there was a second party, the *National Progress Party*, which was created by the government to represent business interests. It took 6 seats.

Uzbekistan

New presidential elections were scheduled to take place in 1996; instead, a referendum was held in March 1995 asking the people to approve an extension of the term of the president until the year 2000. This was supposed to put the elections for the presidency on the same schedule as that for the legislature.

President Karimov was elected to another five–year term in January 2000, winning with 91.9 percent of the vote. His only rival in the elections, Abdulhafiz Dzhalalov was personally selected by President Karimov as the alternate candidate in the election. Dzalalov is head of the *People's Democratic Party*, which Karimov headed until 1996.

Having to run for reelection every five years apparently became burdensome to Karimov, however. In January 2002, he held a national referendum which extended the term of the presidency. Karimov's term as president will now run until December 2007.

Uzbekistan and Militant Islam

Although the political leadership of newly independent Uzbekistan was secular in its orientation, its attitude toward Islam during the first several years of independence was one of tolerance and even encouragement. That changed in December 1997 when four policemen were killed in the city of Namangan, known as a center of Islamic fervency. Although no one claimed responsibility for the killings, the government blamed Islamic militants and launched a massive crackdown. It also enforced a 9:00 p.m. curfew in Namangan and the neighboring city of Andizhan. Following the crackdown, veiled women organized demonstrations before the presidential palace in Tashkent to protest the arrest and detention of their sons and husbands without charges. As one of the demonstrating women said of her husband, "there are no charges. He has a beard, so they accuse him of being a Wahabi." At the time, the watchword was that the government routinely used the word Wahabi as a catch–all pejorative which it applied to all Islamic devotees.

Abid Khan Nazarov, a religious leader expelled in 1995 as the imam of an important mosque in Tashkent, said of the situation, "Government policy is becoming tougher and people are losing their tolerance. There is the danger that the situation will provoke the emergence of some terrorist group."

That happened on February 16, 1999, when militant Islamists set off at least eight car bomb explosions in Tashkent with the apparent target being President Karimov. The explosions were set off as Karimov was being driven to a cabinet meeting at government headquarters. Ka-

rimov was uninjured, but 16 people were killed and another 80 were injured. The government immediately identified religious extremists as the culprits and sealed the borders.

A major trial took place in November 2000. Two men who were tried in absentia—*Islamic Renaissance Movement* leader Takhir Yuldashev and Juma Namangani, founder of the *Islamic Movement of Uzbekistan (IMU)*—were sentenced to death. Ten others received various terms of imprisonment for their role in the bombings. Muhammad Solih, leader of the *Erk* party, was also tried in absentia and given a prison sentence.

At the time, most outside observers thought that the Uzbek Government was exaggerating the threat from radical Islam and few had heard of Juma Namangani,

one of the two men sentenced to death in absentia. That changed soon after the terror attacks of September 11 that led to the American–led war on terrorism and the decision to carry the fight to Afghanistan.

Uzbekistan, with memories of February 1999 fresh before it, became one of the first nations to throw its support behind the American–led war on terrorism. On September 16, President Karimov offered the use of Uzbek airspace and territory for an attack against Afghanistan and Foreign Minister Kamilov said that Uzbekistan was willing to discuss the stationing of United States troops in the country.

Uzbekistan's willingness to participate in a U.S. military coalition surprised some people for Uzbekistan had rejected participating in any military alliances after becoming independent in 1991. However, it

At *Uzbekistan Restaurant* in Tashkent, chef Bikhadyr Iskhakov prepares a traditional Uzbek dish—*lagman*, pasta with mutton

Courtesy: NOVOSTI

joined the U.S.–led war on terrorism because it was already carrying out a similar policy on its own. The Uzbek Government knew, for example, that Juma Namangani, whom it held responsible for the February 1999 explosions, had been in Afghanistan for a number of years and had become a top officer in the Taliban militia. In the fall of 2001, he was the commander in charge of the pivotal northern city of Mazar–i–Sharif and had under him a force of 14,000 soldiers, including Arab, Tajik, Uzbek, and other foreign mercenaries and volunteers. One of those volunteers serving under him was John Walker Lindh, the American Taliban captured when American forces invaded Afghanistan.

Namangani had served in Afghanistan 14 years earlier as an 18–year old conscript in the Soviet military. After his service, he returned to his native city of Namangan and founded the *Islamic Movement of Uzbekistan (IMU)*. The goal of the *IMU* was the formation of an Islamic state uniting the Muslims of Central Asia; from the beginning, the organization ignored the boundaries of existing states and recruited members throughout the region. In 1997, the group began assassinating regional Uzbek officials, in one case leaving the head of one official on the gate post of the home of the Namangan security chief. Namangani himself fled Uzbekistan in 1997 and from that time made his headquarters in Afghanistan, but the focus of his organization continued to be Central Asia. In 1999, armed bands of *IMU* guerrillas launched attacks from Afghanistan into Tajikistan, Kyrgyzstan, and Uzbekistan. Their target was the fertile Fergana River Valley, the most densely populated area of Central Asia. When the 1999 attacks failed, they were launched again in 2000, this time with the purpose of setting up guerrilla camps in the mountains northeast of Tashkent. They made their way into the mountains, but were eventually driven out.

The American invasion of Afghanistan in the fall of 2001 ended the *IMU's* safe haven in Afghanistan and led to the death of Namangani himself. Yet Namangani engendered such fear in Central Asia that Uzbekistan had closed its border with Afghanistan and did not reopen the Friendship Bridge connecting the two countries until December 2001, after it was absolutely certain that Namangani had been killed during the fighting that led up to the fall of Mazar–i–Sharif.

The *IMU* survived Namangani's death, but his death left the organization without a charismatic military leader. The Uzbek Government thus began to focus on the *Hizb ut–Tahrir*, a banned Islamic extremist party committed to uniting all Central Asian Muslims in a single Islamic state by political means, as the new threat to governmental stability. *Hizb ut–Tahrir* does, in fact, represent a threat to secular governments throughout Central Asia, but possibly somewhat less so in Uzbekistan. Here, where a state committee has complete control over religious practice, the Grand Mufti of Tashkent and the Islamic clergy under him present a powerful counterweight to the radical Islamists.

Nevertheless, a series of bombings and attacks that extended from March 28 to April 1, 2004 and included the first known suicide bombings in Uzbekistan were believed to have been organized by Islamic militants. The first of the attacks killed 10 persons in the province of Bukhara; the next morning, female suicide bombers blew themselves up in a children's store in central Tashkent and at a nearby bus stop. As the attacks continued over the next days, the government reported that at least 47 persons had been killed, including ten policemen and 33 militants, seven of them women.

Four months later, on July 30, three suicide bombers blew themselves up outside the Israeli and American Embassies and at the headquarters of the Uzbek chief prosecutor. In this second case, it was eventually established that all three of the bombers were from Kazakhstan.

As the government began rounding up suspected militants, it first laid the blame on *Hizb ut–Tahrir* (which denied any involvement), but it then appeared that the attacks had been organized by a resurgent *Islamic Movement of Uzbekistan*. In fact, it is still not clear who organized and carried out the attacks. Although the government subsequently rounded up numerous suspected militants, it was already holding up to 7,000 Muslims in jail for their religious or political beliefs prior to these attacks.

Responding to the advice of the U. S. State Department that democracy is the best cure for terrorism and the best response to the attacks would be to open up society, Uzbek Foreign Minister Sodik Saforev agreed that

> *more civil society, more democracy, is one of the best ways to secure profound stability and, let's say, public accord in society.*

But, he then added,

> *We believe that what happened in Uzbekistan is part of a global activation of terrorism. We believe that its aim is to sow chaos and systematic instability.*

In May 2005, violence again broke out in Uzbekistan when armed Uzbeks in the town of Andijon attacked a military garrison to obtain additional weapons, then

Students at Alisher Navoi University in Samarkand listen to a lecturer
Courtesy: NOVOSTI

stormed a local prison, freeing 23 businessmen and releasing about 2,000 other prisoners. After the insurgents occupied the regional-administrative building in Andijon, they organized a demonstration in the main square of the city where a number of the freed businessmen spoke.

In response, the Uzbek Government sent in soldiers with tanks who fired on the demonstrators, resulting in the deaths of several hundred individuals. The 23 businessmen had earlier been charged with involvement in an Islamic extremist group, a charge the businessmen denied although they did admit that they had tried to integrate Islamic ethical principles into their business practices.

As more information became available, it became known that the "Islamist extremist" behind the businessmen's actions was Akram Yuldashev, a self-taught spiritual leader who wrote a 44-page tract entitled "The Path of Faith" in 1991. In this sort of self-help tract, Yuldashev advised his readers to place spiritual values ahead of material desires, in accordance with the Koran. Yuldashev was never an advocate of violence and, in fact, it appears that his tract was purely religious with no reference whatsoever to politics; however, the Uzbekistan Government, with its extremely small tolerance for any movement outside of government control, considered his actions and the tract to be seditious.

Uzbekistan

After his arrest, he was given a 17-year sentence, which he is serving in a Tashkent prison.

The businessmen who were arrested for attempting to put Yuldashev's ideas into effect in their business were never accused of advocating violence, but only of being involved with an Islamist extremist group. On the other hand, it is clear that the insurgents involved in breaking the businessmen out of prison in May 2005 were guilty of using violence, though it appears that their motivation for their particular actions was related to their belief that the businessmen were innocent of any crime rather than some particular religious belief. In fact, there has never been any indication that those involved were even aware of Yuldashev's writings.

Andijon, a city of about 300,000 inhabitants located in the Fergana Valley, is in a region that has been experiencing worsening economic problems for a number of years, and it was the scene of at least one other demonstration in September 2004. That demonstration, which lasted several days, was set off after the authorities issued new regulations requiring bazaar sellers who sold imported goods to undergo individual registration. The bazaar sellers, many of whom were women, complained that the new regulations would increase costs to them and require them to raise their prices. Andijon's individual merchants failed to get the regulations withdrawn, however, and nearly 3,000 were left without any work at all. Thus, although the government has blamed the May 2005 events on religious extremism, it appears that economic motivations may have played at least as important a role.

In the actual trials, which took place in November 2005, the defendants all pleaded guilty to the charges and were given prison sentences ranging from 14 to 20 years. One month later, the government organized a second trial of local Uzbek officials—policemen, prison guards, soldiers and medics—who were put on trial for dereliction of duty and negligence in connection with the May 2005 violence. There was also a third trial of 768 individuals charged with direct involvement in the violence. Unlike the first public trial, these trials have taken place behind closed doors. In addition, numerous Uzbek political and rights activists have been arrested and detained by the government since the events of May 2005.

The Uzbek Government has also moved against foreign non-government organizations (NGOs) operating in the country. In June 2006, Uzbek courts ordered the closure of the American Council for Collaboration in Education and Language Study (ACCELS) for numerous violations of Uzbek law. The chief accusation was that ACCELS had sent more than 100 Uzbek students to study in the United States without informing the Uzbek Government. In July, the courts closed the offices of Winrock International, a U.S.-based agricultural NGO. Winrock's crime was that it had financed a publication entitled "Islam and Women," which was found to denigrate national values. In August, the courts closed the Massachusetts-based NGO Partnership in Academics and Development (PAD) for proselytizing among Uzbeks. PAD had been charged with engaging in unlawful missionary activity, offering Internet access without a license, and other "violations."

There was one important exception to this general picture, however. In October 2006, the Tashkent city courts ruled in favor of two U.S. funded NGO—-the Cooperative Housing Foundation International and Mercy Corps—-who had been charged with violating Uzbek law. These verdicts were unusual, however. Virtually all Western-funded NGOs have been closed over the past two years. In November, the Uzbek Government took another step in this direction when it created a special fund to control and manage foreign financial assistance to the country's media outlets. Foreign states and organizations are now forbidden to provide grants directly to Uzbek media.

Foreign Policy

Uzbekistan has been a member of the Commonwealth of Independent States since it came into being and it was a founding member, along with Kazakhstan and Kyrgyzstan, of the Central Asian Customs Union. Although it continues to attend CIS meetings, Uzbekistan has been reluctant to enter into CIS agreements, and particularly economic agreements such as Russia's proposed free trade zone within the CIS.

Until recently, in fact, Uzbekistan has not placed great emphasis on the foreign affairs area, choosing instead to concentrate on domestic affairs. As an exception, it has worked to develop stronger ties with Turkey and it has attempted to maintain good relations with its Central Asian neighbors.

President Karimov's particular fear has been that Russia could continue to dominate the various Central Asian republics. For that reason, Uzbekistan placed a greater emphasis on building up its military forces than any other Central Asian republic. In addition, Uzbekistan—alone among the Central Asian Republics—never permitted Russian border guards to be stationed on its soil. On the other hand, Uzbekistan was always careful to maintain friendly relations with Russia, and even cooperated with the Russian Government on occasion. In June 2000, in fact, Uzbekistan signed new military cooperation agreements that specifically spelled out additional areas of Russian–Uzbek military cooperation. One of those agreements allowed Uzbekistan to use Russian weapons testing facilities. It was also announced at this time that further military agreements were being drafted on the training of Uzbek military personnel in Russia, the repair of all Uzbek military equipment in Russia, and the establishment of a joint venture to manufacture explosives.

A further Uzbek-Russian strategic partnership treaty, signed in June 2004, carried this trend further. The treaty, which calls for beefed-up military cooperation, also made reference to increased cooperation in the political, economic, and commercial

Women doing gold embroidery—a traditional art form—at factory in Bukhara
Photo by Hermine Dreyfuss

spheres. Under the terms of the treaty, Uzbekistan will purchase military hardware from Russia and send Uzbek officers to Russia for training in maintenance and modernization.

Uzbek-Russian commercial ties were enhanced when Russia's LUKoil signed a 35-year production sharing agreement with Uzbekneftegas PSA to develop the Kandym gas field. Under the terms of the agreement, LUKoil will provide 90 percent of the $1 billion investment the projects requires. In addition, Gazprom, Russia's state-run gas monopoly, which will purchase the gas produced by the new consortium, intends to invest a further $1 billion in Uzbekistan to develop gas-condensate fields in the Ustyurt region.

Relations with the United States, correct but not cordial, improved somewhat in 1999 when the two countries negotiated an agreement providing for American aid in dismantling and decontaminating a large chemical weapons testing facility located at Nukus, Uzbekistan. The United States also negotiated a separate agreement with Uzbekistan and Kazakhstan concerning a site on Vozrozhdeniya Island, in the middle of the Aral Sea, where the Soviet Union dumped hundreds of tons of anthrax bacteria in the spring of 1988. Tests performed by American military laboratories have established that the dump still contains live anthrax bacteria and is potentially extremely dangerous. This led to an "implementing arrangement with Uzbekistan," signed on October 22, 2001, in which the United States "agreed to provide technical assistance" and help pay for the removal of thousands of tons of anthrax spores dumped on Vozrozhdeniya Island.

However, the real change in U.S.–Uzbek relations came after the terror attacks against the United States of September 11, 2001 when Uzbekistan became one of the first nations to sign on to the subsequent United States–led war on terrorism. It was also among the first to open its airspace for use by U.S. military planes.

The next several months were a heady time for U.S.-Uzbek relations. During a meeting between President Karimov and Defense Secretary Rumsfeld on October 5, Karimov gave formal approval for the use of an Uzbek military airfield and Rumsfeld provided assurances that America would protect Uzbekistan's security. Less than a week later, nearly 1,000 U.S. troops from the Army's 10th Mountain Division were on the ground at the Hanabad air base in southern Uzbekistan.

On October 30, General Tommy Franks, commander of the military campaign against Afghanistan, visited Tashkent and met with President Karimov, plus the Uzbek defense and foreign ministers. Five days later, Defense Secretary Rumsfeld was back in Tashkent for another meeting with President Karimov. Secretary of State Powell came a month later, on December 9. It was after meeting with Powell that Karimov announced the opening of the Friendship Bridge between Uzbekistan and Afghanistan.

After that, Tashkent seemingly played host to a high–level American delegation every few days. In January, a delegation of nine U.S. Senators was followed five days later by a five person delegation from the House of Representatives, led by Congressman Jim Kolbe. It was Kolbe who announced that the United States had awarded Uzbekistan $100 million in economic and humanitarian assistance. On January 18, another Senatorial delegation headed by Majority Leader Daschle arrived in Tashkent and, like the two previous delegations, met with President Karimov.

On January 22, General Franks arrived back in Tashkent. Franks' visit was marked by a further formalization of the military cooperation between the two nations, including a plan of military visits and exchanges through the remainder of 2002. A day later, Elizabeth Jones, assistant secretary of state for European and Eurasian affairs, arrived in Tashkent for a discussion of future U.S.–Uzbek relations. Since that time, General Richard Myers, chairman of the U.S. Joint Chiefs of Staff, came to Tashkent to meet with President Karimov, followed by a U.S. Congressional delegation led by Congressman Hobson.

President Karimov then made a four–day trip to the United States in March 2002 where he met with President Bush and other U.S. Government officials. The tenor in the relationship at this time can best be summed up by two actions of Secretary Powell on March 12, the same day that President Karimov was meeting with President Bush. Testifying at a congressional hearing, Secretary Powell said that "Karimov has been a solid coalition partner;" but then added, "at the same time, there are problems with respect to human rights in Uzbekistan, and we will not shrink from discussing them." That afternoon, Secretary Powell and his counterpart, Uzbek Foreign Minister Komilov, signed a five–point "Strategic Partner" agreement that spelled out cooperation in the military, political, legal, humanitarian, and economic areas, plus cooperation against nuclear proliferation.

The decision of the Uzbek Government to support U.S. policy in Iraq cemented the relationship even further, especially after President Karimov declared his firm support of the U.S. position in Iraq in March 2003 at the same time that Russia was threatening to veto a United Nations Security Council resolution supporting a military invasion of Iraq. President Karimov even went so far as to characterize an invasion of Iraq as a continuation of the antiterrorist campaign that began in Afghanistan. A month later, when a session of the U.S.–Uzbekistan Security Cooperation Council was held in Washington, the American representatives announced the willingness of the United States to expand defense and military cooperation with Uzbekistan.

The issues of human rights and democratic reform were not dead, however. In July 2004, the U.S. State Department announced that Uzbekistan would be denied $18 million in aid because of a "lack of progress on democratic reform." However, U.S. diplomats afterwards tried to cushion the blow by stressing that, while the United States intended to continue to offer Uzbekistan "advice and assistance" in implementing democratic reforms, the United States Government considered that it was a separate issue from that of cooperation in combating international terrorism. A U.S. delegation headed by Lincoln Bloomfield, Assistant Secretary of State for Political and Military Affairs, and Andy Hoen, Deputy Assistant Secretary of Defense, did visit Tashkent in October 2004 and, after discussing bilateral military cooperation in a series of high level meetings, met with President Karimov.

Uzbekistan had expanded its international relations in other areas as well during this period. In March 2002, the chief of staff of the Turkish armed forces visited Tashkent to discuss bilateral military cooperation. He brought also an offer of $1.2 million in military assistance to Uzbekistan. A few days later, NATO Deputy Secretary–General Speckhard arrived in Tashkent to meet with Defense Minister Gulyamov. The message he brought was

President Islam Karimov

Uzbekistan

View of the city of Khiva, Uzbekistan

that NATO was ready to help Uzbekistan reorganize its military forces. In addition, he brought a NATO offer of 70 research grants to be awarded to Uzbek scientists. In April 2003, NATO held civil–emergency exercises in the Uzbek part of the Fergana Valley. Fourteen countries took part in the exercises. Uzbekistan reciprocated with a promise of full support in logistics, medical assistance, and humanitarian operations to NATO in its operations in Afghanistan.

President Karimov also welcomed German Chancellor Schroeder to Tashkent in May 2002; he then paid a three–day visit to Japan in July, meeting with Prime Minister Koizumi and being received by Emperor Akihito. A total of 14 documents were signed during the visit, including a joint declaration of friendship, cooperation and strategic partnership. Three months later, Karimov welcomed Aleksander Kwasniewski, President of Poland, to Uzbekistan. The two presidents discussed, among other things, bilateral military cooperation to combat terrorism. President Karimov then paid a three–day visit to Spain in January 2003. Although the main purpose of the visit was to boost trade and attract Spanish investment in Uzbekistan, the discussions also covered political and economic cooperation as well as the war against international terrorism and drug trafficking

Up to this time, the world emphasis on fighting terrorism meant that Uzbekistan was getting a great deal out of the new relationships that had developed after September 2001. Then came the first of the "color revolutions" in Georgia in November 2003, which were then followed by the "color revolutions" in Ukraine, and Kyrgyzstan in 2004 and 2005. Now the emphasis had switched from terrorism to democracy and this caused the top Uzbek leadership to question whether it was possible to cooperate with the western na-

tions over terrorism without encouraging the growth of similar democratic movements locally. And then came the violent events of May 2005 in Andijon.

When the United States and the various member countries of the European Union called on an international investigation of the events of May 2005 and its aftermath, the Uzbek Government rejected this approach as interference in its domestic affairs. Even at this time, however, the Uzbek Government leadership had decided that democracy was a greater threat to the regime than terrorism, and that the contamination was coming from the west. The government therefore began to reverse its policies of the previous three or so years and to return to its earlier policy of isolation.

The European Union imposition of sanctions against Uzbekistan in November 2005—which included an embargo on arms and equipment which could be used for internal repression and a ban on travel by officials directly involved in the Andijon crackdown—only reinforced this policy.

Because the United States was as critical of Uzbekistan's handling of the events of May 2005 as the Europeans, its continued presence in Uzbekistan became a potential threat. In June 2005, the Uzbek Government responded by placing new restrictions on United States Government use of the Karshi-Khanabad air base which the United States had been using to support its forces in Afghanistan; one month later, it gave the United States Government a deadline of six months to get out entirely. It also quietly terminated most other forms of cooperation with the United States Government, including counterterrorism and international cultural exchanges. In general, it applied the same new policy to the members of the European Union as well. As part of this new policy, the government also expelled

most international organizations that had been active in Uzbekistan up to this time. These included Freedom House, the Eurasia Foundation, Internews, the BBC, RFE/RL and the Soros Foundation's Open Society Institute. In March 2006, the UN High Commissioner for Refugees was told that it had to leave Uzbekistan within a month.

As part of this realignment, Uzbekistan also reversed its earlier policy of holding Russia at arms length. In September 2005, Russian Defense Minister Ivanov visited Uzbekistan to observe the first ever joint Russian-Uzbek military exercises. In November, Uzbekistan and Russia signed a bilateral treaty providing for long-term cooperation in trade and security. The treaty calls for defense cooperation and intelligence sharing, mutual use of military facilities, and cooperation in battling terrorism and drug trafficking. In speaking about the treaty, President Karimov said that the "consolidation of Russia's presence in Central Asia will be a reliable guarantee of peace and stability in the region." Not coincidentally, Russia's Gazprom and LUKoil announced at about this time that they will be investing as much as $2 billion in Uzbekistan's energy sector over the next several years.

In December 2006, this cooperation was carried a step further when Uzbekistan and Russia signed a new agreement providing Russian forces with basing rights at the Navoi military airfield in Uzbekistan. The agreement gives Russia the right to deploy fighter jets and bombers at the airfield; in return, Russia has agreed to upgrade the airfield's navigation systems and to provide "air-defense weaponry."

Karimov also visited China in the aftermath of Andijon, and here he heard unequivocal support for the Uzbek version of events. While there, he signed a $600 million oil joint venture with China.

In August 2006, Uzbekistan rejoined the Collective Security Treaty Organization (CSTO), which it quit in 1999. CSTO—whose membership includes Russia, Armenia, Belarus, Kazakhstan, Kyrgyzstan, and Tajikistan—promotes military and political cooperation aimed at ensuring the collective security of its member states.

Nature of the Regime

Uzbekistan has a presidential–parliamentary system similar to those found in the other ex–Soviet republics. However, the system has been totally dominated by President Karimov since independence. At first, Karimov ruled through the *Uzbek Communist Party*, merely changing its name to the *People's Democratic Party*. In 1996, then, Karimov resigned as leader of the *People's Democratic Party* and began creating a facade of political pluralism. As a result, five political parties entered the *Oliy Majlis* (parliament). None of these were true opposition parties, however, for all five political parties were created at the initiative of President Karimov.

In January 2002, President Karimov called a national referendum which asked voters two questions: whether a bicameral parliament should be created at the time of the next elections and whether the term of the presidency should be extended from five to seven years. Voters predictably approved both questions by huge margins. Karimov's current term as president thus runs until December 2007.

In December 2004, a new upper house or Senate was set up, consisting of 100 members. Sixteen of the senators were appointed by President Karimov while the remaining 84 were elected at joint meetings of region, district, and city assemblies from among the members of those bodies. Six senators were elected from each of the country's 12 regions plus Karakalpakistan and the city of Tashkent.

The new lower house, called the Legislative Chamber, now has 120 members. Elections to this second body took place on December 26, 2004, with a second round of voting taking place on January 9, 2005. Once again, five (pro-government) political parties were permitted to nominate candidates. In the final tally, the Uzbekistan Liberal Democratic Party took 41 seats, followed by the People's Democratic Party with 28. The Fidorkorlar (Self–Sacrifice) National Democratic Party came third with 18 seats, followed by the Uzbekistan National Rebirth Democratic Party with 11. The Adolat (Justice) Social Democratic Party took 10 seats. The remaining 14 seats went to candidates nominated by non-partisan public organizations.

Culture

Uzbekis are among the most traditional of the Central Asian peoples and national costumes are still often worn. Men wear a robe striped with bright colors and an embroidered skullcap. Women wear bright silk dresses with a shawl over the head. Rugs cover the floors of Uzbeki houses and often folk art decorates the walls. There are also traditional Uzbeki festivals in various times of the year when the people dress up in their finery and there is singing and dancing. Another specialty of the festivals is horse dancing. This is also the time for games and tests of strength, dexterity and skill. And of course food plays a role. Some of the distinctive foods include *d'ighman* (meat with pastry in a strong broth), spicy chopped meat wrapped in a thin dough, and *plov* (rice with meat, vegetables, spices and dried apricots).

Religion also plays a great role in the lives of the Uzbeki people, and attendance at the Friday mosque service has been increasing in recent years. Uzbekis are Sunni Muslims of the Hanafi School. Sufism is also practiced by some, and there is a famous Sufi School, the Naqshbandi or *tariqat–al–Khwajagan*, in Bukhara.

The government has taken an ambivalent attitude toward Islam. Moderate leaders have been wooed, but when 400 Muslims tried to hold a congress in Tashkent, the leaders were arrested and non–Uzbekis were expelled from the republic. On the other hand, no effort is made to discourage the practice of Islam, and new mosques are being built every day. New Islamic seminaries have also been opened.

Tashkent is the Islamic center for Central Asia. The "Spiritual Department of Muslims of Central Asia," headed by the Mufti of Tashkent, is located here. It is allowed to receive large sums of money from Saudi Arabia, which has also do-

A metro station in Tashkent

Courtesy: NOVOSTI

Uzbekistan

nated a million *Korans* for distribution in Central Asia. It also publishes a newspaper, *Dawn of Islam*, and a magazine, *Islamic Faith*.

Uzbekistan has produced a number of writers in the twentieth century. Perhaps the best known is Abdullah Qadiri, famous for two historical novels, Days Gone By and Scorpion from the Pulpit, published in the 1920s. Qadiri was later killed in the Soviet purges of the late 1930s. The novel Sisters, by Asqad Mukhtar, has been translated into English. Uzbeks have also made some original contributions in modern graphic arts. Some of the ancient skills such as ornamental wall painting, wood carving and fabric printing have also been kept alive. There is an Uzbek film studio where films in the Uzbeki language are made, and the republic also has its own radio and television facilities. The Navoi Theater of Opera and Ballet in Tashkent is also famous for its productions.

Economy

Uzbekistan has what is traditionally referred to as a commercial single–crop agricultural economy. What this means is that the republic is heavily dependent on the production of a single agricultural product, cotton. Although Uzbekistan does have some textile manufacturing, the majority of all cotton is exported outside the republic, constituting 41.5 percent of all exports in 2001. In fact, Uzbekistan produces two–thirds of Central Asia's production of cotton. It is also the world's second largest exporter of cotton. In addition, Uzbek farmers produce most of the food consumed within the republic, usually on small individually worked plots.

Almost all agriculture is dependent on irrigation, and practically all irrigated land was organized into huge state farms during the Soviet period whose sole commercial product was cotton. Most of these state farms were transformed into cooperatives or "joint–stock companies" in the first five years after independence but with ownership vested in the state, the management and efficiency of the state farms remained more or less what it had been in Soviet times. New legislation passed in July 1998 improved land use rights and gave greater security of tenure to individual farmers. The government also raised the state procurement prices of cotton and wheat in 1999 and again in 2000. The 1999 legislation wrote off farm debts to the state, simplified the taxation system (providing a tax cut for farms), and gave responsibility for social and community facilities formerly supported by the state farms to local governmental units. These changes have apparently had mixed results; the grain harvest reached a record 4.4 million tons in 2003 but the cot-

ton harvest was the worst it had been in a decade. According to official statistics, agricultural production was up by 9 percent in 2004, but the growth rate was somewhat lower in 2005, reaching only 7.3 percent.

Approximately 60 percent of the population lives in the countryside, but only 44 percent of the labor force are directly employed in agriculture. About a third of the country's annual GDP is derived from agriculture.

In addition to cotton and wheat, silkworms are raised in the Fergana Valley, with mulberry trees planted along the streets and irrigation canals. Orchards of apricots, peaches, figs, and pears, and vineyards, used to produce table grapes, raisins and wine, are found in the Fergana Valley, the Zeravshan oasis and the Chirchik and Agren Valleys.

The republic has the second highest birth rate of Central Asia, which has resulted in a surplus rural population. As a result, farm wages are low and rural unemployment is high. The unemployment rate in the republic was over ten percent even before the collapse of the Soviet system. Although the government is pursuing programs aimed at addressing these problems, the greatest help thus far has been out–migration. The independent Uzbek newspaper *Hurriyat* reported in April 2003 that between 500,000 and 700,000 Uzbeks had gone abroad in search of work. The newspaper also reported that the number of people leaving the country to find jobs is increasing. Government figures on the numbers of unemployed and underemployed in Uzbekistan are considered to be unreliable because of the government's reluctance to publicly admit the scope of the problem.

An indication of the number of Uzbeks working in Russia is found in an August 2006 report by the Russian Central Bank. According to the Bank, Uzbekistan was the largest recipient of remittances from Russia in 2006. According to these figures, remittances to Uzbekistan were running at the rate of $840 million a year.

Uzbekistan has large reserves of natural gas, petroleum and coal. Most local industry uses natural gas. Gas is also exported to Russia via a pipeline that runs from Bukhara to the area of the Urals and then on to European Russia. Petroleum is being produced in the Fergana Valley, in the area around Bukhara, and in the area south of the Aral Sea. The Angren coal field produces coal for local use, but coal deposits have not been developed to any great extent.

Plentiful energy supplies are used to support some industry as well. Uzbekistan produces machines and heavy equipment, its specialty being machinery

for cotton cultivation and harvesting. Machinery for irrigation projects and road construction are also manufactured, plus some for the textile industry.

Uzbekistan also mines gold, copper, zinc and lead ores, plus uranium, tungsten and molybdenum. It also produces fertilizers, cement, cotton textiles, coke and chemicals. Gold made up 9.6 percent of all exports in 2001. The Navoi Combine, which is the country's largest producer of gold, also owns several uranium mines. Several were closed in 1995, but growing world demand and new mining techniques have recently reinvigorated the industry. Uranium production, which was 2,100 tons in 2002, is expected to grow to 3,000 tons by 2010.

Uzbekistan has been the most reluctant of all the Central Asian republics to reform. The first step was taken in February 1994, when President Karimov decreed a package of economic reforms. Designed to set up a market economy, the plan called for the phasing out of subsidies on basic foodstuffs and public transport. Peasant farmers were also granted private plots of land. This brought some improvement in the economy. Inflation decreased somewhat, foreign reserves grew, and there was a bumper cotton crop. A Mercedes–Benz joint venture began turning out its first trucks as well.

When agricultural production fell below expectations in 1995–97, however, the government introduced "centralized purchasing" in August 1997, under which the government controlled sales of flour, sugar, edible oil and butter.

In late 1999, President Karimov began talking about additional moves to develop a market economy as a way of giving a boost to the flagging economy. He promised to extend privatization, promote small businesses, and to free the *som*, the Uzbek currency, and allow it to float. The government did sell 49 percent of the shares in Uzbekneftegaz, the state petroleum company, to foreign investors—and shares in three other petroleum companies, Uzneftegazdobycha, Uzneftepererobatka, and Uzburneftegaz, were also made available to foreign investors—but little else changed.

After Uzbekistan joined the United States–led war on terrorism in the fall of 2001, however, President Karimov suddenly found all sorts of opportunities opening up before him. It began in November when the United States Government offered an aid package worth $100 million to help Uzbekistan's currency become fully convertible. In February 2002, the Government of Uzbekistan announced a new macroeconomic and structural reform plan which it had worked out in consultation with the IMF. The plan called for removal of all restrictions on access to foreign exchange, unification of the exchange rates, agricultural sector reforms, and measures to improve the nation's banking system. In April 2002, the government adopted a new commercial exchange rate which brought it just slightly under the real black market rate; the next step came in October 2003, when the *som* became fully convertible.

When James Wolfensohn, president of the World Bank, met with President Karimov in Tashkent in April 2002, he proposed lending Uzbekistan $350 million over the next two years to fund projects in health, agriculture, banking, and water– resources and offered another $40 million credit agreement for a project to improve water supplies in Samarkand and Bukhara. To put these figures into perspective, Uzbekistan, which joined the World Bank in 1992, received a total of $494 million from the World Bank from 1992 to 2002. In September 2004, the World Bank agreed to provide another $40 million loan to finance a project to improve health care services.

A reversal of sorts occurred in March 2006, when Martin Raiser, the World Bank's country manager for Uzbekistan announced that the World Bank would not offer new loans to the government of Uzbekistan, though it would continue to service existing programs and provide technical assistance. Although Raiser stressed that there were no political reasons behind the World Bank's decision, it is evident that Uzbekistan's turn away from reform since the violent events of May 2005 has had a negative effect on the economy.

In a partial reversal, the World Bank announced in July 2006 that it would pursue an interim strategy of "continued engagement" with Uzbekistan over the next 12–15 months. The Bank indicated that this strategy "reflects the need to strengthen the poverty orientation of public policy, deepen structural reforms, and ensure broader civil society participation." The Bank indicated that the new policy might include limited new lending for global public goods and basic social services." In October 2006, it approved a $40 million credit to Uzbekistan to improve basic education.

Foreign investment in Uzbekistan, already the lowest on a *per capita* basis of any Central Asian republic, may actually be shrinking due to Uzbek Government policy. In August 2006, the Uzbek Government launched a criminal probe of Zarafshan-Newmont, an open-pit gold mining joint venture set up in 1992 by the Colorado-based Newmont Mining Corporation in partnership with the Uzbek State Committee for Geology and Mineral Resources. Two months earlier, the Uzbek Government ordered Zarafshan-Newmont to pay $45 million in back taxes; they next froze the joint venture's assets and seized some of its gold. After declaring Zarafshan-Newmont bankrupt in October, 2006, the government announced in February 2007 that it would be putting the company up for auction with a starting price of $139 million. It is believed that the auction is a formality to allow the government to take control of Newmont's assets in the country.

Four months earlier, the Uzbek Government authorities presented the joint venture Amantaytau Goldfields, half-owned by the British mining company Oxus Gold, with a $224.7 million claim for back taxes. This case has not yet been resolved, but it appears that the Uzbek Government intends to take full control of all gold-mining enterprises in the republic.

According to an official government report, Uzbek GDP rose 7.3 percent in 2007. The rate of inflation was 6.8 percent, a one percent drop over 2005. President Karimov commented that "the high economic growth figures, the drop in inflation, and improvement in the lives of citizens are a result of deeper reforms and the liberalization of the economy." The government did create a $1 billion State Development Fund in May 2006 which, according to the decree which created it, is supposed to focus on "securing dynamic, sustainable, and balanced social and economic development, as well as conducting effective structural and investment policies." Perhaps this insertion of new funds is having some effect.

The Future

Uzbekistan has one long-term problem which appears to be unsolvable—the shrinking Aral Sea—and a second problem related to the first—the fact that the standard of living among the population has been dropping for a number of years. Both are related to an over-dependence on the production of cotton using irrigation. Greater industrialization could provide more jobs for Uzbekis, but they have been reluctant to leave the land. Even today, a majority of jobs in industry is held by ethnic Russians.

Economic discontent has been growing in the country. This has put a great strain on government and helps explain why the country has not made greater progress toward democracy or a market economy. President Karimov had begun moving Uzbekistan in the direction of change, but the series of bombings in 2004 and the riots in early 2005 mean a reversal of this trend for at least the near future.

kalyan-mosque

BIBLIOGRAPHY OF KEY
ENGLISH LANGUAGE BOOKS

WEB SITES
Useful Web Sites on the UN, EU, OECD, NATO and other:
www.un.org (Web site for United Nations. Many links.)
www.unsystem.or (Official UN website)
http://europa.eu.int (EU server site)
http://europa.eu.int/comm (European Commission site)
http://www.euobserver.com (EU news)
http://www.euractiv.com (European news)
www.euractiv.com (Diverse news on EU and Europe)
www.oecd.org/daf/cmis/fdi/statist.htm (OECD site)
www.osce.org (Site of OSCE)
www.nato.int/structur/nids/nids.htm (NATO documentation, NATO Review)
www.nato.org and www.NATO.int (Web sites for NATO. Many links.)
www.wto.org (World Trade Organization site)
www.worldbank.org/html/Welcome.html (World Bank news, publications with
    links to other financial institutions)
www.ceip.org (Carnegie Endowment for International Peace, using a fully inte-
    grated Web-database system)
www.cia.gov/index.html (Central Intelligence Agency)
www.odci.gov/cia (Includes useful CIA publications, such as The World Factbook
    and maps)
www.xe.com/ucc/. (where the reader can check the current exchange rate of
    currencies)
www.state.gov/www/ind.html (U.S. Department of State, including country reports)
lcweb2.loc.gov/frd/cs/cshome.html (Library of Congress with coverage of over 100
    countries)
www.embassy.org/embassies (A site with links to all embassy web sites in Wash-
    ington D.C.)
www.psr.keele.ac.uk\official.htm (Collective site for governments and international
    organizations)
http://usinfo.state.gov (U.S. Department of State)
http://www.duma.ru (Site for Russian Federation parliament)
http://www.government.gov.ru (Russian government site)
http://www.president.kremlin.ru/ (Russian president site)
http://www.eurasianet.org (News for Eurasia)
www.rferl.org/caucasus-report/ (Site for Caucasus)
http://www.foreignpolicy.org.ua (Site for Ukrainian foreign policy)

NEWSPAPERS, JOURNALS AND TELEVISION WITH GOOD COVERAGE ON INTERNATIONAL AFFAIRS:

www.chicagotribune.com (Named best overall US newspaper online service for
    newspapers with circulation over 100,000.)
www.csmonitor.com (Respected U.S. newspaper, *Christian Science Monitor*. Named
    best overall US newspaper online service for newspapers with circulation under
    100,000.)
www.economist.com (British weekly news magazine)
www.nytimes.com (Respected U.S. newspaper, *The New York Times*)
www.washingtonpost.com
www.IHT.com (International Herald Tribune, published and distributed in Europe)
www.Europeanvoice.com (Weekly newspaper with EU and European news)
www.timeeurope.com (European edition of Time)
www.foreignaffairs.org (One of best-known international affairs journal)
www.cnn.com (Latest news with external links)
www.news.BBC.co.uk (British Broadcasting Corporation site)
www.c-span.org (Includes C-SPAN International)

RUSSIA GENERAL

Allensworth, Wayne. *The Russian Question: Nationalism, Modernization, and Post-
    Communist Russia.* Lanham, MD: Rowman & Littlefield Publishers, 1999; 368 p. (pb).
Bermeo, Nancy (ed.). *Liberalization and Democratization: Change in the Soviet Union and
    Eastern Europe.* Baltimore, MD: Johns Hopkins University Press, 1992; 200 p. (pb).
Blum, Douglas W. (ed.). *Russia's Future: Consolidation or Disintegration?* Boulder, CO:
    Westview Press, 1994; 173 p. (pb).

Evtuhov et al. *A History of Russia: People, Legends, Events, Forces.* St. Charles, IL: Houghton Mifflin, 2003.

Kaiser, Robert G. *Russia: The People and the Power.* New York, NY: Pocket Books, 1974; 557 p. (pb).

Lapidus, Gail W. (ed.). *The New Russia.* Boulder, CO: Westview Press, 1994; 280 p. (pb).

Milner-Gulland, Robin R. *The Russians.* NY: Blackwell, 1999.

Remnik, David. *Lenin's Tomb: The Last Days of the Soviet Empire.* New York, NY: Vintage, 1992; 608 p. (pb).

Rozman, Gilbert (ed.). *Dismantling Communism: Common Causes and Regional Variations.* Baltimore, MD: Johns Hopkins University Press, 1992; 304 p. (pb).

Service, Robert. *A History of World Communism.* Cambridge, MA: Harvard University Press, 2007; 624 p.

Smith, Hedrick. *The New Russians.* New York, NY: Avon Books, 1991; 734 p. (pb).

HISTORY

Chamberlin, William Henry. *The Russian Revolution.* 2 vols., New York, NY: Macmillan, 1952.

Daniels, Robert V. *The Conscience of the Revolution: Communist Opposition in Soviet Russia.* Cambridge, MA: Harvard University Press, 1960; 524 p.

Dmytryshyn, Basil. *A History of Russia.* Englewood Cliffs, NJ: Prentice Hall, 1977; 648. p.

Dmytryshyn, Basil. *U.S.S.R.: A Concise History.* New York, NY: Charles Scribner's Sons, 1978; 620 p.

Florinsky, Michael T. *Russia: A History and an Interpretation.* 2 vols, New York, NY: Macmillan, 1954.

Lincoln, W. Bruce. *Sunlight at Midnight. St. Petersburg and the Rise of Modern Russia.* NY: Basic Books, 2002.

Pipes, Richard. *Russia Under the Old Regime.* New York, NY: Charles Scribner's Sons, 1974; 361 p.

Radzinsky, *Alexander II: The Last Great Tsar.* New York: The Free Press, 2005; 462 p.

Riasanovsky, Nicholas. *A History of Russia.* New York, NY: Oxford University Press, 1993; 768 p.

Thompson, John M. *Russia and the Soviet Union.* (3rd ed); Boulder, CO: Westview Press, 1994; 320 p. (pb).

Treadgold, Donald W. *Twentieth Century Russia.* (8th ed); Boulder, CO: Westview Press, 1994; 498 p.

Wren, Melvin C. *The Course of Russian History.* Prospect Heights, IL: Waveland Press, 1994; 617 p. (pb).

THE COMMUNIST ERA

Andrew, Christopher and Vasili Mitrokhin. *The Sword and the Shield: The Mitrokhin Archive and the Secret History of the KGB.* New York: Basic Books, 1999; 700 p.

Applebaum, Anne. *Gulag: A History.* New York, NY: Doubleday, 2003; 736 p.

Arbatov, Georgi. *The System: An Insider's Life in Soviet Politics.* New York, NY: Times Books, 1993; 380 p. (pb).

Bailer, Seweryn. *Stalin's Successors: Leadership, Stability, and Change in the Soviet Union.* Cambridge, England: Cambridge University Press, 1980; 312 p. (pb).

Bailes, Kendall E. *Technology and Society under Lenin and Stalin: Origins of the Soviet Technical Intelligentsia.* Princeton, NJ: Princeton University Press, 1978; 472 p.

Braithwaite, Rodric. *Moscow 1941: A City and Its People at War.* New York: Alfred Knopf, 2006; 416 p.

Breslauer, George W. *Khrushchëv and Brezhnev as Leaders: Building Authority in Soviet Politics.* London, England: Allen Unwin, 1982; 318 p. (pb).

Caute, David. *The Dancer Defects: The Struggle for Cultural Supremacy during the Cold War.* New York: Oxford University Press, 2003; 788 p.

Daniels, Robert V. *Trotsky, Stalin and Socialism.* Boulder, CO: Westview Press, 1991; 208 p.

Daniels, Robert Vincent. *Stalin Revolution: Foundations of Soviet Totalitarianism.* (2nd ed.) Boston, MA: Heath, 1973; 106 p.

Djilas, Milovan. *Conversations with Stalin.* New York, NY: Harcourt Brace World, 1962; 211 p.

Getty, J. Arch and Oleg V. Naumov. *The Road to Terror: Stalin and the Self–Destruction of the Bolsheviks, 1932–1939.* New Haven, CT: Yale University Press, 1999; 688 p.

Goldgeier, James M. *Leadership Style and Soviet Foreign Policy: Stalin, Khrushchëv, Brezhnev, Gorbachëv.* Baltimore, MD: Johns Hopkins University Press, 1994; 192 p.

Gorodetsky, Gabriel. *Grand Illusion: Stalin and the German Invasion of Russia.* New Haven, CT: Yale University Press, 1999; 424 p.

Gorbachëv, Mikhail. *Memoirs*. New York, NY: Doubleday, 1996; 800 p.

Gorbachëv, Mikhail. *Gorbachëv on His Country and the World*; Trans. George Shriver. New York: Columbia University Press, 1999; 499 p.

Hill, Fiona and Clifford G. Gaddy. *The Siberian Curse: How Communist Planners Left Russia Out in the Cold*. Washington D.C.: Brookings, 2003.

Hosking, Geoffrey. *Rulers and Victims: The Russians in the Soviet Union*. Cambridge, MA: Harvard University Press, 2006; 496 p.

Karcz, Jerzy F. *The Economics of Communist Agriculture: Selected Papers*. Bloomington, IN: International Development Institute, 1979; 494 p.

Keep, John. *Last of the Empires: A History of the Soviet Union, 1946–1991*. New York, NY: Oxford University Press, 1997 (pb).

Ligachëv, Yegor. *Inside Gorbachëv's Kremlin*. trans. Catherine A Fitzpatrick, Michele A Berdy, and Dobrochna Dyrcz–Freeman. New York, NY: Pantheon Books, 1993; 369 p.

Linden, Carl. *Khrushchëv and the Soviet Leadership: With an Epilogue on Gorbachëv*. Baltimore, MD: Johns Hopkins University Press, 1990; 304 p. (pb).

Montefiore, Simon Sebag. *Young Stalin*. New York: Knopf, 2007; 432p.

Service, Robert. *Stalin: A Biography*. New York, Macmillan, 2005.

Taubman, William. *Khrushchev: The Man and His Era*. New York: Norton, 2003; 876 p.

Ulam, Adam B. *The Bolsheviks: The Intellectual and Political History of the Triumph of Communism in Russia*. New York, NY: Macmillan, 1965; 598 p.

Viola, Lynne. *Peasant Rebels under Stalin: Collectivization and the Culture of Peasant Resistance*. New York, NY: Oxford University Press, 1999; 328 p. (pb)

Volkogonov, Dmitri. *Autopsy for an Empire*. New York, NY: The Free Press (Simon & Schuster), 1998. 528 p.

Volkogonov, Dmitri. *Lenin: A New Biography*. New York: The Free Press, 1994; 529 p.

Yakovlev, Alexander. *The Fate of Marxism in Russia*. trans. by Catherine A. Fitzpatrick. New Haven, CT: Yale University Press, 1993; 256 p.

SOVIET/RUSSIAN FOREIGN POLICY

Aron, Leon and Kenneth M. Jensen (eds.). *The Emergence of Russian Foreign Policy*. Herndon, VA.: United States Institute of Peace Press, 1994; 221 p. (pb).

Beschloss, Michael R. and Strobe Talbott. *At the Highest Levels: The Inside Story of the End of the Cold War*. Boston, MA: Little, Brown, 1993; 498 p.

Bialer, Seweryn. *The Soviet Paradox–External Expansion, Internal Decline*. New York, NY: Alfred Knopf, 1986; 391 p.

Fischer, Louis. *Russia's Road from Peace to War*. New York, NY: Harper Row, 1969; 499 p.

Fursenko, Aleksandr and Timothy Naftali. *Khrushchev's Cold War: The Inside Story of an American Adversary*. New York: Norton, 2006; 670 p.

Gaddis, John Lewis. *The Cold War: A New History*. New York: The Penguin Press, 2005; 400 p.

Harriman, W. Averill. *Special Envoy to Churchill and Stalin, 1941–1946*. New York, NY: Random House, 1975; 595 p.

Ivanov, Igor S. *The New Russian Diplomacy*. Washington, D.C.: Brookings, 2002.

Jonson, Lena (ed.). *Peacekeeping and the Role of Russia in Eurasia*. Boulder, CO: Westview Press, 1996; 240 p.

Kennan, George F. *Russia and the West under Lenin and Stalin*. Boston, MA: Little, Brown, 1961; 411 p.

McFaul, Michael and James Goldgeiger. *Power and Purpose: U.S. Policy Toward Russia After the Cold War*. Washington: Carnegie Endowment, 2003.

Shearman, Peter (ed.). *Russian Foreign Policy Since 1990*. Boulder, CO: Westview Press, 1995; 320 p. (pb).

Talbott, Strobe. *The Russia Hand: A Memoir of Presidential Diplomacy*. NY: Random House, 2002.

Trenin, Dmitri V. *The End of Eurasia: Russia on the Border Between Geopolitics and Globalization*. Washington: Carnegie Endowment, 2002.

Ulam, Adam B. *Expansion and Coexistence*. New York, NY: Praeger, 1968; 797 p.

Ulam, Adam B. *The Rivals: America and Russia Since World War II*. New York, NY: Viking Press, 1971; 405 p.

Von Bencke, Matthew J. *The Politics of Space: A History of U.S.–Soviet/Russian Cooperation in Space*. Boulder, CO: Westview Press, 1996; 272 p.

Wettig, Gerhard. *Changes in Soviet Policy Toward the West*. Boulder, CO: Westview Press, 1991; 193 p.

COLLAPSE OF COMMUNISM

Balzer, Harley D. (ed.). *Five Years That Shook the World: Gorbachëv's Unfinished Revolution*. Boulder, CO: Westview Press, 1991; 267 p. (pb).

Brown, Archie. *Seven Years that Changed the World: Perestroika in Perspective*. Cambridge, England: Oxford University Press, 2007; 350 p.

Dallin, Alexander and Gail W. Lapidus (eds.). *The Soviet System: From Crisis to Collapse*. Boulder, CO: Westview Press, 1994; 725 p. (pb).

Daniels, Robert V. *Russia's Transformation: Snapshots of a Crumbling System*. Lanham, MD: Rowman & Littlield Publishers, 1997; 256 p. (pb).

Goldman, Marshal I. *USSR in Crisis: the Failure of an Economic System*. New York, NY: Norton, 1983; 210 p. (pb).

Goldman, Marshall I. *What Went Wrong with Perestroika?* New York, NY: Norton, 1991.

Gorbachëv, Mikhail. *The August Coup: The Truth and the Lessons*. New York, NY: HarperCollins, 1991; 127 p.

Jones, Anthony, Walter D. Conner and David E. Powell (eds.). *Soviet Social Problems*. Boulder, CO: Westview Press, 1991; 337 p. (pb).

Kaiser, Robert. *Why Gorbachëv Happened: His Triumphs and His Failures*. New York, NY: Simon Schuster, 1991; 476 p.

Kotkin, Stephen. *Armageddon Averted: The Soviet Collapse 1970–2000*. New York: Oxford University Press, 2001; 258 p.

Kotkin, Stephen. *Steeltown, USSR: Soviet Society in the Gorbachëv Era*. Berkeley, CA: University of California Press, 1991; 269 p.

Kull, Steven. *Burying Lenin: The Revolution in Soviet Ideology and Foreign Policy*. Boulder, CO: Westview Press, 1992; 219 p. (pb).

Odom, William E. *The Collapse of the Soviet Military*. New Haven, CT: Yale University Press, 1998; 480 p.

Shane, Scott. *Dismantling Utopia: How Information Ended the Soviet Union*. Chicago, IL: Ivan R. Dee, Inc., Publisher, 1995; 336 p.

Sharlet, Robert. *Soviet Constitutional Crisis: From De–Stalinization to Disintegration*. Armonk, NY: M. E. Sharpe, 1992; 204 p. (pb).

Solomon, Andrew. *The Irony Tower: Soviet Artists in a Time of Glasnost*. New York, NY: Knopf, 1991; 170 p.

Nahaylo, B. and V. Svoboda. *Soviet Disunion*. New York, NY: Free Press, 1990.

Volkogonov, Dmitri. *Autopsy for an Empire*. New York: The Free Press, 1998; 572 p.

White, Stephen. *Gorbachëv and After*. New York, NY: Cambridge University Press, 1992; 327 p. (pb).

Zaslavskaya, Tatyana. *The Second Socialist Revolution: An Alternative Soviet Strategy*. Bloomington, IN: Indiana University Press, 1990; 241 p. (pb).

POLITICS

Baker, Peter and Susan Glasser. *Kremlin Rising: Vladimir Putin's Russia and the End of Revolution*. New York: A Lisa Drew Book/Scribner, 2005; 453 p.

Barry, Donald D. (ed.). *Towards the Rule of Law in Russia: Political and Legal Reform in the Transition Period*. Armonk, NY: Sharpe, 1992.

Bjorkman, Tom. *Russia's Road to Deeper Democracy*. Washington, D.C.: Brookings, 2003.

Blum, Douglas W. (ed.). *Russia's Future: Consolidation or Disintegration*. Boulder, CO: Westview Press, 1994; 192 p. (pb).

Braithwaite, Rodric. *Across the Moscow River: The World Turned Upside Down*. New Haven: Yale University, 2002.

Brown, Archie and Lilia Shevtsova, eds. *Gorbachev, Yeltsin & Putin. Political Leadership in Russia's Transition*. Washington, D.C.: Brookings, 2001.

Cronberg, Tarja. *Transforming Russia: From a Military to a Peace Economy*. NY: Palgrave, 2003.

Cuchins, Andrew C. (ed.). *Russia After The Fall*. Washington: Carnegie Endowment, 2002.

Davis, Sue. *The Russian Far East: The Last Frontier*. NY: Routledge, 2002.

Dunlop, John B. *Russia Confronts Chechnya: Roots of a Separatist Conflict*. New York, NY: Cambridge University Press, 1998; 248 p. (pb).

Eckstein, Harry *et al*. *Can Democracy Take Root in Post–Soviet Russia?* Lanham, MD: Rowman & Littlefield Publishers, 1998; 406 p. (pb).

Evangelista, Matthew. *The Chechen Wars. Will Russia Go the Way of the Soviet Union?* Washington, D.C.: Brookings, 2002.

Feltbrugge, F.J.M. *Russian Law: The end of the Soviet System and the Role of Law*. Dordrecht, The Netherlands: Martinus Nijhoff, 1993.

Fish, Steven. *Democracy from Scratch*. Princeton, NJ: Princeton University Press, 1996; 312 p. (pb).

Friedgut, Theodore H. and Jeffrey W. Hahn (eds.). *Local Power and Post–Soviet Politics*. Armonk, NY: M. E. Sharpe, 1994; 320 p. (pb).

Gall, Carlotta and Thomas DeWall. *Chechnya: Calamity in the Caucasus*. New York: NYU Press, 2000; 416 p. (pb).

Golosov, Grigorii V. *Political Parties in the Regions of Russia: Democracy Unclaimed*. Boulder, CO: Lynne Rienner, 2004; 307 p.

Hoffmann, David. *The Oligarchs. Wealth and Power in the New Russia*. NY: Public Affairs, 2003.

Hosking, Geoffrey. *Russia and the Russians*. Cambridge, MA: Harvard University, 2003.

Hosking, Geoffrey. *The Russians in the Soviet Union*. Cambridge, MA: Harvard University Press, 2006; 496 p.

Jack, Andrew. *Inside Putin's Russia*. Granta Books, 2004.

Lapidus, Gail W. (ed.). *The New Russia: Troubled Transformation*. Boulder, CO: Westview Press, 1994; 320 p. (pb).

Lempert, David H. *Daily Life in a Crumbling Empire*; 2 vols. New York: Columbia University Press, 1996; 600 p. (each).

Marsh, Christopher. *Russia at the Polls: Voters, Elections, and Democratization*. Washington: CQ Press, 2002.

McFaul, Michael et al. *Between Dictatorship and Democracy: Russian Post-Communist Political Reforms*. Washington D.C.: Brookings, 2004.

Meier, Andrew. *Black Earth: A Journey through Russia After the Fall*. NY: Norton, 2004.

Meier, Andrew. *Chechnya: To the Heart of a Conflict*. New York: Norton, 2005.

Moore, Robert. *A Time to Die. The Kursk Disaster*. London: Bantam, 2003.

Olcott, Martha Brill et al. *Getting It Wrong: Regional Cooperation and the Commonwealth of Independent States*. Washington D.C.: Brookings, 2000.

Politkovskaya, Anna. *A Russian Diary*. New York: Random House, 2007; 272 p.

Politkovskaya, Anna. *Putin's Russia*. Harvill, 2005.

Putin, Vladimir. *First Person*. NY: PublicAffairs, 2000.

Robinson, Neil. *Russia. A State of Uncertainty*. NY: Routledge, 2001.

Ross, Cameron (ed). *Russian politics under Putin*. Manchester: Manchester University Press, 2004.

Ross, Cameron. *Federalism and Democratization in Post-Communist Russia*. Manchester: Manchester University Press, 2003.

Saivetz, Carol R. and Anthony Jones. *In Search of Pluralism: Soviet and Post–Soviet Politics*. Boulder, CO: Westview Press, 1994; 174 p. (pb).

Sakwa, Richard. *Russian Politics and Society*, 3d. ed. NY: Routledge, 2002.

Service, Robert. *Russia: Experiment with a People*. Cambridge, MA: Harvard University, 2003.

Shevtsova, Lilia. *Putin's Russia*. Revised Edition. Carnegie Endowment for International Peace, 2005; 298 p.

Smith, Gordon B. (ed.). *State–Building in Russia: The Yeltsin Legacy and the Challenge of the Future*. Armonk, NY: M. E. Sharpe, 1998; 224 p.

Taylor, Brian D. *Politics and the Russian Army: Civil-Military Relations, 1689–2000*. Cambridge: Cambridge University, 2003.

Treisman, Daniel S. *After the Deluge: Regional Crises and Political Consolidation in Russia*. Ann Arbor, MI: The University of Michigan Press, 1999; 340 p.

Trenin, Dmitri et al. *Russia's Restless Frontier. The Chechnya Factor in Post-Soviet Russia*. Washington D.C.: Brookings, 2004.

Truscott, Peter. *Putin's Progress*. NY: Simon & Schuster, 2004.

Urban, Joan Barth. *Russia's Communists at the Crossroads*. Boulder, CO: Westview Press, 1997; 224 p. (pb).

Waller, J. Michael. *Secret Empire: The KBG in Russia Today*. Boulder, CO: Westview Press, 1994; 375 p. (pb).

Weiler, Jonathon. *Human Rights in Russia: A Darker Side of Reform*. Boulder, CO: Lynne Rienner, 2004.

Yeltsin, Boris. *The Struggle for Russia*. New York, NY: Times Books, 1995; 336 p.

Zyuganov, Gennady A. *My Russia: The Political Autobiography of Gennedy Zyuganov*. Armonk, NY: M.E. Sharpe, Inc, 1997; 224 p.

ECONOMY

Aslund, Anders. *Building Capitalism: The Transformation of the Former Soviet Bloc*. New York: Cambridge University Press, 2001; 536 p.

Aslund, Anders and Richard Layard (eds.). *Changing the Economic System in Russia*. London, England: Pinter, 1993.

Boeva, Irina and Viacheslav Shironin. *Russians Between State and Market*. Glasgow, Scotland: University of Strathclyde Centre for the Study of Public Policy, SPP 205, 1992.

Brady, Rose. *Kapitalizm: Russia's Struggle to Free its Economy*. New Haven, CT: Yale University Press, 1998. 320 p.

Ellman, Michael and Vladimir Kontorovich (eds.). *The Disintegration of the Soviet Economic System*. New York, NY: Routledge, 1994; 281 p. (pb).

Gaddy, Clifford G. and Barry W.Ickes. *Russia's Virtual Economy*. Washington D.C.: Brookings, 2002.

Granville, Brigitte and Peter Oppenheimer. *Russia's Post-Communist Economy*. New York: Oxford University Press, 2001; 570 p.

Gaddy, Clifford G. and Barry W. Ickes. *Russia's Virtual Economy*. Washington, DC: Brookings Institution Press, 1999; 96 p. (pb).

Hill, Fiona and Clifford G. Gaddy. *The Siberian Curse: How Communist Planners Left Russia Out in the Cold*. Washington: Brookings, 2004.

Ioffe, Grigory and Tatyana Nefedova. *Continuity and Change in Rural Russia*. Boulder, CO: Westview Press, 1997; 328 p.

Keren, Michael and Gur Ofer (eds.). *Trials of Transition: Economic Reform in the Former Communist Bloc*. Boulder, CO: Westview Press, 1992; 308 p. (pb).

Kokh, Alfred. *The Selling of the Soviet Empire: Politics & Economics of Russia's Privatization—Revelations of the Principal Insider*. New York, NY: S.P.I. Books, 1999. (pb).

Lane, David (ed.). *The Political Economy of Russian Oil*. Lanham, MD: Rowland & Littlefield Publishers, Inc., 1999; 240 p. (pb)

Lavagne, Marie. *The Economics of Transition: From Socialist Economy to Market Economy*. New York: St. Martin's Press, 1999; 304 p.

McKinnon, Ronald. *The Order of Economic Liberalization: Financial Control in the Transition to a Market Economy*. Baltimore, MD: Johns Hopkins University Press, 1993; 224 p. (pb).

Nelson, Lynn D. and Irina Y. Kuzes. *Property to the People: The Struggle for Radical Economic Reform in Russia*. Armonk, NY: M. E. Sharpe, 1994; 280 p. (pb).

Wegren, Stephen K. *Agriculture and the State in Soviet and Post–Soviet Russia*. Pittsburgh, PA: University of Pittsburgh Press, 1998; 246 p.

CULTURAL

Berlin, Isaiah and Henry Hardy (eds.). *The Soviet Mind. Russian Culture under Communism*. Washington: Brookings, 2004.

Buckley, Mary. *Redefining Russian Society and Polity*. Boulder, CO: Westview Press, 1993; 346 p. (pb).

Davis, Nathaniel. *A Long Walk to Church: A Contemporary History*. Boulder, CO: Westview Press, 1994; 381 p. (pb).

Dunlap, John B. *Russia Confronts Chechnya*. New York: Cambridge University Press, 1998; 248 p.

Goscilo, Helena. *Dehexing Sex: Russian Womanhood During and After Glasnost*. Ann Arbor, MI: University of Michigan Press, 1996; 192 p. (pb).

Hilton, Alison. *Russian Folk Art*. Bloomington, IN: Indiana University Press, 1995; 320 p.

Hosking, Geoffrey A. *Beyond Socialist Realism: Soviet Fiction Since Ivan Denisovich*. New York, NY: Holmes Meier Publishers, 1980; 260 p.

Jones, Anthony (ed.). *Education and Society in the New Russia*. Armonk, NY: M. E. Sharpe, 1994; 360 p. (pb).

Leach, Robert and Victor Borovsky (eds.). *A History of Russian Theatre*. New York, NY: Cambridge University Press, 1998; 425 p.

Marks, Steven G. *How Russia Shaped the Modern World: From Art to Anti-Semitism, Ballet to Bolshevism*. Princeton: Princeton University, 2004.

Orlov, Yuri. *Dangerous Thoughts*. New York, NY: Morrow, 1991; 339 p.

Ramet, Sabrina P. *Nihil obstat: Religion, Politics, and Social Change in East–Central Europe and Russia*. Durham, NC: Duke University Press, 1998; 424 p. (pb).

Ramet, Sabrina P. *Rocking the State: Rock Music and Politics in Eastern Europe and Russia*. Boulder, CO: Westview Press, 1994; 317 p. (pb).

Rand, Robert. *Comrade Lawyer: Inside Soviet Justice in an Era of Reform*. Boulder, CO: Westview Press, 1991; 166 p. (pb).

Scanlan, James P. (ed.). *Russian Thought After Communism*. Armonk, NY: M. E. Sharpe, 1994; 256 p. (pb).

Segal, Harold B. *Twentieth–century Russian Drama: From Gorky to the Present*. New York, NY: Columbia University Press, 1979; 502 p.

Shlapentikh, Vladimir. *Soviet Intellectuals and Political Power*. Princeton, NJ: Princeton University Press, 1991; 321 p.

Shneidman, N.N. *Soviet Literature in the 1970's: Artistic Diversity and Ideological Conformity*. Toronto, Canada: University of Toronto Press, 1979; 128 p.

Smeliansky, Anatoly. *The Russian Theatre After Stalin*. New York: Cambridge University Press, 1999; 270 p. (pb).

Smith, Gerald S. (ed. and trans.). *Contemporary Russian Poetry*. Bloomington, IN: Indiana University Press, 1993; 390 p.

Solzhenitsyn, Alexander *et al. From Under the Rubble*. trans. by A.M. Brock. Boston, MA: Little, Brown, 1975; 308 p.

Solzhenitsyn, Alexander. *The Gulag Archipelago: 1918–1956*. trans. by Thomas R. Whitney. New York, NY: Harper Row, 1974; 640 p. (pb).

Terras, Victor. *A History of Russian Literature*. New Haven, CT: Yale University Press, 1992; 672 p. (pb).

COMMONWEALTH OF INDEPENDENT STATES

Akiner, Shirin. *Islamic Peoples of the Soviet Union*. New York, NY: Routledge Kegan Paul, 1986; 462 p.

Allison, Roy and Lena Jonson, eds. *Central Asian Security. The New International Context*. Washington, D.C.: Brookings, 2001.

Aslund, Anders and Michael McFaul (eds). *Revolution in Orange: The Origins of Ukraine's Democratic Breakthrough*. Washington, D.C.: Carnegie Endowment for International Peace, 2006; 216 p.

Banuazizi, Ali and Myron Weiner (eds.). *New Geopolitics of Central Asia*. Bloomington, IN: Indiana University Press, 1994; 288 p. (pb).

Bissell, Tom. *Chasing the Sea: Lost Among the Ghosts of Empire in Central Asia*. Pantheon, 2003; 416 p.

Bremmer, Ian and Ray Taras (eds.). *Nations and Politics in the Soviet Successor States*. New York, NY: Cambridge University Press, 1993; 577 p. (pb).

Brzezinski, Zbigniew and Paige Sullivan. *Russia and the Commonwealth of Independent States: A Historical and Geopolitical Evolution*. Armonk, NY: M. E. Sharpe, 1996.

Buckley, Mary, *Post–Soviet Women: From the Baltic to Central Asia*. New York, NY: Cambridge University Press, 1997; 333 p. (pb).

Chahin, M. *The Kingdom of Armenia*. New York, NY: Dorset Press, 1987; 332 p.

Coulton, Timothy J. and Robert C. Tucker (eds). *Patterns of Post–Soviet Leadership*. Boulder, CO: Westview Press, 1995; 256 p. (pb).

Dawisha, Karen and Bruce Parrott (eds.). *Conflict, Cleavage and Change in Central Asia and the Caucasus*. New York, NY: Cambridge University Press, 1997; 441 p. (pb).

Denber, Rachel (ed.). *The Soviet Nationality Reader: The Disintegration in Context*. Boulder, CO: Westview Press, 1992; 635 p. (pb).

d'Encausse, Helen Careere. *Decline of an Empire: The Soviet Socialist Republics in Revolt*. trans. Martin Sokolinsky and Henry A. La Farge. New York, NY: Newsweek Books, 1978; 304 p.

Enders, Wimbush S. *Soviet Nationalities in Strategic Perspective*. New York, NY: St. Martin's Press, 1985; 253 p.

Edgar, Adrienne Lynn. *Tribal Nation: The Making of Soviet Turkmenistan*. Princeton: Princeton University, 2004.

Frydman, Roman *et al. The Privatization Process in Russia, Ukraine and the Baltic States*. Budapest, Hungary: Central European University Press, 1993.

Gitelman, Zvi (ed.). *The Politics of Nationality and the Erosion of the USSR*. London, England: Macmillan, 1992.

Gleason, Gregory. *The Central Asian States*. Boulder, CO: Westview Press, 1997; 240 p. (pb).

Hajda, L and M. Beissinger (eds.). *The Nationalities Factor in Soviet Politics and Society*. Boulder, CO: Westview Press, 1990.

Hosking, Geoffrey *et al. The Road to Post–Communism: Independent Political Movements in the Soviet Union 1985–1991*. London, England: Pinter, 1992.

Hunter, Shireen. *Central Asia Since Independence*. New York, NY: Praeger, 1996; 220 p. (pb).

Hunter, Shireen. *The Transcaucasus in Transition: Nation–Building and Conflict*. New York, NY: Praeger, 1994; 240 p. (pb).

Kiev, Anna Reid. *Borderland. A Journey through the History of the Ukraine*. Boulder, CO: Westview, 2000.

Kravchuk, Robert S. *Ukrainian Political Economy. The First Ten Years*. NY: Palgrave, 2003.

Krushelnycky, Askold. *An Orange Revolution: A Personal Journey Through Ukrainian History*. Great Britain: Harvill Secker, 2006; 368 p. (pb)

Kuzio, Taras (ed.). *Contemporary Ukraine: Dynamics of Post–Soviet Transformation*. Armonk, NY: M. E. Sharpe, 1998; 272 p. (pb).

Lentini, Peter. *Political Parties and Movements in the Commonwealth of Independent States*. Manchester, England: Lorton House, 1992.

Lieven, Anatol. *Ukraine and Russia. A Fraternal Rivalry*. Herndon, VA: U.S. Institute of Peace, 1999.

Lynch, Dov. *Engaging Eurasia's Separatist States: Unresolved Conflicts and De Facto States*. Herndon, VA: United States Institute of Peace, 2004.

Mandelbaum, Michael (ed.). *The Rise of Nations in the Soviet Union: American Foreign Policy and the Disintegration of the USSR*. New York, NY: Council on Foreign Relations, 1991; 104 p. (pb).

Marples, David R. *Belarus. A denationalized nation*. Amsterdam: Harwood Academic Publishers, 1999.

Masik, Joseph R. and Robert O. Krikorian. *Armenia at the Crossroads* Amsterdam: Harwood Academic Publishers, 1999.

Miyamoto, Akira. *Natural Gas in Central Asia: Industries, Markets and Export Options of Kazakstan, Turkmenistan and Uzbekistan.* Washington, DC: The Brookings Institute Press, 1998; 100 p. (pb).

Motyl, Alexander J. *Dilemmas of Independence: Ukraine after Totalitarianism.* New York, NY: Council on Foreign Relations, 1993.

Nahaylo, B. and V. Svoboda. *Soviet Disunion.* New York, NY: Free Press, 1990.

Olcott, Martha Brill. *Central Asia's New States: Independence, Foreign Policy, and Regional Security.* Herndon, VA: United States Institute of Peace Press, 1966; 256 p. (pb).

Olcott, Martha Brill. *Central Asia's Second Chance.* Washington, D.C.: Carnegie Endowment for International Peace, 2005; 380 p. (pb).

Olcott, Martha Brill. *Kazakhstan. Unfulfilled Promise.* Washington, D.C.: Brookings, 2002.

Paksoy, H. B. (ed.). *Central Asian Reader: The Rediscovery of History.* Armonk, NY: M. E. Sharpe, 1994; 216 p. (pb).

Peterson, D. J. *Troubled Lands: The Legacy of Soviet Environmental Destruction.* Boulder, CO: Westview Press, 1993; 276 p. (pb).

Rashid, Ahmed. *Jihad: The Rise of Militant Islam in Central Asia.* New York: Penguin Books, 2003; 281 p.

Remington, Thomas F. (ed.). *Parliaments in Transition: The New Legislative Politics in the Former USSR and Eastern Europe.* Boulder, CO: Westview Press, 1994; 246 p. (pb).

Rumer, Boris Z. *Soviet Central Asia: A Tragic Experiment.* Boston, MA: Unwin Hyman, 1989; 204 p. (pb).

Rywkin, Michael. *Moscow's Muslim Challenge: Soviet Central Asia.* Armonk, NY: M. E. Sharpe, 1990; 181 p.

Rywkin, Michael. *Moscow's Lost Empire.* Armonk, NY: M.E. Sharpe, 1994; 230 p. (pb).

Shlapentokh, Vladimir and Munir Sendich (eds.). *The New Russian Diaspora: Russian Minorities in the Former Soviet Republics.* Armonk, NY: M. E. Sharpe, 1994; 248 p. (pb).

Smith, Graham *et al. Nation–Building in the Post–Soviet Borderlands: The Politics of National Identities.* New York, NY: Cambridge University Press, 1998; 312 p. (pb).

Suny, Ronald Grigor. *Looking Toward Ararat: Armenia in Modern History.* Bloomington, IN: Indiana University Press, 1993; 304 p. (pb).

Suny, Ronald Grigor. *The Making of the Georgian Nation.* Bloomington, IN: Indiana University Press, 1994; 448 p. (pb).

Tongeren, Paul van et al, eds. *Searching for Peace in Europe and Eurasia: An Overview of Conflict Prevention and Peacebuilding Activities.* Boulder, CO: Lynne Reinner, 2002.

Walker, Christopher J. *Armenia: The Survival of a Nation.* New York, NY: St Martin's Press, 1990; 476 p.

Wilson, Andrew. *The Ukrainians: Unexpected Nation.* Second Edition. New Haven: Yale University, 2002.

Wolchik, Sharon and Volodymyr Zviglyanich (eds.). *Ukraine: The Search for a National Identity.* Lanham, MD: Rowland & Littlefield Publishers, Inc., 1999; 336 p. (pb)

Wolczuk, Kasia and Roman Wulczuk. *Poland and Ukraine.* Washington, D.C.: Brookings, 2003.

Yalcin, Resul. *Rebirth of Uzbekistan. Politics, Economy and Society in the Post-Soviet Era.* UK: Ithaca Press, 2002.

Zaprudnik, Jan. *Belarus: At a Crossroads in History.* Boulder, CO: Westview Press, 1993; 278 p. (pb).

Zevelev, Igor. *Russia and Its New Diasporas.* Herndon, VA: U.S. Institute of Peace, 2001.